A Sustainable Revolution

A Sustainable Revolution

Let's Go Sustainable to Get our Globe Cleaner

Special Issue Editors

Idiano D'Adamo

Pasquale Marcello Falcone

Michael Martin

Paolo Rosa

MDPI • Basel • Beijing • Wuhan • Barcelona • Belgrade • Manchester • Tokyo • Cluj • Tianjin

Special Issue Editors
Idiano D'Adamo
Sapienza University of Rome
Italy

Pasquale Marcello Falcone
University of Naples Parthenope
Italy

Michael Martin
IVL Swedish Environmental Research Institute
KTH-Royal Institute of Technology
Sweden

Paolo Rosa
Politecnico di Milano
Italy

Editorial Office
MDPI
St. Alban-Anlage 66
4052 Basel, Switzerland

This is a reprint of articles from the Special Issue published online in the open access journal *Sustainability* (ISSN 2071-1050) (available at: https://www.mdpi.com/journal/sustainability/special_issues/Sustainable_Revolution_Globe_Cleaner).

For citation purposes, cite each article independently as indicated on the article page online and as indicated below:

LastName, A.A.; LastName, B.B.; LastName, C.C. Article Title. *Journal Name* **Year**, *Article Number*, Page Range.

ISBN 978-3-03936-455-8 (Hbk)
ISBN 978-3-03936-456-5 (PDF)

Cover image courtesy of Idiano D'Adamo.

Contents

About the Special Issue Editors vii

Idiano D'Adamo, Pasquale Marcello Falcone, Michael Martin and Paolo Rosa
A Sustainable Revolution: Let's Go Sustainable to Get Our Globe Cleaner
Reprinted from: *Sustainability* **2020**, *12*, 4387, doi:10.3390/su12114387 1

Elkhan Richard Sadik-Zada and Mattia Ferrari
Environmental Policy Stringency, Technical Progress and Pollution Haven Hypothesis
Reprinted from: *Sustainability* **2020**, *12*, 3880, doi:10.3390/su12093880 7

Durwin H.J. Lynch, Pim Klaassen, Lan van Wassenaer and Jacqueline E.W. Broerse
Constructing the Public in Roadmapping the Transition to a Bioeconomy: A Case Study from the Netherlands
Reprinted from: *Sustainability* **2020**, *12*, 3179, doi:10.3390/su12083179 27

Giulia Caruso, Emiliano Colantonio and Stefano Antonio Gattone
Relationships between Renewable Energy Consumption, Social Factors, and Health: A Panel Vector Auto Regression Analysis of a Cluster of 12 EU Countries
Reprinted from: *Sustainability* **2020**, *12*, 2915, doi:10.3390/su12072915 47

Chun Jiang, Yi-Fan Wu, Xiao-Lin Li and Xin Li
Time-frequency Connectedness between Coal Market Prices, New Energy Stock Prices and CO_2 Emissions Trading Prices in China
Reprinted from: *Sustainability* **2020**, *12*, 2823, doi:10.3390/su12072823 63

Camelia Delcea, Liliana Crăciun, Corina Ioanăș, Gabriella Ferruzzi and Liviu-Adrian Cotfas
Determinants of Individuals' E-Waste Recycling Decision: A Case Study from Romania
Reprinted from: *Sustainability* **2020**, *12*, 2753, doi:10.3390/su12072753 81

Fernando E. García-Muiña, María Sonia Medina-Salgado, Anna Maria Ferrari and Marco Cucchi
Sustainability Transition in Industry 4.0 and Smart Manufacturing with the Triple-Layered Business Model Canvas
Reprinted from: *Sustainability* **2020**, *12*, 2364, doi:10.3390/su12062364 109

Roberto Rocca, Paolo Rosa, Claudio Sassanelli, Luca Fumagalli and Sergio Terzi
Integrating Virtual Reality and Digital Twin in Circular Economy Practices: A Laboratory Application Case
Reprinted from: *Sustainability* **2020**, *12*, 2286, doi:10.3390/su12062286 129

Mariarosa Argentiero and Pasquale Marcello Falcone
The Role of Earth Observation Satellites in Maximizing Renewable Energy Production: Case Studies Analysis for Renewable Power Plants
Reprinted from: *Sustainability* **2020**, *12*, 2062, doi:10.3390/su12052062 157

Maria Rashidi, Alireza Joshaghani and Maryam Ghodrat
Towards Eco-Flowable Concrete Production
Reprinted from: *Sustainability* **2020**, *12*, 1208, doi:10.3390/su12031208 177

Lisandra Rocha-Meneses, Oghenetejiri Frances Otor, Nemailla Bonturi, Kaja Orupõld and Timo Kikas
Bioenergy Yields from Sequential Bioethanol and Biomethane Production: An Optimized Process Flow
Reprinted from: *Sustainability* **2020**, *12*, 272, doi:10.3390/su12010272 . . . . **195**

Florin-Constantin Mihai and Adrian Grozavu
Role of Waste Collection Efficiency in Providing a Cleaner Rural Environment
Reprinted from: *Sustainability* **2019**, *11*, 6855, doi:10.3390/su11236855 . . . . **215**

Michael Martin, Sofia Poulikidou and Elvira Molin
Exploring the Environmental Performance of Urban Symbiosis for Vertical Hydroponic Farming
Reprinted from: *Sustainability* **2019**, *11*, 6724, doi:10.3390/su11236724 . . . . **237**

Daeheon Choi, Chune Young Chung, Dongnyoung Kim and Chang Liu
Corporate Environmental Responsibility and Firm Information Risk: Evidence from the Korean Market
Reprinted from: *Sustainability* **2019**, *11*, 6518, doi:10.3390/su11226518 . . . . **255**

Mihail Busu
The Role of Renewables in a Low-Carbon Society: Evidence from a Multivariate Panel Data Analysis at the EU Level
Reprinted from: *Sustainability* **2019**, *11*, 5260, doi:10.3390/su11195260 . . . . **265**

Jin Guo and Junhong Bai
The Role of Public Participation in Environmental Governance: Empirical Evidence from China
Reprinted from: *Sustainability* **2019**, *11*, 4696, doi:10.3390/su11174696 . . . . **281**

Francesco Ferella, Valentina Innocenzi, Svetlana Zueva, Valentina Corradini, Nicolò M. Ippolito, Ionela P. Birloaga, Ida De Michelis, Marina Prisciandaro and Francesco Vegliò
Aerobic Treatment of Waste Process Solutions from the Semiconductor Industry: From Lab to Pilot Scale
Reprinted from: *Sustainability* **2019**, *11*, 3923, doi:10.3390/su11143923 . . . . **301**

Rocío González-Sánchez, Davide Settembre-Blundo, Anna Maria Ferrari and Fernando E. García-Muiña
Main Dimensions in the Building of the Circular Supply Chain: A Literature Review
Reprinted from: *Sustainability* **2020**, *12*, 2459, doi:10.3390/su12062459 . . . . **313**

Idiano D'Adamo and Paolo Rosa
A Structured Literature Review on Obsolete Electric Vehicles Management Practices
Reprinted from: *Sustainability* **2019**, *11*, 6876, doi:10.3390/su11236876 . . . . **339**

About the Special Issue Editors

Idiano D'Adamo (Ph.D.) is an associate professor at Sapienza—University of Rome. He completed his Master of Science in Management Engineering in 2008, and his PhD in Electrical and Information Engineering in 2012, both at the University of L'Aquila. He has worked at the University of Sheffield, the National Research Council of Italy, Politecnico di Milano, University of L'Aquila and Unitelma Sapienza University of Rome. His current research interests are bioeconomy, circular economy, renewable energy, sustainability and waste management. During his academic career, Idiano D'Adamo has published 61 papers, which are all listed in the Scopus database; he has reached an h-index of 23. In August 2015, he obtained the Elsevier Atlas Price, with a work published in Renewable and Sustainable Energy Reviews. He received two Excellence Review Awards: Waste Management in 2017, and Resources, Conservation and Recycling in 2018. He is a reviewer for 50 international journals. Idiano currently teaches "Business Management" and "Economics of Technology and Management" at Sapienza University of Rome.

Pasquale Marcello Falcone (MA, MSc, PhD) is an economist, with a strong interest in policy analysis applied to sustainable transitions. He is an assistant professor (tenured) of economic policy at the Department of Business and Economics—University of Naples "Parthenope" (Italy). He completed his MSc in Economics in 2013, at the University of Leicester (UK). He then completed his PhD in Economics (2014) and a MA in Business Economics (2010), both at the University of Foggia (Italy). His research interests span from environmental economics and sustainable development to sustainability transition theory. Recently, he has been exploring the mechanisms through which transitions towards a bio-based economy can be intertwined with socio-economic and policy aspects from the perspective of circular bio-economy. His work regularly appears in prestigious, highly impactful, innovative and environmental economics journals.

Michael Martin (BSc, MSc, Ph.D.) is a senior researcher at IVL Swedish Environmental Research Institute and Affiliated Faculty/Research at the Department of Sustainable Development, Environmental Science and Engineering (SEED) of KTH—Royal Institute of Technology. Dr. Martin has a PhD in Environmental Systems Analysis and Environmental Management, which focused on approaches to quantify the environmental and economic benefits of industrial symbiosis and circular based production in the bio-based sector, using LCA from Linköping University, in 2013. His expertise and current work include quantitative and qualitative research methods applied to understanding the implications of sustainable production and consumption systems through the use of sustainability assessments. His research also specializes in how sustainability assessment information can be improved by, and perceived through, stakeholder dialogue. Furthermore, he is also a member of the Executive Board of the International Society for Industrial Ecology.

Paolo Rosa (Ph.D.) is a post-doctoral researcher at the Manufacturing Group of Politecnico di Milano, Department of Management, Economics and Industrial Engineering. He got his MSc in Management Engineering from Politecnico di Milano in 2009. He spent three years working as a research assistant at Politecnico di Milano and ITIA-CNR in lifecycle simulation, manufacturing business models and end-of-life management areas. Currently, he is conducting his research at Politecnico di Milano, by focusing on product lifecycle management and circular economy. He has been (and is still) involved in industrial, regional and European research projects; he won an H2020 project in 2018 (www.fenix-project.eu). Furthermore, he has been (and is still) a teaching assistant on the Industrial Technologies course at Politecnico di Milano. He has co-authored 29 papers published in international journals and 15 papers presented at international conferences. He is the co-guest editor of a Special Issue and member of the Editorial Board of the *Sustainability* journal, published by MDPI. He was awarded the Elsevier Atlas Award for best paper in August 2015. He received one Excellence in Review Award from Resources, Conservation and Recycling in 2019.

sustainability

MDPI

Editorial

A Sustainable Revolution: Let's Go Sustainable to Get Our Globe Cleaner

Idiano D'Adamo [1,*], Pasquale Marcello Falcone [2], Michael Martin [3,4] and Paolo Rosa [5]

1 Department of Computer, Control and Management Engineering, Sapienza University of Rome, Via Ariosto 25, 00185 Rome, Italy
2 Department of Business and Economics—University of Naples Parthenope, Via Generale Parisi 13, 80132 Napoli, Italy; pasquale.falcone@uniparthenope.it
3 IVL Swedish Environmental Research Institute, Valhallavägen 81, 114 28 Stockholm, Sweden; michael.martin@ivl.se
4 KTH—Royal Institute of Technology, Department of Sustainable Development, Environmental Science and Engineering, Teknikringen 34, 114 28 Stockholm, Sweden
5 Department of Management, Economics and Industrial Engineering, Politecnico di Milano, Piazza L. Da Vinci 32, 20133 Milano, Italy; paolo1.rosa@polimi.it
* Correspondence: idiano.dadamo@uniroma1.it

Received: 22 May 2020; Accepted: 26 May 2020; Published: 27 May 2020

Abstract: The concept of sustainability is a clear blue sea, a snowy mountain, a flowery meadow, in which there is resource sharing that allows us to satisfy human needs without damaging natural resources. The challenge is complex, and we hope to support the decarbonization of our society and mitigate climate changes. This Special Issue aims to outline different approaches in several sectors with a common point of view: seeing our world with a green perception and encouraging a sustainable revolution to provide a cleaner world.

Keywords: circular economy; bioeconomy; green economy; sustainability

1. Introduction

The parties of the United Nations Framework Convention on Climate Change (UNFCCC) reached the Paris Agreement to combat climate change and intensify the actions needed for a sustainable transition towards a low-carbon future. This transition will require holistic approaches and complex societal changes, necessitating solutions and collaboration between private, public, and academic sectors. Many previous studies have identified potential areas for improving societal and environmental impacts of several sectors, including transitioning and improving our energy and food supply and transforming our economic system to deliver more environmentally-friendly products and services through a more circular and bio-based economy.

The term "sustainable revolution" is discussed by McManners [1], in which the revolution is associated with the actions following people's concerns over climate. Sustainability has required a paradigm shift in towards strategic and long-term thinking where organizations are asked to implement practices and daily work based on environmental protection [2]. Sustainability is based on a balanced relationship of the triple bottom line—people, profit and planet [3]. An effective management of people, oriented to see the workforce not as a cost to be minimized or avoided, is able to determine a sustainable competitive advantage [4]. Following this direction, human needs are not always in contrast with the protection of ecosystems. Sustainability requires the development of local, regional and global solutions [5]. For this ambitious goal, a collaboration between technical and social profiles is needed. The concepts of bioeconomy, circular economy and green economy have the common objective of developing a sustainable economy [6].

This Special Issue aims to encourage studies exploring the transition towards a more sustainable future, encompassing and identifying the development and implications of more sustainable options in collaboration with communities, firms, policymakers, and researchers to achieve this transition.

2. Form and Contents of the Thematic Issue

Sustainability issues towards a low carbon economy have been investigated both at the macro and micro levels.

Sadik-Zada and Ferrari [7] reconsider the pollution haven hypothesis with a refined dataset containing observations for 26 OECD member countries and innovative cointegration methods. They found a solid verification of the pollution haven conjecture indicating that, a purely national perspective of the Environmental Kuznets Curve is not always adequate.

Based on macro data, Caruso et al. [8] use a Panel Vector Auto Regression technique applied to a group of European Countries, to show the importance of implementing a stringent policy for the development of renewable energy consumption and its impact towards social aspects (e.g., general public awareness, lobbying activity, etc.).

The relevant role of policymaking has been stressed also by Jiang et al. [9]. Looking at inherent dynamic connectedness among coal market prices, new energy stock prices and carbon emission trading prices (CET) in China, the authors suggest that the policymakers not only should take actions to stabilize China's CET market price, but also should develop the financial function of this market.

In a subsequent paper, Lynch et al. [10] present a conceptual-analytical work aimed at exploring the construction of various publics in the bioeconomy by focusing on a specific case in the Netherlands. Authors emphasized the lack of a single all-encompassing "public perception of the bioeconomy" highlighting the need for a better understanding of different segments of the public in sustainability transitions.

Moreover, focusing on a national setting, Delcea et al. [11] analyze the influence of social media towards the actions taken by the government and nongovernmental organizations in Romania, with the purpose to understand the determinants in the e-waste recycling process. Their results showed that the demographic variables, such as age and gender, impact the predicting residents' pro-e-waste recycling behavior.

The 4.0 industry approach opens new opportunities in terms of sustainable development. García-Muiña et al. [12] explore the introduction of sustainability in the corporate value proposition, through the evolution from a traditional to a sustainable business model by focusing on a ceramic tile producer. The innovation of the business model represents an opportunity not only from an operational perspective but also in terms of the company's value creation.

In the same vein, Rocca et al. [13] provide a laboratory research case to show how the 4.0 industry paradigm can stimulate the adoption of circular economy (CE) practices by virtually testing waste from electrical and electronic equipment (WEEE) employing dedicated simulation tools. When looking at the factory level, service-oriented, event-driven processing and information models could foster the combination of digital and smart solutions.

Innovative technologies are paramount for sustainable development. Argentiero and Falcone [14] introduce, discuss and present a research case based on the role of Earth observation satellites in maximizing renewable energy production. Building on a large database of satellite parameters, results show how to discriminate, in the pre-feasibility phase, the type of installation not efficient for the selected location or not convenient in terms of internal rate of return (IRR) on equity.

Developing innovative approaches to plastic waste disposal that are able to consider both the economy and environmental protection is of paramount importance. Rashidi et al. [15] appraise the impacts of using expired plastic syringes as fine aggregate on fresh and hardened features of flowable concrete as a potential solution to environmental issues. Results show that, at the age of 28 days, using waste aggregates increased the compressive strength of the samples.

The efficient use of local resources is also paramount to achieve sustainable energy systems. Rocha-Meneses et al. [16] explore the potential of employing Napier grass, to produce ethanol via the nitrogen explosive decompression (NED) method at different temperatures. They find that Napier grass is a suitable feedstock for the process, an extensively available grass in Africa, but that the process is influenced by temperature and further refinements will be needed to explore its potential, and market, in Africa.

Wastes, especially household wastes, are important to address. Mihai and Grozavu [17] review the possibility to improve household waste collection and disposal in Romania. By reviewing waste statistics, they show that there are discrepancies in reported household waste collection, and highlight the use of illegal dumping. They suggest that CE based policies should be in place to improve waste collection and recycling through composting, recycling schemes and valorization processes to reuse and upcycle waste streams.

Martin et al. [18] also address urban wastes and residual materials to improve the resource efficiency of urban farming systems. They find that residual streams, such as brewers spent grains (BSG), paper and compost can replace potting soil used in indoor farms producing leafy greens and other plants. Furthermore, digestate from biogas plants, also employing urban bio-based waste, may play an important role in reducing the impacts from fertilizers for these systems.

Choi et al. [19] explore how business can contribute to sustainable development by reviewing socially responsible firms and the effect of their corporate environmental responsibility (CER) information on business. They found that environmental responsibility has importance for profitability by improving information transparency and increasing shareholder value. Such findings are important to promote more socially and environmentally sound businesses and investments.

Busu [20] also discusses the need for more investment in renewables in Europe. Using a multiple linear regression analysis, the study examines the carbon dioxide emissions in the European Union (EU) by testing the relationship to urbanization and population and carbon dioxide mitigation pathways, e.g., renewable energy consumption, biofuel production, resources productivity, bioenergy productivity. The findings further support the role of renewables, encouraging increased policy support to mitigate climate emissions in Europe.

In order to promote more environmentally sound systems, Guo and Bai [21] suggest that the public has an important role in environmental governance to promote changes. They model the potential effects of public participation and identify that the public can have an influence on the important environmental enforcement of polluting enterprises, extending empirical research to promote public involvement in environmental governance.

Directly supporting the reduced potential for pollution, Ferella et al. [22] study the potential for aerobic biodegration of toxic solvents used in the semiconductor industry. The study reviews aerobic biodegration of Tetramethylammonium hydroxide (TMAH), concluding that more than 99.3% of the solvent can be removed through the process, which can significantly improve the reduction in pollutants entering the environment.

An approach often highlighted to achieve sustainability is the adoption of circular economy principles. However, this shift could have complex logistical needs and require the redistribution of materials and resources. González-Sánchez et al. [23] study these changes through supply chain mapping and a literature review. They recommend that support for new supply chains from a circular perspective are needed, including greater intensity in the relationships established in the supply chain, the adaptation of logistics and organizational, disruptive and smart technologies, and a functioning environment.

In the final paper, D'Adamo and Rosa [24] study the potential risks with the growing number of electric vehicles (EV), and their subsequent end-of-life strategies. They conduct a literature review of EV management practices identified in the literature and find that end-of-life strategies have been extensively covered, with a number of potential applications and management systems, especially for the critical materials used in EVs, although the economics have received little focus.

3. Concluding Remarks and Further Issues on the Research Agenda

This Special Issue aimed at collecting studies suggesting innovative ways to cope with the transition from current (consumerist) behaviors to more sustainable lifestyles. Even if the messages of the experts are widely distributed in different ways (depending on their knowledge), the common logic linking all these contributions is the central role of the environment in human activities. No one (neither private nor industrial, nor public actor) can nowadays act on the global market without having a clear perspective and strategy about the environment. Technologies, processes, products, services, policies, and financial activities must consider the sustainability aspect, and, with time, their sustainability level will improve further through advanced performance assessment methods. Sustainability has become a way of reaching a competitive advantage in the market. Its influence has changed the way in which companies act on the market, organize themselves internally, interact with suppliers and customers and innovate their portfolio of products and services. At the same time, Industry 4.0 technologies are supporting companies in managing this transition and exploiting its benefits. The reported contributions offer to managers and common readers a good sample of how researchers are mapping this sustainable (re)evolution.

Author Contributions: All the authors were Guest Editors for this Special Issue and contributed equally to the Editorial. All authors have read and agreed to the published version of the manuscript.

Funding: This research received no external funding.

Acknowledgments: We are very grateful to all authors, reviewers and assistant editors involved in this Special Issue. A special thanks to Leanne Fan and Franck Vazquez. Cover image represents Tremiti islands (Italy).

Conflicts of Interest: The authors declare no conflict of interest.

References

1. McManners, P.J. *Adapt and Thrive: The Sustainable Revolution*; Susta Press: London, UK, 2008; ISBN 0955736900.
2. Andersson, L.; Jackson, S.E.; Russell, S.V. Greening organizational behavior: An introduction to the special issue. *J. Organ. Behav.* **2013**, *34*, 151–155. [CrossRef]
3. Gallagher, V.C.; Hrivnak, M.W.; Valcea, S.; Mahoney, C.B.; LaWong, D. A comprehensive three-dimensional sustainability measure: The 'missing P' of 'people'—A vital stakeholder in sustainable development. *Corp. Soc. Responsib. Environ. Manag.* **2018**, *25*, 772–787. [CrossRef]
4. Pfeffer, J. Producing sustainable competitive advantage through the effective management of people. *Acad. Manag. Exec.* **2005**, *19*, 95–106. [CrossRef]
5. Giannetti, B.F.; Agostinho, F.; Almeida, C.M.V.B.; Yang, Z.; Liu, G.; Wang, Y.; Huisingh, D. Ten years working together for a sustainable world, dedicated to the 6th IWACP: Introductory article. *J. Clean. Prod.* **2019**, *226*, 866–873. [CrossRef]
6. Gregorio, V.F.; Pié, L.; Terceño, A. A systematic literature review of bio, green and circular economy trends in publications in the field of economics and business management. *Sustainability* **2018**, *10*, 4232. [CrossRef]
7. Sadik-Zada, E.R.; Ferrari, M. Environmental Policy Stringency, Technical Progress and Pollution Haven Hypothesis. *Sustainability* **2020**, *12*, 3880. [CrossRef]
8. Caruso, G.; Colantonio, E.; Gattone, S.A. Relationships between Renewable Energy Consumption, Social Factors, and Health: A Panel Vector Auto Regression Analysis of a Cluster of 12 EU Countries. *Sustainability* **2020**, *12*, 2915. [CrossRef]
9. Jiang, C.; Wu, Y.-F.; Li, X.-L.; Li, X. Time-frequency Connectedness between Coal Market Prices, New Energy Stock Prices and CO_2 Emissions Trading Prices in China. *Sustainability* **2020**, *12*, 2823. [CrossRef]
10. Lynch, D.H.J.; Klaassen, P.; van Wassenaer, L.; Broerse, J.E.W. Constructing the Public in Roadmapping the Transition to a Bioeconomy: A Case Study from the Netherlands. *Sustainability* **2020**, *12*, 3179. [CrossRef]
11. Delcea, C.; Crăciun, L.; Ioanăș, C.; Ferruzzi, G.; Cotfas, L.-A. Determinants of Individuals' E-Waste Recycling Decision: A Case Study from Romania. *Sustainability* **2020**, *12*, 2753. [CrossRef]
12. García-Muiña, F.E.; Medina-Salgado, M.S.; Ferrari, A.M.; Cucchi, M. Sustainability Transition in Industry 4.0 and Smart Manufacturing with the Triple-Layered Business Model Canvas. *Sustainability* **2020**, *12*, 2364. [CrossRef]

13. Rocca, R.; Rosa, P.; Sassanelli, C.; Fumagalli, L.; Terzi, S. Integrating Virtual Reality and Digital Twin in Circular Economy Practices: A Laboratory Application Case. *Sustainability* **2020**, *12*, 2286. [CrossRef]
14. Argentiero, M.; Falcone, P.M. The Role of Earth Observation Satellites in Maximizing Renewable Energy Production: Case Studies Analysis for Renewable Power Plants. *Sustainability* **2020**, *12*, 2062. [CrossRef]
15. Rashidi, M.; Joshaghani, A.; Ghodrat, M. Towards Eco-Flowable Concrete Production. *Sustainability* **2020**, *12*, 1208. [CrossRef]
16. Rocha-Meneses, L.; Otor, O.F.; Bonturi, N.; Orupõld, K.; Kikas, T. Bioenergy yields from sequential bioethanol and biomethane production: An optimized process flow. *Sustainability* **2020**, *12*, 272. [CrossRef]
17. Mihai, F.C.; Grozavu, A. Role of waste collection efficiency in providing a cleaner rural environment. *Sustainability* **2019**, *11*, 6855. [CrossRef]
18. Martin, M.; Poulikidou, S.; Molin, E. Exploring the environmental performance of urban symbiosis for vertical hydroponic farming. *Sustainability* **2019**, *11*, 6724. [CrossRef]
19. Choi, D.; Chung, C.Y.; Kim, D.; Liu, C. Corporate Environmental Responsibility and Firm Information Risk: Evidence from the Korean Market. *Sustainability* **2019**, *11*, 6518. [CrossRef]
20. Busu, M. The role of renewables in a low-carbon society: Evidence from a multivariate panel data analysis at the eu level. *Sustainability* **2019**, *11*, 5260. [CrossRef]
21. Guo, J.; Bai, J. The role of public participation in environmental governance: Empirical evidence from China. *Sustainability* **2019**, *11*, 4696. [CrossRef]
22. Ferella, F.; Innocenzi, V.; Zueva, S.; Corradini, V.; Ippolito, N.M.; Birloaga, I.P.; De Michelis, I.; Prisciandaro, M.; Vegliò, F. Aerobic treatment of waste process solutions from the semiconductor industry: From lab to pilot scale. *Sustainability* **2019**, *11*, 3923. [CrossRef]
23. González-Sánchez, R.; Settembre-Blundo, D.; Ferrari, A.M.; García-Muiña, F.E. Main dimensions in the building of the circular supply chain: A literature review. *Sustainability* **2020**, *12*, 2459. [CrossRef]
24. D'Adamo, I.; Rosa, P. A Structured Literature Review on Obsolete Electric Vehicles Management Practices. *Sustainability* **2019**, *11*, 6876. [CrossRef]

sustainability

MDPI

Article

Environmental Policy Stringency, Technical Progress and Pollution Haven Hypothesis

Elkhan Richard Sadik-Zada [1,2,3,4,5,*] and Mattia Ferrari [3,6]

1 Institute of Development Research and Development Policy, Ruhr-University, 44801 Bochum, Germany
2 Centrum für Umwelt, Ressourcen, Energie (CURE), Faculty of Management and Economics, Ruhr-University, 44801 Bochum, Germany
3 Centre for Studies on European Economy (AIM), Azerbaijan State University of Economics (UNEC), Baku 1001, Azerbaijan; mattia.ferrari@rub.de
4 Center for Economic Development and Social Change (CED), 80128 Napoli, Italy
5 Energy Transitions at Cambridge (Visiting), University of Cambridge, Cambridge CB2 1TN, UK
6 European Institute for Innovation–Technology e.V., 73525 Schwäbisch Gmünd, Germany
* Correspondence: Elkhan.R.Sadik-Zada@ruhr-uni-bochum.de; Tel.: +49-(0)-234-32-25153

Received: 17 March 2020; Accepted: 1 May 2020; Published: 9 May 2020

Abstract: The present inquiry provides a common ground for the analysis of two strands of literature, the environmental Kuznets curve (EKC) and the pollution haven hypothesis (PHH). To this end, the study sets out a simple variational model, which identifies the structural composition of the economy and the level of economic development as the primary determinants of the magnitude of the domestic environmental degradation. The juxtaposition of the mentioned literature strands undermines the optimistic view that economic growth, in the long run, leads to the reduction of atmospheric pollution. To assess the empirical validity of the pollution haven conjecture, the study employs the OECD Environmental Policy Stringency Index and the refined data on carbon emissions embodied in imports for the dataset of 26 OECD countries in the time interval between 1995 and 2011. By employing pooled mean group (PMG) estimators, the study, for the first time, accounts for a number of issues mentioned in the literature as factors that confine the inferential power of existing empirical studies on the EKC. The strong and robust confirmation of the pollution haven conjecture indicates that at least in the context of global common pool resources, a purely national perspective of the EKC is not satisfactory.

Keywords: environmental policy stringency; carbon leakage; pollution havens; intensity-of-use hypothesis; development economics; environmental Kuznets curve; calculus of variations; pooled mean group estimator

1. Introduction

OECD countries are occupying the top positions with regards to climate change awareness. More than 90% of the population in the OECD countries are aware of climate change and more than 60% of them deem climate change a serious threat for the sustainable livelihood and international security [1]. An investigation of the European Investment Bank (EIB) shows that 91% of Europeans consider climate change as an existential risk. 72% of the Europeans support the idea of the extension of carbon tax on consumption in order to reduce environmental degradation. A total of 44% of Europeans support stricter pollution controls on industry and especially on the energy sector [2,3]. Despite their relatively low Climate Change Performance Index, which condenses the climate protection performance of 57 countries, the OECD members Australia, Canada and the US belong to the countries with strong awareness of the risks related to climate change, and have relatively stringent environmental regulations in the global comparison. In 2012, Australia introduced an emission trading system (ETS). In 2018,

Canada kicked off a nation-wide ETS. Nine northern US states and California price carbon, whereby only California has a carbon pricing system that covers a substantial share of emissions and has an appropriate carbon price (15 USD per metric ton CO_2). The northern states massively underprice carbon emissions. Nevertheless, the overwhelming majority of Americans support the revenue-neutral carbon tax, i.e., if the collected taxes are used directly to protect and upgrade the natural environment [4].

The awareness on climate change risks and the importance of environmental regulations is steadily increasing in developing countries too [5]. In countries such as Ecuador, Bangladesh, Trinidad and Tobago, and Venezuela, for instance, the level of awareness of climate change risks, with 99%, 98%, 97% and 98%, respectively, is even higher than in some advanced countries [1]. Faure and Partain [5] point out that less developed countries have greater challenges in terms of financial leeway and institutional capacities for the formulation of efficient environmental policies and implementation of the corresponding regulations. The huge gap in the Environmental Performance Index (EPI) between advanced and developing countries shows that rising environmental awareness in the Global South is still not enough for bridging this gap [6].

In tendency, developing countries still have laxer environmental regulations, especially in terms of carbon emissions, which are manifested in the geography of the pricing or taxing emissions. Worldwide, there are only 40 countries that have already introduced or have concrete plans for taxing emissions that emanate from combusting fossil fuels like coal, oil and natural gas. Most of them are high-income countries. None of the low-income countries impose a carbon tax. Developing nations that consider a carbon tax, including China, Mexico, South Africa, Turkey, Indonesia, Kazakhstan and Brazil, are all emerging high to middle-income economies [7].

The differences in the content and stringency of environmental policies in combination with trade liberalization could trigger the relocation of pollution-intensive industries or the divisions of value chains from industrialized economies to the jurisdictions with lax or no environmental regulations. Even with carbon taxing in the respective developing countries, the tax burden in the developing areas, imposed on the same multinational enterprise for the same amount of emissions, is in the developing areas much than in the advanced and emerging economies [3]. This kind of internationalization of the value chains of the pollution-intensive industrial production, dubbed "pollution haven hypothesis" (PHH) or "carbon leakage", has been first proposed by Copeland and Taylor [8].

The central problem in the context of the global climate change is not only the relocation of the "dirty" industries to the countries with lax or no environmental regulations, but rather the net increase of emissions due to lax environmental regulations in the new locations. If so, then outsourcing of the production from the developed to the developing countries has a positive net carbon footprint. One example: the recycling of old batteries in the US is a stringently regulated area because of the health risks related to the lead contained in batteries. Mexico has no regulation of these processes and thus has morphed, at least with regards to the recycling of old batteries, into a pollution haven for the US [9].

In 2015, the contemporary "workshop of the global manufacturing", People's Republic of China initiated eight pioneer ETS projects in Beijing, Shanghai, Guangdong, Hunei, Tianjin, Chongging and Shenzgen. In 2020 China plans to introduce a countrywide ETS system. Could the planned implementation of a China-wide ETS trigger a new wave of relocation of dirty industries from China to other jurisdictions with surplus labor and substantial natural resources, such as Sub-Saharan Africa, Central Asia and South-East Asia? Or would the nation-wide ETS in China rather stimulate carbon-saving innovations? Thus, the upcoming implementation of ETSs in a number of developing and transitioning economies, the increasing environmental stringency in the OECD countries, especially Germany, and the EU's planned carbon border tax all contribute to the topicality of the analysis of the responsiveness of carbon-intensive manufacturing to the increasing tightness of environmental regulations.

The paper at hand reappraises the pollution haven hypothesis (PHH) with a refined dataset for 26 OECD member countries and advanced cointegration methods, which have not been employed for the analysis of the PHH yet. To this end, the study analyzes the nexus between the stringency of environmental policies in the OECD member countries and carbon leakage. The study also accounts for the possibly of the mitigating power of the Porter effect. The Porter effect, also known as Porter hypothesis (PoH), has been suggested by Porter and van der Linde [10]. According to PoH, strict environmental regulation fosters alternative business models, for instance the implementation of resource-efficient production processes based on circular economy and the development of climate mitigating technological advances [11,12]. Under the burden of environmental regulation, the companies develop new production techniques that lead to first-mover advantages and learning by doing effects. Despite its prominence, the empirical validation of the PoH has been confined to the companies striving cost leadership, which have relatively small product portfolios [13].

Despite a large and rigorous corpus of theoretical literature on the PHH, the empirical cross-country literature on the PHH and PoH is rather inconclusive [14–16]. In addition, there is a host of incongruences related to the employed indicators of environmental policy stringency and technological adjustment. Further, with the exception of Jobert et al. [16], there is no known empirical analysis of the PHH that accounts for the time series character of the analyzed data.

The paper contributes to the literature on the PHH in three ways. First, it suggests a tractable analytical model of environmental degradation in the framework of the calculus of variations. The model disentangles the forces determining the magnitude of environmental degradation. Second, the study employs for the first time the Environmental Policy Stringency Index (EPSI), the recycling rate and imported carbon emissions of the OECD for the test of the pollution haven conjecture. The mentioned variables are more precise and yield more reliable estimation results. Previous literature mostly employed rather fuzzy indicators of the PHH, such as gross greenhouse gases (GHGs) or total CO_2 emissions. The third contribution of this inquiry is related to the employed estimation methodology. This is the first study that accounts at the same time for issues such as panel heterogeneity and mixed stationarity in the assessment of the PHH by employing pooled mean group (PMG) estimators proposed by Pesaran et al. [17].

The paper proceeds as follows. Section 2 analyzes the relevant literature. In Section 3 we descriptively illustrate two scenarios, whereby the national reduction of the GHGs is driven by the relocation of the carbon-intensive manufacturing overseas. Section 4 sets out a variational analytical model that identifies, on the theoretical level, the sectoral composition of the economy and the level of economic development as the primary factors that determine the level of pollution in the individual economies. Section 5 is dedicated to the underlying estimation methodology. Section 6 delves into data issues. In Section 7, we present the estimation results, and Section 8 concludes.

2. Structural Change and Environmental Degradation

The discussion on economic activities and pollution dynamics dates back to the early 1970s as the economists of the "Club of Rome" in the *Limits to Growth* reawakened the old views of the classics, David Ricardo and Thomas Malthus, that in the face of the finiteness of the natural resources and environmental endowments, growth of the economies cannot be sustained in the long term [18]. They urged instead for zero-growth steady state economies [19]. This lead to the surge of the theoretical elaborations on optimal growth, abatement policies and trade openness [20–22]. These studies were in line with the recommendations of the "Club of Rome". Nevertheless, there were also critical voices. The most influential of them was Malenbaum [23,24], who strengthened the World Steel Association's Intensity-of-Use (IoU) hypothesis. The IoU hypothesis has been predicated on the analysis of the relationship between metal-intensity and per capita income [25]. He detected an inverted U-shaped relationship between metal-intensity and the average income.

Although Malenbaum [24] points to the improvement of the efficiency of intermediate inputs and structural change, expressed in the tertiarization of the economy, as the cause of the declining material intensity of the GDP, he considers the structural component of the mentioned phenomenon as the primary driver of the declining material intensity. Although Malenbaum [23,24] addressed the increasing efficiency of intermediate input use, he ignored the role of innovation in finding the substitutes. Substitutes like plastics contributed substantially to the reduction of the metal-intensity of modern manufacturing [26]. Hence, the underlying idea behind the IoU hypothesis is deeply rooted in the structuralist paradigm of economic modernization [27–34]. De Bruyn [35] defines structural transformation in the ecological context as "quantitative and qualitative changes in the composition of economic activities that result in different environmental pressures".

At the pre-capitalist stage of economic development, the economy is based on subsistence, i.e., not mechanized agriculture, primitive handicraft, petty trading and domestic service [36]. At this stage, only labor force is the essential production factor. Capital at this stage consists only of the primitive means of production and has a negligible contribution to the value creation, i.e., gross domestic product [37]. The material and energy requirements in the pre-capitalist milieu are low. The initial capital accumulation and burgeoning capitalism hallmark a take-off in terms of economic growth.

The take-off leads to the growth of the material- and energy-intensive activities, such as construction, mining and manufacturing. After the demand for the manufactured goods, houses, factories, transport infrastructure and power generation stations has been satiated, the demand for services starts to increase [25]. This is in line with the predictions of Engel [38] and Pasinetti [39,40]. The tertiary sector is less material- and energy-intensive than manufacturing, mining and construction. Advancing tertiarization leads to the decreasing material and energy use per unit of GDP [41]. Hence, the material and energy intensity of the economy starts to decline.

The seminal contribution of Grossmann and Krueger [42,43] led to the re-awakening and proliferation of Malenbaum's ideas [24]. Their work has been inspired by the foundation of the North American Free Trade Agreement (NAFTA) and its related environmental risks for Mexico. The authors re-detected an inverted U-shaped relationship between the level of the average income and environmental degradation. This gave an impetus for the burgeoning of studies delving into the role of environmental regulations and trade liberalization as the concomitants of the growing level of the average income. Because of its analogy to the Kuznets curve hypothesis suggested by Kuznets Simon [44], Panayoutou [45] dubbed this relationship the environmental Kuznets curve (EKC).

The idea behind EKC is in line with the explanation of the IoU hypothesis, which foregrounds the change of the sectoral structure as the primary explanation of the EKC. In the following, the intensity of the environmental degradation is delineated graphically in Figure 1. The phases of economic development have been separated by the dashed vertical lines. In the pre-capitalist economy, there is an intact environment because of the relatively low intensity of the anthropogenic impact on natural amenities. The economy evolves at a low level of subsistence income. After capitalistic "take off" and the emergence of the manufacturing, mining and market-oriented agriculture, the economy starts to grow at a greater pace. Hence, the slope of the environmental degradation curve becomes steeper in the industrialization phase. Manufacturing is the leading sector that fuels growth in all the sectors by growing itself [46–48].

Economic growth in the industrializing societies correspond with the increasing environmental degradation. A higher level of income and the resulting tertiarization lead to a greater environmental awareness, and pushes cleaner production techniques [49,50]. Services, in contrast to mining and manufacturing, have a much smaller emission factor [51]. This leads to the leveling off and gradual decline of environmental degradation [49]. As depicted in Figure 1, at the last stage the level of degradation starts to decrease. Besides of tertiarization, the rise of the knowledge economy also contributes to a greater material-efficiency of the economy.

A group of influential environmental and resource economists, such as Kenneth Arrow, Bert Bolin, Robert Constanza, Partha Dasgupta, Carl Folke, C.S. Holling, Bengt-Owe Jansson, Simon Levin, Karl-Göran Möler, Chares Perrigs and David Pimentel intervened decisively in the debate on the EKC hypothesis with their joint paper in Arrow et al. [52] in *Science*, and expressed their skepticism concerning the growth optimism in the context of the EKC hypothesis. The authors agreed with the underlying logic behind the cleaning effect of economic growth:

"One explanation of this finding is that poor countries cannot afford to emphasize amenities over material well-being. Consequently, in the earlier stages of economic development, increased pollution is regarded as acceptable side effect of economic growth. However, when a country has attained a sufficiently high standard of living, people give greater attention to environmental amenities. This leads to environmental legislation, new institutions for the protection of environment, and so forth." ([52], p. 106).

Notwithstanding basic agreement with the EKC hypothesis, the authors also mention a number of reasons for caution in interpreting the nonlinear income–environment nexus. The central cause for the skepticism, especially concerning global atmospheric pollution with stock pollutants such as carbon dioxide, is related to the global implications of the emissions. If reduction in the pollutant in one country leads to the transfers of pollutants to other countries, then the net GHG footprint is not necessarily negative. This was the reflection of the awareness about the role of international trade as the catalyst of the pollution haven formation in jurisdictions with lax or no environmental regulations [8].

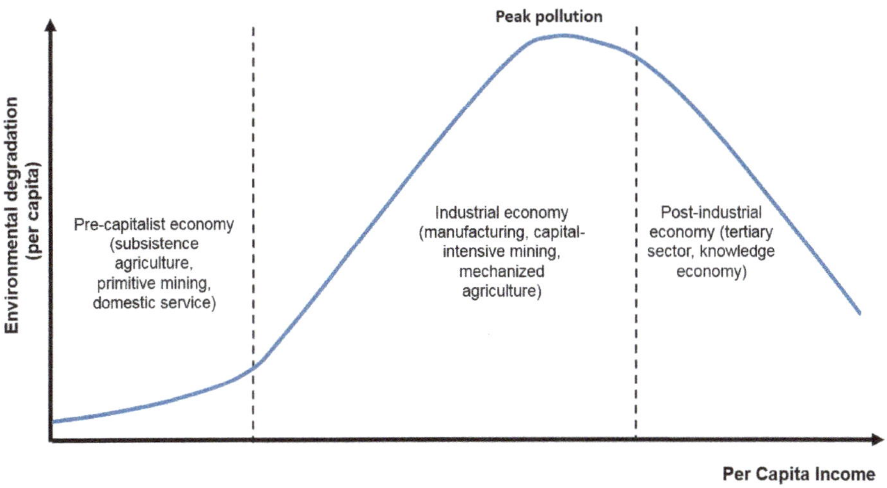

Figure 1. Structuralist approach to the environmental Kuznets curve (EKC).

According to Malenbaum [24], developing countries at the industrialization stage have, similarly to the advanced economies, rapidly increasing emission dynamics. Nevertheless, assuming that South Korea in the early stages of its industrialization in the 1970s repeated the emission intensity of Great Britain in the 1860s is not correct. Due to a substantial progress in knowledge and available technologies, the South Korean steel industry in the 1970s was much cleaner than that of advanced capitalist countries at the end of the nineteenth century. Further, Malenbaum [24] refers also to the contemporary differences in the state of the technology between advanced and developing nations at many instances. Richard Auty [26], in his reference, writes that Malenbaum [24] states that although material usage intensity patterns of the developing countries will be lower than those of rich countries at comparable levels of per capita GDP, they will be unable to fully adopt the best of modern technologies that are mostly available in the technologically advanced economies with stringent environmental policies.

Besides the stringency of environmental regulations and the technology gap, there is also a third essential barrier for the deployment of advanced carbon-saving technologies from the Global North to the Global South. This is the underdevelopment of the intellectual property rights (IPRS) regime, which is regulated by the World Trade Organization Agreement on Trade related Aspects of the IPRs (TRIPS) [53]. Enforcement of IPRs protection does not generate higher transfer of environmental technologies due to the poor governance, the small size of the economies and the low level of the corresponding scale effects [54,55]. Maskus and Reichman [56] indicate the need for a balanced approach to the issue of the attraction of the foreign direct investments(FDI) and carbon-mitigating technology transfers in the context of the Global South. Littleton [53], by contrast, takes the view that in the face of a greater responsibility of the developed countries, this balance has to be tilted towards technology transfer from the Global North to the Global South. In our opinion, the financial and institutional assistance for the transfers of the carbon-saving technologies has to be implemented in the framework of international development cooperation. A larger deployment of climate-friendly technologies in the least developed countries could substantially reduce the negative environmental externalities on the global scale stemming from the relocation of polluting industries.

3. Juxtaposing the Environmental Kuznets Curve and Pollution Haven Hypotheses

In this subsection, by juxtaposing the EKC hypothesis with the PHH, we show graphically that an inverted U-shaped income–environment relationship could be the result of the relocation of carbon-intensive production divisions overseas, i.e., the establishment of pollution havens. Broadening of the perspective from the national EKC to the international or global pollution framework is necessary in the context of the global climate change, whereby atmosphere serves as a global common good as sink for global GHGs.

We illustrate two scenarios whereby the international mobility of the manufacturing value chains imply that in the context of global environment, the observed national EKCs are just artifacts. Furthermore, the national EKCs can incur not only an emission-neutral but also an emission-augmenting effect. The scenarios are illustrated in Figure 2.

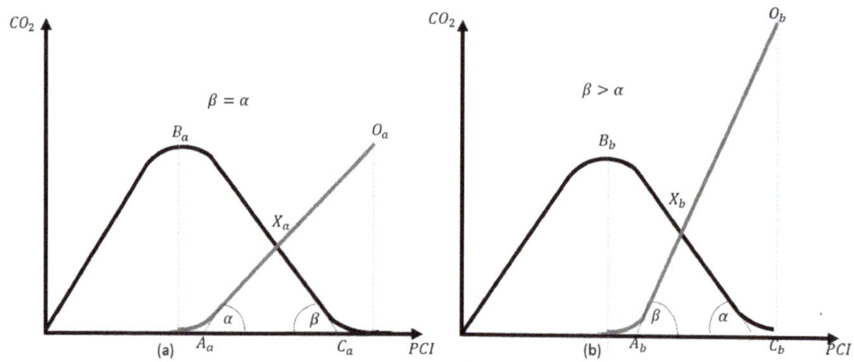

Figure 2. Carbon leakage with (**a**) zero and (**b**) negative net greenhouse gas (GHG) footprint.

The first scenario is a zero-sum relocation, whereby the migration of the dirty industries to the less-developed countries has a zero net effect on carbon emissions. The emissions in one country are now emitted in another country using the same production and abatement technologies (Figure 2a). Under these conditions, the inverted U-shaped income–environment relationship comes to its own via carbon leakage. Hence, this kind of carbon leakage leads to the realization of the spurious environmental upgrading effect and has no effect on the gross carbon intensity for the production of the same amount of goods. Figure 2b depicts a situation whereby the industries are relocating to the jurisdictions, where the output of the same quantity of output requires more carbon emissions than production at home.

Because of the identity of the emission factors under scenario (a), the angles α and β of the triangle $A_aX_aC_a$ are equal. This implies that the carbon leakage equals the reduction of carbon emissions at home. Under scenario (b), the angle β of the triangle $A_bX_bC_b$ is greater than the angle α, i.e., one unit reduction of emissions at home leads to a more than one unit increase of emissions abroad. Hence, this is a scenario with a net positive carbon footprint. The scenario (b) holds if the jurisdictions have different technologies or environmental regulations concerning environmental pollution. The triangle $A_aO_aC_a$ indicates pollution overseas that can be attributed to relocation or outsourcing of the domestic industry in the case of homogenous emission factors. In the case whereby the foreign jurisdiction has a greater emission factor, i.e., scenario (b), the emissions that could be attributed to relocation of outsourcing of the domestic industries are commensurate with the triangle $A_bO_bC_b$. The negative net footprint of this kind of internationalization of production equals the difference between the areas of $A_aO_aC_a$ and $A_bO_bC_b$.

Nevertheless, the assumption of the general technology gap between the heavy industries of developing and developed countries is not straightforward, especially if the countries of interest are not practicing import substitution policies. This holds even more for World Trade Organization (WTO) member states. Most pollution-intensive industries are heavy industries, such as metallurgy, the petroleum industry and cement production. To survive in the global competition, these industries are competing with each other for technological leadership that leads to cost advantage. Labor-technology substitution possibilities are rather limited in these capital-intensive industries. Especially the metallurgy and petroleum industries of the Global South are the "islands of modernity" in the terms of Sir Arthur Lewis [36]. They are comparable to the analogous sectors in the Global North. The only systematic difference with regards to technology that could favor the competitiveness of the developing countries is related to the lax regulations and taxation of polluting activities in the less-developed countries.

4. A Model of Environmental Degradation

We suppose that at t_0 there is a fixed amount, E_0, which is the stock of the natural environment. In the context of the proposed model, we could think of the natural environment as a measure of total natural environment or a specific aspect of it, e.g., the available soil, water or air resources. Johnson et al. [57] confine the natural environment to the part of the total environment that has not been affected by human culture, that is, without anthropogenic intervention. $E(t)$ is the measure of environmental degradation in period t, whereby environmental degradation in contrast to natural or environmental change is a disturbance that sources from the human intervention into the natural environment ([57], p. 584).

In the framework of this investigation we focus on carbon dioxide emissions. Hence, environmental degradation in the framework of this model is related to the extraction of fuel and nonfuel mineral endowments, their refinement and combustion. It is assumed that the exploitation of fossil riches contributes to the gross economic value added of the country. This utility has a monetary value. For the sake of simplicity, we normalize the contribution of one unit of the environmental quality to the value added to $q(t)$. T is the time juncture at which the use of the environmental assets stops due to the depletion or increasing costs related to the degradation of environmental quality or arriving at the critical mass (disutility) concerning air, soil or water quality [58]. Hence,

$$\int_0^T E(t)dt \le E_0 \tag{1}$$

To simplify the presentation, we assume without any loss of generality that there are no extraction costs. The society carries costs, i.e., externalities that are related to the depletion of the natural environments, $C(E(t),t)$. These are the externalities of the manufacturing sector. These costs depend on the magnitude of the resource revenue in period t, $E(t)$. Thus, we denote the costs incurred due to depletion of environmental goods as $C(E(t),\ t)$.

The economic value added (EVA) is related to environmental degradation, commensurate with the following expression:

$$\textit{Economic Value Added} = q(t)E(t) + M(E(t),t) - C(E(t),t) \tag{2}$$

$M(E(t),t)$ is part of the manufacturing output minus costs, i.e., manufacturing value added (MVA), which is attributed to the exploitation of the natural environment. $M(E(t),t)$ is not the total manufacturing sector output. It is its part that can be attributed to the existence of the extractives' sector.

If r is the relevant discount rate then the total discounted EVA in the relevant time horizon, $[0;T]$, is commensurate with

$$\int_0^T EVA_t^E = \int_0^T [q(t)E(t) + M(E(t),t) - C(E(t),t)]e^{-rt}dt \tag{3}$$

We want to find time, T, and the magnitude of environmental degradation, $E(t)$, which maximize Equation (3) subject to the constraint of Equation (1). This problem can be analyzed in the variational framework and yields a tractable result because it is a special case with regards to the functional form and transversality condition [59]. Due to the fact that the terminal point is not fixed, there may be many paths satisfying the Euler equation. To pick up the correct transversality conditions, i.e., the terminal condition that can distinguish the optimal path from those satisfying the Euler equation, we have to figure out the terminal condition [60]. The terminal condition for the problem in Equation (3) is consistent with the following Condition (4) [59–62]:

$$\mathrm{E(t_1) \geq E_1,\ t_1\ free,\ E_1\ fixed} \tag{4}$$

This implies that environmental degradation lasts as long as there is a budget surplus ($E(t_1) \geq E_1$) and there is no restriction on the last time period (*variable-time problem*) with environmental degradation, t_1. The transversality conditions for the terminal condition are expressed in Equation (5a,b):

$$\left(F'_E\right)_{t=t_1} \leq 0\ (= 0\ if\ E^*(t_1) > E_1 \tag{5a}$$

$$(F - EF'_E)_{t=t_1} = 0 \tag{5b}$$

$S(t)$ is the remaining stock of the natural environment at time t, whereby

$$S(t) = E_0 - \int_0^t E(t)dt \tag{6}$$

Thus, $S(t) = -E(t)$ and our problem is as follows:

$$\left.\begin{array}{c} \max\limits_{S(t),T} \int_0^T [-q(t)S(t) + M(S(t),t) - C(-S(t),t)]e^{-rt}dt \\ E(0) = E_0,\ S(T) \geq 0 \end{array}\right\} \tag{7}$$

The integrand Function (7) does not contain all three arguments of the objective functional, $F(t, S(t),\ S(t))$. S(t), the remaining stock of the natural environment, is missing from the integrand function F. This is one of four special cases in the calculus of variations, which yields a special version of the Euler equation ([61], pp. 37–45). This is a special case of the form $F = F(t,S)$ whereby F does not depend on S but rather on its degradation rate, $S(t)$. This implies that $F'_S = 0$. Hence, the Euler equation, $\frac{\partial F}{\partial S} - \frac{d}{dt}\left(\frac{\partial F}{\partial S}\right) = 0$, reduces to $\frac{dF_S}{dt} = 0\ \forall\ t \in [0,\ T]$. This implies that the time derivative of F'_x(t,x) is 0 $\forall\ t \in [0,\ T]$. This, after integration, yields the following solution of the Euler first-order differential equation:

$$\frac{\partial F(t,S)}{\partial S} = constant \tag{8}$$

Applied for our problem, the Euler equation corresponds with the following expression, Equation (9):

$$[-q(t) - M'_E(-S(t),t) + C'_E(-S(t),t)]e^{-rt} = -c \tag{9}$$

whereby c is an arbitrary constant.

According to the transversality condition corresponding to the terminal requirements $(F'_x)_{t=t_1} \leq 0\ (= 0\ if\ x^*(t_1) > x_1)$, the left-hand-side of (9) is equal or less than zero (≤0) at $t = T$. Hence, c ≥ 0, and (9) can be rewritten as:

$$[-q(t) - M'(-S(t),t) + C'_E(-S(t),t)] = -ce^{rt} \tag{10}$$

$$[q(t) + M'(-S(t),t) - C'_E(-S(t),t)] = ce^{rt} \tag{11}$$

The left-hand side of this equation is the marginal contribution of the environmental degradation to EVA ($\frac{\partial EVA(E(t),t)}{\partial E(t)}$). Thus, (12) tells us that in the optimum the marginal contribution of environmental degradation must increase exponentially with a rate equal to the discount factor r [59].

Assuming that the discount factor r is a measure for the marginal returns of capital employed in the activities related to environmental degradation has repercussions on the intensity of environmental degradation. Greater discount rates correspond with a less advanced stage of economic development. This is in line with the Solow model of economic growth, which predicts decreasing returns on capital employed until marginal utility of one unit of additional investment leads to zero growth of the per capita income [63]. This means that in advanced economies, such as Japan or the European Union, with negligibly low or negative interest rates, we could expect zero or negative growth of profits induced by the environmental degradation. Zero growth of profits related to environmental degradation corresponds with environmental conservation and negative profits induced by environmental degradation correspond with environmental upgrading. By contrast, in less-developed countries, which have scarce capital stock, environmental degradation that leads to capital accumulation subsequently has a greater contribution (shadow value) to the economic value added. Hence, we could expect a greater level of the environmental degradation in the less-developed countries.

Equation (5b) represents the second transversality condition corresponding to the terminal requirements of our problem as represented in Equation (6), which is:

$$(F - SF'_S)_{t=t_1} = 0 \tag{12}$$

Applied to Equation (7), the second transversality condition (12) has the following form:

$$\begin{aligned}[-q(T)S(T) + M\quad &(-S(T),T) - C(-S(T),T)]e^{-rT} \\ &-S(T)[-q(T) - M'(-S(T),T) + C'_E(-S(T),T)]e^{-rT} = 0\end{aligned} \tag{13}$$

After some basic transformations, Equation (13) can be reformulated as follows (for a detailed derivation see Appendix A):

$$\frac{\partial C(-S(T),T)}{\partial E}\ \frac{E}{C(-S(T),T)} = 1 + \frac{M(E(t),t)}{C(-S(T),T)}\left(\frac{\partial M(-S(T),T)}{\partial E}\ \frac{E}{M(-S(T),T)} - 1\right) \tag{14}$$

$\frac{\partial M(-S(T),T)}{\partial E}\ \frac{E}{M(-S(T),T)}$ on the right-hand side of Equation (14) is the elasticity of the manufacturing sector with respect to the extraction of natural resources and environmental degradation ε_M.

$$\varepsilon_E^C = \frac{\partial C(-S(T),T)}{\partial E}\ \frac{E}{C(-S(T),T)} = 1 + \frac{M(E(t),t)}{C(-S(T),T)}(\varepsilon_M - 1) \tag{15}$$

Without nature's contribution to the MVA, Equation (14) would have the following form:

$$\varepsilon_E^C = \frac{\partial C(-S(T),T)}{\partial E} \frac{E}{C(-S(T),T)} = 1 \tag{16}$$

This implies that the social optimizer continues exploiting the environment and resources until the juncture at which the elasticity of costs with respect to depletion is unity.

According to Equation (15), in the case with linkages between the manufacturing sector and the exploitation of the environment and resources, extraction stops at a time at which the elasticity of externality related costs with respect to the extraction, ε_E^C, is $\left[1 + \frac{M(E(t),t)}{C(-S(T),T)}(\varepsilon_M - 1)\right]$. The value of this term depends on MVA^E, its ratio to the costs of exploitation, $\frac{M(E(t),t)}{C(-S(T),T)}$ and the value of ε_M. As mentioned above, based on the theoretical elaborations and empirical evidence we expect a positive sign for $(\partial M(E(t),\ t))/(\partial\, E(t)) > 0)$ and consequently for ε_M $(=\left(\frac{\partial M(-S(T),T)}{\partial E} \frac{E}{M(-S(T),T)}\right)$ because $\frac{E}{M(-S(T),T)} \geq 0$. Hence, $(1 - \varepsilon_M)$ and consequently the whole right-hand side of Equation (15) is positive. The magnitude is mostly dependent on the ratio of MVA^E and the costs of exploitation, $\frac{M(E(t),t)}{C(-S(T),T)}$. If the manufacturing sector benefits more from the exploitation of nature, a larger manufacturing sector implies a higher value for ε_E^C. This means that in optimum in an economy with a great contribution of environmental degradation to the MVA, depletion of environmental amenities stops at a greater threshold.

The left-hand side of the elasticity model in Equation (15) indicates the responsiveness of the environment and mineral endowments-related externalities at the subjective optimum of the social optimizer in a hypothetical country. The equation reveals that a greater ratio of environment and resources' contribution to the MVA to externalities corresponds to a greater threshold for ε_E^C if $(\varepsilon_M - 1) > 0$. This means that as long as a one percent increase in the exploitation of nature leads to more than a one percent increase of the MVA^E, then the level of the acceptable degradation is greater than 1. If a one percent increase of the exploitation of natural environment leads to less than one percent of environmental degradation then an increase of exploitation of the environment and minerals by one percent leads to less than a one percent increase of the externalities. In accordance with the law of diminishing returns, increasing use of the natural resources leads to a gradually decreasing yield. This means that at the saturation phase of manufacturing a relatively low value of ε_M can be expected. This would reduce the frontiers of the acceptable pollution from the perspective of the social optimizer.

To assure this level of nature use the government would induce environmental regulations and conservation policies. This threshold is much higher in the more natural resource-based and pollution-intensive industries. Knowledge or tertiary sector-reliant economies are less dependent on the exploitation of natural resources and environmental degradation. Hence, the heavy industry that has the greatest carbon footprint faces a greater regulatory burden in the face of the increasing stringency of environmental regulations than the cleaner tertiary sector or knowledge economy. This has been confirmed in the framework of a multisector elasticity model in Sadik-Zada, Loewenstein and Hasanli [64].

This means that the pollution threshold is endogenous to the stage of economic development, and this threshold can be satisfied by employing cleaner production technologies or by outsourcing dirty industries in the countries that experience the industrialization phase. This decision depends on a myriad of factors.

Whether such costs could really trigger the relocation of the heavy industry overseas is nevertheless a question, which can only be answered after the scrutiny of the individual industry cases. Environmental degradation and related costs are just one of many facets that determine the relocation decision of the individual firms [65–69]. Resource and asset seeking, market seeking and efficiency seeking are three major factors that could trigger the multinational enterprises to relocate their production facilities [69]. Lax environmental regulations are often not a sufficient condition for relocation. Especially the narrowness of the local markets and lack of a skilled labor force could outweigh the advantages provided by lax environmental regulations.

5. Methodology

The literature identifies three problems related to the empirical analysis of issues related to international trade flows, environmental policies and atmospheric pollution. These are aggregation bias, panel heterogeneity and unobserved foreign regulation [16,70,71]. To account for these problems, the study employs pooled mean group (PMG) and dynamic fixed effects (DFE) estimators.

Our empirical strategy is in line with Cavalcanti et al. [72] and is based on the following model specification:

$$\ln PHH_{it} = a_j + \beta_{j1} \ln\_Stringency_{jt} + \beta_{j2} \ln\_PoH_{jt} + \beta_{j3} X_{jt} + u_{ij} \tag{17}$$

where a_j denotes country-specific fixed effects, $\ln\_Stringency_{jt}$ is the indicator for the stringency of environmental policies and $\ln\_PoH_{jt}$ is a proxy for the technological progress induced by environmental regulations for countries $j = \overline{1,J}$ and time periods $t = \overline{1,T}$. The major focus of this study is, nevertheless, on the bivariate relationship between income inequality and fine wine imports. The advantage of the parsimoniousness of the model is that the broad number of country-specific time-irreversible factors is captured by the country-specific deterministic factor. The same holds for u_{ij} with respect to the unobserved common factors [72].

The unit root tests indicate that the variables of interest are a mixture of stationary at level, I(0), and first difference, I(1). Hence, the fixed effect, random effect or generalized method of moments (GMM) estimators requiring the stationarity of all time series are not efficient in this case. In addition, the pooling of the individual groups in the fixed effects, random effects and GMM implies the identity of all the slope coefficients across countries. As shown in Pesaran et al. [17], this assumption is mostly statistically inconsistent.

For the mixture of the I(0) and I(1) series, the autoregressive distributed lag (ARDL) based mean group (MG) or PMG procedure are the feasible methodology. The model crashes if one of the estimation variables is a I(2) process [17]. (P)MG also solves the endogeneity problem by taking into consideration the feedback effects. The endogeneity issue, nevertheless, is not the central issue, in the estimations because it is plausible to assume that wine imports do not influence the level of income inequality or wealth concentration nor the level of income in the respective countries. Due to the mixture of I(0) and I(1) series, panel heterogeneity and cross-sectional dependence, we employ the panel analysis techniques suggested in Pesaran et al. [17]. The choice between MG and PMG estimators has to be made based on the Hausman test. PMG yields homogenous long-run coefficients, but allows for country-specific intercepts, short-run coefficients (adjustment speed) and error variances [73]. Based on the Hausman test statistics for the case of Dataset 2, we conclude that the PMG estimator, the efficient estimator under the null hypothesis, is preferred. Due to missing values, the implementation of the MG estimation in the case of the Dataset 1 was not feasible. For this reason, the results for Dataset 1 are confined to the presentation of the PMG estimators.

6. Data

In contrast to the existing empirical literature on the environmental regulation–trade nexus, the study does not employ gross imports as a measure of strength of the PHH; and per capita GDP, energy efficiency, returns on energy invested of gross greenhouse gas emissions, rule of law or other institutional variables are employed as the measure of environmental regulations [74,75]. As a measure of the PHH intensity we employ the novel methodology for the approximation of the carbon emissions from fossil fuel combustion in imports in megatons of CO_2 ($MtCO_2$). This methodology has been suggested in Wiebe and Yamano [76]. They combine the OECD Inter-Country Input–Output (ICIO) database with statistics on carbon emissions. The data have been generated on the basis of a computable input–output model translated into carbon terms by multiplying the values by carbon emission factors.

To quantify the emission multiplier for final demand, carbon intensities are combined with the Leontief inverse of the ICIO. The fuel combustion database of the International Energy Agency (IEA) provided the data on carbon emissions from fossil fuels.

The data are available for 26 OECD countries for the time interval between 1995 and 2011. The countries are the following: Australia, Austria, Belgium, Canada, Czech Republic, Denmark, Finland, France, Germany, Greece, Hungary, Ireland, Italy, Japan, Korea, Netherlands, Norway, Poland, Portugal, Slovak Republic, Spain, Sweden, Switzerland, Turkey, UK, and the US. To assure its compatibility with the PHH, the approximations of the quantity of the carbon emissions embodied in trade are calculated under the equal carbon intensity (ECI) assumption, because taking the emission factors of the developing countries with inferior environmental technologies would substantially overstate the magnitude of the pollution haven effect. Because of its congruence with the PHH, Garsous [75] himself suggests employing carbon emissions embodied in the trade indicator as an instrument for the strength of the PHH. Table 1 below shows the description of the data used in this study.

Table 1. Description of data.

Variable	Description/Transformation	Source
Carbon emissions embodied in imports	This indicator reports the per capita carbon emissions from fossil fuel combustion embodied in imports and exports in for 63 countries and 34 industries between 1995 and 2011.	OECD (2020)
Recycling rate	The share of the recycled municipal waste. This dataset shows data provided by member countries' authorities through the questionnaire on the state of the environment (OECD/Eurostat). They were updated or revised on the basis of data from other national and international sources available to the OECD Secretariat, and on the basis of comments received from national delegates (OECD 2020).	OECD (2020)
Environmental policy stringency	The OECD Environmental Policy Stringency Index (EPS) is a country-specific and internationally comparable measure of the stringency of environmental policy. Stringency is defined as the degree to which environmental policies put an explicit or implicit price on polluting or environmentally harmful behavior.	OECD (2020)
Trade openness	Trade is the sum of exports and imports of goods and services measured as a share of gross domestic product.	WB WDI (2020)
Environmentally adjusted multifactor productivity (EAMFP)	EAMFP growth measures the residual growth in the joint production of both the desirable and the undesirable outputs that cannot be explained by changes in the consumption of factor inputs (including labor, produced capital and natural capital). Therefore, for a given growth of input use, EAMFP increases when GDP increases or when pollution decreases.	OECD (2020)
Per capita GDP	Average GDP in constant 2010 US Dollars	WB WDI (2020)
Openness	Trade is the sum of exports and imports of goods and services measured as a share of gross domestic product.	WB WDI (2020)

7. Estimation Results

The PMG estimators compiled in Table 2 reveal that the stringency of environmental regulations have no statistically significant short-term effect on carbon imports. The estimations reveal, nevertheless, a strong and statistically significant robust long-run impact of environmental policy stringency on carbon leakage: in the long run, a one percent increase of the level of the environmental policy stringency leads to a 0.304–0.775 percent increase of carbon emissions embodied in imports. The short-run effect of environmental policy stringency vanishes if we control for other variables.

To assess the impact of trade liberalization on carbon leakage, the study employed the share of trade volumes (openness), i.e., the sum of the imports and exports, to GDP, as an independent variable. The estimations show that in the long-run, a one percent increase of trade openness leads to a 0.496–1.012 percent increase of carbon emissions embodies in imports (Models 2 and 3). The results with regards to the short-term effects are not unambiguous: the statistical significance of the positive short-term effect in Model 2 vanishes if we control for the level of the per capita income.

Table 2. Pooled mean group (PMG) estimators.

Dependent variable: Per capita carbon emissions embodied in imports										
VARIABLES	Model 1		Model 2		Model 3		Model 4		Model 5	
	ec	Short Run	ec	Short Run	ec	Short Run	ec	Short Run	ec	Short Run
ec		−0.231 ***		−0.177 ***		−0.193 ***		−0.203 ***		−0.203 ***
		(0.0480)		(0.0454)		(0.0636)		(0.0385)		(0.0385)
D.lnStringency		−0.199 ***		−0.0714		−0.0404		−0.0156		−0.0156
		(0.0540)		(0.0589)		(0.0488)		(0.0381)		(0.0381)
lnStringency	0.775 ***		0.621 ***		0.480 ***		0.304 **		0.304 **	
	(0.0383)		(0.0320)		(0.0357)		(0.123)		(0.123)	
lnOpen			1.012 ***		0.496 ***					
			(0.115)		(0.0702)					
D.lnOpen				0.260 **		0.108				
				(0.108)		(0.0739)				
ln_PCI					0.981 ***		3.101 ***			
					(0.145)		(0.526)			
D.ln_PCI						2.873 ***		2.281 ***		
						(0.309)		(0.251)		
Open							0.000281		0.000281	
							(0.000391)		(0.00039)	
ln_RECLNG							−0.145 **		−0.145 **	
							(0.0678)		(0.0678)	
D.Open								3.06*e* − 05		3.06*e* − 05
								(8.15*e* − 05)		(8.15*e* − 05)
D.ln_RECLNG								−0.0274		−0.0274
								(0.0231)		(0.0231)
lnPCI2									1.550 ***	
									(0.263)	
D.lnPCI2										1.140 ***
										(0.125)
Constant		1.156 ***		−0.0775		−1.583 ***		−5.480 ***		−5.480 ***
		(0.227)		(0.0528)		(0.533)		(1.093)		(1.093)
Observations	400	400	384	384	384	384	.	.	.	.

Standard errors in parentheses. *** $p < 0.01$, ** $p < 0.05$, * $p < 0.1$.

We found that per capita income has a robust statistically significant positive short- and long-run effect on carbon emissions embodied in imports. The long-term elasticity ranges between 0.981 and 3.101 percent. The short-term elasticity ranges between 2.281 and 2.873 percent (Models 3 and 4). We controlled also for the squared value of the natural logarithm of PCI, PCI^2, and found a robust positive relationship between this variable and carbon imports. The long-run coefficient of $(PCI)^2$ is 1.550 and the short-run coefficient of $(PCI)^2$ is 1.140 (Model 5).

To account for the PoH, we employed the recycling rate of the municipal waste as a possible proxy for the development of the carbon-saving technologies and found that their deployment has a statistically significant robust negative impact on carbon imports: in the long term, a one percent increase of the recycling rate leads to a 0.145 percent decrease of carbon emissions embodied in imports. We detected no statistically significant short-term effect of the recycling rate on carbon imports (Models 4 and 5).

Controlling for a more comprehensive proxy for the PoH, the EAMFP, which is, in contrast to the recycling rate, more relevant but less precise, reveals that an increasing EAMPF corresponds with a slight decrease of the long-run carbon imports: a one percent increase of the EAMFP (environmentally adjusted multifactor productivity) leads to a −0.0441 percent decrease of carbon imports (Table A2). To account for the effect of tertiarization, we controlled for the share of the services sector in GDP. The estimations revealed a weak negative long-run effect of tertiarization on carbon imports, whereby the result is not robust (Tables A1 and A2). This could be the consequence of the shortness of the available time series data. Economic structure changed insignificantly between 1995 and 2011.

To address the tertiarization hypothesis, the employment of a longer time series data would be more conclusive.

8. Concluding Remarks

The atmosphere in its function as a sink for GHGs is definitely a global common pool resource. Hence, at least in the context of climate change, a purely national perspective on the environmental Kuznets curve is not satisfactory. The juxtaposition of the two strands of literature—the literature on the EKC on the one side and the pollution haven conjecture on the other side—enabled a substantial broadening of the perspective on the income–environment relationship. The analysis of the income–environment relationship has been extended from a purely national to international perspective.

The relevance of carbon leakage from strictly regulated jurisdictions towards the jurisdictions with lax environmental standards has been emphasized immediately after the proliferation of the EKC hypothesis in the early 1990s by the leading environmental and resource economists [52]. Despite an early impetus to consider the relocation of the pollution-intensive industries overseas, both theoretical and empirical literature ignored the limitations of the purely national perspective. Empirical validation of the inverted U-shaped income–environment relationship for the individual countries and country groups led not only to the empowerment of the EKC to one of most cited stylized facts of the economics discipline, but also to the establishment of the growth optimism with regards to environmental upgrading [77]. The studies to test the pollution haven hypothesis and its antipode, the Porter effect, evolved separately, and not in the context of the environmental Kuznets curve paradigm [16,78].

To address the challenge of merging two concepts—the inward-oriented EKC hypothesis and the pollution haven hypothesis—this study embedded both concepts within the framework of the structuralist paradigm of development economics [27,28,37,79]. To this end, the study set out a simple variational model of environmental degradation. Due to its special case with respect to the transversality conditions, the model yields tractable results in the framework of the calculus of variations [59].

The model revealed that, at least on the theoretical level, the ratio of the absolute utility from environmental degradation to the absolute costs related to environmental degradation, and the elasticity of the manufacturing output with respect to environmental degradation are the determinants of the magnitude of environmental degradation. This has two implications. First, the countries whose manufacturing sector enjoys greater linkages from polluting activities have a greater pollution threshold (peak pollution). Second, the countries that carry greater losses induced by environmental degradation tend to get peak pollution at a lower magnitude of environmental degradation. The crux of the matter is, however, the ratio of the utility to externalities related to environmental degradation.

In addition, the elasticity of the manufacturing sector value added to environmental degradation plays an important role in terms of the actual optimal level of environmental degradation. If a one percent increase in the magnitude of environmental degradation leads to less than a one percent increase of the manufacturing value added, then such an economy does not experience environmental degradation but rather environmental upgrading and follows conservation policies. If we think about this in terms of the Solow model of economic growth, then the economies at the relatively mature stages of economic development have low growth multiplier effects that emanate from the depletion of environmental amenities.

The central implication of this theoretical model is not the determination of the numeric value of the threshold of pollution but rather the recognition of the fact that countries at different stages of economic development have different thresholds of environmental degradation. The stringency of environmental policies is endogenous to this threshold, This result is predicated on the sectoral interaction patterns and sectoral structure of the respective economies. This implies that the same pollution activity could be economically and socially inappropriate for the developed settings and desirable in the less developed settings. These differences provide a basis for the emergence of the pollution havens.

The central argument against the pollution haven hypothesis is related to the small weight of the environmental costs in the share of total costs and the significance of other factors like market and efficiency seeking as determinants of FDI flows. The largest steel companies did not relocate from the advanced countries to the less developed countries. The advantages of the large market size, natural resource base, human capital etc. could countervail the disadvantage of the strict environmental regulations. Under such conditions, deployment of advanced carbon-saving technologies makes more sense than relocating to developing countries. This is the logic behind the Porter hypothesis [11,13,68,80].

The revolution in the time series econometrics in the late 1990s [17], and especially the proliferation of the autoregressive distributed lag models, led to a surge of empirical assessments of the income–environment relationship, and especially the EKC hypothesis for the individual country cases and groups of countries [81]. None of these studies, however, accounted for carbon leakage. The panel estimations, based on the usual fixed or random effects, mostly ignored the time series characteristics of the underlying data, endogeneity issues and heterogeneity of the countries in the dataset. The empirical literature on pollution havens has been employing rather fuzzy instruments to approximate the carbon leakage.

To address all of these issues, the study employed pooled mean group estimators that account both for nonstationarity, endogeneity and panel heterogeneity issues. In addition, the study employs, for the first time, more precise indicators of the environmental policy stringency. pollution haven and Porter effects [72,73].

The pooled mean group estimators provide a strong validation for the pollution haven conjecture. Environmental policy stringency leads to carbon leakage. The limitation of the pollution haven effect by the deployment of the novel carbon-saving technologies is rather weak. Tertiarization, per capita income and trade openness are also drivers of carbon leakage.

The confirmation of the pollution haven hypothesis shows that environmental stringency, which is confined to the boarders of the national state, or even regional integration blocks could lead to sub-optimal solutions in terms of global climate change. Hence, the proposal of the European Commission concerning the EU border carbon tax, if well designed, could contribute to the reduction of the carbon leakage and enhance carbon-saving innovations [82]. This kind of policies has, nevertheless, to be combined with the developmental considerations in developing and especially low-income countries. Because of the decreasing FDI influx owing to the carbon border tax, carbon tariffs could have negative indirect repercussions for the poverty and employment in the developing countries.

Empirical validation of the strong pollution haven and weak Porter effects shows that in reality, the inverted U-shaped income–environment relationship is not an indication for the long-run upgrading of environmental quality or prevention of environmental degradation. Environmental upgrading within advanced economies could be the result of the relocation of dirty industries to the developing areas with lax environmental standards. If so, then the net GHG-emission effect of this kind of relocation is positive. This implies that the national EKC is just an artifact.

Author Contributions: Conceptualization, E.R.S.-Z.; Empirical methodology, E.R.S.-Z. and M.F.; Writing—original draft preparation, E.R.S.-Z. and M.F.; Writing—review and editing, M.F. and E.R.S.Z.; Supervision, E.R.S.-Z. All authors have read and agreed to the published version of the manuscript.

Funding: This research received no external funding.

Acknowledgments: We would like to express our deep gratitude to Wilhelm Loewenstein for his guidance, enthusiastic encouragement and useful critiques of this research work. I would also like to thank Kamiar Mohaddes from the University of Cambridge for his advice on the employment of the pooled mean group approach. We are also grateful to the managing editors and three anonymous reviewers for their helpful comments and suggestions.

Conflicts of Interest: The authors declare no conflict of interests.

Appendix A. Derivation of Equation (14)

$$M(-S(T),T) - C(-S(T),T) - \frac{\partial M(-S(T),T)}{\partial E} \cdot E + \frac{\partial C(-S(T),T)}{\partial E} \cdot E = 0$$

$$\frac{\partial C(-S(T),T)}{\partial E} \cdot E = \frac{\partial M(-S(T),T)}{\partial E} \cdot E + C(-S(T),T) - M(-S(T),T) \qquad \Big| \div C$$

$$\frac{\partial C(-S(T),T)}{\partial E} \frac{E}{C(-S(T),T)} = 1 - \frac{M(-S(T),T)}{C(-S(T),T)} + \frac{\partial M(-S(T),T)}{\partial E} \frac{E}{C(-S(T),T)}$$

$$\Leftrightarrow$$

$$\frac{\partial C(-S(T),T)}{\partial E} \frac{E}{C(-S(T),T)} = 1 - \underbrace{\frac{M(-S(T),T)}{C(-S(T),T)}} + \frac{\partial M(-S(T),T)}{\partial E} \frac{E}{M(-S(T),T)} \underbrace{\frac{M(-S(T),T)}{C(-S(T),T)}}$$

$$\Leftrightarrow$$

$$\frac{\partial C(-S(T),T)}{\partial E} \frac{E}{C((18) - S(T),T)} = 1 + \frac{M(E(t),t)}{C(-S(T),T)} \left(\frac{\partial M(-S(T),T)}{\partial E} \frac{E}{M(-S(T),T)} - 1 \right)$$

Table A1. Multivariate pooled mean group estimator.

	(1)	(2)
VARIABLES	ec	SR
ec		−0.347 ***
		(0.0576)
D.lnStringency		0.0491 **
		(0.0208)
L3D.lnSERV		−0.0256 **
		(0.0116)
D.lnEAMPF		0.0112 *
		(0.00590)
D.ln_PCI		0.698 *
		(0.383)
L2D.lnPCI2		0.185 ***
		(0.0657)
lnStringency	−0.164 ***	
	(0.0589)	
L3.lnSERV	0.0331	
	(0.0287)	
lnEAMPF	−0.0441 *	
	(0.0244)	
ln_PCI	−0.273	
	(0.676)	
L2.lnPCI2	0.345	
	(0.351)	
Constant		−0.773
		(0.701)
Observations	.	.

Standard errors in parentheses. *** $p < 0.01$, ** $p < 0.05$, * $p < 0.1$.

Table A2. Multivariate pooled mean group estimator.

Dependent Variable: Carbon Emissions Embodies in Imports		
VARIABLES	**ec**	**SR**
ec		−0.402 ***
		(0.0518)
D.lnStringency		0.0459 **
		(0.0204)
LD.SERVICES		0.000265
		(0.000189)
D.lnEAMPF		0.00815
		(0.00506)
D.ln_PCI		0.888 ***
		(0.226)
D.ln_RECYCLING		−0.00308
		(0.0116)
lnStringency	−0.125 ***	
	(0.0450)	
L.SERVICES	−0.000525 *	
	(0.000302)	
lnEAMPF	−0.0465 **	
	(0.0193)	
ln_PCI	0.442 ***	
	(0.153)	
ln_RECYCLING	−0.00503	
	(0.0186)	
Constant		0.912
		(0.617)

Standard errors in parentheses. *** $p < 0.01$, ** $p < 0.05$, * $p < 0.1$.

References

1. Lee, T.M.; Markowitz, E.M.; Howe, P.D.; Ko, C.-Y.; Leiserowitz, A.A. Predictors of public climate change awareness and risk perception around the world. *Nat. Clim. Chang.* **2015**, *5*, 1014–1020. [CrossRef]
2. Baristow, J. Majority of Europeans want stricter measures on air quality. *Energy Live News*, 4 December 2019.
3. Mavrokefalidis, D. EU poll shows 72% of EU citizens would back a carbon tax on air travel. *Connectin Energy*, 14 March 2020.
4. Coren, M.J. Americans: We need a carbon tax, but keep the change. *Quartz*, 22 January 2019.
5. Faure, M.G.; Partain, R.A. *The Role of Environmental Law in Developing Countries*; Cambridge University Press (CUP): Cambridge, UK, 2019; pp. 292–314.
6. Conrad, E.; Cassar, L.F. The Environmental Performance Index. In *Routledge Handbook of Sustainability Indicators*; Routledge: Abingdon, UK, 2018; pp. 294–307. [CrossRef]
7. World Bank Carbon Pricing Dashboard. Available online: carbonpricingdashboard.worldbank.org (accessed on 31 January 2020).
8. Copeland, B.R.; Taylor, M.S. Trade, Growth, and the Environment. *J. Econ. Lit.* **2004**, *42*, 7–71. [CrossRef]
9. Rosenthal, E. Lead from old U.S. Batteries sent to Mexico raises risks. *New York Times*, 8 December 2011.
10. Porter, M.E.; Van Der Linde, C. Toward a New Conception of the Environment-Competitiveness Relationship. *J. Econ. Perspect.* **1995**, *9*, 97–118. [CrossRef]
11. D'Adamo, I.; Gastaldi, M.; Rosa, P. Recycling of end-of-life vehicles: Assessing trends and performances in Europe. *Technol. Forecast. Soc. Chang.* **2020**, *152*, 119887. [CrossRef]
12. D'Adamo, I.; Falcone, P.M.; Ferella, F. A socio-economic analysis of biomethane in the transport sector: The case of Italy. *Waste Manag.* **2019**, *95*, 102–115.
13. Frohwein, T.; Hansjürgens, B. Chemicals Regulation and the Porter Hypothesis: A Critical Review of the New European Chemicals Regulation. *J. Bus. Chem.* **2005**, *2*. Available online: https://papers.ssrn.com/sol3/papers.cfm?abstract_id=757645 (accessed on 23 July 2005).

14. Lindahl, S. Environmental Regulations and Pollution Havens. An Empirical Study of the Most Polluting Industries. Master's Thesis, Goteborgs University, Gothenburg, Sweden, 2016.
15. McWilliams, B.; Zachmann, G. A European Carbon Border Tax- Much Pain, Little Gain. *Policy Contrib.* **2020**. Available online: https://www.bruegel.org/wp-content/uploads/2020/03/PC-05-2020-050320v2.pdf (accessed on 15 March 2020).
16. Jobert, T.; Karanfil, F.; Tykhonenko, A. Degree Of Stringency Matters: Revisiting The Pollution Haven Hypothesis Based On Heterogeneous Panels And Aggregate Data. *Macroecon. Dyn.* **2018**, *23*, 2675–2697. [CrossRef]
17. Pesaran, M.H.; Shin, Y.; Smith, R.P. Pooled Mean Group Estimation of Dynamic Heterogeneous Panels. *J. Am. Stat. Assoc.* **1999**, *94*, 621–634. [CrossRef]
18. Ayres, R.; Ayres, L. A Handbook of Industrial Ecology. In *A Handbook of Industrial Ecology*; Edward Elgar Publishing: Cheltenham, UK, 2002.
19. Meadows, D.H.; Meadows, D.L.; Randers, J.; Behrens, W.W. The limits to growth. In *Green Planet Blues: Critical Perspectives on Global Environmental Politics*; Taylor & Francis: Abingdon-on-Thames, Oxfordshire, UK, 1972; ISBN 9780429962295.
20. Baumol, W.J. *Environmental Protection, International Spillovers and Trade*; Almqvist and Wiksell: Stockholm, Sweden, 1971.
21. Markusen, J.R. International externalities and optimal tax structures. *J. Int. Econ.* **1975**, *5*, 15–29. [CrossRef]
22. Siebert, H. Environmental quality and the gains from trade. *Kyklos* **1977**, *30*, 657–673. [CrossRef]
23. Malenbaum, W. *Material Requirements in the United States and abroad in the Year 2000*; US National Commission on Materials Policy; University of Pennsylvania: Philadelphia, PA, USA, 1973.
24. Malenbaum, W. *World Demand for Raw Materials in 1985 and 2000*; McGraw-Hill: New York, NY, USA, 1978.
25. Wårell, L. Trends and developments in long-term steel demand—The intensity-of-use hypothesis revisited. *Resour. Policy* **2014**, *39*, 134–143. [CrossRef]
26. Auty, R. Materials intensity of GDP. *Resour. Policy* **1985**, *11*, 275–283. [CrossRef]
27. Fisher, A.G.B. Production, Primary, Secondary and Tertiary. *Econ. Rec.* **1939**, *15*, 24–38. [CrossRef]
28. Rosenstein-Rodan, P.N. Problems of Industrialisation of Eastern and South-Eastern Europe. *Econ. J.* **1943**, *53*, 202. [CrossRef]
29. Marc, M.S.; Fourastié, J. Le grand espoir du XXe siècle. *Sociétés* **1997**, *57*, 81–90. [CrossRef]
30. Ragnar, N. Problems of Capital Formation in Underdeveloped Countries (1953). In *Trade and Development*; United Nations Conference on Trade and Development: Geneva, Switzerland, 2012.
31. Hirschman, A. *The Strategy of Economic Development*; Yale University Press: New Haven, CT, USA, 1958.
32. Huntington, S.P. Political Development and Political Decay. *World Polit.* **1965**, *17*, 386–430. [CrossRef]
33. Eisenstadt, S. *Modernization: Protest and change (Modernization of Traditional Society)*; Prentice Hall: Upper Saddle River, NJ, USA, 1967.
34. Myint, R.B.H. Asian Drama: An Inquiry into the Poverty of Nations. *Swed. J. Econ.* **1968**, *70*, 242. [CrossRef]
35. Bruyn, S.M. The environmental Kuznets curve hypothesis. In *Economy and Ecology: Towards Sustainable Development*; Kluwer Academic Publishers: Dordrecht, The Netherlands, 2000; Volume 18, pp. 77–98.
36. Lewis, W.A. Economic Development with Unlimited Supplies of Labour. *Manch. Sch.* **1954**, *22*, 139–191. [CrossRef]
37. Loewenstein, W.; Bender, D. Labour Market Failure, Capital Accumulation, Growth and Poverty Dynamics in Partially Formalised Economies: Why Developing Countriess Growth Patterns are Different. *SSRN Electron. J.* **2017**. [CrossRef]
38. Engel, E. Die Productions-und Consumtionsverhältnisse des Königreichs Sachsen. *Zeitschrift Statistischen Bureaus Königlich Sächsischen Ministeriums Innern* **1857**, *8*, 1–54.
39. Pasinetti, L. *Structural Change and Economic Growth*; Cambridge University Press: Cambridge, UK, 1981.
40. Pasinetti, L. *Structural Economic Dynamics*; Cambridge University Press (CUP): Cambridge, UK, 1993.
41. Radetzki, M.; Tilton, J. Conceptual and methodological issues. In *World Metal Demand*; Resources for the Future: Washington, DC, USA, 1990.
42. Grossman, G.; Krueger, A. Environmental Impacts of a North American Free Trade Agreement. In *Environmental Impacts of a North American Free Trade Agreement*; National Bureau of Economic Research: Cambridge, MA, USA, 1991. [CrossRef]

43. Grossman, G.M.; Krueger, A.B. Economic Growth and the Environment. *Q. J. Econ.* **1995**, *110*, 353–377. [CrossRef]
44. Kuznets, S. Economic growth and income inequality. *Am. Econ. Rev.* **1955**, *45*, 1–28.
45. Panayotou, T. Demystifying the environmental Kuznets curve: Turning a black box into a policy tool. *Environ. Dev. Econ.* **1997**, *2*, 465–484. [CrossRef]
46. Singh, A. UK Industry and the World Economy: A Case of de-Industrialization? In *Welfare Aspects of Industrial Markets*; Springer Science and Business Media LLC: Berlin, Germany, 1977; pp. 183–214.
47. Black, G.; Kaldor, N. Further Essays on Economic Theory. *South. Econ. J.* **1980**, *47*, 245. [CrossRef]
48. Tregenna, F. Characterising deindustrialisation: An analysis of changes in manufacturing employment and output internationally. *Camb. J. Econ.* **2008**, *33*, 433–466. [CrossRef]
49. Dinda, S. Environmental Kuznets Curve Hypothesis: A Survey. *Ecol. Econ.* **2004**, *49*, 431–455. [CrossRef]
50. Kaika, D.; Zervas, E. The Environmental Kuznets Curve (EKC) theory—Part A: Concept, causes and the CO2 emissions case. *Energy Policy* **2013**, *62*, 1392–1402. [CrossRef]
51. Congregado, E.; Feria-Gallardo, J.; Golpe, A.A.; Iglesias, J. The environmental Kuznets curve and CO2 emissions in the USA. *Environ. Sci. Pollut. Res.* **2016**, *23*, 18407–18420. [CrossRef]
52. Arrow, K.; Bolin, B.; Costanza, R.; Dasgupta, P.; Folke, C.; Holling, C.; Jansson, B.-O.; Levin, S.; Maler, K.-G.; Perrings, C.; et al. Economic growth, carrying capacity, and the environment. *Environ. Dev. Econ.* **1996**, *1*, 104–110. [CrossRef]
53. Littleton, M. The TRIPS Agreement and transfer of climate-change-related technologies to developing countries. *Nat. Resour. Forum* **2009**, *33*, 233–244. [CrossRef]
54. Blyde, S.; Acea, C. How Does Intellectual Property Affect Foreign Direct Investment in Latin America? *Integr. Trade J.* **2003**, *7*, 135–152.
55. Smith, P.J. How do foreign patent rights affect U.S. exports, affiliate sales, and licenses? *J. Int. Econ.* **2001**, *55*, 411–439. [CrossRef]
56. Maskus, K.E.; Reichman, J.H. The globalization of private knowledge goods and the privatization of global public goods. *J. Int. Econ. Law* **2004**, *7*, 279–320. [CrossRef]
57. Johnson, D.L.; Ambrose, S.H.; Bassett, T.J.; Bowen, M.L.; Crummey, D.E.; Isaacson, J.S.; Lamb, P.; Saul, M.; Winter-Nelson, A.E.; Johnson, D.N. Meanings of Environmental Terms. *J. Environ. Qual.* **1997**, *26*, 581–589. [CrossRef]
58. Agrawal, A.; Gopal, K. *Biomonitoring of Water and Waste Water*; Springer: Berlin/Heidelberg, Germany, 2013.
59. Becker, R.A.; Sierstad, A.; Sydsæter, K.; Sydsaeter, K. Optimal Control Theory with Economic Applications. *Scand. J. Econ.* **1989**, *91*, 175. [CrossRef]
60. Kamihigashi, T. Transversality conditions and dynamic economic behaviour. In *The New Palgrave Dictionary of Economics*; Research Institute for Economics & Business Administration, Kobe University: Kobe, Hyogo, Japan, 2008.
61. Chiang, A.C. *Elements of Dynamic Optimization*; Waveland Pr Inc.: Long Grove, IL, USA, 1992; ISBN 157766096X.
62. Derakhshan-Nou, M. *Mathematical Economics and Control Theory: Studies in Policy Optimization*; Department of Economics, University of London: London, UK, 1996.
63. Solow, R.M. A Contribution to the Theory of Economic Growth. *Q. J. Econ.* **1956**, *70*, 65. [CrossRef]
64. Sadik-Zada, E.R.; Loewenstein, W.; Hasanli, Y. Commodity Revenues, Agricultural Sector and the Magnitude of Deindustrialization: A Novel Multisector Perspective. *Economies* **2019**, *7*, 113. [CrossRef]
65. Yee-Cheong, J.L. *Innovation: Applying Knowledge in Development*; UN Millenium Project; Earthscan: London, UK, 2005.
66. Matsushita, M.; Schoenbaum, T.J.; Mavroidis, P. *The World Trade Organization: Law, Practice, and Policy*; Oxford International Law Library: Oxford, UK, 2016.
67. Fischer, C.; Greaker, M.; Rosendahl, K.E. Robust technology policy against emission leakage: The case of upstream subsidies. *J. Environ. Econ. Manag.* **2017**, *84*, 44–61. [CrossRef]
68. Greaker, M. Spillovers in the development of new pollution abatement technology: A new look at the Porter-hypothesis. *J. Environ. Econ. Manag.* **2006**, *52*, 411–420. [CrossRef]
69. Boehringer, C.; Balistreri, E.J.; Rutherford, T.F. The role of border carbon adjustment in unilateral climate policy: Overview of an Energy Modeling Forum study (EMF 29). *Energy Econ.* **2012**, *34*, S97–S110. [CrossRef]
70. Levinson, A.; Taylor, M.S. Unmasking the pollution haven effect. *Int. Econ. Rev.* **2008**, *49*, 223–254. [CrossRef]

71. Grether, J.-M.; De Melo, J. *Globalization and Dirty Industries: Do Pollution Havens Matter?* NBER Working Paper Series; NBER: Cambridge, MA, USA, 2003.
72. Cavalcanti, T.V.D.V.; Mohaddes, K.; Raissi, M. Growth, development and natural resources: New evidence using a heterogeneous panel analysis. *Q. Rev. Econ. Finance* **2011**, *51*, 305–318. [CrossRef]
73. Mohaddes, K.; Raissi, M. Do sovereign wealth funds dampen the negative effects of commodity price volatility? *J. Commod. Mark.* **2017**, *8*, 18–27. [CrossRef]
74. Millimet, D.L.; Roy, J. Empirical Tests of the Pollution Haven Hypothesis When Environmental Regulation is Endogenous. *J. Appl. Econ.* **2015**, *31*, 652–677. [CrossRef]
75. Garsous, G. *Trends in Policy Indicators on Trade and Environment*; OECD Trade and Environment Working Papers; 2019; Available online: https://www.oecd-ilibrary.org/trade/trends-in-policy-indicators-on-trade-and-environment_b8d2bcac-en (accessed on 1 March 2019). [CrossRef]
76. Wiebe, K.S.; Yamano, N. *Estimating CO2 Emissions Embodied in Final Demand and Trade Using the OECD ICIO 2015: Methodology and Results*; OECD Science, Technology and Industry Working Papers No. 2016/05; 2016; Available online: https://www.oecd-ilibrary.org/science-and-technology/estimating-co2-emissions-embodied-in-final-demand-and-trade-using-the-oecd-icio-2015_5jlrcm216xkl-en (accessed on 3 September 2016).
77. Mikayilov, J.I.; Galeotti, M.; Hasanov, F.J. The impact of economic growth on CO2 emissions in Azerbaijan. *J. Clean. Prod.* **2018**, *197*, 1558–1572. [CrossRef]
78. D'Agostino, L.M. How MNEs respond to environmental regulation: Integrating the Porter hypothesis and the pollution haven hypothesis. *Econ. Polit.* **2015**, *32*, 245–269. [CrossRef]
79. Fischer, C. Emissions pricing, spillovers, and public investment in environmentally friendly technologies. *Energy Econ.* **2008**, *30*, 487–502. [CrossRef]
80. Rutqvist, J. Porter or Pollution Haven? An Analysis of the Dynamics of Competitiveness and Environmental Regulation. Master's Thesis, Uppsala University, Uppsala, Sweden, 2009.
81. Ozturk, I.; Al-Mulali, U. Investigating the validity of the environmental Kuznets curve hypothesis in Cambodia. *Ecol. Indic.* **2015**, *57*, 324–330. [CrossRef]
82. Karl, H.; Ranne, O. European environmental policy between decentralization and uniformity. *Intereconomics* **1997**, *32*, 159–169. [CrossRef]

sustainability

MDPI

Article

Constructing the Public in Roadmapping the Transition to a Bioeconomy: A Case Study from the Netherlands

Durwin H.J. Lynch [1,*], Pim Klaassen [1], Lan van Wassenaer [2] and Jacqueline E.W. Broerse [1]

1 Athena Institute for Research on Innovation and Communication in Health and Life Sciences, Faculty of Science, Vrije Universiteit Amsterdam, 1081 HV Amsterdam, The Netherlands; p.klaassen@vu.nl (P.K.); j.e.w.broerse@vu.nl (J.E.W.B.)

2 Wageningen Economic Research, Droevendaalsesteeg 4, 6708 PB Wageningen, The Netherlands; Lan.vanWassenaer@wur.nl

* Correspondence: d.lynch@vu.nl

Received: 16 March 2020; Accepted: 10 April 2020; Published: 15 April 2020

Abstract: In recent years there has been increasing attention to the transition toward a bioeconomy. From comparable transitions toward sustainability, we know that transitions require integral, inclusive approaches toward developing a long-term strategy, focusing not only on technological innovation, but also on involving the public. This is not easy. Public engagement encompasses diverse forms of public and civil society participation, and it is crucial to understand the specificities of these interactions and their effects on potential transition pathways. We present a conceptual-analytical paper where the focus lies on understanding sense-making practices in the construction of publics in the bioeconomy. Using a case-study approach, this article describes five partialities of the constructed public in the bioeconomy and analyzes the orchestration, productive dimensions and effects of these constructions. Our analysis offers a new perspective on, and appreciation of, the partiality of different forms of public participation, and varying degrees in which possibilities of system change in the bioeconomy transition are inclusive or exclusive toward differentially constructed publics. This offers an alternative, constructive way of exploring actor dynamics and politics in system change. We aim to contribute to a more nuanced and integral interpretation of public engagement in sustainability transitions, which is relevant to actors from academia, policy, industry and other spheres relevant to the bioeconomy transition.

Keywords: public engagement; bioeconomy; transition management; STS; participative collective; public construction; sustainability transition; participatory mechanism; coproduction; the Netherlands

---

1. Introduction

Over the last two decades, there has been increasing interest in the bioeconomy. Making the transition to a bioeconomy is perceived as being able to address various challenges, including those concerning energy security and worsening environmental conditions—the most prominent of which is climate change induced by greenhouse gases (GHG) [1–3]. Acknowledging that there are many definitions for the bioeconomy [4], in this paper we build on McCormick and Kautto [5], who define the bioeconomy as '*an economy where the basic building blocks for materials, chemicals, and energy are derived from renewable biological resources*'. The bioeconomy is generally portrayed as a positive, stimulating economic development with significant potential, for instance for agriculture, the production of food and beverages, pharmaceuticals, agro-industrial products and energy production [6]. Nonetheless, there are concerns about possible negative social and environmental side effects. For instance, scaling up the bioeconomy potentially comes with controversial practices, such as promoting monocultures and land grabbing [7,8]. Its polarizing potential warrants an exploration of the—possibly critical—public perceptions of the bioeconomy.

Although there has been an increase in literature on the transition to a bioeconomy, this revolves mainly around technological, chemical and biological issues entailed in the transition [9–11]. Less attention has been paid to its social, ethical and economic aspects, and the voice of the public regarding such matters. For a transition to a bioeconomy to take place, however, the bioeconomy should not only be technically and economically [12] viable, but also socially desirable and ethically acceptable [1,7,9]. Indeed, it has been argued that a successful transition to a bioeconomy requires system-wide changes involving society, academia, governments and industry [13]. If political and innovation developments (continue to) ignore ongoing social debates, this could hamper the transition [4]. Transitions not only entail systemic changes in modes of production and consumption, but are also accompanied by changes in beliefs, values and governance [14]. It has been argued that there is a need for broader social dialogues on the bioeconomy, as well as more attention paid to social studies focusing on its non-technological aspects, giving voice to a broader array of social stakeholders, including citizens [7,9,15]. Such broader dialogues can take different forms and formats—for instance, stakeholders and citizens can be brought together directly or indirectly [16,17]. What these different forms and formats of participation actually signify for the bioeconomy transition, however, remains unclear.

A few studies have attempted to close this knowledge gap [17–21]. Mustahalati [18] explored the need to include citizens in a responsive forest-based bioeconomy and discussed the fact that responsive governance involves several key aspects of change, such as citizens' values, interests, know-how and environmental entitlements. This requires an interactive collaborative approach that enables citizens and institutions to meet and debate the development of living environments. One important challenge is to develop strategies that prevent powerful actors from dominating the discussion, hampering ordinary citizens from expressing their values in, and opinions on, this transition. Stern et al. investigated the social perspectives on the bioeconomy in Austria [17]. They argued that the current discourse has mainly been driven from a strategic top-down level, which leads to the failure to include social actors, and consequently to the acceptance of reduced engagement. Their study sheds light on sustainable consumption—a topic the participants in the study considered important, and which is of particular interest for creating an inclusive bioeconomy by focusing on consumers' active involvement.

Since public engagement encompasses diverse forms of civil society participation, it becomes crucial to understand the specificities of different forms of interaction and their impacts on potential transition pathways. All forms of participation are by definition exclusive, partial, framed in particular ways and subject to overflows. Having a solid understanding of their details provides opportunities to optimize public engagement in the bioeconomy transition, in such a way that, in addition to attempting to be inclusive, it is also responsive to public input. In this article, to contribute to this effort, we build on constructivist work in Science and Technology Studies (STS) and pay close attention to the construction, performance, productive dimensions and effects of what we will refer to as "collectives of participation" [22,23].

This study aims to explore the construction of various publics in the bioeconomy by drawing on a specific case, the "Societal Roadmap for the Bioeconomy in the Netherlands" project. We reflect on two public engagement elements of this project: (1) seven Focus Group Discussions (FGDs) in which 57 citizens participated, and (2) three multi-stakeholder workshops in which 29 representatives from academia, industry, government and civil society participated. First, we analyze how the publics were orchestrated, by looking at the enrollment processes and how these participatory collectives were mediated. Here we ask which actors and (related) knowledge remain excluded and what competing visions emerge. Second, we seek to understand the productive dimensions and effects of these participatory collectives. Here we ask how issues are defined, different visions valued, and how they are integrated in the transition pathway. Moreover, we analyze what identities the constructed publics come to embody.

2. Toward an Understanding of the Construction of Publics

There are several established theoretical branches pertinent to sustainability transitions, for example the Multi-level Perspective, Strategic Niche Management, Transition Management and Technological Innovation systems. What these theories have in common is that they focus on explaining how technical configurations become stabilized and how transitions can be steered. They also share a relatively technocratic and expert-oriented nature, thereby potentially obscuring possible influences on the dynamics of transitions by the public (e.g., ordinary citizens, Civil Society Organizations (CSOs), consumers). Various scholars call for more inclusive sustainability transition processes, highlighting particularly the relative lack of attention to the general public [24–26]. Smith [27] argued that public engagement encompasses diverse forms of public and social participation, and calls for more detailed work on these different forms, seeking to understand their interactions and effects on potential transition pathways.

Public engagement is often approached through political science and theories of democracy, emphasizing its normative surplus as a way of legitimizing the outcomes of research or policy-making. A constructivist perspective on public engagement, rooted in STS, takes a slightly different angle. Whereas the former tends to focus more on elements of procedural justice and normative principles that define predetermined models of what constitutes good deliberation and participation, constructivist approaches view all forms of participation as emergent co-productionist phenomena and as social experiments in themselves. Approaching public engagement from an STS perspective, then, entails paying close attention to the construction, performance, productive dimensions and effects of particular instances of practicing public engagement [28–30]. An assumption in this constructivist perspective is that all forms of participation are simultaneously shaped by, and actively shape, human subjectivities, objects of concern and models of participation.

This paper presents such a constructivist approach to public engagement. Our focus is on a case-study conducted to facilitate the development of a societal roadmap to the bioeconomy, a central element of which was to give a voice to the public in general, as well as to specific stakeholders. The analytical framework used is inspired by the work of Chilvers and Longhurst [22,31], who have studied the construction of the public in the energy transition.

All collectives of participation start with the inclusion or exclusion of actors via mechanisms of enrollment. Consequently, the constitution of these actors highlights the productive ways in which approaches to mediation construct *objects* (or issues), *subjects* (or publics/participants) and *models of participation* (or procedural formats/configurations). Chilvers and Longhurst present a framework (Figure 1) in which the mutual interaction between these three dimensions is presented as constitutive of their own emergent and co-produced features. Furthermore, they highlight that the settings in which situated participatory collectives emerge are shaped by (and in turn shape) existing orders (systemic, institutional and constitutional states relating to the three dimensions). Concretely, this boils down to interpreting how "public" actors become involved, how the design of the participatory mechanisms used comes about and what their effects are. As such, we study how actors come to be included or excluded, what mechanisms of enrollment are in place and what this means for the public identity assumed.

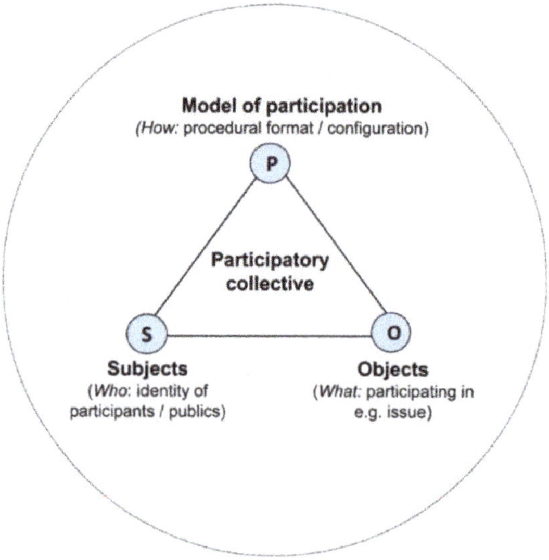

Figure 1. Socio-material participatory collectives emerge in the co-productive relationships existing between models of participation, subjects and objects, and in relation with their specific context. Adapted from Chilvers and Longhurst (2016), p. 590.

According to Chilvers and Longhurst [22], understanding participation as emergent and co-produced offers a number of analytical possibilities, including gaining insight into the *orchestration* and *the productive dimensions and effects* of emergent participatory collectives. First, the orchestration of a collective of participation focuses on processes of enrollment and mediation. Here, *enrollment* refers to the way different actors are drawn into a particular form of participatory collective practice and definition of the issue at stake. Mechanisms of enrollment can be highly centralized and controlled by a small number of actors in the collective. This is especially true for formalized "technologies of participation" such as citizen panels, focus groups or other established deliberative participatory techniques which have standardized designs. Enrollment can also be more distributed and fluid, as viewed in informal and citizen-led forms of engagement. *Mediation* refers to the way in which a participatory collective is held together by different devices, processes, skills or technologies of participation. All forms of participation by definition lead to exclusions, are always partial, framed in particular ways and subject to overflows.

Second, the *productive dimensions and effects* of emergent participatory collectives. This means a focus on the ways in which diverse collectives of participation construct particular definitions of (1) models of participation), (2) the public and (3) the issue at stake. First, the relations between actors and participants in a participatory collective create a particular model of participation, which can range from consensual to antagonistic. Emergent collectives produce publics through constructing particular identities of the actors involved, such as "naïve" citizens or "pure" publics (assumed to have limited prior knowledge or simply being representative of a wider public), or "interested" or "affected" citizens (with a personal attachment to the object of participation; or more active or innovative citizens, who are expected to bring about forms of distributed action). Finally, issues can be subject to powerful framing effects, especially in institutionally orchestrated processes.

The theoretical notions described above highlight that "the public" is not static, nor can it be easily captured, since it does not exist in a pregiven natural state. Rather, it is actively constructed, orchestrated, mediated and interpreted.

3. Methods and Materials

3.1. Case Selection and Description

In order to empirically explore the constructions of the public in the bioeconomy we draw on a case called "Societal Roadmap for the Bioeconomy in the Netherlands". This case is chosen because of its unique and innovative methodological approach, involving the public in governance toward the bioeconomy transition in the Netherlands. The case is therefore helpful for understanding more about the participatory mechanisms, the productive elements and the complexities that arise when taking an inclusive and holistic approach to long-term strategy development.

The project was a formal and discrete state-sponsored exercise of participation on the issue of bioeconomy in the Netherlands, and was conducted in 2014–2015. It involved a range of actors from academia, industry, government, non-governmental organizations (NGOs) and the general public, who came together to identify non-technological opportunities, threats and other considerations relevant for the governance of the transition toward a bioeconomy. The project focused on three distinctive technological applications in the bioeconomy: (1) biomaterials, (2) biorefineries and (3) biojetfuels. Two paths ran in parallel in the project. The first path focused on citizens' perceptions of the bioeconomy, while the second focused on the views of several stakeholder groups on governance issues entailed in the transition toward it.

The purpose of the first path was to identify Dutch citizens' perceptions of the bioeconomy. For this, a qualitative research approach was used, with FGDs as the primary research method. In FGDs, participants respond to, and build on, the views expressed by other participants, stimulating shared creative thinking and providing an opportunity to gain in-depth insight into the participants' ideas, values, wishes and concerns [32]. This is particularly relevant for complex topics that require a process of familiarization and opinion forming. Three concrete bio-based technologies—bioplastics, small-scale biorefineries and biojetfuels—were selected as topics for in-depth exploration in the FGDs. The choice to focus on specific bioeconomic applications was made because discussions on something as abstract and poorly delineated as "the bioeconomy" was seen as risking only vague and superficial deliberations. Participants were selected from the general public, based on a diversity with respects to citizens' relationships with the technologies (direct consumers, residents and indirect consumers). In total, 57 Dutch citizens participated in seven FGDs, three of which dealt with bioplastics, two concerned (small-scale) biorefineries and two focused on biojetfuels. For a more elaborate overview of the participant selection, the structure of the FGDs and the analysis, see [16].

The purpose of the second path was to explore perceptions and evaluations of policy scenarios. To this end, three multi-stakeholder workshops with 29 participants from academia, NGOs, industry and government were held, on the topics of biomaterials, biorefineries and biojetfuels. Using the participatory Multi-Criteria Analysis (pMCA) method, the workshops explored how different scenarios are valued according to a large set of criteria that are weighted differently by different stakeholders (e.g., NGOs may assign more weight to CO_2 reduction than to economic growth than the private sector). The participatory element entails the inclusion of different stakeholders in the workshops. The pMCA workshops followed the FGDs on the same technology routes. The researchers in the project aimed to incorporate the outcomes of the FGDs with citizens in the pMCA workshops.

3.2. Case-Study

In exploring this case, we are interested in two specific analytical themes developed by Chilvers and Longhurst (2016) and presented in Section 2 above. Thus, we first analyzed how the public was *orchestrated*, by looking at the enrollment processes and how the participatory collective was mediated. This entailed answering the questions about which actors and forms of knowledge were excluded, and what emerging competing visions could be identified. And second, we sought to understand the *productive dimensions and effects* of these participatory collectives. To this end, we posed several more questions: What was the model of participation? What identities do the constructed publics come to embody? How are issues defined and different visions valued and integrated in the transition pathway?

To answer these questions, we drew on a variety of materials: the FGD designs, transcripts of the audio recorded FGDs, the analysis of the FGDs (which has been published [16]), pMCA workshop designs, the outcomes of the workshops, informal participant evaluations at the end of the workshops and the project's final synthesis report [33]. Furthermore, email communication between the project team members and recruitment agencies were used to extract relevant justifications of the choices made. Personal reflective notes which were made after the FGDs and workshops, and during and after project meetings through participant observations, were also analyzed. An additional qualitative analysis of documentary grey and academic literature sources was used to deepen the analysis of the FGDs and pMCA workshops. These materials were coded against the two main analytical themes just outlined: the orchestration and the productive dimensions and effects of the participatory collective.

4. Results

In this section we discuss the construction of the public for the three different bioeconomy technologies—biomaterials, biorefineries and biojetfuels—and the two different objects, i.e., the general public's perception of each of these technologies and the stakeholders' views on appropriate governance models for the transition toward a bioeconomy in which these technologies are featured. In this project, the public was involved in two ways. First, citizens, as members of the public, were invited to discuss "public perceptions" of three bioeconomy technologies in designated FGDs—so *citizens with citizens*. Second, NGOs, as entities representing "the public", were invited to discuss strategic governance related to three bioeconomy technologies in designated pMCAs—so *NGOs with other stakeholders*. We focus primarily on the construction of *the public* in the bioeconomy, i.e., the citizens involved in the FGDs and the NGOs in the pMCA workshops. Specific results related to the other stakeholders' (academia, industry and government) perceptions of the issues are not incorporated in our analysis of how the issue was constructed by the public in this participatory collective.

4.1. The Orchestration of the Public

4.1.1. Enrollment and Mediation

Enrollment refers to the way different actors are drawn into a particular form of participatory collective practice and definition of the issue at stake. For the FGDs, enrollment was centrally organized via a recruitment agency, which was requested to follow a standardized design for selecting a "representative" sample of Dutch citizens. Two different recruitment agencies were involved, each with its own recruitment strategy. The first agency, which recruited for the FGDs on bioplastics, used its Facebook page to invite participants. It also used the snowballing technique, as recruited participants were invited to further recruit other participants. However, as a result, one of the FGDs comprised three acquaintances among the total number of six participants, heavily weighing on the FGD's internal dynamic; these three participants dominated the discussion and occasionally shared insider jokes. The second agency, which recruited for the FGDs on biorefineries and biojetfuels, actively matched participants from its own member database. This was, however, challenging for the FGDs on bio-refineries, as there was the additional criterion that participants had to come from the "De Achterhoek" (a rural region in the province of Gelderland) and live within 5 km distance of a farm. For all FGDs, participants received a standard reimbursement of €30–40. The only information the participants received upfront was that the FGD would be related to the topic of sustainability, and in order to participate they should have an interest in this. No further information on the bioeconomy or any of the three technological applications was given. This was done to avoid the possibility of participants informing themselves beforehand. A brief introduction to the technology was provided in a PowerPoint presentation during the FGD.

The enrollment of the public in the pMCA workshops was also institutionally centralized, as this was controlled by key stakeholders of the project team. The aim was to have representatives of four stakeholder groups in each workshop: NGOs, academia, industry and government. Most of these stakeholders were already engaged in the bioeconomy, as most had previously signed a bioeconomy Manifesto (Retrieved from: https://www.biobasedeconomy.nl/wp-content/uploads/2011/10/Manifest-BBE-def-29-sep.pdf, see also Section 4.2.3, Box 1, for an excerpt). In addition, several other people from a specific selection of organizations were invited to attend the workshop. The selected participants knew beforehand that they were invited because they represented a particular stakeholder group and had expertise in bioeconomy. Although NGOs can be considered to be representative of the public (including citizens), they were not invited with the explicit (pregiven) task to do so. The project was led by an NGO, which attended all three workshops, although each time represented by a different individual. The aim was to have representatives from two NGOs in each of the three workshops (the project leader and one other). For the pMCA on biojetfuels, however, the additional NGO dropped out at the last minute, leaving only the project leader to represent the NGOs.

Mediation refers to the way in which a participatory collective is held together by different devices, processes, skills or technologies of participation. In order to capture and provide exposure to the citizens' distinctive voice in the bioeconomy, and to prevent them from being potentially overshadowed by more dominant expert discussions, the deliberations with citizens were organized separately from those with stakeholders. The decision to keep these two groups—experts and non-experts—separate simultaneously meant designing and implementing different modes of participation. Furthermore, as the concept of bioeconomy is broad and encompasses a variety of technologies, applications and dimensions, each FGD and pMCA workshop dealt with one of the three bioeconomy technologies. Both the deliberations with citizens and those with stakeholders were mediated by professional facilitators from two research institutes that formed part of the project team: the FGDs by the Vrije Universiteit Amsterdam, and the pMCA workshops by Wageningen University. The research team from each university was independently responsible for the organization, implementation and analysis of their deliberations. Regular finetuning and reflection between the two teams took place to align the two paths.

4.1.2. Exclusion and Resistance

Since all forms of participation by definition lead to exclusion, are always partial, framed in particular ways and subject to overflows, we reflect in this section on which actors—and consequently on what knowledge—were consciously or inadvertently excluded, or resisted taking part in the participatory collective.

It could be argued that for the FGDs there was, to a certain extent, exclusion in terms of achieving a geographically representative sample of the population. This is mostly related to the practical and organizational decision-making aspects that arise when working in research projects that have a fixed timeline and budget to carry out the activities. For example, the FGDs on bioplastics and biojetfuels were held at the Vrije Universiteit, in Amsterdam, at a fixed time in the evening, during the week, which made it less convenient for potential citizens from other regions in the Netherlands to participate. The FGDs on biorefineries in De Achterhoek were held at a central location in the city of Doetinchem, but at a place that was less accessible for anyone using public transport. So, in order to be part of "the public", participants had to be (1) in the crossline of the recruitment agencies, (2) be willing to travel to the location at a specified date and time, and (3) in the case of biorefineries, also live close to a farm in the region of De Achterhoek. The exclusion does not, however, render the outcomes of the FGDs less valid, irrelevant or non-representative. It simply highlights that organizing FGDs comes with delineations, and this automatically causes exclusion of the general public.

In order to make the FGDs more "accessible" to all Dutch citizens, the project could have worked with campaigns and self-enrollment possibilities. However, the project organizers deliberately wanted to avoid attracting citizens who were already familiar with the topic, either because of their work or hobby, and whose views were therefore not representative of those of "the general public". Needless to say, the aim of FGDs was to elucidate diversity (breadth) and in-depth exploration of opinions, and not to achieve generalizable outcomes.

Similarly to the FGDs, the pMCA workshops excluded certain actors in their model of participation. First, it could be argued that the involved NGOs dealt primarily with environmental topics (Stichting Natuur & Milieu, Milieu Centraal, IUCN NL), thereby excluding other NGOs or CSOs dealing with, for example, more health-related topics or consumer interests. Both practical and substantial reasons explain this. A practical reason is that a pMCA workshop can be conducted only with a limited number of participants, otherwise it will become harder to facilitate, so the organizers have to select, and therefore exclude. In order to achieve a wide variety of stakeholders' perspectives, this was limited to around 10–12 participants divided over four stakeholder groups. The majority of the selected stakeholders, including the NGOs, had signed the Manifesto. To a certain extent, these parties were "on the same page" on a variety of aspects related to the bioeconomy. However, within the bioeconomy there are also polarizing groups (see, e.g., [7]), and it seems that these different perspectives were excluded from the participatory collective in this project.

On a different note, and as will become evident from the model of participation (see Section 4.2.1), the pMCA workshops dealt with transition governance, and the commissioner of the project (Ministry of Economic affairs) attended all three workshops. The design of the workshops was focused on input from participants well acquainted with the bioeconomy and policy-making. It could therefore be argued that the general public was excluded from the pMCA process. At the same time, ensuring proper facilitation remains key, which requires keeping the workshop manageable in terms of the number of participants and safe in terms of potential power-plays. However, this set-up did jeopardize the inclusion of public perceptions of the bioeconomy as explored in the FGDs.

4.2. The Productive Dimensions and Effects of Emerging Participatory Collectives

4.2.1. Model of Participation

For the deliberations with citizens, the FGD method was used as a model of participation, and the FGDs were facilitated by researchers from the Vrije Universiteit Amsterdam. As the invited participants were not expected to prepare anything beforehand, the facilitators carefully designed and structured a script for the FGDs, in consultation with the project team (one NGO and two universities). For each of the three selected technological bioeconomy applications, a slightly different approach was taken, but, in general, each FGD consisted of five activities (see Table 1) and lasted for two hours.

In line with FGD guidelines, each FGD had on average eight participants, providing enough room to discuss in depth a variety of opinions related to the topic. Since the FGDs aimed at elucidating citizens' perceptions of the bioeconomy technologies, each design contained elements in which information on the technology was provided to the participants. The first activity provided more information on the technology via a PowerPoint presentation with neutral and factual information on how it relates to larger social challenges and what the technology entails. In the case of bioplastics, there were actual bioproducts that the participants could hold in their hands. This step is necessary, as it triggers participants to become acquainted with the technology by asking questions, giving reactions and thereby developing their opinion. Other activities discussed concrete examples of the technology. First, participants were requested to individually reflect on arguments in favor of, and against, the technology; second, they were asked to discuss this with each other. This enabled other participants to understand different perspectives and perhaps adjust their own perceptions. Collectively, participants were then asked to formulate important considerations for a successful development and implementation of the technology. Although the FGDs did not aim for participants to reach consensus, the final activity aimed at determining which considerations the participants collectively prioritized in each particular FGD.

Table 1. General structure of the FGDs.

Activity	Description
1	*Getting acquainted with the bio-based technology:* In order to assess the starting level of knowledge, the participants were individually asked if they were familiar with the bio-based technology in question and what their first thoughts or associations were. Subsequently, a short PowerPoint presentation containing basic factual information on the subject was provided to the participants in order to acquaint them with the subject.
2	*Inventory of arguments for and against the bio-based technology:* The participants were individually asked to write down arguments for and against the bio-based technology, after which each was asked to clarify their arguments. We stimulated their thinking process by telling them that they could also write "opportunities" and "concerns" related to the bio-based technology. The arguments were all collected and clustered on a flip chart, according to the wishes of the participants.
3	*Individual prioritization of arguments:* For this exercise, each participant received three prioritization stickers. They were asked to express their acceptance of the bio-based technology by individually prioritizing arguments. Afterwards, a facilitated discussion took place to find out why people prioritize certain arguments rather than others.
4	*Formulate considerations for the bio-based technology:* During this step, participants were asked to identify criteria for a successful implementation of bio-based technologies. The facilitator wrote down these considerations on a flip chart.
5	*Closure:* At the end of the FGD, the participants were asked to reflect on the discussions and how they had experienced the FGD.

A central aspect of each pMCA workshop, facilitated by researchers from Wageningen University, was to discuss three policy scenarios in relation to the bioeconomy technological applications. The first was a demand-pull scenario in which the government supports bioeconomy developments by introducing incentives, such as green public procurement and subsidies that would increase demand. For the second scenario, technology-push, the government would stimulate technological bioeconomy developments by providing financial support for research and development (R&D) and pilot and demonstration projects. In the third scenario, market-driven, the government would intervene less and allow the market to take initiatives with innovation strategies. All pMCA workshops followed a general structure (see Table 2) and lasted for three hours. Although the workshops contained elements of individually assigning weights and scores to indicators, these were used as a means to explore possibilities and discuss governance strategies in a collective way. Therefore, the model of participation can best be described as consensual.

The pMCA workshops were one-off events with no additional participatory configurations before or after the workshop. While most stakeholders' organizations were present only once, two organizations attended all the workshops. These were the commissioning party (Ministry of Economic affairs) and the NGO acting as project leader (Stichting Natuur & Milieu). As a stakeholder group, Wageningen University and another government stakeholder (Rijksdienst voor Ondernemend Nederland, EN: *Netherlands Enterprise Agency*) were present in two of the three workshops. Therefore, only the latter two were able to contribute to the workshops by taking insights from the previous ones into account. Despite this possibility, there were varying representatives of these organizations at the workshops.

After each workshop there was a short informal evaluation with the participants and the project team, which served to improve the following workshop. For example, the first workshop (on biomaterials) was considered too abstract, and more concrete examples and delineation of the scenarios was considered desirable. The preliminary list of criteria was also considered too complex, and simplification was proposed. These aspects were considered for the design of the workshops on biorefineries and biojetfuels, so the methodology was refined over time. This shows that the topic of the bioeconomy is rather abstract and vague, not only for citizens. Even expert stakeholders, who are already engaged and involved in this topic, require concrete examples in order to properly discuss governance strategies.

Table 2. General structure of the pMCA workshops.

Activity	Description
1	*Discuss the policy scenarios* Determine if the three scenarios were relevant and appropriate, and whether some scenarios had to be adapted, removed or new scenarios should be added.
2	*Discuss criteria and indicators* Determine whether the predefined criteria and indicators were appropriate, ensure that everybody had the same understanding of these, and if necessary discuss modifications, additions and removals.
3	*Assign weights to criteria* All participants individually assigned weights between 1 and 5 to the criteria.
4	*Assign scores to indicators* All participants assigned scores (between 1 and 5) to the expected effects of the different scenarios on the criteria. Lower scores corresponded to negative effects, higher scores to positive effects.
5	*Discuss scores* Plenary discussion of considerations of the different scenarios.
6	*Discuss scenario preferences* Discuss the implementation of the most preferred scenario.

4.2.2. Defining the Public: Many Partialities

This section will reflect on how the public was constructed through particular identities of the stakeholders and citizens involved in the participatory collective. Here we incorporate the work of Michael [34] and Braun and Schultz [35] on constructions of the public.

First, the FGD participants were invited to take part as "citizen members" of the Dutch public. This corresponds to what Michael calls the Public-in-General: " ... *an undifferentiated whole that is distinguished from science that is itself characterized globally in terms of some key dimension.*" At the beginning of each FGD it was made clear to the participants that they were invited as the Public-in-General. However, each FGD also contained a particular activity in which the participants were asked to interpret aspects of the bioeconomy from a more specific identity. This is in line with what Michael defined as Publics-in-Particular: " ... *those publics that have an identifiable stake in particular scientific or technological issues or controversies.*" As Public-in-Particular, three roles were distinguished. The FGD on bioplastics asked participants to discuss their willingness to buy two concrete bioplastics, so playing the role of *direct consumers*, while the FGDs on biorefineries asked participants to perceive this technology from the perspective of *residents*. The FGDs on biojetfuels asked participants to discuss these from the perspective of *indirect consumers*. It was unclear which identity the participants embodied, or reacted from, when, for the final activity, they were asked to propose and prioritize general considerations for the development and implementation of the biotechnology.

The results of the FGDs [16] showed that participants easily switched between the identities, perhaps as a result of the guided process. What can be observed here is that as particular public identities are assigned to, and embodied by, citizen participants, they experience a more personal connection with the given technology. This enables them to reflect on different personal values that matter most, and to frame their perception accordingly. This perception is then shared with other participants, enabling knowledge integration. While in all FGDs the participants started on a positive note toward the bioeconomy technology, issues of personal costs and benefits became more important as they took up the particular, secondary identities. This will be further elaborated in Section 4.2.3.

It was a deliberate choice to exclude citizens from taking part in the pMCA workshops. However, in line with Braun and Schultz [35], in the conceptualization of publics in governance arrangements, NGOs can be considered as the "Partisan Public": " … *organisations (not individuals) who hold strong collective opinions on the issue [at stake] or have a particular interest. They are also referred to as stakeholders or lobbyists*." Therefore, we argue that the NGOs in the pMCA workshops represented not only their particular interest, discussing transition governance on an equal footing with other "expert" stakeholders, but also a different partiality of the public. On the other hand, citizens were framed as relevant actors for a successful bioeconomy transition. This can be seen through the defined criteria and indicators which were used to discuss the different policy scenarios. Table 3 presents the ranking of these criteria in each of the workshops. For the workshop on biomaterials, it shows that the "*citizens' acceptance*" was seen as an important, highly valued indicator, and related to the "*willingness to buy*". In the other workshops, "*citizens' acceptance*" and "*health and wellbeing*" were considered relevant, but of less importance.

Table 3. Rankings of the criteria indicators defined in the three pMCAs.

Rank	Biomaterials	Biorefinery	Biojetfuels
1	Carbon footprint	Carbon footprint	Carbon footprint
2	**Citizens' acceptance**	Profit	Supply chain availability
3	Biodiversity	Environmental impact	Job opportunities
4	Production costs	Level playing field	Energy efficiency
5	**Consumer willingness to buy**	Biodiversity	Profit
6	Quality of products	Job opportunities	Competitive position NL
7	Profit	Policy consistency	Level playing field
8	Policy consistency	**Citizens' acceptance**	**Citizens' acceptance**
9	Job opportunities	**Health and wellbeing**	Public investments
10	Level playing field	Quality	Biodiversity
11	Market share	Administration costs	Administration costs
12	Administration costs		

The input of citizens (as the Public-in-General) was limited to formulating criteria for a successful bioeconomy transition. Although NGOs can be considered as Partisan Public, only a few NGOs (with a strong focus on environmental issues) were involved. Other, more or less organized sectors of the public were not seen as stakeholders with the same "privileges", invited to discuss transition governance. For the first workshop (biomaterials), the highlights of the outcomes of the corresponding FGDs were presented orally to the stakeholders by the facilitator of the FGDs. The rationale of this was to provide a more nuanced view of public concerns, wishes and conditions for the stakeholders to consider when discussing the policy scenarios. However, since there were no citizens present to "own" to these outcomes, and all stakeholders were mainly focused on their own interests, the perceptions of citizens, and therefore also other partialities of the public, remained excluded from the discussions during the pMCA workshops. It was, however, mentioned to the participants that the final reporting to the commissioner would attempt to integrate insights from the FGDs with the outcomes of the pMCA workshops. This will be further reflected upon in Section 4.3.

4.2.3. Defining Issues of the Bioeconomy

Issues can be subject to powerful framing effects, especially in institutionally orchestrated processes. Although the concept of "bioeconomy" was not discussed as such with the FGD participants, they were able to substantiate their perceptions of the three concrete technologies that were introduced. The majority of the participants expressed positive associations with these technologies, linking these to notions such as sustainability, environmental friendliness, naturalness and green feeling. However, there were also negative associations, such as genetic modification, higher prices and improper land use. These framings were the result of a guided process of knowledge articulation undergone by the citizens.

Overall, there seemed to be acceptance of the three applications of the bioeconomy technologies and the sustainability purpose they served (i.e., replacing fossil-based products). Citizens enjoyed being engaged in the discussions on this transition, as they find topics related to sustainability relevant. They were, however, more critical regarding how these applications would be framed and presented to the public. This became more evident when participants were asked to perceive the technology from a particular public perspective. For example, in the concrete case of a bio-based bottle for a specific drink, participants felt they were still buying "the drink" and not a sustainable bottle. As can be seen in the quote below, they became less willing to "pay more" as consumers, as this was seen more as greenwashing.

> *[the manufacturer] actually wants me to buy the beverage, they don't want me to buy the bottle. I won't buy the drink just because it is in a bioplastic.*
>
> (Bioplastics, FG1, P3)

In the case of a biobag, which could be used for shopping, participants were more interested in its quality, price and how it was made. Here the application of the technology was regarded as more positive. This is illustrated with the quote below.

> *It suggests a green and good intention of the producer, and such endeavors should be supported.*
>
> (Bioplastics, FG3, P6)

It is important to mention here that, contrary to the participants of the pMCA workshops, the FGD participants did not have a chance to study the topic beforehand. The FGD participants were therefore dependent on the information provided to them in the FGD to form an opinion. It is likely that the content of this information, as well as the way it was communicated, had some framing effect. While the FGD setting provided an opportunity to study this process of opinion forming in a more or less controlled environment, opinions can also be formed independently, without the mediating context of an FGD. Citizens are increasingly empowered and self-sufficient, and find ways to inform themselves through the internet and informal discussions, and form their opinions at their own pace.

The pMCA workshops did not devote particular attention to the framing of the bioeconomy by the different stakeholders. Therefore, not much can be said about how it was framed through the participatory collective. However, by enrolling stakeholders who previously signed the Manifesto, it can be assumed that these stakeholders were, to a certain degree, "on the same page". In Box 1 the main points of this Manifesto are presented, to give insight into the position to which they were signatory.

Box 1. Excerpt from the Dutch *Biobased Economy Manifesto*.

In conclusion, we, the signatories of this Manifesto:

- Commit ourselves in the pursuit of a sustainable bio-based economy that supports ecosystems and acknowledges people's basic necessities as preconditions;
- Commit ourselves to enter into partnerships to make the bio-bases economy come to practice in line with the stated principles;
- Agree as much as possible within legal frameworks, to inform each other about lessons learned, dilemmas and aspirations in order to build on the frameworks of a bio-based economy that offers opportunities for people, the environment and sustainable economic growth;
- Ask the Dutch government to:
    - actively promote and communicate the stated principles nationally and internationally and to support in policy and associated financial instruments,
    - promote monitoring of the bio-based economy progress, including labour market and sustainability related information.
    - be take an open approach, and contribute to initiatives arising from our partnerships

4.3. *Knowledge Integration: A Persistent Challenge*

4.3.1. A Revised Configuration of the Participatory Collective

In this section we briefly reflect on the model of Chilvers and Longhurst [22] and describe the co-productive relationships between the model of participation (P), subjects (S) and objects (O) in the participatory collective. The case studied in this article shows a unique additional dimension to this model: a multiplicity of collectives of participation. Since the public was involved in two related—yet separate—paths, the participatory collective became more enriched, yet complex and problematic. Below (Figure 2) we present this dual configuration, in which it becomes evident that not all relationships can be considered relational and co-productive. For the two models of participation, in this case FGDs (P1) and pMCA workshops (P2), the relation has been co-productive: there was regular finetuning and contemplation between the researchers designing these models of participation. The subjects, however, experienced less co-production: both the FGD participants (S1) and the pMCA workshop participants (S2) were kept separate from each other, and this implied less opportunities for learning and co-creation between the "non-expert" citizens and the "expert" stakeholders. Consequently, the objects were also less relational: discussing the desirability of three bioeconomy technologies (O1) versus discussing criteria and indicators for transition governance (O2).

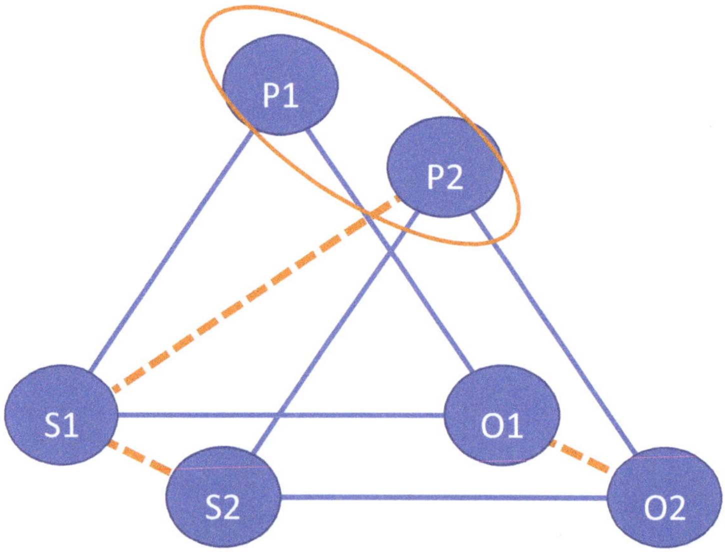

Figure 2. A configuration of dual models of participation.

In the project's final synthesis report these two paths were presented in two separate chapters, one focusing on the FGD outcomes and the other on the pMCA workshop outcomes. As becomes evident, certain partialities of the constructed public remained excluded from the actual decision-making arena, in this particular case taking an active part in the governance discussion of the transition toward a bioeconomy. While the Partisan Public (as one of the Publics-in-Particular) was considered appropriate to discuss governance strategies with other "expert" stakeholders, this was not the case for citizens (as the Public-in-General). As a result, although the project was inclusive with regard to the public, it cannot be said that the resulting roadmap on the bioeconomy is supported by the public. For the government, the license to operate remains therefore only partially supported, which means that the the roadmap may be less responsive to the public.

4.3.2. Striving for a Meaningful Deliberation

In the case studied, the involved researchers regularly reflected on the process and results of the previous steps to realize a meaningful deliberation. This happened in different ways. First, the outcomes of the FGDs with citizens served as input for the design of the pMCA workshops. It was also attempted by including preliminary results of the FGD on bioplastics in the deliberations during the pMCA workshop on biomaterials. However, the stakeholders participating in the workshop were more interested in framing and portraying their own, and other experts' perceptions than in trying to understand and integrate the perspectives of citizens. They were directly integrating their co-constructions on the object through a particular model of participation—a model that lies closer to actual decision-making, thus having an increased chance of having a direct impact. The citizens' framing (as members of the Public-in-General) was reduced to "*citizens' acceptance*" and "*consumers' willingness to buy*", indicating a traditional way of positioning lay citizens exclusively as end-users, instead of co-creators of the transition process.

5. Discussion

5.1. Main Findings

In this paper, we explored the orchestration, the production dimensions and the effects of involving the public in the transition to a bioeconomy. One of our main conclusions from the FGDs is that, overall, citizens can be very supportive of the bioeconomy—relating it to visions of sustainability, reduction of GHG emissions, alternatives to depleting fossil-fuels—and yet still have varying degrees of resistance to certain applications of bioeconomy technologies, particularly by the industry. Furthermore, the public, as a broad and non-homogenous group, entertains widely diverging thoughts on a wide palette of aspects of the bioeconomy. There is no singular all-encompassing "public perception of the bioeconomy". In addition, in the project, the researchers perceived and valued the public differently. The public was implicitly and explicitly enrolled in one of five identity roles [34]:

- members of the *general public*, who possess commonsense knowledge and can discuss their appreciation of bioeconomy technologies in relation to social challenges;
- *direct consumers* of two different bioplastic applications, whereby citizens discussed desirability in relation to the willingness to buy;
- *indirect consumers* of biojetfuels, whereby the willingness to pay more for biotickets was explored;
- the *affected public*, possessing experiential knowledge by living near a farm where a small-scale bio-refinery could potentially be installed; and
- the *partisan public*, such as an organized group (NGO), expected to represent social concerns and wishes in expert-based discussions on transition governance.

These show five partialities of the constructed public, resulting from two models of participation. These models of participation, with their corresponding definitions of the issues at stake, are constantly being co-produced through the construction of collectives of participation. Moreover, regardless of how the public embodied these identity roles in the FGDs, experts in the pMCA workshops constructed "the public" in their own way—mostly as receptive end-users (or consumers) of the bioeconomy, whose acceptance of the bioeconomy needs to be monitored. This construction appears to emerge as a by-product both of the self-definition of these stakeholders *as experts* on one or another element pertinent to the transition toward a bioeconomy, which also brings along a delineated group of non-experts that is "the public", as well as the design of the arena in which they make sense of the public in relation to the governance of a transition toward a bioeconomy.

Our analysis highlights a tension between the inclusion and exclusion of participants. While the case studied in this article aimed to be inclusive, the overall participatory collective that was formed was partially framed and subject to "overflows" [36]. This means that certain actors and definitions of the issues were excluded. For example, excluded actors included stakeholders with an opposing standpoint to those who signed the Manifesto and citizens who were not in the crossline of the recruitment agencies or interested in sustainability issues. In some cases, these exclusions were deliberate and purposive, in others they were the unintended consequence of the orchestration.

Unlike experts from academia, industry or policy, or partisan public bodies, such as NGOs, citizens are not *already and continuously engaged* in the transition toward a bioeconomy. When thinking of engaging citizens as members of the Public-in-General, the focus is placed specifically on those citizens who are not educated on the topic, but who possess commonsense and experiential knowledge, as well as a value scheme in relation to socio-political and technological developments that is not specifically colored by their investment in the bioeconomy. It is such a heterogeneous and unstable group whose ways of giving meaning to the bioeconomy one would generally want to explore. These citizens need to go through a process of knowledge articulation, which entails familiarization for deliberate opinion forming. As a consequence, and because of time and resource constraints, their articulated, unique and distinctive knowledge became siloed, and their embodied identities were excluded from the process of knowledge integration with others—experts, stakeholders, policymakers—when criteria and preferences for transition governance were discussed. This is an important decision-making aspect of defining the societal transition pathway, where involved stakeholders participate and interact in order to develop support for policies (i.e., license to operate) and to engage actors in reframing problems and solutions through social learning [37]. We argue that this could ultimately hamper the overall effectiveness of integral, holistic transition governance, as policy-makers are now tasked with integrating the separately collected knowledge themselves, while lacking a clear license to operate granted by the "general public".

This case-study has shown how easily certain partialities of the public that have a substantial stake in the transition, but have less power, remain "ignored" or are framed according to specific interpretations. This highlights the need for a better, more substantial, involvement of the heterogeneous public, as also stressed by a number of other studies [7,9,10,38]. Chilvers and Longhurst [22] have called for a better analysis of the relationship between the way in which collectives of participation are configured and political openings/closings that occur with respect to models, publics and objects of participation. Our study responds to this call, showing how the configuration of FGDs and pMCA workshops in the bioeconomy can lead to political closing for a number of partialities of the constructed public.

5.2. *Strengths, Limitations and Future Perspectives*

The findings of our study are contextualized by many factors that are specific to the political and innovation culture of the Netherlands [39]. The governance approach to bioeconomy in this country focuses on co-creating a long-term vision that informs short-term action, on facilitating bottom-up, regional clusters and on promoting radical innovation through stimulating the cooperation between players with vested interests and frontrunners [37]. Since we are dealing with a transition that needs to happen in contexts that vary widely with regards to political and innovation cultures, as well as biocapacity [40], it becomes pertinent to investigate how such differences in culture weigh into what can or should be expected from how participative collectives are constituted [30]. Whereas in some contexts, such as the Netherlands, it is considered straightforward that public engagement is a prerequisite for a successful bioeconomy transition [37], in others it might not—or with different enactments [23]. The transition to a bioeconomy requires actions on a global scale, yet regional efforts are needed to demonstrate progress and to identify useful indicators that monitor the performance of a sustainable bioeconomy [41,42]. It is a challenge that takes on many forms to ensure that public participation does not turn into a meaningless or stripped-down strategic practice, in which official authorities pretend to listen to citizens while continuing the pursuit of their own vested interests and exerting their own power [23]. Contextualized case studies, such as the one presented in this article, can serve to shed light both on good practices as well as on blind spots or open-ended challenges—such as for instance knowledge integration. It is in this capacity that such studies can contribute to a more sustainable and inclusive transition to a bioeconomy [43].

Our analysis offers a new perspective on, and appreciation of, the partiality of different forms of public participation, and varying degrees by which possibilities of system change in the transition to a bioeconomy are inclusive or exclusive with regard to these publics. We are simultaneously being reminded of the complexities, or even the impossibility, of putting into practice anything even vaguely like a situation of ideal dialogue, of the importance, in our efforts to engage with them, to attend to the public with an ethics of care, and, as researchers, doing what we can to emancipate the voice of those who are affected but are not in the driver's seat. This offers a promising way of exploring actor dynamics and politics in system change. With this, we aim to contribute to a more sensitive, sensible and integral interpretation of public engagement in sustainability transitions—one that is relevant to actors from academia, policy, industry and other spheres relevant to the bioeconomy transition.

Our work adds to the growing body of literature focused on explaining transition actor dynamics, such as Farla et al. [44], where there is a particular interest in a greater understanding of designing and implementing innovative participation collectives and spaces of intervention in system change in transitions. Actors in transitions need to be reflexively aware of the partialities of the public and the impact that potential exclusions can have. Stakeholders have diverging views and priorities with regard to the policy objectives and interventions. Citizens are often interested in technological change [45] and progress toward more sustainable societies, but enrolling them in participatory collectives does require an appropriate participatory approach to make sense of current developments and to form an opinion on the developments and desirable futures [23,31,46]. Understanding this can help us design more effective or targeted policy interventions (be it with incentives such as subsidies, public procurement or behavioral "nudging" to induce changes).

6. Conclusions

Our case-study shows that there is no single all-encompassing "public perception of the bioeconomy". The constructed "public" has various partialities, thus highlighting the need for a better acknowledgement and involvement of diverse segments of the public in sustainability transitions. This requires appropriate experimentation with participatory research—an approach that takes time, provides room for contemplation, creativity and reflexivity, and that stimulates curiosity and appreciation toward the distinctiveness of non-expert knowledge and how this could substantially contribute to the transition pathways. By focusing on the latter, we will be able to develop technologies and policies that are not only inclusive, but also accepted by society. Although our case study was limited to the transition to a bioeconomy in the Netherlands, the findings are also likely to be applicable to other policy themes and, to some extent, to other countries.

Author Contributions: Conceptualization, P.K., J.E.W.B. and D.H.J.L.; Methodology, D.H.J.L., L.v.W. and J.E.W.B.; Analysis D.H.J.L. and P.K.; Data Curation, D.H.J.L.; Writing—Original Draft Preparation, D.H.J.L.; Writing—Review & Editing, D.H.J.L., P.K., L.v.W. and J.E.W.B.; Visualization, P.K.; Supervision, J.E.W.B.; Project Administration, J.E.W.B.; Funding Acquisition, J.E.W.B. All authors have read and agreed to the published version of the manuscript.

Funding: This research was supported by BE-BASIC, an international public–private partnership (PPP) that develops industrial bio-based solutions to build a sustainable society (http://www.be-basic.org). This project was carried out under the Flagship "Embedding Biobased Economy in Society" of the BE-Basic program, funded by the Dutch Government's FES program.

Acknowledgments: The authors would like to thank Deborah Eade for English editing. In addition, the authors wish to thank the editor and the two anonymous reviewers for their constructive comments and suggestions for improving this manuscript.

Conflicts of Interest: The authors declare no conflicts of interest. The funders had no role in the design of the study; in the collection, analyses or interpretation of data; in the writing of the manuscript or in the decision to publish the results.

References

1. Langeveld, J.W.A.; Dixon, J.; Jaworski, J.F. Development Perspectives Of The Biobased Economy: A Review. *Crop Sci.* **2010**, *50* (Suppl. 1), 142. [CrossRef]
2. Priefer, C.; Jörissen, J.; Frör, O. Pathways to shape the bioeconomy. *Resources* **2017**, *6*, 10. [CrossRef]
3. Pfau, S.F.; Hagens, J.E.; Dankbaar, B.; Smits, A.J.M. Visions of sustainability in bioeconomy research. *Sustainability* **2014**, *6*, 1222–1249. [CrossRef]
4. Meyer, R. Bioeconomy strategies: Contexts, visions, guiding implementation principles and resulting debates. *Sustainability* **2017**, *9*, 1031. [CrossRef]
5. Mccormick, K.; Kautto, N. The Bioeconomy in Europe: An Overview. *Sustainability* **2013**, *6*, 2589–2608. [CrossRef]
6. Scarlat, N.; Dallemand, J.F.; Monforti-Ferrario, F.; Nita, V. The role of biomass and bioenergy in a future bioeconomy: Policies and facts. *Environ. Dev.* **2015**, *15*, 3–34. [CrossRef]
7. Mukhtarov, F.; Gerlak, A. Away from fossil-fuels and toward a bioeconomy: Knowledge versatility for public policy ? *Environ. Plan. C Politics Space* **2017**, *35*, 1010–1028. [CrossRef]
8. Butler, C.; Demski, C.; Parkhill, K.; Pidgeon, N.; Spence, A. Public values for energy futures: Framing, indeterminacy and policy making. *Energy Policy* **2015**, *87*, 665–672. [CrossRef]

9. Bugge, M.M.; Hansen, T.; Klitkou, A. What is the bioeconomy? A review of the literature. *Sustainability* **2016**, *8*, 691. [CrossRef]
10. Aquilani, B.; Silvestri, C.; Ioppolo, G.; Ruggieri, A. The challenging transition to bio-economies: Towards a new framework integrating corporate sustainability and value co-creation. *J. Clean. Prod.* **2018**, *172*, 4001–4009. [CrossRef]
11. Haider, T.P.; Völker, C.; Kramm, J.; Landfester, K.; Wurm, F.R. Plastics of the Future? The Impact of Biodegradable Polymers on the Environment and on Society. *Angew. Chem. Int. Ed.* **2019**, *58*, 50–62. [CrossRef] [PubMed]
12. Reim, W.; Parida, V.; Sjödin, D.R. Circular business models for the bio-economy: A review and new directions for future research. *Sustainability* **2019**, *11*, 2558. [CrossRef]
13. De Besi, M.; McCormick, K. Towards a bioeconomy in Europe: National, regional and industrial strategies. *Sustainability* **2015**, *7*, 10461–10478. [CrossRef]
14. Kern, F.; Smith, A. Restructuring energy systems for sustainability? Energy transition policy in the Netherlands. *Energy Policy* **2008**, *36*, 4093–4103. [CrossRef]
15. Wesseler, J.; Von Braun, J. Measuring the Bioeconomy: Economics and Policies. *Annu. Rev. Resour. Econ.* **2017**, *9*, 275–298. [CrossRef]
16. Lynch, D.H.J.; Klaassen, P.; Broerse, J.E.W. Unraveling Dutch citizens' perceptions on the bio-based economy: The case of bioplastics, bio-jetfuels and small-scale bio-refineries. *Ind. Crops Prod.* **2017**, *106*, 130–137. [CrossRef]
17. Stern, T.; Ploll, U.; Spies, R.; Schwarzbauer, P.; Hesser, F.; Ranacher, L. Understanding perceptions of the bioeconomy in Austria-An explorative case study. *Sustainability* **2018**, *10*, 4142. [CrossRef]
18. Mustalahti, I. The responsive bioeconomy: The need for inclusion of citizens and environmental capability in the forest based bioeconomy. *J. Clean. Prod.* **2018**, *172*, 3781–3790. [CrossRef]
19. Sanz-Hernández, A.; Sanagustín-Fons, M.V.; López-Rodríguez, M.E. A transition to an innovative and inclusive bioeconomy in Aragon, Spain. *Environ. Innov. Soc. Trans.* **2019**, *33*, 301–316. [CrossRef]
20. Sanz-Hernández, A.; Esteban, E.; Garrido, P. Transition to a bioeconomy: Perspectives from social sciences. *J. Clean. Prod.* **2019**, *224*, 107–119. [CrossRef]
21. Hempel, C.; Will, S.; Zander, K. Societal perspectives on a bio-economy in Germany: An explorative study using Q methodology. *Int. J. Food Syst. Dyn.* **2019**, *10*, 21–37.
22. Chilvers, J.; Longhurst, N. Participation in transition(s): Reconceiving public engagements in energy transitions as co-produced, emergent and diverse. *J. Environ. Policy Plan.* **2016**, *18*, 585–607. [CrossRef]
23. Carvalho, A.; Pinto-Coelho, Z.; Seixas, E. Listening to the Public–Enacting Power: Citizen Access, Standing and Influence in Public Participation Discourses. *J. Environ. Policy Plan.* **2019**, *21*, 563–576. [CrossRef]
24. Jasanoff, S. A mirror for science. *Public Underst. Sci.* **2014**, *23*, 21–26. [CrossRef]
25. Hendriks, C.M.; Grin, J. Contextualizing reflexive governance: The politics of Dutch transitions to sustainability. *J. Environ. Policy Plan.* **2007**, *9*, 333–350. [CrossRef]
26. Walker, G.; Cass, N. Carbon reduction, "the public" and renewable energy: Engaging with socio-technical configurations. *Area* **2007**, *39*, 458–469. [CrossRef]
27. Smith, A. Civil society in sustainable energy transitions. In *Governing the Energy Transition: Reality, Illusion, or Necessity*; Verbong, G., Loorbach, D., Eds.; Routledge: New York, NY, USA, 2012; pp. 180–202.
28. Irwin, A. The politics of talk: Coming to terms with the "new" scientific governance. *Soc. Stud. Sci.* **2006**, *36*, 299–320. [CrossRef]
29. Irwin, A. Constructing the scientific citizen: Science and democracy in the biosciences. *Public Underst. Sci.* **2001**, *10*, 1–18. [CrossRef]
30. Hagendijk, R.; Irwin, A. Public deliberation and governance: Engaging with science and technology in contemporary Europe. *Minerva* **2006**, *44*, 167–184. [CrossRef]
31. Chilvers, J.; Kearnes, M. Remaking Participation in Science and Democracy. *Sci. Technol. Hum. Values* **2019**, *45*, 347–380. [CrossRef]
32. Krueger, R.A.; Casey, M.A. *Focus Groups: A Practical Guide for Applied Research*; SAGE Publications, Inc.: London, UK, 2009.
33. Ransdorp, S.; Osseweijer, P. *Maatschappelijke Roadmap voor de Biobased Economy*; Stichting BE-Basic: Delft, The Netherlands, 2016.

34. Michael, M. Publics performing publics: Of PiGs, PiPs and politics. *Public Underst. Sci.* **2009**, *18*, 617–631. [CrossRef]
35. Braun, K.; Schultz, S. " . . . a certain amount of engineering involved": Constructing the public in participatory governance arrangements. *Public Underst. Sci.* **2010**, *19*, 403–419. [CrossRef] [PubMed]
36. Callon, M.; Lascoumes, P.; Barthe, Y. *Acting in an Uncertain World: An Essay on Technical Democracy*; MIT Press: Cambridge, MA, USA, 2009.
37. Bosman, R.; Rotmans, J. Transition Governance towards a Bioeconomy: A Comparison of Finland and The Netherlands. *Sustainability* **2016**, *8*, 1017. [CrossRef]
38. Hausknost, D.; Schriefl, E.; Lauk, C.; Kalt, G. A transition to which bioeconomy? An exploration of diverging techno-political choices. *Sustainability* **2017**, *9*, 669. [CrossRef]
39. Van der Molen, F.; Ludwig, D.; Consoli, L.; Zwart, H. Global challenges, Dutch solutions? The shape of responsibility in Dutch science and technology policies. *J. Responsib. Innov.* **2019**, *6*, 340–345. [CrossRef]
40. Liobikiene, G.; Chen, X.; Streimikiene, D.; Balezentis, T. The trends in bioeconomy development in the European Union: Exploiting capacity and productivity measures based on the land footprint approach. *Land Use Policy* **2020**, *91*, 104375. [CrossRef]
41. Falcone, P.M.; González García, S.; Imbert, E.; Lijó, L.; Moreira, M.T.; Tani, A.; Tartiu, V.E.; Morone, P. Transitioning towards the bio-economy: Assessing the social dimension through a stakeholder lens. *Corp. Soc. Responsib. Environ. Manag.* **2019**, *26*, 1135–1153. [CrossRef]
42. Liobikiene, G.; Balezentis, T.; Streimikiene, D.; Chen, X. Evaluation of bioeconomy in the context of strong sustainability. *Sustain. Dev.* **2019**, *27*, 955–964. [CrossRef]
43. Fevolden, A.M.; Coenen, L.; Hansen, T.; Klitkou, A. The role of trials and demonstration projects in the development of a sustainable bioeconomy. *Sustainability* **2017**, *9*, 419. [CrossRef]
44. Farla, J.; Markard, J.; Raven, R.; Coenen, L. Sustainability transitions in the making: A closer look at actors, strategies and resources. *Technol. Forecast. Soc. Chang.* **2012**, *79*, 991–998. [CrossRef]
45. D'Adamo, I.; Gastaldi, M.; Rosa, P. Recycling of end-of-life vehicles: Assessing trends and performances in Europe. *Technol. Forecast. Soc. Chang.* **2020**, *152*, 119887. [CrossRef]
46. Lynch, D.; Kupper, F.; Broerse, J. Toward a socially desirable EU research and innovation agenda on urban waste: A transnational EU citizen consultation. *Sustainability* **2018**, *10*, 1641. [CrossRef]

sustainability

MDPI

Article

Relationships between Renewable Energy Consumption, Social Factors, and Health: A Panel Vector Auto Regression Analysis of a Cluster of 12 EU Countries

Giulia Caruso [1,*], Emiliano Colantonio [2] and Stefano Antonio Gattone [2]

[1] Department of Neuroscience, Imaging and Clinical Sciences, University G. d'Annunzio Chieti-Pescara, Via L. Polacchi n. 11, 66100 Chieti, Italy

[2] Department of Philosophical, Pedagogical and Economic-Quantitative Sciences, University G. d'Annunzio Chieti-Pescara, V.le Pindaro n. 42, 65127 Pescara, Italy; colantonio@unich.it (E.C.); gattone@unich.it (S.A.G.)

* Correspondence: giulia.caruso@unich.it

Received: 13 March 2020; Accepted: 3 April 2020; Published: 6 April 2020

Abstract: One of the key indicators of a population's well-being and the economic development of a country is represented by health, the main proxy for which is life expectancy at birth. Some factors, such as industrialization and modernization, have allowed this to improve considerably. On the other hand, along with high global population growth, the factor which may jeopardize human health the most is environmental degradation, which can be tackled through the transition to renewable energy. The main purpose of our study is to investigate the relationship between renewable energy consumption, social factors, and health, using a Panel Vector Auto Regression (PVAR) technique. We explore the link between some proxy variables for renewable energy consumption, government policy, general public awareness, the market, lobbying activity, the energy dependence on third countries, and health, spanning the period from 1990 to 2015, for a cluster of 12 European countries characterized by common features. Specifically, our analysis shows the importance of having a stringent policy for the development of renewable energy consumption and its influence over other social factors, rather than the existence of causal relationships between health and renewable energy consumption for the analyzed countries. This kind of analysis has a great potential for policy-makers. Further, a deeper understanding of these relationships can create a more effective decision-making process.

Keywords: renewable energy consumption; CO_2; health; PVAR; low carbon economy; environmental policy; hydrocarbon economy; clean energy development

1. Introduction

The increasing concern over issues related to energy security, climate change, global warming, environmental degradation, and the depletion of fossil fuels represent a threat to Europe and the whole world, propelling the need to make systemic changes to a shift towards a more sustainable economy [1]. Furthermore, the report of the Second UN Environment Conference states that approximately seven million people worldwide die from air pollution every year [2].

Moreover, the agenda of the European Union (EU) stresses the importance of sustainable development as a means of development, capable of improving living conditions, developing better conditions for companies, and increasing countries' competitiveness [3].

To this extent, government policies must urgently implement sustainable transportation, waste management strategies [4–9], sustainable tourism [10,11], and develop low-carbon economies [8].

Concerning the latter, the increasing interest in renewable energy is also due to Europe's dependency on foreign energy sources and to the recent concerns over the volatility of the price of crude oil [8].

Moreover, we are currently witnessing an ongoing debate over how to balance the relationships between human health, environmental concerns, and economic development [12–14].

In this regard, in December 2019 the European Commission presented the European Green Deal, which establishes that the European Union needs to transform itself into a resource-efficient and competitive economy with zero net emissions of greenhouse gases by 2050, and its economic growth should detach itself from resources use. The main objective is to boost the efficient use of resources by moving to a clean, circular economy, and, consequently, stopping climate change, cutting pollution, and improving the health of population [12].

Moreover, European Union member countries launched, at the beginning of 2005, the CO_2 emissions trading scheme. Setting environmental taxes is very useful for two reasons. First, they represent an incentive for companies to research and invest in more environmentally friendly technologies, or to deploy fewer resources. Secondly, the increased fiscal revenue resulting from higher tax collection can be used to reduce taxes on labor, savings, and capital, thereby favoring higher investment in environmental conservation [13].

Health, the main proxy for which is life expectancy at birth, certainly represents one of the key indicators of a population's well-being and the economic development of a country [14]. Some factors, such as industrialization and modernization, have allowed life expectancy to improve considerably. According to some scholars, economic development leads to reductions in the impact on the environment. Thus, the search for economic growth would also have the positive effect of improving sustainability [9]. Furthermore, many past studies suggest that development reduces infant mortality and increases life expectancy throughout the world [9,15].

Research on the economic factors influencing human health have flourished recently [3,12,16,17], whereas the literature on the relationships between health, renewable energy consumption, and socio-economic factors is rather poor. The International Energy Agency [17] underlined the importance of the promotion of clean energy globally, pointing out that all countries can dispose of at least one renewable energy source, the development of which requires significant investment, creating job opportunities and improving new technologies. Mazur [18] analyzed energy consumption and various human well-being indicators for a sample of high-income nations from 1980 to 2006, but he registered a higher life expectancy independent of the increase or decrease in per capita energy consumption levels.

According to Firebaugh and Beck [19], economic development reduces infant mortality and increases life expectancy worldwide. However, Brady et al. [10] highlight that the effects of development registered a moderate reduction over time in less developed nations, and Preston [20] emphasizes that economic development is not the only factor influencing changes in human well-being.

The Stern Report [21], commissioned by the UK Treasury, revealed the negative impacts that climate change may have on health and economic growth. It stated that the average temperature of greenhouse gases would rise in the next 50 years by between 2 °C and 3 °C, posing a threat to human life with regards to access to water, food production, land use, environment, and health. In regard to health, accelerating global warming is expected to worsen the impact of diseases such as malaria and malnutrition, mainly affecting poor countries [22–24]. Furthermore, it increases the formation of ozone, which has negative effects on respiratory and cardiovascular health and favors the intensification of heat waves [24], which contribute to increasing numbers of heart attacks. Moreover, increasing sea levels [25,26] have negative effects on population health and crops, causing changes in nutrition and increased instances of infectious diseases.

Fossil fuels, as is well known, are the main source of air pollutants, and many papers have shown their damaging effects on human health, including cardiovascular and respiratory diseases. To this extent, Pablo-Romero et al. [27] reviewed the exploitation of renewable energy sources.

They highlighted that the direct result of the use of renewables is the reduction of fossil fuels and of related air pollutant emissions, generating positive effects on human health.

Some of the studies that analyzed the impact of climate change on health [28,29] show that it has the worst effect in societies characterized by exiguous resources, little technology, and inadequate infrastructure. Historically, indeed, higher temperatures have reduced economic growth mainly in poor countries, with a noticeable effect on agriculture, industry, and political stability [22]. In particular, a study [30] shows that greenhouse gas emissions by fossil electricity generation have the highest impact on human health, whereas nuclear and renewables technologies have a noticeable lower one. Therefore, since the use of fewer pollutant energies leads to a decrease in emissions, it follows that there will result a reduction of diseases, consequent lower economic costs to society, and less dependence on fossil fuels in third countries.

Since understanding the relationship between renewable energy consumption and health is crucial, and, given the poor scientific literature on their bilateral relationship, the main purpose of our study is to evaluate this, thereby filling this gap in knowledge. All nations share the same fight against climate change and environmental degradation, but not all EU member states start from the same position [12]; thus, we identified twelve countries sharing common features: Austria, Belgium, Finland, France, Germany, Greece, Ireland, Italy, the Netherlands, Portugal, Spain, and Sweden. They have in common that they are historical members, energy importers, and among the richest countries in the EU. Naturally, the drivers of climate change and biodiversity loss are not limited to European borders; thus, the EU should also use its influence to mobilize its neighbors to join in its efforts [31].

We explored the link between some proxy variables for renewable energy consumption, government policy, the market, general public awareness, lobbying activity, the dependence on third countries, and health, spanning the period from 1990 to 2015. Specifically, our analysis shows the importance of adopting a stringent policy for the development of renewable energy consumption and its influence over other social factors, rather than the existence of causal relationships between health and renewable energy consumption for the analyzed countries. This kind of analysis has a great importance for policy-makers. Further, a deeper understanding of these relationships can create a more effective decision-making process.

The remainder of this paper is organized as follows. Section 2 describes the data, the methodology used, and the econometric specification, estimating the impact of the variables of interest. The empirical results are presented in Section 3. Section 4 summarizes the main findings of the study, and the final Section outlines our conclusions.

2. Materials and Methods

The main purpose of this study was to investigate the role that socio-technical factors can play in the transition to a renewable-energy-based economy in a group of 12 European countries (Austria, Belgium, Finland, France, Germany, Greece, Ireland, Italy, the Netherlands, Portugal, Spain, and Sweden) that are energy importers. For this purpose, we used annual data from 1990 to 2015. Given that the process of transition to a renewable energy economy is a dynamic one, we tried to use the longest time span possible. Our empirical strategy uses a Panel Vector Auto Regression (PVAR) technique. In the wake of the work of Sung & Park [1,32], this methodology combines the traditional VAR approach, in which all the variables in the system are endogenous, with the panel data approach, which allows to borrow strength from the cross-sectional dimension and focus on bidirectional effects.

In Table 1 the name, definition, and source of the raw variables are presented.

The first variable is renewable energy consumption (REC), which is measured by the percentage contribution of renewables to total energy generation. It proxies the degree of transition to a renewable-energy economy [1].

EPS (Environmental Policy Stringency Index) represents government policy, since it is used as an indicator of the stringency of environmental regulations. It proxies pressure exercised by government, and, since it is a mighty force, it is able to promote change [1].

Table 1. Description of the raw variables.

Variable	Definition	Source
REC	Renewable energy consumption (% of total final energy consumption)	World Bank
EPS	Environmental Policy Stringency Index	OECD
GDPc	GDP per capita, PPP (current international $)	World Bank
CO_2	CO_2 emissions (metric tons per capita)	World Bank
OGCN	Electricity production from oil, gas, coal, and nuclear sources (% of total)	World Bank
IMP	Energy imports, net (% of energy use)	World Bank
LIFE	Life expectancy at birth, total (years)	World Bank

This composite index does not only include market-based instruments, but also non-market-based ones. The first component contains market-based instruments such as taxes, trading schemes, and feed-in tariffs. The second instead includes government expenditure in R&D for renewable technologies, or the emissions limit standards for greenhouse effect gases [1].

CO_2 is a proxy for general public awareness, and it is measured in metric tons of emissions per capita. Greenhouse gases consists of water vapor, carbon dioxide, methane, ozone, nitrous dioxide, chlorofluorocarbons, and hydrofluorocarbons, which are directly responsible for global warming and climate change. Thus, it is essential to act as swiftly as possible to reduce these kind of emissions [1].

GDP is an indicator of the economic growth of a country and is an important factor affecting both CO_2 emissions and REC. Thus, in their analysis, Durmuşoğlu et al. [33] assumed that GDP is a key factor to development. Indeed, economic growth has an important effect on many indexes, and is undoubtedly essential to achieving sustainable development.

According to the Kuznets curve hypothesis [34–37], pollution increase is linked to income at low income levels. At a higher income level, instead, a turning point is reached, and further growth leads to lower pollution levels [37]. Some researchers [38,39], on the contrary, state that the relationship between development and pollution is monotonically rising.

Many studies have analyzed the relationship between REC and GDP, concluding that there is a relationship between them. Sadorsky [40] has shown that increasing GDP has a positive and statistically significant impact on REC. In the long term, a 1% increase in per capita income is related to an increase in per capita REC by approximately 3.5%.

Apergis et al. [41] have analyzed the long-run causality between REC and GDP using the Canning and Pedroni [42] long-run causality test, finding a strong bidirectional causality. Renewable energy has a crucial role with regards to economic growth, which, in turn, increases the use of renewable energy sources. Also Sebri et al. [43], examining this relationship, found a bidirectional causality between variables.

In their analysis, Bakirtas et al. [44,45] found a long-run cointegration between renewable energy and economic growth and a causality from economic growth to renewable energy.

Özşahin et al. [45,46] found a positive long-run relationship between REC and economic development and Inglesi-Lotz [47] found a statistically significant positive effect of REC on economic growth. Menyah et al. [48], exploring the causal relationship between CO_2 emissions, REC, nuclear energy consumption, and GDP, found a causality from economic growth to REC. Tugcu et al. [49] have analyzed the long-run and causal relationships between REC, non-renewable energy consumption, and economic growth, finding that both REC and non-REC are important for economic growth.

Lin et al. [50] have examined the relationship between REC and economic growth in China, finding a bi-directional long-term causality between them. This indicates that the growing economy of China is favorable to boosting the development of the renewable energy sector, which, in turn, increases economic growth. Ocal and Aslan [51] found that REC has a negative impact on GDP, and that there is unidirectional causality from economic growth to REC. In their study, Ben-Sahla et al. [52] detected the presence of a bi-directional causality between GDP and REC. It positively impacts GDP and, in turn, is positively affected by GDP. This suggests that REC exerts negative effects on CO_2 emissions; thus, the promotion of renewable energy in developing countries may reduce the use of non-renewable energy consumption. Furthermore, it appears that REC positively impacts the GDP, and CO_2 emissions negatively affect REC, and that the latter is only affected by GDP.

The variable electricity production from oil, gas, coal, and nuclear sources (OGCN) instead relates to lobbying pressure, and is measured as the percentage contribution of traditional energy sources, such as oil, gas, coal, and nuclear, to overall electricity generation. Lobbying power is directly proportional to the contributions of traditional energy sources, which discourage the development of the renewable energy sector. For this reason, the contributions of traditional energy sources lend themselves well as proxies for the power exerted by their relevant interest groups.

Net energy imports (IMP) proxy a country's dependency on energy imported from third countries, and can be measured by the ratio of imported energy to the total energy supply. The relevance of this factor lies in the fact that a higher import dependency should induce investments in a country's own renewable resources, increasing the contribution of renewables to the total energy supply [9].

Life expectancy at birth (LIFE) proxies health. It denotes the average number of years that a newborn infant is likely to live, assuming that prevailing patterns of mortality at the moment of its birth remain unchanged throughout its life [9].

The data on REC, CO_2, GDPc, OGCN, IMP and LIFE were extracted from the World Development Indicator database of World Bank, whereas the data on EPS were obtained from the Organisation for Economic Co-operation and Development (OECD).

The existing literature, especially on renewable energy, has contributed to the discussion on the roles and interactions of factors and has helped us to determine and focus upon the main identified factors and determine the relationships between them. By proposing a systematic panel approach, we identified the importance of each factor and defined its influence.

The use of percentage values was due to the fact that they are capable of removing distortions produced by country size.

Following the recent empirical literature, Love and Zicchino [53] proposed an estimator that allows for the presence of stationary endogenous variables and unobserved individual heterogeneity. The specification of the PVAR model used in this empirical analysis follows the specification of Equation (1):

$$X_{it} = f_i + \Gamma(L)X_{it} + \varepsilon_t \tag{1}$$

where X_{it} represents the vector of stationary variables in our analysis, f_i denotes the vector of deterministic fixed effects, $\Gamma(L)X_{it}$ is a square matrix polynomial in the lag operator, and ε_t is the random error term.

Integration within the EU has induced closer ties among member states, so that variations in the energy sector of a country may influence that of others. As a consequence, cross-national endogenous interactions must be taken into account.

Interdependencies among variables may take three forms [54]:

(1) Dynamic interdependencies spanning over time, due to the presence of the lagged variables on the right-hand side of the model.
(2) Within-countries interdependencies, arising as the elements of X may affect each other at the national level.
(3) Between-countries interdependencies, arising as the elements of X may affect each other across the national borders.

The descriptive statistics of the variables are presented in Table 2.

Macroeconomic variables are usually characterized by non-stationarity, and this may affect the econometric analysis of time series and panels since the use of non-stationary variables gives spurious results. When the variables in the model are non-stationary, the first-difference transformation may be used to overcome this problem. The first step of the empirical analysis was to examine the stationarity of the different series using various unit root tests. Two classes of test allow the investigation of the presence of a unit root. The first-generation unit root tests are based on the hypothesis of cross-sectional independence between panel units; among others, we have the Levin, Lin and Chu (LLC) tests [55], the Im, Pesaran and Shin (IPS) tests [56,57], and the Fisher's type tests [58]. The main limitation of these tests is that they are all constructed under the assumption that the individual time series in the panel are cross-sectionally independently distributed, while, on the contrary, a large amount of literature provides evidence of the co-movements between economic variables, and, as argued by Banerjee et al. [59], panel unit root tests may be biased if the panel units are cross-cointegrated. To overcome this difficulty, a second generation of unit root tests has been proposed that relax the assumption of cross-sectional independence, allowing for a variety of dependence across the different units; among others, we have the Pesaran tests, based on the Cross-Sectional Augmented Dickey–Fuller [60].

Table 2. Descriptive statistics.

Variable	Mean	Std. Dev.	Min	Max
REC	16.484	12.900	0.940	53.248
EPS	1.991	0.835	0.646	4.133
GDPc	28.871	9.514	11.763	50.302
CO_2	8.111	2.283	4.239	13.261
OGCN	72.974	21.561	17.721	98.583
IMP	56.769	19.441	0.573	86.340
LIFE	78.846	1.963	73.966	83.229
dREC	0.361	1.336	−3.415	5.216
dEPS	0.086	0.265	−0.633	1.000
dGDPc	0.982	0.889	−2.217	3.506
dCO_2	−0.055	0.486	−2.417	2.155
dOGCN	−0.635	4.576	−17.560	16.088
dIMP	0.115	2.615	−9.917	15.252
dLIFE	0.220	0.226	−0.449	1.444

d denotes the first difference operator.

To analyze the order of the integration of our variables, the IPS tests, the Maddala and Wu (MW) tests, and the Pesaran tests were used. All tests were characterized by a null hypothesis that assumes a unit root. The results of these panel unit root tests are shown in Table 3 (variables in levels) and Table 4 (variables in first differences). At conventional levels of significance, the results show that all variables were non-stationary in levels, since the null hypothesis is usually not rejected. However, all the selected variables were stationary after the first difference: all the series were integrated of order one I(1).

Table 3. Unit root tests: variables in level.

Variable	IPS W-t-bar	MW	Pesaran Z-t-bar
REC	7.846	25.944	4.727
EPS	1.933	22.613	0.025
GDPc	2.193	4.825	0.523
CO_2	6.343	29.568	0.387
OGCN	6.212	58.144	−0.603
IMP	−1.201	60.223	1.610
LIFE	3.687	33.939	−0.640

* $p < 0.1$; ** $p < 0.05$; *** $p < 0.01$.

Table 4. Unit root tests: variables in first differences.

Variable	IPS W-t-bar	MW	Pesaran Z-t-bar
dREC	−10.765 ***	285.755 ***	−9.981 ***
dEPS	−13.420 ***	332.459 ***	−7.584 ***
dGDPc	−12.753 ***	254.233 ***	−3.536 ***
dCO_2	−8.309 ***	352.629 ***	−11.022 ***
dOGCN	−11.628 ***	428.891 ***	−12.003 ***
dIMP	−10.007 ***	322.048 ***	−9.026 ***
dLIFE	−17.780 ***	539.268 ***	−9.858 ***

* $p < 0.1$; ** $p < 0.05$; *** $p < 0.01$.

Table 5 shows the results of the cointegration tests developed by Westerlund [61]. The null hypothesis of these tests is the absence of cointegration. The G_τ and G_α statistics test whether cointegration exists for at least one panel unit. The P_τ and P_α statistics test whether cointegration exists for the panel as a whole. To take account of cross-section interdependence the robust *p*-value was computed through bootstrapping with 100 replications. As shown by the robust *p*-value, the null hypothesis of no cointegration cannot be rejected by all four tests. Therefore, the empirical properties of the variables examined require estimation in first differences, since no cointegration relationships exist between the (non-stationary) variables (in level).

Table 5. Cointegration tests.

Statistic	Value	Z-Value	*p*-Value	Robust *p*-Value
G_τ	−1.485	2.918	0.998	0.90
G_α	−2.733	4.217	1.000	0.74
P_τ	−5.337	1.160	0.877	0.50
P_α	−2.897	2.568	0.995	0.75

p-value are robust critical values obtained through bootstrapping with 100 replications.

The correlation matrix and the Variance Inflation Factor (VIF) have been analyzed to check the presence of collinearity and multicollinearity. The correlation matrix and the VIF statistics are reported in Table 6 (dREC has been considered as dependent variable). Given the low correlation values and the low VIF and mean VIF values, we can conclude that collinearity and multicollinearity were not a concern.

Table 6. Correlation matrix and variance inflation factor (VIF) statistics.

	dREC	dEPS	dGDPc	dCO_2	dOGCN	dIMP	dLIFE
dREC	1.000						
dEPS	−0.021	1.000					
dGDPc	0.068	−0.109	1.000				
dCO_2	−0.460	0.085	0.082	1.000			
dOGCN	−0.824	−0.007	−0.0431	0.4031	1.000		
dIMP	−0.360	0.124	0.0518	0.376	0.336	1.000	
dLIFE	−0.093	0.062	0.112	−0.0009	0.1179	−0.0075	1.000
VIF		1.05	1.32	1.05	1.06	1.05	1.04
Mean VIF	1.17						

Before the PVAR estimation, the last preliminary step was the lag order selection. Selecting the appropriate number of lags is crucial for PVAR: too few lags fail to capture the system's dynamics, leading to omitted variable bias; too many lags cause a loss of degrees of freedom, with consequent over-parameterization. The results can be seen in Table 7. The Hansen's J statistics test the null hypothesis that the model specification is over-identified, or, in other words, that the included instruments were valid instruments and that they were uncorrelated with the error term, while the excluded instruments were correctly excluded [62]. After passing the Hansen's J test, following the econometric literature, the optimal lag length should be the one that minimizes the moment model selection criteria developed by Andrews and Lu (2001): Moment Bayesian Information Criterion (MBIC), Moment Akaike's Information Criterion (MAIC), and Moment Hannan and Quinn Information Criterion (MQIC). These criteria are very similar to the maximum likelihood-based information criteria AIC, BIC and HQIC. Based on the three model selection criteria by Andrews and Lu (2001), a first-order PVAR was the preferred model.

Table 7. Lag order selection criteria.

Lag	J	J *p*-Value	MBIC	MAIC	MQIC
1	111.29	0.17	−399.24	−84.71	−212.20
2	46.27	0.58	−208.99	−51.73	−115.47

The deterministic fixed effects f_i in Equation (1) were removed by applying the first difference transformation. This procedure, however, may generate the well-known Nickell bias [63], due to the correlation between the first-differenced lag and the first-differenced error term (both depend on ε_{it-1}). In this context, estimating the dynamic panel equation by OLS will produce biased and inconsistent estimates [64]. To overcome this problem, we used forward mean-differencing, also known as the Helmert procedure [53,65]. This procedure removes the forward mean from each observation, i.e., the mean of all the future observations available for each unit and available years. As a result, the orthogonality between transformed variables and lagged regressors was preserved. The system may thus be estimated by the Generalized Method of Moments (GMM), with the lags of the regressors as instrumental variables.

3. Results and Discussion

The PVAR was estimated using one lag and with the GMM-style option [36], which replaces the missing values with zeroes and is capable of producing more efficient estimates. The first-order PVAR results are listed in Table 8. The stability of the PVAR was checked and confirmed since the eigenvalues are strictly less than 1 (see Table 9). Figure 1 shows that none of the roots are outside of the unit circle, indicating that the PVAR model is stable; this also indicates that our variables are stationary [66].

Table 8. PVAR results.

	Dependent Variables						
Independent Variables	**dREC**	**dEPS**	**dGDPc**	**dCO_2**	**Dogcn**	**dIMP**	**dLIFE**
dREC	0.250 ***	−0.030 **	0.243 ***	−0.178 ***	−0.309	−0.822 ***	0.052 ***
dEPS	3.686 ***	−0.182 ***	−0.371 **	−0.173 *	−17.393 ***	−1.536 **	−0.142 ***
dGDPc	0.236	−0.028 *	0.141 ***	−0.011	−1.892 ***	0.118	−0.060 ***
dCO_2	−0.025	−0.029	0.429 ***	−0.271 ***	0.941	−0.456	0.136 ***
dOGCN	0.157 ***	0.007	0.049 ***	−0.027 **	−0.593 ***	−0.142 **	0.000
dIMP	−0.084 **	−0.016 **	0.055 ***	−0.002	0.197	−0.196 **	−0.005
dLIFE	4.092 ***	−0.617 ***	−0.438 **	−1.277 ***	−14.974 ***	−6.667 ***	−0.144 **

* $p < 0.1$; ** $p < 0.05$; *** $p < 0.01$.

Table 9. Eigenvalue stability condition.

Eigenvalue		
Real	**Imaginary**	**Modulus**
−0.690	0.000	0.690
−0.125	−0.373	0.394
−0.125	0.373	0.394
0.346	0.000	0.346
−0.256	−0.028	0.258
−0.256	0.028	0.258
0.110	0.000	0.110

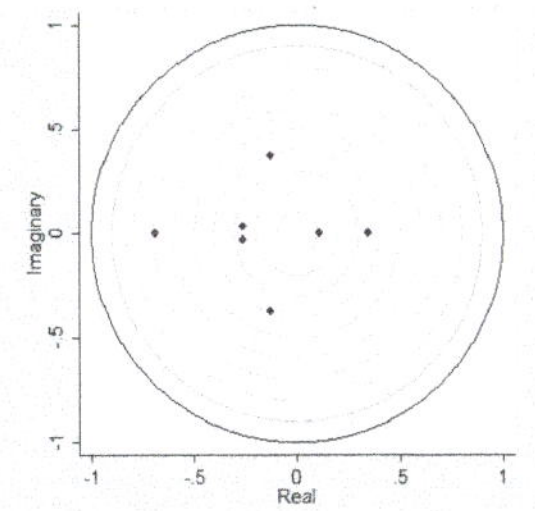

Figure 1. Roots of the companion matrix.

After the first-order PVAR estimation and its stability check, we performed the Granger causality test [67], based on the Wald test. The null hypothesis is the absence of Granger causality. The results of the Granger causality test are shown in Table 10. The presence of endogeneity is confirmed by the blocks of exogeneity analysis (ALL).

For the examined group of countries, Table 8 shows that a more stringent environmental policy should have a positive direct effect on REC and could be used by policy-makers to stimulate the transition to a renewable-energy economy. Based on the estimations, an increase in EPS would also generate a reduction of both OGCN and CO_2 emissions. The decrease in OGCN, in turn, seems not to generate a positive effect on REC, likely due to its relatively low weight in such economies (higher energy importers). In other words, this result does not necessarily mean that traditional energy sources are not important for the improvement of REC; rather, the effects of those factors are not sufficiently large to influence REC.

An increase in EPS can also produce a decrease in GDPc at first. Therefore, policy-makers should make significant efforts to develop instruments that can synergistically support the environment and market expansion, to further promote the transition to a renewable-energy-based economy. The analysis, however, shows that positive bidirectional casual relationships between GDPc and REC exist for this group of countries. First, an increase in GDPc can generate an increase in the demand for energy, including from renewable sources; second, an increase in the consumption of energy from renewable sources, perhaps generated by policy stringency, can subsequently generate an increase in GDPc. Apergis et al. [68] have also documented a positive effect of REC on GDPc. This result is the opposite of the finding of Fei et al. [69], who highlight a negative relationship between REC and GDPc.

Markets may have a significantly positive effect in promoting sustainability and the transition to a renewable-energy economy. This implies that policy-makers should encourage the economy to be renewable-friendly by promoting the renewable energy technology sector. The promotion of the consumption of renewable energy could be very important for guaranteeing market competitiveness and for creating better opportunities for potential investors.

Table 10. Granger causality test.

Equation Variable	Excluded Variables	Chi2	*p*-Value
dREC	dEPS	34.127	0.000
	dGDPc	2.360	0.125
	dCO_2	0.021	0.884
	dOGCN	9.821	0.002
	dIMP	4.274	0.039
	dLIFE	22.002	0.000
	ALL	72.545	0.000
dEPS	dREC	3.064	0.080
	dGDPc	2.720	0.099
	dCO_2	1.195	0.274
	dOGCN	1.460	0.227
	dIMP	4.225	0.040
	dLIFE	21.728	0.000
	ALL	50.575	0.000
dGDPc	dREC	25.037	0.000
	dEPS	5.484	0.019
	dCO_2	33.919	0.000
	dOGCN	13.997	0.000
	dIMP	8.385	0.004
	dLIFE	4.740	0.029
	ALL	83.204	0.000
dCO_2	dREC	24.115	0.000
	dEPS	3.003	0.083
	dGDPc	0.096	0.757
	dOGCN	6.194	0.013
	dIMP	0.029	0.864
	dLIFE	41.386	0.000
	ALL	80.084	0.000
dOGCN	dREC	0.174	0.677
	dEPS	42.340	0.000
	dGDPc	8.884	0.003
	dCO_2	1.562	0.211
	dIMP	1.169	0.280
	dLIFE	18.094	0.000
	ALL	58.776	0.000
dIMP	dREC	19.339	0.000
	dEPS	6.341	0.012
	dGDPc	0.439	0.507
	dCO_2	2.146	0.143
	dOGCN	5.774	0.016
	dLIFE	39.492	0.000
	ALL	97.128	0.000
dLIFE	dREC	14.554	0.000
	dEPS	23.856	0.000
	dGDPc	31.779	0.000
	dCO_2	68.036	0.000
	dOGCN	0.001	0.976
	dIMP	2.248	0.134
	ALL	124.179	0.000

A decrease in CO_2 seems to generate an increase in REC. If positive results in the reduction of CO_2 emissions are achieved, there will be further improvement in people's behaviour, thus generating an increase in REC. Hence, to support this, policy measures should also be directed towards promoting public awareness and emphasize the role of REC in achieving a sustainable growth for society. Furthermore, this study shows that there is a dynamic effect (path dependence), demonstrating that the input of REC and GDPc observed in previous periods generate effects on it in the present period. From a political-economy perspective, the results suggest that public awareness as well as the market (competitive) forces should be involved in promoting the transition to a renewable-energy economy. However, an increase in REC could cause a lightening in policy stringency (moreover EPS does not show a path dependence). This means that, to support REC, the political efforts in the social system must be consistently preserved.

Our findings show that, as expected, there is a negative causal relationship between REC and CO_2 for the examined group of countries. The results imply that the transition to renewable-energy economies should mitigate the carbon dioxide emissions and their negative consequences in terms of global warming and climate change. In addition, an increase in the consumption of energy from renewable sources should cause a reduction in OGCN and IMP, in this case favouring a substitution effect compared to traditional sources and imported energy.

Finally, this study found that LIFE has a significant direct influence on REC, which in turn positively influences LIFE. This means that individual well-being and public awareness could stimulate a greater demand for energy from renewable sources. Moreover, an increase in REC should in turn favour the improvement of public health. Hence, policy-makers should implement a combination of policy instruments to promote sustainable development within society and public awareness about the essential transition to renewable-energy economies, keeping in mind that those efforts need time and are a dynamic process. Particularly, national governments are called to affect public awareness by working in schools, training institutions, and universities. In this sense, it is reasonable that policy-makers start to implement actions to develop and assess knowledge, skills, and attitudes on climate change and sustainable development, providing supporting materials and facilitating the exchange of good practices.

The variance decomposition and the impulse response functions resulting from the PVAR model are shown below. Particularly, Table 11 reports the variance decomposition, which allows the assessment of the relative importance of shocks in one variable on fluctuations in other variables over time. The forecast error variance decomposition followed the Cholesky decomposition and were performed using 1000 Monte Carlo simulations for 10 periods. The Cholesky decomposition assumes that series that come earlier in the ordering affect the following variables contemporaneously, as well as with a lag, whereas the series listed successively in the VAR order affect those listed first only through their lags. The variables that appear earlier in the system are thus considered to be more exogenous. The table shows that each variable is mainly influenced by its lag. Unsurprisingly, each variable depends closely on its history.

Table 11. Variance decomposition analysis.

	Impulse Variables						
Response Variables	**dREC**	**dEPS**	**dGDPc**	**dCO_2**	**dOGCN**	**dIMP**	**Dlife**
dREC	0.497	0.197	0.053	0.047	0.039	0.009	0.157
dEPS	0.045	0.787	0.025	0.006	0.002	0.004	0.132
dGDPc	0.009	0.022	0.886	0.038	0.019	0.014	0.013
dCO_2	0.236	0.019	0.065	0.488	0.034	0.005	0.153
dOGCN	0.401	0.224	0.066	0.054	0.096	0.005	0.154
dIMP	0.209	0.050	0.044	0.043	0.047	0.418	0.189
dLIFE	0.086	0.087	0.053	0.095	0.020	0.017	0.642

Variation in response variables explained by the impulse variables in the columns (10 periods ahead).

Table 11 shows that each variable is primarily influenced by its lag (with the exception of OGCN). Specifically, REC is mainly determined by EPS (19.7%) and LIFE (15.7%) on average during a 10-year period, while OGCN is mostly influenced by shocks in EPS (22.4%).

The impulse response functions (Figure 2) illustrate the reaction of one variable to the shocks in another variable in the system, while holding all other shocks equal to zero (a Gaussian approximation based on a 200 Monte Carlo simulation was used to estimate the impulse response functions, which in this case also followed the Cholesky decomposition).

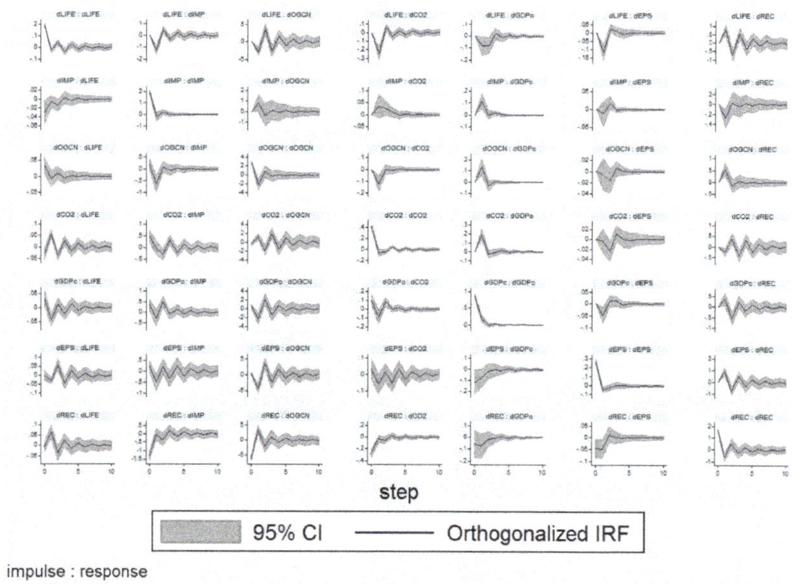

Figure 2. Impulse Response Analysis.

Specifically, when a positive shock is exerted on EPS in the current stage, REC and OGCN exhibit positive and negative responses during the early periods, respectively.

4. Conclusions

This study investigated the relationship between REC, social factors, and health in a group of 12 European countries selected on the basis of common characteristics, such as being historical members, importers, and among the richest countries in the EU. Since the process of transition to a renewable-energy economy is a dynamic one, we tried to use the longest time span possible, namely using annual data from 1990 to 2015. We used a PVAR technique that combines the traditional VAR approach, which treats all the variables in the system as endogenous, with the panel data approach, which allows to borrow strength from the cross-sectional dimension and focus on bidirectional effects. We can draw the following conclusions from our study.

First, we found that the implementation of a more stringent environmental policy has positive direct effects on REC. On the contrary, a decreasing use of OGCN seems not to generate a positive effect on REC; indeed, since the analyzed countries are high energy importers, this factor is not strong enough.

We also found that a more stringent environmental policy is linked to a reduction of OGCN and, consequently, of CO_2 emissions. Since, at least initially, a reduction of per capita GDP is also registered, governments should try to simultaneously support both the environment and market expansion.

Another finding is the existence of a positive bidirectional causal relationship between GDPc and REC. Indeed, at the beginning, an increasing per capita GDP is linked to an increase in the demand for energy in general; then, an increase in REC, maybe generated by a stringent policy, can subsequently generate an increase in per capita GDP. Markets may have a significant positive effect in boosting the transition to a renewable-energy economy. Thus, in order to guarantee their competitiveness and to create better investment opportunities, policy-makers should promote the sector related to renewable energy technology.

We also, predictably, found that lower levels of CO_2 seem to be linked to a higher REC. To this end, policy-makers should promote public awareness of the importance of the role of REC in achieving sustainable growth. Within this framework, the European Commission recently presented the European Green Deal [12], main goals of which are to stop climate change, cut pollution, and improve the health of population through an efficient use of resources.

Furthermore, we found a path dependence between REC and GDPc, since the input of REC and GDPc observed in previous periods generate effects on it in the present period. This highlights that, to boost the transition to a renewable-energy economy, it is necessary to involve both public awareness and market forces.

A higher REC could lead to a less need for a stringent policy. Furthermore, since EPS does not show a path dependence, constant political efforts should be made to support REC.

As expected, the result demonstrated the existence of a negative causal relationship between REC and CO_2. The transition to clean economies should reduce CO_2 levels and, consequently, global warming and climate change. Moreover, an increasing REC should be linked with a reduction in OGCN and IMP.

Finally, another important finding is that LIFE has a significant direct influence on REC, which in turn positively influences it. This means that individual well-being and public awareness could generate a greater demand for renewable energy.

Moreover, an increased REC should in turn improve public health, and is expected to generate significant implications on the macroeconomic environment, too, influencing the employment rate and overall economic development [70]. Society is increasingly demanding environment-friendly businesses. The development of regulations, by imposing sustainable criteria, could limit the discretion of companies in order to protect the environment and the cycle of waste [71–73], water [74], and emissions [10,75].

The novelty of our work lies in the fact that the literature on this topic is quite limited and the methodology adopted is rather new. Furthermore, the results on the relationship between renewable energy consumption and health are very interesting.

It may be argued that life expectancy is a poor variable to synthesize health, and that it is a long-term proxy, but there is no availability of a sufficiently long series associated with health.

Since the model could be extended to other clusters, this kind of analysis has a great potential for policy-makers. In addition, they are expected to gain from the resulting empirical findings [76]. Hence, they should promote sustainable development and public awareness about the essential transition to renewable-energy economics, not forgetting that those efforts need time and are a dynamic process.

Particularly, governments should raise public awareness by implementing informative campaigns in schools, training institutions, and universities, providing supporting materials to develop and assess knowledge, skills, and attitudes on climate change and sustainable development.

Author Contributions: Conceptualization, G.C. and E.C.; methodology, E.C.; formal analysis, E.C.; writing—original draft preparation, G.C. and E.C.; writing—review and editing, G.C.; supervision, S.A.G. All authors have read and agreed to the published version of the manuscript.

Funding: This research received no external funding.

Conflicts of Interest: The authors declare no conflict of interest.

References

1. Sung, B.; Park, S.D. Who drives the transition to a renewable-energy economy? Multi-actor perspective on social innovation. *Sustainability* **2018**, *10*, 448. [CrossRef]
2. Han, D.; Li, T.; Feng, S.; Shi, Z. Application of threshold regression analysis to study the impact of clean energy development on China's carbon productivity. *Int. J. Environ. Res. Public Health* **2020**, *17*, 1060. [CrossRef] [PubMed]
3. Vasylieva, T.; Lyulyov, O.; Bilan, Y.; Streimikiene, D. Sustainable economic development and greenhouse gas emissions: The dynamic impact of renewable energy consumption, GDP, and corruption. *Energies* **2019**, *12*, 3289. [CrossRef]
4. D'Adamo, I.; Rosa, P. A structured literature review on obsolete electric vehicles management practices. *Sustainability* **2019**, *11*, 6876. [CrossRef]
5. Taddeo, R.; Simboli, A.; di Vincenzo, F.; Ioppolo, G. A bibliometric and network analysis of Lean and Clean(er) production research (1990/2017). *Sci. Total Environ.* **2019**. [CrossRef]
6. Ruiz-kahia, I.; Molina-Moreno, V.; Cortés-García, F.J.; Núñez-Cacho, P. Prediction of the impact on air quality of the cities receiving cruise tourism: The case of the Port of Barcelona. *Heliyon* **2019**. [CrossRef]
7. Falcone, P.M. Tourism-based circular economy in Salento (South Italy): A SWOT-ANP analysis. *Soc. Sci.* **2019**. [CrossRef]
8. Omri, A.; Nguyen, D.K. On the determinants of renewable energy consumption: International evidence. *Energy* **2014**. [CrossRef]
9. Jorgenson, A.K.; Alekseyko, A.; Giedraitis, V. Energy consumption, human well-being and economic development in central and eastern European nations: A cautionary tale of sustainability. *Energy Policy* **2014**. [CrossRef]
10. Brady, D.; Kaya, Y.; Beckfield, J. Reassessing the effect of economic growth on well-being in less-developed countries, 1980–2003. *Stud. Comp. Int. Dev.* **2007**. [CrossRef]
11. Gilpin, R.; Gilpin, J.M. *Global Political Economy: Understanding the International Economic Order*; Princeton University Press: Princeton, NJ, USA, 2011.
12. European Commission. *The European Green Deal*; European Commission: Brussels, Belgium, 2019. [CrossRef]
13. Rubio, E.V.; Rubio, Q.; Manuel, J.; Molina-Moreno, V. Convergence analysis of environmental fiscal pressure across EU-15 Countries. *Energy Environ.* **2015**. [CrossRef]
14. Caruso, G.; Fortuna, F. Mediterranean diet Patterns in the Italian Population: A functional data analysis of Google Trends. In *Decision and Trends in Social Systems, Innovative and Integrated Approaches of Care Services*; Springer International Publishing: Cham, Switzerland, 2020.
15. Beaglehole, R.; Bonita, R. Global public health: A scorecard. *Lancet* **2008**. [CrossRef]
16. Bobak, M.; Pikhart, H.; Rose, R.; Hertzman, C.; Marmot, M. Socioeconomic factors, material inequalities, and perceived control in self-rated health: Cross-sectional data from seven post-communist countries. *Soc. Sci. Med.* **2000**. [CrossRef]
17. International Energy Agency (IEA). *Medium Term Market Report*; IEA: Paris, France, 2014.
18. Mazur, A. Does increasing energy or electricity consumption improve quality of life in industrial nations? *Energy Policy* **2011**. [CrossRef]
19. Firebaugh, G.; Beck, F.D. Does economic growth benefit the masses? Growth, dependence, and welfare in the Third World. *Am. Sociol. Rev.* **1994**. [CrossRef]
20. Preston, S.H. The Changing Relation between Mortality and level of Economic Development. *Popul. Stud. (N.Y.)* **1975**. [CrossRef]
21. Stern, N. *The Economics of Climate Change: The Stern Review*; Cambridge University Press: New York, NY, USA, 2007.
22. Dell, M.; Jones, B.F.; Olken, B.A. Temperature shocks and economic growth: Evidence from the last half century. *Am. Econ. J. Macroecon.* **2012**. [CrossRef]
23. Akachi, Y.; Goodman, D.; Parker, D. *Global Climate Change and Child Health: A Review of Pathways, Impacts and Measures to Improve the Evidence Base*; UNICEF Innocenti Research Centre, Innocenti Discussion Papers: Florence, Italy, 2009.
24. GEA Writing Team. Global Energy Assessment: Towards a Sustainable Future. *Manag. Environ. Qual. Int. J.* **2013**. [CrossRef]
25. Hansen, J.E. Scientific reticence and sea level rise. *Environ. Res. Lett.* **2007**. [CrossRef]

26. Allison, I.; Bindoff, N.L.; Bindschadler, R.A.; Cox, P.M.; de Noblet, N.; England, M.H.; Francis, J.E.; Gruber, N.; Haywood, A.M.; Karoly, D.J.; et al. *Updating the World on the Latest Climate Science*; UNSW Climate Change Research Centre: Sydney, Australia, 2009.
27. De Pablo-Romero, M.; Román, R.; Sánchez-Braza, A.; Yñiguez, R. Renewable Energy, Emissions, and Health. In *Renewable Energy—Utilisation and System Integration*; IntechOpen: Rijeka, Croatia, 2016.
28. Campbell-Lendrum, D.; Woodruff, R. *Climate Change: Quantifying the Health Impact at National and Local Levels*; Environmental Burden of Disease Series no. 14; World Health Organization: Geneva, Switzerland, 2007.
29. Portier, C.; Tart, K.; Carter, S.; Dilworth, C.; Grambsch, A.; Gohlke, J.; Hess, J.; Howard, S.; Luber, G.; Lutz, J.; et al. A Human Health Perspective on Climate Change: A Report Outlining Research Needs on the Human Health Effects of Climate Change. *Environ. Health Perspect.* **2010**. [CrossRef]
30. Treyer, K.; Bauer, C.; Simons, A. Human health impacts in the life cycle of future European electricity generation. *Energy Policy* **2014**. [CrossRef]
31. European Commission Website. Available online: https://ec.europa.eu/commission/presscorner/detail/en/IP_19_6691 (accessed on 14 December 2019).
32. Kahia, M.; Kadria, M.; Aissa, M.S.B. What impacts of renewable energy consumption on CO_2 emissions and the economic and financial development? A panel data vector autoregressive (PVAR) approach. In Proceedings of the IREC 2016 7th International Renewable Energy Congress, Hammamet, Tunisia, 22–24 March 2016. [CrossRef]
33. Durmuşoğlu, B.; Selam, A.A.; Fırat, S.Ü.O. A Comparative Study on the Relations among Sustainability Focused Indexes with REC, CO2, and GDP. *Am. Sci. Res. J. Eng. Technol. Sci.* **2017**, *34*, 81–94.
34. Kuznets, S. Economic growth and income inequality. *Am. Econ. Rev.* **1955**, *45*, 1–28.
35. Grossman, G.M.; Krueger, A.B. Economic Growth and the Environment. 1994. Available online: https://ssrn.com/abstract=227961 (accessed on 14 December 2019).
36. Holtz-Eakin, D.; Newey, W.; Rosen, H.S. Estimating Vector Autoregressions with Panel Data. *Econometrica* **1988**. [CrossRef]
37. Panayotou, T. Environmental Degradation at Different Stages of Economic Development. In *Beyond Rio*; ILO Study Series; St. Martin's Press: New York, NY, USA, 1995; pp. 13–36.
38. Cole, M.A. Limits to growth, sustainable development and environmental Kuznets curves: An examination of the environmental impact of economic development. *Sustain. Dev.* **1999**. [CrossRef]
39. Stern, D.I. The Rise and Fall of the Environmental Kuznets Curve. *World Dev.* **2004**. [CrossRef]
40. Sadorsky, P. Renewable energy consumption and income in emerging economies. *Energy Policy* **2009**. [CrossRef]
41. Apergis, N.; Danuletiu, D.C. Renewable energy and economic growth: Evidence from the sign of panel long-run causality. *Int. J. Energy Econ. Policy* **2014**, *4*, 578–587.
42. Canning, D.; Pedroni, P. Infrastructure, long-run economic growth and causality tests for cointegrated panels. *Manchester Sch.* **2008**. [CrossRef]
43. Sebri, M.; Ben-Salha, O. On the causal dynamics between economic growth, renewable energy consumption, CO_2 emissions and trade openness: Fresh evidence from BRICS countries. *Renew. Sustain. Energy Rev.* **2014**. [CrossRef]
44. Bakirtaş, İ.; Çetin, M.A. Yenilenebilir Enerji Tüketimi İle Ekonomik Büyüme Arasındaki İlişki: G-20 Ülkeleri. *Sosyoekonomi* **2016**. [CrossRef]
45. Kahran, G. Does Renewable Energy increase growth? Evidence from EU-19 Countries. *Int. J. Energy Econ. Policy* **2019**, *9*, 341.
46. Özşahin, Ş.; Mucuk, M.; Gerçeker, M. Yenilenebilir enerji ve ekonomik büyüme arasındaki ilişki: BRICS-T ülkeleri üzerine Panel ARDL analizi. *Siyaset Ekon. Yönetim Araştırmaları Derg.* **2016**, *4*, 111–130.
47. Inglesi-Lotz, R. The impact of renewable energy consumption to economic growth: A panel data application. *Energy Econ.* **2016**. [CrossRef]
48. Menyah, K.; Wolde-Rufael, Y. CO_2 emissions, nuclear energy, renewable energy and economic growth in the US. *Energy Policy* **2010**. [CrossRef]
49. Tugcu, C.T.; Ozturk, I.; Aslan, A. Renewable and non-renewable energy consumption and economic growth relationship revisited: Evidence from G7 countries. *Energy Econ.* **2012**. [CrossRef]
50. Lin, B.; Moubarak, M. Renewable energy consumption—Economic growth nexus for China. *Renew. Sustain. Energy Rev.* **2014**. [CrossRef]

51. Ocal, O.; Aslan, A. Renewable energy consumption-economic growth nexus in Turkey. *Renew. Sustain. Energy Rev.* **2013**. [CrossRef]
52. Ben-Salha, O.; Sebri, M. A multivariate analysis of the causal flow between renewable energy consumption and GDP in Tunisia. *Econ. Bull.* **2014**, *34*, 2396–2410.
53. Love, I.; Zicchino, L. Financial development and dynamic investment behavior: Evidence from panel VAR. *Q. Rev. Econ. Financ.* **2006**. [CrossRef]
54. Crociata, A.; Agovino, M.; Furia, D.; Osmi, G.; Mattoscio, N.; Cerciello, M. Impulse and time persistence of disaggregate welfare expenditure on growth in the EU. *Econ. Polit.* **2019**. [CrossRef]
55. Levin, A.; Lin, C.F.; Chu, C.S.J. Unit root tests in panel data: Asymptotic and finite-sample properties. *J. Econom.* **2002**. [CrossRef]
56. Im, K.S.; Pesaran, M.H. On the Panel Unit Root Tests Using Nonlinear Instrumental Variables. *SSRN Electron. J.* **2011**. [CrossRef]
57. Im, K.S.; Pesaran, M.H.; Shin, Y. Testing for unit roots in heterogeneous panels. *J. Econom.* **2003**. [CrossRef]
58. Maddala, G.S.; Wu, S. A Comparative Study of Unit Root Tests with Panel Data and a New Simple Test. *Oxf. Bull. Econ. Stat.* **1999**. [CrossRef]
59. Banerjee, A.; Marcellino, M.; Osbat, C. Testing for PPP: Should we use panel methods? *Empir. Econ.* **2005**. [CrossRef]
60. Pesaran, M.H. A simple panel unit root test in the presence of cross-section dependence. *J. Appl. Econom.* **2007**. [CrossRef]
61. Westerlund, J. Testing for error correction in panel data. *Oxf. Bull. Econ. Stat.* **2007**. [CrossRef]
62. Hansen, L.P. Large Sample Properties of Generalized Method of Moments Estimators. *Econometrica* **1982**. [CrossRef]
63. Nickell, S. Biases in Dynamic Models with Fixed Effects. *Econometrica* **1981**. [CrossRef]
64. Baltagi, B.H. *Econometric Analysis of Panel Data*, 3rd ed.; Wyley: Weinheim, Germany, 2005.
65. Arellano, M.; Bover, O. Another look at the instrumental variable estimation of error-components models. *J. Econom.* **1995**. [CrossRef]
66. Lütkepohl, H. *New Introduction to Multiple Time Series Analysis*; Springer: Berlin, Germany, 2005.
67. Abrigo, M.R.M.; Love, I. Estimation of panel vector autoregression in Stata. *Stata J.* **2016**. [CrossRef]
68. Apergis, N.; Payne, J.E. The renewable energy consumption-growth nexus in Central America. *Appl. Energy* **2011**. [CrossRef]
69. Fei, Q.; Rasiah, R.; Shen, L.J. The clean energy-growth nexus with CO_2 emissions and technological innovation in Norway and New Zealand. *Energy Environ.* **2014**. [CrossRef]
70. Markaki, M.; Belegri-Roboli, A.; Michaelides, P.; Mirasgedis, S.; Lalas, D.P. The impact of clean energy investments on the Greek economy: An input-output analysis (2010–2020). *Energy Policy* **2013**. [CrossRef]
71. Caruso, G.; Gattone, S.A. Waste management analysis in developing countries through unsupervised classification of mixed data. *Soc. Sci.* **2019**. [CrossRef]
72. D'Adamo, I.; Gastaldi, M.; Rosa, P. Recycling of end-of-life vehicles: Assessing trends and performances in Europe. *Technol. Forecast. Soc. Chang.* **2020**. [CrossRef]
73. D'Adamo, I.; Rosa, P.; Terzi, S. Challenges in waste electrical and electronic equipment management: A profitability assessment in three European countries. *Sustainability* **2016**, *8*, 633. [CrossRef]
74. Di Battista, T.; Fortuna, F.; Maturo, F. Parametric functional analysis of variance for fish biodiversity assessment. *J. Environ. Inform.* **2016**. [CrossRef]
75. Singlitico, A.; Goggins, J.; Monaghan, R.F.D. The role of life cycle assessment in the sustainable transition to a decarbonised gas network through green gas production. *Renew. Sustain. Energy Rev.* **2019**. [CrossRef]
76. Caruso, G.; di Battista, T.; Gattone, S.A. A Micro-level Analysis of Regional Economic Activity Through a PCA Approach. In *Advances in Intelligent Systems and Computing*; Springer International Publishing: Cham, Switzerland, 2020.

sustainability

MDPI

Article

Time-frequency Connectedness between Coal Market Prices, New Energy Stock Prices and CO_2 Emissions Trading Prices in China

Chun Jiang [1], Yi-Fan Wu [1], Xiao-Lin Li [2] and Xin Li [2,*]

[1] Department of Finance, School of Economics and Management, Wuhan University, Wuhan 476411, China; jiangchwhuedu@163.com (C.J.); wuyifan93@163.com (Y.-F.W.)

[2] Department of Finance, School of Economics, Ocean University of China, Qingdao 266100, China; smileman2004@126.com

* Correspondence: lixin9462@stu.ouc.edu.cn

Received: 15 March 2020; Accepted: 1 April 2020; Published: 2 April 2020

Abstract: This paper aims to examine whether there is inherent dynamic connectedness among coal market prices, new energy stock prices and carbon emission trading (CET) prices in China under time- and frequency-varying perspectives. For this purpose, we apply a novel wavelet method proposed by Aguiar-Conraria et al. (2018). Specifically, utilizing the single wavelet power spectrum, the multiple wavelet coherency, the partial wavelet coherency, also combined with the partial phase difference and the partial wavelet gains, this paper discovers the time-frequency interaction between three markets. The empirical results show that the connectedness between the CET market price and the coal price is frequency-varying and mainly occur in the lower and higher frequency bands, while the connectedness between the CET market price and the new energy stock price mainly happen in the middle and lower frequency bands. In the high-frequency domain, the CET market price is mainly affected by the coal price, while the CET market price is dominated by the new energy stock price in the middle frequency. These uncovered frequency-varying characteristics among these markets in this study could provide several implications. Main participants in these markets, such as polluting industries, governments and financial actors, should pay close attention to the connectedness under different frequencies, in order to realize their goal of the production, the policymaking, and the investment.

Keywords: carbon emission trading market; coal price; new energy stocks; multivariate wavelet analysis; partial wavelet gains

1. Introduction

The global climate warming has brought a series of environmental problems during the last two decades. In response to the increased climate change concerns, policymakers in nearly all countries have makes great efforts to reduce CO_2 emissions. From the financial market perspective, the development of the international carbon market is on the track, and the carbon emission trading (CET) markets have been growing rapidly since the Kyoto Protocol formally came into force in February 2005 [1]. Moreover, the Paris Agreement coming into effect in November 2016, further promises to control the global average temperature increase within 2 degrees Celsius in this century. These commitments of CO_2 emissions reduction and the establishment of the CET scheme might play important roles in improving the situation of global climate warming.

China, as the largest emerging market, has witnessed a huge economic development since the reform and opening up in 1978. The process of industrialization and rapid economic development inevitably bring with huge energy consumptions, especially coal consumptions (According to the BP

Energy Outlook's data, the consumption shares of coal, oil and natural gas in China accounted for 61.8%, 19%, and 6.2%, respectively in 2016, while non-fossil energy consumption accounted for 13%), leading to large amounts of CO_2 emissions in China. In fact, China has still remained the coal-based energy consumption structure and become the world's largest CO_2 emitter since 2006 [2], which makes China undertaking dual pressure from domestic environment problems and external carbon emission commitments. Therefore, aiming to optimize the energy consumption structure and realize the goal of CO_2 emission reduction, the Chinese government makes continuous efforts to set up regional CET scheme pilots and foster the development of new energy in recent years (Until now, there are eight CET market pilots in China's provinces and cities, namely as, Beijing, Shanghai, Guangdong, Shenzhen, Chongqing, Tianjin, Hubei and Fujian). Under this circumstance, understanding the dynamic nexus between China's CET market, the energy market, and the development of new energy companies is of policy importance.

The purpose of the paper is to examine the dynamic interactions and price transmission nexus among China's CET market, coal market, and new energy market. Understanding the linkages and transmission among these markets has operational and political significance highly relevant to the main participants in the Chinese energy markets: polluting industries, governments and financial actors. Previous studies have contributed to explaining this issue by employing several conventional time-domain techniques such as the vector autoregressive (VAR) approach, the autoregressive distribution lag (ARDL) model, the GARCH model, the multivariate empirical mode decomposition (MEMD) model, the Granger causality test, the cointegration test, and among others [3–9]. Until now, to our knowledge, there are only two studies considering this interaction in the frequency domain. Sousa et al. [10] rely on a multivariate wavelet method to investigate the correlation between the U.S. carbon emission trading (U.S. CET) market and several energy prices (the gas, coal, and electricity prices). Wavelet analysis is also adopted by Ortas and Álvarezb [11] and they reveal the interaction between the European carbon emission trading (EU CET) market and the main energy commodities in time and frequency domains. These studies provide robust evidence that the frequency-varying feature is important not only since energy commodity prices tend to be sticky in the short-run and perfectly flexible in the long-run but also since the information on the interactions in different frequencies provides implications for different players in the energy markets. In general, financial actors are more likely to be interested in understanding high-frequency interactions between energy commodities prices, while the polluters and regulators are also interested in lower frequencies. Considering these arguments, this paper further investigates the time- and frequency-varying feature of the interactions among the three markets, utilizing a novel multivariable wavelet method, especially in the China context, the largest developing economy in the world.

The contribution of this study to the existing literature mainly lies in the following two parts. For one thing, different from a wild range of existing research placing more weight on the EU or U.S. CET markets, we try to fill the research gap in the China context given that the Chinese CET market, despite its rapid development in the latest years, exhibits manifest structural differences from the developed markets. Furthermore, growing empirical evidence in terms of the EU CET and U.S. CET scheme has confirmed that CET allowances and energy markets are closely linked. Nevertheless, their connection with the new energy market is still a topic that remains largely unstudied. Especially for China recently undertaking the period of green economic transformation, which drives benign changes in energy consumption. Changes in energy consumption concepts and the commitment to the reduction of carbon emission both promote the rapid development of new energy industries. In view of this, this paper tries to investigate whether there exists inherent connectedness of the new energy market with the CET market and the coal market. For another, unlike the previous literature mainly considering these interactions in a time dimension, this paper adopts a novel multivariate wavelet analysis to explore the time-variation as well as the frequency-variation relationship of the CET allowances prices with coal market prices and new energy stock prices, which might shed new light on the existing literature. To the best of our knowledge, this study might be one of the first studies to employ a time- and frequency-dimension method to analyze this subject in China.

The remainder of this paper proceeds as follows. Section 2 reviews the related literature. Section 3 explains the methodology. Section 4 describes the data and does a preliminary statistical analysis. Section 5 discusses the empirical results. Finally, Section 6 concludes this paper.

2. Literature Review

The issue of dynamic interactions between fossil energy consumption, the CO_2 emission trading allowance, and the development of new energy companies arouses much attention in academia during the last near decades. Different studies take different research perspectives and there exist two main fields of literature on detecting the relationship between them.

The first strand of the literature has concentrated on the linkage between the energy market and the CET market. Among these researches, a large number of studies focus on the European carbon emissions trading market and investigate the underlying determinants of the EU CET market price. Their empirical results show that fuel prices (i.e. coal, crude oil, and natural gas price), especially crude oil prices, are the main factor influencing the price of the EU CET market (see, for example, [4,12–16]). The possible reason is that fossil fuel energy demand will be adjusted according to changes in its price. Changes in fossil fuel consumption will lead to changes in carbon dioxide emissions, which may change the carbon demand in the CET market and ultimately affect the CET market price. Different from the literature concerning the traditional fossil fuel energy, D'Adamo [17] notes that new energy, such as photovoltaic resources, could drive the clean global economy of the future and also affect the price of EU CET market. Besides, Chen et al. [18] find that CET future market prices could exert an influence on the spot market price too. Through a linear regression model analysis, D'Adamo [19] reveals that the relationship between the circular economy and the price of CO_2 is currently low. Moreover, there is also a handful of researches investigating the latent factors of U.S CET market prices. Kim and Koo [3] rely on a linear ARDL model to examine the response of U.S. CET market price to the changes of energy price and their findings indicate that the coal price has an effective influence on the U.S. CET price over the long-term rather than short-term. Hammoudeh et al. [20] utilize a quantile regression model to investigate the interaction between energy price and U.S. CET price and their empirical results show that the fluctuation of U.S. CET prices can be attributed to the natural gas, the crude oil, and the electricity prices. Marimoutou and Soury [21] show that the relationships between the energy market and the CO_2 emission market fluctuate over time. Hammoudeh et al. [22] claim that the negative changes in coal prices can interpret the carbon market price better than the impact of positive changes in the short-term.

In recent years, several types of research start to pay attention to China's CET market. Among these, Zhang and Zhang [23] find that there is a long-term negative nexus between the Shanghai CET market prices and the coal price. However, they also notice that it exists a positive interplay across different quantiles. Zeng et al. [24] rely on a SVAR model to detect the relationship between energy price and CET market price and drew a conclusion that the coal prices show a negative impact on the price of the Beijing CET market. However, Fan and Todorova [25] notice that there is no statistically significant relationship between energy indices and carbon allowance prices in the Beijing CET market and attribute it to the initial development stages of China's carbon market. Chang et al. [26] utilize GARCH models to investigate the asymmetric clustering and regime-switching behaviors of the CET market in China. Furthermore, Chang et al. [7] apply a cointegration test to examine the dynamic interactions between the CET market and energy price. Lin and Jia [27] apply a computable general equilibrium model to detect the underlying determinants of CET market price and analyze the impact mechanism in China. Besides, Yang et al. [28] use the difference-in-differences model to investigate the impact of the policy of China's CO_2 CET on the carbon price and they find that this policy plays an important role in the stabilization of carbon price. Wang et al. [29] find that the CET pilot policy undertaken in China could contribute to CO_2 abatement in the pilot provinces. Through applying the data envelopment model-slack based measurement method and difference-in-differences model, Zhang et al. [30] also examine the impact of the CET policy on environmental efficiency in China and find that the policy has significantly improved environmental efficiency in the pilot regions.

The second strand of the literature has attempted to examine the relationship between the CET market and the stock market of new energy firms. Henriques and Sadorsky [31] indicate that there does not exist significant interactions between the stock market of clean energy firms and EU CET market prices. Kumar et al. [32] also draw a similar conclusion. More recently, Jiménez-Rodríguez [33] finds the impacts of the European stock markets on the EU CET market prices. In China context, Zhu and Kong [34] apply a VAR model to detect this relationship and find that the interplays between the Shenzhen CET market price and the stock prices of new energy firms are ineffective. Different from these findings, Qin [6] claims that China's CET market prices have a certain influence on the stock price of new energy firms and further indicates that the nexus between them is positively correlated. It is can be noticed that the interaction between these market prices still exists argues in academia, due that these findings do not consist of each other. Therefore, it is a worthy investigating issue, especially in China which has not much enough analysis on this topic before.

Compared with numerous researches that pay attention to investigating the CET price and energy price (especially crude oil price) in EU and U.S. markets, fewer studies have focused on China's CET market. However, in order to realize the goal of CO_2 emission reduction, China's CET market is developing rapidly in recent years. Therefore, studies of China's CET market can give us a better understanding of the current development in this market. In terms of empirical methods, Caruso et al. [35] suggest that mathematical models need to be applied in the related research to evaluate the economic aspects of CET price. However, a large body of research merely considers these interactions in the time domain, not including frequency analysis, which might bias the understanding of the nexus. Hence, this paper re-examines relationships between China's CET market, the coal market, and the stock market of the new energy firms under time-and frequency-varying perspectives, trying to shew new light on previous researches.

3. Methodology

3.1. Continuous Wavelet Transformation

In order to investigate the dynamic links among China's CET market, coal prices, and stock market of new energy companies across time and frequency domain, we apply an innovative multivariate wavelet method proposed by Aguiar-Conraria et al. [36], which can help us to detect dynamic interaction among variables from two dimensions of time-varying and frequency-varying [37].

Considering a time series x (t), its continuous wavelet transformation (CWT) with a considered wavelet ψ is a function of two variables $W_x(\tau, s)$ scaling by s and translation by τ:

$$W_x(\tau, s) = \frac{1}{\sqrt{|s|}} \int_{-\infty}^{\infty} x(t)\overline{\psi}(\frac{t-\tau}{s})dt \tag{1}$$

where $\tau, s \in \mathbb{R}, s \neq 0$. When $|s| < 1$, the windows of function $W_x(\tau, s)$ become narrower, indicating that it is in a higher frequency. Similarly, for $|s| > 1$, the windows become larger, implying a function with lower frequency.

3.2. Wavelet Power Spectrum and Bivariate-wavelet Tools

In a wavelet domain, the wavelet power spectrum (WPS) is a key concept denoted by $(WPS)_x$ which can be expressed as:

$$(WPS)_x = W_x\overline{W_x} = \left|\overline{W_x}\right|^2 \tag{2}$$

The WPS can give us a measure of the time-series' variance at each time-frequency. Due to the wavelet ψ is complex-valued, the W_x is also a complex value, and this transform can be represented by a polar formlike $W_x = |W_x|e^{i\phi_x}, \phi_x \in (-\pi, \pi]$. The angle ϕ_x is called the (wavelet) phase.

Given two time-series, x (t) and y (t), the cross-wavelet transform W_{yx} is represented by:

$$W_{yx} = W_y \overline{W_x} \tag{3}$$

where W_x and W_y are the wavelet transforms of x and y. The absolute value $|W_{yx}|$ is called the cross-wavelet power, which indicates the covariance between x and y across time and frequency.

The complex wavelet coherency of two time-series, x (t) and y (t) are defined by:

$$\vartheta_{yx} = \frac{S(W_{yx})}{\left[S\left(|W_y|^2\right)S\left(|W_y|^2\right)\right]^{1/2}} \tag{4}$$

where S denotes a smoothing operator in scale and time. For simplicity, we denote $S_{yx} = S(W_{yx})$ and respectively use σ_x and σ_y to represent $\sqrt{S(|W_x|^2)}$ and $\sqrt{S\left(|W_y|^2\right)}$, (i.e., $\sigma_x = \sqrt{S(|W_x|^2)} = \sqrt{S_{xx}}$ and $\sigma_y = \sqrt{S\left(|W_y|^2\right)} = \sqrt{S_{yy}}$). Therefore, the complex wavelet coherency of two variables can be written simply as:

$$\vartheta_{yx} = \frac{S_{yx}}{\sigma_x \sigma_y} \tag{5}$$

The wavelet coherency is the absolute value of the complex wavelet coherency (R_{yx}), which can be represented by $R_{yx} = |\vartheta_{yx}| = \frac{|S_{yx}|}{\sigma_x \sigma_y}$.

With a complex-valued wavelet, we are able to compute the wavelet phases of two time-series, x(t) and y(t). Moreover, we can further capture the possible leading-lag relationship between x(t) and y (t) by computing their phase-difference (ϕ_{yx}) at each time and frequency. Specifically, the two time-series are in the phase and y leads x if $\phi_{yx} \in [0, \pi/2]$, and x leads y when $\phi_{yx} \in [-\pi/2, 0]$. Similarly, the series is in anti-phase and x leads y for $\phi_{yx} \in [\pi/2, \pi]$ while y leads x if $\phi_{yx} \in [-\pi, -\pi/2]$. Finally, the complex wavelet gain of y over x is defined by $\mathcal{G}_{yx}$, as follows:

$$\mathcal{G}_{yx} = \frac{S_{yx}}{S_{xx}} = \vartheta_{yx} \frac{\sigma_y}{\sigma_x} \tag{6}$$

In addition, according to Aguiar-Conraria et al. [36], we refer wavelet gain of y over x, and define the modulus of $\mathcal{G}_{yx}$ as G_{yx}, which can be written as:

$$G_{yx} = \frac{|S_{yx}|}{S_{xx}} = R_{yx} \frac{\sigma_y}{\sigma_x} \tag{7}$$

3.3. Multivariate Wavelet Tools

This section introduces the formulas for multivariate wavelet tools, namely, multiple and partial wavelet coherency, partial wavelet phase-difference, and partial wavelet gain, considering three variables, y, x, and z.

The squared multiple wavelet coherency among these variables are denoted by $R^2_{y(xz)}$ which is represented by:

$$R^2_{y(xz)} = \frac{R^2_{yx} + R^2_{yz} - 2\Re\left(\vartheta_{yx}\vartheta_{xz}\overline{\vartheta_{yz}}\right)}{1 - R^2_{xz}} \tag{8}$$

and we define that the multiple wavelet coherency among these three variables $R_{y(xz)}$ is the positive square root of $R^2_{y(xz)}$.

In term of partial wavelet coherency, after controlling for z, we obtain the complex partial wavelet coherency between y and x, that is,

$$\vartheta_{yx|z} = \frac{\vartheta_{yx} - \vartheta_{yz}\overline{\vartheta_{xz}}}{\left[(1 - R_{yz}^2)(1 - R_{xz}^2)\right]^{1/2}} \tag{9}$$

Moreover, after controlling for z, we can obtain the partial wavelet coherency ($R_{yx|z}$) and partial phase-difference ($\phi_{yx|z}$) between y and x, which is the absolute value and the angle of $\vartheta_{yx|z}$.

Last, similarly, after controlling for z, we can obtain the complex partial wavelet gain between series y and x which can be expressed as:

$$\mathcal{G}_{yx|z} = \frac{\vartheta_{yx} - \vartheta_{yz}\overline{\vartheta_{xz}}}{(1 - R_{xz}^2)}\frac{\sigma_y}{\sigma_x} \tag{10}$$

In addition, we define that the partial wavelet gain $G_{yx|z}$ is the absolute value of $\mathcal{G}_{yx|z}$, that is,

$$G_{yx|z} = \frac{\left|\vartheta_{yx} - \vartheta_{yz}\overline{\vartheta_{xz}}\right|}{(1 - R_{xz}^2)}\frac{\sigma_y}{\sigma_x} \tag{11}$$

As observed before, the partial wavelet gain can give us a measure of the degree of influence among variables, which is different from the traditional wavelet method.

4. Data and Preliminary Statistical Analysis

4.1. Data

This paper aims to examine the dynamic connectedness among the CET market, coal prices, and the new energy market in China. Given that China's eight regional CET scheme pilots are still in the developing stage, this study adopts the Beijing CET market as a proxy for China's CET market, which has been running smoothly compared to other pilots since its establishment [38]. Besides, considering the fact that China's energy consumption structure dominated by coal and steam coal is the main power consumption for many industries, we select the steam coal price to represent China's coal market price [38]. Meanwhile, in light of Sun et al. [39], we choose future price not spot price as a proxy for two reasons. First, the spot price of the steam coal may fluctuate frequently due to it only pays attention to the short-run demand and supply and the price. Second, the future price has the advantage to find forward prices, which can better represent the true value of coal prices. Therefore, this study selects the coal future price to reflect China's coal market price [39]. Moreover, in order to realize the goal of CO_2 emission reduction and response to problems of the environment, the Chinese government has promoted the development of new energy in recent decades. To some extent, the new energy market is an important strategic industry in China. Since the performance of new energy development can be effectively measured by stock price movements [40], this study makes use of the China New Energy Index (CNI) to a proxy for the development of the new energy firms.

The data of CET price can be obtained from the Carbon Emissions trading network of China (www.tanpaifang.com), the steam coal future contracts prices are chosen from the Zhengzhou Commodity Exchange (ZCE), and the CNI price is selected from databases provided by Wind Information Co., Ltd. (WIND). Instead of utilizing daily data, this study works with weekly averages. The data sampling period ranges from the 49th week of 2013 (early-December, 2013) to the 23rd week of 2019 (early-June, 2019), and a total of data has 283 observations. The beginning point is determined by the data availability of China's CET market.

The details of the sampling price movement of the CET, Coal, and CNI are registered in Figure 1. The three market prices reflect different degrees of fluctuation during the sample period. It can be obviously noticed in Figure 1a that CET market prices have changed sharply from late-June to late-August in 2014. It can be contributed to the reason that the Beijing CET market becomes available to individuals to invest during this period. Different market participates might alter the demand and supply of the carbon emission allowance, which finally reflects on the fluctuation of market prices. In recent two years, the change in this market price starts to appear more fluctuating. Moreover, Figure 1b shows that the coal price witnesses a huge roaring from December 2015 to December 2016. The reason behind this can be interpreted by the Chinese government implemented policies to cut overcapacity for all industries during this period, especially for the coal industry [32]. The short-supply of coal pushes the coal price soaring. The coal prices appeared fewer fluctuations in subsequent years. Besides, Figure 1c illustrates the movement of the new energy stock price. Due to the Chinese government fostering the development of new energy industries, a large number of investment funds poured into the market and the stock price of new energy companies soared hugely before middle-June 2015. However, the Chinese stock market went through a great crisis in June 2015, and imperfect new energy storage technology leads to a relatively slow development of new energy, therefore, the stock price of new energy firms appeared a decreasing tendency in subsequent years. Since 2017, the new energy stock price reflected fewer fluctuations.

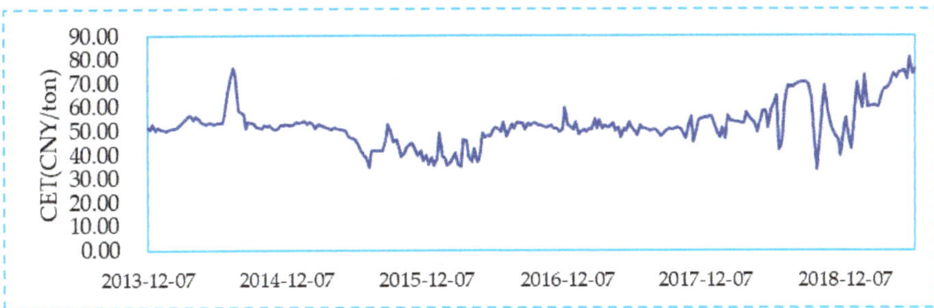

(a) The price movement of the Carbon Emission Trading Market

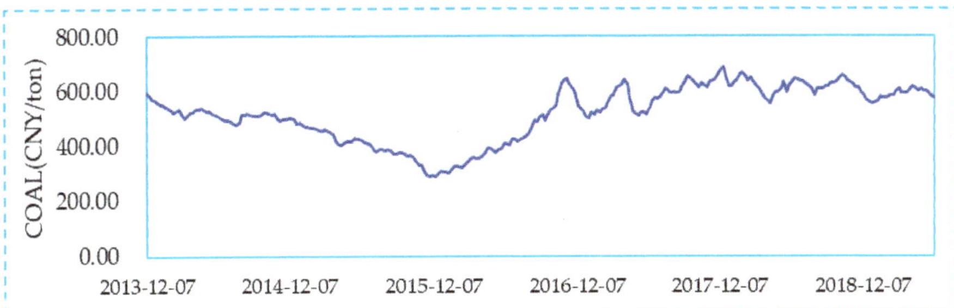

(b) The price movement of the Coal Market

Figure 1. *Cont.*

(c) The price movement of the New Energy Firms Stock Market

Figure 1. The price movement of the Carbon Emission Trading Market, Coal market, and New Energy Firms Stock Market.

4.2. Preliminary Statistical Analysis

Due to the price returns have better statistical characteristics than the original prices, which are more suitable for the econometric analysis, this paper utilizes the logarithm returns of the series calculated as $\mathrm{Ln}(P_t) - \mathrm{Ln}(P_{t\text{-}1})$, where P_t representing the weekly prices of the CET market, the coal market, and the new energy market. Table 1 displays the descriptive statistics of the weekly returns of variables in this study. It can be obviously noticed that price returns of three markets all near to zero and all variables reject the null hypothesis of subjecting to a normal distribution. In addition, the standard deviation of the CET market shows the largest, implying the fluctuation of this market price is fiercer than others.

Table 1. Descriptive statistics of variables in this study.

Variable	Mean	Max.	Mini.	Std. Dev.	Skewness	Kurtosis	*J-Brea*
RCET	0.001	0.473	−0.426	0.089	0.236	9.652	522.564 ***
RCOAL	0.000	0.070	−0.090	0.025	−0.235	4.212	19.839 ***
RNEWSTOCK	0.001	0.108	−0.218	0.044	−1.100	6.370	190.321 ***

Note: asterisks *** represent significance levels of 1%.

Moreover, in light of Aguiar-Conraria et al. [29], we also do a preliminary statistical analysis across time and frequency domain, utilizing the single wavelet power spectrum, which is different from the traditional descriptive statistics of variables. The novel approach might allow us to capture deeper features about time-series, where are ignored by the traditional method. The corresponding results are registered in Figure 2.

On the left-hand side, Figure 2(a.1–a.3) displays the weekly returns of the CET market price, the coal market, and the new energy stock market. On the right-hand side, Figure 2(b.1–b.3) illustrate each wavelet power spectrum, which reflects the intensity of the time-series variance for each time and frequency. Specifically, in terms of CET market prices, we can notice that the volatility is more significant at higher frequencies (smaller than 15 weeks) during the second half of 2018. Moreover, in the case of coal market price, it can be obviously found that there exist four dominant volatility regions. Three of them appear at high frequencies (around 20 weeks), which is happened from the second half of 2016 to early 2018. Another cycle appears around 80 weeks (about one and half-years), indicating that the coal market also has a significant volatility cycle area at low frequencies. Last, in the case of the new energy stock price, we can find that the volatility regions are mainly concentrated in the first half of the whole sample, between the second half of 2014 to early 2016. And the significant cycle areas across 20 weeks to 40 weeks, mainly in the middle frequencies.

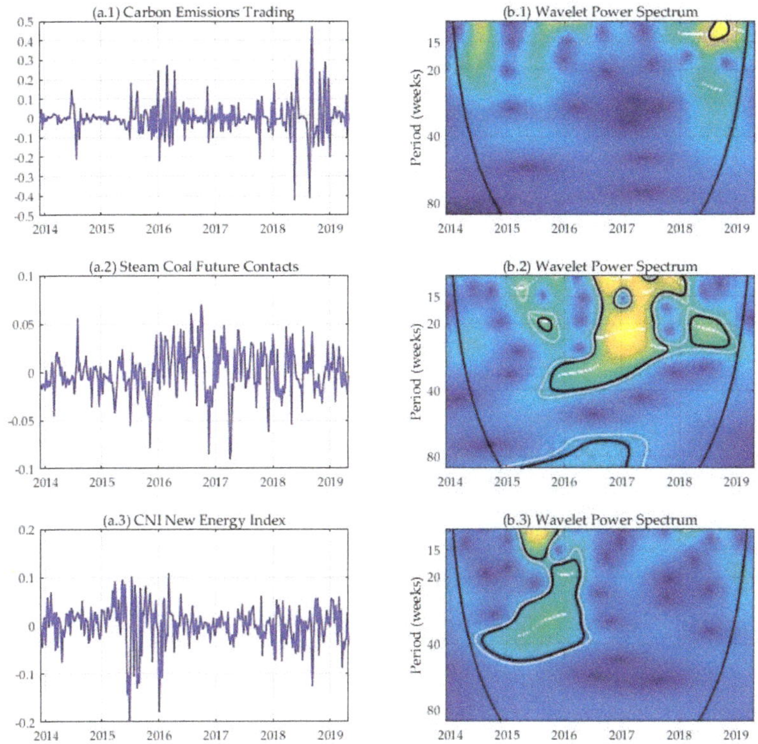

Figure 2. (**a**) Represents the weekly return of each market. (**b**) plots each wavelet power spectrum. The significance level of 10% (5%) is depicted by the thick gray (black) curve. The white broken line indicates the maximum of the local wavelet power spectrum for each variable. The black contour near the edge is the cone-of-influence, implying the edge effects. The different color spectrum distinguishes the degree of variability, ranging from blue (low variability) to yellow (high variability).

From the traditional statistical analysis and wavelet power spectrum analysis of three market prices, we can notice that the results of the two methods are mutually reinforcing. However, compared with the traditional method, the wavelet power spectrum analysis has more advantages, because it could further reveal the high-frequency-vary features of the three market fluctuations. Therefore, the novel approach can capture the features of time series better than the traditional one. Despite this, it is still difficult to discover any interaction between them from the single wavelet power spectrum. In the next section, we will apply multivariate continuous wavelet tools to catch their possible interplays both across time and frequency domain.

5. Empirical Results

In this section, we will utilize multivariate continuous wavelet tools to investigate the interaction between the CET market, the coal market, and the new energy stock market. The wavelet analysis results between three markets are illustrated in Figures 3–6, which can help us to capture the strongest interplays among them across time- and frequency domain. Note that the significance level of 10% (5%) is depicted by the thick gray (black) curve. The black contours near the edge are cones of influence (COI) in which edge effects exist, indicating unreliable indications of co-movement and causality beyond the COI (Readers can see Grinsted et al. [41] and Torrence and Compo [42] for more details on the COI). Moreover, the different color spectrum distinguishes the degree of coherency, ranging from cold color (low coherency-close to blue) to warm color (high coherency-close to yellow). In addition, we define a high-frequency band between 15–20 weeks, a middle-frequency region between 20–40 weeks, and a low-frequency area between 40–80 weeks to facilitate the interpretation of their interactions at each frequency band.

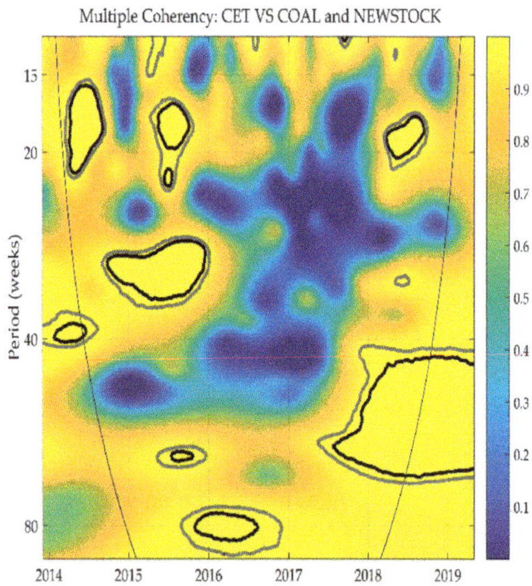

Figure 3. Wavelet Multiple Coherency between CET market price and coal price and new energy firms stock price. The significance level of 10% (5%) is depicted by the thick gray (black) curve. The color code distinguishes the different coherency, ranging from blue (low coherency) to yellow (high coherency).

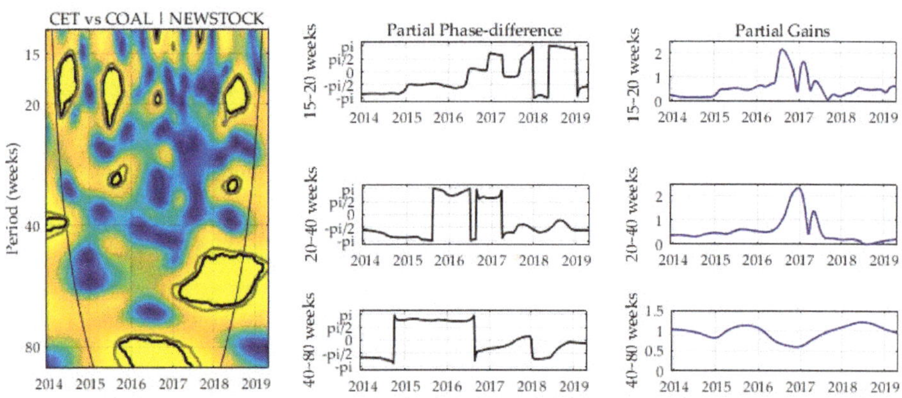

Figure 4. On the left-hand side, it plots the partial wavelet coherency between the CET market price and the coal price. The significance level of 10% (5%) is depicted by the thick gray (black) curve. The color code distinguishes the different coherency, ranging from blue (low coherency) to yellow (high coherency). **In the middle,** it displays partial phase-difference. **On the right-hand side,** it indicates the partial wavelet gain.

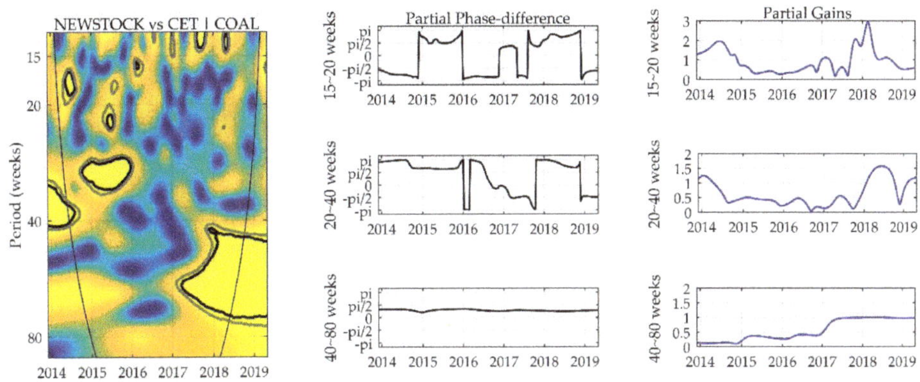

Figure 5. On the left-hand side, it plots the partial wavelet coherency between the CET market price and the new energy firm's stock price. The significance level of 10% (5%) is depicted by the thick gray (black) curve. The color code distinguishes the different coherency, ranging from blue (low coherency) to yellow (high coherency). **In the middle**, it displays partial phase-difference. **On the right-hand side**, it indicates the partial wavelet gain.

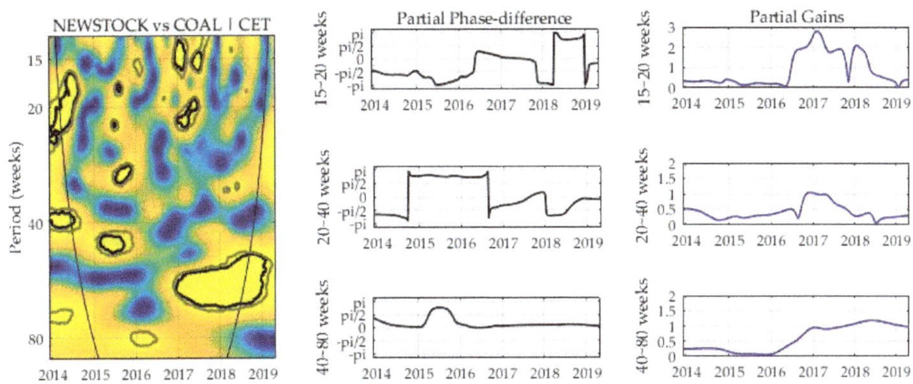

Figure 6. On the left-hand side, it plots the partial wavelet coherency between the coal price and the new energy firm's stock price. The significance level of 10% (5%) is depicted by the thick gray (black) curve. The color code distinguishes the different coherency, ranging from blue (low coherency) to yellow (high coherency). **In the middle**, it displays partial phase-difference. **On the right-hand side**, it indicates the partial wavelet gain.

Figure 3 reports the multivariate wavelet coherencies among three markets. According to Figure 3, it can be clearly noticed that there are six main locations with high coherency at the significance level of 5%, which indicates that the three market prices are jointly significant to affect each other. In the 40–80 weeks frequency band, we find the most important one, which starts from the second half of 2017 to the middle of 2018. Also, in this frequency band, another high coherency runs from the late-2016 to the third quarter of 2017. Moreover, in the 20–40 weeks frequency areas, there is a large region with high coherency starting from the fourth quarter of 2014 to the end of 2015. Finally, the remaining three significant coherency areas are concentrated in the 15–20 weeks. Specifically, one starts from the second quarter of 2014 to the third quarter of 2014. The following one runs from the second quarter of 2015 to the third quarter of 2015. The last one starts in the second quarter of 2018 to the third quarter of 2018.

Although the multiple coherencies can detect the strong relationship between the CET market, the coal market, and the new energy stock market, it is still unable for us to distinguish the different impacts of each market. Therefore, we rely on the partial coherence, combined with the partial phase-difference, and the partial gains to further differentiate the influence of each market price after controlling another variable. The corresponding results are registered in Figures 4–6.

Figure 4 displays the partial wavelet coherency between the CET market price and the coal price (left), the corresponding partial phase-differences (mid), and the partial wavelet gains (right). Figure 4 denotes that there are main five regions with high interactions. In the 15–20 weeks frequency band, we find three areas with significantly high coherency. The first two regions are in the second and third quarters of 2014 and 2015, respectively. In both areas, the partial phase differences are between $-\pi$ and $-\pi/2$, which indicate that two market price returns are out-phase (i.e. negative relationship) with coal market price leading. Therefore, the financial actors in the CET market should also pay attention to the increase in coal price in the short-term, in order to avoid the loss of assets. Moreover, according to partial wavelet gains, we can clearly observe that the effect of coal market price changing on the CET market price is larger in 2015 than that of 2014. Similarly, the third one runs from the second quarter to the third quarter of 2018. The phase difference is between $\pi/2$ and π, implying that the relationship between them is still negative, however, with CET market price leading. The magnitude of the impact of the CET market price on the coal market price is as same as that of 2015. The possible reason behind is that when the CET market price increases in the short-term, in order to reduce CO_2 emissions costs, the companies might tend to rely on cleaner energy, therefore, the demand for fuel with higher CO_2 emissions (like coal) will be cut down, which generally brings the lower price of the coal market price.

At a lower frequency band (corresponding to 40–80 weeks), we notice that there are two regions with significantly high coherency. Both areas are located between late 2015 to the end of 2018. For the former region, the phase differences are between $\pi/2$ and π, suggesting that the nexus between two market prices are still negative, with the CET market price leading. Moreover, the partial wavelet gains show that the relationship is stable in both regions, with a value close to 1. In the case of the latter region, we find that the phase differences are between $-\pi$ and $-\pi/2$, implying that the coal price negatively affects the CET market. The economic implication behinds these findings are as follows. In the long-term, the decreasing coal price will cut the production costs of industries that heavily depend on coal consumption (i.e. heating power industries and power generation industries). Therefore, these industries might tend to consider more demand for coal. Increasing coal consumption will inevitably increase carbon emissions, which in turn drives up the demand for carbon emission allowances, therefore making the CET market price increase.

Similarly, Figure 5 represents the partial wavelet coherency between the CET market price and the new energy stock price, the corresponding partial phase-differences, and the partial wavelet gains. Figure 5 indicates that there are two main high coherency regions at the middle and low-frequency bands, except for a region in the COI. The first one is located in the 20–40 weeks frequency band, running from the fourth quarter of 2014 to the end of 2015. The corresponding partial phase differences are between $\pi/2$ and π, which indicates that the relationship between two market price returns is negative, with the new energy stock price leading. Moreover, according to the partial wavelet gain, we can notice that the magnitude of the impact of the new energy stock price on the CET market price is around 0.5. The reason behind is that the cleaner energy will replace fossil energy, due to the development of new energy (economically, reflected in the value of the stock), which results in reduced CO_2 emissions. Therefore, the demand for the CO_2 emissions allowance is dropped and finally leads to the CET market price decreasing. The second is located in the 40-80 weeks frequency band and starts from the first quarter of 2017 to the second quarter of 2018. And the phase difference is between 0 and $\pi/2$, implying that the relationship between two market prices is positive, with the CET market price leading. Moreover, the corresponding partial wavelet gain shows that this high coherency relationship is stable and the coefficient appears to be 1. The economic implication of this finding indicates that increasing the CET market price means the pressure of the huge demand for CO_2 emissions. However, in order to implement green economic development and meet the goal of CO_2 emissions reduction, the government might take initiatives to cultivate the growth of new energy companies. Better future prospects make new energy company stock prices rise.

In addition, Figure 6 illustrates the partial wavelet coherency between the coal price and the new energy stock price (left), the corresponding partial phase-differences (mid), and the partial wavelet gains (right). It can be found that there are major three regions with high interactions. Specifically, in the 15–20 weeks frequency band, we find the first one that begins from the second quarter of 2014 to the third quarter of 2014. Combined with the partial phase-difference, it is clear that the coal price negatively leads to the new energy stock price. In the 40–80 weeks frequency band, we notice that there are two regions with high linkages, running from the second quarter of 2015 to the third quarter of 2015 and the first quarter of 2017 to the second quarter of 2018. Moreover, the partial wavelet gains of significant regions indicate that the connection between new energy stock prices and the coal price is stronger than others from 2017 to 2018. In the former region, the partial phase differences are between $\pi/2$ and π, which indicates that the change of new energy company stock prices will negatively alter the coal prices. The economic implication behind this is that there is an obvious substitution effect between these markets. And the continuing development of new energy will reduce the consumption of coal, therefore, the demand for coal and their prices will decline. However, in the latter region, with the help of partial phase-difference, we find the coal price positively affects the new energy firm's stock price. The reason behind this is that when coal prices rise, the demand for coal will fall, while demand for new energy, as an alternative product, will increase, which in turn forces the research and development of new energy products. The prospect of new energy makes the stock price increase.

To facilitate the presentation, we summarize the above results in Table 2, which can help us to observe the relationship more clearly and further catch the different influences of each market. It can be clearly found that after controlling the new energy stock price, the relationship between the CET market price and the coal price is negative at both higher frequency (i.e. 15–20 weeks) and lower frequency (40–80 weeks). In addition, these connections are shorter in the higher frequency (in the short-term), while lasting longer in the lower frequency (in the long-term). In the case of the relationship between the CET market price and the new energy stock price, after controlling the coal price, we can obtain a similar finding. In the region of middle frequency, the new energy stock price has a negative impact on the CET market price. Besides, in the region of lower frequency, changes in the CET market price lead changes in the new energy stock price, however, the relationship is altered to be positive. Finally, after controlling the CET market price, we notice that the relationships between the coal price and the new energy company stock price are mixed. The coal price positively affects the new energy company stock price, while the new energy company stock price shows a negative impact on the coal price in the lower frequency. Compared to each partial wavelet gain, we can conclude that the partial wavelet gain in the lower frequency is larger than the middle or higher frequency, which indicates the connectedness among three markets is stronger in the long-term. According to these uncovered time- and frequency-varying characteristics, main participants in these markets, such as polluting industries, governments and financial actors, should pay close attention to the different connectedness among three markets under different frequency, in order to realize the goal of the production, the policymaking, and investment.

Table 2. Summary of the empirical results on the relationship between the CET market price, the coal price, and the new energy stock price in this study.

Frequency Band	Time Span	Partial Co-movement	Wavelet Gains Coefficient	Partial Causality
Panel A: Results between CET and COAL | NEWSTOCK				
15-20 weeks	2Q-2014 to 3Q-2014	Negative	About 0.2	Coal→CET
	2Q-2015 to 3Q-2015	Negative	About0.5	Coal→CET
	2Q-2018 to 3Q-2018	Negative	About0.5	CET→Coal
40-80 weeks	4Q-2015to 4Q-2016	Negative	About 0.75	CET→Coal
	1Q-2017 to 2Q-2018	Negative	About 1	Coal→CET
Panel B: Results between CET and NEWSTOCK | COAL				
20-40 weeks	4Q-2014 to 4Q-2015	Negative	About 0.5	Newstock→CET
40-80 weeks	1Q-2017 to 2Q-2018	Positive	About 1	CET→Newstock
Panel C: Results between COAL and NEWSTOCK | CET				
15-20 weeks	2Q-2014 to 3Q-2014	Negative	About 0.5	Coal→Newstock
40-80 weeks	2Q-2015 to 3Q-2015	Negative	About 0.5	Newstock→Coal
	1Q-2017 to 2Q-2018	Positive	About 1	Coal→Newstock

6. Conclusions

The issue of environment and the dynamic interactions between fossil energy consumption, CO_2 emission trading allowance, and the development of new energy companies arouse much attention in academia during the last near decades. This paper adopts a novel multivariate wavelet analysis to explore the time-frequency co-movement and causality among them in China over the sampling period from the 49th week of 2013 (early-December, 2013) to the 23rd week of 2019 (early-June, 2019). Given that each market might have a different impact on others, we utilize the multiple wavelet coherency and the partial wavelet coherency, combined with partial phase difference and the partial wavelet gains to catch the time-frequency interaction between them.

The empirical evidence suggests that there are substantial time- and frequency-varying interactions between three market prices, suggesting that only considering time-domain model estimations performed by previous literature are not suitable to seize the actual nexus. First, the multiple wavelet coherency results suggest that there exists high coherency between the CET markets price and the coal price and the new energy stock price across each frequency band. Besides, there are more and shorter regions at a higher frequency band. Second, the findings of the partial wavelet coherency further help us to find the different impacts of each market price. Specifically, the interaction between the CET market price and the coal price is time-varying and both occur in the lower and higher frequency bands, while the co-movement between the CET market price and the new energy stock price both happen in the middle and lower frequency bands. Moreover, the co-movement between the coal price and the new energy stock price mainly exists in the lower and higher frequency band.

The findings of the current study provide several important implications. First, the presence of time- and frequency-varying features should not be ignored in future research when studying the interaction between the CET market, the coal price, and the new energy stock price. Moreover, this study further provides a better understanding of the dynamic linkages between the three markets for market regulators. For example, the CET market price is affected by the coal price and the new energy stock prices in the short- and middle-term, but in turn, it has limited impact. Therefore, in order to foster the development of the national CET market, the policymakers not only should take initiatives to stabilize China's CET market price, but also should improve the financial function of the CET market in China, making it could impact related energy prices. In addition, for financial actors that mainly focus on the short-term connectedness among energy commodities prices, those findings might help them understand the high-frequency interactions and accordingly alter the different energy asset allocations in the short-term to avoid the price volatility risk. Besides, the interaction between the coal market price and the CET market in the lower frequencies suggests that polluting industries that heavily depend on coal consumption should pay attention to the changes of CET market prices in the long-term. Moreover, these polluters need to reduce their coal energy dependence through increasing research and development of new energy, which can not only reduce costs of carbon emissions and thus help them achieve their goal of the production but also make China's environmental quality improved. The improvement of energy dependence structure in these polluting industries will inevitably decrease the demand for carbon emission allowances, therefore making the CET market price decrease.

However, this paper also has some shortcomings. For example, the model employed in the current paper cannot unravel asymmetric interactions among the three variables. The relationship between the CET market price and the other energy prices, such as coal prices and new energy prices, may differ when the CET market prices undergo positive or negative changes. Therefore, different methods could be applied to address this shortcoming in future research. An in-depth analysis of this motivation could give more profound implications.

Author Contributions: Conceptualization, C.J., and X.-L.L.; methodology, X.L; formal analysis, Y.-F.W.; data curation, X.L.; writing—original draft preparation, Y.-F.W. and X.-L.Li. All authors have read and agreed to the published version of the manuscript.

Funding: This research was funded by the Qingdao Social Science Planning Project (Grant number: QDSKL1801008).

Acknowledgments: We thank Professors Aguiar-Conraria and Soares for providing the wavelet package to plot the corresponding results.

Conflicts of Interest: The authors declare no conflict of interest.

References

1. Zhang, Y.J.; Sun, Y.F. The dynamic volatility spillover between European carbon trading market and fossil energy market. *J. Clean. Prod.* **2016**, *112*, 2654–2663. [CrossRef]
2. Zhang, Y.J.; Peng, Y.L.; Ma, C.Q.; Shen, B. Can environmental innovation facilitate carbon emissions reduction? Evidence from China. *Energy Policy* **2017**, *100*, 18–28. [CrossRef]
3. Kim, H.S.; Koo, W.W. Factors affecting the carbon allowance market in the US. *Energy Policy* **2010**, *38*, 1879–1884. [CrossRef]
4. Creti, A.; Jouvet, P.A.; Mignon, V. Carbon price drivers: Phase I versus Phase II equilibrium? *Energy Econ.* **2012**, *34*, 327–334. [CrossRef]
5. Chen, X.; Wang, Z.; Wu, D.D. Modeling the Price Mechanism of Carbon Emission Exchange in the European Union Emission Trading System. *Hum. Ecol. Risk Assess.* **2013**, *19*, 1309–1323. [CrossRef]
6. Qin, T. The Prices of the Conventional Energy and Carbon Emissions Trading as well as the Stock Price of the New Energy—Based on the Analysis of VAR and CAPM-GARCH Model. Technol. *Econ. Manage. Rese.* **2014**, *12*, 120–124.
7. Chang, K.; Ge, F.; Zhang, C.; Wang, W. The dynamic linkage effect between energy and emissions allowances price for regional emissions trading scheme pilots in China. Renew. *Sustain. Energy Rev.* **2018**, *98*, 415–425. [CrossRef]
8. Zhu, B.; Ye, S.; Han, D.; Wang, P.; He, K.; Wei, Y.M.; Xie, R. A multiscale analysis for carbon price drivers. *Energy Econ.* **2019**, *78*, 202–216. [CrossRef]
9. Zhou, K.; Li, Y. Influencing factors and fluctuation characteristics of China's carbon emission trading price. *Phys. A Stat. Mech. its Appl.* **2019**, *524*, 459–474. [CrossRef]
10. Sousa, R.; Aguiar-Conraria, L.; Soares, M.J. Carbon financial markets: A time-frequency analysis of CO_2 prices. *Phys. A Stat. Mech. its Appl.* **2014**, *414*, 118–127. [CrossRef]
11. Ortas, E.; Álvarez, I. The efficacy of the European Union Emissions Trading Scheme: Depicting the co-movement of carbon assets and energy commodities through wavelet decomposition. *J. Clean. Prod.* **2016**, *116*, 40–49. [CrossRef]
12. Keppler, J.H.; Mansanet-Bataller, M. Causalities between CO_2, electricity, and other energy variables during phase I and phase II of the EU ETS. *Energy Policy* **2010**, *38*, 3329–3341. [CrossRef]
13. Rickels, W.; Görlich, D.; Peterson, S. Explaining European emission allowance price dynamics: Evidence from phase II. *Ger. Econ. Rev.* **2015**, *16*, 181–202. [CrossRef]

14. Yu, L.; Li, J.; Tang, L.; Wang, S. Linear and nonlinear Granger causality investigation between carbon market and crude oil market: A multi-scale approach. *Energy Econ.* **2015**, *51*, 300–311. [CrossRef]
15. Ji, Q.; Zhang, D.; Geng, J.B. Information linkage, dynamic spillovers in prices and volatility between the carbon and energy markets. *J. Clean. Prod.* **2018**, *198*, 972–978. [CrossRef]
16. Wang, Y.; Guo, Z. The dynamic spillover between carbon and energy markets: New evidence. *Energy* **2018**, *149*, 24–33. [CrossRef]
17. D'Adamo, I. The Profitability of Residential Photovoltaic Systems. A New Scheme of Subsidies Based on the Price of CO_2 in a Developed PV Market. *Soc. Sci.* **2018**, *7*, 148. [CrossRef]
18. Chen, H.; Liu, Z.; Zhang, Y.; Wu, Y. The Linkages of Carbon Spot-Futures: Evidence from EU-ETS in the Third Phase. *Sustainability* **2020**, *12*, 2517. [CrossRef]
19. D'Adamo, I.; Gastaldi, M.; Rosa, P. Recycling of end-of-life vehicles: Assessing trends and performances in Europe. *Technol. Forecast. Soc. Chang.* **2020**, *152*, 119887. [CrossRef]
20. Hammoudeh, S.; Nguyen, D.K.; Sousa, R.M. Energy prices and CO_2 emission allowance prices: A quantile regression approach. *Energy Policy* **2014**, *70*, 201–206. [CrossRef]
21. Marimoutou, V.; Soury, M. Energy markets and CO_2 emissions: Analysis by stochastic copula autoregressive model. *Energy* **2015**, *88*, 417–429. [CrossRef]
22. Hammoudeh, S.; Lahiani, A.; Nguyen, D.K.; Sousa, R.M. An empirical analysis of energy cost pass-through to CO_2 emission prices. *Energy Econ.* **2015**, *49*, 149–156. [CrossRef]
23. Zhang, J.; Zhang, L. Impacts on CO_2 emission allowance prices in China: A quantile regression analysis of the Shanghai emission trading scheme. *Sustainability* **2016**, *8*, 1195. [CrossRef]
24. Zeng, S.; Nan, X.; Liu, C.; Chen, J. The response of the Beijing carbon emissions allowance price (BJC) to macroeconomic and energy price indices. *Energy Policy* **2017**, *106*, 111–121. [CrossRef]
25. Fan, J.H.; Todorova, N. Dynamics of China's carbon prices in the pilot trading phase. *Appl. Energy* **2017**, *208*, 1452–1467. [CrossRef]
26. Chang, K.; Pei, P.; Zhang, C.; Wu, X. Exploring the price dynamics of CO_2 emissions allowances in China's emissions trading scheme pilots. *Energy Econ.* **2017**, *67*, 213–223. [CrossRef]
27. Lin, B.; Jia, Z. What are the main factors affecting carbon price in Emission Trading Scheme? A case study in China. *Sci. Total Environ.* **2019**, *654*, 525–534. [CrossRef]
28. Yang, B.; Liu, C.; Gou, Z.; Man, J.; Su, Y. How Will Policies of China's CO_2 ETS Affect its Carbon Price: Evidence from Chinese Pilot Regions. *Sustainability* **2018**, *10*, 605. [CrossRef]
29. Wang, Q.; Gao, C.; Dai, S. Effect of the Emissions Trading Scheme on CO_2 Abatement in China. *Sustainability* **2019**, *11*, 1055. [CrossRef]
30. Zhang, Y.; Li, S.; Zhang, F. Does an Emissions Trading Policy Improve Environmental Efficiency? Evidence from China. *Sustainability* **2020**, *12*, 2165. [CrossRef]
31. Henriques, I.; Sadorsky, P. Oil prices and the stock prices of alternative energy companies. *Energy Econ.* **2008**, *30*, 998–1010. [CrossRef]
32. Kumar, S.; Managi, S.; Matsuda, A. Stock prices of clean energy firms, oil and carbon markets: A vector autoregressive analysis. *Energy Econ.* **2012**, *34*, 215–226. [CrossRef]
33. Jiménez-Rodríguez, R. What happens to the relationship between EU allowances prices and stock market indices in Europe? *Energy Econ.* **2019**, *81*, 13–24. [CrossRef]
34. Zhu, D.; Kong, Y. A Study on the Relationship between Stock Prices of Companies of Low Carbon Economy & New Energy and the Price of Carbon Allowances. *Ecology Eco.* **2016**, *32*, 52–57.
35. Caruso, G.; Di Battista, T.; Gattone, S.A. A. A Micro-level Analysis of Regional Economic Activity Through a PCA Approach. In *Decision Economics: Complexity of Decisions and Decisions for Complexity*; Bucciarelli, E., Chen, S.H., Corchado, J., Eds.; Springer: Cham, Switzerland, 2019; pp. 227–234. [CrossRef]
36. Aguiar-Conraria, L.; Martins, M.F.; Soares, M.J. Estimating the Taylor rule in the time-frequency domain. *J. Macroecon.* **2018**, *57*, 122–137. [CrossRef]
37. Aguiar-Conraria, L.; Azevedo, N.; Soares, M.J. Using wavelets to decompose the time-frequency effects of monetary policy. *Phys. A Stat. Mech. Appl.* **2008**, *387*, 2863–2878. [CrossRef]
38. Lin, B.; Chen, Y. Dynamic linkages and spillover effects between CET market, coal market and stock market of new energy companies: A case of Beijing CET market in China. *Energy* **2019**, *172*, 1198–1210. [CrossRef]

39. Sun, C.; Ding, D.; Fang, X.; Zhang, H.; Li, J. How do fossil energy prices affect the stock prices of new energy companies? Evidence from Divisia energy price index in China's market. *Energy* **2019**, *169*, 637–645. [CrossRef]
40. Ewing, B.T.; Malik, F.; Ozfidan, O. Volatility transmission in the oil and natural gas markets. *Energy Econ.* **2002**, *24*, 525–538. [CrossRef]
41. Grinsted, A.; Moore, J.C.; Jevrejeva, N.R. Application of the cross wavelet transform and wavelet coherence to geophysical time series. *Nonlinear Process. Geophys.* **2004**, *11*, 561–566. [CrossRef]
42. Torrence, C.; Compo, G. A practical guide to wavelet analysis. *Bull. Am. Meteorol. Soc.* **1998**, *79*, 61–78. [CrossRef]

sustainability

MDPI

Article

Determinants of Individuals' E-Waste Recycling Decision: A Case Study from Romania

Camelia Delcea [1,*], Liliana Crăciun [2], Corina Ioanăș [3], Gabriella Ferruzzi [4] and Liviu-Adrian Cotfas [1]

1 Department of Economic Informatics and Cybernetics, Bucharest University of Economic Studies, 010552 Bucharest, Romania; liviu.cotfas@ase.ro
2 Department of Economics and Economic Policies, Bucharest University of Economic Studies, 010552 Bucharest, Romania; liliana.craciun@softscape.ro
3 Department of Accounting, Bucharest University of Economic Studies, 010552 Bucharest, Romania; corina.ioanas@softscape.ro
4 Department of Industrial Engineering, University of Naples Federico II, 80125 Naples, Italy; gabriella.ferruzzi@unina.it
* Correspondence: camelia.delcea@csie.ase.ro

Received: 9 March 2020; Accepted: 29 March 2020; Published: 1 April 2020

Abstract: Due to the increase of the amount of electrical and electronical equipment waste (e-waste), the understanding of individual consumers' main decision triggers represents a key point in increasing the quantity of recycled e-waste. A series of studies from the literature have shown a positive relationship between the consumers' attitude, awareness, self-efficacy, social norms, and their e-waste recycling intention, as well as the positive influence between the intention and the manifested behavior. Additional to these determinants, in the present study, the influence of social media was analyzed along with the actions taken by the government and nongovernmental organizations, with the purpose to include and to capture, as much as possible, a high amount of determinants in the e-waste recycling process. Nevertheless, the demographic or socio-economic variables, such as age, gender, income, education, number of family members, etc., have shown over time to have a contribution to predicting the consumers' pro-recycling behavior. As on one side, in the research literature, the opinions related to which of the demographic or socio-economic factors can have an impact on the recycling behavior have been divided and, on another side, a series of researchers believe that the discrepancies in the findings of different studies can be due to culture in various countries, in this paper we conducted such an analysis with reference to the Romania's case. The results have shown that the demographic variables, such as age and gender, can have a contribution to predicting residents' pro-e-waste recycling behavior. Based on these findings, the policymakers can gain a better understanding of the e-waste recycling phenomenon and on its main triggers, with results in creating better policies for sustaining a proper e-waste managing system.

Keywords: e-waste recycling; consumers' decisions; recycling behavioral intention; structural equation modeling; Romania; social media influence

1. Introduction

E-waste (waste electrical and electronical equipment, WEEE) refers to any discarded products that have a battery or a plug, and have ceased to represent value to their users or no longer satisfy their initial purpose [1]. Various types of waste products can be included in the e-waste category, such as, but not limited to: washing machines, dishwashers, air conditioners, refrigerators, microwaves, toasters, coffee machines, appliances for toothbrushing, shaving, hair drying, laptops, personal computers, notebooks, telephones, cell phones, printers, electronical and electronic tools, leisure equipment, medical devices, monitoring and control instruments, automatic dispensers, etc.

A high amount of e-waste is currently generated worldwide at an estimated annual growth rate between 4% and 5%, and with an expected amount of more than 50 million tons in 2021 [2]. Blade et al. [3] determined that in 2016, Asia generated almost 40.7% of the global e-waste, followed by Europe with 27.4% of the global waste, and America with 25.3%. Smaller percentages have been brought by Africa (5%) and Oceania (1.6%). Regarding the percentage of collected e-waste, Europe collected almost 35% of the e-waste generated in the countries, followed by America with 17%, and Asia with 15%. Even in this case, Oceania collected a small amount, with a rate of 6%, while for Africa, the numbers presented a 0% collected rate (representing in absolute value 0.004 million tons) [3].

Considering the numbers for Europe, according to Eurostat [4], in 2017 the recycling rate of e-waste has been below 50% for most European countries, except for Estonia, Bulgaria, Iceland, Hungary, and Austria, which passed the 50% e-waste recycling threshold, and Croatia and Liechtenstein, which hit scores above 80%. The smallest e-waste recycling rates have been recorded in Greece, Lithuania, and Poland. Figure 1 presents the recycling rate of the e-waste in 2017 only for the countries for which this information was available on the database offered by Eurostat.

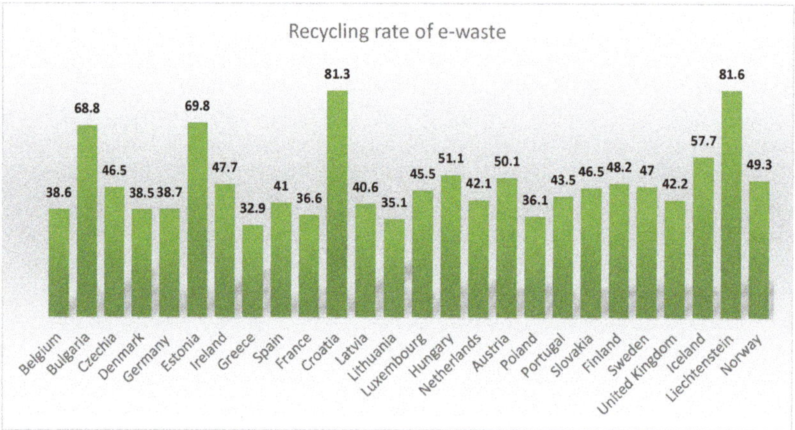

Figure 1. Recycling rate of e-waste in Europe in 2017 (source: Eurostat [4]).

Regarding the volume of e-waste generated in the European Union, including Norway and Switzerland, it is estimated that in 2020 it will reach 10,960,799 tons [5]. By categories (considering six main categories) of e-waste, the highest value is being recorded for large equipment (3,656,468 tons) and small equipment (3,392,044 tons). The temperature exchange equipment e-waste is estimated at 1,853,605 tons, while screens at 1,083,991 tones. Lower values are estimated for small IT (900,695 tons) and lamps (73,996 tons) [5].

Not only does the weight or the quantity of the yearly generated e-waste represent a high level of pressure for the environment and for the measures needed to be taken in order to properly recycle the electronic products, but the damage that the e-waste produces in the environment is also significant. From this point of view, even though globally the e-waste represents almost 5% of all municipal solid waste [1], the toxicity brought to the environment by this type of waste is high, representing almost 70% of our overall toxic waste [6]. The environmental and health impacts of the e-waste have been largely discussed in the research literature attached to this field [7–10]. Also, Shevchenko et al. [11] underlined that more than 1000 different substances are included in the e-waste category, many of them toxic to both human health and environment, while 70% of the cadmium and mercury present in the USA's landfills are from e-waste.

In this context, the environmental and health protection is a key point in the current economy, and measures should be taken for encouraging the e-waste recycling process as a part of the overall recycling process. The need to have a clean environment is widely acknowledged in the scientific literature [12–14]. Moreover, extensive efforts have been made for the optimization of the environmental bioprocess on the path towards a green economy [15]. Guidelines for adopting a circular economy are presented in [16].

Due to issues connected to the management system of the e-waste handling, households deal with higher challenges in the recycling process of e-waste than companies [17–19]. Nevertheless, households play an important role in participating to this process, and besides the awareness, attitude, responsibility, self-efficacy, and other aspects that can contribute to individuals' intention of recycling the e-waste, the occurrence of social media and of the actions taken by the government and NGOs (nongovernmental organizations) might have a positive impact on the overall e-waste recycling process [20].

In January 2020, the penetration rate of the social media recorded high values for countries in Eastern Asia (71%), Northern America (69%), Northern Europe, and Southern America (67%) [21]. Smaller penetration rates have been recorded for different parts of Africa (between 6%–39%), contributing to a global social media penetration rate of 49% [21]. Considering the areas with the highest e-waste production, it can be observed that these are also the areas in which social media has succeed to penetrate at a higher rate.

As the topic of e-waste recycling is vast, a series of papers have addressed this problem in different countries contexts such as: Brazil [22], Canada [23], China [24–28], Costa Rica [29], Ghana [30,31], Greece [32], Hong Kong [24], India [33], Italy [34], Japan [26], Mexico [35,36], New Zealand [7], Nigeria [19,37], South Korea [26], Sri Lanka [38], Taiwan [26,39], United Kingdom [40], United States [41], Vietnam [42], etc., by studying various aspects related to the e-waste recycling process in the context of the behavior of the consumers' located in these areas.

Given the fact that, to the best of our knowledge, there is little evidence regarding the e-waste determinants in the case of Romania, the current study aimed to analyze these determinants from multiple points of view. In order to underline more the importance of the e-waste recycling process in the context of Romania, it should be mentioned that even though efforts have been made in this direction (as there are over 2000 collection points in commercial networks [43]), Romania is facing serious problems regarding the e-waste management [43]. According to Păceșilă et al. [43], the total amount of electrical and electronic equipment was about 25–30 kg/capita in 2016, while the e-waste collected in the same period was 1.6 kg/capita [44], lower than the European Union average of 8.9 kg/capita.

Projected data from Urban Mine Platform [45] for 2020 show that 12.81 kg/capita of waste will be generated in Romania (higher than the 12.56 kg/capita in 2019), most of it belonging to large equipment (4.53 kg/capita), small equipment (3.09 kg/capita), and temperature exchange equipment (3.01 kg/capita), while small amounts come from small IT (0.59 kg/capita) and lamps (0.12 kg/capita).

In this context, the paper aimed to identify the main factors that can influence consumers' behavior towards e-waste recycling and to analyze whether some of the demographic and/or socio-economic variables can have an effect on the e-waste recycling and intention.

The remainder of the paper is structured as follows: Section 2 provides a literature review on the topic of e-waste and how different aspects related to it have been addressed in the scientific literature. Section 3 presents the methodology associated to this study, highlighting the elements considered in the questionnaire and stating the main hypotheses of the study. Section 4 provides the results gathered through the use of the questionnaire and analysis of them in terms of demographic and socio-economic variables. The paper ends with a concluding remarks section, in which the limitations of this study are discussed.

2. Literature Review

The recorded population growth combined with the rapid changes and advances in technologies has facilitated the increase of the waste generated worldwide [37,46–49], among which, e-waste plays an important role due to the harmful effects on both environment and health.

A broad range of research has been written in the area of e-waste recycling, addressing the issue from different point of views. Wang et al. [50] underlined the fact that when e-waste recycling is done with responsibility, it does not only reduce the quantity of waste that is disposed in landfills but it is also a beneficial process in recovering the valuable materials, such as nonprecious metals (aluminum, steel, copper, iron, etc.), precious metals (such as platinum, gold, silver, etc.), and plastic. In a recent study, Vaccari et al. [51] conducted an overview study considering both the environmental pollution and the health consequences, and showed that high levels of pollutants have been discovered in the bodies of the persons living or working in the areas with informal e-waste treatment. The authors have shown that not only the human health suffered from the informal working activity related to the e-waste treatment, but even the soil, air, and water have been contaminated with heavy metals and organic contaminants [51].

Arain et al. [52] showed in a recent work that the consumers' behavior is critical in managing and reducing the e-waste. In order to better shape the consumers' behavior, the authors have conducted a study in a university environment and have observed that lack of consumer knowledge about products and disposal sites plays an important role in consumer decisions. Even more, the free access to disposal and recycling facilities within a reasonable distance positively influences the consumers' decision to participate in the recycling process [52]. Even more, recycling opportunities and reduced distance to collection points have been named as underlying factors for e-waste recycling by [53–55]. Rousta et al. [54] have determined that a decreased distance to drop-off points resulted in improved sorting of recyclables, while the missorted fraction depended on the proper information received by the recycling persons.

Also, consumers' awareness has been proved to have a direct relationship with the willingness of e-waste recycling [56]. The role of households' awareness is underlined by Miner et al. [19], who believed that a well informed and aware population can make better decisions related to handling the e-waste. Along with the awareness manifested by the consumer, a pro-recycling attitude has been determined to have a major contribution to the recycling behavior [40].

Intrinsic factors, such as personal and social norms and understanding the consequences of a given behavior, are triggers for the peoples' intention, having at the same time a mediated influence on behavior [40,57].

The importance of the government and NGOs has been stated in [29]. The authors presented in their work the steps followed in Costa Rica in order to develop a better e-waste management system and the role played by different organizations in promotion and increasing the population awareness regarding their responsibility in the e-waste management process [29]. Also, D'Adamo et al. [58], focusing on end of life vehicles, have shown that it is important for carbon price to increase in order to promote recycling.

By focusing on the e-waste recycling process and considering the presence of the online environment and its influence on the e-waste recycling process, Wang et al. [59] explored the factors influencing this process and identified that subjective norms, economic motivation, the level of income and education, the perceived behavioral control, and behavioral attitudes affect the online recycling intention in a positive manner.

With the development of social media, a series of studies have presented the role of consumers' influence on these networks [60–65], proving that the social influence positively affects the people's behavior when adopting a pro-environment attitude [49,66]. Sujata et al. [20] analyzed in their study the determinants of recycling intention behavior for the general public. Using a questionnaire approach, the authors have observed a positive relation between attitude, social norms, self-efficacy, social media usage, and recycling intention. Even more, the authors have considered the role of government and NGOs from the recyclers' perspective and have extracted the feelings the respondents had with regard to the actions taken by the government and NGOs. As a result, it has been observed that the recyclers' intention and their opinion upon the NGOs activity influence the recycling behavior, while the moderating role of the government seemed not to be significant to the recycling behavior of the consumers [20].

Considering a broad range of papers, Shevchenko et al. [11] have analyzed consumers' recycling behavior determinants by considering 27 papers written on different continents (Europe, America, Asia, and Africa). Among the most listed determinant, one can highlight the awareness and knowledge level, followed by convenience and economic incentives. Other determinants considered in the selected studies are: gender, current habits, legislative norms and trustworthiness, mentality and attitude, income, age, and educational level [11]. Piligrimiene et al. [67] have divided the factors influencing the consumer engagement into two main categories: internal factors (environmental attitude, perceived responsibility, perceived behavioral efficiency) and external factors (conditions for sustainable conditions, social environment, and promotion of sustainable conditions).

Other areas of study related to the e-waste recycling process have addressed, but are not limited to: stress and occupational noise exposure in the case of e-waste recycling workers [31,68], public awareness regarding the informal sector's involvement in managing e-waste [33], developing an e-waste sorting methodology [69], the effect of macroeconomic and social factors on illegal e-waste trade [70], the link between gross domestic product (GDP) and e-waste [71].

3. Material and Methods

3.1. Survey Design

Based on the papers mentioned above and by considering a series of other studies from a broader range of papers referring to the general recycling process and the way humans actions can be influenced (such as [72–81]), a 54-questions survey was generated. Due to the validation process of the questionnaire, the number of questions was reduced due to low loadings as suggested by [20], with a 41-questions construction remaining after the validation. The questions included in the validated construction are presented in Appendix A (Table A1). The main focus was to keep in the survey the elements that seemed to have an influence on the e-waste recycling intention and on the behavior associated to e-waste recycling.

For this purpose, the aspects considered in the case of consumers' e-waste recycling process were: attitude (AT), awareness (AW), self-efficacy (SE), responsibility (RESP), social norms (SN), social influence (SI), social media (SM), government and NGOs' actions (GNGO), recycling intention (RI), convenience (CONV), government measures (GM, compressing ideas related to the legislative actions the government should make), and recycling behavior (RB)—Figure 2. The considered aspects were inspired by the elements analyzed in various research papers written in the literature associated with the consumer recycling behavior (as presented in the literature review section). All the questions in these categories have been valuated using a 5-point Likert scale, with 1—strongly disagree, 2—disagree, 3—neutral, 4—agree, and 5—strongly agree [82].

Besides the questions associated with these categories, some demographic data were also extracted, along with information related to ownership and knowledge of the e-waste products and the degree of usage of social media platforms, time spent on these platforms, and the degree to which the respondent can be influenced by the posts, videos, links, advertisements, and friends' attitudes on these platforms. These questions allowed the respondents to choose one or more option from a list of possible options or asked the respondents to write their answers inside text fields.

3.2. Distribution

The questionnaire was created and hosted using Google Forms and was distributed through a series of social media platforms. All the questions were marked as "mandatory" in order to submit the form, assuring in this way that we were not faced with an empty data case.

The questionnaire was available for three weeks in the fall of 2019. No incentives were given for participation. A number of 532 valid questionnaires were filled in.

3.3. Data Analysis

Data gathered through the questionnaire were analyzed using IBM SPSS Amos version 22 [83]—Figure 3.

Descriptive statistics and analysis were run over the data set. The results obtained through this analysis are presented in detail in the next section of the paper.

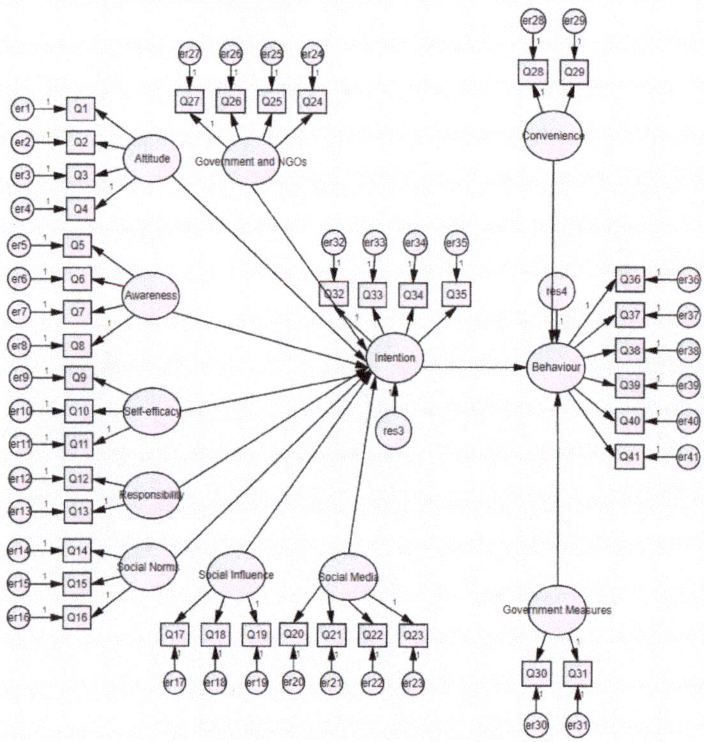

Figure 2. The considered construction.

The questionnaire was validated through a confirmatory factor analysis [84]. This analysis was conducted using IBM SPSS Amos 22. The unidimensionality, feasibility, convergent validity, and similarity validity were considered in accordance with the recommendations [85] from the field.

The standardized regression weights were used in order to test the unidimensionality. For a proper validation of the unidimensionality, all these factor loading values should exceed 0.5. In our model, all the standardized regression weights were above this threshold, except for the one between the self-efficacy and responsibility, which was close to this value, but slightly below, reaching 0.492.

Feasibility and convergent validity are tested through average variance extracted (AVE) and construct reliability (CR). The used software does not offer the possibility to automatically compute the values corresponding to these indicators. AVE and CR were manually computed using the formulas in [84] and their associated values can be found in Table 1. As a general rule, the values recorded for CR should be greater than 0.7 in order to suggest a good feasibility (other studies suggest that a value between 0.6 and 0.7 is also acceptable [42,85]). Considering the values for the CR presented in Table 1, it can be observed that all of them exceeded the imposed threshold value, even more, all the values for the CR were above 0.7. Regarding the expected values for AVE, it is acknowledged that a value above 0.5 proves a good convergent validity [42,85]. Values between 0.4 and 0.5 might also prove a good convergent validity if the associated CR values are above 0.6, according to [42,86]. In our case, three of the twelve constructions considered had values for the AVE in the 0.4–0.5 range, while all the others were hitting values above the imposed threshold of 0.5. Based on the research literature, we could conclude that given the values obtained for AVE and CR, the feasibility and convergent validity criterion were passed.

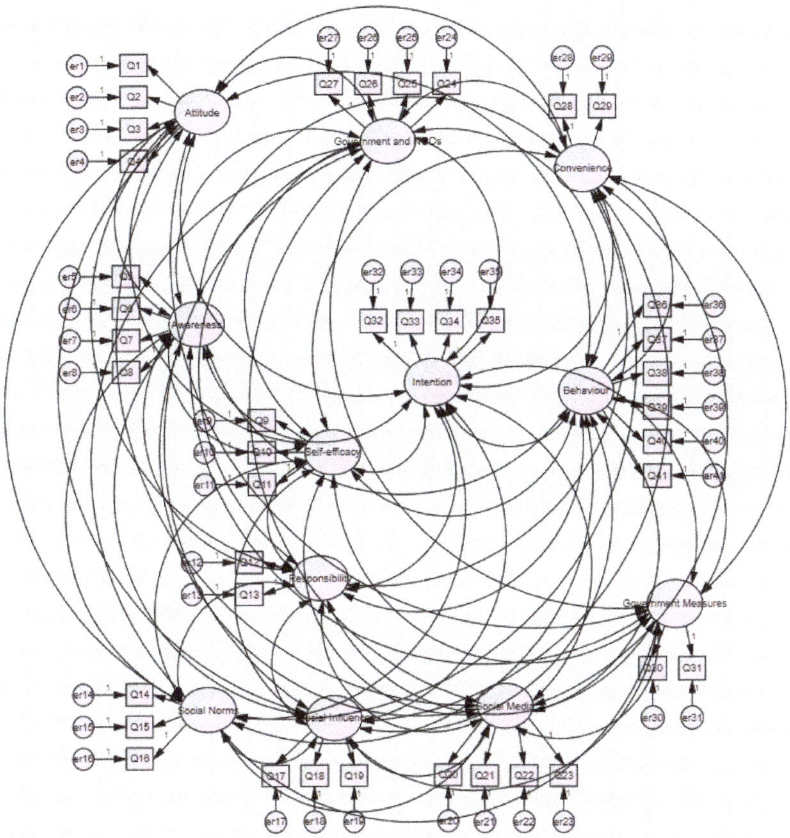

Figure 3. The individual components validation process.

The goodness of fit (GOF) measures were used for validating the construct similarity. These measures are listed under the "model fit summary" section in IBM SPSS Amos. The fit indexes can take values up to a maximum value of 1, being recommended to reach values above 0.9–0.95. In our case, the comparative fit index (CFI) reached a value of 0.922, which is considered acceptable given the size of the sample, the high number of individual construction components, and the number of questions.

Also, for a more in-depth analysis, it is recommended to check the values for the normed fit index (NFI) [87], which in our case was 0.851. Even more, the values for relative fit index (RFI) [87] should be considered, having in our case a value of 0.833. Last, the incremental fit index (IFI) [87] was 0.923, which is considered adequate given the size of the model.

Table 1. Standardized regression weights, average variance extracted (AVE), and construct reliability (CR).

	AT	AW	SE	RESP	SN	SI	SM	GNGO	CONV	GM	RI	RB
Q1	0.796											
Q2	0.848											
Q3	0.723											
Q4	0.835											
Q5		0.580										
Q6		0.732										
Q7		0.856										
Q8		0.876										
Q9			0.864									
Q10			0.853									
Q11			0.691									
Q12				0.786								
Q13				0.773								
Q14					0.609							
Q15					0.726							
Q16					0.556							
Q17						0.713						
Q18						0.794						
Q19						0.797						
Q20							0.749					
Q21							0.573					
Q22							0.667					
Q23							0.616					
Q24								0.518				
Q25								0.837				
Q26								0.781				
Q27								0.812				
Q28									0.603			
Q29									0.837			

Table 1. *Cont.*

	AT	AW	SE	RESP	SN	SI	SM	GNGO	CONV	GM	RI	RB
Q31										0.652		
Q32											0.904	
Q33											0.600	
Q34											0.737	
Q35											0.658	
Q36												0.838
Q37												0.833
Q38												0.868
Q39												0.848
Q40												0.549
Q41												0.692
AVE	0.643	0.593	0.651	0.608	0.402	0.591	0.428	0.560	0.532	0.472	0.538	0.634
CR	0.928	0.906	0.907	0.846	0.763	0.884	0.829	0.892	0.787	0.750	0.884	0.936

Even more, Brown [87] and Byrne [88] recommended the use of the Tucker–Lewis index (TLI), which should be around the value of 0.95. For our model, the Tucker–Lewis index was 0.912, also acceptable considering the size of the model.

A root mean square error of approximation (RMSEA) below 0.06 signifies a good model fit according to Hu and Bentler [89], Harrington [90], and Paswan [91]. In our case the RMSEA of 0.059 < 0.06, within the imposed threshold value. Even more, Paswan [91] recommended a threshold value of 0.085 for the LO90 and HI90 intervals. For the model under investigation, the LO90 was 0.054, while HI90 was 0.064, being in the imposed range.

3.4. Hypotheses

Based on the literature presented in Section 2, the following hypotheses have been considered:

Hypothesis (H1): *Attitude towards e-waste recycling positively affects consumers' e-waste recycling intention.*

Hypothesis (H2): *E-waste recycling awareness positively affects consumers' e-waste recycling intention.*

Hypothesis (H3): *Self-efficacy positively affects consumers' e-waste recycling intention.*

Hypothesis (H4): *Responsibility positively affects consumers' e-waste recycling intention.*

Hypothesis (H5): *Social norms have a positive impact on e-waste recycling intention.*

Hypothesis (H6): *Social influence positively affects individuals' e-waste recycling intention.*

Hypothesis (H7): *Social media has a positive impact on individuals' e-waste recycling intention.*

Hypothesis (H8): *Government and NGOs' actions positively contribute to consumers' e-waste recycling intention.*

Hypothesis (H9): *Recycling intention positively affects the recycling decision in the case of e-waste.*

Hypothesis (H10): *Government measures have a positive impact on consumers' e-waste recycling decision.*

Hypothesis (H11): *Convenience positively affects the consumers' e-waste recycling decision.*

The considered hypotheses are summarized in Figure 4.

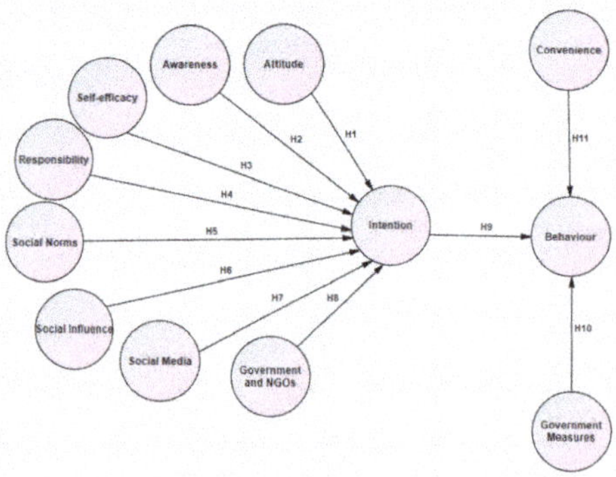

Figure 4. The hypotheses framework.

4. Case Study

4.1. Demographic and Socio-Economic Characteristics

The research focused both on the elements stated in the literature that might contribute to consumers' intention or decision to participate in the e-waste recycling, such as attitude, awareness, self-efficacy, responsibility, social norms, and convenience, but also on the elements related to the emergence of social media and the influence exerted among the consumers due to their online activity and the actions made by the government and NGOs.

As the questionnaire was distributed to the online social platforms, it ensured that all the respondents had access to social media platforms, therefore, none of the valid questionnaires had to be removed from the completed questionnaire database. As a result, a number of 532 questionnaires were validated and used for the analysis. The demographic and socio-economic characteristics of the respondents are presented in Table 2.

Table 2. Demographic and socio-economic profile of respondents (n = 532 persons).

Demographic and Socio-Economic Variables	Group/Components	Frequency	Percentage
Gender	Female	317	59.59%
	Male	215	40.41%
Age	18–30	198	37.22%
	30–50	251	47.18%
	≥50	83	15.60%
Educational level	Secondary education	157	29.51%
	University	294	55.26%
	Post-university	81	15.23%
Residential area	Urban	385	72.37%
	Rural	147	27.63%
Marital status	Single	169	31.77%
	Married	363	68.23%
Occupation	Services	207	38.91%
	Production	144	27.07%
	Student	102	19.17%
	Others	79	14.85%
Family size	1–2 persons	162	30.45%
	3–4 persons	259	48.68%
	≥5 persons	111	20.87%
Income (per month)	≤500 €	130	24.44%
	500–1000 €	327	61.46%
	≥1000 €	75	14.10%
Number of years in e-waste recycling	Do not practice	112	21.05%
	≤1 year	106	19.92%
	1–3 years	223	41.92%
	≥3 years	91	17.11%

Table 2. *Cont.*

Demographic and Socio-Economic Variables	Group/Components	Frequency	Percentage
Number of hours spent on social media	≤1 h	92	17.29%
	1–2 h	154	28.95%
	3–4 h	271	50.94%
	≥5 h	15	2.82%
Most frequently used social media	Facebook	237	44.55%
	Twitter	57	10.71%
	Instagram	199	37.41%
	LinkedIn	36	6.77%
	Others	3	0.56%

Regarding the period of engagement in e-waste recycling, 21.05% marked that they had not previously engaged in the e-waste recycling process, while the vast majority, 41.92%, were practicing it for 1–3 years. A smaller number of respondents, 91 persons (17.11%), marked the fact that they were engaged in the e-waste recycling for more than 3 years.

The use of social media was measured through the number of hours spent by the respondents on various sites. The great majority of the respondents spent 3–4 h on social media (50.94%), while 28.95% of the respondents spent 1–2 h. Among the most popular social networks, Facebook represented the most used platform (44.55% of the respondents marking it as their most frequently used social media platform), followed by Instagram (37.41%) and Twitter (10.71%).

4.2. E-Waste Behavior

The respondents' behavior related to the e-waste products recycling is analyzed in the following. Besides the answers to the questions presented in Appendix A, in this section, few other aspects will be presented related to the degree to which the respondents know how to recognize the products that can be included in the e-waste category, the level of ownership of these products, and how social media influence is manifested in their case, namely how prone to be influenced by the opinions expressed by other persons in these environments they are.

4.2.1. Attitude and Awareness of E-Waste Recycling

The items related to consumers' attitude regarding the e-waste recycling have showed that, in general, the respondents possessed a good opinion related to the whole e-waste recycling process.

It was observed that 74.06% of the respondents marked that e-waste recycling is a part of a responsible citizen's life, while only 8.27% disagreed or strongly disagreed with this idea, 17.67% having no particular opinion on the subject—Figure 5.

A similar percentage, 76.88% of the respondents believed that a pro-environment behavior is necessary given the current development conditions, while only 10.53% disagreed with this statement.

Regarding their own actions, 61.84% of the respondents believed that his/her own behavior contributes a lot to a healthy environment, while 56.20% affirmed that they have a positive attitude and that they feel good when they engage in the e-waste recycling.

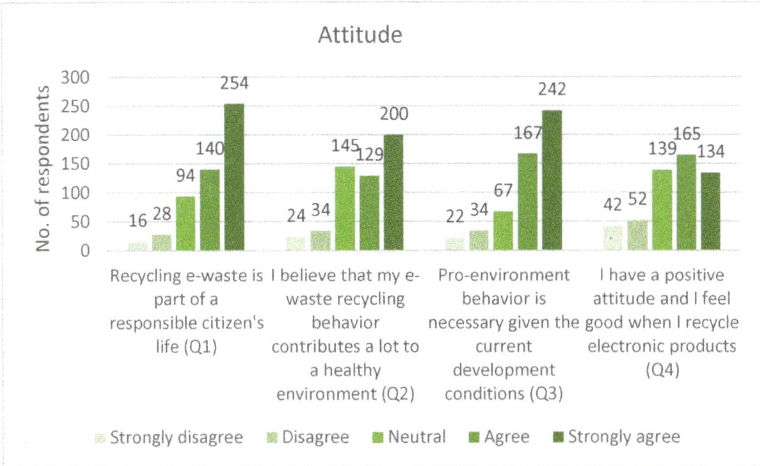

Figure 5. The distribution of the answers received for attitude.

As for the awareness, it was observed that a great part of the respondents knew that the electronic products contain potentially toxic substances (76.32%) and that not recycling e-waste can cause environment pollution (82.71%). Even more, 75.19% of the respondents were aware of the fact that the way we manage e-waste can harm the human health. A lower percentage of respondents (47.93%) were aware of the benefits e-waste recycling can have—Figure 6.

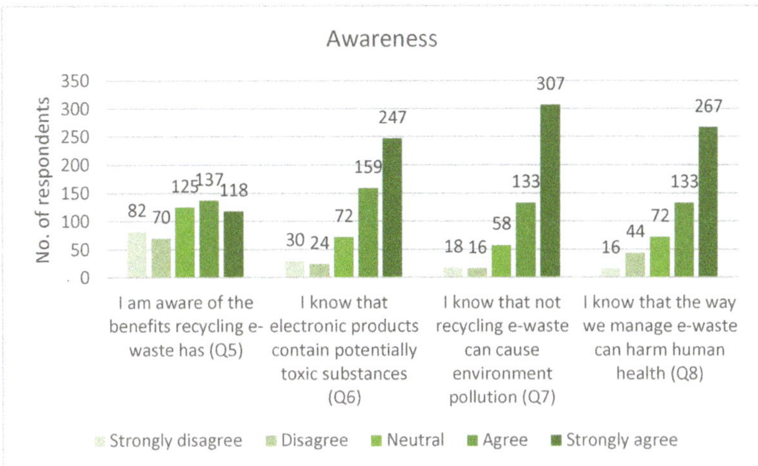

Figure 6. The distribution of the answers received for awareness.

4.2.2. Self-efficacy and Responsibility in the E-Waste Recycling Context

Self-efficacy, which reflects an individual's perception regarding his/her ability to perform e-waste-minimizing activities [92], has been measured through the answers received to three questions related to the knowledge associated to the items that can be recycled, to the e-waste recycling centers, and to the easiness to participate in the e-waste recycling activities. The vast majority of the respondents marked "agree" or "strongly agree" on these questions, demonstrating a good self-efficacy level—Table 3.

As for the responsibility, 77.25% of the respondents felt responsible to take actions in order to manage the level of e-waste they generate, while 71.79% of the respondents felt responsible for the environment pollution due to e-waste generation—Table 3.

Table 3. Summary of the answers received for self-efficacy and responsibility.

Issue	Questions	Strongly Disagree	Disagree	Neutral	Agree	Strongly Agree
SE	I know which are the items that can be recycled in e-waste recycling process (Q9)	10 (1.88%)	16 (3.01%)	53 (9.96%)	149 (28.01%)	304 (57.14%)
	I know where to take my e-waste for recycling (Q10)	21 (3.95%)	32 (6.02%)	86 (16.17%)	172 (32.33%)	221 (41.54%)
	I find it easy to participate in the e-waste recycling activities (Q11)	20 (3.76%)	30 (5.64%)	89 (16.73%)	178 (33.46%)	215 (40.41%)
RESP	I feel responsible to take actions in order to manage the level of e-waste I generate (Q12)	12 (2.26%)	18 (3.38%)	91 (17.11%)	170 (31.95%)	157 (45.30%)
	I feel responsible for the environment pollution due to e-waste generation (Q13)	16 (3.01%)	16 (3.01%)	117 (21.99%)	157 (29.51%)	226 (42.48%)

4.2.3. Social Norms, Social Influence, and Social Media

Considering the three questions included in the social norms construction, it was observed that, on average, only 23.12% of the respondents said that their family, friends, and other persons to whom they are in contact expect them to engage in e-waste activities, while 31.58% have not expressed any opinion regarding this aspect. The vast majority of respondents, 45.30% of the respondents, marked that their friends, family, and acquaintances do not expect them to engage in e-waste recycling behavior.

As for the social influence, only 27.44% of the respondents marked that their family, friends, and/or acquaintances talk to them about engaging into e-waste recycling activities, and 25.19% of respondents said that their friends, families, and other people they interact would appreciate if they engage into e-waste recycling activities. Even more, 32.14% of the respondents affirmed that the opinion of their family, friends, and other people they interact with regarding e-waste recycling matters to them.

Social media influence was measured through the occurrence of links, discussions, commercials, and videos in the respondents' social media newsfeed—Figure 7. Comparing the answers received on the four categories, it was observed that the highest occurrence was in the links category (40.04% of the respondents marked that links related to e-waste appear in their newsfeed), followed by discussions (33.46%) and commercials (32.33%). Videos represent the category with the smallest amount of appearance, in only 24.06% of the cases.

Additionally, the degree to which the respondent can be influenced by the posts, videos, links, advertisements, and friends' attitudes on these platforms was extracted—29.14% of the respondents marked that they can be influenced to a certain extent by other persons' opinions and posts on social media, while 32.71% affirmed that the videos, advertisements, and the links with information related to the e-waste can make them change their opinion.

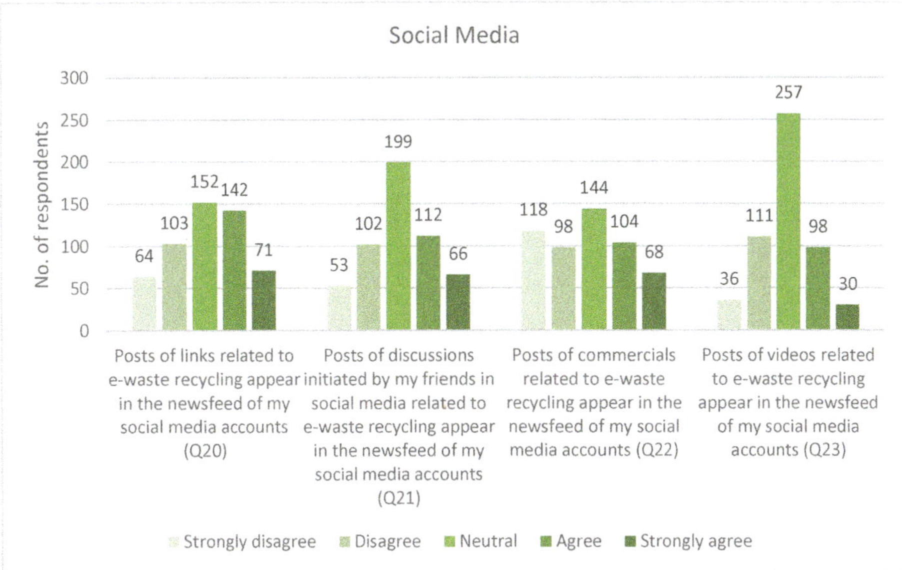

Figure 7. The distribution of the answers received for Social Media.

4.2.4. Government and NGOs' Actions vs. Government Measures

Regarding the government's actions, the great majority of the respondents, representing 56.95%, marked that they believe that a program made by the authorities in order to ease the e-waste recycling process would be beneficial, while most of them said that they are not happy with the measures taken by the government for encouraging e-waste collection (56.20%). Also, NGOs have been seen as the main actors to encourage the e-waste collection process by 51.50% of the respondents.

As for the government's measures, the opinions were split among the respondents as 31.58% manifested no opinion, 34.40% thought that a series of specific laws and enforcements rules would be beneficial, while the rest of 34.02% disagreed with the introduction of such measures.

4.2.5. Convenience

The need for e-waste recycling points was observed in the answers provided by 64.66% of the respondents, while only 19.36% of the respondents affirmed that it is easy to find a curbside for e-waste pick-ups.

4.2.6. Ownership and Knowledge of the E-Waste Products

The knowledge of the e-waste products was measured by asking the respondents to name some of the electronic devices they have, along with the number of these devices. Based on the received answers, it was observed that all the respondents had the needed knowledge related to identifying the e-waste products, as each respondent named at least one category.

Regarding the ownership of e-waste products, 90.60% of the respondents named cell phones, followed by television 85.53%, refrigerators 77.26%, computers and laptops 74.81%, kitchen products 50.94%, personal care devices 35.34%, other devices 14.47%.

4.2.7. E-Waste Recycling Intention and Recycling Behavior

Recycling intention was measured through the answers received to four questions as presented in Figure 8. Considering the distribution of the answers, it can be observed that, in general, the respondents manifested a good e-waste recycling intention, 63.16% of them saying that they plan on recycling e-waste even though it will not necessarily be easy, 40.79% plan to participate to e-waste recycling activities advocated on social media, while 56.95% intend to buy electronic products that can be easily recycled. A percentage of 58.08% plan to put more effort into the actions related to e-waste recycling process.

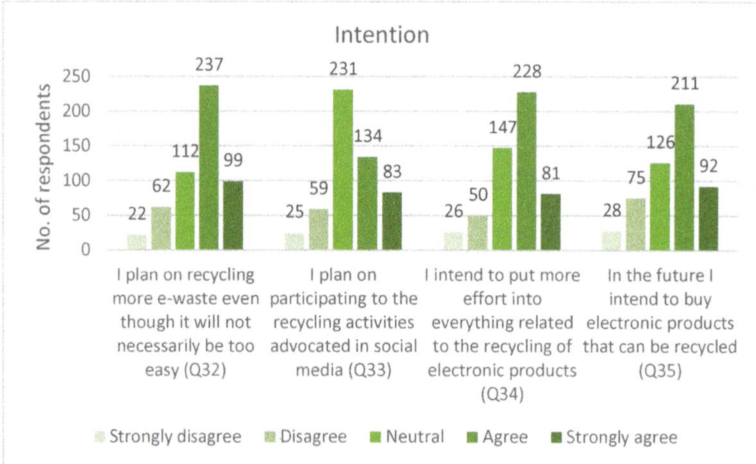

Figure 8. The distribution of the answers received for e-waste recycling intention.

Regarding the recycling of different e-waste products categories, 46.43% of the respondents mentioned that they have recycled information technology and telecommunications equipment, 41.35% have recycled consumer equipment, 33.08% have recycled large household appliances, 26.69% have recycled small household appliances, while light equipment has been recycled by 18.23%. E-waste not listed in the above categories and included in "other" section has been recycled by 10.53%.

4.3. Structural Model's Results

Based on the research hypotheses, the structural modelling was performed. Table 4 summarizes the determined structural path coefficients and the decision taken with regard to each of the formulated hypotheses.

Table 4. Structural path coefficients and hypotheses test results.

Hypotheses	Relationship	Structural Path Coefficients	Decision
H1	Attitude -> Intention	0.277 ***	Supported
H2	Awareness -> Intention	0.202 **	Supported
H3	Self-efficacy -> Intention	0.121 **	Supported
H4	Responsibility -> Intention	0.083 **	Supported
H5	Social norms -> Intention	0.075 *	Supported
H6	Social influence -> Intention	0.102 ***	Supported
H7	Social media -> Intention	0.071 **	Supported
H8	Government and NGOs -> Intention	0.024 +	Supported
H9	Intention -> Behavior	0.608 **	Supported
H10	Government measures -> Behavior	0.057 *	Supported
H11	Convenience -> Behavior	0.026 +	Supported

Note: $^{+}$ $p < 0.10$, * $p < 0.05$, ** $p < 0.01$, *** $p < 0.001$.

From the data listed in Table 4 it can be seen that all of the hypotheses were supported, but at different levels of significance. Considering the data, it was observed that the factors with significant influence on the e-waste recycling intention were the consumers' attitude and awareness, followed by self-efficacy and social influences. Referring to other studies in the field, the result achieved for the attitude effects on intention was expected [20,37,42,79,93]. Also, self-efficacy has been proved in previous studies to have a direct positive influence on consumers' recycling behavior, therefore the outcome has been in line with previous findings from the research literature [20,42]. As for the social influence, Nguyen et al. [42] considered a similar construction named "social pressure" which has been proven to have positive impact on the recycling intention.

Social media, social norms, and responsibility scored positive, but small values in comparison with other factors considered in the model. These findings are in line with the ones provided by Sujata et al. [20] in their study, which underlined the fact that social media appeared to be a weak predictor of intention.

Last, government and NGOs' actions seems to have little influence on consumers' intention to recycle, this being a possible consequence of the reduced activity carried on by these organizations.

As for the elements influencing the consumers' behavior to engage in e-waste recycling processes, the main trigger was found to be the e-waste recycling intention. The results obtained a high level of significance. Even in this case the results were consistent with past studies from the research literature [20,94–96]. Government measures seemed to have a small direct positive effect on the recycling decision, while convenience exerted even a smaller effect.

4.4. Contribution of Demographic Variables

Demographic or socio-economic variables have shown over the time to have a contribution to predicting the consumers' pro-recycling behavior. The opinions related to which of the demographic or socio-economic factors have an impact on the recycling behavior have been divided in the literature.

For example, age was one of the most discussed aspects for which no mutual agreement has been reached. A series of researchers believed that age has a contribution to recycling [77,97–102], most of them underlying the fact that seniors are more prone to recycling actions, while others did not find any connection between recycling and age [42,103–105].

Gender was another demographic variable considered in the research literature. While most of the researchers found a connection between gender and recycling, stating that women showed more readiness to recycle than men [42,102,106,107], there are also studies proving the contrary [105,108,109]. Even more, Darby and Obara [110] found that for US consumers, men were more likely to visit the CA sites, while Arcury et al. [111] suggested that women are usually associated to this process as traditionally they play an important role in every household's domestic activities.

Other demographic and socio-economic variables considered to influence the recycling decisions have been: education level [77,102,112], family size [77,107,112,113], income [77,98,103,110,112,113], ethnicity [107,114], and residence type [115].

Additionally, Husmann et al. [116] believed that the discrepancies in the findings of different studies can be due to culture in various countries.

As a result, in the present study we considered all the demographic and socio-economic variables extracted through the questionnaire. After running the structural equations analysis, differences were found among different categories based on only gender and age. These differences are presented and discussed below.

4.4.1. Gender Contribution

The relationship between attitude, awareness, self-efficacy, social influence, and social media seems to have a significant positive impact on e-waste recycling intention for both male and female respondents—Table 5. Compared to females, males showed a higher effect of awareness and self-efficacy on the intention, while females' attitude had a higher effect on intention. Social media influence was slightly higher in the case of female respondents, while social influence seemed to have a higher influence in the case of the male respondents.

Also, responsibility and social norms were significant only in the case of females, while the government and NGOs' actions seemed to be significant in the case of the male persons.

Regarding the e-waste recycling behavior, intention was the main trigger in the case of both male and female participants in the study, with higher values scored in the case of men. At the same time, convenience and government measures scored positive for the e-waste recycling behavior only in the case of male respondents.

Table 5. Structural path coefficients and hypotheses test results based on gender.

Hypotheses	Relationship	Structural Path Coefficients		Significance
		Female	Male	
H1	Attitude -> Intention	0.307 ***	0.261 **	Both
H2	Awareness -> Intention	0.147 *	0.198 **	Both
H3	Self-efficacy -> Intention	0.063 *	0.156 ***	Both
H4	Responsibility -> Intention	0.104 **	0.031	Female
H5	Social norms -> Intention	0.095 *	0.061	Female
H6	Social influence -> Intention	0.098 **	0.087 **	Both
H7	Social media -> Intention	0.064 **	0.070 *	Both
H8	Government and NGOs -> Intention	0.011	0.032 *	Male
H9	Intention -> Behavior	0.549 **	0.606 ***	Both
H10	Government measures -> Behavior	0.029	0.063 **	Male
H11	Convenience -> Behavior	0.014	0.057 *	Male

Note: * $p < 0.05$, ** $p < 0.01$, *** $p < 0.001$.

4.4.2. Age Contribution

Based on age, it was observed that all the three considered categories (≤30; 30–50; ≥50) manifested an effect of attitude, awareness, and social influence on the e-waste recycling behavior—Table 6. Higher values were reported for the "30–50" category in terms of the influence of awareness on e-waste recycling intention when compared to the other two age categories.

Responsibility and social norms were important factors in e-waste recycling behavior for persons in the "30–50" and "≥50" age categories, while social media influence manifested more in the cases of the "≤30" and "30–50" categories. Also, the government and NGOs' actions seemed to have an influence in the case of the persons in the "≤30" category.

The influence of intention on e-waste recycling behavior was observed in all the three categories under investigation, with high values in the case of "≥50" category. Even more, the government measures seemed to have an effect on the recycling decision only in the case of the "≥50" category, while convenience scored relevant values for the recycling behavior in the case of the "30–50" category.

Table 6. Structural path coefficients and hypotheses test results based on age.

Hypotheses	Relationship	Structural Path Coefficients			Significance
		≤30	30–50	≥50	
H1	Attitude -> Intention	0.251 *	0.284 ***	0.265 *	All
H2	Awareness -> Intention	0.174 **	0.222 *	0.180 *	All
H3	Self-efficacy -> Intention	0.147 *	0.104	0.087	≤30
H4	Responsibility -> Intention	0.033	0.091 **	0.102 *	30–50; ≥50
H5	Social norms -> Intention	0.062	0.094 **	0.091 *	30–50; ≥50
H6	Social influence -> Intention	0.134 ***	0.097 **	0.083 *	All
H7	Social media -> Intention	0.088 ***	0.064 *	0.049	≤30; 30–50
H8	Government and NGOs -> Intention	0.042 *	0.011	0.008	≤30
H9	Intention -> Behavior	0.583 **	0.596 **	0.611 ***	All
H10	Government measures -> Behavior	0.040	0.063	0.059 *	≥50
H11	Convenience -> Behavior	0.019	0.031 *	0.024	30–50

Note: * $p < 0.05$, ** $p < 0.01$, *** $p < 0.001$.

5. Conclusions

The present paper tried to model the potential influence of various determinants on e-waste recycling intention and behavior. The need for this study exists both in the context of highly generated amounts of e-waste every year, but also due to the different influences the determinant factors can have over the decision variables.

The study focused on some of the elements already stated in the literature as main determinants for the e-waste recycling intention and decisions, while adding some new factors that emerged from the occurrence and high use of the social media environments. Also, the activity conducted by the government was captured by splitting the activity made by the organization into actions and measures. While government actions have been assumed to influence the consumers' e-waste recycling intention, the government measures have been assumed to have a direct impact on the consumers' final behavior in relation with the recycling decision. Beside the government, the actions carried on the by the NGOs have been assumed to have an impact on the e-waste recycling intention.

For capturing all the dimensions related to the determinant factors, a questionnaire was created and validated. A structural equation model was used for analyzing this complex situation.

Even more, the demographic and socio-economic variables were analyzed as, in the research literature, there was no common ground regarding their influence on the e-waste recycling behavior.

Among the findings, the positive effect of all the considered variables on the e-waste recycling intention can be underlined. The analysis revealed that attitude and awareness towards e-waste recycling were the primary influencing factors for the intention to recycle, which underlines more the need for campaigns that contribute to increasing people's understanding over the harmful influence on environmental and human health.

Also, the self-efficacy and social influence have a contribution to the e-waste recycling intention, which makes us believe that the campaigns must be designed based on an educative ground that will make consumers better understand which are the items to be recycled and what are the needed steps to be taken for recycling, making this process as easy as possible. As for the social influence, the increase in knowledge related to this phenomenon might enhance the diffusion system of information among various participants to the economic life, including families, friends, and acquaintances, with a direct result on the increase in e-waste recycling intention.

Even other determinant factors that scored positive but smaller values, such as social media and social norms, can make their contribution through a proper communication program related to the e-waste recycling process. Considering the high amount of time spent on social media, some campaigns designed especially for diffusion in this environment can encourage consumers' to participate in the recycling process.

Boosting the consumers' intention has been proven to have a direct and positive impact on their e-waste recycling behavior. Government measures and convenience scored lesser, but positive, scores, which shows that there is still a place for changes in these determinant factors.

Nevertheless, the analysis provided, featuring the gender and age demographic variables' contribution to boosting the recycling intention and decision, has showed that a more in-depth analysis can provide additional information related to the determinant factors for each of the considered categories. Even though the main determinants have remained the same among the selected categories, the secondary determinant factors can offer more insight to the policy-makers on the channels they can use and the actions they can take in order to boost the e-waste recycling behavior.

The study has its limitations, given by the size of the sample, the fact that it only contained respondents that used social media, and by the specificity, as it applied to Romanian citizens.

In order to better shape the interactions among the consumers, the study was aimed to be extended by including the results gathered from the questionnaire in an agent-based model. By creating intelligent agents that act similarly to real persons engaged in the recycling process, the behavior of the consumers can be better analyzed and the outcome can be more easily observed when little changes are made to the input variables. Also, combined effects can be easier to observe in an agent-based environment.

Author Contributions: Conceptualization, C.D. and L.C.; data curation, C.D. and L.-A.C.; formal analysis, C.D. and G.F.; investigation, G.F. and L.-A.C.; methodology, C.D. and L.-A.C.; software, G.F. and L.-A.C.; supervision, C.D.; validation, L.C. and C.I.; visualization, L.C. and C.I.; writing—original draft, C.D.; writing—review and editing, C.I., G.F., and L.-A.C. All authors have read and agreed to the published version of the manuscript.

Funding: This research received no external funding.

Acknowledgments: The results included in this work are part of the project FutureWeb, supported by the Romanian Ministry of Research and Innovation, CCCDI-UEFISCDI, project number PN-III-P1-1.2-PCCDI-2017-0800/86PCCDI/2018-FutureWeb, within PNCD III.

Conflicts of Interest: The authors declare no conflict of interest.

Appendix A

Table A1. Research questionnaire.

Issue	Acronym	Questions	Strongly Disagree	Disagree	Neutral	Agree	Strongly Agree
Attitude	AT	Recycling e-waste is part of a responsible citizen's life (Q1)	□	□	□	□	□
		I believe that my e-waste recycling behavior contributes a lot to a healthy environment (Q2)	□	□	□	□	□
		Pro-environment behavior is necessary given the current development conditions (Q3)	□	□	□	□	□
		I have a positive attitude and I feel good when I recycle electronic products (Q4)	□	□	□	□	□

Table A1. *Cont.*

Issue	Acronym	Questions	Strongly Disagree	Disagree	Neutral	Agree	Strongly Agree
Awareness	AW	I am aware of the benefits recycling e-waste has (Q5)	□	□	□	□	□
		I know that electronic products contain potentially toxic substances (Q6)	□	□	□	□	□
		I know that not recycling e-waste can cause environment pollution (Q7)	□	□	□	□	□
		I know that the way we manage e-waste can harm human health (Q8)	□	□	□	□	□
Self-efficacy	SE	I know which are the items that can be recycled in e-waste recycling process (Q9)	□	□	□	□	□
		I know where to take my e-waste for recycling (Q10)	□	□	□	□	□
		I find it easy to participate in the e-waste recycling activities (Q11)	□	□	□	□	□
Responsibility	RESP	I feel responsible to take actions in order to manage the level of e-waste I generate (Q12)	□	□	□	□	□
		I feel responsible for the environment pollution due e-waste generation (Q13)	□	□	□	□	□
Social Norms	SN	My family expect me to engage in e-waste recycling behavior (Q14)	□	□	□	□	□
		My friends expect me to engage in e-waste recycling behavior (Q15)	□	□	□	□	□
		Other persons with whom I am in contact expect me to engage in e-waste recycling behavior (Q16)	□	□	□	□	□
Social Influence	SI	Family/friends/people around me talk about e-waste recycling and/or recommend me to engage in e-waste recycling (Q17)	□	□	□	□	□
		Family/friends/people around me would appreciate if I engage in an e-waste recycling behavior (Q18)	□	□	□	□	□
		The opinions of family/friends/people around regarding e-waste recycling matters to me (Q19)	□	□	□	□	□

Table A1. *Cont.*

Issue	Acronym	Questions	Strongly Disagree	Disagree	Neutral	Agree	Strongly Agree
Social Media	SM	Posts of links related to e-waste recycling appear in the newsfeed of my social media accounts (Q20)	☐	☐	☐	☐	☐
		Posts of discussions initiated by my friends on social media related to e-waste recycling appear in the newsfeed of my social media accounts (Q21)	☐	☐	☐	☐	☐
		Posts of commercials related to e-waste recycling appear in the newsfeed of my social media accounts (Q22)	☐	☐	☐	☐	☐
		Posts of videos related to e-waste recycling appear in the newsfeed of my social media accounts (Q23)	☐	☐	☐	☐	☐
Government and NGOs	GNGO	The actions made by the government and/or NGOs for encouraging e-waste collection makes me happy (Q24)	☐	☐	☐	☐	☐
		The services offered by the government ease the e-waste recycling process (Q25)	☐	☐	☐	☐	☐
		NGOs are one of the main actors that encourage the e-waste recycling process (Q26)	☐	☐	☐	☐	☐
		A program by the authorities for collecting electronic products for recycling from people's houses would be useful (Q27)	☐	☐	☐	☐	☐
Convenience	CONV	Near my house there are many recycling centers for electronic products (Q28)	☐	☐	☐	☐	☐
		I found it to be easy and convenient to access the curbside pick-ups for the e-waste (Q29)	☐	☐	☐	☐	☐
Government Measures	GM	Some specific laws on the recycling of electronic products would make me recycle more (Q30)	☐	☐	☐	☐	☐
		I believe that if the government enforced the rules for e-waste more electronics product will be recycled (Q31)	☐	☐	☐	☐	☐
Recycling Intention	RI	I plan on recycling more e-waste even though it will not necessarily be too easy (Q32)	☐	☐	☐	☐	☐
		I plan on participating in the recycling activities advocated in social media (Q33)	☐	☐	☐	☐	☐
		I intend to put more effort into everything related to the recycling of electronic products (Q34)	☐	☐	☐	☐	☐
		In the future I intend to buy electronic products that can be recycled (Q35)	☐	☐	☐	☐	☐

Table A1. *Cont.*

Issue	Acronym	Questions	Strongly Disagree	Disagree	Neutral	Agree	Strongly Agree
Recycling Behavior	RB	I recycle large household appliances (e.g., washing machines, dishwashers, air conditioners, refrigerators, microwaves, etc.) (Q36)	□	□	□	□	□
		I recycle small household appliances (e.g., toasters, vacuum cleaners, coffee machines, appliances for toothbrushing, shaving, hair drying, etc.) (Q37)	□	□	□	□	□
		I recycle information technology and telecommunications equipment (e.g., laptops, personal computers, notebooks, telephones, cell phones, printers, etc.) (Q38)	□	□	□	□	□
		I recycle consumer equipment (e.g., video recorders, stereo recorders, musical instruments, radios, televisions, etc.) (Q39)	□	□	□	□	□
		I recycle light equipment (Q40)	□	□	□	□	□
		I recycle other categories of e-waste (not listed above, e.g., electronical and electronic tools, leisure equipment, medical devices, monitoring and control instruments, automatic dispensers, etc.) (Q41)	□	□	□	□	□

References

1. Gill, G.N. Electronic Waste. Available online: https://www.britannica.com/technology/electronic-waste (accessed on 4 March 2020).
2. LeBlanc, R. Learn More about E-Waste Recycling with These Facts and Figures. Available online: https://www.thebalancesmb.com/e-waste-recycling-facts-and-figures-2878189 (accessed on 4 March 2020).
3. Blade, C.P.; Forti, V.; Gray, V.; Kuehr, R.; Stegmann, P. The Global E-Waste Monitor. 2017. Available online: https://www.itu.int/en/ITUD/Climate-Change/Documents/GEM%202017/Global-E-waste%20Monitor%202017%20.pdf (accessed on 22 February 2019).
4. Eurostat Statistics Eurostat. Available online: https://ec.europa.eu/eurostat/databrowser/view/cei_wm050/default/table?lang=en (accessed on 4 March 2019).
5. Huisman, J.; Leroy, P.; Tertre, F.; Söderman, M.L., Chancerel, P.; Cassard, D.; Løvik, A.N.; Wäger, P.; Kushnir, D.; Rotter, V.S.; et al. Prospecting Secondary Raw Materials in the Urban Mine and Mining Wastes (ProSUM). Available online: http://prosumproject.eu/sites/default/files/DIGITAL_Final_Report.pdf (accessed on 4 March 2019).
6. The World Counts. Electronic Waste Facts. Available online: https://www.theworldcounts.com/stories/Electronic-Waste-Facts (accessed on 4 February 2020).
7. Blake, V.; Farrelly, T.; Hannon, J. Is Voluntary Product Stewardship for E-Waste Working in New Zealand? A Whangarei Case Study. *Sustainability* **2019**, *11*, 3063. [CrossRef]
8. Jaiswal, A.; Samuel, C.; Patel, B.S.; Kumar, M. Go Green with WEEE: Eco-friendly Approach for Handling E-waste. *Procedia Comput. Sci.* **2015**, *46*, 1317–1324. [CrossRef]
9. Kiddee, P.; Naidu, R.; Wong, M.H. Electronic waste management approaches: An overview. *Waste Manag.* **2013**, *33*, 1237–1250. [CrossRef] [PubMed]

10. Robinson, B.H. E-waste: An assessment of global production and environmental impacts. *Sci. Total Environ.* **2009**, *408*, 183–191. [CrossRef]
11. Shevchenko, T.; Laitala, K.; Danko, Y. Understanding Consumer E-Waste Recycling Behavior: Introducing a New Economic Incentive to Increase the Collection Rates. *Sustainability* **2019**, *11*, 2656. [CrossRef]
12. El-Mously, H. Innovating green products as a mean to alleviate poverty in Upper Egypt. *Ain Shams Eng. J.* **2018**, *9*, 2039–2056. [CrossRef]
13. De Medeiros, J.F.; Ribeiro, J.L.D. Environmentally sustainable innovation: Expected attributes in the purchase of green products. *J. Clean. Prod.* **2017**, *142*, 240–248. [CrossRef]
14. Zhang, W.; He, Y. Optimal policies for new and green remanufactured short-life-cycle products considering consumer behavior. *J. Clean. Prod.* **2019**, *214*, 483–505. [CrossRef]
15. Dobrowolski, J.W.; Bedla, D.; Czech, T.; Gambuś, F.; Górecka, K.; Kiszczak, W.; Kuźniar, T.; Mazur, R.; Nowak, A.; Śliwka, M.; et al. Integrated Innovative Biotechnology for Optimization of Environmental Bioprocesses and a Green Economy. In *Optimization and Applicability of Bioprocesses*; Purohit, H.J., Kalia, V.C., Vaidya, A.N., Khardenavis, A.A., Eds.; Springer: Singapore, 2017; pp. 27–71. ISBN 978-981-10-6863-8.
16. D'Adamo, I. Adopting a Circular Economy: Current Practices and Future Perspectives. *Soc. Sci.* **2019**, *8*, 328. [CrossRef]
17. Liu, X.; Tanaka, M.; Matsui, Y. Electrical and electronic waste management in China: Progress and the barriers to overcome. *Waste Manag. Res.* **2006**, *24*, 92–101. [CrossRef]
18. Wang, W.; Tian, Y.; Zhu, Q.; Zhong, Y. Barriers for household e-waste collection in China: Perspectives from formal collecting enterprises in Liaoning Province. *J. Clean. Prod.* **2017**, *153*, 299–308. [CrossRef]
19. Miner, K.J.; Rampedi, I.T.; Ifegbesan, A.P.; Machete, F. Survey on Household Awareness and Willingness to Participate in E-Waste Management in Jos, Plateau State, Nigeria. *Sustainability* **2020**, *12*, 1047. [CrossRef]
20. Sujata, M.; Khor, K.-S.; Ramayah, T.; Teoh, A.P. The role of social media on recycling behaviour. *Sustain. Prod. Consum.* **2019**, *20*, 365–374. [CrossRef]
21. Statista. Social Media Penetration Rate Worldwide. 2019. Available online: https://www.statista.com/statistics/269615/social-network-penetration-by-region/ (accessed on 5 March 2020).
22. Rodrigues, A.C.; Boscov, M.E.G.; Günther, W.M.R. Domestic flow of e-waste in São Paulo, Brazil: Characterization to support public policies. *Waste Manag.* **2020**, *102*, 474–485. [CrossRef]
23. Kumar, A.; Holuszko, M. Electronic Waste and Existing Processing Routes: A Canadian Perspective. *Resources* **2016**, *5*, 35. [CrossRef]
24. Wong, N.W.M. Electronic Waste Governance under "One Country, Two Systems": Hong Kong and Mainland China. *Int. J. Environ. Res. Public Health* **2018**, *15*, 2347. [CrossRef]
25. Steuer, B. What Institutional Dynamics Guide Waste Electrical and Electronic Equipment Refurbishment and Reuse in Urban China? *Recycling* **2016**, *1*, 286. [CrossRef]
26. Lee, S.; Na, S. E-Waste Recycling Systems and Sound Circulative Economies in East Asia: A Comparative Analysis of Systems in Japan, South Korea, China and Taiwan. *Sustainability* **2010**, *2*, 1632–1644. [CrossRef]
27. Xue, R.; Zhang, F.; Tian, F. A System Dynamics Model to Evaluate Effects of Retailer-Led Recycling Based on Dual Chains Competition: A Case of e-Waste in China. *Sustainability* **2018**, *10*, 3391. [CrossRef]
28. Wang, Z.; Wang, Q.; Chen, B.; Wang, Y. Evolutionary game analysis on behavioral strategies of multiple stakeholders in E-waste recycling industry. *Resour. Conserv. Recycl.* **2020**, *155*, 104618. [CrossRef]
29. Abarca-Guerrero, L.; Roa-Gutiérrez, F.; Rudín-Vega, V. WEEE Resource Management System in Costa Rica. *Resources* **2018**, *7*, 2. [CrossRef]
30. Daum, K.; Stoler, J.; Grant, R.J. Toward a More Sustainable Trajectory for E-Waste Policy: A Review of a Decade of E-Waste Research in Accra, Ghana. *Int. J. Environ. Res. Public Health* **2017**, *14*, 135. [CrossRef] [PubMed]
31. Asante, K.A.; Agusa, T.; Biney, C.A.; Agyekum, W.A.; Bello, M.; Otsuka, M.; Itai, T.; Takahashi, S.; Tanabe, S. Multi-trace element levels and arsenic speciation in urine of e-waste recycling workers from Agbogbloshie, Accra in Ghana. *Sci. Total Environ.* **2012**, *424*, 63–73. [CrossRef] [PubMed]
32. Aidonis, D.; Achillas, C.; Folinas, D.; Keramydas, C.; Tsolakis, N. Decision Support Model for Evaluating Alternative Waste Electrical and Electronic Equipment Management Schemes—A Case Study. *Sustainability* **2019**, *11*, 3364. [CrossRef]
33. Radulovic, V. Portrayals in Print: Media Depictions of the Informal Sector's Involvement in Managing E-Waste in India. *Sustainability* **2018**, *10*, 966. [CrossRef]

34. Isernia, R.; Passaro, R.; Quinto, I.; Thomas, A. The Reverse Supply Chain of the E-Waste Management Processes in a Circular Economy Framework: Evidence from Italy. *Sustainability* **2019**, *11*, 2430. [CrossRef]
35. Cruz-Sotelo, S.E.; Ojeda-Benítez, S.; Jáuregui Sesma, J.; Velázquez-Victorica, K.I.; Santillán-Soto, N.; García-Cueto, O.R.; Alcántara Concepción, V.; Alcántara, C. E-Waste Supply Chain in Mexico: Challenges and Opportunities for Sustainable Management. *Sustainability* **2017**, *9*, 503. [CrossRef]
36. Cordova-Pizarro, D.; Aguilar-Barajas, I.; Romero, D.; Rodriguez, C.A. Circular Economy in the Electronic Products Sector: Material Flow Analysis and Economic Impact of Cellphone E-Waste in Mexico. *Sustainability* **2019**, *11*, 1361. [CrossRef]
37. Nduneseokwu, C.; Qu, Y.; Appolloni, A. Factors Influencing Consumers' Intentions to Participate in a Formal E-Waste Collection System: A Case Study of Onitsha, Nigeria. *Sustainability* **2017**, *9*, 881. [CrossRef]
38. Gunarathne, N.; de Alwis, A.; Alahakoon, Y. Challenges facing sustainable urban mining in the e-waste recycling industry in Sri Lanka. *J. Clean. Prod.* **2020**, *251*, 119641. [CrossRef]
39. Cheng, C.; Lin, C.; Wen, L.; Chang, T. Determining Environmental Costs: A Challenge in a Governmental E-Waste Recycling Scheme. *Sustainability* **2019**, *11*, 5156. [CrossRef]
40. Tonglet, M.; Phillips, P.S.; Read, A.D. Using the Theory of Planned Behaviour to investigate the determinants of recycling behaviour: A case study from Brixworth, UK. *Resour. Conserv. Recycl.* **2004**, *41*, 191–214. [CrossRef]
41. Kahhat, R.; Kim, J.; Xu, M.; Allenby, B.; Williams, E.; Zhang, P. Exploring e-waste management systems in the United States. *Resour. Conserv. Recycl.* **2008**, *52*, 955–964. [CrossRef]
42. Thi Thu Nguyen, H.; Hung, R.-J.; Lee, C.-H.; Thi Thu Nguyen, H. Determinants of Residents' E-Waste Recycling Behavioral Intention: A Case Study from Vietnam. *Sustainability* **2019**, *11*, 164. [CrossRef]
43. Păcesilă, M.; Ciocoiu, C.; Colesca, S.E.; Burcea, S. Current Trends in WEEE Management in Romania. *Theor. Empir. Res. Urban Manag.* **2016**, *11*, 46–60.
44. Eurostat Waste Statistics. Electrical and Electronic Equipment—Statistics Explained. Available online: https://ec.europa.eu/eurostat/statistics-explained/index.php?title=Waste_statistics_-_electrical_and_electronic_equipment&oldid=470242 (accessed on 8 March 2020).
45. Urban Mine Platform. Waste Generated. Available online: http://www.urbanmineplatform.eu/urbanmine/eee/weightpercapita (accessed on 8 February 2020).
46. Lakatos, E.; Cioca, L.-I.; Dan, V.; Ciomos, A.; Crisan, O.; Barsan, G. Studies and Investigation about the Attitude towards Sustainable Production, Consumption and Waste Generation in Line with Circular Economy in Romania. *Sustainability* **2018**, *10*, 865. [CrossRef]
47. Kianpour, K.; Jusoh, A.; Mardani, A.; Streimikiene, D.; Cavallaro, F.; Nor, K.M.; Zavadskas, E. Factors Influencing Consumers' Intention to Return the End of Life Electronic Products through Reverse Supply Chain Management for Reuse, Repair and Recycling. *Sustainability* **2017**, *9*, 1657. [CrossRef]
48. Meng, Q.; Zhu, H.; Li, Z.; Du, J.; Wang, X.; Jeong Kim, M. How Green Building Product Decisions from Customers Can Be Transitioned to Manufacturers: An Agent-Based Model. *Sustainability* **2018**, *10*, 3977. [CrossRef]
49. Delcea, C.; Cotfas, L.-A.; Trică, C.; Crăciun, L.; Molanescu, A. Modeling the Consumers Opinion Influence in Online Social Media in the Case of Eco-friendly Products. *Sustainability* **2019**, *11*, 1796. [CrossRef]
50. Wang, F.; Huisman, J.; Meskers, C.E.M.; Schluep, M.; Stevels, A.; Hagelüken, C. The Best-of-2-Worlds philosophy: Developing local dismantling and global infrastructure network for sustainable e-waste treatment in emerging economies. *Waste Manag.* **2012**, *32*, 2134–2146. [CrossRef]
51. Vaccari, M.; Vinti, G.; Cesaro, A.; Belgiorno, V.; Salhofer, S.; Dias, M.I.; Jandric, A. WEEE Treatment in Developing Countries: Environmental Pollution and Health Consequences—An Overview. *Int. J. Environ. Res. Public Health* **2019**, *16*, 1595. [CrossRef]
52. Arain, A.L.; Pummill, R.; Adu-Brimpong, J.; Becker, S.; Green, M.; Ilardi, M.; Van Dam, E.; Neitzel, R.L. Analysis of e-waste recycling behavior based on survey at a Midwestern US University. *Waste Manag.* **2020**, *105*, 119–127. [CrossRef] [PubMed]
53. Meneses, G.D.; Palacio, A.B. Recycling Behavior: A Multidimensional Approach. *Environ. Behav.* **2016**, *37*, 837–860. [CrossRef]
54. Rousta, K.; Bolton, K.; Lundin, M.; Dahlén, L. Quantitative assessment of distance to collection point and improved sorting information on source separation of household waste. *Waste Manag.* **2015**, *40*, 22–30. [CrossRef] [PubMed]

55. Ylä-Mella, J.; Keiski, R.L.; Pongrácz, E. Electronic waste recovery in Finland: Consumers' perceptions towards recycling and re-use of mobile phones. *Waste Manag.* **2015**, *45*, 374–384. [CrossRef] [PubMed]
56. Sivathanu, D.B. User's Perspective: Knowledge and Attitude towards E-Waste. *Int. J. Appl. Environ. Sci.* **2016**, *11*, 413–423.
57. Klöckner, C.A. A comprehensive model of the psychology of environmental behaviour—A meta-analysis. *Glob. Environ. Chang.* **2013**, *23*, 1028–1038. [CrossRef]
58. D'Adamo, I.; Gastaldi, M.; Rosa, P. Recycling of end-of-life vehicles: Assessing trends and performances in Europe. *Technol. Forecast. Soc. Chang.* **2020**, *152*, 119887. [CrossRef]
59. Wang, B.; Ren, C.; Dong, X.; Zhang, B.; Wang, Z. Determinants shaping willingness towards on-line recycling behaviour: An empirical study of household e-waste recycling in China. *Resour. Conserv. Recycl.* **2019**, *143*, 218–225. [CrossRef]
60. Doha, A.; Elnahla, N.; McShane, L. Social commerce as social networking. *J. Retail. Consum. Serv.* **2019**, *47*, 307–321. [CrossRef]
61. Asim, Y.; Malik, A.K.; Raza, B.; Shahid, A.R. A trust model for analysis of trust, influence and their relationship in social network communities. *Telemat. Inf.* **2019**, *36*, 94–116. [CrossRef]
62. Kujur, F.; Singh, S. Engaging customers through online participation in social networking sites. *Asia Pac. Manag. Rev.* **2017**, *22*, 16–24. [CrossRef]
63. Lim, H.; Kumar, A. Variations in consumers' use of brand online social networking: A uses and gratifications approach. *J. Retail. Consum. Serv.* **2017**, *51*, 450–457. [CrossRef]
64. Wang, F.; Jiang, W.; Li, X.; Wang, G. Maximizing positive influence spread in online social networks via fluid dynamics. *Future Gener. Comput. Syst.* **2018**, *86*, 1491–1502. [CrossRef]
65. Delcea, C.; Popa, C.D.S.; Boloş, M. Consumers' Decisions in Grey Online Social Networks. *J. Grey Syst.* **2015**, *27*, 12–27.
66. Chen, C.-C.; Chen, C.-W.; Tung, Y.-C. Exploring the Consumer Behavior of Intention to Purchase Green Products in Belt and Road Countries: An Empirical Analysis. *Sustainability* **2018**, *10*, 854. [CrossRef]
67. Piligrimienė, Z.; Žukauskaitė, A.; Korzilius, H.; Banytė, J.; Dovalienė, A. Internal and External Determinants of Consumer Engagement in Sustainable Consumption. *Sustainability* **2020**, *12*, 1349. [CrossRef]
68. Burns, K.N.; Sun, K.; Fobil, J.N.; Neitzel, R.L. Heart Rate, Stress, and Occupational Noise Exposure among Electronic Waste Recycling Workers. *Int. J. Environ. Res. Public Health* **2016**, *13*, 140. [CrossRef]
69. Barletta, I.; Larborn, J.; Mani, M.; Johannson, B. Towards an Assessment Methodology to Support Decision Making for Sustainable Electronic Waste Management Systems: Automatic Sorting Technology. *Sustainability* **2016**, *8*, 84. [CrossRef]
70. Efthymiou, L.; Mavragani, A.; Tsagarakis, K.P. Quantifying the Effect of Macroeconomic and Social Factors on Illegal E-Waste Trade. *Int. J. Environ. Res. Public Health* **2016**, *13*, 789. [CrossRef]
71. Kusch, S.; Hills, C.D. The Link between e-Waste and GDP—New Insights from Data from the Pan-European Region. *Resources* **2017**, *6*, 15. [CrossRef]
72. Ramayah, T.; Lee, J.W.C.; Lim, S. Sustaining the environment through recycling: An empirical study. *J. Environ. Manag.* **2012**, *102*, 141–147. [CrossRef] [PubMed]
73. Oakley, R.L.; Salam, A.F. Examining the impact of computer-mediated social networks on individual consumerism environmental behaviors. *Comput. Hum. Behav.* **2014**, *35*, 516–526. [CrossRef]
74. Park, N.; Yang, A. Online environmental community members' intention to participate in environmental activities: An application of the theory of planned behavior in the Chinese context. *Comput. Hum. Behav.* **2012**, *28*, 1298–1306. [CrossRef]
75. Keramitsoglou, K.M.; Tsagarakis, K.P. Public participation in designing a recycling scheme towards maximum public acceptance. *Resour. Conserv. Recycl.* **2013**, *70*, 55–67. [CrossRef]
76. Barr, S.; Gilg, A.W.; Ford, N.J. Differences between household waste reduction, reuse and recycling behaviour: A study of reported behaviours, intentions and explanatory variables. *Environ. Waste Manag.* **2001**, *4*, 69–82.
77. Sidique, S.F.; Lupi, F.; Joshi, S.V. The effects of behavior and attitudes on drop-off recycling activities. *Resour. Conserv. Recycl.* **2010**, *54*, 163–170. [CrossRef]
78. Knussen, C.; Yule, F.; MacKenzie, J.; Wells, M. An analysis of intentions to recycle household waste: The roles of past behaviour, perceived habit, and perceived lack of facilities. *J. Environ. Psychol.* **2004**, *24*, 237–246. [CrossRef]

79. Zhang, D.; Huang, G.; Yin, X.; Gong, Q. Residents' Waste Separation Behaviors at the Source: Using SEM with the Theory of Planned Behavior in Guangzhou, China. *Int. J. Environ. Res. Public Health* **2015**, *12*, 9475–9491. [CrossRef]
80. Gonul Kochan, C.; Pourreza, S.; Tran, H.; Prybutok, V.R. Determinants and logistics of e-waste recycling. *Int. J. Logist. Manag.* **2016**, *27*, 52–70. [CrossRef]
81. Xu, L.; Ling, M.; Lu, Y.; Shen, M. Understanding Household Waste Separation Behaviour: Testing the Roles of Moral, Past Experience, and Perceived Policy Effectiveness within the Theory of Planned Behaviour. *Sustainability* **2017**, *9*, 625. [CrossRef]
82. Falcone, P.M.; Tani, A.; Tartiu, V.E.; Imbriani, C. Towards a sustainable forest-based bioeconomy in Italy: Findings from a SWOT analysis. *For. Policy Econ.* **2020**, *110*, 101910. [CrossRef]
83. IBM. IBM SPSS Amos. Available online: https://www.ibm.com/ro-en/marketplace/structural-equation-modeling-sem (accessed on 6 March 2020).
84. Spanos, Y.E.; Lioukas, S. An examination into the causal logic of rent generation: Contrasting Porter's competitive strategy framework and the resource-based perspective. *Strateg. Manag. J.* **2001**, *22*, 907–934. [CrossRef]
85. Delcea, C.; Bradea, I.-A. Patients' perceived risks in hospitals: A grey qualitative analysis. *Kybernetes* **2017**, *46*, 1408–1424. [CrossRef]
86. Fornell, C.; Larcker, D.F. Evaluating Structural Equation Models with Unobservable Variables and Measurement Error. *J. Mark. Res.* **1981**, *18*, 39–50. [CrossRef]
87. Brown, T.A. *Confirmatory Factor Analysis for Applied Research*, 2nd ed.; Methodology in the Social Sciences; The Guilford Press: New York, NY, USA; London, UK, 2015; ISBN 978-1-4625-1779-4.
88. Byrne, B.M. *Structural Equation Modeling With AMOS: Basic Concepts, Applications, and Programming*, 3rd ed.; Routledge: Abigdon, Great Britain, 2016; ISBN 978-1-317-63312-9.
89. Hu, L.; Bentler, P.M. Cutoff criteria for fit indexes in covariance structure analysis: Conventional criteria versus new alternatives. *Struct. Equ. Model. Multidiscip. J.* **1999**, *6*, 1–55. [CrossRef]
90. Harrington, D. *Confirmatory Factor Analysis*; Pocket Guides to Social Work Research Methods; Oxford University Press: Oxford, NY, USA, 2009; ISBN 978-0-19-533988-8.
91. Paswan, A.; D'Souza, D.; Zolfagharian, M.A. Toward a Contextually Anchored Service Innovation Typology. *Decis. Sci.* **2009**, *40*, 513–540. [CrossRef]
92. Bandura, A. *Social Foundations of Thought and Action: A Social Cognitive Theory*, 1st ed.; Prentice Hall: Englewood Cliffs, NJ, USA, 1985; ISBN 978-0-13-815614-5.
93. Wang, Z.; Guo, D.; Wang, X. Determinants of residents' e-waste recycling behaviour intentions: Evidence from China. *J. Clean. Prod.* **2016**, *137*, 850–860. [CrossRef]
94. Ma, J.; Hipel, K.W.; Hanson, M.L.; Cai, X.; Liu, Y. An analysis of influencing factors on municipal solid waste source-separated collection behavior in Guilin, China by Using the Theory of Planned Behavior. *Sustain. Cities Soc.* **2018**, *37*, 336–343. [CrossRef]
95. Chan, L.; Bishop, B. A moral basis for recycling: Extending the theory of planned behaviour. *J. Environ. Psychol.* **2013**, *36*, 96–102. [CrossRef]
96. Khan, F.; Ahmed, W.; Najmi, A. Understanding consumers' behavior intentions towards dealing with the plastic waste: Perspective of a developing country. *Resour. Conserv. Recycl.* **2019**, *142*, 49–58. [CrossRef]
97. Ewing, G. Altruistic, Egoistic, and Normative Effects on Curbside Recycling. *Environ. Behav.* **2001**, *33*, 733–764. [CrossRef]
98. Vining, J.; Ebreo, A. What Makes a Recycler? A Comparison of Recyclers and Nonrecyclers. *Environ. Behav.* **1990**, *22*, 55–73. [CrossRef]
99. Derksen, L.; Gartrell, J. The Social Context of Recycling. *Am. Sociol. Rev.* **1993**, *58*, 434–442. [CrossRef]
100. Margai, F.L. Analyzing Changes in Waste Reduction Behavior in a Low-Income Urban Community Following a Public Outreach Program. *Environ. Behav.* **1997**, *29*, 769–792. [CrossRef]
101. Scott, D. Equal Opportunity, Unequal Results: Determinants of Household Recycling Intensity. *Environ. Behav.* **1999**, *31*, 267–290. [CrossRef]
102. Saphores, J.-D.M.; Nixon, H.; Ogunseitan, O.A.; Shapiro, A.A. Household Willingness to Recycle Electronic Waste: An Application to California. *Environ. Behav.* **2006**, *38*, 183–208. [CrossRef]
103. Oskamp, S.; Harrington, M.J.; Edwards, T.C.; Sherwood, D.L.; Okuda, S.M.; Swanson, D.C. Factors Influencing Household Recycling Behavior. *Environ. Behav.* **1991**, *23*, 494–519. [CrossRef]

104. Corral-Verdugo, V. Dual 'realities' of conservation behavior: Self-reports vs. Observations of re-use and recycling behavior. *J. Environ. Psychol.* **1997**, *17*, 135–145. [CrossRef]
105. Werner, C.M.; Turner, J.; Shipman, K.; Shawn Twitchell, F.; Dickson, B.R.; Bruschke, G.V.; von Bismarck, W.B. Commitment, behavior, and attitude change: An analysis of voluntary recycling. *J. Environ. Psychol.* **1995**, *15*, 197–208. [CrossRef]
106. Schultz, P.W.; Oskamp, S.; Mainieri, T. Who recycles and when? A review of personal and situational factors. *J. Environ. Psychol.* **1995**, *15*, 105–121. [CrossRef]
107. Johnson, C.Y.; Bowker, J.M.; Cordell, H.K. Ethnic Variation in Environmental Belief and Behavior: An Examination of the New Ecological Paradigm in a Social Psychological Context. *Environ. Behav.* **2004**, *36*, 157–186. [CrossRef]
108. Gamba, R.J.; Oskamp, S. Factors Influencing Community Residents' Participation in Commingled Curbside Recycling Programs. *Environ. Behav.* **1994**, *26*, 587–612. [CrossRef]
109. Do Valle, P.O.; Reis, E.; Menezes, J.; Rebelo, E. Behavioral Determinants of Household Recycling Participation: The Portuguese Case. *Environ. Behav.* **2004**, *36*, 505–540. [CrossRef]
110. Darby, L.; Obara, L. Household recycling behaviour and attitudes towards the disposal of small electrical and electronic equipment. *Resour. Conserv. Recycl.* **2005**, *44*, 17–35. [CrossRef]
111. Arcury, T.A.; Scollay, S.J.; Johnson, T.P. Sex differences in environmental concern and knowledge: The case of acid rain. *Sex Roles* **1987**, *16*, 463–472. [CrossRef]
112. Wang, Z.; Zhang, B.; Yin, J.; Zhang, X. Willingness and behavior towards e-waste recycling for residents in Beijing city, China. *J. Clean. Prod.* **2011**, *19*, 977–984. [CrossRef]
113. Domina, T.; Koch, K. Convenience and Frequency of Recycling: Implications for Including Textiles in Curbside Recycling Programs. *Environ. Behav.* **2002**, *34*, 216–238. [CrossRef]
114. Perry, G.D.R.; Williams, I.D. The participation of ethnic minorities in kerbside recycling: A case study. *Resour. Conserv. Recycl.* **2007**, *49*, 308–323. [CrossRef]
115. Granzin, K.L.; Olsen, J.E. Characterizing Participants in Activities Protecting the Environment: A Focus on Donating, Recycling, and Conservation Behaviors. *J. Public Policy Mark.* **1991**, *10*, 1–27. [CrossRef]
116. Hansmann, R.; Bernasconi, P.; Smieszek, T.; Loukopoulos, P.; Scholz, R.W. Justifications and self-organization as determinants of recycling behavior: The case of used batteries. *Resour. Conserv. Recycl.* **2006**, *47*, 133–159. [CrossRef]

sustainability

MDPI

Article

Sustainability Transition in Industry 4.0 and Smart Manufacturing with the Triple-Layered Business Model Canvas

Fernando E. García-Muiña [1,*], María Sonia Medina-Salgado [1], Anna Maria Ferrari [2] and Marco Cucchi [3]

1 Department of Business Administration (ADO), Applied Economics II and Fundamentals of Economic Analysis, Rey-Juan-Carlos University, 28032 Madrid, Spain; sonia.medina@urjc.es

2 Department of Sciences and Methods for Engineering, University of Modena and Reggio Emilia, 42122 Reggio Emilia, Italy; annamaria.ferrari@unimore.it

3 Gruppo Ceramiche Gresmalt, Via Mosca 4, 41049 Sassuolo, Italy; marco.cucchi@gresmalt.it

* Correspondence: fernando.muina@urjc.es

Received: 29 February 2020; Accepted: 16 March 2020; Published: 18 March 2020

Abstract: Sustainability transition is becoming increasingly relevant at a manufacturing level, especially for resource- and energy-intensive industries. In addition, the 4.0 industry paradigm opens new opportunities in terms of sustainable development. The aim of this research is to analyze the introduction of sustainability in the corporate value proposition, through the evolution from a traditional to a sustainable business model. The business model innovation will be investigated in the case of a ceramic tile producer in the district of Sassuolo, Italy. The company has introduced several sustainability practices over the years and, through investments in Industry 4.0 technologies, is able to conduct impact assessments of its production process. The applied tool for the business model transition will be the Triple-Layered Business Model Canvas by Joyce and Paquin. The results illustrate the new company's sustainable value proposition, considering all three pillars of sustainability: environment, economy, and society. Despite the limitations resulting from the individual case study, the findings can be easily adapted to other ceramic tile companies in the sector. Besides, the paper could inspire other manufacturing companies in the drafting of a sustainable business model. The paper explores the still limited literature on the application of sustainable business models in operational scenarios.

Keywords: Industry 4.0; sustainability; manufacturing; business model canvas

1. Introduction

In recent years, the theme of sustainability in manufacturing contexts has been assuming a primary role in the political agendas of many states and public opinion, the latter increasingly sensitive to the commitment of companies on this issue [1]. In response to this pressure, manufacturing companies have reacted by introducing new sustainability pathways in their production processes and they have increased the level of communication of these practices to customers and stakeholders [2].

In support of manufacturing enterprises, industry 4.0 technologies have made production processes more efficient and less impacting [3]. In addition, the new industry 4.0 management and data collection tools, which are able to collect timely process data, can facilitate companies in the evaluation of the sustainability practices introduced [4]. This sustainable transition process, facilitated by the industry 4.0 paradigm, is naturally based on the successful operational introduction of sustainability practices, but it cannot disregard the strategic evolution of the company in terms of value creation. In this regard, the implementation of sustainability is usually a complex process, which requires a medium-long term strategic vision and effective communication between top management and operational business units and between the company and its stakeholders [5]. In order to address these challenges, the topic of sustainable business models, as tools to represent sustainability within the value proposition of companies, has become extremely widespread in the academic literature [6]. The business model represents the value that a company promises to deliver to customers if they choose to purchase its product. Sustainability, if properly introduced and communicated, can change this value proposition and differentiate the product or brand from the competition [7].

The purpose of this paper is to explore the literature on sustainable business models and to contribute through the implementation of a model within an operational case. Despite the great interest in the subject, there are still few articles that apply formal business models in operational contexts [8]. In addition, researches that analyze implementations of business models in manufacturing contexts tend to focus on the environmental aspect, not investigating the economic and social dimension of sustainability in a triple bottom line perspective [9]. In order to address these issues, the model selected for the study is the Triple-Layered Business Model Canvas (TLBMC) published by Joyce and Paquin [10]. The model consists of three separate business model canvas, one for each pillar of sustainability. By consequence, the model integrates the three pillars of sustainability and does not limit the analysis of the value proposition to the mere economic aspect. The company taken as a reference is one of the main producers of ceramic tiles in the ceramic Sassuolo district, in Italy, which has reached a high level of automation and control of the production process due to investments in industry 4.0. Through the drafting of a sustainable business model, the paper tries to offer a framework for future research on the operational innovation of business models within manufacturing contexts and for the introduction of sustainability into business strategies.

The paper is organized as follows: Section 2 deals with an analysis of the academic literature on the concept of the business model and its innovation in terms of sustainability. Section 3 deals with the methodology applied in the drafting of the new company's business model. Section 4 focuses on the company under analysis and the sectoral context in which the company operates. Section 5 deals with the results and the new sustainable value proposition of the company. Finally, Sections 6 and 7 offers some concluding remarks.

2. Theoretical Background

2.1. Business Model Concept

In order to outline the process of value creation, the business model has been considered for years as an essential tool in business activities. From an academic perspective, the concept of a business model (BM) has aroused much interest among researchers [11]. Despite the numerous papers published on the subject, the studies on the field are still in an early stage and there is still no univocal definition of a BM [12].

With the growth of technology and internet-based business, Amit and Zott [13] stated that "A BM depicts the content, structure, and governance of transactions designed so as to create value through the exploitation of business opportunities". In this case, the BM was considered as a construct that could be used to explain and predict value creation in an e-business context. In 2005, Shafer, Smith, and Linder [14] addressed the problem of defining a unique BM concept, not influenced by different business contexts. The authors defined BM as "a representation of a firm's underlying core logic and strategic choices for creating and capturing value within a value network". Following the authors, the BM was a tool that reflected the company's strategic choices, which must lead to creating value and consequently generate profit. The BM not only concerned the company itself but also involved the stakeholders who interact with it.

Some authors, in identifying the concept of BM, extended their analysis by specifying the difference between BM and strategy. In order to explain the two concepts, Magretta [15] considered the example of Walmart as a company which, starting from the BM of the discount supermarket also used by competitors, created a competitive advantage through its strategy of offering national brands at low prices. On the other hand, other authors like Massa, Tucci, and Afuah [11] argued instead that the business model was not a new field but simply an extension of the concept of strategy. The BM relaxed some of the assumptions that were implicitly present in traditional strategic management theories (such as Resource-Based View), considering, in addition, externalities and the lack of perfect information for customers. By consequence, the BM simply extended the breadth of the strategy field.

In parallel with the definitions, studies were also being developed on how to formally represent a business model. In this respect, one of the most common representations of BMs has been the Business Model Canvas (BMC), firstly introduced by Osterwalder, Pigneur and Clark [16]. The BMC is simple and intuitive, but it does not oversimplify the complexity related to companies' functions. In specific, the BMC describes through nine blocks (key partners, key activities, key resources, value proposition, customer relationships, customer segments, channels, cost structure, and revenue streams) the logic of how a company expects to generate profit. The value proposition is the heart of the BMC and it explains the benefit that the company creates for the client and why he should choose that company among many others [11]. BMC is one of the many alternatives present in the literature. Gassmann, Frankenberger and Csik [17] illustrated a model representation based on four dimensions: who, what, how, why. The model is represented as a triangle in which the customer is at the center (who). At the corners, there are the value proposition (what), the value chain (how) and the profit mechanism (why). The reason why these three aspects are at the corner of a triangle is that the modification of one of the three aspects requires, therefore, the modification of the other two as well. Some authors, even without offering a business model representation, offered some guidelines regarding BM design. Zott and Amit [18] argued that the BM must be based on the interdependence of activities that span the company's boundaries. Weiller and Neely [19] claimed that the design of business models must necessarily be centered on the ecosystem in which the company operates.

The notion of BM was initially considered from a static perspective. In more recent times, several authors have considered the dynamic evolution of business models, through processes of business model innovation [20]. Specifically, one of the most relevant research topics in the last years has been the relationship between business models and sustainability [21]. The introduction of sustainability practices requires companies to rethink their process of value creation. In this regard, sustainable business models allow for the introduction of sustainability practices into the business value creation process [22]. The paragraph leads to the following proposition:

Proposition 1 (P1). *Business models describe the value proposition of the company and can be a useful instrument for the integration of sustainability.*

2.2. Business Model Innovation through Industry 4.0

The literature on business model innovation (BMI) has developed independently from the more extensive business model theory. BMI is generally referred to as a process addressed to reduce costs, optimize processes, access new markets or improve financial performances [23]. Compared to product and process innovation, BMI consists of a systemic change that affects the companies' values proposition and how this value is generated. If the BMI is successful, the innovation process should lead to a positive company's transformation and renewal [24]. The development of a BMI process is usually linked to a stimulus deriving from a change in the competitive environment, as, for instance, the pressure caused by the introduction of new disruptive technology [25]. This transformation is also fostered by the choices of policymakers, who in turn monitor the company's business model evolution to understand how to stimulate innovation within a sector [26].

Among the disruptive technologies which are affecting the business value creation model, the transition to industry 4.0 in manufacturing companies should be analyzed. Industry 4.0 is an approach, first developed in Germany, based on the exploitation of four new technological paradigms:

Cyber-Physical Systems, Internet of Things, Internet of Services, and Smart Factory [27,28]. In contrast to previous industrial revolutions, industry 4.0 acts in several different areas and focuses on an exchange of information between people and digital tools and between tools among themselves [29]. Industry 4.0 concept is based on the principle of Smart Manufacturing, a flexible system in which production lines are adaptable to product diversity and changing conditions [30].

The adoption of industry 4.0 technologies is leading enterprises to an increase in productivity and a higher level of awareness of the mechanisms that drive production processes [31]. In this context, the higher productivity, namely the provision of the highest level of output with the lowest amount of resources, is made possible by the efficiency and flexibility offered by cyber-physical systems, which allow a continuous optimization of resource and energy consumption [32]. In connection with productivity, the impact of industry 4.0 also concerns the reduction of industrial costs, in particular production, logistic and quality management costs [28].

Industry 4.0 technologies can also increase the perception of the customer with reference to the product value. The implementation of identification and tracking technologies enable the manufacturer to collect information throughout the product life cycle and to exploit its content to communicate the value of the product [29]. This kind of product, manufactured in a smart factory context and linked to technologies that allow interconnection with the user, can be defined as a smart product [33]. These products provide a significantly different role for the user, who is actively involved and can participate in the product design process [34]. In addition to the topic of smart products, industry 4.0 is affecting competition rules between companies in the same sector, because digital technologies provide customers with new digital options and highly personalized products [35]. The competitive advantage of the enterprise resulting from the implementation of industry 4.0 depends on its ability to exploit the amount of data available and its capacity to manage a wide range of heterogeneous devices [36].

The implementation of industry 4.0 technologies, other than generating numerous benefits for companies, requires them to transform their value proposition through a business model innovation process [3,37,38]. The business model innovation process can be of a limited entity if the introduction of industry 4.0 consists of incremental innovation. On the other hand, in the case of radical innovations, the process can lead to a total reconfiguration of the company's value proposition [39]. In this regard, in recent years, the appearance of a high number of disruptive technologies in the context of industry 4.0 has led many companies to abandon traditional business models in favor of more complex digital market models [40].

Business model innovation through industry 4.0 can, therefore, generate many advantages, intensifying customer relationships and bringing them to mutually positive medium and long-term relationships. At the same time, however, this innovation leaves many open challenges, including the increasing need for a qualified workforce, financial resources and consumer resistance to change.

One of these challenges for manufacturing companies is to leverage the benefits of industry 4.0 to integrate sustainability into traditional business models [39,41]. Industry 4.0 can be considered as a new business mindset, helping companies in their sustainable transition [42]. In specific, industry 4.0 offers opportunities both in environmental terms by increasing the efficiency of the production process and in social terms, for instance by improving working time models and increasing employee satisfaction and productivity [43]. Other environmental advantages of industry 4.0 implementation are related to waste reduction, a decrease in resource consumption and energy requirements and an increase of circular economy practices [44]. The intertwining of industry 4.0 and sustainability must be reflected within a strategic business model context, which can no longer be limited to considerations of economic factors but must also include environmental and social factors, in line with the Triple Bottom Line of sustainability [45]. In this respect, the very role of the company itself cannot be disregarded, as industry 4.0 could be beneficial to introduce sustainable business models, but it could also be an inhibiter if merely used in a traditional business model perspective [46].

From the above discussion, we derive:

Proposition 2 (P2). *The business model innovation is a process that allows to internalize, from a strategic perspective, the external changes of the company's competitive environment.*

Proposition 3 (P3). *In manufacturing, industry 4.0 leads to greater efficiency and control of production processes and provides new opportunities in terms of sustainability introduction and impact assessment.*

2.3. From Traditional to Sustainable Business Models

From a business perspective, the introduction of sustainability into manufacturing production processes is usually analyzed according to the lower industrial costs. Recently, however, the impact of sustainability is increasingly considered from a triple bottom line angle, simultaneously assessing the environmental, economic and social benefits [47]. Regarding companies' value proposition, the development of sustainability practices should not influence the importance of providing value for customers but should complement it with environmental and social objectives [22]. Furthermore, the impact of sustainability practices should not be merely limited to an internal company viewpoint but should also involve stakeholders, especially those directly affected by these changes.

From a strategic perspective, the inclusion of sustainability within a traditional business model leads to the creation of what is defined in the literature as a sustainable business model, namely a model which create competitive advantage through premium customer value, with attention to the implementation of all the pillars of sustainability: environmental, economic and social [48]. Sustainable business models are a topic increasingly covered in the literature and increasingly applied operationally in different sectors [49]. The introduction of a sustainable business model should be based on three main considerations: sustainable value (based on the three pillars of sustainability), pro-active multi-stakeholder management and long-term perspective [50].

Among sustainable business models, a specific strand of research focused on circular business models. Linder and Williander [51] define a circular business model (CBM) as "a business model in which the conceptual logic for value creation is based on utilizing economic value retained in products after use in the production of new offerings". In a CBM, there is a return flow of value from users to manufacturers, which frequently passes through intermediaries. At the basis of the flow is the philosophy of the circular economy, whose concept is in turn based on the principles of reuse, recycling, and recovery [52].

The shift to a circular business model generally offers many advantages for the company that applies it, consisting of cost-saving through waste reduction, lower sensitivity to resource price volatility, and better relationships with customers [53]. The latter can result in long term relationships in which the customer can have an active role in the company's value creation. On the other hand, a circular model can be not viable because of the lack of profitability or excessive financial effort involved in it [54]. The lack of financial resources and the lack of support of public institutions are two relevant barriers in the adoption of CBMs, especially in small and medium enterprises. In addition to the financial issue, Linder and Williander [51] identify some other challenges and limitations. The first are the customer type restrictions (not all the customers would accept remanufactured products), followed by technological knowledge/expertise and the return flow challenges (predictability of the return flow). In addition, there is the risk of restrictions (products not suitable for remanufacturing) and the risk of cannibalization of the new sustainable products on the old ones.

In conclusion, the possibility that some circular practices may prove unsustainable under the three pillars of sustainability leads to the conclusion that circular business models cannot always be qualified as a subcategory of sustainable business models. [50] The possibility that circularity may not coincide with sustainability is mitigated in a case of industrial symbiosis, consisting of the sharing, between dissimilar companies, of materials (including waste), services and skills. The main reason for companies to collaborate is to share the burden of environmental investment, thereby reducing business risk. [55] The following propositions thus emerge:

Proposition 4 (P4). *The introduction of sustainability must be associated with a strategic evolution of the value proposition, through the transition to a sustainable business model.*

Proposition 5 (P5). *With reference to the three pillars of sustainability, not all circular business practices (and circular business models), without adequate assessment tools, can be considered as sustainable.*

2.4. Building a Conceptual Framework

As a conclusion of the literature analysis, a conceptual framework has been drawn, which is shown in Figure 1. The model represents the theoretical link of the five propositions listed in the previous paragraphs.

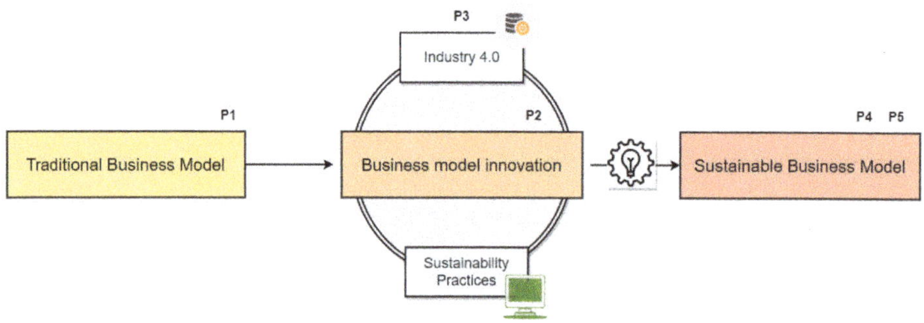

Figure 1. Conceptual framework (own elaboration).

The model illustrates the transition from a traditional business model to a sustainable business model, within a manufacturing context.

The baseline is a traditional business model, which does not consider sustainability in the company's value proposition. The first step in the transaction to a sustainable business model is the introduction of some sustainability practices within the production process. In parallel, any sustainability practice should be evaluated with environmental, economic and social sustainability assessment tools, to assess its feasibility. Some sustainability practices could lead to a reduction of environmental impacts but at the same time, they may not be economically feasible. In a manufacturing context, the assessment of sustainability is facilitated by industry 4.0 paradigms, which have enabled companies to increase production efficiency and monitor their production process.

The successful implementation of sustainability practices, in addition to an operational process change, also requires strategic evolution. This evolution occurs through innovation in the business model, namely a change in the value proposition of a company. A sustainable business model must represent the sustainability practices that a company has decided to implement. At the same time, the new model must also represent how the sustainable practices introduced impacts on the company's customers and all stakeholders involved in the value creation process.

3. Methodology

In order to evaluate the transition from a traditional to a sustainable model, it has been decided to consider one of the largest producers of tiles in the Sassuolo ceramic district as a case study to test the conceptual model [56].

This research uses the theoretical approach of grounded theory [57] with the qualitative approach of case-based research [58] which is particularly appropriate in exploratory studies, like the one of Harrison et al. [59]. In fact, empirical studies on the application of the Triple-Layered Business Model Canvas are still scarce, so the conceptual model that was built theoretically required validation in a real situation.

The company under analysis is one of the leading players in the ceramic sector in Italy for square meters produced, with five locations, over 130 million in turnover and cutting-edge technology. Starting from a traditional business model, the sustainability and circularity practices introduced by the company are considered and are integrated into a strategic context of value creation. The new value proposition, in terms of sustainability, is represented by a business model innovation that results in the drafting of a sustainable business model.

The tool selected to represent the new sustainable business model of the company is the triple-layered business model canvas, created by Joyce and Paquin [10]. This model consists of three separate business model canvas, one for each pillar of sustainability. The economic pillar must be represented by a traditional business canvas model, therefore the traditional (and linear) model already developed in the paper of Garcia Muiña [60] is considered. This model, subsequently represented in Figure 2, refers to the same company as this paper case study and focuses on the economic side of the value proposition.

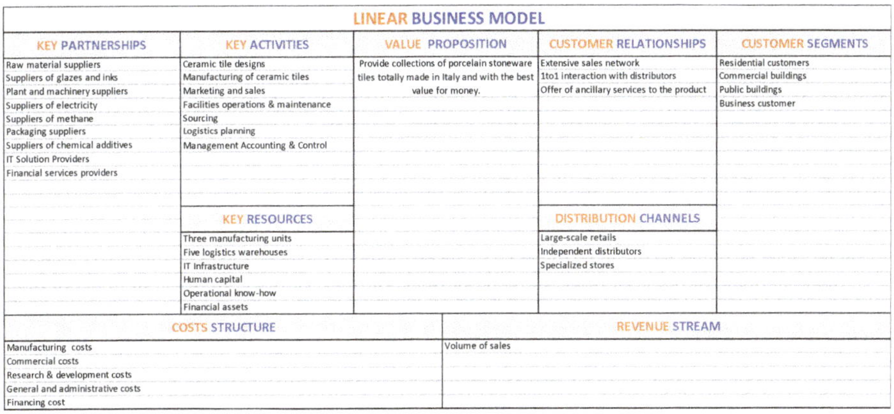

Figure 2. Linear Business Model Canvas (BMC) of the production process in a ceramic tile company [60].

Regarding the remaining two pillars of sustainability, different methodologies have been followed. For the environmental pillar, the compilation of the business model canvas items is based on the environmental impact analysis that the company is conducting on its production process. The company under study, due to the incentives that the Italian government provided, has implemented various technologies within industry 4.0 [60]. Part of these technologies concerns the installation of sensors and meters for the collection of production process data. Through the Life Cycle Assessment (LCA) methodology, and thanks to data collection tools, it was possible to implement an environmental impact assessment model of the production process. The items in the environmental TLBMC all correspond to the information needed to compile an environmental impact LCA tool. In parallel to the LCA analysis, the business model was therefore also compiled.

In order to include the social dimension in the new business model, the semi-structured interview technique [61] was applied to identify the company's main stakeholders. To this end, twenty-one apical positions were selected from the board of directors and top and middle management to conduct an interview following the interpretive method described by Settembre Blundo et al. [62].

From an operational point of view, the managers of the different functions (see Table 1) were met and each was asked to identify the categories of people and organizations that from their perspective can be considered stakeholders with respect to the company's activities. They were then asked to aggregate the individual stakeholders into groups, in descending order of importance, based on three criteria: (1) Interest, (2) Power, and (3) Priority. The aim of the interviews conducted with top and middle managers was to obtain a view, from their perspective, of stakeholders relevant to the company. The interviews were audited and then digitally transcribed for subsequent evaluation of the results. The approach followed to interpret the results of the interviews was a phenomenological hermeneutical one inspired by Gadamer's vision [63] and applied by Settembre-Blundo et al. (2019) [64] using a hermeneutical circle as a tool to interpret reality. The interpretation process involved three stages:

- Phase 1—*Understanding*: A first construction of the reality provided by the texts of the interviews was made by the authors based on their own knowledge and experience. In this phase, a first hierarchical list of stakeholders was built.
- Phase 2—*Interpretation*: In this phase, the authors compared their first construction of reality (phase 1) with the individual perspectives offered by the interviewees. In this phase, a hierarchical list of stakeholders was constructed for each interviewee, assigning to each one a weighting index.
- Phase 3—*Application*: The lists have been merged together, respecting the weighting criteria to obtain a construction of reality that comes as close as possible to the vision that the company has of its stakeholders.

Table 1. Framework for carrying out the interviews.

Business Function	Job Position	Topics
Board of Directors	Chief Executive Officer	INTEREST: Which stakeholders have an interest in the company's business? POWER: Which stakeholders have the power to influence the company's business? PRIORITY: Depending on the level and type of stakeholder involvement, what priority should be given to their needs?
Top Management (C-Level)	Chief Financial Officer B2B Sales Director B2C Sales Director Procurement Director Technical Director	
Management (B-Level)	Innovation Manager Marketing Manager Administrative Manager Controller Manager HR Manager IT Manager Credit Manager Sourcing Manager Logistic Manager Security Manager Quality Manager R&D Manager Plant Manager 1 Plant Manager 2 Plant Manager 3	

In addition to the identification of stakeholders, the interview continued with a second phase related only to the company's top management (C-Level). Starting with the identified stakeholders, who are the basis of the social business model canvas model, information was collected on the other items of the model. On the basis of the stakeholders that were identified, and the additional information collected for each of them, the other items of the social business model canvas were then compiled.

The methodological model of the hermeneutical circle is simple and easy to apply one, but it has the limit of the subjectivity of conducting the analysis: one's personal experience and the criteria adopted for the fusion of the interpretative horizons [65] of the people interviewed, due to their subjective nature, can influence the factual construction of reality. However, the adoption of a multiple analysis perspective, which takes into account the individual visions of the interviewees, mitigates this bias. From a procedural point of view, this approach can be easily replicated to any other organizational reality.

4. Case Study

The case study on which this paper is based concerns a major tile producer in the ceramic district of Sassuolo, Italy. The ceramic district of Sassuolo is one of the most important industrial entities in the Emilia Romagna region and in Italy itself. In this territory, the ceramic sector comprises over 90 companies that employ more than 17,000 people, contributing to the economic and social development of the region [66]. The district, born around the 1950s, has evolved significantly in a relatively short time, experiencing several disruptive innovations such as the transition to a single firing process or the tile decoration by digital printing. Although innovation and industry 4.0 have made the production process increasingly efficient, the ceramic industry has always been considered a polluting industry. In order to limit the environmental impact of production, the ceramic industry has constantly invested in the field of sustainability to the point of turning the ceramic production process into excellence, according to European parameters. Despite the growing production values, the collaboration between the companies of the district and the dialogue between companies and public bodies has generated a strong commitment to sustainability and has made it possible to reconcile sustainable development with greater process efficiency [67].

Focusing on strategic analysis, the business model canvas in Figure 2 offers a first perspective on the functioning of the ceramic producer and its value creation process.

The value proposition of the ceramic tile producer is to provide "made in Italy" ceramic tiles collections for the best value for money. The customer segments are residential customers, commercial and public buildings and business customers. These customer groups generally expect a high-quality product but are also extremely price-sensitive, aware of the different competitors offering quality ceramic tile products. In customer relations, the strength of the company is a quality sales network, in close contact with distribution and able to offer after-sales services of a high level and highly appreciated by customers. The distribution channels are different and range from large-scale retails to specialized stores. As far as company resources are concerned, the company has three production plants, five logistic warehouses, an IT structure with cloud servers, human capital and know-how of production processes and, finally, a solid financial structure. The main activity that distinguishes the company is the production of porcelain stoneware tiles. The group also has purchasing, accounting, quality and management control, sales and marketing offices and research laboratories for the design of new tiles. The main partners with which the group interacts are the suppliers of raw materials, glazes, and inks. These are added the suppliers of machinery and of electricity and methane, which are fundamental for the ceramic production process. Finally, there are the suppliers of financial and IT services. In conclusion, it is necessary to evaluate the cost and revenue flows for the company. The main costs identified in the model are manufacturing, commercial, research, and development, administrative and financing costs. Revenues, on the other hand, given a generally standardized sales price, are almost entirely based on the sales volumes that can be achieved.

Focusing on industry 4.0, the company under analysis has invested during the last few years in various technologies within the 4.0 industry paradigm. In addition to the automation of part of the production process, resulting in a consequent increase in productivity and reduction of industrial costs, an important part of the investments has concerned the equipment of sensors and meters for the collection of process data. As highlighted in the literature analysis, one challenge companies face with the introduction of these technologies is the capacity to exploit the amount of data resulting from the production process. The ceramic producer under study opted to exploit the data available for a sustainability assessment of the production process, evaluating the three pillars of sustainability:

environment, economy, and society. This evaluation was conducted with the Life Cycle Sustainability Assessment (LCSA) methodology, one of the most widely recognized methodologies in sustainability evaluation [68]. In particular, the environmental analysis conducted through LCA was the one that benefited most from the implementation of Industry 4.0. Due to the data acquisition tools, it was possible to collect important process data that allowed us to complete the inventory analysis, on the basis of the LCA environmental impact analysis. The presence of a company ERP system easily connected to the company data collection systems has also facilitated economic impact assessments, through the Life Cycle Costing tool and social impact assessment, through the Social Life Cycle Assessment tool [69].

Industry 4.0, with the role of supporting the manufacturing process impact assessment, has thus favored the implementation of sustainability within the company analyzed. The sustainability practices implemented by the company can in this way be evaluated and communicated externally to the stakeholders involved and interested in them. Despite the importance of these practices, the implementation of sustainability is not strategically perceived through the use of a traditional business model. In this regard, the following paragraph will consider the transition from a traditional business model to a sustainable business model, highlighting the path of sustainable development pursued by the company.

5. Results

5.1. The Triple Layered Business Model Canvas

The traditional business model canvas is a tool that analyses value creation by focusing on an economic perspective. However, the perspective of a traditional business model canvas does not allow the reader to intuitively perceive the path of sustainability that a company is undertaking. Specifically, the environmental and social pillars of sustainability assume a secondary role, being concealed by an analysis that remains merely economic. The partial analysis of sustainability and a lack of harmonization of the three pillars enables to exploit only part of the benefits resulting from a sustainable transition [70].

In order to extend the analysis to all the three pillars of sustainability, an instrument adopting a triple bottom line perspective is needed. In this regard, the TLBMC created by Joyce and Paquin [10] is a comprehensive choice to better represent also the environmental and social point of view. This model consists of three separate business model canvas, one for each pillar of sustainability. The economic pillar is represented by the traditional canvas while the other two are organized on different items. The following paragraphs, therefore, deal with the environmental and social layer of the TLBMC, entering the specifics of each item.

5.2. The Environmental Layer

The environmental layer of the TLBMC is based on a view of the entire life cycle from a life cycle assessment perspective. The fundamental purpose of this model is to understand the environmental benefits deriving from the company's sustainability path and the major environmental impacts deriving from the product's life cycle. The advantage of this model is the possibility to understand the most critical environmental issues of the company and the most important practices of circularity and sustainability that the company is undertaking [10].

Figure 3 below shows the result of the environmental layer:

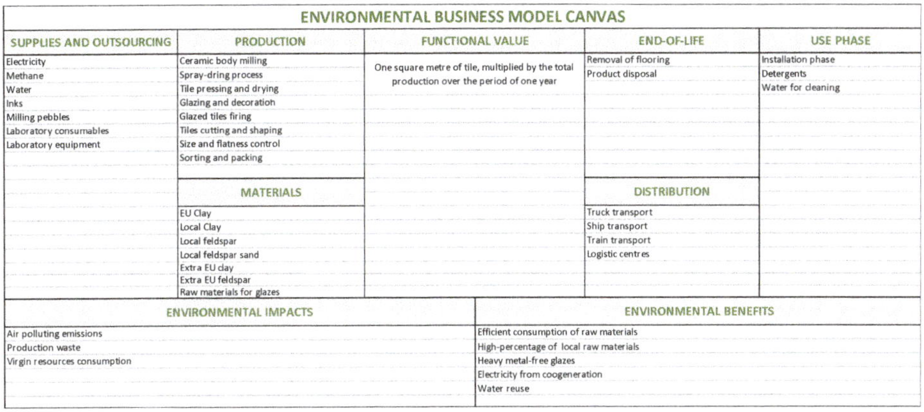

Figure 3. Environmental layer of the Triple-Layered Business Model Canvas (TLBMC) in a ceramic tile company (own elaboration from [10]).

The functional value of Figure 3 describes the output of the production process being analyzed. This value corresponds to the functional unit used in the LCA analysis conducted on the company. In the case of the company under analysis, this value corresponds to the square meter of tile which, multiplied by the total production, allows the value of the company's annual production to be obtained.

The heading "materials" of Figure 3 represents the components of the key resource of the traditional business model canvas, from a more detailed perspective. In the company case study, it was decided to focus on the main raw materials used by the company to produce the ceramic body. The materials selected are (with different percentages) the same used by most ceramic manufacturing companies for ceramic body compositions. These materials are therefore EU clay, local clay, local feldspar, local feldspar sand, non-EU clay, and non-EU feldspar. Local raw materials are considered raw materials sourced from Italian territory.

The heading "production" incorporates the key activities of the traditional business model and focuses on the activities of transforming material inputs into a finished product output. In the case of the ceramic tile manufacturer, it was decided to divide the production process into process steps following the literature on the subject [69]. The selected process steps are ceramic body milling, atomization, drying, glazing and decoration, firing, cutting and shaping, flatness control and sorting and packing.

"Supplies and outsourcing" refer to all materials and production activities that are necessary for the production process but cannot be defined as central to the organization. In this regard, raw materials for bodies and glazes have been considered as "materials" and the other main resources have been reported under the heading "supplies and outsourcing". In this section, therefore, the main items reported are water, energy, methane and packaging materials.

"Distribution", as in the traditional canvas model, refers to the transport of the finished product. In the environmental layer, this heading focuses on the main transport modes used by the company. For these reasons, this section includes the means of transport with which distribution takes place: trucks, trains, and ships.

The "use phase" includes the necessary resources that the customer must employ for the use and maintenance of the product. In the case of ceramic tiles, it is possible to consider the installation phase and the cleaning and maintenance phases, with consequent consumption of water and detergent.

The last phase is the end-of-life phase. In this context, it should be considered how the end of life is managed by the customer. The ceramic manufacturer rarely has data on this aspect and the ceramic product, being composed of several layers, is difficult to recycle or reuse.

In conclusion, instead of costs and revenues, environmental benefits and impacts are considered. As for benefits, namely all actions taken in favor of sustainability, the actions that emerged in the previous paragraphs are selected. As a result, it has been included energy co-generation, water reuse, the choice of local raw materials and the choice of raw materials for glazes that do not contain heavy metals. These represent the main sustainability and circularity practices introduced by the company, whose positive effects on the environment have been verified through the LCA instruments. As far as environmental impacts are concerned, the sources of the greatest environmental impact of the ceramic production process are highlighted, respectively air-polluting emissions, production waste, and virgin resources consumption.

5.3. The Social Layer

The social layer of the TLBMC represents the social pillar of sustainability and it investigates the relationship between stakeholders and the organization. The objective of the model is to understand the major social impacts arising from relations with key stakeholders [10].

Figure 4 below shows the result of the social layer:

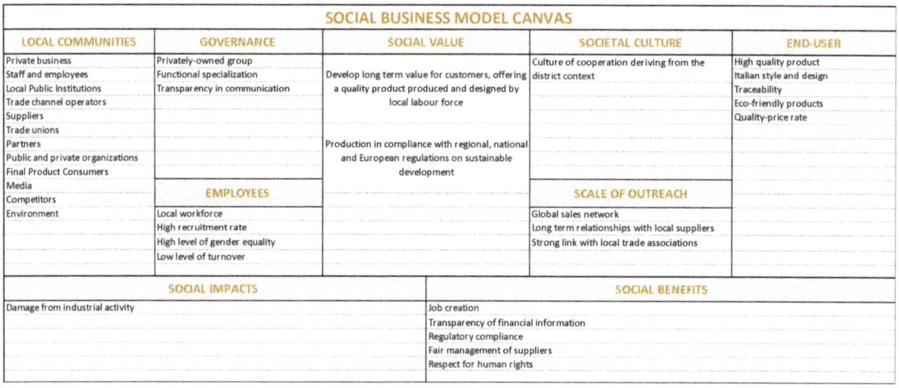

Figure 4. Social layer of the TLBMC in a ceramic tile company (own elaboration from [10]).

The heading "local community" must be the first to be analyzed, because it concerns the relationship established between the company and the stakeholders present on the company's territory, including suppliers. The stakeholders identified from the semi-structured interviews for each individual interviewee were merged into a single list that optimally represented the reality of the stakeholders with whom the company interacts. The list is represented in the social business model canvas and the order of stakeholders is hierarchical by importance.

The heading "social value" is the part of the corporate mission that focuses on how to create benefits for stakeholders and society. There is always a social value within an organization, even though the company may appear to be solely profit-driven. In the company case study, the social values that have been identified are, first of all, the development of long-term value for customers, offering a quality product produced and designed by the local labor force. Secondly, another value is to produce in compliance with regional, national and European regulations on sustainable development.

Employees are a key aspect of the social pillar of a company and are treated in a separate section. This aspect concerns the characteristics and management of the workforce. In this case, the most important factors highlighted in this analysis are the high percentage of the local workforce and the high levels of recruitment rates, given by the favorable financial performance of the company. Furthermore, it is relevant to underline the high level of gender equality reached by the ceramic company during the last years.

The heading "governance" explains the organizational structure of the company under analysis. It is possible to consider different structure frameworks, such as functional specialization v. unit specialization, privately-owned companies v. publicly traded companies, etc. The company consists of a privately-owned group, managed by the two sons of the first company's owner. The group is characterized by a functional specialization, with different offices for the various areas of marketing, administration, sales, etc. In addition, the ceramic company is characterized by a high level of transparency in communication, with high degrees of inter-office communication.

The heading "societal culture" represents the potential impact of an organization on society. The focus is on the potential actions of the company that can positively or negatively influence society. As for the paper case study, a positive impact that has been highlighted is the cooperative culture that the company adopts in interaction with other organizations in the district.

The scale of outreach provides information on the breadth and depth of the relationship between the company and its stakeholders. This relationship could be based on the short-term interest of both parties or could be focused on a long-term perspective. Another factor to consider is the outreach in terms of geographical area. The company could be focused on the local territory or it could act from a global perspective. In this connection, the ceramic company has strong links with the local territory for what concerns production and design, but it presents a global sales network. Furthermore, the positive relationship with trade unions allows to enlarge the company's network and facilitate the dialogue with other stakeholders.

Finally, the heading "end-user" consists of the subject who consumes the value proposition offered by the company. In the ceramic context, the client can be different from the end-user. The ceramic company, for instance, sells the major part of its final products to large scale retailers who act as intermediaries between the producer and the end customer. Regarding ceramic tiles, the end-user expectations are to buy a high-quality product based on Italian style and design. At the same time, the interest is also directed to the level of sustainability of the product and the traceability of the production chain. In the end, one of the most important aspects is undoubtedly the selling price, which has a strong impact on the choice of one product over another.

Social impacts and social benefits are the last two headings of the model and they represent the core of the social business model canvas. Regarding social benefits, it was highlighted the increasing ability to create jobs for the local community, the transparency of financial information, compliance with laws in the field of production, the fair management of suppliers and the respect for human rights. At the same time, the most important social impacts consist of pollution deriving from the production process and traffic congestion.

6. Discussion

This paper illustrates the theme of the transition from a traditional business model to a sustainable business model in a manufacturing context. The literature analysis highlights the business model innovation process that leads to the drafting of a sustainable business model. This process is theorized by several authors who have investigated the introduction of sustainability within the company's value proposition [21,41,48,49,71]. Furthermore, the paper explores the role and importance of industry 4.0 in the sustainable transition of enterprises. This topic has also been extensively covered in the literature, with emphasis on the advantages offered by industry 4.0 and the possible barriers that companies face when introducing these technologies [36,41,44,45,71]. Despite numerous contributions to sustainable business model innovation and industry 4.0, there are still few papers that provide a visual representation of a sustainable business model within a manufacturing context. Moreover, there are almost no papers that address this issue with reference to the ceramic tile production sector, which has an important impact on European and global levels [37]. In order to bridge the gap in scientific research, the previous paragraphs present the triple-layered business model canvas tool [32]. This TLBMC model represents, with one single model each, the three pillars of sustainability.

Regardless of the success of this model, very few authors have attempted to apply and adapt it to a manufacturing context.

The application of the TLBMC in this paper concerns a ceramic tile manufacturer from the Sassuolo district in Italy, chosen as a case study. The district is formed by companies that are extremely virtuous in terms of sustainability, as there have been strict regulations and sustainability practices in production processes for years. In many cases, however, companies lack greater awareness of the reduced environmental impact of their processes, the ability to assess their level of sustainability and the inclusion of sustainability in their value creation process. In the context of the Sassuolo ceramic district, the implementation of sustainability is facilitated by industry 4.0 tools, which allow for greater efficiency in manufacturing processes and the possibility of dynamically monitoring production processes. The implementation of process data collection tools has allowed the company under analysis to exploit this information in the evaluation of environmental, economic and social impacts. The factory sensors and meters, connected to the company ERP management system, provided the database for environmental impact analysis through LCA tools and supported economic and social assessments. The introduction and evaluation of sustainability have led the company first to the drafting of a circular business model [60] and, through this paper, to the drafting of a more comprehensive sustainable business model that assesses sustainability in terms of the triple bottom line.

Looking at the results obtained, in the model concerning the environmental pillar, important details of the ceramic production process are highlighted, including the raw materials used, the distribution channels and the process phases throughout the entire life cycle. In addition, the main environmental impacts created by the production activity and the greatest benefits in environmental terms, deriving from sustainability practices undertaken by the company analyzed, are considered. The simultaneous reading of the traditional and environmental business model allows the reader to have a much more detailed picture of the company's activity. In particular, it reveals how the company has individually engaged in a path of sustainability that not all other companies in the sector may have chosen to pursue. This choice can be exploited by the company to create value for its finished product, no longer based solely on price or quality. The business model represented in this way is already an intuitive tool that can be communicated externally in this respect.

In the model concerning the social pillar, instead, the functional structure of the company, the company's governance and the main stakeholders involved are specified, with a focus on employees and the end-user. Furthermore, the main social impacts and benefits deriving from business activity are also analyzed. In this situation, the social model added to the other two further increases the information provided to the reader. In particular, the model provides details of the social benefits that the company generates, which could be important information to share with the company's main stakeholders. In addition, the social model provides guidance for a possible social audit by the company's authorities or clients or for the preparation of a sustainability report that also includes the company's social commitment.

In summary, the results show the company's value proposition in a revised and significantly more detailed form than the previous traditional business model. From the results of the paper, the sustainability path undertaken emerges and the reader perceives the awareness that the company has of its production process and the environmental impact it creates. In parallel, the considerations on the social sustainability dimension are also relevant. The environmental damage produced by industrial activity inevitably has social repercussions, particularly in the territory in which the company operates. At the same time, however, no less important are the social benefits that the company generates, especially in creating several jobs in the area and in communicating transparently and ethically with suppliers and customers. The absence of the transition to a sustainable business model tool such as the triple-layered business model canvas, which highlights the creation of social value, does not allow the company to become aware of the social benefits it generates and, by consequence, these benefits are also not communicated to customers and stakeholders.

7. Conclusions

The transition from traditional to sustainable business models and the revision of value proposition is a complex but fundamental step to become aware of the sustainability path that a company is undertaking. The sustainability transition of enterprises should be based on sustainability objectives formulated by top management in a long-term orientation [72]. Furthermore, the sustainable objectives should not be limited to an environmental analysis but should include the three pillars of sustainability in a triple bottom line perspective [9]. Despite the importance of strategic analysis, manufacturing companies very frequently introduce sustainability practices on the basis of an economic benefit, regulatory imposition or other external factors [73] without being aware of the environmental and social benefits generated by these choices. In the ceramic tile sector, an example of this process concerns the reuse of water consumed in production processes, which has a reduced cost compared to water from aqueducts or wells. In addition to the economic advantage, this circular economy practice brings a high environmental benefit which, with the use of impact assessment methodologies, can be properly quantified. The innovation of the business model allows these practices to be considered not only from an operational perspective but also in the company's value creation strategy.

In addition to enriching the increasingly comprehensive literature on sustainable business models, the paper offers interesting insights into managerial implications. As far as ceramic tile companies are concerned, the importance of a correct impact assessment of sustainability practices emerges. Impact assessment case studies already exist in the literature, although they tend to concentrate solely on the environmental pillar of sustainability [74–76]. In particular, ceramic companies that have implemented data collection systems based on industry 4.0 paradigms have the opportunity to create dynamic monitoring systems of the impact of their processes. The issue of impact assessment also concerns other manufacturing companies in other sectors, as corporate social responsibility programs are playing an increasingly important role in generating social legitimacy, trustworthy relationships with stakeholders and improved reputation [77]. Another area of interest regards the top management of manufacturing companies which, in the introduction of a sustainable development path, should carefully assess the evolution of the value proposition of the company through a shift to a sustainable business model. In this regard, the TLBMC consists of an intuitive and easy to implement tool, which allows companies to better understand their value creation process and to evaluate at the same level the three pillars of sustainability. In order to be truly effective, however, the sustainable business model should not be considered as static but should be continuously updated according to the sustainable transition of the enterprise.

Despite the good degree of detail achieved by TLBMC and the progress compared to previous research, the results show some limitations. First, the major limitation of this paper derives from the single company case study in a specific sector such as ceramic tiles. Nevertheless, the case study remains valuable because, in addition to the importance of the sector worldwide, ceramic companies in the most important European districts have very similar production processes, the same type of machinery suppliers and similar sustainability practices implemented within the processes. In particular, the similarity of production processes within the Italian (Sassuolo) and Spanish (Castellon) ceramic district makes the model a useful reference for further studies of sustainable business models within the sector. Secondly, other limitations are those related to the TLBMC itself and they are already highlighted by the authors of the model. Although the model is comprehensive, it remains an instrument that cannot individually assess the potential of innovation and should subsequently be followed by more extensive analysis [10]. Finally, regarding the social pillar, unlike the environmental pillar based on LCA impact studies, the results were based on semi-structured interviews with a limited number of respondents.

In conclusion, future research could be dedicated to integrating the circular business model developed previously in the same case study with the results of this article [60]. In addition, another area of research could concern a fourth dimension that is frequently omitted, namely the technological dimension concerning the technological performance of the product. In the ceramic tile sector, as in other manufacturing sectors, the introduction of sustainability into the processes must maintain the technological characteristics of the product, otherwise, the risk arises of creating a product of a lower quality or not complying with national and international regulations. Finally, future research will be devoted to the implementation of the TLBMC model in other manufacturing realities within the ceramic supply chain.

Author Contributions: Conceptualization, F.E.G.-M.; methodology, M.S.M.-S.; supervision, A.M.F. and writing—review and editing, M.C. All authors have read and agree to the published version of the manuscript.

Funding: This research was co-funded by the European Union under the LIFE Programme (LIFE16 ENV/IT/000307: LIFE Force of the Future-Forture), under which a research grant has been activated at the Department of Sciences and Methods for Engineering (DISMI) of University of Modena and Reggio Emilia, Italy.

Acknowledgments: The authors would like to acknowledge the editor and the two anonymous reviewers for their helpful suggestions to improve the paper.

Conflicts of Interest: The authors declare no conflict of interest.

References

1. Carvalho, N.; Chaim, O.; Cazarini, E.; Gerolamo, M. Manufacturing in the fourth industrial revolution: A positive prospect in Sustainable Manufacturing. *Procedia Manuf.* **2018**, *21*, 671–678. [CrossRef]
2. Misopoulos, F.; Michaelides, R.; Salehuddin, M.; Manthou, V.; Michaelides, Z. Addressing Organisational Pressures as Drivers towards Sustainability in Manufacturing Projects and Project Management Methodologies. *Sustainability* **2018**, *10*, 2098. [CrossRef]
3. Müller, J.; Buliga, O.; Voigt, K. The role of absorptive capacity and innovation strategy in the design of industry 4.0 business Models-A comparison between SMEs and large enterprises. *Eur. Manag. J.* **2020**. [CrossRef]
4. Peukert, B.; Benecke, S.; Clavell, J.; Neugebauer, S.; Nissen, N.F.; Uhlmann, E.; Lang, K.-D.; Finkbeiner, M. Addressing Sustainability and Flexibility in Manufacturing via Smart Modular Machine Tool Frames to Support Sustainable Value Creation. *Procedia CIRP* **2015**, *29*, 514–519. [CrossRef]
5. Hong, P.; Jagani, S.; Kim, J.; Youn, S. Managing sustainability orientation: An empirical investigation of manufacturing firms. *Int. J. Prod. Econ.* **2019**, *211*, 71–81. [CrossRef]
6. Lüdeke-Freund, F.; Carroux, S.; Joyce, A.; Massa, L.; Breuer, H. The sustainable business model pattern taxonomy—45 patterns to support sustainability-oriented business model innovation. *Sustain. Prod. Consum.* **2018**, *15*, 145–162.
7. Gupta, S.; Czinkota, M.; Melewar, T. Embedding knowledge and value of a brand into sustainability for differentiation. *J. World Bus.* **2013**, *48*, 287–296. [CrossRef]
8. Ritala, P.; Huotari, P.; Bocken, N.; Albareda, L.; Puumalainen, K. Sustainable business model adoption among S&P 500 firms: A longitudinal content analysis study. *J. Clean. Prod.* **2018**, *170*, 216–226. [CrossRef]
9. Giddings, B.; Hopwood, B.; O'Brien, G. Environment, economy and society: Fitting them together into sustainable development. *Sustain. Dev.* **2002**, *10*, 187–196. [CrossRef]
10. Joyce, A.; Paquin, R. The triple layered business model canvas: A tool to design more sustainable business models. *J. Clean. Prod.* **2016**, *135*, 1474–1486. [CrossRef]
11. Massa, L.; Tucci, C.L.; Afuah, A. A critical assessment of business model research. *Acad. Manag. Ann.* **2017**, *11*, 73–104. [CrossRef]
12. Moggi, S.; Cantele, S.; Vernizzi, S.; Beretta Zanoni, A. The Business Model Concept and Disclosure: A Preliminary Analysis of Integrated Reports. In Proceedings of the 9th Annual Conference of the EuroMed Academy of Business, Warsaw, Poland, 14–16 September 2016.
13. Amit, R.; Zott, C. Value creation in E-business. *Strateg. Manag. J.* **2001**, *22*, 493–520. [CrossRef]
14. Shafer, S.; Smith, H.; Linder, J. The power of business models. *Bus. Horiz.* **2005**, *48*, 199–207. [CrossRef]
15. Magretta, J. Why Business Models Matter. *Harv. Bus. Rev.* **2002**, *80*, 86–92, 133.
16. Osterwalder, A.; Pigneur, Y.; Clark, T. *Business Model Generation*; John Wiley & Sons: Hoboken, NJ, USA, 2010.
17. Gassmann, O.; Frankenberger, K.; Csik, M. *The Business Model Navigator*; Pearson: London, UK, 2010.
18. Zott, C.; Amit, R. Business Model Design: An Activity System Perspective. *Long Range Plan.* **2010**, *43*, 216–226. [CrossRef]

19. Weiller, C.; Neely, A. *Business Model Design in an Ecosystem Context*; University of Cambridge, Cambridge Service Alliance: Cambridge, UK, 2013.
20. Wirtz, B.W.; Pistoia, A.; Ullrich, S.; Gottel, V. Business models: Origin, development and future research perspectives. *Long Range Plan.* **2016**, *49*. [CrossRef]
21. Evans, S.; Vladimirova, D.; Holgado, M.; Van Fossen, K.; Yang, M.; Silva, E.A.; Barlow, C.Y. Business model innovation for sustainability: Towards a unified perspective for creation of sustainable business models. *Bus. Strategy Environ.* **2017**, *26*, 597–608. [CrossRef]
22. Yang, M.; Evans, S.; Vladimirova, D.; Rana, P. Value uncaptured perspective for sustainable business model innovation. *J. Clean. Prod.* **2017**, *140*, 1794–1804. [CrossRef]
23. Foss, N.; Saebi, T. Fifteen Years of Research on Business Model Innovation. *J. Manag.* **2016**, *43*, 200–227. [CrossRef]
24. Velu, C. Business Model Innovation and Third-Party Alliance on the Survival of New Firms. *Technovation* **2015**, *35*, 1–11. [CrossRef]
25. Lee, J.; Suh, T.; Roy, D.; Baucus, M. Emerging Technology and Business Model Innovation: The Case of Artificial Intelligence. *J. Open Innov. Technol. Mark. Complex.* **2019**, *5*, 44. [CrossRef]
26. Falcone, P.; Lopolito, A.; Sica, E. Instrument mix for energy transition: A method for policy formulation. *Technol. Forecast. Soc. Chang.* **2019**, *148*, 119706. [CrossRef]
27. Bartodziej, C.J. The concept industry 4.0. In *The Concept Industry 4.0*; Springer Gabler: Wiesbaden, Germany, 2017.
28. Rojko, A. Industry 4.0 Concept: Background and Overview. *Int. J. Interact Mob. Technol.* **2017**, *11*, 77. [CrossRef]
29. Ślusarczyk, B. Industry 4.0—Are we ready? *Pol. J. Manag. Stud.* **2018**, *17*, 232–248. [CrossRef]
30. Frank, A.; Dalenogare, L.; Ayala, N. Industry 4.0 technologies: Implementation patterns in manufacturing companies. *Int. J. Prod. Econ.* **2019**, *210*, 15–26. [CrossRef]
31. Agrawal, A.; Schaefer, S.; Funke, T. Incorporating Industry 4.0. in Corporate Strategy. *Adv. Bus. Inf. Syst. Anal.* **2018**, 161–176. [CrossRef]
32. Kagermann, H.; Helbig, J.; Hellinger, A.; Wahlster, W. Recommendations for Implementing the strategic initiative. In *INDUSTRIE 4.0: Securing the Future of German Manufacturing Industry*; Final report of the Industrie 4.0 working group; Forschungsunion: München, Germany, 2013.
33. Ślusarczyk, B.; Haseeb, M.; Hussain, H. Fourth industrial revolution: A way forward to attain better performance in the textile industry. *Eng. Manag. Prod. Serv.* **2019**, *11*, 52–69. [CrossRef]
34. Zheng, P.; Wang, H.; Sang, Z.; Zhong, R.; Liu, Y.; Liu, C.; Mubarok, K.; Yu, S.; Xu, X. Smart manufacturing systems for Industry 4.0: Conceptual framework, scenarios, and future perspectives. *Front. Mech. Eng.* **2018**, *13*, 137–150. [CrossRef]
35. Dalenogare, L.S.; Benitez, G.B.; Ayala, N.F.; Frank, A.G. The expected contribution of Industry 4.0 technologies for industrial performance. *Int. J. Prod. Econ.* **2018**, *204*, 383–394. [CrossRef]
36. Xu, L.; Xu, E.; Li, L. Industry 4.0: State of the art and future trends. *Int. J. Prod. Res.* **2018**, *56*, 2941–2962. [CrossRef]
37. Arnold, C.; Kiel, D.; Voigt, K.I. Innovative business models for the industrial internet of things. *BHM Berg-und Hüttenmännische Mon.* **2017**, *162*, 371–381. [CrossRef]
38. Parida, V.; Sjödin, D.; Reim, W. Reviewing Literature on Digitalization, Business Model Innovation, and Sustainable Industry: Past Achievements and Future Promises. *Sustainability* **2019**, *11*, 391. [CrossRef]
39. Ibarra, D.; Ganzarain, J.; Igartua, J.I. Business model innovation through Industry 4.0: A review. *Procedia Manuf.* **2018**, *22*, 4–10. [CrossRef]
40. Pereira, A.; Romero, F. A review of the meanings and the implications of the Industry 4.0 concept. *Procedia Manuf.* **2017**, *13*, 1206–1214. [CrossRef]
41. Stock, T.; Seliger, G. Opportunities of Sustainable Manufacturing in Industry 4.0. *Procedia CIRP* **2016**, *40*, 536–541. [CrossRef]
42. Luthra, S.; Mangla, S. Evaluating challenges to Industry 4.0 initiatives for supply chain sustainability in emerging economies. *Process Saf. Environ. Prot.* **2018**, *117*, 168–179. [CrossRef]
43. Müller, J.; Kiel, D.; Voigt, K. What Drives the Implementation of Industry 4.0? The Role of Opportunities and Challenges in the Context of Sustainability. *Sustainability* **2018**, *10*, 247. [CrossRef]

44. Varela, L.; Araújo, A.; Ávila, P.; Castro, H.; Putnik, G. Evaluation of the Relation between Lean Manufacturing, Industry 4.0, and Sustainability. *Sustainability* **2019**, *11*, 1439. [CrossRef]
45. Birkel, H.; Veile, J.; Müller, J.; Hartmann, E.; Voigt, K. Development of a Risk Framework for Industry 4.0 in the Context of Sustainability for Established Manufacturers. *Sustainability* **2019**, *11*, 384. [CrossRef]
46. Man, J.; Strandhagen, J. An Industry 4.0 Research Agenda for Sustainable Business Models. *Procedia CIRP* **2017**, *63*, 721–726. [CrossRef]
47. Abdul-Rashid, S.; Sakundarini, N.; Raja Ghazilla, R.; Thurasamy, R. The impact of sustainable manufacturing practices on sustainability performance. *Int. J. Oper. Prod. Manag.* **2017**, *37*, 182–204. [CrossRef]
48. Bocken, N.; Boons, F.; Baldassarre, B. Sustainable business model experimentation by understanding ecologies of business models. *J. Clean. Prod.* **2018**, *208C*, 1498–1512. [CrossRef]
49. Nosratabadi, S.; Mosavi, A.; Shamshirband, S.; Kazimieras Zavadskas, E.; Rakotonirainy, A.; Chau, K. Sustainable Business Models: A Review. *Sustainability* **2019**, *11*, 1663. [CrossRef]
50. Geissdoerfer, M.; Vladimirova, D.; Evans, S. Sustainable business model innovation: A review. *J. Clean. Prod.* **2018**, *198*, 401–416. [CrossRef]
51. Linder, M.; Williander, M. Circular Business Model Innovation: Inherent Uncertainties. *Bus. Strategy Environ.* **2015**, *26*, 182–196. [CrossRef]
52. D'Adamo, I.; Gastaldi, M.; Rosa, P. Recycling of end-of-life vehicles: Assessing trends and performances in Europe. *Technol. Forecast. Soc. Chang.* **2020**, *152*, 119887. [CrossRef]
53. Lahti, T.; Wincent, J.; Parida, V. A Definition and Theoretical Review of the Circular Economy, Value Creation, and Sustainable Business Models: Where Are We Now and Where Should Research Move in the Future? *Sustainability* **2018**, *10*, 2799. [CrossRef]
54. Ferella, F.; D'Adamo, I.; Leone, S.; Innocenzi, V.; De Michelis, I.; Vegliò, F. Spent FCC E-Cat: Towards a Circular Approach in the Oil Refining Industry. *Sustainability* **2018**, *11*, 113. [CrossRef]
55. Aranda-Usón, A.; Portillo-Tarragona, P.; Marín-Vinuesa, L.; Scarpellini, S. Financial Resources for the Circular Economy: A Perspective from Businesses. *Sustainability* **2019**, *11*, 888. [CrossRef]
56. Klymenko, O.; Nerger, A.J. Application of the Triple Layered Business Model Canvas-A Case Study of the Maritime and Marine Industry. Master's Thesis, Institutt for internasjonal forretningsdrift, Norwegian University of Science and Technology, Gjøvik, Norway, 2018.
57. Nie, Y. Combining Narrative Analysis, Grounded Theory and Qualitative Data Analysis Software to Develop a Case Study Research. *J. Manag. Res.* **2017**, *9*, 53. [CrossRef]
58. Verner, J.; Abdullah, L. Exploratory case study research: Outsourced project failure. *Inf. Softw. Technol.* **2012**, *54*, 866–886. [CrossRef]
59. Harrison, H.; Birks, M.; Franklin, R.; Mills, J. Case Study Research: Foundations and Methodological Orientations. *Forum Qual. Soc. Res.* **2017**, *18*, 19. [CrossRef]
60. Garcia-Muiña, F.; González-Sánchez, R.; Ferrari, A.; Settembre-Blundo, D. The Paradigms of Industry 4.0 and Circular Economy as Enabling Drivers for the Competitiveness of Businesses and Territories: The Case of an Italian Ceramic Tiles Manufacturing Company. *Soc. Sci.* **2018**, *7*, 225. [CrossRef]
61. Kallio, H.; Pietilä, A.M.; Johnson, M.; Kangasniemi, M. Systematic methodological review: Developing a framework for a qualitative semi-structured interview guide. *J. Adv. Nurs.* **2016**, *72*, 2954–2965. [CrossRef]
62. Settembre Blundo, D.; García-Muiña, F.; Pini, M.; Volpi, L.; Siligardi, C.; Ferrari, A. Sustainability as source of competitive advantages in mature sectors: The case of Ceramic District of Sassuolo (Italy). *Smart Sustain. Built Environ.* **2019**, *8*, 53–79. [CrossRef]
63. Fleming, V.; Robb, Y. A critical analysis of articles using a Gadamerian based research method. *Nurs. Inq.* **2019**, *26*, e12283. [CrossRef]
64. Settembre Blundo, D.; Maramotti Politi, A.; Fernández del Hoyo, A.; García Muiña, F. The Gadamerian hermeneutics for a mesoeconomic analysis of Cultural Heritage. *J. Cult. Herit. Manag. Sustain. Dev.* **2019**, *9*, 300–333. [CrossRef]
65. Vessey, D. Gadamer and the Fusion of Horizons. *Int. J. Philos. Stud.* **2009**, *17*, 531–542. [CrossRef]
66. Confindustria Ceramica. *Osservatorio Previsionale sul Mercato Mondiale delle PIASTRELLE di Ceramica: Italia e Principali Competitori a Confronto*; Confindustria Ceramica: Sassuolo, Italy, 2018.
67. Confindustria Ceramica. *L'evoluzione del Comparto Ceramico tra Innovazione, Sostenibilità e Nuove Sfide*; Arpae Emilia-Romagna: Ecoscienza, Italy, 2018.

68. Finkbeiner, M.; Schau, E.; Lehmann, A.; Traverso, M. Towards Life Cycle Sustainability Assessment. *Sustainability* **2010**, *2*, 3309–3322. [CrossRef]
69. Garcia-Muiña, F.E.; González-Sánchez, R.; Ferrari, A.M.; Volpi, L.; Pini, M.; Siligardi, C.; Settembre-Blundo, D. Identifying the equilibrium point between sustainability goals and circular economy practices in an Industry 4.0 manufacturing context using eco-design. *Soc. Sci.* **2019**, *8*, 241. [CrossRef]
70. Kiel, D.; Müller, J.; Arnold, C.; Voigt, K. Sustainable Industrial Value Creation: Benefits and Challenges of Industry 4.0. *Int. J. Innov. Manag.* **2017**, *21*, 1740015. [CrossRef]
71. Bocken, N.; Short, S.; Rana, P.; Evans, S. A literature and practice review to develop sustainable business model archetypes. *J. Clean. Prod.* **2014**, *65*, 42–56. [CrossRef]
72. Chofreh, A.; Goni, F. Review of Frameworks for Sustainability Implementation. *Sustain. Dev.* **2017**, *25*, 180–188. [CrossRef]
73. Bossle, M.; De Barcellos, M.; Vieira, L.; Sauvée, L. The drivers for adoption of eco-innovation. *J. Clean. Prod.* **2020**, *113*, 861–872. [CrossRef]
74. Ye, L.; Hong, J.; Ma, X.; Qi, C.; Yang, D. Life cycle environmental and economic assessment of ceramic tile production: A case study in China. *J. Clean. Prod.* **2018**, *189*, 432–441. [CrossRef]
75. Souza, D.; Lafontaine, M.; Charron-Doucet, F.; Bengoa, X.; Chappert, B.; Duarte, F.; Lima, L. Comparative Life Cycle Assessment of ceramic versus concrete roof tiles in the Brazilian context. *J. Clean. Prod.* **2015**, *89*, 165–173. [CrossRef]
76. Almeida, M.; Dias, A.; Demertzi, M.; Arroja, L. Environmental profile of ceramic tiles and their potential for improvement. *J. Clean. Prod.* **2016**, *131*, 583–593. [CrossRef]
77. Siano, A.; Vollero, A.; Conte, F.; Amabile, S. "More than words": Expanding the taxonomy of greenwashing after the Volkswagen scandal. *J. Bus. Res.* **2017**, *71*, 27–37. [CrossRef]

sustainability

MDPI

Article

Integrating Virtual Reality and Digital Twin in Circular Economy Practices: A Laboratory Application Case

Roberto Rocca *, Paolo Rosa, Claudio Sassanelli, Luca Fumagalli and Sergio Terzi

Department of Management, Economics and Industrial Engineering, Politecnico di Milano, Piazza L. da Vinci 32, 20133 Milan, Italy; paolo1.rosa@polimi.it (P.R.); claudio.sassanelli@polimi.it (C.S.); luca1.fumagalli@polimi.it (L.F.); sergio.terzi@polimi.it (S.T.)

* Correspondence: roberto.rocca@polimi.it; Tel.: +39-02-2399-2729

Received: 13 December 2019; Accepted: 8 March 2020; Published: 14 March 2020

Abstract: The increasing awareness of customers toward climate change effects, the high demand instability affecting several industrial sectors, and the fast automation and digitalization of production systems are forcing companies to re-think their business strategies and models in view of both the Circular Economy (CE) and Industry 4.0 (I4.0) paradigms. Some studies have already assessed the relations between CE and I4.0, their benefits, and barriers. However, a practical demonstration of their potential impact in real contexts is still lacking. The aim of this paper is to present a laboratory application case showing how I4.0-based technologies can support CE practices by virtually testing a waste from electrical and electronic equipment (WEEE) disassembly plant configuration through a set of dedicated simulation tools. Our results highlight that service-oriented, event-driven processing and information models can support the integration of smart and digital solutions in current CE practices at the factory level.

Keywords: virtual reality; digital twin; circular economy; industry 4.0; disassembly; laboratory application case

1. Introduction

Today, manufacturing companies are coping with two types of "instabilities" influencing industrial markets. First, customers are becoming even more aware of the effects of both climate change and the depletion of natural resources. This issue pushed the European Union (EU) and other intranational institutions to define even more restrictive guidelines to be adopted by companies in terms of product and process sustainability. During the last few decades, these guidelines have been translated in the Circular Economy (CE) paradigm, or a synergistic view between ecological and economic systems [1,2]. Second, the intrinsic complexity of current industrial markets (e.g., shorter product lifecycles and higher mass customization) is even more dependent on automated and digital solutions supporting companies for meeting with customer's needs. Trying to include all these digital solutions under the same umbrella, the paradigm of Industry 4.0 (I4.0) has been recently invented, entailing the development of high-tech strategies and internet-based technologies enabling the creation and delivery of added value for organizations and society [3]. Together, CE and I4.0 are forcing companies to re-think their business strategies and models, since both these strategies are complementary, and synergistic effects can be established between them [4]. However, despite many works dealing with the interaction between I4.0 and CE [5], the way in which digital technologies can favor the transition toward CE has been rarely assessed in a real context [6]. Previous studies [4] have looked at various aspects of the CE and digital transformation, structuring a work frameworks under the principles of the CE and the pillars of sustainability and proposing the development of standardization of the CE as a paradigm for sustainability under the potential offered by digital transformation. The proposed framework is composed by four dimension of interest (i.e., product, process, facilities, and business) and by three levels—(i) CE strategy standards; (ii) CE standards; (iii) CE maturity norms. Starting from this, the present work wants to practically demonstrate how digital technologies can support CE by presenting a laboratory application case. To this aim, attention has been paid to disassembly processes (i.e., process dimension) for triggering better End-of-Life (EoL) strategies for the valuable product component recovery and on the third analysis level (i.e., CE maturity norms), intended as the degree of maturity in the implementation of the CE in an organization through the incorporation of digital technologies to enable circular industrial metabolism 4.0. Here, I4.0-based technologies support current CE practices by virtually and practically testing a waste from electrical and electronic equipment (WEEE) disassembly plant configuration through a set of dedicated simulation tools and a fully automatized manufacturing line. The paper is organized as follows: Section 2 presents the research methodology adopted within this paper, the adopted I4.0 technologies, and similar laboratory application cases by pointing out the interaction between I4.0 technologies and CE. Section 3 shows the results coming from different tests. Section 4 discusses the obtained results. Finally, Section 5 offers some concluding remarks and potential future research trends.

2. Materials and Methods

In 1992, the physicist Robert Frosh [7] introduces the concept of an analogy between natural ecosystems and industrial ecosystems—the "industrial ecology." For the first time, the ecosystem concept was applied to the industrial sphere, connecting the metabolism between industries [8]. Industrial ecology allows researchers to focus on the facility level, on the inter-firm level, and on the regional or global level [9]. Referring to a manufacturing system, the linear model is based on a static view of the flows that characterize the logistics-production chain, which starts from raw materials supplying and processing, up to the finished product disposal. On the other hand, the Circular Economy (CE) systems provide for a more efficient and more effective use of resources, where the flows are not static and bound by one-directionality, but they fall circularly in the upstream phases of the production system [10]. In order to mitigate the damages of linear systems, environmental policies have so far focused their attention on pollution and emissions. Nevertheless, this "end-of-pipe" policy, which is now obsolete, is integrated into a new sustainability perspective that focuses on the exploitation of renewable raw materials and energies to offset the inputs of non-renewables [11]. Eco-efficient techniques try to minimize the volume, speed, and toxicity of material flows but are unable to alter their linear progression. Besides these, the concept of eco-efficacy proposes the transformation of products and related material flows in order to establish a support relationship with ecological systems and future economic growth.

The CE, according to the definition given by Ellen MacArthur Foundation [12], acts with a logic that, in addition to achieving sustainability in the production mechanisms and consumption, provides for the reconstruction of social and natural capital. This concept is combined with change in the behavior of the final consumer. It also provides multiple value creation mechanisms that are decoupled from the consumption of finite resources [12]. For this reason, the "cradle to cradle" philosophy characterizes these systems. In this way, it is possible to extend the final phase of the product life cycle, for example, through a different reuse. It is also possible to stretch the entire cycle by enhancing the efficiency and the efficacy of the individual phases due to the circular flow reintegration. This approach focuses on understanding how resource flows can have a positive impact on the environment, rather than thinking about how to reduce negative impacts. The aim of the circular model is to have integrated processes between technical and biological flows and their interconnected use minimizing or eliminating waste [13]. What is important in the transition from a linear to a circular economy remains the creation of a sustainable system and the ability to capture the value that would normally be lost with linearity, which would then result in an economic loss in the long run.

As evidenced in Section 1, many works have already assessed the interaction between I4.0 and CE. Trying to put together the sustainability-oriented and technology-oriented views under the same umbrella, the concept of Smart Sustainability has been proposed by experts as a new way for making goods and managing production processes in a more sustainable way by exploiting smart technologies. As pointed out by the authors of reference [5], experts consider four main ways to describe the relation between I4.0 and the CE:

(i) digitalization of the CE, considering I4.0 technologies as a set of opportunities supporting enterprises in increasing their circular degree;
(ii) the role that I4.0 technologies have in enabling circular business models related to the stakeholder's involvement (e.g., customers);
(iii) other CE-related aspects (e.g., resource efficiency and lifecycle management), where I4.0 technologies are enablers of innovative ways for monitoring and optimizing resources performances;
(iv) disassembly and supply chain management with I4.0 technologies as element for developing and managing supplier–customer relationships.

Similarly, the integration of smart and digital (I4.0-based) technologies in manufacturing plants inspired the definition of new terms such as "Smart Manufacturing" and—within company boundaries—"Smart Factory" [3]. Together, all these technologies are changing the classic approach of industrial processes supporting the storage, transportation, and transformation of raw materials into useful products. Therefore, the International Standards of Automation set of standards (ISA-95) [14]—containing all the commonly agreed definitions of the automation pyramid's layers—must also evolve (see Figure 1, below). However, this evolution through I4.0 technologies can maintain the old pyramid intact by acting on the ways different layers can interact, gather information from the field, and store data [15–17]. This is possible thanks to the Cyber Physical Systems (CPSs) connection among the layers, allowing a more flexible pyramid exploitation.

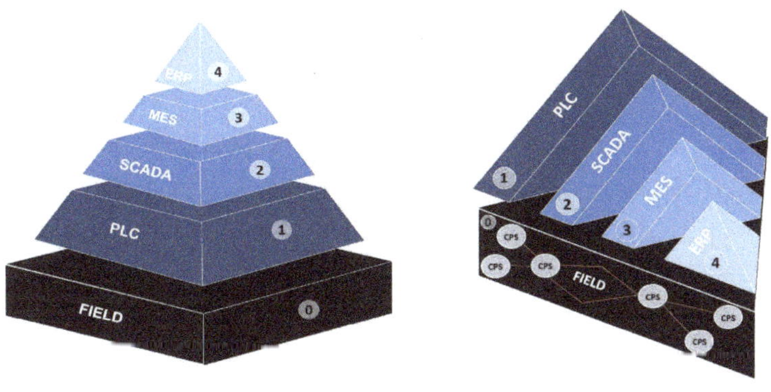

(a) (b)

Figure 1. ISA-95 automation pyramid (**a**) and flexible automation pyramid (**b**).

The enabling 4.0 technologies exploited in the laboratory application case presented in this work are described below. Subsequently, the detailed description of the experiment that has been developed is described, presenting some application results with the scope to practically demonstrate within a laboratory pilot plant the I4.0 technologies exploitation for the digitalization of the disassembly processes. The first application result is related to the monitoring and optimization of energy performance, while the second regards the integration between the MES software and the facility, closing the information flow between the physical and digital parts of the system.

2.1. Enabling Technologies

Considering these technological tendencies, it can be argued that a knowledge gap exists in terms of how organizations can develop integrated smart and sustainable operations in view of a more general I4.0-supported CE strategy. Fortunately, the advent of I4.0 technologies provided immense opportunities for unlocking the potential of CE practices through a higher level of connectivity and efficiency [18]. The following sub-sections describe in detail all the I4.0 technologies and techniques adopted within this paper. The technologies described below have been chosen for their potential in the field of the experiment presented in this work. Moreover, they are the most suitable among those present in Industry 4.0 Lab of Politecnico di Milano, where the experiment was conducted.

2.1.1. Cyber Physical Systems

Cyber Physical Systems (CPSs) are ICTs systems [15] integrating computation, networking, and physical processes [19–21]. They represent the key object linking together all I4.0 technologies, by enabling a real improvement of goods and services. CPSs integrate a cyber space with physical processes and objects by connecting machine tools and devices as a network, thus monitoring and exchanging real-time data for decision making. They represents a new way to enable either better lifecycle management of products and services (e.g., for maintenance reasons) or to optimize remanufacturing practices or multi-agent systems for managing the extraction of natural resources [5]. This way, resources (products, material, energy) can be allocated efficiently based on intelligent cross-linked value creation modules [22]. Together with the Internet of Things (IoT) and Cloud Computing (CC), CPSs can inform users either about components and materials embedded into products or disassembly and recycling procedures [23] in order to enable a more efficient reintroduction into new product value chains.

2.1.2. Internet of Things

Internet of Things (IoT) is the digital technology that can be most easily integrated in CE practices [18,24,25]. Its role lies in collecting data from the field and then transferring that data (for example, through CPS [3]) to other I4.0 technologies (e.g., Big Data & Analytics (BDA) and CC) tools that are able to analyze them and extrapolate information for better decision-making at either the product or process level [18,26–28]. Under this perspective, IoT may intrinsically increase resource efficiency, extend product lifespan, and close the loop [24]. By collecting and analyzing product-related data through IoT, they can be redesigned, maintained, upgraded, disassembled, or recycled more easily [25,29]. In addition, IoT also provides process-related data by optimizing remanufacturing and recycling practices and enabling better production planning and control [24,28]. For these reasons, IoT adoption in CE practices can enable (i) new waste management strategies, (ii) improvement of the processes circularity level, and (iii) creation of smart industrial environments or dynamic feedback control loops [5,30,31].

2.1.3. Simulation

Within the I4.0 paradigm, simulation is used to replicate real world behaviours in virtual environments. This way, physical and virtual dimensions coexist and are synchronized in real-time [19]. However, synchronization requires full data models of alternative scenarios to be simulated [32–34]. This issue led to the concept of Digital Twin (DT), or a virtual representation of physical objects coping their behaviour through a real-time data acquisition from the field [16,35]. A DT not only allows a prognostic assessment at design stage (static perspective), but also a real-time synchronization and optimization of the virtual object (dynamic perspective) [36]. From a CE perspective, simulation is logically related to either better management of complex supply chains (e.g., closed-loop chains through disassembly process optimization within EoL phase) or the remanufacturing of complex products [5]. Even if DT could be easily adaptable to CE practices, only a few papers have dealt with this topic. For example, Wang et al. [37] described the idea of adopting a DT in different CE practices, either for the virtual optimization of disassembly (e.g., monitoring materials and energy consumptions) or recycling and remanufacturing processes (e.g., storing knowledge about components and materials embedded into products). Another example of simulation is based on the concept of Augmented Reality (AR) and Virtual Reality (VR). Considering what was reported by the authors of reference [29], AR/VR could represent a valuable element for improving disassembly and remanufacturing processes.

2.1.4. Autonomous Robots

The last I4.0 solution evaluated in this literature review is represented by autonomous robots. For many decades, robots have been used in manufacturing processes for complex assignments. However, the latest developments in robotics have made them even more autonomous, flexible, and cooperative. The disassembly of products is a key process in the treatment of WEEE. When performed efficiently, it enables the maximization of resources re-usage and a minimization of pollution. Despite this, currently employed automation solutions are mainly custom-oriented and not quite suited to cope with the dynamic nature of the disassembly environment resulting from the wide variety of products to be disassembled as well as their general shape at their disposal (e.g., scratches and fractions) [38]. Within the I4.0 paradigm, collaborative robots (co-bots) can safely interact with humans and learn from them. This flexibility makes them suitable for supporting current CE practices, especially during disassembly and remanufacturing operations [39].

2.1.5. Generic Application Cases: I4.0 Technologies Supporting CE Practices

The literature reports some examples of generic application cases linking I4.0 technologies with current CE practices, especially for remanufacturing, maintenance, and disassembly (ordered by number of works). Considering remanufacturing and disassembly processes, some examples are available. Yang et al. [18] presented two case studies showing how I4.0 technologies can increase performance in remanufacturing processes. A smart remanufacturing cell (focused on repairing activities) of Computer Numerical Control (CNC) machine tools has been simulated by gathering data from the field through smart sensors. A CPS was thus developed for the real-time monitoring of CNC machines and the definition of maintenance activities. French et al. [40] described the use of robots, BDA, and IoT for improving remanufacturing performances in the aerospace industry. By incorporating machine vision systems for characterization, inspection, and fault detection, alongside advanced real-time sensor data acquisition for monitoring and evaluating the welding process, manual remanufacturing can become a smart process.

Other experts focus more on the usage phase of products, especially on maintenance activities. Barbosa et al. [41] show how CPSs can be integrated into products via two industrial cases (trains and washing machines manufacturing), covering production, use, and maintenance lifecycle phases. In the first case, CPSs were used for monitoring, gathering data from different lifecycle stages and improve the capitalized knowledge on products. In the second case, CPSs were adopted to improve both production efficiency and product quality through constant monitoring and optimization of the production processes. Lee et al. [19] described the exploitation of CPSs and simulation tools for developing a DT for CNC machines by monitoring product quality and system reliability in real-time, improving the capitalized knowledge of the whole system, and increasing the resiliency of manufacturing equipment. Hehenberger et al. [42] presented a case study where CPS and IoT have been integrated in wind turbines for condition monitoring reasons. Here, a Genetic Algorithm (GA) was exploited to reduce the number of variables to be managed by the CPS. Finally, Schroeder et al. [43] exploited CPSs and simulation (under the form of a DT) for monitoring the health level of a valving system. Subsequently, Schroeder et al. [44] upgraded the original model by exploiting AR and web services for supervising an oil tank.

2.1.6. Featured Application Cases: I4.0 Technologies Supporting WEEE Management Practices

WEEE and CE are emerging topics attracting great interest in the fields of environmental science and engineering [45,46]. In order to strengthen the value of the current work, application cases focused on the same sector have been grouped in this sub-section. Here, the experts focus on remanufacturing and disassembly. Goodall et al. [47] developed a discrete-event simulation approach to predict material flow behavior within remanufacturing operations, by utilizing data coming from digital manufacturing systems for updating and automatically modifying the simulated model and reflect the real system state. The simulation approach has been tested in a WEEE remanufacturing facility and data have been gathered through radio-frequency identification (RFID) traceability systems. Alqahtani et al. [48] discussed an advanced remanufacturing system based on a discrete-event simulation model. Here, a smart refrigerator—with embedding sensors and network connectivity for gathering and exchanging data—was monitored in order to plan its refurbishing and repair. Subsequently, Joshi et al. [49] upgraded the original remanufacturing system by also considering the disassembly stage. RFIDs have been exploited for recovering data from obsolete laptops and, basing on that, for deciding the best EoL strategy to adopt through a multi-criteria decision-making model based on linear physical programming. Bressanelli et al. [24] explored how CPS, IoT, and BDA can improve remanufacturing performances in terms of monitoring, data gathering and process optimization of washing machines. Marconi et al. [50] presented a method for calculating the disassembly times of target components in washing and coffee machines. Data mining has been used to derive corrective factors that are useful in designing new products. Sharpe et al. [51] described the adoption of CPSs in WEEE management processes. Here, RFID tags were exploited for gathering data from the cores and subsequently sent to graphical user interfaces (GUIs) to monitor and control their refurbishment. Finally, Wang et al. [37] discussed a novel DT-based system for WEEE recovery that supported manufacturing/remanufacturing operations. DT was exploited to develop a reliable cloud-based avatar of WEEE, thus constituting a CPS.

In trying to summarize the most important topics from the literature review presented above, it is possible to say that there are clear perspectives about how I4.0 technologies can be integrated in current CE practices by contributing to strategic decision-making processes, data collection, and sharing [22,23,28]. However, there is a clear lack of real application cases (e.g., adopting simulation tools, CPSs, IoT, and robots together) supporting WEEE management practices. Attention has been voluntarily focused on WEEE and these four I4.0 technologies, given the potential benefits coming from their integration in achieving better performances during disassembly, remanufacturing, and recycling processes. The following sections will present a real application case going in this direction, where simulation (under the form of VR and DT models) and a robot interact to optimize a WEEE disassembly process. Before presenting the model conceptualization and development, the results of the literature review related to the interaction between advanced simulation tools and CE practices is reported.

2.2. *Model Conceptualization*

Among the main effects of simulation on CE practices, the literature underlines (i) support on products remanufacturing—for example, in the form of decision-support tools—and (ii) improvement of efficiency in exploiting natural resources through the calculation of eco-efficiency indexes [5,37,52,53].

According to Smith et al. [54], it is possible to identify two main categories of simulation applications in the manufacturing sector—(i) manufacturing system design simulation and (ii) manufacturing system operation simulation. These two categories are based on the same interpretation of the concept of simulation, only differing in the way they are used within a manufacturing environment. From one side, manufacturing systems design (furtherly subdivided into general system/facility design/layout and material handling design) mainly refers to long-term decisions with large impacts on costs and efficiency of manufacturing operations. From the other side, manufacturing system operation applications (furtherly subdivided in operations planning/scheduling and real-time control) refers to short-term decisions. Following this categorization, the paper presents the development of two simulation models for a disassembly process optimization (see Figure 2, below):

- A simulation model belonging to the manufacturing system design category (i.e., a virtual reality (VR)-based disassembly process configuration model);
- A simulation model belonging to the manufacturing system operation category (i.e., a digital twin (DT)-based real-time process optimization tool)

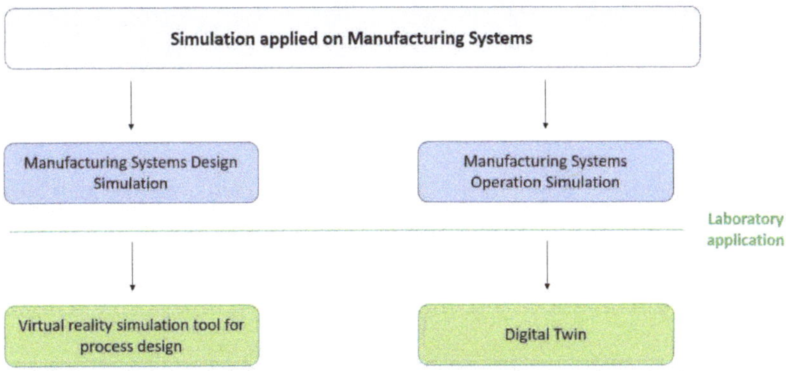

Figure 2. Simulation models schematization.

The first model focuses on facilities design, an important factor influencing the general performance of a manufacturing system. Facility layout design deals with the allocation of machines in a plant and can have a large impact on the effectiveness and efficiency of disassembly processes, increasing the ability to recover resources, and enabling their usage in new product value chains. An effective layout can reduce manufacturing costs and improve the system's performance. Discrete event simulation is an appropriate tool for evaluating the current layout, thus showing potential areas of improvement by evaluating different layout alternatives [54,55]. The second model focuses on the real-time control of a manufacturing system. This way, simulation is used as a tool for monitoring what happens in the system during the disassembly process, trying to optimize energy consumption and valuable materials recovery. Here, the simulation is exploited for easing real-time decision making. However, the use of simulation as a basis for a real-time system control is still a hard task due to response time, data collection, and aggregation issues, making it an emerging field of research within manufacturing systems [55–57].

2.3. *Models Development*

2.3.1. The Industry 4.0 Lab of Politecnico di Milano

The reference application case described in this paper was implemented at the Industry 4.0 Lab of Politecnico di Milano, pertaining to the research activities funded by the H2020 FENIX project. The Industry 4.0 Lab is one of the few pilot plants in Italy fully focused on demonstrating the benefits coming from the introduction of I4.0 technologies in manufacturing. The core of the lab is constituted by a fully automated assembly (manufacturing) line developed by Festo® Didactics(Esslingen, Germany) [58], which is able to assemble a simplified version of a smartphone. This product is made up of several components:

- Front cover;
- Back cover;
- Fuses;

- Printed circuit board (PCB).

The assembly line is made up of seven modular workstations, each of them controlled by a programmable logic controller (PLC). Here, services can be instantiated on each component and phase, both in terms of operations (by interacting with the MES) and energy consumptions (by interacting with the energy server). Different CPS and IoT infrastructures (infrared sensors, inductive sensors, RFIDs, quick response (QR) codes and barcode systems, and VR/AR system) allow users to track and trace the production flow in terms of single component or pallet.

Within the H2020 FENIX project, the Industry 4.0 Lab has been exploited for demonstrating how CPSs, IoT, AR/VR, DT, and robots can be used together for testing, managing and optimizing a WEEE disassembly process. In order to ease its description, the application case has been split into two configuration tools:

- a VR-based configuration tool supporting the disassembly process reconfiguration and implementation; and
- a DT-based configuration tool for a real-time disassembly process monitoring and control.

2.3.2. The VR-Based Configuration Tool

Trying to fill in the existing gap regarding application cases matching together I4.0 and CE, a VR-based configuration tool was developed for supporting disassembly processes reconfigurability and implementation. The process reconfigurability allows the user to improve the ability to manage a higher product variety for disassembly, thus achieving better materials recovery. The baseline idea was to exploit a virtual environment in which to simulate and optimize a disassembly process before efficiently replicating it on the real world. To this aim, CIROS® Studio 6.0 was selected as the reference software [59]. The virtual disassembly process configuration tool was implemented following five steps:

- Disassembly line modelling;
- Disassembly process design;
- Robotic disassembly program coding;
- Disassembly workplan creation within the MES software and process simulation;
- Disassembly configuration uploading on the real system.

Disassembly Line Modelling

CIROS® Studio 6.0 embeds all the libraries for simulating each workstation constituting the real line (including conveyors), plus those related to other workstations that could be added in the future. This way, when all the workstations have been modelled, it is possible to combine them and virtually replicate and test the real line. In addition, smartphone components and robot tools have been added in the model. Figure 3 shows both virtual and real lines at the Industry 4.0 Lab.

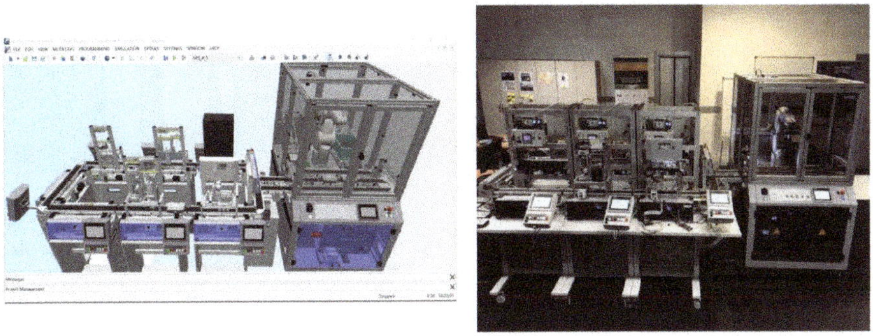

(**a**) (**b**)

Figure 3. Virtual (**a**) and real (**b**) configuration of the line.

Disassembly Process Design

Starting from the final product (constituted by front cover, PCB, fuses, and back cover)—and considering constraints related with each workstation of the line—the disassembly process has been designed as follows:

- Step 1—Manual operation: this step refers to the manual removal of back cover and fuses by an operator, by interacting with the line through a human–machine interface (HMI). Given the initial structure of the line (originally designed for assemble products), it was not possible to remove the pressed-back cover. Specifically, robot tools do not currently allow for the removal of the pressed-back cover because it is needed to fix the product on the pallet.
- Step 2—Unscrewing: This step is performed by the drilling station, through the unscrewing of the front cover from the PCB.
- Step 3—PCB removal: This step is performed by the robot station by disassembling the PCB from the front cover and positioning it in a dedicated box. This step enables valuable components recovery (i.e., PCB), making it available for further remanufacturing and recycling activities. This represents the core of the disassembly process, since the program performing this operation has been directly developed and tested in the simulation environment.
- Step 4—Final inspection: The last step is performed by the camera inspection station, which is responsible for checking if the PCB has been correctly removed from the front cover.

Robotic Disassembly Program Coding

The robot station is the most flexible one. According to specific types of production needed, it is possible to easily reconfigure it in CIROS®. Considering the disassembly process, a dedicated code has been implemented in order to control the robot working cycle through a series of moving instructions. To this aim, Melfa-Basic V [59] has been selected as the reference robot programming language. Once the code was tested and validated in the virtual environment, it was uploaded to the real robot. In order to program the robot, it was important to understand which positions, tools, and movements are needed to perform the correct removal of PCBs.

Figure 4 shows the most relevant positions that can be assumed by the robot and the tools to which the robot arm can be jointed.

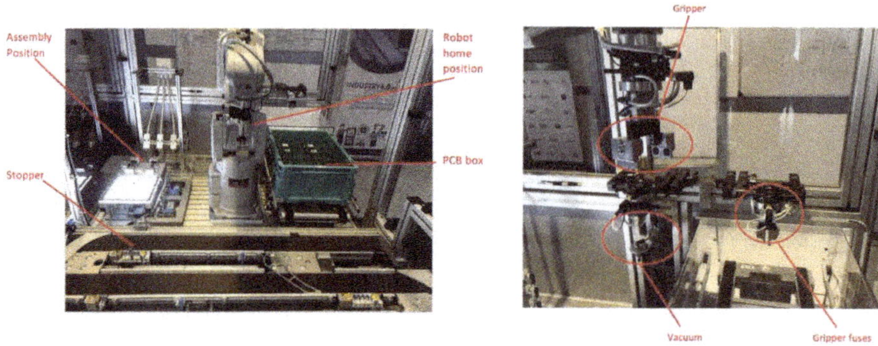

(a) (b)

Figure 4. Positions (**a**) and tools (**b**) within the robot cell.

Disassembly Workplan Creation within the MES Software and Process Simulation

Coherently with the automation pyramid presented in Section 1, within the Industry 4.0 Lab, a MES is responsible for creating, managing, controlling, and launching the workplans. The Industry 4.0 Lab MES has many functions that enable the planning field of the automation pyramid. Substantially, this MES is specially prepared with a peculiar design for I4.0 learning platforms. It features an open database, and it can be written by external programs and read via Structured Query Language (SQL) commands by external programs. Furthermore, the individual controllers can communicate with the MES via Transmission Control Protocol/Internet Protocol (TCP/IP) communication protocol. The MES can be exploited for several purposes:

(i) Define and edit work order flows and process plans;
(ii) Read orders and update status;
(iii) Write allocation of the goods carriers to the order;
(iv) Create warehouse data and material buffer;
(v) Overall equipment effectiveness (OEE) calculation;
(vi) PLC and malfunction report generation, including graphic representation.

According to these points, before starting any kind of production, it is necessary to plan and develop a new workplan using the MES software. Within the virtual environment, the MES is responsible for launching orders. This is the reason why CIROS® is provided with its own MES, which communicates with the virtual line. In order to start the simulation, the creation of a disassembly work plan and its uploading to the MES is required. The disassembly workplan created within the MES reflects the four steps described for the disassembly process design.

Once the line is virtualized and the disassembly program of the robot is coded, the disassembly process can be simulated in CIROS® by running the dedicated workplan uploaded within the MES. This way, it is possible to test and control the sequential operations constituting the workplan, both in terms of errors present in the workplan (if so, the simulation stops) and moving instructions sent to the robot (automatically optimized by the software).

Disassembly Configuration Uploading on the Real System

Once the code and process have been virtually optimized, CIROS® allows a direct connection between virtual and real contexts, by setting out the communication port. This way, the code can be transferred from virtual to real environments. At the same time, the workplan uploaded within the MES starts the production on the real system.

The adoption of a VR-based simulation tool together with advanced manufacturing systems allows us to comprehend how it is possible to support the transition toward CE practices with I4.0

technologies, reconfiguring a fully automatized manufacturing line originally designed for assembly processes. After having focused the attention on design and optimization, the following sub-section will describe in detail how to develop a DT simulation tool.

2.3.3. The DT-Based Real-Time Process Optimization Tool

The real value of the I4.0 paradigm is the new way through which information is managed across the different automation pyramid levels. To this aim, CPS can lead to this transformation without changing the whole perspective [15]. A CPS-based structure of an automated system can follow the 5C (connection, conversion, cyber, cognition, and configuration) architecture available in the literature [19], constituted by two functional elements:

- Advanced connectivity, ensuring real-time data acquisition from the physical world and information feedback from the cyber space;
- Intelligent data management, analytics, and computational capability, constructing the cyber space.

According to reference [19], the 5C levels shown in Figure 5.enable the implementation of a CPS starting from the data acquisition stage.

- Connection—data are acquired from machines and their components;
- Conversion—acquired data are transformed into useful information;
- Cyber—information is exploited for building a virtual copy of the real system;
- Cognition—the acquired knowledge is shown to expert users and compared with available information for a self-comparing capability, which improves the decision-making process;
- Configuration—the feedback layer acts on the real system as supervisory control.

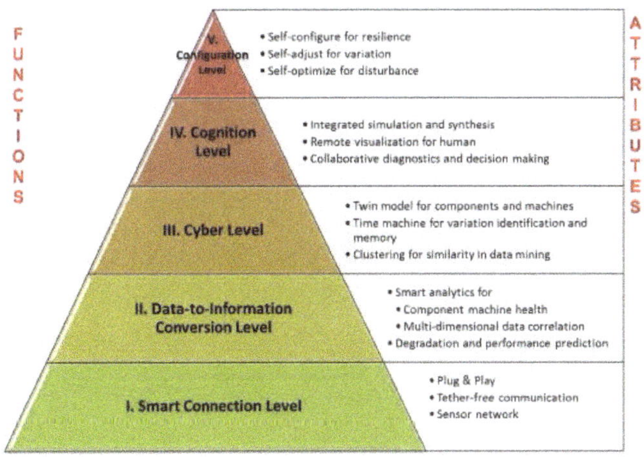

Figure 5. Cyber Physical System (CPS) 5C Architecture [19].

CPS being at base of the pyramid (field level) leads to a convergence of physical and digital worlds within the Digital Twin [15] by allowing a real-time simulation of processes, material flows, and energy consumptions [60]. The Industry 4.0 Lab DT has been developed by exploiting the OLE for Process Control (OPC) Unified Architecture (OPC-UA) communication protocol. This is a Machine-to-Machine (M2M) communication protocol compliant with the IEC 62541 standard allowing a real-time information exchange with sensors and actuators of the real system between machines and an external simulation environment [61]. OPC is a technology commonly used in PLC, Distributed Control System (DCS), and Supervisory Control and Data Acquisition (SCADA) devices as a basic communication platform for integrating, supervising and controlling data. OPC-UA uses client-server architecture with clearly assigned roles:

- Servers are applications sharing information basing on the OPC-UA information model. Each server defines an address space containing nodes of the OPC-UA model. These nodes represent physical or software objects.
- Clients are applications retrieving information from servers, by browsing and querying the information model.

This way, the OPC-UA protocol enables communication between the industrial equipment and systems for a continuous data collection and control by creating a virtual mirror of the system. This mirror is the cyber part of the physical plant through which machine data can flow, and the process simulation can be carried out. Moreover, the information flow coming (going) from (to) the field (e.g., sensors states and variables values) can be read and managed in real-time also through generic numerical computing and engineering tools, such as MATLAB® and Simulink®. Since all the modules in the Industry 4.0 Lab are equipped with PLCs representing OPC-UA nodes, it is possible to

- Create a real-time connection with workstations—by exploiting the OPC-UA Toolbox in MATLAB®—by accessing to live and historical data directly from MATLAB® and Simulink®;
- Read, write and log in OPC-UA directly from PLCs.
- In general terms, through the Industry 4.0 Lab DT it is possible to
- Identify possible machine states (e.g., errors, failures and downtimes). It is possible to consider CPS as a way to enable either better lifecycle management of products or the development of new services, especially for maintenance reasons [62];
- Identify sensors and actuators states/values (e.g., presence of products, temperature or air consumption), allowing a better monitoring of resource usage within disassembly process (e.g., energy consumption, scrap rates and waste management);
- Monitor and control operations performances;
- Real-time analysis of signals;
- Define maintenance plans of machines;
- Store all the gathered data;
- Execute data analytics on operational and energy parameters.

As an example, in Table 1, the path identification of a specific node (sensor xBG1) of the Magazine Front Station (IP address: 10.48.134.20) through UA Expert is reported. This sensor is used to know if the carrier is in a working position within the station.

Table 1. Command steps to find and connect an OLE for Process Control Unified Architecture (OPC-UA) variable in MATLAB®.

Command Step	Practical Step
serverList = opcuaserverinfo ('10.48.134.20:4840')	Connect to the server with the right IP address data
uaClient = opcua(serverList)	Creation of the client
connect(uaClient)	Connect the created client to the server

f = getNamespace(uaClient)
b = findNodeByName(f,'plcMagazineFront','once');
k = findNodeByName(b, 'Inputs','-once');
I = findNodeByName(k, 'xBG1','-once');
	Using the address founded in UA Expert, the user knows the sequence of node to reach the right variable

Once the connection for the variable real-time reading is done, the next step is to try to extract these values using the MATLAB® function in Simulink®. To do this, Level-2 MATLAB® S-functions are used. This kind of function allows us to create custom blocks with multiple input and output ports capable of handling any type of signal produced by a Simulink® model. The MATLAB® function comprises a set of call-back methods that the Simulink® model invokes when updating or simulating the model. The implementation of this call-back method, in turn, determines the blocks attributes (e.g., ports, parameters and states) and behavior (e.g., the block outputs as function of time and the block inputs, states and parameters). In this specific case three types of call-back methods are used, which are the ones that allow the extraction of the values of the sensors and actuators present on the line and the creation of the blocks related to this sensor and actuators in the Simulink® environment. These blocks compose the DT model of the line. The three main parts used in the Level-2 MATLAB® S-functions are

(i) Setup—in this part, the number of inputs and outputs of the function, their datatype, complexity, and dimensions are defined. Since the model crated is a Discrete Event Simulation, this method includes also the specification of the sample time required for the lecture of sensors values.
(ii) Start—this part performs the initialization activities that the S-function requires, such as allocating memory and setting up user data. This method, as reported in Table 1, allows the connection to the server of interest only at the start of the simulation in Simulink®. Then, after having properly defined the address of each node that it is required to extract from the server, this step allows Simulink® to relate to the specific nodes in real-time.
(iii) Outputs—this part calculates the S-function's outputs at the current time step and store the results in the run-time object's OutputPort(n).Data property.

The Level-2 MATLAB® S-functions that has been used to read the Carrier ID is reported in Figure 6. Using this function in Simulink®, it is possible to monitor in real-time the state of these sensors and actuators in this virtual environment. Hence, in order to create the DT of the production line, it is possible to combine the sensors and actuators values using simple MATLAB® functions to reproduce, for example, the machine states (idle, working, energy saving, etc.) or to evaluate the energy consumption of each station.

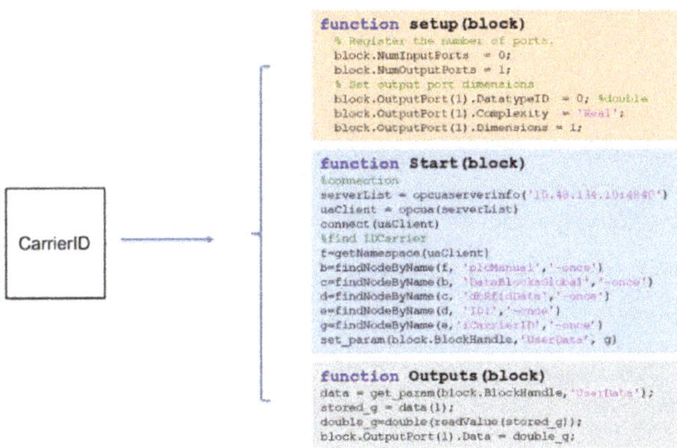

Figure 6. Level 2 MATLAB® S-Function code to read the Carrier ID value from the server.

The sequence of activities needed to do that is the same for all stations and can be summarized as follows:

1. Identification of the possible machine states;
2. Identification of sensors and actuators useful in order to reproduce the machine states identified in the previous step and their combination for the model;
3. Analysis of the signal in real-time;
4. Storage of the data.

Table 2 summarized the five different states that have been identified with the correspondent identification number.

Table 2. Machine stat.

Machine State	Description	Output
Idle	The conveyor is moving but no operation is performed. The machine is waiting for a piece to be processed.	1
Working	The machine is performing an operation.	2
Error	For each of the station of the line, a specific kind of fault have been identified. The machine is blocked due to abnormal behavior and shows an error message in the Human-Machine Interface (HMI). Only when the fault is fixed and the operator respond to the error message on the HMI, the working resumes.	3
Emergency button	State of the machine that can be classified as a fault state, in which the normal behavior of the machine is stopped due to the fact that the operator has triggered the emergency button.	4
Energy-saving mode	The machine is on, but the belt is not moving to save energy when there is no piece to work immediately.	5

The sensors belonging to the belt system of the stations used for the identification of the machines states are described in table below (see Table 3).

Table 3. Belt system sensors.

Sensor	Description	Values
xQA_A1	Sensor used to know if the belt is moving or not	1 if the belt is moving
xBG1	Sensor used to know if the carrier is in the working position of the station	1 when the carrier is ready to be processed
xBG5	Entrance sensor of the machine's belt	1 when carrier moves over it
xBG6	Exit sensor of the machine's belt	1 when carrier moves over it
xMB1	Stopper sensor, that releases the carrier from working position	1 when activated

Then, MATLAB® functions have been implemented in order to combine these sensors and reproduce a specific machine state. The example of the emergency button state with the combination of its related sensors, is described in Table 4. The emergency button can be used by the operator to immediately stop the station when it is needed (see Table 5).

Table 4. Emergency button sensors.

Sensor	Description
xPF1	It is set to 1 until the operator checks the error on the HMI
xPF3	When is set to 1, the green light of the 'Start' is turned on to show that the operator must press it to resume the work
xSF5	Set to 1 when the emergency button is released

Table 5. Actions definitions of emergency button triggering.

xSF5	xPF1	xPF3	Action	Em.Button
0	0	0/1	Button triggered	1
1	0	0/1	Button released	1
1	0/1	1	Wait for start	0
1	1	0	Start triggered	0

The sensors and actuators identified are common to all the stations. This implies that the schematization of the idle, working, and emergency Button states is the same for all the machines. What differs from one station to another is the definition of the error state, since each of the stations of the line performs a specific operation on the product. This means that different failure modes are linked.

Once all these steps have been done for each of the seven stations of the line, the combination of all the models allows us to create the final DT of the line exploiting the Simulink® SimEvent® blocks. In this way, it is possible to have a graphical representation of the assembly-disassembly line. It is also possible to see, for each station the number of worked pieces, if there is any piece working and the number of pieces attending to be worked, as reported. Moreover, the DT represents a useful tool that allows for the exploitation of a database for post-processing of data to compute KPIs needed to make decisions.

3. Results

3.1. *Energy Consumption Optimization*

3.1.1. Energy Data Acquisition

The model was developed in a practice environment with the aim of obtaining the final consolidated Waste from Electrical and Electronic Equipment (WEEE) disassembly process optimization. Among the waste sources produced by human activity, electronic waste (e-waste) is one of the most important, in terms of both volume and growth [45]. This was the first research field where the simulation models were tested regarding their energy efficiency (understood as process energy consumption optimization through digital solution). One of the problematic issues that the industrial sector faces as the largest consumer of electricity is CO_2 production and its related environmental impacts. For this reason, the energy sustainability of disassembly processes helps to justify their implementation instead of different solutions within the product's EoL phase (e.g., incinerator or landfill). However, limited resources and high costs lead energy production not to grow at same ratio, resulting in a demand-supply mismatch. Considering this gap, energy suppliers and consumer are working to keep demand at a secure level. As an energy consumer, the industrial sector can use the available energy more efficiently.

Since each of the stations of the Industry 4.0 Lab is provided with two PLCs (one responsible to manage the process and one responsible for monitoring energy parameters), it is possible to connect the DT to the energy server to gather energy consumption data from each station. The energy server connections are possible through the Level-2 MATLAB® S-function. From this server three data are extracted—the instantaneous power consumed by the station (rActivePower), the pneumatic system pressure of the station (rPressure), and the air flow rate during the working condition (rFlow).

These variables have been identified to monitor and control the energy consumption and the working condition of the line. At this point, in order to match the machine states with the respective energy consumption, we created an accumulator function. This function allows us to associate the respective energy consumption to each one of the five machine states identified in the model. The function takes as input the machine state, the instantaneous power consumed by the energy box and the sample frequency of the simulation. It gives as outputs

- The time spent by the machine in each state t_i [s];
- The mean value of the power consumed in each state during the simulation P_i [W];
- The energy consumption in each machine state (Idle, Working, Fault, and Energy Saving) during the simulation $E_i = P_i \times t_i$.

3.1.2. Energy Data Analysis

The simulation can improve efficiency when exploiting resources—for example, through the calculation of eco-efficiency indexes. In this way, the DT allows for the real-time interaction with the system in order to monitor and control the line. Basically, it uses data extracted directly from the shop-floor, enabling their collection. Then, data analysis can be applied to these data, giving benefit to the decision-making process. An energy management application exploiting the two simulation tools presented in this paper has been created by developing a proper energy consumption indicator whose value has been elaborate through the DT disassembly simulation runs. To achieve these objectives, an energy-based Overall Equipment Effectiveness (OEE) was developed and tested. The DT simulation and energy-based OEE need a proper graphical user interface to be more user friendly and support easier decision making. The energy Graphical User Interface (e-GUI) development allowed for the real-time monitoring of the stations, enabling the immediate identification of what happens in the production line. Finally, these energy tools have been applied to different production processes in order to evaluate their results and differences.

From the literature, it has emerged that many KPIs are continuously calculated in order to evaluate production system performance. In particular, reference [63] underlines that the OEE is a widely used performance indicator in manufacturing industries. As reported in their work, the increasing industrialization provides means to automatically acquire manufacturing data and analyze them. Therefore, companies are investing in MES where the OEE measurement is a central part, as happens also with the MES of Industry 4.0 Lab. The OEE is a KPI developed to investigate the performance of the production system considering the speed, quality, and breakdown of the systems. It is a time-based approach aiming to measure the direct time related to the production pieces with respect to the total production time.

Starting from the definition of OEE, an energy-based OEE (e-OEE) applied to the line, in order to evaluate its energetic performance, has been introduced. The definition of the e-OEE derives from the definition of the classic OEE, with an effort in translating the time-based indexes presented before into energy-based indexes. In order to introduce this concept, a distinction between the type of energy consumed in the line is necessary. The following two types of energy have been identified:

- Active energy—this is the energy from which, in theory, is possible to extract added value for the final product (both for assembly and disassembly processes); and
- Passive energy—this is the energy wasted by the line, i.e., it does not produce any added value to the final product.

Active energy includes types of energy consumption related to three machine states—Idle, Working, and Failure energy consumption. During the daily working cycle, the overall energy consumption of the stations in the Industry 4.0 Lab is equal to the sum of different contributes, both active and passive, as it is possible to see from Figure 7.

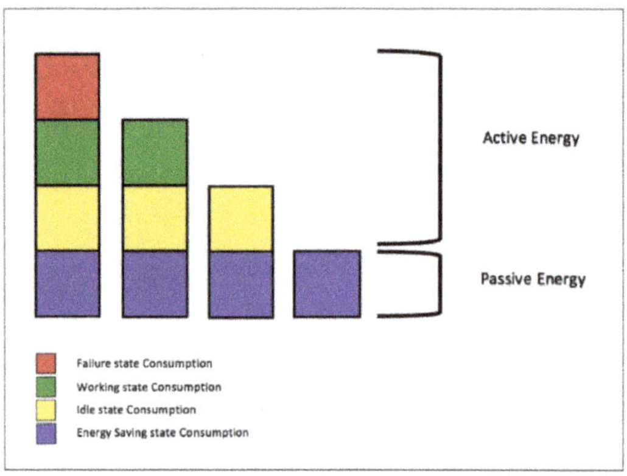

Figure 7. Graphical representation of energies type.

The traditional time-based OEE is composed of three terms—availability, performance, and quality. At the basis of this KPI there are three important time concepts—planned production time, run time, and working time. From an energetic perspective, these concepts are substituted with

- Total energy consumption—this is equal to the overall energy consumed by the line (or a machine if applied to a single station). It is the sum of all the four components shown in Figure 7.
- Operative energy consumption—this is equal to the Total energy consumption minus the passive energy. in other words, it is the sum of the active energy;
- Working energy consumption—this is the sum of the energy consumption in the working state (or the working consumption of the single machine).

It is also possible to define the different coefficients that are used to calculate the e-OEE:

- e-Availability—under the energetic perspective, the availability evaluates how much of the total energy consumption is used to perform active operation on the processed piece. The availability is equal to

$$\text{e-Availability} = (\text{Operative Energy Consumption})/(\text{Total Energy Consumption}) \tag{1}$$

- e-Performance—from an energetic perspective, the performance evaluates how much of the active power is effectively used to perform operations on the processed product. The performance is equal to

$$\text{e-Performance} = (\text{Working Energy Consumption})/(\text{Operative Energy Consumption}) \tag{2}$$

- Quality—defined in the same way as for the time-based perspective so as the ratio between accepted product over the number of products produced:

$$\text{Quality} = (\text{Accepted products})/(\text{N. of produced/disassembled products}) \tag{3}$$

The e-OEE indicator is calculated as

$$\text{e-OEE} = \text{e-Availability} \times \text{e-Performance} \times \text{Quality} \tag{4}$$

e-OEE is defined as the ratio between the energy consumed for producing goods of approved quality and the overall energy consumption of the line. As previously discussed, the e-OEE can be applied both to the whole line or to a single station according to the analysis. In fact, if applied to the whole line, this KPI can monitor overall energy consumption, giving an overview on how much of the energy consumed in each time period is effectively used for the production and not wasted. Also, the calculation of the e-OEE for different processes gives us the opportunity to understand which are the most performing under an energy-based approach, giving the possibility to understand which are the critical ones that require some kind of improvement for their optimization.

On the other hand, the e-OEE is thought also to be applied to each station in order to make a comparison between them. In fact, fixing the monitoring time, it results in the e-OEE being normalized to each station since all the coefficients presented in the formula are only function of the station in which it is applied. In this way, it is possible to evaluate which is the critical station from an energetic point of view. Once it has been identified, some improvements could be identified in order to optimize its energetic behavior.

3.1.3. Energy Data Interface

In order to link together what has been discussed regarding the energy monitoring and management application, a Graphical User Interface has been developed using the MATLAB® GUI. The GUI is connected to the DT of the line, and it can give the user an overview of the most relevant data for the process control. This links together the main scope of the two simulation tools introduced because, once the disassembly process has been updated on the real line, the GUI is able to show and extract from the DT the data related to this type of configuration in a user-friendly way. It also calculates the e-OEE for both assembly and disassembly processes, giving the possibility to evaluate which is the most performing from an energetic point of view.

The developed GUI contains

- Start and Stop buttons—by clicking these two buttons, it is possible to start and to stop the simulation with the DT while data are extracted;
- Analyze button—when the simulation is stopped, it is possible to calculate the e-OEE;
- Energy button—with this button, it is possible to gain access to a graphical interface that plots the power absorbed by each station as function of the time;
- Machine values—for each machine, it shows the state, the CarrierID on which the piece is processed, the number of the process (given from the MES), the actual power consumption, and all the energy consumption discussed before. Also. the result of the camera inspection is available;
- Database generator—this button is available for each station and allows for the generation of the excel file with data gathered.

Figure 8 shows how the GUI appears. It is a user-friendly interface where each section is referred to a machine of the line. The main advantages of the GUI are

1. The data are clearer, more readable, and do not require the user to be able to read the code that lead to the creation of the DT;
2. It is possible to keep the stations under control in real-time and identify immediately what is happening in the production line;
3. It is possible to have a direct evaluation of the energetic performance of the line.

Together with the GUI, an interface that monitors the energy consumption of the line in real-time has been also developed. It is possible to plot this energy monitoring interface using the energy button of the GUI. Basically, it gives the same information of the previous interface, but it allows the user to have a graphical plot of the energy consumption as function of the time, if required. This interface is a tool linked to the DT since it is related to the data extracted from it. It is linked to the actual energy consumption of each station.

3.2. Test of the Disassembly Process

The process monitoring tool described above has been tested through different production plans within the Industry 4.0 Lab. The validation activity was carried out through different test, regarding both assembly and disassembly processes. In order to evaluate all the possible scenarios, a simulation with an error state for some stations has also been included. Here, the disassembly process is considered, exploiting in this way both the simulation tools presented in this paper. Starting from a generic production plans composed of three products already assembled, the disassembly process was performed to test the system reconfigurability. The main difference between the assembly and disassembly processes implemented on the line is that, in the second scenario, not all the stations are exploited. For this reason, it is expected that the e-OEE will be lower if compared to the one of the first configurations, since three station are not used in the production cycle of the processed pieces. Then, the e-OEE of this station will be equal to 0. Figure 8 shows the results obtained at the end of the simulation through the GUI.

As expected, the e-OEE of the magazine front cover, magazine back cover, and press stations is equal to 0 since these stations do not perform any kind of operations, and the energy consumed by these stations is wasted. Overall, the disassembly process is more energy consuming compared to assembly, resulting in a lower value of e-OEE. This is justified by the fact that the line has been designed to perform the assembly process, and so the disassembly process it is not optimized from an energetic point of view.

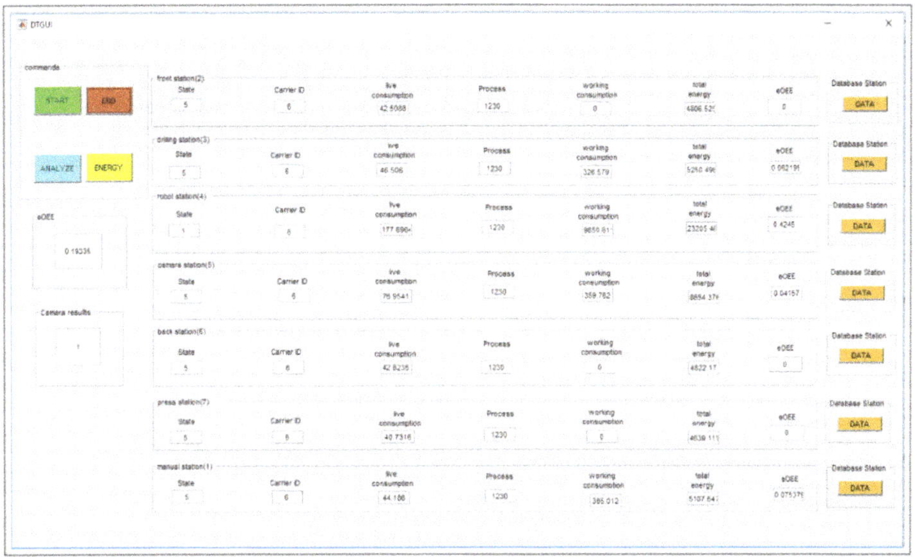

Figure 8. Disassembly process graphical user interface (GUI).

Since disassembly is an important part of remanufacturing systems for reuse and recycling purposes, automation and digitalization have a growing number of applications in the area of WEEE. For this reason, reconfigurability of disassembly systems represents an important paradigm of automated disassembly system that uses reconfigurable manufacturing technology for fast adaptation to changes in the quantity and mix of products to disassemble [64]. However, there are still many barriers in reverse production process adoption due to the complexity of the most of manufacturing systems and to the high number of product and components to be treated. As pointed out in reference [65], system reconfigurability can be classified in terms of the levels where the reconfigurable actions are taken—(i) at lower levels is mainly achieved by changing hardware resources and (ii) at the higher levels when is mainly achieved by changing software resources and/or by choosing alternatives methods or organization structures by flexible people. As demonstrated by the experiments, the changes at lower levels can imply a process performance decrease, representing a technical barrier to CE adoption at the factory level.

3.3. MES Integration

In the literature, few studies focus on either disassembly or reuse, apart from a few papers that are related to I4.0 technologies in general as good support for disassembly [5]. Among these, digital technologies are exploited for disassembly process optimization and disassembly sequence planning. Coherently with this, an application that aims to integrate the MES software with the DT in order to close the information flow between the simulation tool and the shop-floor has been created. This integration introduces bi-lateral communication, enabling the possibility to have control capability from the digital side to the physical side of an asset. In this way, not only is it possible to monitor real-time the process and gather the data in order extrapolate information, but they can also act autonomously on the process. This can enrich the simulation models with decision-making ability related to shop-floor level events in the production facility.

First, a way to send commands to the MES and get information by it was performed manually in MATLAB®. Second, the focus switched on developing the same functions on Simulink®. Using this tool, a way to automatically communicate with the MES from the DT was conceived. The procedure of sending information to the MES via MATLAB® is one of the easiest and the most immediate to implement, since the only steps to follow are first, create a TCP/IP object to connect to the MES server; and second, send the relative string to request the performing of a specific task to the MES.

As in the MATLAB® library, the use of the TCP/IP-embedded function was needed [66]. The use of strings can be done for any communication using the standards on the library available.

The operation to get the information that the PLC sends back is more delicate and needs more steps. The basic flow to send information to the MES server, and so to the PLC, is exactly the same as the one reported in Table 6.

Table 6. Basic steps to send commands to the Programmable Logic Control (PLC) via Transmission Control Protocol/Internet Protocol TCP/IP communication protocol in MATLAB®.

Step	Code	Description
1	t = tcpip ("RemoteHost", Remote Port);	Creation of TCP/IP object, connected to a remote host (IP address of the MES server) with a remote port
2	fopen (t);	Connect the TCP/IP object to the host
3	fprintf (t,sprint(" ... "));	Write in the TCP/IP object (t) the formulation of the string by creating a string variable (sprintf)

The difference lies in the fact that the third step should contemplate a string capable to "get" information. A block-based sequence of the process to get information is given in Figure 9. If the "send" type just transmits control data to the PLC, the "get" kind can interrogate the PLC about some specific information, storing it in a certain object for it to be retrieved by the user in a second moment. So, by applying the procedure in Table 5 with the proper string, the TCP/IP object will be created and stored on the MATLAB® workspace.

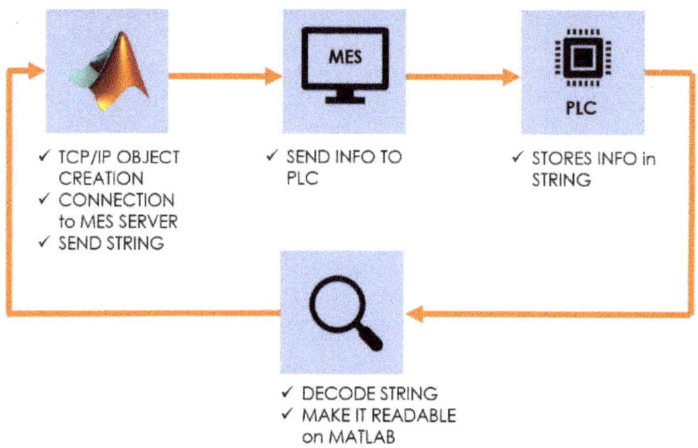

Figure 9. Operations performed by the "get" information model.

Moreover, the creation of a connection through which the DT can communicate with its physical counterpart in both directions is proposed with the definition of an optimization framework. The optimization aims for disassembly processes that can be reached using the VR-based simulation model, and the DT that is tightly integrated to its physical counterpart. This re-scheduling and disassembly framework proposes an integration of physical and digital sides with the objective to optimize the production process in terms of reactive disassembly in cases in which compliance with respect to certain production standards is not respected. Even in this case, the modelling of a tailored simulation-based DT is proposed to deal with the reactive scheduling of disassembly processes. The purpose of this application framework is to practically demonstrate the integration of I4.0 technologies for the disassembly process optimization and digitalization in order to improve the rates of waste generation and product components restoration.

In this case, the framework in Figure 10 has a simpler way of working:

- The order, already assembled, arrives at the station in charge of checking compliance. If conformity is verified, the process continues, otherwise it does not.
- When compliance is not verified, the DT aborts the current work plan and acts by reactively scheduling a disassembly plan on the same piece.
- For this framework, optimization lies in the autonomous reactive scheduling of a disassembly plan, whether certain compliance conditions are not met.
- An overall scrap reduction with the possibility of materials recovery.

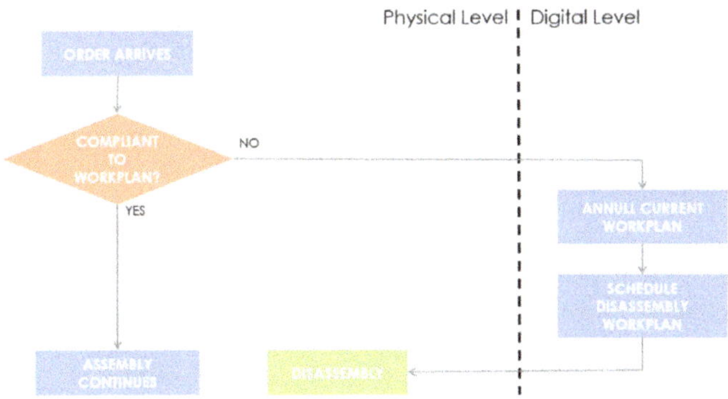

Figure 10. Framework of integrated management of disassembly with the simulation tool.

The function to be embedded in the DT is one that processes the values coming from the other function of the DT and identifies the conditions in which the reactive scheduling of a disassembly process is necessary. In fact, in order to avoid the scrapping of a component that is not compliant with some standards, a disassembly work plan can be reactively scheduled. This greatly reduces the risk of discarding non-compliant productions exploiting the reactive reconfigurability of the system.

Within the Industry 4.0 Lab, this kind of activity can be performed by properly modelling the DT tool based on the workstation whose task is to check compliance with quality standards—the camera inspection station. This workstation is placed right after the Robot Assembly cell and checks whether the assembly work done so far is compliant with respect to the work plan requirements. The carrier passes through the workstation, where a camera, together with light beam, checks the conformity. The workstation does not stop the working process if these standards are not satisfied, but it is able to detect it using specific embedded sensors values. The final aim of this station, as it is meant in the framework application, is to be able to reactively schedule a disassembly order that is going to be performed by the robot assembly. The latter, in fact, can be easily configured to perform several activities, both of assembly and of disassembly nature, as previously described.

The steps to effectively run this peculiar simulation model are hereby described:

- A work order that plans the assembly of a front cover with a PCB and one or more fuses is planned and launched.
- The Simulink® MATLAB® function checks at every sampled instant if the xResult variable (sensor that detects if the assembly process done so far is compliant to the work plan; this Boolean variable is true if there is compliance, whilst it is false if not) changes its value from true to false.
- When the order approaches the camera inspection workstation and this condition is verified, the xResult becomes false. This means that the work order that is being assembled is not compliant with the workplan expectations. The case analyzed is relative to the work plan that assembles, inside the covers of the prototypical phone, a PCB and one or more fuses. The xResult changing

its value to false indicates the lack of fuses on the assembled component, detecting the presence of only the front cover and PCB on the pallet and that at least a fuse is missing from the assembled product. Thus, the simulation code aborts the order that just passed by the camera inspection station thanks to a specific string command sent to the MES.

- As soon as this task is done, a further order with the disassembly work plan is immediately rescheduled on the same pallet, where the front cover with the assembled PCB lies. This work plan has been created and optimized through the first simulation tool described in previous sections.

This kind of work plan is automatically planned by the DT in order to avoid scrapping of material due to the found quality inconsistencies. At this point the whole operation can be considered done and the output changes value. Based on this, thanks to a feedback loop to the Level-2 MATLAB® S-Function, the xResult value is set back to true; otherwise, it would remain false.

The proposed DT, thanks to its high integration level with respect to its physical part given by the MES integration, can be exploited for both the EoL disassembly process and for the scheduling of a new work orders as a reaction to peculiar shop-floor situations. The main objective and benefit that has been proven is the ability of the proposed DT to reactively schedule a disassembly work plan based on certain conditions that can be detected by the embedded sensor system. This outcome is a further validation of the possibility to reconfigure the system and react to shop-floor events that do not block production flow. In fact, the production keeps running, but the lack of compliance with the assembly standards is automatically identified by the DT, and the disassembly work plan is automatically scheduled. According to a broader perspective, this kind of activity allows the possibility to reduce scraps in the facility in which this application is performed. In fact, the pieces that are not compliant with certain standards are usually scrapped, causing potential money loss and inefficiencies for the company. With the use of a DT that is able to perform the activity of disassembly reconfiguration and reactive disassembly, a more sustainable approach can be applied to the manufacturing environment. Accordingly, the materials are not scrapped, but they can be recovered and later re-used according to the application of a CE policy.

4. Discussion

The aim of the FENIX project was to demonstrate how the adoption of Circular Economy (CE) principles can enable more sustainable supply chains by increasing the quality, market value, and alternative exploitation of secondary materials. In parallel, a long-lasting European leadership in innovative manufacturing plants engineering will be enabled. Among the FENIX pilots, POLIMI's Industry 4.0 Lab is dedicated to the disassembly of Waste from Electrical and Electronic Equipment (WEEE). This demonstrative, lab-scaled manufacturing process must be adequately reconfigured for managing the selected kind of obsolete products constituting the source of materials to be recovered during FENIX.

Considering the work presented in this paper and developed within the FENIX context, both a VR-based simulation tool and a DT-based simulation tool for assembly and disassembly processes at POLIMI's Industry 4.0 Lab have been tested and optimized, achieving the following summarized results:

1. Reconfiguration of the line (originally designed to perform an assembly process) in order to execute EoL disassembly processes, through virtual design, simulation, and optimization with the CIROS® software and its uploading on the real system. System reconfigurability at lower levels has been mainly achieved by changing hardware resources (i.e., change of robot tools for disassembly activities), while at the higher levels, it has been mainly achieved by changing software resources (i.e., robot program coding).
2. Creation of a DT of the line, where the data acquired from the field and analyzed in real-time are used to simulate the behavior of the system and allows to evaluate in real-time the energetic performance of the line. This tool allowed possibility for exploiting the IoT for the digitalization

of CE practices, by implementing smart disassembly process and dynamic feedback control loops [31].

3. Introduction of an energy-based KPI (e-OEE) able to evaluate the energetic performance of the system. This indicator has been introduced in the DT, which is able to extract all the values for real-time energy consumption using an accumulator function. At the end, thanks to the GUI, it is possible to have a clearer and readable way to find useful information for energy management. In this case, CPS and data analytics on energy consumption have been exploited for improving disassembly process performances.
4. Integration of the MES to the DT by using a communication protocol, which is able to give commands to the MES from external sources. With this integration, the monitoring DT became a bi-lateral communication-based DT.
5. Real validation of application models. The disassembly framework concerns the ability to react to a lack of conformity with respect to work orders. When this predicament occurs, the DT is modelled to abort the non-compliant order and re-schedule a disassembly order to avoid scraps.

With the DT, data can be used for different purposes (e.g., applications, analysis, etc.). The OPC-UA communication protocols allows the user to open a gateway to the available data, which is exactly the concept of IoT integration described by the I4.0 paradigm. As presented, the DT is a flexible tool that can be applied both to assembly and disassembly processes without the need of any kind of changes. In this way, the DT allows the evaluation of the behavior of a real system in real-time, enabling the collection of data that can be then used for decision-making process. Through the introduction of an energy-based KPI, and thanks to the exchange of information with the real system in real-time, the platform is able give an overview of the energetic performance of the line in a user-friendly way. The tests reported show how all the data available in the GUI are acquired in order to evaluate the energy consumption of each station of the line in real-time. This is applied to both assembly and disassembly processes with the aim of evaluating their energetic performance.

5. Conclusions

Results coming from the literature review show that, even if the intersections between I4.0 technologies and CE have been assessed by describing the valuable benefits achievable (e.g., optimizing forward and reverse material flows), a real demonstration of these benefits is rarely presented by the experts, especially in the WEEE management field. Furthermore, even if IoT and CPS are described as the most integrated I4.0 technologies able to support the transition toward CE, none of the experts adopted them together with AR/VR and DT simulation tools and robots. The intent of this paper is therefore to present an application case exploiting all these I4.0 technologies together for managing and optimizing a WEEE disassembly process.

Thanks to a new integrated data management along the automation pyramid and thanks to the industrial automation improvements introduced by the fourth industrial revolution, this work proposes an introduction to the following main benefits that I4.0 allows to reach for boosting CE:

- Digitalization of the CE, considering I4.0 technologies as a set of opportunities supporting enterprises in increasing their circular degree through the digital optimization of disassembly processes, increasing their capacity to recover valuable components, and improving materials restoration.
- Process effectiveness, whose goal is not to minimize the flow of materials from the BoL to the EoL but to generate a cyclic metabolism, allowing the materials to maintain their original state, thus being continuously used as input for production systems. This is implemented in this work with the exploitation of VR simulation software applied to advanced manufacturing system for the implementation of disassembly processes.
- CE-related aspects (e.g., resource efficiency and lifecycle management), where I4.0 technologies are enablers of innovative ways for monitoring and optimizing resources performances. The aim is to

minimize volume and consumption of both energy and material resources. This is implemented in this work by energy data collection and KPI systems creation for decision making process.

The exploitation of these tools and techniques is made possible thanks to the introduction of CPS and I4.0 technologies, making the automation pyramid more flexible and representing the way to create powerful simulation models and a better resource monitoring tool to digitalize CE practice. The intention was to practically demonstrate through a laboratory experiment the incorporation of digital technologies to enable circular industrial metabolism 4.0. The main benefits presented allows for the optimized use of resources for increasing the production cycles sustainability, bringing benefits along the entire product lifecycle. They represent technological boost for the creation of more sustainable and circular business models.

Author Contributions: Conceptualization, R.R., P.R., C.S., L.F., and S.T.; methodology, R.R. and C.S.; formal analysis, R.R. and P.R.; data curation, R.R.; software, R.R.; validation, R.R.; writing—original draft preparation, R.R. and P.R.; writing—review and editing, R.R. and P.R.; visualization, R.R. and P.R.; supervision, L.F. and S.T. All authors have read and agreed to the published version of the manuscript.

Funding: This research was funded by the European Union's Horizon 2020 research and innovation program, grant number 760792. In any case, the present work cannot be considered as an official position of the supporting organization, and it reports only the point of view of the authors.

Conflicts of Interest: The authors declare no conflict of interest.

Abbreviations

AR	Augmented Reality
BDA	Big Data & Analytics
BoL	Beginning of Life
CC	Cloud Computing
CNC	Computer Numerical Control
CPS	Cyber-Physical Systems
CE	Circular Economy
DES	Discrete Event Simulation
DT	Digital Twin
e-GUI	energy-Graphical User Interface
e-KPI	energy-Key Performance Indicator
EoL	End of Life
EU	European Union
GA	Genetic Algorithm
HMI	Human Machine Interface
ICT	Information & Communication Technology
IoT	Internet of Things
ISA	International Standards of Automation
I4.0	Industry 4.0
MES	Manufacturing Execution System
M2M	Machine-to-Machine
OEE	Overall Equipment Effectiveness
OPC-UA	OLE for Process Control-Unified Architecture
KPI	Key Performance Indicator
PCB	Printed Circuit Board
PLC	Programmable Logic Controller
RFID	Radio-Frequency IDentification
SCADA	Supervisory Control And Data Acquisition
SD	System Dynamics
VR	Virtual Reality
WEEE	Waste from Electrical and Electronic Equipment

References

1. Cucchiella, F.; D'Adamo, I.; Lenny Koh, S.C.; Rosa, P. Recycling of WEEEs: An economic assessment of present and future e-waste streams. *Renew. Sustain. Energy Rev.* **2015**, *51*, 263–272. [CrossRef]
2. Rosa, P.; Terzi, S. Comparison of current practices for a combined management of printed circuit boards from different waste streams. *J. Clean. Prod.* **2016**, *137*, 300–312. [CrossRef]
3. Roblek, V.; Meško, M.; Krapež, A. A complex view of industry 4.0. *SAGE Open* **2016**, *6*, 2. [CrossRef]
4. Ávila-Gutiérrez, M.J.; Martín-Gómez, A.; Aguayo-González, F.; Córdoba-Roldán, A. Standardization framework for sustainability from circular economy 4.0. *Sustainability* **2019**, *11*, 6490. [CrossRef]
5. Rosa, P.; Sassanelli, C.; Urbinati, A.; Chiaroni, D.; Terzi, S. Assessing relations between Circular Economy and Industry 4.0: A systematic literature review. *Int. J. Prod. Res.* **2019**, *58*. [CrossRef]
6. Nobre, G.C.; Tavares, E. Scientific literature analysis on big data and internet of things applications on circular economy: A bibliometric study. *Scientometrics* **2017**, *111*, 463–492. [CrossRef]
7. Frosch, R.A. Industrial ecology: A philosophical introduction. *Proc. Natl. Acad. Sci. USA* **1992**, *89*, 800–803. [CrossRef]
8. Anderberg, S. Industrial metabolism and the linkages between economics, ethics and the environment. *Ecol. Econ.* **1998**, *24*, 311–320. [CrossRef]
9. Chertow, M.R. Industrial symbiosis: Literature and taxonomy. *Annu. Rev. Energy Environ.* **2000**, *25*, 313–337. [CrossRef]
10. Yuan, Z.; Bi, J.; Moriguchi, Y. The circular economy: A new development strategy in China. *J. Ind. Ecol.* **2006**, *10*, 4–8. [CrossRef]
11. Florin, N.; Madden, B.; Sharpe, S.; Benn, S.; Agarwal, R.; Perey, R.; Giurco, D. *Shifting Business Models for a Circular Economy: Metals Management for Multi-Product-Use Cycles*; UTS: Sydney, Australia, 2015.
12. The Ellen MacArthur Foundation. *Towards a Circular Economy: Business Rationale for an Accelerated Transition*; The Ellen MacArthur Foundation: Cowes, UK, 11 March 2015. Available online: https://www.ellenmacarthurfoundation.org/assets/downloads/TCE_Ellen-MacArthur-Foundation_9-Dec-2015.pdf (accessed on 11 March 2020).
13. MacArthur, E. Circularity Indicators: An Approach to Measuring Circularity. *Methodology* **2015**. [CrossRef]
14. ANSI/ISA. *Enterprise-Control System Integration—Part 1: Models and Terminology*; American National Standards Institute: Washington, DC, USA, 2010.
15. Pathfinder project. Pointing out research priorities leading to the next generation of simulation and forecasting technologies. 2014. Available online: https://pathfinderproject.eu/downloads/results/Pathfinder_WhitePaper1.pdf (accessed on 11 March 2020).
16. Negri, E.; Fumagalli, L.; Macchi, M. A review of the roles of digital twin in CPS-based production systems. *Procedia Manuf.* **2017**, *11*, 939–948. [CrossRef]
17. Fumagalli, L.; Pala, S.; Garetti, M.; Negri, E. *Ontology-Based Modeling of Manufacturing and Logistics Systems for a New MES Architecture*; Springer: Berlin/Heidelberg, Germany, 2014; pp. 192–200.
18. Yang, S.; Raghavendra, M.R.A.; Kaminski, J.; Pepin, H. Opportunities for industry 4.0 to support remanufacturing. *Appl. Sci.* **2018**, *8*, 7. [CrossRef]
19. Lee, J.; Bagheri, B.; Kao, H.-A. A cyber-physical systems architecture for industry 4.0-based manufacturing systems. *Manuf. Lett.* **2015**, *3*, 18–23. [CrossRef]
20. Jazdi, N. Cyber physical systems in the context of industry 4.0. In Proceedings of the 2014 IEEE International Conference on Automation, Quality and Testing, Robotics, Cluj-Napoca, Romania, 22–24 May 2014. [CrossRef]
21. Baheti, R.; Gill, H. Cyber-physical systems. *Impact Control Technol.* **2011**, *12*, 161–166.
22. Stock, T.; Seliger, G. Opportunities of sustainable manufacturing in industry 4.0. *Procedia CIRP* **2016**, *40*, 536–541. [CrossRef]
23. Jabbour, A.B.L.D.S.; Jabbour, C.J.C.; Filho, M.G.; Roubaud, D. Industry 4.0 and the circular economy: A proposed research agenda and original roadmap for sustainable operations. *Ann. Oper. Resour.* **2018**, *270*, 273–286.
24. Bressanelli, G.; Adrodegari, F.; Perona, M.; Saccani, N. Exploring how usage-focused business models enable circular economy through digital technologies. *Sustainability* **2018**, *10*, 639. [CrossRef]
25. Pagoropoulos, A.; Pigosso, D.C.A.; McAloone, T.C. The emergent role of digital technologies in the circular economy: A review. *Procedia CIRP* **2017**, *64*, 19–24. [CrossRef]

26. Davis, J.; Edgar, T.; Porter, J.; Bernaden, J.; Sarli, M. Smart manufacturing, manufacturing intelligence and demand-dynamic performance. *Comput. Chem. Eng.* **2012**, *47*, 145–156. [CrossRef]
27. Lee, J.; Kao, H.; Yang, S. Service innovation and smart analytics for Industry 4.0 and big data environment. *Procedia CIRP* **2014**, *16*, 3–8. [CrossRef]
28. De Man, J.C.; Strandhagen, J.O. An industry 4.0 research agenda for sustainable business models. *Procedia CIRP* **2017**, *63*, 721–726. [CrossRef]
29. Chang, M.M.L.; Ong, S.K.; Nee, A.Y.C. Approaches and challenges in product disassembly planning for sustainability. *Procedia CIRP* **2017**, *60*, 506–511. [CrossRef]
30. Hatzivasilis, G.; Fysarakis, K.; Soultatos, O.; Askoxylakis, I.; Papaefstathiou, I.; Demetriou, G. The industrial Internet of things as an enabler for a circular economy Hy-LP: A novel IIoT protocol, evaluated on a wind park's SDN/NFV-enabled 5G industrial network. *Comput. Commun.* **2018**, *119*, 127–137. [CrossRef]
31. Reuter, M.A. Digitalizing the circular economy: Circular economy engineering defined by the metallurgical internet of things. *Metall. Mater. Trans. B Process Metall. Mater. Process. Sci.* **2016**, *47*, 3194–3220. [CrossRef]
32. Weyer, S.; Meyer, T.; Ohmer, M.; Gorecky, D.; Zühlke, D. Future modeling and simulation of CPS-based factories: An example from the automotive industry. *IFAC PapersOnLine* **2016**, *49*, 97–102. [CrossRef]
33. Legat, C.; Seitz, C.; Lamparter, S.; Feldmann, S. Semantics to the shop floor: Towards ontology modularization and reuse in the automation domain. *IFAC Proc. Vol.* **2014**, *47*, 3444–3449. [CrossRef]
34. Negri, E.; Fumagalli, L.; Garetti, M.; Tanca, L. Computers in industry requirements and languages for the semantic representation of manufacturing systems. *Comput. Ind.* **2016**, *81*, 55–66. [CrossRef]
35. Posada, J.; Toro, C.; Barandiaran, I.; Oyarzun, D.; Stricker, D.; de Amicis, R.; Pinto, E.B.; Eisert, P.; Döllner, J.; Vallarino, I. Visual computing as a key enabling technology for industrie 4.0 and industrial internet. *IEEE Comput. Graph. Appl.* **2015**, *35*, 26–40. [CrossRef]
36. Cimino, C.; Negri, E.; Fumagalli, L. Review of digital twin applications in manufacturing. *Comput. Ind.* **2019**, *113*, 103130. [CrossRef]
37. Wang, X.V.; Wang, L. Digital twin-based WEEE recycling, recovery and remanufacturing in the background of Industry 4.0. *Int. J. Prod. Res.* **2019**, *57*, 3892–3902. [CrossRef]
38. Merdan, M.; Lepuschitz, W.; Meurer, T.; Vincze, M. Towards ontology-based automated disassembly systems. In Proceedings of the IECON 2010—36th Annual Conference on IEEE Industrial Electronics Societyp, Glendale, AZ, USA, 7–10 November 2010. [CrossRef]
39. PricewaterhouseCoopers (PWC), Making business and economic sense of climate change: Pwc sustainability and climate change blog. Available online: https://www.pwc.com/gx/en/services/sustainability.html. (accessed on 13 March 2020).
40. French, R.; Benakis, M.; Marin-Reyes, H. Intelligent sensing for robotic re-manufacturing in aerospace—An industry 4.0 design based prototype. In Proceedings of the IRIS 2017—5th IEEE International Symposium on Robotics and Intelligent Sensors, Ottawa, ON, Canada, 5–7 October 2017; pp. 272–277. [CrossRef]
41. Barbosa, J.; Leitão, P.; Trentesaux, D.; Colombo, A.W.; Karnouskos, S. Cross benefits from cyber-physical systems and intelligent products for future smart industries. In Proceedings of the INDIN 2016—14th IEEE International Conference on Industrial Informatics, Poitiers, France, 19–21 July 2016; pp. 504–509. [CrossRef]
42. Hehenberger, P.; Vogel-Heuser, B.; Bradley, D.; Eynard, B.; Tomiyama, T.; Achiche, S. Design, modelling, simulation and integration of cyber physical systems: Methods and applications. *Comput. Ind.* **2016**, *82*, 273–289. [CrossRef]
43. Schroeder, G.N.; Steinmetz, C.; Pereira, C.E.; Espindola, D.B. Digital twin data modeling with automationml and a communication methodology for data exchange. *IFAC PapersOnLine* **2016**, *49*, 12–17. [CrossRef]
44. Schroeder, G.N.; Rodrigues, R.; Espindola, D.; Garcia, N.; Muller, I. Visualising the digital twin using web services and augmented reality. In Proceedings of the INDIN' 16—14th IEEE International Conference on Industrial Informatics, Poitiers, France, 19–21 July 2016; pp. 522–527. [CrossRef]
45. D'Adamo, I.; Ferella, F.; Gastaldi, M.; Maggiore, F.; Rosa, P.; Terzi, S. Towards sustainable recycling processes: Wasted printed circuit boards as a source of economic opportunities. *Resour. Conserv. Recycl.* **2019**, *149*, 455–467. [CrossRef]
46. Ji, L.; Liu, C.; Huang, L.; Huang, G. The evolution of Resources Conservation and Recycling over the past 30 years: A bibliometric overview. *Resour. Conserv. Recycl.* **2018**, *134*, 34–43. [CrossRef]
47. Goodall, P.A.; Sharpe, R.G.; West, A.A. A data-driven simulation to support remanufacturing operations. *Comput. Ind.* **2019**, *105*, 48–60. [CrossRef]

48. Alqahtani, A.Y.; Gupta, S.M.; Nakashima, K. Warranty and maintenance analysis of sensor embedded products using internet of things in industry 4.0. *Int. J. Prod. Econ.* **2019**, *208*, 483–499. [CrossRef]
49. Joshi, A.D.; Gupta, S.M. Evaluation of design alternatives of End-Of-Life products using internet of things. *Int. J. Prod. Econ.* **2019**, *208*, 281–293. [CrossRef]
50. Marconi, M.; Germani, M.; Mandolini, M.; Favi, C. Applying data mining technique to disassembly sequence planning: A method to assess effective disassembly time of industrial products applying data mining technique to disassembly sequence planning: A method to assess effective disassembly time of industry. *Int. J. Prod. Res.* **2018**, *57*, 599–623. [CrossRef]
51. Sharpe, R.G.; Goodall, P.A.; Neal, A.D.; Conway, P.P.; West, A.A. Cyber-physical systems in the re-use, refurbishment and recycling of used electrical and electronic equipment. *J. Clean. Prod.* **2018**, *170*, 351–361. [CrossRef]
52. Kuik, S.S.; Kaihara, T.; Fujii, N. Product recovery configuration decisions for achieving sustainable manufacturing. *Procedia CIRP* **2016**, *41*, 258–263. [CrossRef]
53. Rönnlund, I.; Reuter, M.; Horn, S.; Aho, J.; Aho, M.; Päällysaho, M.; Ylimäki, L.; Pursula, T. Eco-efficiency indicator framework implemented in the metallurgical industry: Part 1—A comprehensive view and benchmark. *Int. J. Life Cycle Assess.* **2016**, *21*, 1473–1500. [CrossRef]
54. Smith, J.S. Survey on the use of simulation for manufacturing system design and operation. *J. Manuf. Syst.* **2013**, *22*, 157–171. [CrossRef]
55. Negahban, A.; Smith, J.S. Simulation for manufacturing system design and operation: Literature review and analysis. *J. Manuf. Syst.* **2014**, *33*, 241–261. [CrossRef]
56. Mourtzis, D.; Doukas, M.; Bernidaki, D. Simulation in manufacturing: Review and challenges. *Procedia CIRP* **2014**, *25*, 213–229. [CrossRef]
57. Taraman, S.R.; Lee, D.G. Manufacturing Lines Design and Analysis Utilizing Systems Simulation—A Case Study. In Proceedings of the 1983 ASME International Computers In Engineering Conference, Chicago, IL, USA, August 1983; pp. 99–105.
58. Festo® Didactics—Festo SE & Co. KG, Ruiter Straße 82, 73734, Esslingen, Germany. Available online: https://www.festo.com/cms/it_it/index.htm (accessed on 13 March 2020).
59. Festo® Didactics—CIROS software. 2018. Available online: https://www.festo-didactic.com/int-en/learning-systems/software-e-learning/ciros/?fbid=aW50LmVuLjU1Ny4xNy4yMC4xMTEw (accessed on 13 March 2020).
60. Rosen, R.; Von Wichert, G.; Lo, G.; Bettenhausen, K.D. About the importance of autonomy and digital twins for the future of manufacturing. *ScienceDirect* **2015**, *48*, 567–572. [CrossRef]
61. Colombo, A.W.; Bangemann, T.; Stluka, P.; Harrison, R.; Jammes, F. Industrial cloud-based cyber-physical systems. *Imc Aesop Approach* **2014**, *22*, 4–5.
62. Caggiano, A. Cloud-based manufacturing process monitoring for smart diagnosis services. *Int. J. Comput. Integr. Manuf.* **2018**, *31*, 612–623. [CrossRef]
63. Hedman, R.; Subramaniyan, M.; Almström, P. Analysis of critical factors for automatic measurement of OEE. *Procedia CIRP* **2016**, *57*, 128–133. [CrossRef]
64. Eguia, I.; Lozano, S.; Racero, J.; Guerrero, F. A methodological approach for designing and sequencing product families in reconfigurable disassembly systems. *J. Ind. Eng. Manag.* **2011**, *4*, 418–435. [CrossRef]
65. Bi, Z.M.; Lang, S.Y.T.; Shen, W.; Wang, L. Reconfigurable manufacturing systems: The state of the art. *Int. J. Prod. Res.* **2008**, *46*, 967–992. [CrossRef]
66. MATLAB®, "MATLAB® Library—TCP/IP Function. Available online: https://it.mathworks.com/help/instrument/tcpip.html (accessed on 11 March 2020).

sustainability

MDPI

Article

The Role of Earth Observation Satellites in Maximizing Renewable Energy Production: Case Studies Analysis for Renewable Power Plants

Mariarosa Argentiero [1] and Pasquale Marcello Falcone [2,*]

1. Department of Law and Economics, Unitelma Sapienza University of Rome, Viale Regina Elena, 295, 00161 Rome, Italy; mariarosaargentiero@gmail.com
2. Department of Business and Economics, University of Naples Parthenope, Via Generale Parisi, 13, 80132 Naples, Italy

* Correspondence: pasquale.falcone@unipathenope.it

Received: 9 February 2020; Accepted: 5 March 2020; Published: 7 March 2020

Abstract: This paper is based on a novel approach towards clean energy production, i.e., space innovative applications toward sustainable development. Specifically, the role of Earth observation (EO) satellites in maximizing renewable energy production is considered to show the enormous potential in exploiting sustainable energy generation plants when the Earth is mapped by satellites to provide some peculiar parameters (e.g., solar irradiance, wind speed, precipitation, climate conditions, geothermal data). In this framework, RETScreen clean energy management software can be used for numerical analysis, such as energy generation and efficiency, prices, emission reductions, financial viability and hazard of various types of renewable-energy and energy-efficient technologies (RETs), based on a large database of satellite parameters. This simplifies initial assessments and provides streamlined processes that enable funders, architects, designers, regulators, etc. to make decisions on future clean energy initiatives. After describing the logic of life cycle analysis of RETScreen, two case studies (Mexicali and Toronto) on multiple technologies power plant are analyzed. The different results obtained, when projecting the two scenarios, showed how the software could be useful in the pre-feasibility phase to discriminate the type of installation not efficient for the selected location or not convenient in terms of internal rate of return (IRR) on equity.

Keywords: renewable energy; space industry; RETScreen

1. Introduction

Finding an effective way to deal with current resource depletion and climate change will require soon a complete transformation of existing unsustainable energy systems [1]. The space industry has come to represent an icon of knowledge-creation processes in technology-intensive industries [2]. The industry is not merely comprised of launches and satellites, but now includes direct consumer applications and personal entertainment [3]. Therefore, the space industry has some history of expansion, and its growth is expected to accelerate [4]. An input-output analysis is useful for predicting which industries will benefit from their growth and to inform the government, which may want to use this information for policy making or investment decisions [5]. For example, space tourism is becoming a topic of great media interest thanks to technological evolution in the aerospace sector and with the reduced costs of access to space [6]. Moreover, space-based applications are already helping emerging nations in reaching social equity, but often their demands come after the excellent attempts taken in industrialized nations to guarantee that all helpful space-based information and features are put to greatest use for social reasons [7]. Space applications are mainly based on closed-loop systems (i.e., circular), due to two main reasons: (i) to guarantee a satellite mission, the platform should be autonomously powered; (ii) then, the spatial missions need regenerative processes to deal with limited available resources, for example air and water. Moreover, the very high costs for projecting and producing space technologies become more affordable when the system is reusable (to give an example, this is what happens for new launchers project). Therefore, the space industry is a clear example of a circular economy model.

The circular economy (CE) approach has the ambition of making better use of resources/materials through reuse, recycling and recovery with the aim of minimizing the energy and environmental impact of resource extraction and processing [8,9]. This mission is mainly pursued by redesigning the life cycle of the product, in order to have minimal input and minimal production of system waste [10]. A transition to a circular economy is required, not only because we need to overcome the limits of a linear economy, but also because scarcity of resources usually required a dependence on foreign countries on supply and a strong impact on environmental conditions due to virgin material extractions and "old" manufacturing process with no recycling objectives [11]. CE drives sustainable consumption and steers public and private investment, which eventually lead to sustainable development [12]. The sustainable development goals (SDGs) convey worldwide aspirations and urge all potential donors to help meet their difficulties [13]. Given the significant part that the space domain has already performed in growth initiatives and the excellent chance to increase its input, space operators are called on to take advantage of the momentum of the SDGs, not only to concentrate on how they can further participate, but also how they can become a more integrated component of a society struggling with growth in a wider global sense, thereby optimizing efficiency and input [14].

The following mapping, shown in Table 1, may be suggested to evaluate the space potential in order to pursue SDGs.

Table 1. Space contribution to SDGs [15].

SDG Topic	Actual or Possible Contribution of Space
SDG 1: No Poverty	Improved communications and more environmental data as a driver of growth, better logistics management by the use of sat/nav
SDG 2: Zero Hunger	EO data for optimized agriculture and livestock management, more efficient crop markets, better delivery systems using sat/nav
SDG 3: Good Health and Well-Being	E- health including telemedicine and medical tele-training and learning
SDG 4: Quality Education	Tele-learning
SDG 5: Gender Equality	Female empowerment by telecoms links to the information society, tele-learning, telecoms enabling small businesses of women
SDG 6: Clean Water and Sanitation	EO data for water management, water detection, and water pollution monitoring
SDG 7: Affordable & Clean Energy	EO data for renewable energy management, grid management
SDG 8: Decent Work and Economic Growth	Space services as enabler of economic growth and high quality jobs in all economic sectors
SDG 9: Industry, Innovation and Infrastructure	Space as enablers of innovation both in own sector and others, space based data and communication abilities key for industrial processes, space telecoms compensates for lack of terrestrial networks, EO for lack of in-situ stations, sat/nav important for best use of transport infrastructure and banking systems
SDG 10: Reduced Inequalities	Access to information society through telecoms is a leveler, fosters transparency and hence helps fight against corruption, space services as an enabler of work opportunity
SDG 11: Sustainable Cities and Communities	EO data for pollution monitoring, energy management and land use planning, sat/nav for traffic management, telecoms for efficient information exchange

Table 1. *Cont.*

SDG Topic	Actual or Possible Contribution of Space
SDG 12: Responsible consumption and production	EO data for optimized supply management, energy management, sat/nav for logistics management in production
SDG 13: Climate Action	EO data key for climate change monitoring and definition of mitigation strategies
SDG 14: Life below Water	EO data key for monitoring the health of oceans and other water systems, for fisheries management and policing
SDG 15: Life on Land	EO data for bio-diversity monitoring, pollution monitoring, land use management and policing
SDG 16: Peace Justice and Strong Institutions	Telecoms empower civil society by connecting to the information society, e-voting enabled by telecoms, legal evidence, treaty compliance monitoring, security management through EO systems
SDG 17: Partnerships	Space community is a part of an international fabric of partnerships. Possibilities of reinforcement of links with development actors

Space technology has quickly followed and performed a significant part in economic development initiatives (coping with the majority of SDGs content) [16]. This is true in both emerging and industrialized countries. In emerging nations, where terrestrial infrastructure is often inadequate or missing, space-based applications give excellent benefits as they mainly eliminate the need for such infrastructure [17]. EO satellites are among the most relevant source of data even in industrialized countries, and they are often essential to guide policy governance providing information that is fundamental to watershed and fisheries management and to tracking pollution areas [18].

Through its SDG7 (affordable and clean energy) initiatives, the European Space Agency (ESA) promotes initiatives to guarantee inexpensive, safe, viable and contemporary energy for all. ESA is using its satellite technologies to create safe power alternatives that can substitute natural emissions producing greenhouse gasses that account for at least 70% of worldwide warming caused by human activity. Through the agency and its utility suppliers' extensive cloud booking operations conducted by ESA, consumers can build networks to support sustainable development in multiple industries, including energy, and assist in making the 17 SDGs a fact by 2030 [19].

Outside the European area, the National Aeronautics and Space Administration (NASA) has made a significant contribution to our awareness of Earth and the need for modern, greener technology in many ways. NASA's commitment to Earth, the atmosphere and green technologies continues today through solar arrays and fuel cells projects, EO satellite applications, more powerful spaceships, more efficient climate models and air, water and waste recycling processes. This is giving a strong enhancement for our planet's clean energy programs while advancing in highly technological research for science, aeronautics and space exploration tasks [20].

When talking about space technologies for clean energy generation, it is necessary to look at EO satellites for maximizing renewable energy production [21]. Satellites for EO provide a distinctive basis of data for anyone designing, implementing or assessing sustainable development initiatives. They can assist in reconstructing a sequence of occurrences by displaying a series of pictures over the span of a moment. High-resolution pictures can be used during a particular timeframe to investigate extremely focused phenomenon with a limited range of sight. In portraying national events that may involve more systemic and repeated compilation, low precision photography is easier.

Copernicus is the European Union (EU) EO and monitoring program, which looks to our planet and its environment for the ultimate benefit of all European citizens. It aims at providing accurate and easily accessible data to improve environment management and understanding of climate change effects [22]. Copernicus primarily draws on data collected from EO satellites, but it also depends on a large amount of information gathered in situ (meaning on-site or local) measurement systems made available by the Member States of the EU to the programme.

In Figure 1, the Sentinel family is displayed, which constitutes the space segment of the Copernicus program.

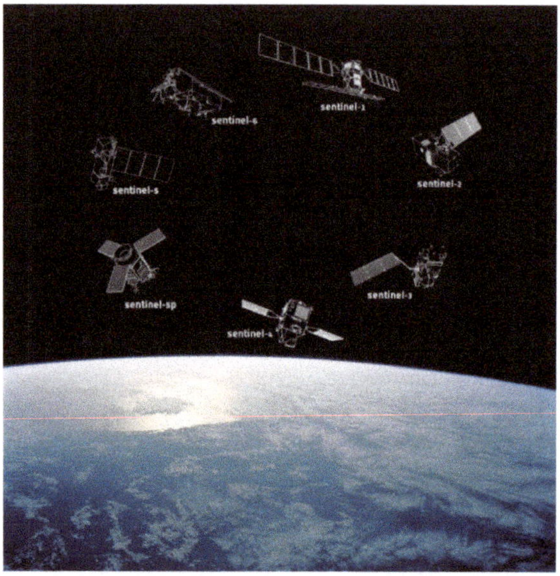

Figure 1. Copernicus EO satellite constellation [23].

Satellite programs for collecting climate data and, in general, for Earth monitoring are among the key sustainable development initiatives for SDGs, but this is not the end of the process: telemetry data properly post-processed are inserted in databases in order to allow very accurate analysis for certain type of project. For this scope, many software and tools have been developed with user-friendly interfaces, going from a basic-user level (a family that wants a domestic photovoltaic installation) to an advanced-user level (engineers working for investors in power plants or smart building programs). RETScreen, being the oldest tool conceived for exploiting databases of typical sets of data for Earth monitoring and consequently analyzing the feasibility of a power plant installation (traditional or renewable), has been adopted for describing how useful satellite missions are for renewable energy optimization in power plants, already existing or not [24].

The peculiarity of this study is to show how space-based research could produce significant enhancements to sustainability and, in particular, to renewable energy generation. Specifically, the novelty of this work comes from the emphasis given to one of the most innovative fields of study (i.e., space research) for finding solutions for our environment by trying to exploit already existing technologies to propose an innovative approach to clean energy generation. Our analyses show the results of two scenarios. The first one included a case study mixing multiple renewable technologies in a single installation; as a result, power, cost analysis, pollution analysis, financial analysis and risk analysis have been provided. The second scenario compared two equivalent (in terms of location and capacity) power plants, one provided with wind turbine and the other with photovoltaic technology.

The rest of the work is organized as follows. Section 2 introduces the materials and methods, Section 3 presents the results, whereas Section 4 discusses the findings; finally, Section 5 concludes.

2. Materials and Methods

Parameters should be accurately estimated in order to provide a reliable evaluation of renewable energy power plant installation. In Table 2, a typical set of data of the most significant parameters needed to evaluate Earth's conditions in order to better manage renewable resource plants is shown.

Table 2. Typical set of data for Earth monitoring [25].

Parameter Category	Specific Parameters
SOLAR GEOMETRY	• Solar noon • Daylight hour • Hourly solar angles from horizon
RADIATION	• All-sky insolation (Average, Min, Max) • Diffuse horizontal radiation (Average, Min, Max) • Direct normal radiation (Average, Min, Max) • Clear-sky insolation • Clear-sky days
ILLUMINANCE	• Illuminance on tilted surfaces at available GMT times • Illuminance on tilted surfaces over 24 hour period
SURFACE ALBEDO	• Surface albedo
CLOUDS	• Daylight cloud amount • Cloud amount at available GMT times • Frequency of cloud amount at available GMT times
METEOROLOGY (WIND)	• Wind speed at 50 m (Average, Min, Max) • Percent of time for ranges of wind speed at 50 m • Wind speed at 10 m for terrain similar to airports
METEOROLOGY (TEMPERATURE)	• Air temperature at 10 m • Daily temperature Range at 10 m • Dew point temperature at 10 m • Cooling degree days above 18 °C • Heating degree days below 18 °C • Earth skin temperature • Frost days
PRECIPITATION	• Precipitation

These data are not easy to exploit. First, you will need to receive telemetry collected by sensors on-board the satellite. Then, you need to implement statistical and numerical models and choose the best in describing a specifying phenomenon, In the end, you will give as an input to the model, satellite data in a proper format (data normalization is always required). Only when you reach the final point, can the output data be collected in a larger database and help you in designing and optimizing energy plants and sustainable buildings.

In recent times, a spread of tools and software has been noticed, providing the evidence to how sustainability and, specifically, renewable energies are becoming relevant in our modern circular economy.

For example, Google, with its "Project sunroof" tool, allows you in a user-friendly interface to evaluate if it is convenient to build photovoltaic panels in a certain area, by using satellite data. It is not relevant to this point to list the high number of clean energy software that have been developed across the years, but it's important to speak about the most relevant ones and the way in which they provide useful results for an accurate analysis of renewable energies plants, thanks to the availability of large amount of satellite data (all of the Earth's surface is mapped with more than one sensor).

HOMER (Hybrid Optimization Modeling Software) is able to design and analyze the power systems combining traditional and renewable technologies. This tool is very accurate, but it requires too much input data to build a proper scenario, so it is mainly used not for the feasibility study phase, but for the manufacturing phase [26].

Further tools have been developed, as databases or atlases, depicting only a small set of parameters; among these tools, we found the NASA Prediction of Worldwide Energy Resource (POWER) project aimed to improve the current renewable energy data set and to create a new database from new satellite systems. The POWER project is mainly addressed to renewable and sustainable energy [27].

In the European area, the S2S4E Decision Support Tool (DST) has been developed as an operational climate service for clean energy. The DST generates climate information adapted through energy indicators derived from climatic variables such as wind speed, solar radiation, precipitation, temperature and pressure reduced to the average sea level. These indicators provide information on the expected variability in hydroelectric, solar and wind energy production, as well as on electricity demand in the future.

Last, but not least, one of the oldest and largest adopted tools for clean energy management is RETScreen, developed by the Canadian Government with NASA cooperation. In 1996, RETScreen clean energy management software was developed by Natural Resources Canada; after that, in 1998 the software package was carried on by the Canadian government.

The tool can be used for numerical analysis in areas such as energy generation and efficiency, prices, emission reductions, financial viability and hazards of various types of clean energy and energy-efficient technologies. This simplifies initial assessments and provides streamlined processes that enable funders, architects, designers, regulators, etc. to make decisions on future clean energy initiatives. This software is able to exploit post-processed satellite data and guides you through a very simple path from system project to cost analysis, in order to understand if, for example, some smart building or energy plant realization is feasible or not. It includes modelling for many renewable energy systems and the expected costs for the plant characteristics so you will be able to have an approximate, but flexible, estimate on the project you are working on.

The tool has already been used for projecting many installations all over the world: (i) to validate the techno-economic and environmental sustainability of solar PV technology in Nigeria [28], (ii) to evaluate and compare economic policies to increase energy generation capacity in the Iranian household consumption sector [29], (iii) to provide a technical, financial, economic and environmental pre-feasibility study of geothermal power plants in Ecuador [30] and (iv) to provide a preliminary determination of the optimal size for renewable energy resources in buildings [31].

RETScreen Expert software in its latest available version (7.0) has been adopted to provide useful case studies of projects involving renewable energies in contrast with standard power production. The open-source version (only viewer mode) has limited features, but it is still reliable for feasibility analysis of many projects, starting from smart buildings to power plants [32].

The first case study to be proposed is a multiple technologies power plant, combining geothermal and hydric power [33], as shown in Figure 2. In particular, water and geothermal power have been exploited in different percentages, so that the combination can provide 35,033 MWh as electricity export to the grid, reducing CO2 emissions by 15,676 tCO2 (equivalent tons of CO2).

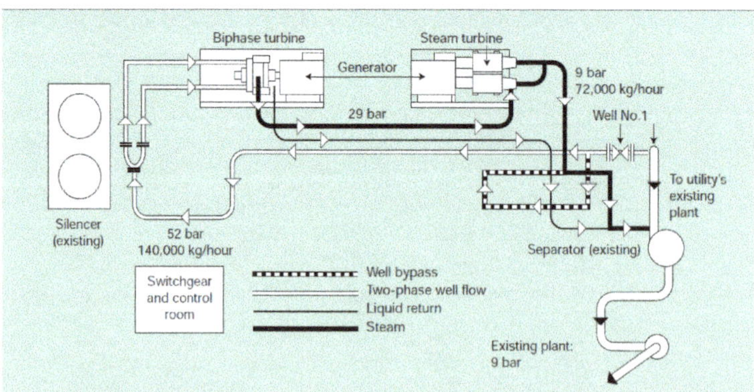

Figure 2. Schematic of the integrated biphase back-pressure system [26].

The type of power plant and the location are the first step choices to go through. For this case study, the installation place is in Mexico.

Mexico's renewable energy contributes 26% of Mexico's electricity generation. The majority of renewable energy adoption comes from hydro, geothermal, solar and wind power. Long-term efforts are being made to increase the use of renewable sources of energy. The sum of geothermal energy used and extracted ranks Mexico as number four in the world.

Starting from a template of RETScreen software, latitude, longitude and altitude of both selected location (Mexicali) and the facility to be set is provided. The climate zone is individuated automatically to be that of Ensenada (the closest place to the facility being mapped for climate reference).

Mexicali is the capital of the Mexican state of Baja California. It covers an area of more than 13,000 km^2 and it counts more than 900,000 inhabitants. The city is located on the border with the United States of America; in fact, its name is a crasis that derives from the union of the words México and California.

Thanks to having plenty of water, gas and electricity, Mexicali counts two major power plants, Cerro Prieto Power Station, one of the world largest installed geothermal power plants, and Sempra Thermoelectric, a combined-cycle gas turbine (CCGT) power plant with two gas turbines, a steam turbine and a heat recovery steam generator (HRSG).

This case study is inspired by a biphase turbine installed in Cerro Prieto to maximize a geothermal well that produces power from both the steam and the water. It has increased the power production of the plant by more than 40%.

On August 20, 1997, this biphase turbine was synchronized with the Commission Federal de Electricidad electrical grid. From that time until May 23, 2000, a period of two years and nine months, the power plant was in operation. The grid was supplied by a total of 77,549 kWh.

Pending replacement of the rotor with a newly designed, higher power rotor and replacement of the bearings and seals, the power plant was subsequently put in a standby state.

In Table 3, location details for the selected location (Mexicali) have been divided into different categories, expressing respectively the climate data for the location area (Ensenada), the climate data for the selected facility (Mexicali) and the origins of the climate data.

Table 3. Location details for Mexicali.

Parameter	Unit	Location Area	Facility Location	Source of Data
Latitude	N.A.	31.9	32.6	N.A.
Longitude	N.A.	−116.6	−115.5	N.A.
Climate zone	N.A.	3B-Warm-Dry		NASA
Elevation	M	270	2	NASA-Map
Heating design temperature	°C	7.0	N.A.	NASA
Cooling design temperature	°C	30.5	N.A.	NASA
Earth temperature amplitude	°C	17.9	N.A.	NASA

After evaluating the type of plant and the location, the software displays the target to be achieved with this project, in terms of electricity to export to the grid, the total revenue and the emissions reduction, shown in Table 4.

Table 4. Target to be reached with the proposed case.

Electricity Exported to Grid (MWh)	Electricity Export Revenue (USD)	GHG Emission Reduction (tCO_2)
35,033	1,471,400	15,767

After defining climate data related to the installation we decided to build, we have to deal with the benchmark module.

Benchmark metrics may derive from the RETScreen Benchmark Database index, company benchmarking initiatives, organisational expectations, market trends or any other relevant measure to better align the facility to performance goals.

The benchmark database collects indicative minimum and maximum energy production costs (also known as the "levelized cost of electricity" or LCOE) of different types of power generation systems; these costs come from considering the system operating conditions, the installation technology, the location and the operation and maintenance (O&M) costs of typical power plants already installed worldwide. There are also main factors used to measure the minimum and maximum range of values, for example fuel cost rate (for combustion power systems) and capacity factor (for renewable energy systems).

An example of benchmark analysis is provided in Figure 3:

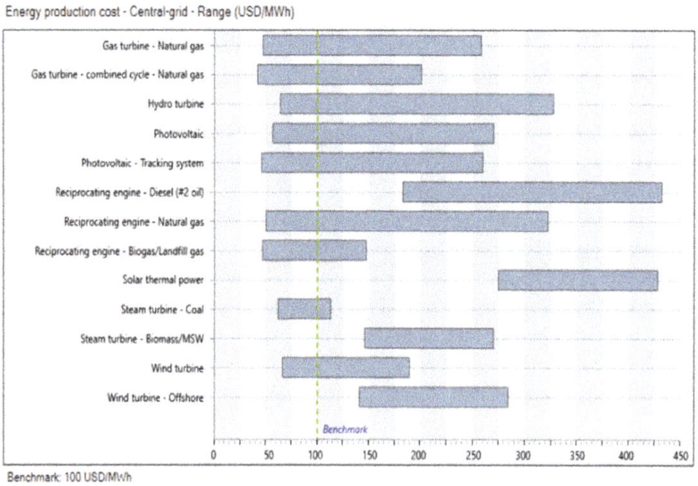

Figure 3. Benchmark setting for energy production (screenshot by authors using RETScreen).

After completion of this high-level benchmark assessment, the user can then conduct a more comprehensive viability report to better estimate the facility energy savings, elimination of greenhouse gases (GHG) pollution, cost savings and/or output capacity.

The system partition for this case study is depicted in Table 5.

Table 5. Definition of the system partition.

POWER SYSTEM – TOTAL	
Capacity	4167 kW
Electricity	35,033 MWh
GEOTHERMAL POWER	
Capacity	3167 kW
Electricity	26,273 MWh
HYDRO TURBINE	
Capacity	1000 kW
Electricity	8760 MWh

Toronto was chosen as the reference location, mainly because a lot of data are available and updated for Canadian territories (usually case studies or templates involving other countries are no more reliable especially for costs analysis). The city has both ground and satellite data to accurately map its territory characteristics. Moreover, Toronto is located in the extreme south-east of Canada, capital of the province of Ontario and most populous center of Canada with its 3,120,668 inhabitants. The city has shown its strong engagement in sustainable development, and in 2013, the City Council introduced a mandate to produce at least 5% of the electricity from renewable energy sources for all new installations. The use of solar photovoltaic, solar thermal, geothermal and biomass supports the environmental, energetic and economic objectives of the city.

Many initiatives have been set up for education and training of the community and even for helping in designing new smart buildings for commercial and personal use.

In Table 6, geographic and climate data for Toronto are provided.

Table 6. Location details for Toronto.

Parameter	Unit	Location Area	Facility Location	Source of Data
Latitude	N.A.	43.7	43.7	N.A.
Longitude	N.A.	−79.4	−79.4	N.A.
Climate zone	N.A.	6A-Cold-Humid		Ground+NASA
Elevation	M	107	91	Ground-Map
Heating design temperature	°C	−17.1	N.A.	Ground
Cooling design temperature	°C	28.8	N.A.	Ground
Earth temperature amplitude	°C	21.4	N.A.	NASA

Wind turbine and photovoltaic plants, both of 1,000 kW, are considered.

For the wind turbine system, the electricity produced will be around 3,000 MWh.

As a benchmark for energy production costs, RETScreen values are quite accurate for many installations in Canada, so it was automatically set at 100 CA$/MWh.

A benchmark analysis for the wind turbine case located in Toronto is shown in Figure 4.

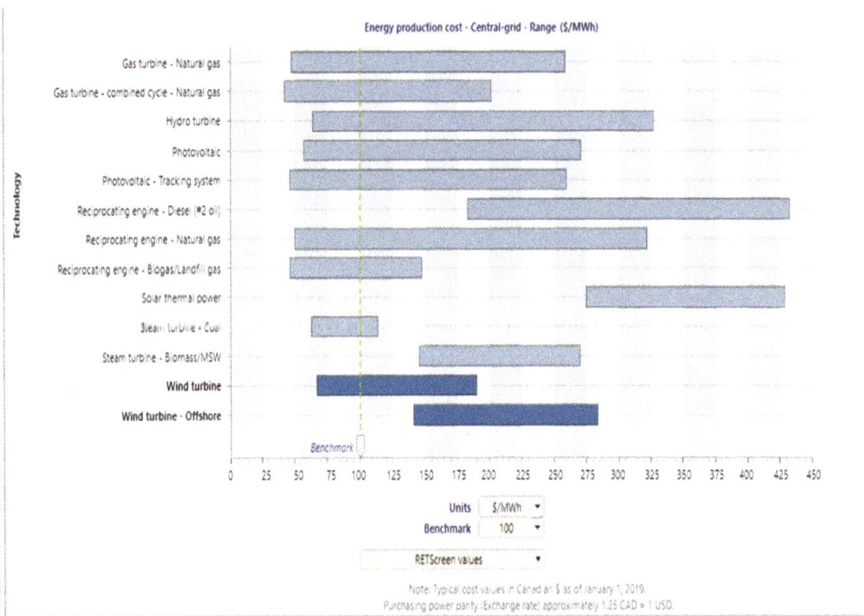

Figure 4. Benchmark setting for energy production (screenshot by author using RETScreen).

Below, in Table 7, the initial target values of the proposed case are presented.

Table 7. Target to be reached with the proposed case.

Electricity Exported to Grid (MWh)	Electricity Export Revenue (USD)	GHG Emission Reduction (tCO_2)
3197	319,740	302

The model of the wind turbine used for this project was manufactured by a Danish company, VESTAS. Many VESTAS turbines have been exported to Canada, as a symbol of European engagement in renewable energies.

The plant, using this wind turbine model, is able to produce 3197 MWh with initial costs of 2,309,703 CA$ (CA$/kW value is scaled with respect to the plant capacity and data are available in the software for defined range).

The electricity export rate value has been changing across the years. To give an example, many countries started with incentives for renewable energies investors, by rewarding them with a feed-in tariff or feed-in premium. In this way, the electricity was paid more for than the real cost per unit of the electricity exported to the central grid. Nowadays, this scenario is no longer relevant because bonuses for renewable energy plants have been largely reduced, so the actual price paid per MWh to sustainable power plants is similar to all other energy source plants.

Finally, the choice to put the electricity export rate at the same value as the benchmark energy production cost is good enough for an approximate evaluation.

Details about tailoring the wind turbine system are presented in Figure 5.

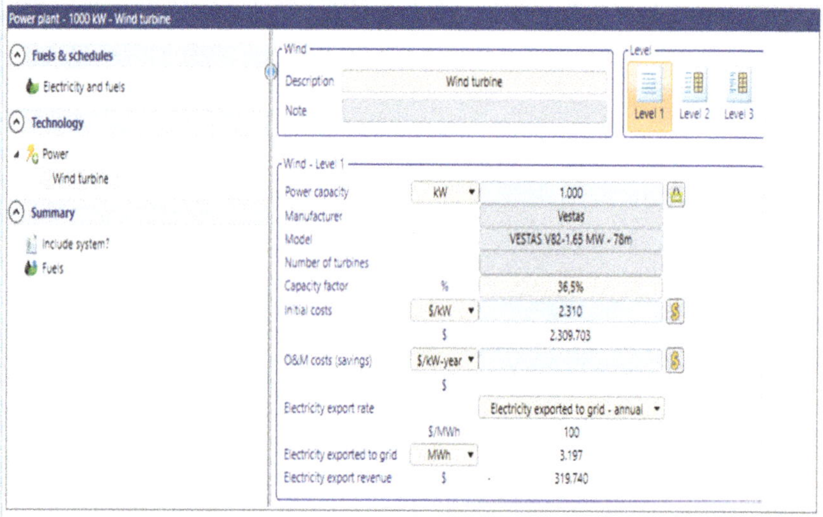

Figure 5. Tailoring the wind turbine system (screenshot by author using RETScreen).

For the photovoltaic system, the electricity produced will be around 1200 MWh and the benchmark value will be the same with respect to the previous project.

The initial target values of the proposed case are presented in Table 8.

Table 8. Target to be reached with the proposed case.

Electricity Exported to Grid (MWh)	Electricity Export Revenue (USD)	GHG Emission Reduction (tCO_2)
1218	121,764	120

In Figure 6, a benchmark analysis for the photovoltaic case located in Toronto is shown.

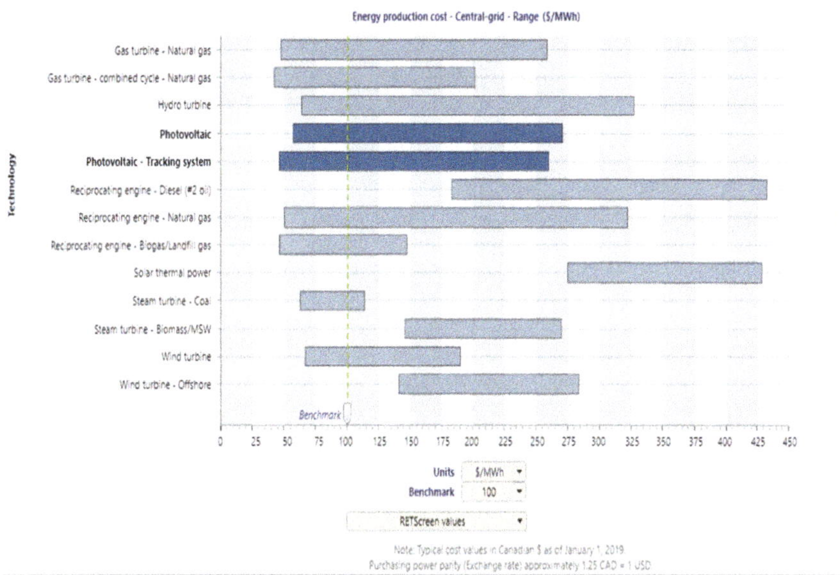

Figure 6. Benchmark setting for energy production (screenshot by author using RETScreen).

The solar cells for this photovoltaic installation are made of mono-crystalline silicon. This system performs with a higher efficiency in terms of energy production and space occupied; moreover, this type of solar cell guarantees the longest lifetime for the whole project. On the other hand, this technology is more expensive than polycrystalline solar panels, and it could be damaged in the case of dirt, shadow or snow or sometimes it might not work properly in very hot locations. In addition, during the production process, a large part of the material becomes waste, so depending on the dimension of the project it could become unsustainable even if it is a renewable energy project.

Details about tailoring the photovoltaic system are presented in Figure 7.

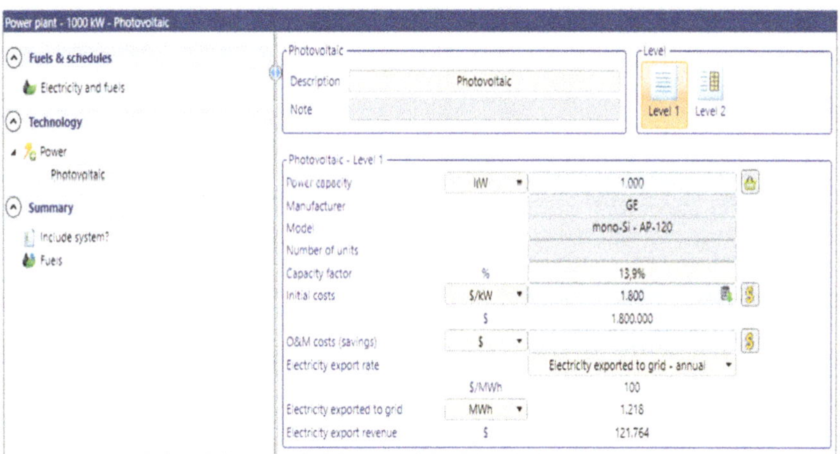

Figure 7. Tailoring the photovoltaic system (screenshot by author using RETScreen).

3. Case Study Results

3.1. Case Study 1

Results are derived from a model comparison between the baseline scenario with the proposed alternative showing the difference in GHG emissions ("Gross annual GHG emission reduction"). Transmission and distribution (T&D) losses are automatically evaluated thanks to the largely populated database embedded in the software. An equivalence is shown in Figure 8 to better understand how much emission is being reduced (almost like 3,000 cars not used).

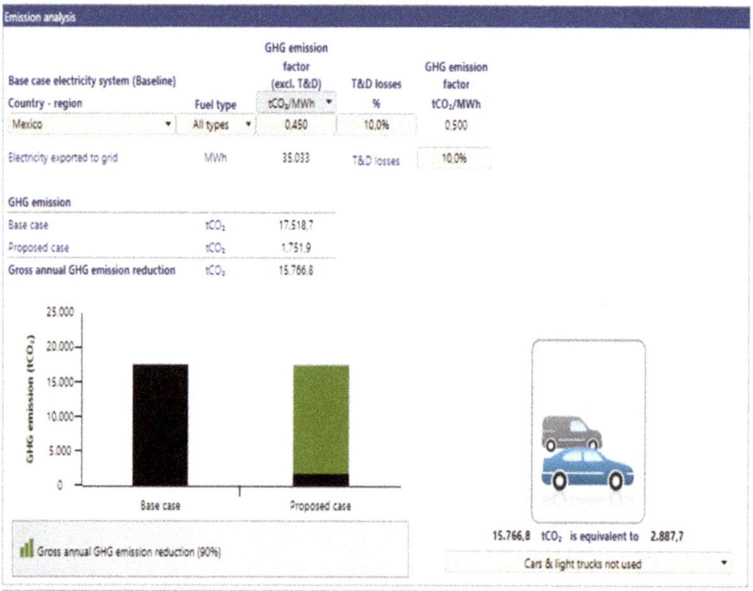

Figure 8. Emission analysis chart (screenshot by author using RETScreen).

A financial analysis is provided as a final step of this pre-feasibility study. Some parameters have been defined such as inflation rate, project lifetime, debt ratio, debt interest rate and debt duration. User-defined costs usually include O&M for the project lifetime or manpower for the installation. Incentives could be inserted, if available for the specific project.

The software gives four outcomes for evaluating financial viability:

- the pre-tax internal rate of return (IRR) on equity, in percentage, represents the true interest yield provided by the project equity through its lifetime (before applying taxes). It is calculated using the pre-tax yearly cash flows and the project duration. To simplify its meaning, it can be linked to the return on equity (ROE) or return on investment (ROI). IRR on equity of the project is used by the organisation as a comparison to the company IRR and to decide if the investment is convenient or not. For a project which requires cash injections during its lifetime, with amounts that are similar to the project annual earnings, the IRR estimate may become inaccurate.
- the pre-tax internal rate of return (IRR) on assets (%) is described as the true interest yield provided by the project assets over its lifetime (pre-tax). It can be reconnected to the return on assets (ROA) meaning.

- the simple payback (in years) formula considers the estimated initial costs, the total annual costs (excluding debt payments) and the total annual benefits and income. This indicator represents how long it takes for a certain plant to cover its initial cost. The simple payback method has the meaning of evaluating the desirability of an investment: if the time to cover the initial cost is short enough, the investment could be considered convenient. This index could be adopted to compare different projects' profitability. This indicator is of secondary importance to evaluate the risk of an investment, especially because it disregards important aspects, such as the impact of inflation during the project lifetime, but it could be useful for small companies which should prefer short-term payback projects, even though they have lower IRR with respect to other ones.
- the equity payback, which represents the duration it takes for the plant owner to cover its own initial investment (equity) out of the project cash flows generated. Equity payback takes into account the cash flow of the company from its start as well as the equity (debt level) of the business, which allows it a better time measure of the value of the project than the previous indicator (simple payback). The model uses the year number and the accumulated post-tax cash flows to measure this value.

As a result, financial feasibility is provided in Figure 9, together with the cumulative cash flow graph. Less than one year is needed to reach the equity payback.

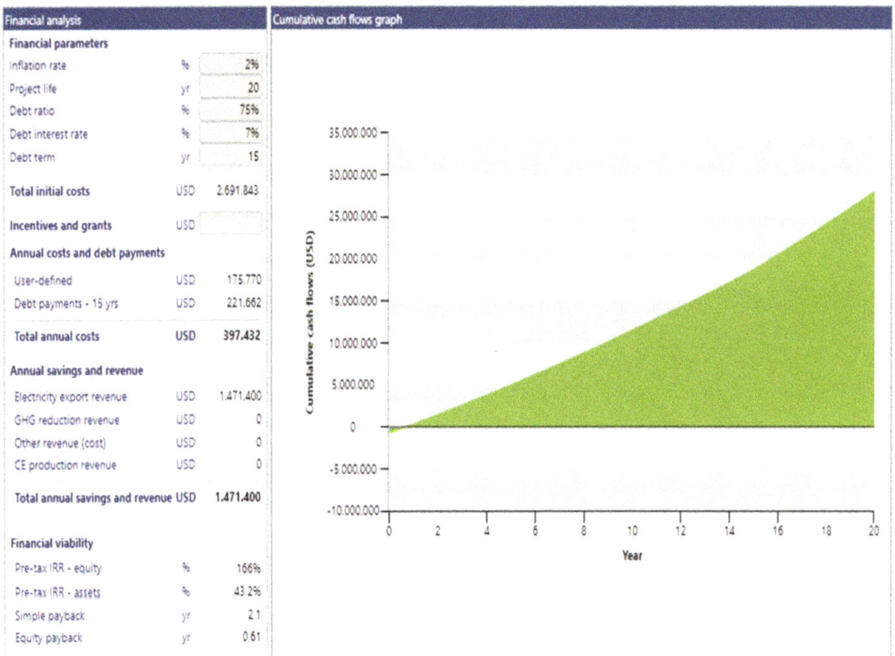

Figure 9. Financial analysis chart (screenshot by author using RETScreen).

For risk analysis, the Monte Carlo method is applied. The possible combinations of input variables range from 500 to 5,000 values of pre and after-tax IRR equity, pre and after-tax IRR assets, equity payback, net present value (NPV) or energy production cost. The risk analysis allows the user to determine whether or not the volatility of the financial metric is appropriate by looking at the range of possible results. An excessive variance would imply the need to make further effort to reduce the volatility associated with the input variables that have been identified as having the greatest impact on the financial metric.

The applicant should enter an appropriate level of risk for the financial metric under consideration. The rate of risk feedback is used to assess the confidence interval (defined by the maximum and minimum limits) within which the financial predictor is expected to fall. The level of risk reflects the possibility that the financial predictor may slip outside this confidence interval.

Limits of the confidence interval are generally determined on the basis of the median value and the risk rate and are shown as "Minimum within the confidence level" and "Maximum within the confidence level". It is recommended that the individual reach a maximum risk level of 5%–10%, which are common values for the generic risk analysis.

The histogram lays out the array of possible values for the financial metric arising from the Monte Carlo simulation. The height of each bar reflects the rate (percent) of values that drop within the scope specified by the width of each bar. The value corresponding to the center of each range is plotted on the X axis.

Looking at the distribution of the financial metric, the consumer is able to quickly determine the volatility of the variable. In some instances, there is a lack of data to accurately map the graph. In the case of equity payback reached instantaneously, the outcome is the "n/a" (not applicable) symbol, and therefore this analysis will be missing.

3.2. Case Study 2

For this case study, we will analyze two sets of results depending on the system adopted (wind turbine or photovoltaics).

For the wind turbine case, the gross annual GHG emission reduction is 93%, comparable to 55 cars (traditionally fueled) no longer used.

Financial analysis shows, in Figure 10, that equity payback for the wind turbine power plant is reached after 3.5 years of the 25 years of the project's lifetime, but it should be taken into consideration that this analysis does not involve any incentive due to the rapid evolution of regulations, that it is progressively converting the initiatives for funding clean energy generation with initiatives for help in designing sustainable systems.

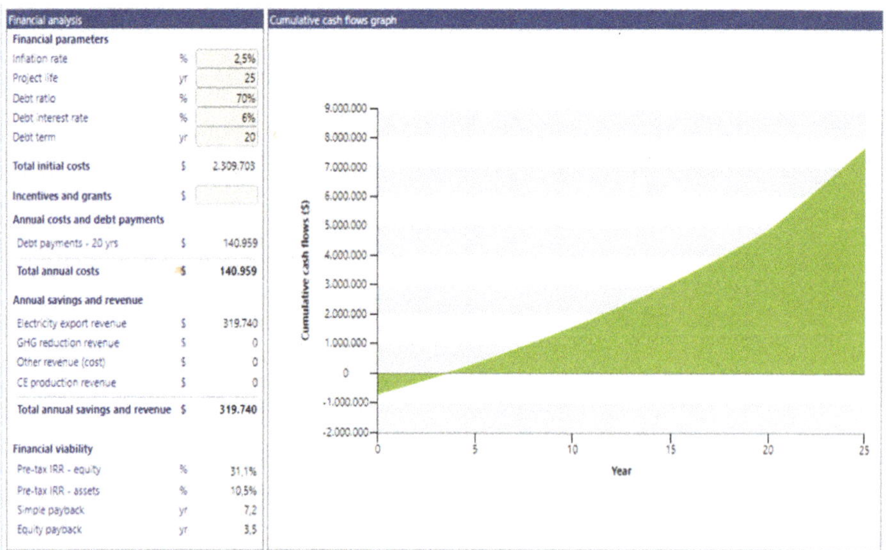

Figure 10. Financial analysis chart (screenshot by author using RETScreen).

For photovoltaic installation, the gross annual GHG emission reduction is 96%, comparable to 22 cars (traditionally fueled) no longer used. Even though the percentage is greater than the wind turbine case, we should consider that the electricity produced with photovoltaics is around one third of that produced by the other system, so effectively the CO_2 reduction is minor.

Financial analysis shows, in Figure 11, that equity payback for the photovoltaic case is reached after 16.7 years of the 25 years of project's lifetime. For incentives and grants, the same consideration made for wind turbine system has been evaluated.

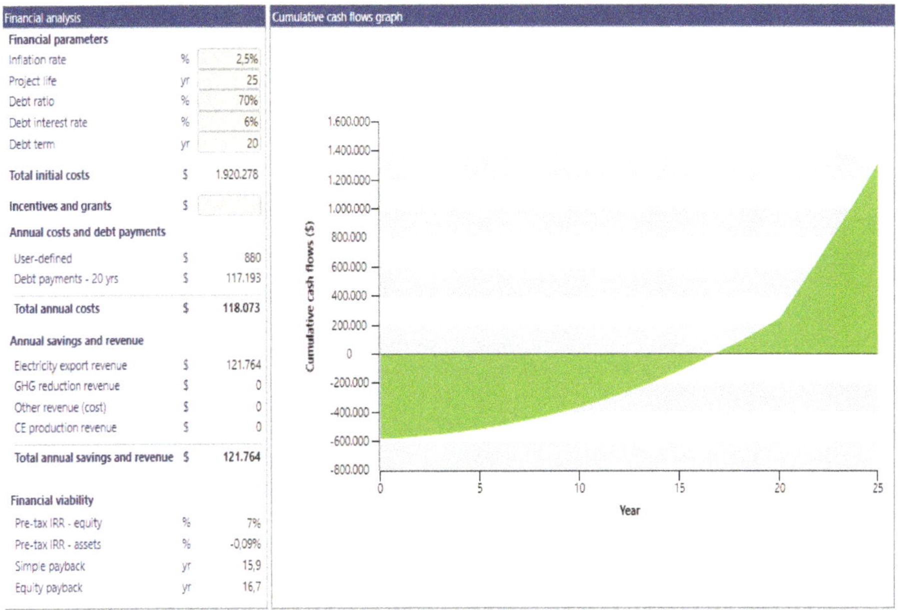

Figure 11. Financial analysis chart (screenshot by author using RETScreen).

4. Discussion

The first case study was only aimed at showing how RETScreen is powerful, even mixing different renewable technologies in one single power plant, optimizing the project on the base of the location characteristics. The second case study provided more evidence, reported in Table 9. The different outputs of the two installations (i.e., wind turbine vs. photovoltaic) are provided.

Table 9. Wind turbine vs photovoltaic in RETScreen.

	Wind Turbine	Photovoltaic
Location	TORONTO	
Capacity	1000 kW	
Project life	25 yr	
Electricity export rate	100 CA$/MWh	
Electricity	3197 MWh	1218 MWh
Gross annual GHG emission reduction	302 tCO_2	120 tCO_2
Total initial costs	2,309,703 CA$	1,920,278 CA$
Pre-tax IRR-equity	31.1%	7%
Equity payback period	3.5 yr	16.7 yr

It is possible to notice that, starting from a common baseline (same location, same power plant capacity, same project life and same evaluation for electricity export rate), that the electricity produced by the two power plants is sensibly different; in fact, the wind turbine system is much more efficient than the photovoltaics. Due to its higher efficiency in producing electricity, the correspondent gross annual emission reduction of greenhouse gases is bigger for the wind turbine with respect to the photovoltaic case. Findings emerged from our investigation can represent useful insights for policy makers. Specifically, besides looking at policy of direct regulations, other policy instruments that can indirectly support deployment of renewable energy resources in the long term should be adequately taken into account. These indirect strategies can be in the form of environmental taxes or of emission permits for energy produced by non-renewable sources, as well as the removal of subsidies given to fossil fuel generation [34]. Moreover, even though the total initial cost for the photovoltaic power plant is lower than for the wind turbine installation, it can be inferred from the financial indicators that the investment is much more convenient for the wind turbine project, which is able to cover its initial costs in a time 14% of the total lifetime; on the other side, with photovoltaics installation you will cover the costs after 70% of the project lifetime. Another aspect for policy makers to consider is looking at the financial issues that might prevent investment decisions. In this perspective, enhancing the green finance—i.e., the financing of investments that provide environmental benefits in the broader context of environmentally sustainable development [35]—may significantly contribute to guaranteeing capital flow in renewable energy sectors [36] so as to enhance the sustainability of the overall financial system [37] as well as to improve corporate planning strategies [38].

Overall, the aim of this study is not to evaluate which renewable technology is more affordable or efficient (it is very easy to find wind turbine for high-capacity systems and, on the contrary, projecting photovoltaic installation is usually aimed at small-capacity systems, such as houses), but to understand how the RETScreen software could be successfully adopted in decision-making processes in an early stage (e.g., pre-feasibility analysis), to effectively exclude inconvenient choices under determined constraints. From this perspective, a technique for optimizing a renewable energy network is developed using RETScreen software tool. It is built to maximize the size of an integrated hybrid energy system in buildings. Case studies for a single and an integrated renewable energy program may research the efficiency of the methods [39]. Another example of using RETScreen is to provide a techno-economic assessment of a certain type of renewable energy installation only after evaluating the environmental consequences of the selected energy systems through comprehensive life cycle assessment (LCA) with a more accurate tool [40]. To provide evidence for how it is valuable to move from traditional energy resources to renewable ones, another case study using RETScreen described how urban photovoltaic installations could improve sustainability in Saudi Arabia [41].

The significant number of analyses carried out with RETScreen is all thanks to the worldwide satellite missions providing data for Earth monitoring, even mapping areas where no ground-based information is available, due to territorial constraints (islands, mountains, etc.).

5. Conclusions

At the Conference of the Parties in December 2015 (Paris Agreement), 195 countries agreed to take urgent action to combat climate change by limiting global warming to well below 2 °C and pursuing efforts to limit it to 1.5 °C. The space industry, and related applications and tools, gives rise to a significant and innovative approach to clean energy generation; it is enough to think that starting from satellite missions, providing more and more accurate weather information, we are able to map every area of the globe, overcoming data limitation due to the lack of meteorological ground stations.

The novelty of this work comes from the emphasis given to one of the most innovative fields of study (i.e., space research) for finding solutions for our environment by trying to exploit already existing technologies, such as EO satellites or deep space exploration applications (them being mostly circular systems). Applying RETScreen software could be useful in the pre-feasibility phase to discriminate the type of installation that is not efficient for the selected location or not convenient in terms of IRR on equity. Results of our analysis indicate that, looking at the geographical context of our case studies, the wind turbine system is much more efficient than the photovoltaics in terms of financial indicators as well as the annual emission reduction of greenhouse gases.

There is a need to expand research based upon space exploration applications to develop capacity building and create less uncertainty for financing long-term projects to accelerate the circular economy framework. Governments and industry must increase R&D efforts to reduce costs and ensure space-based technologies' readiness for rapid deployment, while also supporting longer-term technology innovations.

Author Contributions: Conceptualization, M.A. and P.M.F.; methodology, M.A.; software, M.A.; validation, P.M.F., formal analysis, M.A.; investigation, M.A.; resources, M.A.; data curation, M.A.; writing—original draft preparation, M.A.; writing—review and editing, P.M.F.; visualization, M.A.; supervision, P.M.F.; project administration, P.M.F. All authors have read and agreed to the published version of the manuscript.

Funding: This research received no external funding.

Conflicts of Interest: The authors declare no conflict of interest.

Abbreviations

CCGT	combined-cycle gas turbine
CE	circular economy
DST	decision support tool
EO	earth observation
ESA	European Space Agency
EU	European Union
GHG	greenhouse gases
HRSG	heat recovery steam generator
IRR	internal rate of return
LCOE	levelized cost of electricity
NASA	National Aeronautics and Space Administration
NPV	net present value
O&M	operation and maintenance
RETs	renewable-energy and energy-efficient technologies
ROA	return on assets
ROE	return on equity
ROI	return on investments
SDGs	sustainable development goals
T&D	transmission and distribution

References and Note

1. Majidi Nezhad, M.; Groppi, D.; Rosa, F.; Piras, G.; Cumo, F.; Garcia, D.A. Nearshore wave energy converters comparison and Mediterranean small island grid integration. *Sustain. Energy Technol. Assess.* **2018**, *30*, 68–76. [CrossRef]
2. Bi, J.; Sarpong, D.; Botchie, D.; Rao-Nicholson, R. From imitation to innovation: The discursive processes of knowledge creation in the Chinese space industry. *Technol. Forecast. Soc. Chang.* **2017**, *120*, 261–270. [CrossRef]
3. Whealan George, K. The Economic Impacts of the Commercial Space Industry. *Space Policy* **2019**, *47*, 181–186. [CrossRef]
4. Bockel, J.-M. *The Future of the Space Industry*; NATO Parliamentary Assembly: Brussels, Belgium, 2018.
5. Friel, M. Tourism as a driver in the space economy: New products for intrepid travellers. *Curr. Issues Tour.* **2019**, 1–6. [CrossRef]
6. Forganni, A. The potential of space tourism for space popularisation: An opportunity for the EU Space Policy? *Space Policy* **2017**, *41*, 48–52. [CrossRef]

7. Esterhazy, D. The role of the space industry in building capacity in emerging space nations. *Adv. Space Res.* **2009**, *44*, 1055–1057. [CrossRef]
8. Ardolino, F.; Arena, U. Biowaste-to-Biomethane: An LCA study on biogas and syngas roads. *Waste Manag.* **2019**, *87*, 441–453. [CrossRef]
9. D'Adamo, I.; Gastaldi, M.; Rosa, P. Recycling of end-of-life vehicles: Assessing trends and performances in Europe. *Technol. Forecast. Soc. Chang.* **2020**, *152*, 119887. [CrossRef]
10. D'Amato, D.; Droste, N.; Allen, B.; Kettunen, M.; Lähtinen, K.; Korhonen, J.; Leskinen, P.; Matthies, B.D.; Toppinen, A. Green, circular, bio economy: A comparative analysis of sustainability avenues. *J. Clean. Prod.* **2017**, *168*, 716–734. [CrossRef]
11. Werning, J.P.; Spinler, S. Transition to circular economy on firm level: Barrier identification and prioritization along the value chain. *J. Clean. Prod.* **2020**, *245*, 118609. [CrossRef]
12. Tseng, M.-L.; Lin, S.; Chen, C.-C.; Sarmiento, L.S.C.; Tan, C.L. A causal sustainable product-service system using hierarchical structure with linguistic preferences in the Ecuadorian construction industry. *J. Clean. Prod.* **2019**, *230*, 477–487. [CrossRef]
13. Lin, W.; Hong, C.; Zhou, Y. Multi-Scale Evaluation of Suzhou City's Sustainable Development Level Based on the Sustainable Development Goals Framework. *Sustainability* **2020**, *12*, 976. [CrossRef]
14. Popović, B.; Janković Šoja, S.; Paunović, T.; Maletić, R. Evaluation of Sustainable Development Management in EU Countries. *Sustainability* **2019**, *11*, 7140. [CrossRef]
15. United Nations Office for Outer Space Affairs. *European Global Navigation Satellite System and Copernicus: Supporting the Sustainable Development Goals*; United Nations Office for Outer Space Affairs: Vienna, Austria, 2018.
16. Boyd, D.S.; Jackson, B.; Wardlaw, J.; Foody, G.M.; Marsh, S.; Bales, K. Slavery from space: Demonstrating the role for satellite remote sensing to inform evidence-based action related to UN SDG number 8. *ISPRS J. Photogramm. Remote Sens.* **2018**, *142*, 380–388. [CrossRef]
17. Ayad, A.; Matthews, R.; Vitanov, I. Evaluation of Knowledge Flow from Developed to Developing Countries in Small Satellite Collaborative Projects: The Case of Algeria. *Space Policy* **2020**, *51*, 101360. [CrossRef]
18. Dai, Y.; Feng, L.; Hou, X.; Choi, C.-Y.; Liu, J.; Cai, X.; Shi, L.; Zhang, Y.; Gibson, L. Policy-driven changes in enclosure fisheries of large lakes in the Yangtze Plain: Evidence from satellite imagery. *Sci. Total Environ.* **2019**, *688*, 1286–1297. [CrossRef]
19. Morone, P.; Falcone, P.M.; Tartiu, V.E. Food waste valorisation: Assessing the effectiveness of collaborative research networks through the lenses of a COST action. *J. Clean. Prod.* **2019**, *238*, 117868. [CrossRef]
20. Smith, J.; Bazar, D.; Buchan, W. Greenspace: Leveraging NASA Capabilities for a Cleaner, Greener Earth. In Proceedings of the 7th International Energy Conversion Engineering Conference, Denver, CO, USA, 2–5 August 2009; p. 4583.
21. Leibrand, A.; Sadoff, N.; Maslak, T.; Thomas, A. Using Earth Observations to Help Developing Countries Improve Access to Reliable, Sustainable, and Modern Energy. *Front. Environ. Sci.* **2019**, *7*, 123. [CrossRef]
22. Nezhad, M.M.; Groppi, D.; Marzialetti, P.; Fusilli, L.; Laneve, G.; Cumo, F.; Garcia, D.A. Wind energy potential analysis using Sentinel-1 satellite: A review and a case study on Mediterranean islands. *Renew. Sustain. Energy Rev.* **2019**, *109*, 499–513. [CrossRef]
23. Sener Aeroespacial Copernicus. Available online: http://www.aerospace.sener/products/copernicus (accessed on 15 January 2020).
24. Mirzahosseini, A.H.; Taheri, T. Environmental, technical and financial feasibility study of solar power plants by RETScreen, according to the targeting of energy subsidies in Iran. *Renew. Sustain. Energy Rev.* **2012**, *16*, 2806–2811. [CrossRef]
25. Friedl, L. Benefits Assessment of Applied Earth Science. In *Satellite Earth Observations and Their Impact on Society and Policy*; Springer: Singapore, 2017; pp. 73–79.
26. HOMER Energy. *Homer Pro Version 3.7 User Manual*; HOMER Energy: Boulder, CO, USA, 2016.
27. Stackhouse, P.W., Jr.; Zhang, T.; Westberg, D.; Barnett, A.J.; Bristow, T.; Macpherson, B.; Hoell, J.M.; Hamilton, B.A. *POWER Release 8.0. 1 (with GIS Applications) Methodology (Data Parameters, Sources, & Validation)f.*
28. Owolabi, A.B.; Nsafon, B.E.K.; Roh, J.W.; Suh, D.; Huh, J.-S. Validating the techno-economic and environmental sustainability of solar PV technology in Nigeria using RETScreen Experts to assess its viability. *Sustain. Energy Technol. Assess.* **2019**, *36*, 100542. [CrossRef]

29. Zandi, M.; Bahrami, M.; Eslami, S.; Gavagsaz-Ghoachani, R.; Payman, A.; Phattanasak, M.; Nahid-Mobarakeh, B.; Pierfederici, S. Evaluation and comparison of economic policies to increase distributed generation capacity in the Iranian household consumption sector using photovoltaic systems and RETScreen software. *Renew. Energy* **2017**, *107*, 215–222. [CrossRef]
30. Moya, D.; Paredes, J.; Kaparaju, P. Technical, financial, economic and environmental pre-feasibility study of geothermal power plants by RETScreen—Ecuador's case study. *Renew. Sustain. Energy Rev.* **2018**, *92*, 628–637. [CrossRef]
31. Lee, K.-H.; Lee, D.-W.; Baek, N.-C.; Kwon, H.-M.; Lee, C.-J. Preliminary determination of optimal size for renewable energy resources in buildings using RETScreen. *Energy* **2012**, *47*, 83–96. [CrossRef]
32. Ganoe, R.D.; Stackhouse, P.W., Jr.; DeYoung, R.J. *RETScreen Plus Software Tutorial*; National Aeronautics and Space Administration: Washington, DC, USA, 2014.
33. Oropeza, A.; Hays, L. *Small Biphase Wellhead Plant for the Cerro Prieto Mexico Geothermal Field*; Geothermal Resources Council: Davis, CA, USA, 1996.
34. Falcone, P.M.; Lopolito, A.; Sica, E. Instrument mix for energy transition: A method for policy formulation. *Technol. Forecast. Soc. Chang.* **2019**, *148*, 119706. [CrossRef]
35. Falcone, P.M. Green investment strategies and bank-firm relationship: A firm-level analysis. *Econ. Bull.* **2018**, *38*, 2225–2239.
36. Wu, C.-M.; Hu, J.-L. Can CSR reduce stock price crash risk? Evidence from China's energy industry. *Energy Policy* **2019**, *128*, 505–518. [CrossRef]
37. Liebreich, M. *Towards a Green Climate Finance Framework*; Bloomberg New Energy Finance: London, UK, 2011.
38. Lee, Y.-M.; Hu, J.-L. Integrated approaches for business sustainability: The perspective of corporate social responsibility. *Sustainability* **2018**, *10*, 2318. [CrossRef]
39. Milousi, M.; Souliotis, M.; Arampatzis, G.; Papaefthimiou, S. Evaluating the Environmental Performance of Solar Energy Systems Through a Combined Life Cycle Assessment and Cost Analysis. *Sustainability* **2019**, *11*, 2539. [CrossRef]
40. Kyriakopoulos, G. Evaluation of the Energy Efficiency of Renewable Biomass Fuels: An Environmental and Financial Approach. In Proceedings of the World Summit on Knowledge Society, Athens, Greece, 24–26 September 2008; Springer: Berlin/Heidelberg, Germany, 2008; pp. 125–136.
41. Asif, M. Urban scale application of solar PV to improve sustainability in the building and the energy sectors of KSA. *Sustainability* **2016**, *8*, 1127. [CrossRef]

sustainability

MDPI

Article

Towards Eco-Flowable Concrete Production

Maria Rashidi [1,*], Alireza Joshaghani [2,*] and Maryam Ghodrat [1]

[1] Centre for Infrastructure Engineering, Western Sydney University, Penrith, NSW 2751, Australia; m.ghodrat@westernsydney.edu.au

[2] Zachry Department of Civil Engineering, Texas A&M University, College Station, TX 77840, USA

* Correspondence: m.rashidi@westernsydney.edu.au (M.R.); joshaghani@tamu.edu (A.J.)

Received: 20 December 2019; Accepted: 3 February 2020; Published: 7 February 2020

Abstract: Environmental concerns have increased due to the amount of unused/expired plastic medical waste generated in hospitals, laboratories, and other healthcare facilities, in addition to the fact that disposing of such wastes with extremely low degradation levels causes them to remain in the environment for extended periods of time. These issues have led researchers to develop more environmentally friendly alternatives for disposing of plastic medical waste in Australia. This study is an attempt to assess the impacts of using expired plastic syringes as fine aggregate on fresh and hardened characteristics of flowable concrete, which might provide a solution to environmental concerns. Six mixtures of flowable concrete with water-to-cement ratios of 0.38 were studied. It was found that using recycled aggregate in up to 20% can improve the workability and increase the V-funnel values of flowable concrete mixtures. However, using waste aggregates in more than 30% caused an inapt flowability. Adding waste aggregate at the 30%–50% replacement level led to a decrease in the L-box ratio. To verify the utility and the efficacy of this experiment, the connections between different rheological test measurements were also compared by implementing the Pearson correlation function. The mechanical properties of the mixes containing recycled aggregates were decreased at the age of seven days; however, at later ages, waste aggregates increased the strength at the 10%–30% replacement levels.

Keywords: flowable concrete; expired plastic syringes; rheological properties; mechanical behavior

---

1. Introduction

Numerous plastic products are being consumed with the development of society. However, large amounts of plastic waste pose a threat to the environment due to the very low biodegradability of plastic. It is necessary to develop a rational approach to waste disposal which addresses both the economy and environmental protection [1]. The use of recycled plastic aggregates in concrete can reduce the cost, alleviate an environmental problem, and save energy. In the last few decades, the recycling of waste materials has been a serious concern due to the boundaries of landfill spaces and the growing expenses. Based on a national report in 2016, Australia produced 59,000 tons of medical waste each year (Australia's report to the Basel Convention) [2]; disposable syringes made up a large proportion of the overall medical waste production. Plastic syringes contain a high percentage of plastic (about 90%), which means that they have high potential to be recycled. Currently, the main method instated by hospitals for expired plastic syringes is to pass expired plastic syringes through collection agencies, who dump them into landfills. However, recently, there have been significant increases in landfill levees, raising the price of non-recycled waste such as waste syringes.

There are opportunities for using these wastes in other fields, particularly in the construction industry. The field of research on the assessment of the application of plastic waste in concrete mixtures has gained popularity in the last few decades. The use of waste plastic bottles [3], waste PVC pipe [4], and shredded and recycled plastic waste [5–9] has been investigated by various researchers.

Numerous studies have also been carried out on the usage of scrap rubber in both mortar and concrete [10,11]. In fact, using recycled plastic can improve concrete durability when used as fiber. It has also been found that using waste plastic as fiber in concrete leads to a growth in flexural and splitting-tensile strength [12,13]; at the same time, shrinkage and permeability decreased [14]. Other groups of researchers reported that increasing the amount of plastic waste causes a reduction in splitting-tensile, flexural, and compressive strength [15,16]. The main reason for this behavior is the incompatibility between the cement paste and plastic particles [15]. In addition, some researchers found that the shape of the plastic particles is a definitive parameter, in that sharp edges lead to a reduction in slump value [17]. On the other hand, adding plastic particles with a spherical shape enhances fluid ability.

It is observed that previous studies are mainly aimed at the properties of plastic waste as an aggregate substitution in ordinary concrete. Work related to self-compacting concrete containing plastic particles is relatively scarce. Just a few studies are found about the effect of plastic waste on the properties of self-compacting concrete. Overall, based on the detailed survey in the literature, it has been perceived that most of the research carried out so far is on assessing the implementation of plastic waste as a substitution for aggregate in ordinary concrete. There are relatively few studies found on fresh properties of flowable concrete with plastic particles; however, just a few studies have been done on the impact of plastic medical waste on properties of flowable concrete. This oversight is particularly unfortunate considering that flowable concrete has been increasingly used in stay-in-place formwork structures, concrete-filled steel columns, and prefabricated PVC walls and columns because of their light weight, construction simplicity, and their lower noise levels [18,19].

This study focused on integrating the expired plastic syringes into the matrix of flowable concrete mortar as a replacement for fine aggregate. The objective is to reduce the environmental footprint of expired plastic syringes and to avoid sending them into landfills. Recycled medical waste aggregate is produced from expired plastic syringes. This experimental study was done to evaluate the fresh and hardened properties of the flowable concrete with different proportions of fine aggregate substituted by shredded expired plastic syringes.

2. Experimental Study

The experimental study aims to promote the use of sustainable forms of flowable concrete by incorporating recycled aggregates from shredded expired plastic syringes and to develop information on their fresh and hardened mechanical properties.

2.1. Materials and Mix Properties

Cement type I with a fineness of 2850 cm^2/gr and a specific gravity of 3.16 was added to the mixture as the main cementitious material. The chemical composition of the cement is shown in Table 1. The natural coarse aggregate was limestone gravel with a nominal maximum size of 12.5 mm. The specific gravity and water absorption of the coarse aggregate in flowable concrete were 2.82 and 1.95%, respectively. As a fine aggregate, concrete aggregate with a maximum size of 4.75 mm was added to the mixture. In addition, the fine aggregate had a specific gravity and water absorption of 2.67 and 2.51%, respectively. The physical properties of the aggregates are shown in Table 2. The natural aggregate gradation is shown in Figure 1 with black lines. Moreover, the recycled coarse and fine aggregates are shown in Figure 1 with solid and dashed red lines, respectively. a High-Range Water-Reducing Admixture (HRWRA) with a polycarboxylic-ether base and a specific gravity of 1.09 was used in this study. The HRWRA was used in flowable concrete mixes to reach the flowability target, i.e., the initial slump flow of 650 ± 25 mm.

Table 1. Chemical and physical properties of Type I cement.

Chemical Properties	(wt. %)
SiO_2	20.03
Al_2O_3	5.53
Fe_2O_3	3.63
CaO	62.25
MgO	3.42
SO_3	2.23
K_2O	0.73
Na_2O	0.3
Specific gravity (kg/m^3)	3150
Specific surface area (m^2/kg)	290

Table 2. Physical properties of aggregates.

Properties	Coarse Aggregate	Fine Aggregate	Plastic Waste
Specific Gravity	2.82	2.67	0.97
Water Absorption (%)	1.95	2.51	0.1
Maximum Size (mm)	12.5	4.75	4.75

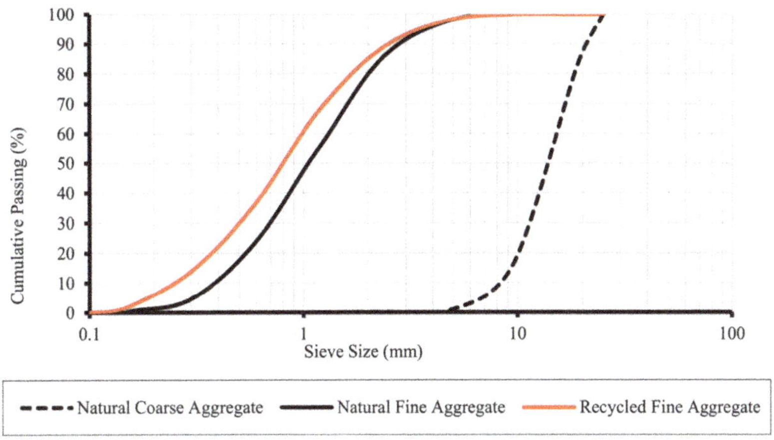

Figure 1. Sieve analysis of coarse and fine aggregates for both natural and recycled aggregates.

2.2. Preparation of Expired Plastic Syringe Aggregate

The flowable concrete mixes of the experimental program were produced using natural aggregates and aggregates from shredded expired plastic syringes. The recyclability of the syringes' bodies and needle attachments were considered initially; this provided a relatively wide scope of materials, e.g., plastic, metal, and rubber. Plastic syringes (50 and 10 mL used in this study) have a high plastic content (around 90%). About 400 expired 50 and 10 mL plastic syringes with different brands and manufacturers were collected from hospitals, laboratories, and dental clinics all around the greater Sydney region. The unused syringes were then shredded by a 1.5 kW jaw crusher, as shown in Figure 2a; the steel needle parts were then removed by a 2 ton Beaver Permanent Magnet Lifter (Figure 2b).

(**a**) The jaw crusher (**b**) The magnet lifter for removing steel needle parts

Figure 2. Waste plastic sample preparation.

Figure 3 represents the plastic types that exist in expired plastic syringes: Rubber, white, green, and crystal plastic. As can be seen from Figure 3, the crushed particles of the rubber plunger are bigger in size when compared with other plastic particles. The microstructural properties of the four plastic types were examined in order to understand the elements that exist in each type.

Crystal plastic particles Green plastic particles Rubber particles White plastic particles

Figure 3. Types of plastic in the expired plastic syringes collected from hospitals and vet clinics.

2.3. *Microstructural Properties of Waste Plastic Syringe Composites*

Scanning electron microscopy (SEM) and energy-dispersive spectroscopy (EDS) tests of ground expired plastic syringes were carried out to analyze the elements existing in these wastes. Four types of plastic particles, including rubber, crystal plastic, green plastic, and white plastic were visually detected and examined. The elemental analyses of these four plastic particles are reported in Figure 4. Samples were X-ray mapped using a JEOL JXA-8600 super probe SEM with an "AMPTEK" EDS silicon drift detector [20]. SEM allows greater magnification, resolution, and depth-of-field than those of an optical microscope. X-ray microanalysis was used to identify, locate, and quantify the elements that compose a specimen, as shown in Figure 4. The results showed the elemental differences between the different plastic particles in expired syringes. As can be seen from Figure 4, carbon is the dominant element in all plastic particle types detected in expired syringes except rubber particles, in which SiO_2 plays a governing role, followed by CaO and SO_3. Previous studies displayed that adhesion between rubber parts and the cement paste seems to be substantial for the product properties [21].

	SEM Image	XRD from EDS Microanalysis
Crystal plastic	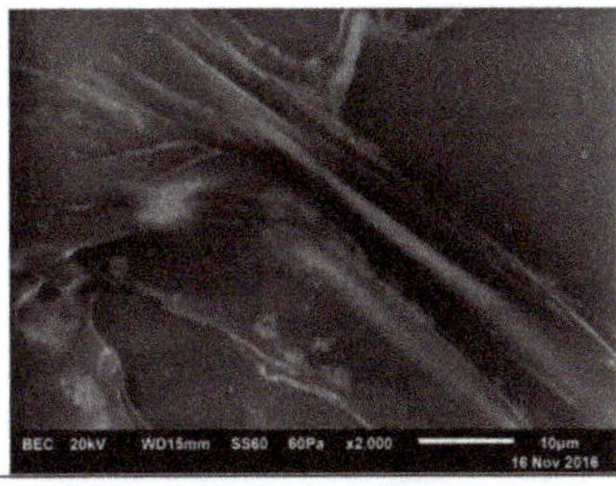	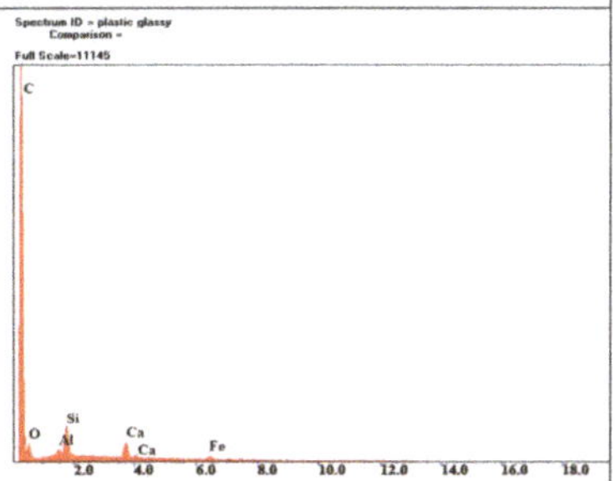
Green plastic	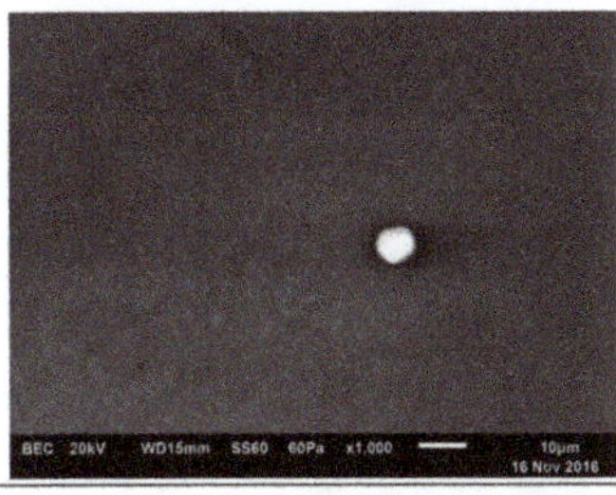	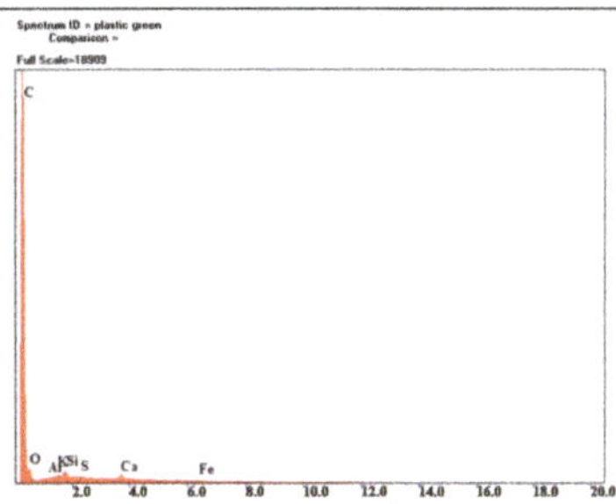
Rubber	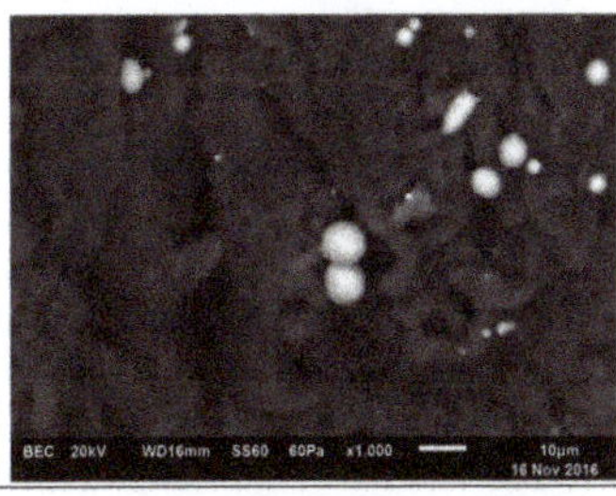	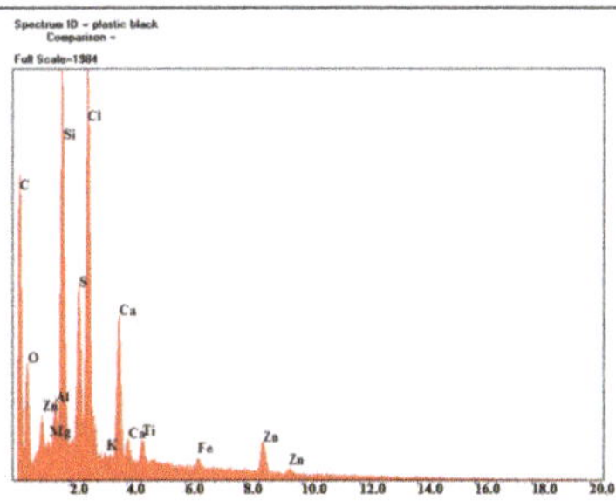
White plastic	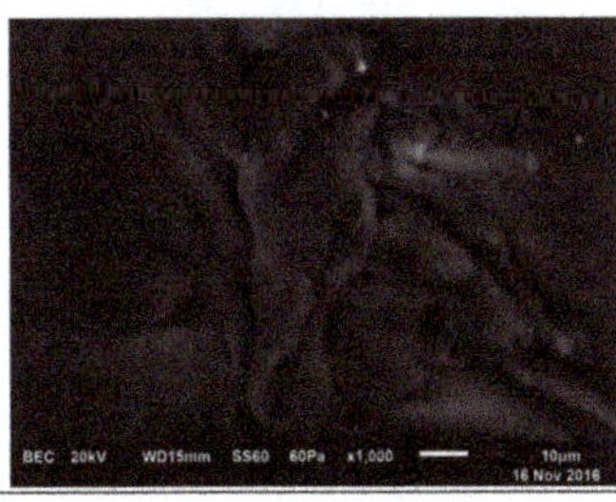	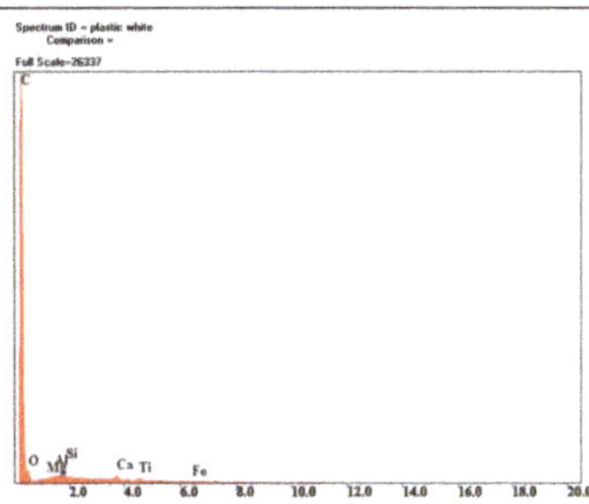

Figure 4. Scanning electron microscopy (SEM) micrographs and energy-dispersive spectroscopy (EDS) microanalysis of materials in expired/waste plastic syringes.

2.4. Mixture Proportion

The binder content for this study was 500 kg/m^3 with a constant water-to-cement ratio of 0.36. In this experimental study, different series of flowable concrete mixtures incorporating expired plastic syringe particles as a replacement for aggregates were designed. Replacement levels for waste materials were 10%–50% of the fine aggregate weight. The mixture proportions of the flowable concrete with recycled aggregates are presented in Table 3. The mix ID consists of two parts: The number is the replacement percentage and R is the sign of replacement. For example, 20R denotes the mixture with the recycled aggregate replacement of 20% of the weight of the sand.

Table 3. Mix proportion of flowable concrete using natural and recycled aggregates (kg/m^3).

Name	Cement	Water	CA	FA	SP	RA
Control	500	180	486	1139	1.2	0
10R	500	180	486	1025	1.2	114
20R	500	180	486	911.2	1.3	227.8
30R	500	180	486	797.3	1.2	341.7
40R	500	180	486	683.4	1.2	455.6
50R	500	180	486	569.5	1	569.5

SP: Superplasticizer, RA: Recycled aggregate, CA: Natural coarse aggregate, and FA: Natural fine aggregate.

ASTM C 192 [22] allows aggregates to be dried to the saturated-surface-dry (SSD) condition instead of oven-dried. In this study, towels were used to dry the surface moisture from aggregates to add them into the mix in the SSD condition. The dosage of HRWRA is presented with respect to the cementitious material content (by weight) in Table 3. In addition, Figure 5 displays the procedure of the mixing used to prepare the flowable concrete mixes. Natural and recycled aggregates were mixed before batching the concrete mixture.

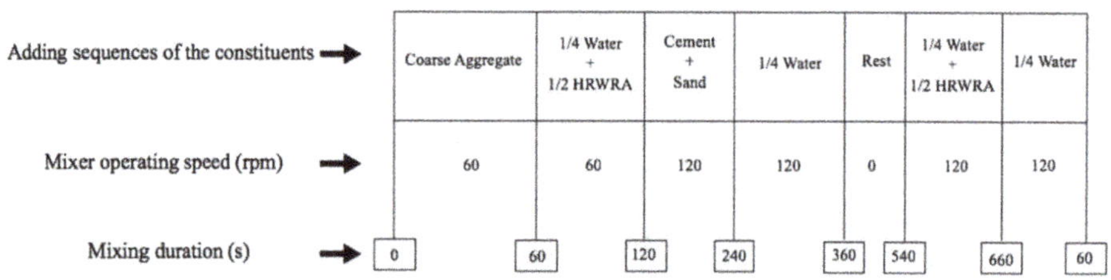

Figure 5. Details of the mixing procedure for flowable concrete with recycled aggregates.

During the first 24 h after pouring, samples were covered with a wet towel at room temperature. Afterward, samples were placed in a lime-saturated water bath at 23 ± 2 °C, where they were kept until the test day. On the test day, specimens were removed from the water bath and brought to SSD condition before they were tested.

2.5. Test Practices

2.5.1. Workability Measurements

The superplasticizer (SP) was adjusted in order to prepare a homogeneous mix with a slump flow diameter of 650 ± 25 mm, as described in the ASTM C 1611 standard [23]. The slump flow T500 test was carried out to take the measurement of the flowable concrete flowability with no obstructions. The purpose of this test was to measure both the flow speed and flow time [24,25]. The T500 time can present the viscosity of the flowable concrete. After preparing the base plate and clean cone, the cone was filled with no agitation or roding. After 30 seconds, the cone was picked up vertically with no interference with the concrete flow, as shown in Figure 6a. To measure the T500 time, the time is started right after the cone case is in contact with the base plate, and timekeeping is continued until the concrete reaches a diameter of 500 mm. The greatest diameter of the flow spread was recorded as the slump flow [26].

(a) Slump flow test (b) V-funnel test

Figure 6. Workability tests: (**a**) Slump flow and (**b**) V-funnel.

The V-funnel was tested based on the BS EN 12350 standard to take a measurement of the flowability through a confined area with no blockage under its own weight. Then, the time that the concrete took to flow through the apparatus (T_V) was recorded. Figure 6b presents the method of performing the V-funnel test.

The J-ring test was also used to measure the passing ability of flowable concrete to fill spaces within the formwork. The J-ring setup includes a slump cone in the middle of a cage of rebar, as shown in Figure 7. This test method was conducted based on the EFNARC specifications and ASTM C1621 [27,28]. The slump cone is filled with concrete and lifted, and the circular flow of concrete is measured. The J-ring flow test represents the passing ability by measuring the difference in the concrete flow diameters (d_2–d_1)) [29].

Figure 7. The J-ring test apparatus for testing the passing ability.

In addition, the L-box test was used as a measurement of the workability of flowable concrete in the presence of obstacles by reinforcing bars in accordance with the BS EN 12350 standard. The L-box test setup has an L-shaped rectangular-section box, as shown in Figure 8. The horizontal and vertical parts are separated by a gate, which is removed after the upright part is filled with flowable concrete. The concrete heights at the vertical part (H_1) and at the end of the horizontal part (H_2) were recorded. The magnitude of H_2/H_1 represents the flowable concrete flowability in the presence of obstacles.

Figure 8. The L-box setup for workability measurement.

The European Federation of National Associations Representing for Concrete (EFNARC) specification defines specific requirements for the flowable concrete material, its composition, and its application. The test procedures that are applied to characterize the properties of flowable concrete have upper and lower limits, as shown in Table 4. The reason is that all flowability limits should be evaluated to fulfill all requirements.

Table 4. Flowable concrete property requirements according to the European Federation of National Associations Representing for Concrete (EFNARC) [27].

Test Method	Unit	Property	Minimum Range	Maximum Range
Slump flow	mm	Filling ability	650	850
T500 slump flow	s	Filling ability	2	5
J-ring	mm	Passing ability	550	750
V-funnel	s	Filling ability	6	12
L-Box	(H_2/H_1)	Passing ability	0.8	1.0

2.5.2. Mechanical Tests

The compressive strengths of flowable concrete specimens were measured at the ages of 7, 28, and 91 days based on ASTM C39. The flowable concrete was cast in 100 × 200 mm cylinders. Concrete specimens with dimensions of 300 × 100 × 100 mm were cast for flexural strength tests (using a beam with three-point loading) based on the committee C-9 of ASTM C78 [30]. Finally, cylinders with a diameter and height of 100 and 200 mm, respectively, were cast for splitting-tensile tests based on the ASTM C496 [31].

3. Experimental Results

3.1. Fresh Properties

Figure 9 illustrates the required HRWRA dosage to reach the slump flow target, 650 ± 25 mm, in each mix. However, the horizontal free flow was changed for flowable concrete mixtures with recycled aggregates. The incorporation of 50% of recycled aggregate caused the highest demand for HRWRA. There was a greater water absorption by using more waste plastic aggregate. For flowable concrete specimens with 30% or more plastic content, the water absorption percentage was significantly greater than those of other specimens with no waste materials. Therefore, samples with greater replacement percentages tended to absorb more water on their surfaces and consequently increased the water demand of the mixtures. Therefore, the lubricant effect of water decreased and the cohesion of flowable concrete mixes increased, which required a higher level of HRWRA to yield the anticipated slump flow. The average slump flows for 10%–20% recycled aggregate replacements were equal to or greater than that of the control sample. This shows the advantages of using recycled aggregate to improve the workability of flowable concrete by only adding up to 20% waste materials. However, 30%–50% replacement decreased the slump flow in comparison with that of the control sample. Al-Hadithi and Hilal reported that slump flow diameters ranging from 650 to 780 mm were obtained for the Self Compacting Concrete (SCC) with plastic waste replacement [32].

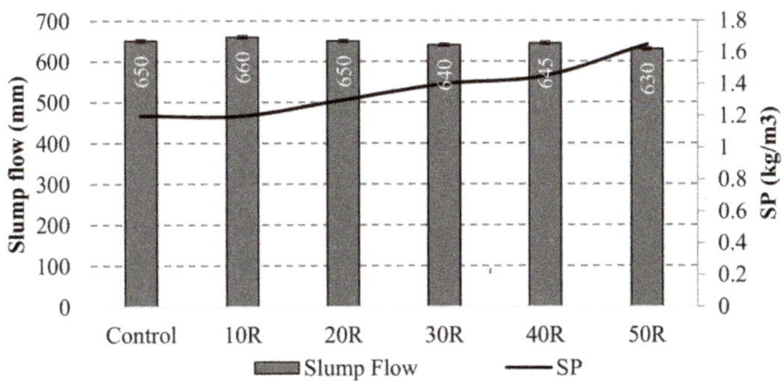

Figure 9. The SP dosage of flowable concrete mixtures to achieve target slump flow.

For all the mixes, although the HRWRA percentage increased with an increased amount of waste aggregate to maintain an acceptable slump, a reduction in the slump flow was seen with increasing waste material content. In addition, the time that the concrete took to achieve the slump flow of 500 mm was measured (T500). Figure 10 shows that the T500 increased from 2.02 seconds for the control flowable concrete to 2.12, 2.26, 2.15, 2.73, and 3.34 for flowable concrete with 10%–50% replacements. Although the plastic waste aggregate did not change the slump flow excessively, the homogeneity of the concrete decreased. The comparison between the T500 and V-funnel flow times of the control sample and flowable concrete at different replacement ratios confirmed that adding waste aggregate significantly increased the flow time.

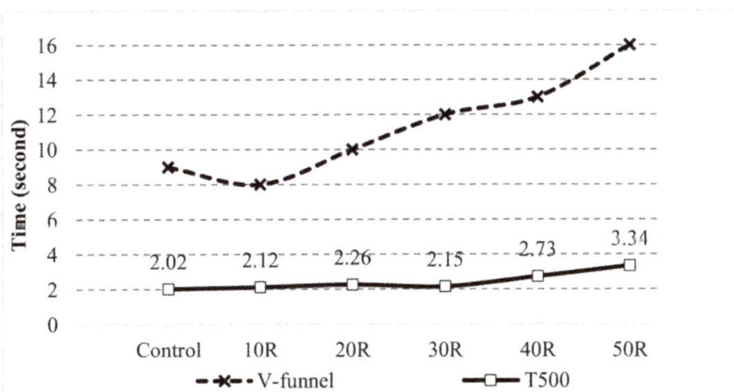

Figure 10. Results of the T500 and V-funnel tests.

The viscosity of flowable concrete was measured by the V-funnel test. Based on the specifications, a longer V-funnel flow time indicates a flowable concrete with greater viscosity. Moreover, those mixtures with shorter V-funnel flow times (i.e., low viscosities) are prone to having segregation [33]. As shown in Figure 10 with a dashed line, using waste aggregates increased the

V-funnel flow time of flowable concrete; thus, the viscosity of SCC would be increased. The minimum value for the V-funnel was 8 seconds, which corresponded with a 10% aggregate replacement. Therefore, all of the flowable concrete mixtures were greater than the minimum EFNARC requirement (i.e., 6 seconds). However, using waste aggregates for more than 30% kept the V-funnel values greater than 12 seconds, which indicated an inappropriate flowability and a viscosity too high for being flowable. Al-Hadithi and Hilal found that the addition of waste plastic increases both T500 slump flow and V-funnel flow times [32].

Figure 11 shows the results of the L-box test. In this test, the L-box values of the mixes, indicating the flowabilities of the mixes, ranged between 0.8 and 1. The mixes with the lower waste aggregate replacement ratios had higher L-box ratio than those with the higher replacement ratios, indicating higher flowability and workability of the mixtures. Addition of waste aggregate at a 30%–50% replacement level decreased the L-box ratio in comparison to that of the control specimen. According to Albano et al., having a higher absorption capacity in mixtures with plastic aggregates can influence the porosity [34]. This behavior can cause an increase in viscosity, as is evident from the reduced L-box ratio magnitudes. The L-box ratio of the mix 10R was greater than those of other mixtures, which indicates that 10% replacement of waste aggregate was more successful in improving workability in comparison with other replacements. Al-Hadithi and Hilal also reported the same trend in L-box testing [32].

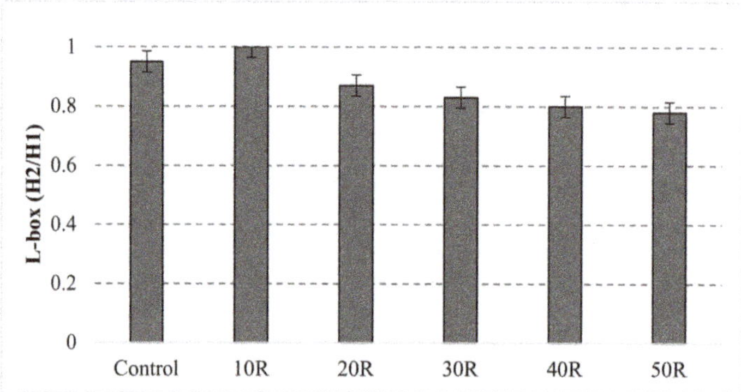

Figure 11. The L-box test results.

The results of the J-ring test also confirmed the results obtained by the L-box, V-funnel, and slump flow tests (see Figure 12). The maximum reduction of mixtures in slump flow in the J-ring test was not higher than 50 mm, except with 50R. Brameshuber and Uebachs [35] reported that a flowable concrete mixture with an acceptable passing ability should have a blocking index (difference between J-ring flow and slump flow) of less than 50 mm to not see any blockage. Figure 12 demonstrates the influences of recycled aggregate on the J-ring flow results; i.e., the passing ability was decreased for 20%–50% replacements as the J-ring flow decreased. On the contrary, the J-ring flow was improved at the 10% waste aggregate replacement level, which shows a greater passing ability compared to that of the control sample. The higher percentage of waste materials made the concrete less workable and increased the potential of blocking. Due to the angularity and rough surface texture of the waste aggregate, the passing ability of flowable concrete was decreased by its friction. Safiuddin et al. reported the same behavior when using construction waste aggregates [36].

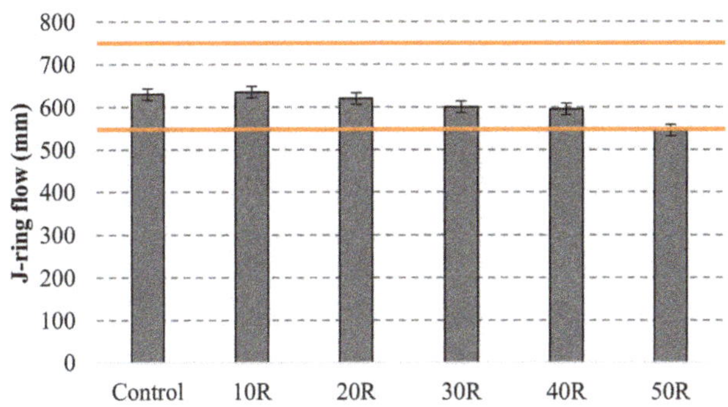

Figure 12. Results of the recycled aggregate on the J-ring flow of concrete.

In order to verify the utility and efficacy of using waste plastic materials, the correlations between different rheological test measurements were calculated by employing the Pearson correlation method, as shown in Table 5. The correlation coefficient is a number between −1 and +1. This number can specify how strongly two factors are correlated to each other. Coefficients of -1 and +1 designate great negative and positive correlations, respectively [37]. In this study, an absolute value of a correlation coefficient of greater than 0.8 was considered as a robust correlation. In addition, a correlation coefficient of less than 0.5 was considered as a weak correlation.

Table 5. Pearson correlation numbers of fresh properties.

	Slump Flow	J-Ring	V-funnel	T500	L-Box
Slump Flow	1	-	-	-	-
J-Ring	0.935	1	-	-	-
V-funnel	−0.942	−0.982	1	-	-
T500	−0.765	−0.931	0.906	1	-
L-Box	0.8761	0.848	−0.923	−0.745	1

The correlation coefficients between the slump flow, J-ring, L-box, and V-funnel were greater than 0.8, which shows a strong correlation. However, the T500 test was weakly correlated with other rheological factors. These relationships between the fresh properties were considered as a strong correlation. The effects of using the waste aggregate in flowable concrete by different levels of replacement were identical. In other words, the rheological properties (stability, mobility, and compactability) were improved in the same manner.

3.2. Mechanical Tests

The compressive strengths of samples were measured at the ages of 7, 28, and 91 days. As can be seen in Figure 13, at the age of 7 days, samples containing recycled aggregates resulted in lower compressive strength values than that of the control sample. However, at the age of 28 days, using waste aggregates increased the compressive strengths of the samples beyond those of the control mix, except for the 30%–50% replacement percentages. Safi et al. reported that the compressive strength of self-compacting mortars decreased with the increase in plastic waste content at all curing times [38]. At 30% and 50% substitution of waste, the percentages of reduction of compressive strength were 15% and 33%, respectively. Other authors found that, compared to control mixes, up to 72% reductions in compressive strength were observed for concrete with 20% replacement [39,40].

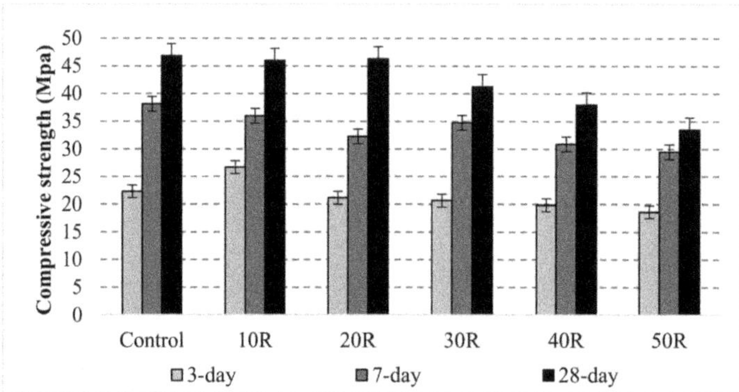

Figure 13. Results of the compressive strength test.

The same trend was seen in the tensile test. As shown in Figure 14, using waste materials as aggregates reduced the splitting-tensile strength of SCC excessively. By using waste products instead of natural aggregates, in comparison with the control sample, the splitting-tensile strengths of samples decreased by 22.3% by adding 50% waste. In addition, Figure 15 shows that the average value for the flexural strength test of the control samples was higher than for other samples except 40R after 7 days. However, after 28 days, for flexural strength, there was a great improvement in 20%–50% replacement percentages, as shown in Figure 15. The highest increase was in the SCC samples by adding 40% waste materials, as the flexural strength increased by 25.8%. Adding 10% waste materials did not change the flexural strength and decreased it insignificantly. The flexural strength decreased by 35% by adding 10% waste products. Other authors reported that the flexural tensile strength decreases with the increase in plastic waste content. Authors found that this is due to the low resistance of the waste [41].

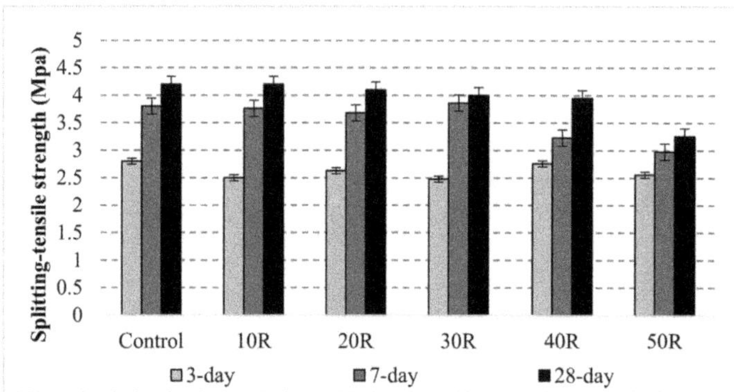

Figure 14. Results of the splitting-tensile strength test.

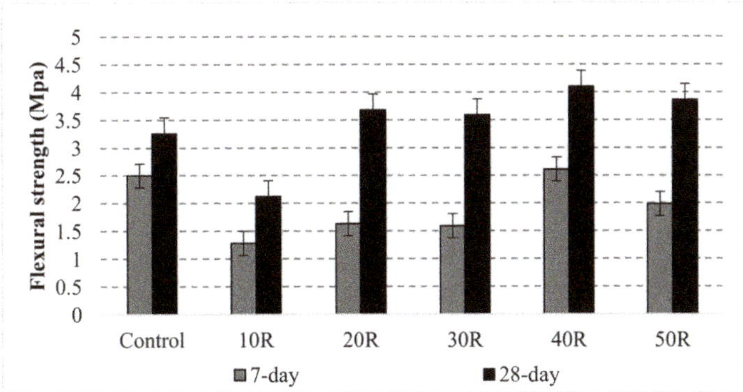

Figure 15. Results of the flexural strength test.

The analysis of variance (ANOVA) is shown in Table 6, which indicates whether the strength differences between samples containing waste replacement and the control sample are significant. As this evaluation was done within the samples in one group, it is called an omnibus test. Based on a defined level of 0.05, when the significance factor with waste materials is less than or equal to 0.05, there is a significant difference between this and the strength of the control sample. Otherwise, samples with significance factors of higher than 0.05 have an insignificant difference with the control sample [42,43]. When adding waste materials, the compressive strengths and splitting-tensile strengths of flowable concrete samples were decreased, but the magnitudes of strength did not change noticeably at small replacement levels. Table 6 shows that the percentage reduction of 50R compared to the control sample was significant for both compressive and splitting-tensile strengths. Based on statistical analysis, all significance factors are larger than 0.05 for replacing waste materials up to 40%. This indicates that almost all compressive and splitting-tensile strength values were in the same range. Based on ANOVA, adding 10% waste materials decreased the flexural strength significantly compared to that of the control sample. While using waste materials to replace more than 10% of the fine aggregates had a slight impact on the flexural strength compared to that of control sample, no notable changes were observed in improving the flexural strength at 28 days.

Table 6. Effects of waste materials on the compressive, splitting-tensile, and flexural strengths of flowable concrete samples after 28 days.

Mixture ID	Waste Replacement (%)	Compressive Strength		Splitting-Tensile Strength		Flexural Strength	
		Std Dev.	Sig. *	Std Dev.	Sig.	Std Dev.	Sig.
Control	0	1.19	-	0.56	-	0.38	-
10R	10	0.92	1.000	0.42	1.000	0.26	0.013
20R	20	1.20	1.000	0.26	1.000	0.14	1.000
30R	30	1.12	0.292	0.49	0.968	0.17	1.000
40R	40	0.78	0.081	0.18	0.477	0.10	0.877
50R	50	1.51	0.002	0.41	0.032	0.08	0.995

* The mean difference is significant at the 0.05 level.

4. Limitations and Future Directions

The legal requirements for different management methods of plastic medical waste along with additional recommended controls and explanations are considered as the key limitations for efficient management of these kinds of wastes.

The lack of strategic planning among the responsible organizations is a big issue, and there is minimal level of awareness among some hospital staff regarding the risks to the environment resulting from inappropriate management of unused plastic medical waste.

The future avenues for efficient waste management at healthcare facilities would include the better education of healthcare workers and standardized sorting of medical waste streams; hence, further research is required given the trend in increased medical waste production with increasing global GDP.

Role towards Sustainability

The main role of this research with respect to sustainability is to introduce a more sustainable method of the usage of expired/unused plastic medical waste and puts forward appropriate countermeasures for the acting facilities operation, performance management and other aspects. The environmental and economic burden related to the management of unused plastic medical waste is huge. The data presented in this research pointed out that using expired plastic syringes as fine aggregate in the production of flowable concrete might provide a solution to environmental concerns, in addition to mediating the cost of the waste treatment.

There are a number of moves that governments could make to improve expired plastic syringe treatment and disposal. Firstly, governments should standardize explicit classification of expired plastic/glass syringes and IDUs (injection drug units) and tightly regulate the disposal of each type to prevent their dumping. In addition, governments need to provide healthcare facilities with incentives for reducing sharp production through adequate procurement of staff training and putting into place an accurate database regarding the level of demands that each hospital has in order to avoid over-ordering syringes and other medical devices. Lastly, governments should increase research funding in the area of medical waste reduction and treatment though research grants and industry research partnerships.

5. Conclusions

This study explored the properties of flowable concrete made with shredded waste plastic syringes as fine aggregate. The following conclusions can be drawn:

- The amount of water absorption was increased with the incorporation of expired plastic aggregate. Thus, the incorporation of 50% recycled aggregate caused the highest demand for HRWRA due the greater absorption of water on their surface.
- Using recycled aggregate for up to 20% can improve the workability of fresh flowable concrete. Therefore, the HRWRA percentage increased with an increased amount of waste aggregate to maintain an acceptable slump.
- Using waste aggregates increased the V-funnel results of flowable concrete mixes; thus, the viscosity of the SCC increased. However, using waste aggregates for more than 30% made an inappropriate flowability and made the mixes too viscous to be flowable.
- Addition of waste aggregate at a 30%–50% replacement level decreased the L-box ratio in comparison to that of the control sample. The 10% replacement of waste aggregate was more successful in improving workability.
- The results of the J-ring test also confirmed the results obtained by the slump flow, L-box, and V-funnel tests. The correlation coefficients between the slump flow, V-funnel, J-ring, and L-box tests indicate a strong correlation.
- At the age of seven days, the samples containing recycled aggregates showed a lower compressive strength than that of the control sample. However, at the age of 28 days, using waste aggregates increased the compressive strength of the samples (except 30%–50% replacements). The same trend was seen in the splitting-tensile and flexural tests.

Author Contributions: Formal analysis, A.J. and M.G.; Funding acquisition, M.R.; Investigation, M.R.; Methodology, A.J. and M.G.; Writing—original draft, A.J. and M.G.; Writing—review and editing, M.R. All authors have read and agreed to the published version of the manuscript.

Funding: This research received no external funding.

Conflicts of Interest: The authors declare no conflict of interest.

References

1. Duque-Acevedo, M.; Belmonte-Ureña, L.J.; Cortés-García, F.J.; Camacho-Ferre, F. Agricultural waste: Review of the evolution, approaches and perspectives on alternative uses. *Glob. Ecol. Conserv.* **2020**, *22*, e00902. [CrossRef]
2. Elmer, J. The Basel Convention: Effect on the Asian secondary lead industry. *J. Power Sources* **1996**, *59*, 1–7. [CrossRef]
3. Akçaözoğlu, S.; Atiş, C.D.; Akçaözoğlu, K. An investigation on the use of shredded waste PET bottles as aggregate in lightweight concrete. *Waste Manag.* **2010**, *30*, 285–290. [CrossRef] [PubMed]
4. Mohammed, A.A.; Mohammed, I.I.; Mohammed, S.A. Some properties of concrete with plastic aggregate derived from shredded PVC sheets. *Constr. Build. Mater.* **2019**, *201*, 232–245. [CrossRef]
5. Hama, S.M.; Hilal, N.N. Fresh properties of self-compacting concrete with plastic waste as partial replacement of sand. *Int. J. Sustain. Built Environ.* **2017**, *6*, 299–308. [CrossRef]
6. Gesoglu, M.; Güneyisi, E.; Hansu, O.; Etli, S.; Alhassan, M. Mechanical and fracture characteristics of self-compacting concretes containing different percentage of plastic waste powder. *Constr. Build. Mater.* **2017**, *140*, 562–569. [CrossRef]
7. Sadrmomtazi, A.; Dolati-Milehsara, S.; Lotfi-Omran, O.; Sadeghi-Nik, A. The combined effects of waste Polyethylene Terephthalate (PET) particles and pozzolanic materials on the properties of self-compacting concrete. *J. Clean. Prod.* **2016**, *112*, 2363–2373. [CrossRef]
8. Pouranian, M.R.; Notani, M.A.; Tabesh, M.T.; Nazeri, B.; Shishehbor, M. Rheological and environmental characteristics of crumb rubber asphalt binders containing non-foaming warm mix asphalt additives. *Constr. Build. Mater.* **2020**, *238*, 117707. [CrossRef]
9. Gonzalez-Sanchez, J.F.; Fernandez-Alvarez, J.M.; Alvarez, J.I.; Navarro-Blasco, I.Í. Solidification/Stabilization of hazardous wastes from the mine La Prieta in Hidalgo del Parral, Chihuahua, México. Available online: https://dadun.unav.edu/bitstream/10171/43879/1/2017-04-06-X%20JICES-Poster-Fidel.pdf (accessed on 12 January 2020).
10. Thomas, B.S.; Gupta, R.C. a comprehensive review on the applications of waste tire rubber in cement concrete. *Renew. Sustain. Energy Rev.* **2016**, *54*, 1323–1333. [CrossRef]
11. Gupta, T.; Chaudhary, S.; Sharma, R.K. Assessment of mechanical and durability properties of concrete containing waste rubber tire as fine aggregate. *Constr. Build. Mater.* **2014**, *73*, 562–574. [CrossRef]
12. Asokan, P.; Osmani, M.; Price, A. Assessing the recycling potential of glass fibre reinforced plastic waste in concrete and cement composites. *J. Clean. Prod.* **2009**, *17*, 821–829. [CrossRef]
13. Boadella, I.L.; Gayarre, F.L.; González, J.S.; Gómez-Soberón, J.M.; Pérez, C.L.-C.; López, M.S.; De Brito, J. The influence of granite cutting waste on the properties of ultra-high performance concrete. *Materials* **2019**, *12*, 634. [CrossRef] [PubMed]
14. Kim, J.-H.J.; Park, C.-G.; Lee, S.-W.; Lee, S.-W.; Won, J.-P. Effects of the geometry of recycled PET fiber reinforcement on shrinkage cracking of cement-based composites. *Compos. Part B Eng.* **2008**, *39*, 442–450. [CrossRef]
15. Kou, S.; Lee, G.; Poon, C.; Lai, W. Properties of lightweight aggregate concrete prepared with PVC granules derived from scraped PVC pipes. *Waste Manag.* **2009**, *29*, 621–628. [CrossRef] [PubMed]
16. Gadea, J.; Rodríguez, A.; Campos, P.; Garabito, J.; Calderón, V. Lightweight mortar made with recycled polyurethane foam. *Cem. Concr. Compos.* **2010**, *32*, 672–677. [CrossRef]
17. Lei, Z.; Bahia, H.; Yi-qiu, T.; Ling, C. Effects of refined waste and bio-based oil modifiers on rheological properties of asphalt binders. *Constr. Build. Mater.* **2017**, *148*, 504–511. [CrossRef]
18. Khayat, K.H.; Meng, W. *Design and Performance of Stay-in-Place UHPC Prefabricated Panels for Infrastructure Construction*; Center for Transportation; Missouri University of Science and Technology: Rolla, MO, USA, 2014.
19. Labuschagne, J.-C. *Formwork Pressures by Self-Compacting Concrete: a Practical Perspective*; Stellenbosch University: Stellenbosch, South Africa, 2018.

20. Salek, S.; Samali, B.; Murphy, T.; Wuhrer, R.; Adam, G. Comparative study between microstructure of a novel durable concrete and normal concrete subjected to harsh environments. In Proceedings of the 9th International Conference on Fracture Mechanics of Concrete and Concrete Structures, San Francisco, CA, USA, 29 May–1 June 2016.
21. Karakurt, C. Microstructure properties of waste tire rubber composites: An overview. *J. Mater. Cycles Waste Manag.* **2015**, *17*, 422–433. [CrossRef]
22. American Society for Testing and Materials. *C192 Standard Practice for Making and Curing Concrete Test Specimens in the Laboratory*; ASTM International: West Conshohocken, PA, USA, 2002.
23. American Society for Testing and Materials. *C1611 Standard Test Method for Slump Flow of Self-Consolidating Concrete*; ASTM International: West Conshohocken, PA, USA, 2009.
24. Ardalan, R.B.; Joshaghani, A.; Hooton, R.D. Workability retention and compressive strength of self-compacting concrete incorporating pumice powder and silica fume. *Constr. Build. Mater.* **2017**, *134*, 116–122. [CrossRef]
25. Joshaghani, A. *Workability Retention and Mechanical Properties of Self-Compacting Concrete (SCC) with Sugar Cane Bagasse Ash (SCBA) and Rice Husk Ash (RHA)*; Nova Science Publishers: New York, NY, USA, 2017; pp. 233–258.
26. Ardalan, R.B.; Emamzadeh, Z.N.; Rasekh, H.; Joshaghani, A.; Samali, B. Physical and mechanical properties of polymer modified self-compacting concrete (SCC) using natural and recycled aggregates. *J. Sustain. Cem. Based Mater.* **2019**. [CrossRef]
27. Efnarc, S. *Guidelines for Self-Compacting Concrete*; Efnarc Association House: Farnham, UK, 2002; pp. 1–32. Available online: www.efnarc.org.
28. Russell, H.G. ASTM Test Methods for Self-Consolidating Concrete. *HPC Bridge Views* **2008**, *50*, 1–11.
29. Askarian, M.; Fakhretaha Aval, S.; Joshaghani, A. a comprehensive experimental study on the performance of pumice powder in self-compacting concrete (SCC). *J. Sustain. Cem. Based Mater.* **2018**, *7*, 340–356. [CrossRef]
30. ASTM International. *Standard Test Method for Flexural Strength of Concrete (Using Simple Beam with Third-Point Loading)*; Committee C09 on Concrete and Concrete Aggregates: West Conshohocken, PA, USA, 2016.
31. Norma, A. C496/C496M-11. In *Standard Test Method for Splitting Tensile Strength of Cylindrical Concrete Specimens*; ASTM International: West Conshohocken, PA, USA, 2004; pp. 469–490.
32. Al-Hadithi, A.I.; Hilal, N.N. The possibility of enhancing some properties of self-compacting concrete by adding waste plastic fibers. *J. Build. Eng.* **2016**, *8*, 20–28. [CrossRef]
33. Karein, S.M.M.; Joshaghani, A.; Ramezanianpour, A.; Isapour, S.; Karakouzian, M. Effects of the mechanical milling method on transport properties of self-compacting concrete containing perlite powder as a supplementary cementitious material. *Constr. Build. Mater.* **2018**, *172*, 677–684. [CrossRef]
34. Albano, C.; Camacho, N.; Hernandez, M.; Matheus, A.; Gutierrez, A. Influence of content and particle size of waste pet bottles on concrete behavior at different w/c ratios. *Waste Manag.* **2009**, *29*, 2707–2716. [CrossRef]
35. Brameshuber, W.; Uebachs, S. Practical experience with the application of self-compacting concrete in Germany. In Proceedings of the 2nd International Symposium on Self-Compacting Concrete, Tokyo, Japan, 3–5 October 2001; pp. 687–696.
36. Safiuddin, M.; Salam, M.; Jumaat, M. Effects of recycled concrete aggregate on the fresh properties of self-consolidating concrete. *Arch. Civ. Mech. Eng.* **2011**, *11*, 1023–1041. [CrossRef]
37. Joshaghani, A.; Bhardwaj, R.; Zollinger, D.G.; Mukhopadhyay, A.K. Investigating the Effects of Curing Quality on Key Concrete Pavement Surface Properties. *Transp. Res. Rec.* **2019**. [CrossRef]
38. Safi, B.; Saidi, M.; Aboutaleb, D.; Maallem, M. The use of plastic waste as fine aggregate in the self-compacting mortars: Effect on physical and mechanical properties. *Constr. Build. Mater.* **2013**, *43*, 436–442. [CrossRef]
39. Ferreira, L.; de Brito, J.; Saikia, N. Influence of curing conditions on the mechanical performance of concrete containing recycled plastic aggregate. *Constr. Build. Mater.* **2012**, *36*, 196–204. [CrossRef]
40. Saikia, N.; De Brito, J. Use of plastic waste as aggregate in cement mortar and concrete preparation: a review. *Constr. Build. Mater.* **2012**, *34*, 385–401. [CrossRef]
41. Rai, B.; Rushad, S.T.; Kr, B.; Duggal, S.K. Study of waste plastic mix concrete with plasticizer. *ISRN Civ. Eng.* **2012**, *2012*, 1–5. [CrossRef]

42. Tabatabaeian, M.; Khaloo, A.; Joshaghani, A.; Hajibandeh, E. Experimental investigation on effects of hybrid fibers on rheological, mechanical, and durability properties of high-strength SCC. *Constr. Build. Mater.* **2017**, *147*, 497–509. [CrossRef]
43. Jafari, K.; Tabatabaeian, M.; Joshaghani, A.; Ozbakkaloglu, T. Optimizing the mixture design of polymer concrete: An experimental investigation. *Constr. Build. Mater.* **2018**, *167*, 185–196. [CrossRef]

sustainability

MDPI

Article

Bioenergy Yields from Sequential Bioethanol and Biomethane Production: An Optimized Process Flow

Lisandra Rocha-Meneses [1,*], Oghenetejiri Frances Otor [2], Nemailla Bonturi [3], Kaja Orupõld [4] and Timo Kikas [1]

1. Institute of Technology, Estonian University of Life Sciences, 51006 Tartu, Estonia; Timo.Kikas@emu.ee
2. School of Engineering, Tallinn University of Technology, 19086 Tallinn, Estonia; otorfrances@gmail.com
3. Institute of Technology, University of Tartu, 50411 Tartu, Estonia; Nemailla.Bonturi@ut.ee
4. Institute of Agricultural and Environmental Sciences, Estonian University of Life Sciences, 51006 Tartu, Estonia; Kaja.Orupold@emu.ee

* Correspondence: lisandra.meneses@emu.ee

Received: 30 November 2019; Accepted: 23 December 2019; Published: 29 December 2019

Abstract: This study investigates the potential of different stages of the bioethanol production process (pretreatment, hydrolysis, and distillation) for bioethanol and biomethane production, and studies the critical steps for the liquid and the solid fractions to be separated and discarded to improve the efficiency of the production chain. For this, Napier grass (a fast-growing grass) from Effurun town of Delta State in Nigeria was used and the novel pretreatment method, nitrogen explosive decompression (NED), was applied at different temperatures. The results show that the lowest glucose (13.7 g/L) and ethanol titers (8.4 g/L) were gained at 150 °C. The highest glucose recovery (31.3 g/L) was obtained at 200 °C and the maximum ethanol production (10.3 g/L) at 170 °C. Methane yields are higher in samples pretreated at lower temperatures. The maximum methane yields were reported in samples from the solid fraction of post-pretreatment (pretreated at 150 °C, 1.13 mol CH4/100 g) and solid fraction of the post-hydrolysis stage (pretreated at 150 °C, 1.00 mol CH4/100 g). The lowest biomethane production was noted in samples from the liquid fraction of post-pretreatment broth (between 0.14 mol CH4/100 g and 0.24 mol CH4/100 g). From the process point of view, samples from liquid fraction of post-pretreatment broth should be separated and discarded from the bioethanol production process, since they do not add value to the production chain. The results suggest that bioethanol and biomethane concentrations are influenced by the pretreatment temperature. Napier grass has potential for bioethanol and further biomethane production and it can be used as an alternative source of energy for the transportation sector in Nigeria and other countries rich in grasses and provide energy security to their population.

Keywords: anaerobic digestion; biofuel; lignocellulose; sidestreams; zero-waste

1. Introduction

The worldwide economic advancements and population growth have been contributing to the increased demand for the electricity generation capacity. About 82% of the gross inland energy consumption in the world still derives from petroleum (32%), coal (28%), and natural gas (22%) [1]. The same trend is evident in different continents and countries around the world, including Nigeria which is one of the major economies in Sub-Saharan Africa and the largest oil producer in Africa. Its total primary energy consumption comes from traditional solid biomass and waste (80%) [2]. The fossil fuels utilised in Nigeria are mainly being consumed in the transportation sector (100% oil), productive (17% gas and 16% oil), and residential uses (3% oil). Nigerian power generation comes mainly from gas (62%), oil (33%), and hydro (5%) [3]. Therefore, there is a need for affordable alternative sources of energy that will decrease the share of fossil fuels utilised in the transportation sector and productive uses, reduce environmental concerns caused by the extensive utilization of these resources (e.g., climate change and global warming), increase energy security, and improve the access of the population to electricity. Renewable energy sources from lignocellulosic biomass have been reported as promising solutions to these problems [4]. Nowadays, biomass itself is responsible for 10% primary energy consumption worldwide [5] and it can be used as a promising feedstock for biofuel production. The sustainability of wastes and by-products as a biofuel for the transportation sector in a circular economy has been studied in the literature, in order to make the biogas–biomethane chain more sustainable [6–8]. These studies show the positive impact of biofuels in the transportation section in Europe. However, further research needs to be done in order to apply circular economy models to emerging economies.

Sub-Saharan Africa has great potential to develop renewable energy sources, such as wind, biomass, solar, and hydro. Just in Nigeria, the biomass potential is about 144 million tonnes per year and the potential of its lignocellulosic agricultural waste varies between 0.4 and 2.3 t/ha, as reported in previous publications [9]. However, the utilisation of biomass resources for electricity, biofuel, or biogas generation has not been extensively utilised or studied in most African countries [9–11]. From the different lignocellulosic materials currently available in Nigeria, Napier grass has been reported to be a particularly attractive feedstock for production of biofuels and bio-based products mainly due to its high cellulose content (34.2–40%), high yields per unit area, tolerance to drought, and a good water use efficiency (ratio of water used by the crop to water lost by evapotranspiration) [12–17].

Napier grass is a perennial C4 plant endemic to Sub-Saharan Africa with a high heating value biomass (16.58 MJ/kg) [18]. This crop is mainly used to feed cattle, but it can also be used for grazing, silage, or hay production or fish food [15]. In moderate climates, it can be harvested up to four times per year [19,20]. However, in most of the cases, Napier grass is a neglected crop that exists in the wild and that does not need to be cultivated [21,22], making it a particularly attractive feedstock for biogas and bioethanol production. Sawasdee and Pisutpaisal [23] studied the potential of Napier grass for biogas production. At 5% total solids, the authors obtained the highest kinetics rate for biogas production and concluded that this feedstock can be grown for this purpose. Narinthorn et al. [13] also investigated the biomethane potential of Napier grass. For this, the authors applied combined alkaline and biological pretreatment methods as a strategy to enhance biomethane yields from Napier grass. The results reveal that alkaline pretreatment method increased the anaerobic digestibility from 49% (untreated grass) to 77% and improved the biomethane yields by about 34%. Janejadkarn and Chavalparit [24] quantified biogas production from Napier grass. The results indicated that with a 2% volatile solids content and an organic load rate of 0.57 kg VS/m^3, it is possible to achieve the maximum biogas yield (0.529 m^3/kg VS). Under the same conditions, the methane production was 0.242 m^3/kg VS added. All this suggests that Napier grass can be successfully converted into biogas by means of anaerobic digestion.

Liu et al. [25] investigated the potential of Napier grass for bioethanol production by using dilute-alkali and dilute-acid pretreatment methods. The results show that, for a feeding concentration of 10 g/L, the theoretical conversion rate of this feedstock is about 12.6%, and for a feeding concentration of 15 g/L its conversion rate increased to 23%. The authors concluded that agricultural waste had potential for bioethanol production. Wongwatanapaiboon et al. [26] analysed the potential of Napier grass as feedstock for lignocellulosic bioethanol production by using alkaline peroxide as a pretreatment method. The ethanol yields from Napier grass produced by simultaneous saccharification and cofermentation (SSCF) are 1171.69 L/ha/year, indicating that Napier grass has potential for cellulosic ethanol production.

Although bioethanol production from lignocellulosic materials has been widely studied, its production still has environmental, economic, and energetic constraints. From the environmental perspective, the sidestream generated after the distillation stage has a high pollutant potential and the best handling options still need to be studied. Economically, the energy costs required in the pretreatment stage are still high, making biofuel production less competitive compared to fossil fuels. Energetically, ethanol from biomass has a low-energy return on energy invested (ERoEI) when compared to coal, oil, and gas. Therefore, solutions to add value to the bioethanol production chain to make its production more competitive are needed. Having this in mind, anaerobic digestion (AD) has been proposed as a handling option for waste recovery from biodegradable waste and bioethanol sidestreams [4,8,27].

As the Nigerian biofuel sector is in a developing stage, this paper aims at evaluating the potential of Nigerian Napier grass for bioethanol and biogas production and at investigating its reliability as an alternative source of energy for the transportation sector in Nigeria and other African countries with high availability of this grass. For this, samples taken from different stages of bioethanol production (pretreatment, hydrolysis, and distillation) and bioethanol sidestream were used. These samples went through a separation process (solid and liquid fractions) and different production pathways in order to enhance bioenergy yields, improve the efficiency of the production chain, decrease the energy and water requirements, and reduce the sidestream volume generated at the end of process.

2. Materials and Methods

2.1. Bioethanol Production

2.1.1. Biomass

The *Penisetum purpurum* (Napier grass) grew in the wild and was harvested near Effurun town of Delta State in Nigeria. It was harvested in the Harmattan period in early January of 2019 and allowed to dry naturally in the sun. After drying, the biomass was shipped to Estonia where all the experiments were carried out. The samples were milled and sieved to the size of 3 mm or smaller in the Cutting Mill SM 100 Comfort (from Retsch GmbH).

2.1.2. Pretreatment

The Napier grass was pretreated with the nitrogen explosive decompression (NED) method. For pretreatment, 100 g of raw material were added into the 2 L non-stirred pressure vessel and soaked in 800 g of distilled water. The vessel was closed, and the samples were heated up from room temperature (23 °C) up to 150 °C, 170 °C, 190 °C, or 200 °C, under constant pressure (30 bar), for the retention time of one minute. Once the desired temperature was reached, the reactor was cooled down to approximately 80 °C and the pressure was released in an explosive manner using the pressure release valve. Figure 1 illustrates the pretreatment system utilised in these experiments. After the pretreatment process, the samples were cooled down to 50 °C for the following enzymatic hydrolysis.

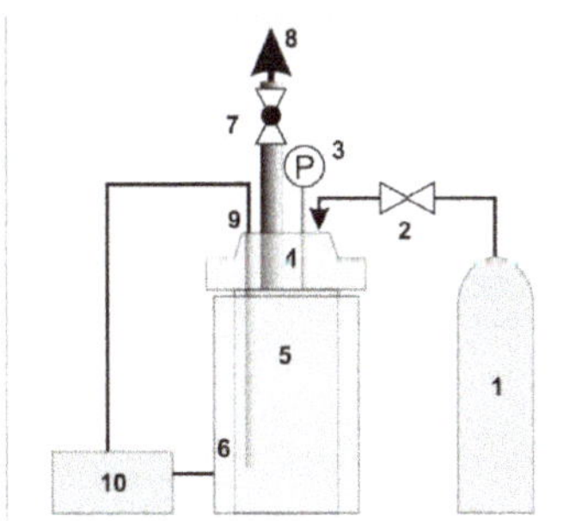

Figure 1. Schematic diagram of the 2 L pressure vessel system (series 4600) for NED pretreatment: 1—nitrogen tank; 2—pressure control valve; 3—manometer; 4—modified pressure vessel cap; 5—Parr instruments pressure vessel; 6—ceramic contact heater; 7—pressure release valve; 8—ventilation system; 9—thermocouple; 10—temperature controller unit [28].

2.1.3. Hydrolysis

The material obtained from the pretreatment process was added into a 1000 mL shake flask for enzymatic hydrolysis. For this, 30 FPU g/cellulose of the cellulase complex Accelerase 1500 (DuPont de Nemours) was added into the suspension, and the flask was filled up with distilled water to 1000 mL (working volume). The process was carried out in an orbital shaker (IKA®-Werke GmbH & Co. KG, Staufen im Breisgau, Germany) (KS 4000 I control) during a 24 h period, at temperature of 50 °C and rotation speed of 250 rpm.

2.1.4. Fermentation

Glucose in the hydrolysate was converted into ethanol in the following fermentation step. The fermentation process was performed in glass bottles with a working volume of 1000 mL, using 2.5 g of the commercial yeast *Saccharomyces cerevisiae* (Turbo yeast T3). After adding the yeast, the glass bottles were closed with an airlock and the fermentation process was carried through for seven days, at room temperature.

2.1.5. Distillation

After the fermentation, the samples went through a distillation process at 175 mbar using a rotating evaporation system designed for ethanol separation, Buchi R-210 Rotavapor System from BÜCHI Labortechnik (Flavil, Switzerland). The material obtained after the distillation process (bioethanol production sidestream) was analysed in terms of its potential for biomethane production in the biomethane potential assay (BMP).

2.2. *Biomethane Potential (BMP)*

Samples from the solid and liquid fractions of different stages of bioethanol production process (pretreatment, hydrolysis, and distillation) were used as a feedstock. Figure 2 illustrates the different production pathways utilised in this study. The BMP was measured in untreated Napier grass (pathway 1), samples from the solid fraction of post-pretreatment broth (pathway 2) and post-hydrolysis broth (pathway 4), and samples from the liquid fraction of post-pretreatment broth (pathway 3), post-hydrolysis broth (pathway 5) and post-distillation broth (pathway 6).

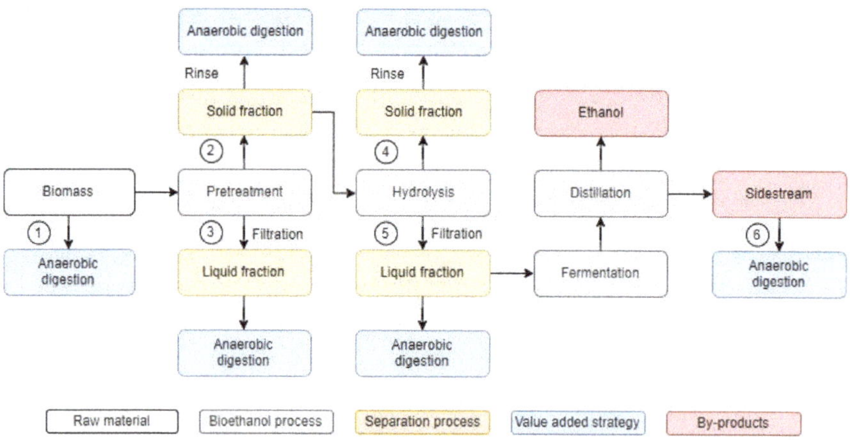

Figure 2. Different production pathways utilised in this study to evaluate the potential of *Pennisetum purpureum* for bioethanol and biogas production by means of solid–liquid separation. 1—untreated Napier grass; 2—samples from the solid fraction of post-pretreatment broth; 3—samples from the liquid fraction of post-pretreatment broth; 4—samples from the solid fraction of post-hydrolysis broth; 5—samples from the liquid fraction of post-hydrolysis broth; 6—samples from post-distillation broth.

The BMP assay utilised in these experiments is based on a modified version of the methods reported by Owen et al. [29] and Angelidaki et al. [30]. The inoculum sludge utilised in this study was obtained from the local wastewater treatment plant (Tartu, Estonia). Prior to use, the inoculum was stabilized for four days in an incubator at 36 °C, so the residual organic matter would be consumed, and the dissolved gases would be removed by a process of degasification. The assays were performed in 575 mL glass bottles, with a working volume of 200 mL, headspace volume of 375 mL and VS substrate/VS inoculum ratio of 0.25 (based on the volatile solids content that characterizes the quantity of organic material available in the solid). Before sealing the bottles, nitrogen gas was purged into the headspace of the flasks for approximately three minutes to ensure anaerobic conditions. The bottles were further sealed with rubber stoppers and aluminium caps, mixed, and incubated for 42 days, under mesophilic conditions (37 °C ± 1 °C) until the methane production was less than 1% of the total amount produced. The bottles were mixed daily by shaking. The experiments were performed in triplicates and a blank test with inoculum sludge only was also prepared in order to determine the methane production from the inoculum sludge itself, which was later utilised in the calculations of methane gas produced.

The biogas production was evaluated by measuring the increase of the total headspace pressure in the test flasks before and after the gas chromatograph (GC) analysis with a pressure meter WAL BMP-Testsystem (from WAL Mess-und Regelsysteme GmbH, Germany).

The pH of all the samples was measured at the end of the experiments with a SevenMulti™ S47-dual pH/conductivity meter to ensure that the anaerobic digestion was performed under optimum conditions (pH of 6.8–7.2) from the beginning until the end of the process [31]. The biomethane results are reported in moles of methane per 100 g of raw material using standard conditions to understand the amount of methane that can be obtained from the original raw material, and in L CH_4/kg VS.

2.3. Analytical Methods

The composition of the samples in terms of cellulose, hemicellulose, and lignin (fibre analysis) was determined using an ANKOM 2000 analyzer (ANKOM Technology, Macedon, NY, USA). The percentage of moisture in the samples was analysed in the Kern MLS-50-3D moisture analyser from Kern & Sohn GmbH.

The active volume of substrate and inoculum was determined from the analysis of the total solids (TS) and volatile solids (VS) content, which were determined according to the method 1684 from the U.S. Environmental Protection Agency (EPA). The methane content in the biogas was measured chromatographically using the GC (CP-4900 Micro-GC, Varian Inc., Palo Alto, CA, USA). The gas chromatograph was equipped with a thermal conductivity detector, a Molsieve 5A Backflush heated column (20 m × 0.53 mm) and a PoraPLOT U heated column (10 m × 0.53 mm). Argon was used as a carrier gas in column 1, and the operational conditions of this column were as follows: injection temperature 110 °C, column temperature 120 °C, and column pressure 50 Psi. In column 2, the carrier gas was helium and the injection temperature, column temperature, and column pressure were set to 110 °C, 150 °C, and 22 Psi, respectively.

The samples of solid and liquid fractions investigated in this study were obtained from different stages of the bioethanol production process (pretreatment, hydrolysis, and distillation) with a separation process using the pathway illustrated in Figure 2. For this, post-pretreatment broth and post-hydrolysis broth were collected and centrifuged using Thermo Scientific Heraeus Megafuge at a rotational speed of 10,000 rpm for 20 min until the solid and liquid fractions were fully separated. To ensure a full separation of the supernatant (liquid fraction) and the retentate (solid fraction), the samples were separated using vacuum filtration. After that, samples from the solid fraction were rinsed with distilled water to remove residual solubles and dried at 40 °C to a moisture content of 4.5% (or less). Both fractions were analysed for BMP.

Glucose, xylose, galactose, arabinose, mannose, glycerol, acetic acid, and ethanol were quantified with a high pressure liquid chromatography [32] using fractions after hydrolysis and fermentation steps.

2.4. Calculations

The quantity of methane gas (initial) produced in the test flask $[CH_{4\ I}]$ (mol CH_4) is given by Equation (1):

$$[CH_{4\ I}] = MF\frac{P_I V_{HS}}{R(273.15 + T)} \tag{1}$$

where P_I (Pa) is the total pressure at the headspace determined prior to the GC analysis, V_{HS} (m^3) is the volume of the headspace of the bottle, MF is the methane fraction determined by the GC in the current period of time, R is the ideal gas constant (8314 $Jmol^{-1}\ K^{-1}$), and T is the temperature in the incubator (°C).

The quantity of methane gas (final) in the headspace of the test flask $[CH_{4\ F}]$ (mol CH_4) is determined by Equation (2):

$$[CH_{4\ F}] = MF\frac{P_F V_{HS}}{R(273.15 + T)} \tag{2}$$

where P_F (Pa) is the total pressure at the headspace determined following the GC analysis.

The cumulative methane produced in the current period of time $[CH_{4\ C}]_t$ (mol CH_4) is defined by Equation (3):

$$[CH_{4\ C}]_t = ([CH_{4\ I}]_t - [CH_{4\ F}]_{t-1}) + [CH_{4\ C}]_{t-1} \tag{3}$$

where $[CH_{4\ I}]_t$ (mol CH_4) is the quantity of methane in the headspace of the flask (initial) in the current period of time, $[CH_{4\ F}]_{t-1}$ (mol CH_4) is the quantity methane in the headspace of the test bottle (final) in the prior period of time, and $[CH_{4\ C}]_{t-1}$ (mol CH_4) is the quantity of cumulative methane gas produced in the prior period of time.

The results of methane gas produced were modelled in the statistics software GraphPad Prism 5.0 using a nonlinear regression model that was further fitted in an exponential first-order association model (Equation (4) [19,20]:

$$B = B_{max}(1 - e^{-kt}) \tag{4}$$

where B is the cumulative methane produced (mol CH_4/100 g) at time interval (t), B_{max} is the maximum methane yield (mol CH_4/100 g), k is the kinetics rate constant (d^{-1}).

2.5. Statistics

The statistical analysis was performed with the software GraphPad Prism 5. The Shapiro-Wilk's normality test was utilised to determine the normal distribution of the variables. The Kruskal–Wallis test and the post hoc test Dunn's multiple comparison test were used to investigate the differences between the variables. The results are represented with the respective error bars and intervals that denote one standard deviation. The results were considered significantly different when the *p*-value was inferior to $p < 0.05$.

2.6. Napier Grass Availability, Production, and Growth

The estimated biomass yields (of all the feedstocks with exception of Napier grass) were obtained from FAO (Food and Agriculture Organisation of UN) bioenergy and food security rapid appraisal tool (Excel-based tools) and represent a ten-years average of annual production at country level [33]. The different Napier grass yields were obtained from the literature [34–36].

3. Results

3.1. Napier Grass Availability, Production and Growth

Although Nigeria has been reported as an emerging economy for biofuel production [37], a study by Rocha-Meneses et al. [38] shows that the country is only 19th out of 27 in the equatorial Africa with more potential available for bioenergy production. The study reported the utilization of agricultural waste as barley, wheat, millet, oat, rice, rye, sorghum, and maize for bioenergy production. Besides agricultural residues, Nigeria has a large quantity of neglected feedstocks that can be further utilised for bioenergy production. Napier grass is one of these substrates.

Napier grass is a perennial crop native to Africa with low input requirements (e.g., low nutrient, fertilizer, and water requirements) and fast-growing characteristics. Its heating value is relatively high, varying between 16.21 MJ/kg (leaves) and 18.12 MJ/kg (stems). The heating value of the full plant is about 16.58 MJ/kg [39]. In addition, Napier grass has a great soil carbon sequestration potential, it can grow in marginal lands, but it is largely available in the wild, decreasing the competition with arable lands and therefore reducing the food versus fuel competition [40]. These unique characteristics make Napier grass one of the most prospective renewable energy sources for biofuel production in this region [36]. Under suitable conditions, Napier grass can grow up to 2–4.5 m tall and has a production of 40–60 t/DM/ha. In temperate climates, it can be harvested up to four times per year. Napier grass can be harvested as soon as three to four months after planting and it can continue in periods of six to eight weeks for up to five years [35,36]. From unfertilized stands, the dry matter yields of Napier grass are between 2 and 10 t/ha. Its dry matter production varies between 4.6 and 20.5 t/ha/year in Ethiopia, 12.1 and 19 t/ha/year in Kenya and 90 t/ha/year in Zimbawe [34].

Figures 3 and 4 represent the distribution of Napier grass in the different countries of Sub-Saharan Africa, and the land suitability for Napier grass production in Nigeria, respectively. As it can be seen from the figures, the majority of the Nigerian territory is highly suitable for Napier grass production. Particularly, the South East zone (SE) and the North central (NC) have the highest land suitability in the country. In the south of Nigeria, South West (SW) is the zone with more potential for Napier grass cultivation. Regarding the productivity of this grass in Nigeria, research has shown that the NC zone is the most productive zone of the country, followed by the North East (NE), and North West (NW) [41]. In terms of bioethanol production, Chukwu (2018) [41] predicted that the NC zone has the highest potential for cellulosic bioethanol production, followed by the NE zone.

Table 1 represents the energy output from Napier grass at different production rates (2 t/ha, 10 t/ha, 20 t/ha, 30 t/ha, 40 t/ha, and 60 t/ha) in comparison with other feedstocks currently available in Nigeria. The results show that even at low production yield (2 t/ha), Napier grass has higher energy yields than some well-known crops such as maize, rice, groundnut, wheat, coffee, sorghum, soybean, and millet. At high production yields, Napier grass has the highest energy yields, followed by sugarcane (bagasse and leaves), coconut (shells and husk), and oil palm (straw/pods). These results show that independent of the production yields, Napier grass is among the top 10 crops in Nigeria with higher energy yields, indicating the potential of this feedstock for further bioenergy production.

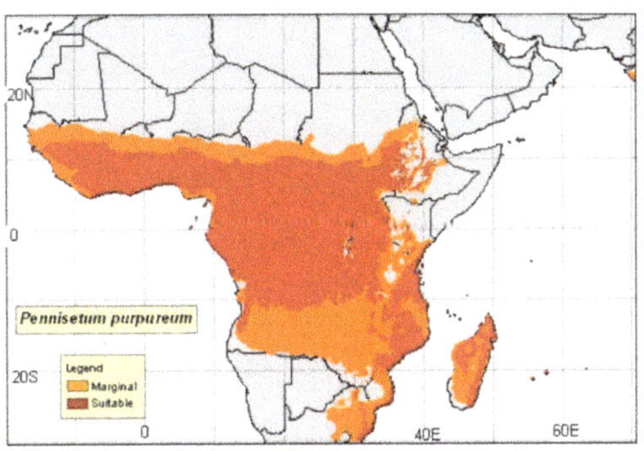

Figure 3. Napier grass distribution in Sub-Saharan Africa (inclusive Nigeria) [42].

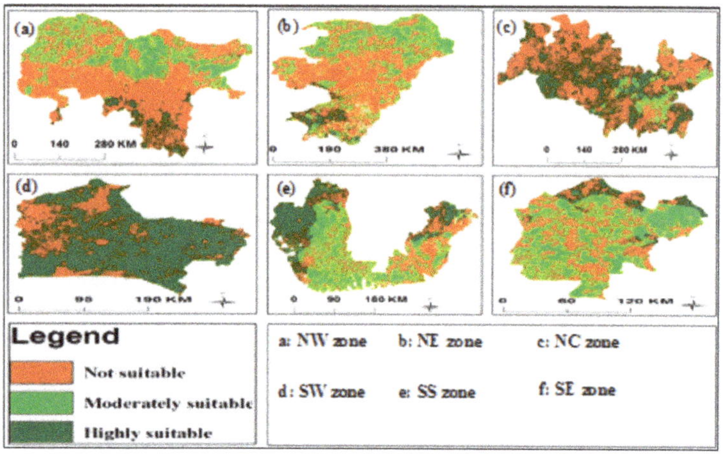

Figure 4. Land suitability for Napier grass production in Nigeria (by geopolitical zone) [41].

Table 1. Estimated energy yield from Napier grass and different agricultural residues available in Nigeria.

Feedstocks	Estimated Production Yield (t/ha) [33–36]	Calorific Value (MJ/kg)	Estimated Energy Yield (MJ/kg)/ha
Napier grass	60	16.58 [43]	994,800
Napier grass	40	16.58 [43]	663,200
Napier grass	30	16.58 [43]	497,400
Sugarcane bagasse	23.72	15.62 [44]	370,506
Napier grass	20	16.58 [43]	331,600
Sugarcane leaves	23.72	9.11 [44]	216,089
Napier grass	10	16.58 [43]	165,800
Coconut shells	6.26	17.9 [45]	112,054
Coconut husk	6.26	9.8 [45]	61,348
Oil palm (straw/ponds)	2.60	18–21 [46]	46,800–54,600
Napier grass	2	16.58 [43]	33,160
Maize cob	1.76	15.4 [46]	27,104
Rice husk/straw	1.75	14.44 [47]	25,270
Groundnut husk	1.30	18.81 [47]	24,453
Wheat straw	1.37	15.2 [45]	20,824
Coffee husk	1.28	16.00 [45]	20,480
Sorghum straw/stalk	1.21	16.00 [47]	19,360
Soybean husk	0.93	16.48 [44]	15,326
Millet straw	1.19	12.48 [47]	14,851

3.2. Chemical Composition

The structural composition of the Napier grass is presented in Table 2. The Napier grass contains 35.69% of cellulose, 26.9% of hemicellulose, 5.2% of lignin, and 9.6% of ash. The proportion of cellulose is relatively low, being 8.5% to 17% lower than the values that were described in the literature, while the hemicellulose content is 25% to 35% higher. The percentage of lignin is particularly low (81% lower) in comparison with the values reported in the available bibliography [43,48]. The ash content is 79% lower than the values reported in the literature [43,48]. These differences in the proportions of cellulose, hemicellulose, and lignin may be due to the growing, harvesting, and drying conditions of the samples. The Napier grass used in this study grew in the wild, it was harvested in early January (possibly the plant was not fully matured) and dried naturally in the sun, while in the studies of Mohammed et al. [43] and Nascimento and Rezende [48] the growing, harvesting, and drying conditions were closely monitored, ensuring the maximum growth and the optimal composition of the substrate. Although the cellulose content was lower than the values reported in the literature, the lignin percentage is also very low, making the delignification process easier. This means that less energy input should be required to break the plant cell wall, and thus making the cellulose easily accessible, degradable, and convertible into sugars. Research has shown that high lignin content leads to low digestibility of the biomass. Therefore, low lignin content is a desirable condition for bioethanol and biomethane production [4,49].

Table 2. Composition of untreated Napier grass.

Component	Composition (%)
Cellulose	35.7 ± 0.3
Hemicellulose	26.9 ± 1.2
Lignin	5.2 ± 0.5
Ash	9.6 ± 0.0
Moisture	6.1 ± 0.3

Table 3 represents the total solids (TS) and volatile solids (VS) content for untreated Napier grass, samples from the solid and liquid fraction from different steps of bioethanol production chain, pretreated with NED at different temperatures. The TS content of untreated material was 956 g/kg. For samples of the solid fraction the TS content varied between 966 g/kg and 987 g/kg, and for samples from the liquid fraction between 13.4 g/kg and 37.4 g/kg. Statistically significant differences were found between TS content of samples from the solid and liquid fractions pretreated at different temperatures. These results show that the solid fraction had higher TS content than liquid fraction. High TS content is particularly important since it indicates there is more substrate available for the anaerobic digestion process, leading to higher methane and biogas yields [50].

Table 3. Total solids and volatile solids content of untreated material, samples from different fractions and stages pretreated at 150 °C, 170 °C, 190 °C, and 200 °C.

Fraction	Stage	Temperature	TS g/kg	VS g/kgTS
Untreated	-	-	956 ± 2	898 ± 1 ^{a,b,c}
Solid fraction	Post-pretreatment broth	150 °C	973 ± 2 ^{a,b,c,d}	938 ± 4 ^{d,e,f}
		170 °C	972 ± 2	931 ± 3 ^{g,h,i}
		190 °C	986 ± 3 ^{e,f,g,h,i,j}	930 ± 4 ^{j,k,l,m,n,o,p}
		200 °C	987 ± 2 ^{k,l,m,n,o,p,q}	929 ± 4 ^{q,r,s,t,u,v,w}
	Post-hydrolysis broth	150 °C	966 ± 2	930 ± 6 ^{x,y,z,aa,bb,cc,dd}
		170 °C	973 ± 6 ^{r,s,t,u}	972 ± 5
		190 °C	971 ± 3 ^{v,w,x,y}	970 ± 2 ^{ee,ff,gg}
		200 °C	976 ± 4 ^{z,aa,bb,cc,dd,ee}	975 ± 2.9 ^{hh,ii}
Liquid fraction	Post-pretreatment broth	150 °C	15.7 ± 2.2 ^{e,k,z}	995 ± 1
		170 °C	20.9 ± 0.7 ^{l}	994 ± 0
		190 °C	22.6 ± 0.8	994 ± 0
		200 °C	15.7 ± 1.7 ^{a,f,m,r,v,aa}	996 ± 1
	Post-hydrolysis broth	150 °C	22.2 ± 2.4	999 ± 0 ^{j,q,x}
		170 °C	32.0 ± 0.7	1000 ± 0 ^{a,d,g,k,r,y,ee}
		190 °C	34.9 ± 0.2	1000 ± 0 ^{b,e,h,l,s,z,ff,hh}
		200 °C	37.4 ± 3.1	1000 ± 0 ^{f,l,m,t,aa,gg,ii}
	Post-distillation broth	150 °C	15.4 ± 0.5 ^{b,g,n,s,w,bb}	998 ± 0
		170 °C	16.8 ± 0.5 ^{h,o,cc}	999 ± 0 ^{n,u,bb}
		190 °C	13.4 ± 0.9 ^{c,i,p,t,x,dd}	999 ± 0 ^{o,v,cc}
		200 °C	13.9 ± 2.2 ^{d,j,q,u,y,ee}	999 ± 0 ^{p,x,dd}

The superscripts designate statistically significant differences ($p < 0.05$) between the variables inside the column.

The VS content of untreated Napier grass was 889 g/kg. For samples of the solid fraction the TS content varied between 929 g/kg and 975 g/kg, and for samples from the liquid fraction between 994 g/kg and 1000 g/kg. Statistically significant differences were found between VS content of samples from the solid and liquid fractions pretreated at different temperatures. The VS content is an indicator of the biodegradability of the samples and represents the portion of substrate that can be converted into biogas and biomethane. Research has shown that high VS content is a desirable condition in the anaerobic digestion process since it leads to higher biogas and biomethane yields [51,52].

3.3. Sugar Composition from Different Stages of the Liquid Fraction and Ethanol Production from Hydrolysates

Monosaccharide concentrations present in all the post-treatment broths were low (>1.0 g/L, Table 4) indicating that sugars were in the form of oligomers non-detected by the methodology employed. Higher temperatures during pretreatment resulted in higher concentrations of glucose after hydrolysis, reaching up to 31.56 g/L when 200 °C was used (Table 4). Regarding the fermentation step, at least 98.9% of all glucose was consumed (as glucose was detected, but the concentration was below the limit of quantification, 0.25 g/L) in all hydrolysates as substrates. The highest ethanol titer was 10.3 g/L (Table 5), 90% of theoretical yield (0.51 g ethanol/g glucose) from the fermentation using the hydrolysate from the pretreatment at 170 °C. The post fermentation broth from the pretreatment at 150 °C contained 8.45 g/L of ethanol, indicating that the cellulases continued the hydrolysis process during the fermentation process as the yield was 28% over the theoretical one (0.66 g ethanol/g glucose). Using temperatures over 170 °C for the pretreatment resulted in decrease in ethanol yields, 0.33 g ethanol/g glucose (190 °C) and 0.18 g ethanol/g glucose (200 °C), probably due to the presence of inhibitors such as acetic acid and furfurals coming from the degradation of hemicellulose.

Table 4. Concentrations of sugars (g/L) for samples from the liquid fraction post-pretreatment and post-hydrolysis broth pretreated at 150 °C, 170 °C, 190 °C, and 200 °C.

Fraction	Stage		Cellobiose	Glucose	Xylose	Galactose	Arabinose	Mannose
Liquid fraction	Post-pretreatment broth	150 °C	0.28 ± 0.05	0.78 ± 0.05	n.d	0.30 ± 0.02	0.12 ± 0.02	0.85 ± 0.01
		170 °C	>0.25	0.41 ± 0.01	n.d	>0.25	0.22 ± 0.02	0.53 ± 0.07
		190 °C	>0.25	0.31 ± 0.02	0.43 ± 0.04	>0.25	>0.25	0.31 ± 0.05
		200 °C	>0.25	0.31 ± 0.02	0.30 ± 0.03	>0.25	>0.25	>0.25
	Post-hydrolysis broth	150 °C	0.49 ± 0.01	13.7 ± 1.16	2.10 ± 0.23	>0.25	0.34 ± 0.02	n.d
		170 °C	0.46 ± 0.04	23.41 ± 0.60	3.01 ± 0.19	>0.25	0.26 ± 0.02	n.d
		190 °C	0.80 ± 0.12	25.07 ± 0.92	2.24 ± 0.13	n.d	0.27 ± 0.08	>0.25
		200 °C	0.57 ± 0.15	31.56 ± 1.37	2.57 ± 0.25	n.d	>0.25	0.26 ± 0.05

n.d: non detected.

Table 5. Concentration of glucose, xylose, glycerol, acetic acid, and ethanol (g/L) for samples from the liquid fraction of post-fermentation broth pretreated at 150 °C, 170 °C, 190 °C, and 200 °C.

Fraction	Stage	Temperature	Glucose	Xylose	Glycerol	Acetic acid	Ethanol
Liquid fraction	Post-fermentation broth	150 °C	>0.25	2.11 ± 0.17	0.46 ± 0.11	1.56 ± 0.95	8.45 ± 1.28
		170 °C	>0.25	2.43 ± 0.36	0.84 ± 0.16	0.72 ± 0.11	10.3 ± 0.89
		190 °C	>0.25	2.25 ± 0.21	0.90 ± 0.07	0.44 ± 0.22	8.49 ± 1.22
		200 °C	>0.25	2.02 ± 0.57	0.95 ± 0.50	0.60 ± 0.00	5.68 ± 0.20

3.4. Methane Recovery

Figures 5–10 represent the maximum methane yield (B_{max}) of untreated Napier grass and samples from different fractions of bioethanol production process pretreated at 150 °C, 170 °C, 190 °C, and 200 °C. The methane yield of untreated material was 1.18 mol CH_4/100 g. For samples from the solid fraction of post-pretreatment broth, the methane yields were highest at 150 °C (1.13 mol CH_4/100 g), followed by samples pretreated at 170 °C (1.04 mol CH_4/100 g), 190 °C (1.00 mol CH_4/100 g), and 200 °C (0.90 mol CH_4/100 g). A similar trend was seen in samples from the solid fraction of post-hydrolysis broth. The samples pretreated at 150 °C had the highest methane yields (1.00 mol CH_4/100 g) while samples pretreated at 200 °C had the lowest methane yields (0.70 mol CH_4/100 g). For samples from the liquid fraction of post-pretreatment broth, the methane yields were highest for samples pretreated at 190 °C (0.27 mol CH_4/100 g), followed by samples pretreated at 170 °C (0.24 mol CH_4/100 g), 150 °C (0.17 mol CH_4/100 g), and 200 °C (0.14 mol CH_4/100 g). The methane yields for samples from the liquid fraction of post-hydrolysis broth varied between 0.41 CH_4/100 g (150 °C) and 0.57 CH_4/100 g (200 °C), and for samples from the liquid fraction of post-distillation broth between 0.25 CH_4/100 g (200 °C) and 0.41 CH_4/100 g (190 °C).

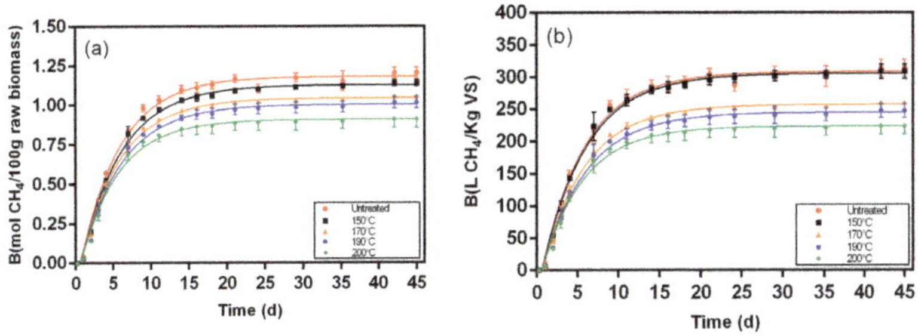

Figure 5. Biochemical methane results and respective fitting curves for samples from the solid fraction of post-pretreatment broth pretreated at 150 °C, 170 °C, 190 °C, and 200 °C. (**a**) results in mol CH4/100 g raw biomass; (**b**) results in L CH4/Kg VS.

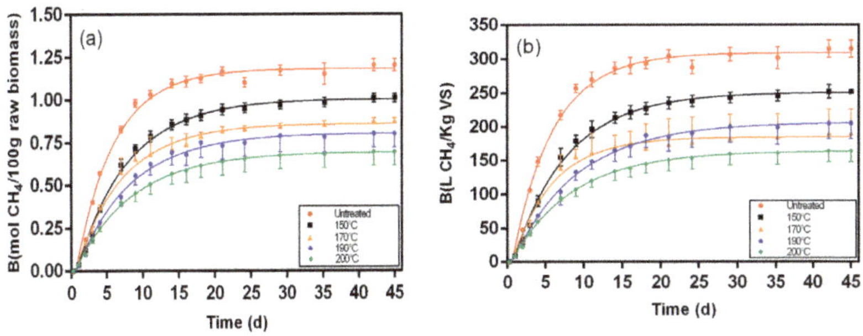

Figure 6. Biochemical methane results and respective fitting curves for samples from solid fraction of post-hydrolysis broth pretreated at 150 °C, 170 °C, 190 °C, and 200 °C. (**a**) results in mol CH4/100 g raw biomass; (**b**) results in L CH4/Kg VS.

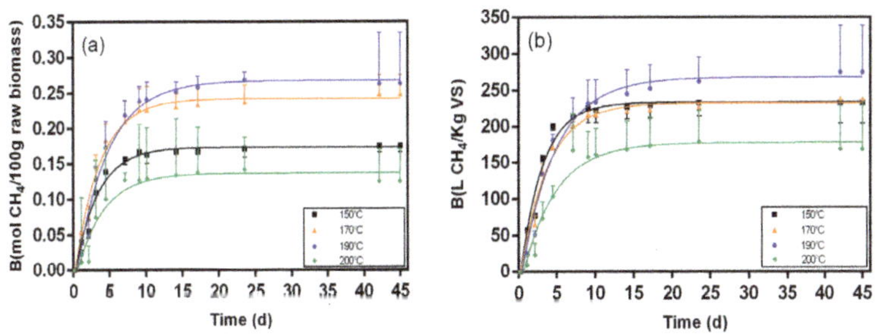

Figure 7. Biochemical methane results and respective fitting curves for samples from the liquid fraction of post-pretreatment broth pretreated at different temperatures (150 °C, 170 °C, 190 °C, and 200 °C). (**a**) results in mol CH4/100 g raw biomass; (**b**) results in L CH4/Kg VS.

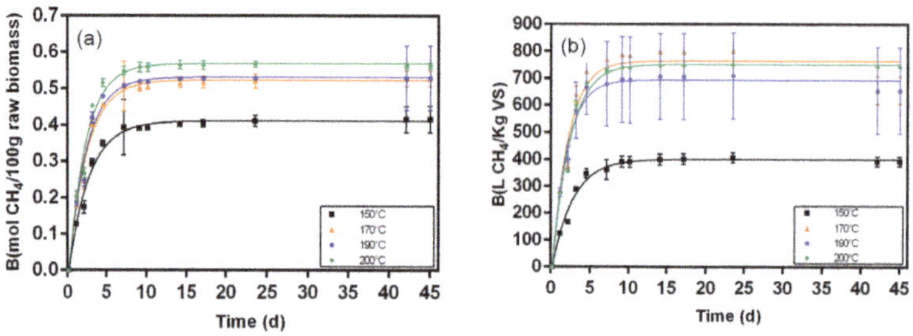

Figure 8. Biochemical methane results and respective fitting curves for samples from the liquid fraction post-hydrolysis broth pretreated at different temperatures (150 °C, 170 °C, 190 °C, and 200 °C). (**a**) results in mol CH4/100 g raw biomass; (**b**) results in L CH4/Kg VS.

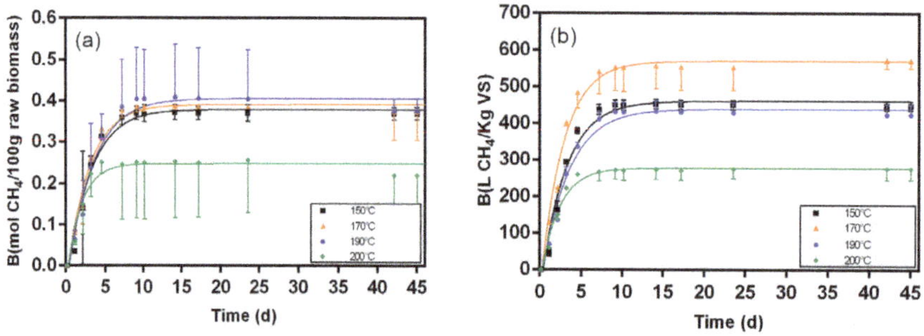

Figure 9. Biochemical methane results and respective fitting curves for samples from the liquid fraction post-distillation broth pretreated at different temperatures (150 °C, 170 °C, 190 °C, and 200 °C). (**a**) results in mol CH4/100 g raw biomass; (**b**) results in L CH4/Kg VS.

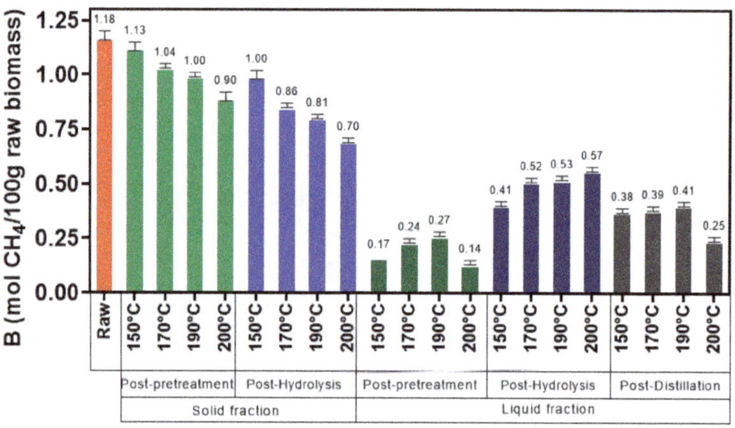

Figure 10. Maximum methane yield (B_{max}) of the fitting curves of samples from the solid and liquid fractions.

Statistically significant differences were found between methane yields of samples from the solid and liquid fractions and between samples pretreated with different temperatures (Table 6).

Table 6. Statistically significant results between the variables investigated in the methane recovery analysis.

Fraction	Stage	Temperature	B_{max} mol CH_4/100 g
Untreated	-	-	1.18 ± 0.02 ^{a}
Solid fraction	Post-pretreatment broth	150 °C	1.13 ± 0.02 ^{b}
		170 °C	1.04 ± 0.01 ^{c}
		190 °C	1.00 ± 0.01 ^{d}
		200 °C	0.90 ± 0.02 ^{a,b,e,f}
	Post-hydrolysis broth	150 °C	1.00 ± 0.02 ^{a,g}
		170 °C	0.86 ± 0.01 ^{a,b,c,h}
		190 °C	0.81 ± 0.01 ^{a,b,c,d,g,i}
		200 °C	0.70 ± 0.01 ^{a,b,c,d,g,j}
Liquid fraction	Post-pretreatment broth	150 °C	0.17 ± 0.00 ^{a,b,c,d,f,g,h,i,j,k}
		170 °C	0.24 ± 0.01 ^{a,b,c,d,f,g,h,i,j,l}
		190 °C	0.27 ± 0.01 ^{a,b,c,d,f,g,h,i,j,m}
		200 °C	0.14 ± 0.01 ^{a,b,c,d,f,g,h,i,j,m,n}
	Post-hydrolysis broth	150 °C	0.41 ± 0.01 ^{a,b,c,d,f,g,h,i,j,k,l,m,n,o}
		170 °C	0.52 ± 0.01 ^{a,b,c,d,f,g,h,i,k,l,m,n,p}
		190 °C	0.53 ± 0.01 ^{a,b,c,d,f,g,h,k,l,m,n,o,q}
		200 °C	0.57 ± 0.01 ^{a,b,c,d,e,f,g,k,l,m,n,o,r}
	Post-distillation broth	150 °C	0.38 ± 0.01 ^{a,b,c,d,f,g,h,i,j,k,l,n,p,q,r}
		170 °C	0.39 ± 0.01 ^{a,b,c,d,f,g,h,i,j,k,l,n,p,q,r,s}
		190 °C	0.41 ± 0.01 ^{a,b,c,d,f,g,h,i,j,k,l,m,n,q,r,t}
		200 °C	0.25 ± 0.01

The superscripts designate no statistically significant differences ($p < 0.05$) between the variables.

As it can be seen from Figure 10 (for samples from the solid fraction), higher pretreatment temperatures tend to decrease the biomethane yields. This may be because higher pretreatment temperatures can reduce the amount of VS available in the solid material, thus leading to lower biomethane yields [53]. Also, research has shown that higher temperatures can produce inhibitory components (such as furan derivatives) that can inhibit the microbial process and lead to lower biomethane yields [54,55].

Overall, samples from the solid and liquid fractions have distinct biomethane yields, mainly due to the composition of the biomaterial. Samples from the solid fraction have higher methane yields than samples from the liquid fraction mainly due to its composition in terms of cellulose and lignin. Samples from the liquid fraction have mainly hemicellulose in its composition, therefore the reaction speed will be faster (as there is no lignin) than in samples from the solid fraction, but the sugar release will be lower (since the amount of cellulose is negligible). From the process point of view, the performance of the solid and liquid fractions in different stages of the bioethanol production chain is also distinct. Samples from the liquid fraction from the post-pretreatment broth have the lowest methane yields, followed by samples from the post-distillation broth and post-hydrolysis broth. Due to its low potential, samples from the liquid fraction from the post-pretreatment broth that contains inhibitory component of the anaerobic digestion process and reduces the efficiency of the process, should be separated and discarded from the bioethanol production process. Sidestream from bioethanol production brings added costs to the production chain since it has a high BOD and COD and needs to be properly handled [4]. When compared with samples from the liquid fraction of post-pretreatment broth, samples from the liquid fraction of post-hydrolysis broth have higher biomethane yields. This is due to the glucose produced during the hydrolysis stage. Biomethane yields in samples from the liquid fraction of post-distillation broth tend to decrease because most of the glucose was fermented during the process or due to the presence of inhibitory compounds such as lignin degradation products generated after the hydrolysis stage [56]. However, this stage still presents some potential for biomethane production mainly due to cellulose, hemicellulose, enzymes, and yeast left in the broth at the end of the process and that creates additional sources for biogas production.

The biomethane yields obtained in this study were improved when compared with the methane yields from samples that have not been through the optimization process [57]. However, further research needs to be done and mass balances should be performed in order to quantify gains from the optimized process.

The results suggest that samples from the liquid fraction still have potential for biomethane production, it is of interest to add further steps to the pathway proposed in this study and investigate new strategies to improve the digestibility of the samples by the anaerobic microorganisms.

3.5. Kinetic Evaluation of Biomass Bioconversion and Digestion Time

Figure 11 represents the kinetic rate constant (k) and the goodness-of-fit (R^2) for samples from different fractions of bioethanol production process pretreated at 150 °C, 170 °C, 190 °C, and 200 °C. As it can be seen from the figure, the kinetic rate of untreated material was 0.185 (d^{-1}), while for samples from the solid fraction of post-pretreatment broth it varied between 0.181 (d^{-1}) (samples pretreated at 150 °C) and 0.196 (d^{-1}) (samples pretreated at 200 °C). For samples from the solid fraction of post-hydrolysis, the kinetic rate constant of the bioconversion was higher for samples pretreated at 170 °C (0.150 d^{-1}), followed by samples pretreated at 150 °C (0.138 d^{-1}), 190 °C (0.130 d^{-1}), and 200 °C (0.123 d^{-1}). Regarding samples from the liquid fraction of post-pretreatment broth, the kinetic rate constant varied between 0.224 d^{-1} (samples pretreated at 190 °C) and 0.314 d^{-1} (samples pretreated at 150 °C). For samples from the liquid fraction of post-hydrolysis broth, the kinetic rate constant was higher for samples pretreated at 200 °C (0.444 d^{-1}), followed by samples pretreated at 190 °C (0.437 d^{-1}), 170 °C (0.422 d^{-1}), and 150 °C (0.380 d^{-1}). Concerning samples from the liquid fraction of post-distillation broth the kinetic rate constant was lower for samples pretreated at 190 °C (0.302 d^{-1}), and higher for samples pretreated at 200 °C (0.532 d^{-1}). The goodness of the fitting curves varied between 0.9517 and 0.9984.

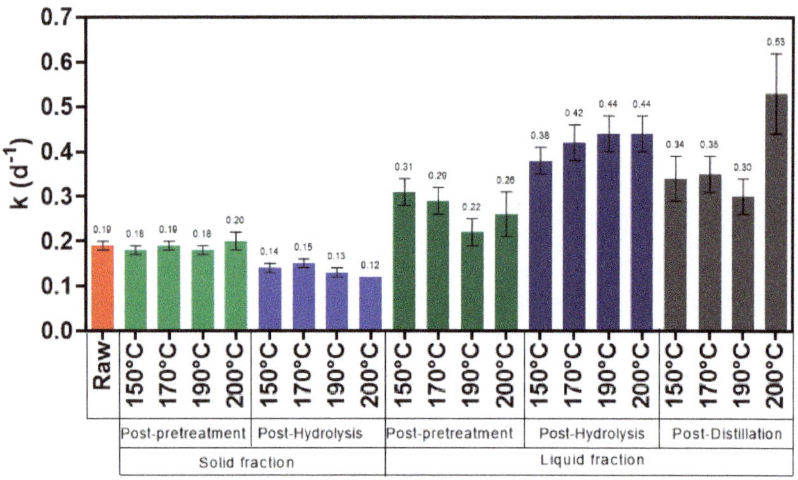

Figure 11. Kinetic constant and correlation coefficient of the fitting curves of samples from solid and liquid fraction.

As it can be seen from Figure 11, the kinetic rate is slower in samples from the solid fraction, and faster in samples from the liquid fraction. The digestion time (85% B_{max} and 95% B_{max}) of the biomaterial is represented in Table 7. The time needed for untreated Napier grass to achieve 85% B_{max} and 95% B_{max} is ~11 days (1.00 CH_4/100 g) and ~17 days (1.12 CH_4/100 g), respectively. Samples from the solid fraction of post-pretreatment broth pretreated at 200 °C had the shortest digestion time. It achieved 85% B_{max} 7 days, and 95% B_{max} 5 days before samples from raw Napier grass. Samples from the solid fraction of post-pretreatment broth pretreated at 170 °C also achieved 85% B_{max} and 95% B_{max} before untreated samples (1 day). On the other hand, the digestion time (85% B_{max} and 95% B_{max}) of samples from the solid fraction of post-hydrolysis broth was 2.2 to 7.6 days longer than untreated Napier grass. Considering the different temperatures, it can be seen that samples pretreated at 170 °C had the shortest digestion time (t = 13.1 days), followed by samples pretreated at 150 °C (t = 14.4 days), 190 °C (t = 15.1 days) and 200 °C (t = 15.7 days). Samples from the liquid fraction of post-pretreatment broth reached 85% B_{max} and 95% B_{max} 1.9 to 7 days before untreated material. As it can be seen from Table 7, samples pretreated at 150 °C had the shortest digestion time (t = 6.3 days), followed by 170 °C (t = 6.9 days), 190 °C (t = 9.0 days), and 200 °C (t = 7.9 days). The opposite trend was noted in samples from the liquid fraction of the post-hydrolysis broth, where pretreated material at 200 °C had the shortest digestion time (t = 4.5 days), followed by samples pretreated at 190 °C (t = 4.6 days), 170 °C (t = 4.7 days), and 150 °C (t = 5.2 days). The samples from this stage had a digestion times 5.7 to 9.9 days shorter than that of untreated Napier grass. Finally, samples from the liquid fraction of post-distillation broth had digestion times 4.2 to 10.9 days shorter than those of the raw material. Samples pretreated at 200 °C had the shortest digestion time (t = 3.9 days), while samples pretreated at 190 °C had the longest digestion time (6.7 days).

Table 7. Digestion time (85% B_{max} and 95% B_{max}) for samples from different fractions of bioethanol production process pretreated at 150 °C, 170 °C, 190 °C, and 200 °C.

Fraction	Stage	Temperature	85% B_{max} mol CH_4/100 g	Days	95% B_{max} mol CH_4/100 g	Days
Untreated	-	-	1.00	10.9	1.00	10.9
Solid fraction	Post-pretreatment broth	150 °C	0.96	11.1	0.96	11.1
		170 °C	0.89	10.8	0.89	10.8
		190 °C	0.85	11.0	0.85	11.0
		200 °C	0.77	10.3	0.77	10.3
	Post-hydrolysis broth	150 °C	0.85	14.4	0.85	14.4
		170 °C	0.73	13.1	0.73	13.1
		190 °C	0.69	15.1	0.69	15.1
		200 °C	0.59	15.7	0.59	15.7
Liquid fraction	Post-pretreatment broth	150 °C	0.15	6.3	0.15	6.3
		170 °C	0.20	6.9	0.20	6.9
		190 °C	0.23	9.0	0.23	9.0
		200 °C	0.12	7.9	0.12	7.9
	Post-hydrolysis broth	150 °C	0.35	5.2	0.35	5.2
		170°C	0.44	4.7	0.44	4.7
		190 °C	0.45	4.6	0.45	4.6
		200 °C	0.48	4.5	0.48	4.5
	Post-distillation broth	150 °C	0.32	6.1	0.32	6.1
		170 °C	0.33	5.7	0.33	5.7
		190 °C	0.35	6.7	0.35	6.7
		200 °C	0.21	3.9	0.21	3.9

These results show that when compared to samples from the solid fraction, samples from the liquid fraction had a better performance in terms of time needed to degrade the biomaterial. This is due to the composition of the samples (solid vs. liquid fractions). On the other hand, samples from the solid fraction had higher methane production. Samples that were pretreated at 200 °C had shorter digestion times. This may be due to the effect of the pretreatment method. High pretreatment temperatures will be more effective in disrupting the biomass, removing lignin, and making the cellulose more accessible for the hydrolysis [58]. When the cellulose is easily accessible, the microbial degradation starts faster, and the overall efficiency of the hydrolysis and fermentation processes is improved.

Production of energy in the form of biogas–methane can contribute to the reduction of greenhouse gas emissions and be utilised as a replacement for fossil fuels, especially in the transportation sector [8]. These green gases (biogas–biomethane) can help developed societies to achieve decarbonisation from fossil fuels, and support emerging societies to achieve their energetic independence.

4. Conclusions

This study investigated the effect of NED pretreatment method (physio-chemical pretreatment) on bioethanol and biomethane yields from Nigerian Napier grass (*Pennisetum purpureum*) by means of solid–liquid separation. For this, different pretreatment temperatures were applied (150 °C, 170 °C, 190 °C, and 200 °C) and samples from different stages (pretreatment, hydrolysis, and sidestream) and fractions (solid and liquid) of the bioethanol production process were used. The results show that the lowest glucose yields (13.7 g/L) and the lowest ethanol yields (8.4 g/L) were gained at 150 °C. Samples that were pretreated at 200 °C had the highest glucose titer (31.3 g/L), while samples that were pretreated at 170 °C had the highest bioethanol concentration (10.3 g/L). The kinetic rate constant of the anaerobic digestion process was higher in samples from the liquid fractions (between 0.22 d^{-1} and 0.53 d^{-1}) and lower in samples from the solid fractions (between 0.12 d^{-1} and 0.20 d^{-1}). The maximum methane yields were reported in samples from the solid fraction of post-pretreatment broth at 150 °C (1.13 mol CH_4/100 g) and samples from the solid fraction of post-hydrolysis broth pretreated at 150 °C (1.00 mol CH_4/100 g). The lowest methane yields were reported in samples from the liquid fraction of post-pretreatment broth at 200 °C (0.14 mol CH_4/100 g). Nigerian *Pennisetum purpureum* is a promising feedstock for bioethanol and biomethane production. The bioethanol and biomethane productions are influenced by the pretreatment temperatures. From the different stages and fractions of the bioethanol production process, samples from the post-pretreatment stage (liquid fraction) have the lowest methane yields. From the process point of view, the results suggest that the liquid fraction after the pretreatment stage should be separated and discarded from the bioethanol production process, since it has inhibitory compounds in its composition and does not add value to the production chain. Further research needs to be done and additional strategies weighed in order to further optimise the mass flow and maximise the added value to the process. Further research needs to be done in order to apply circular economy models to emerging economies especially because environmentally friendly fuel sources are not on the agenda of developing economies. It is not reasonable to wait for emerging countries to fully develop and only then invest in their decarbonisation. There is an urge to accelerate the worldwide bioeconomy.

Author Contributions: Conceptualization, L.R.-M. and T.K.; methodology, L.R.-M., O.F.O. and N.B.; software, L.R.-M.; validation, L.R.-M.; formal analysis, L.R.-M. and N.B.; investigation, L.R.-M., O.F.O. and N.B.; resources, L.R.-M., O.F.O., N.B., K.O. and T.K.; data curation, L.R.-M. and N.B.; writing—original draft preparation, L.R.-M. and N.B.; writing—review and editing, L.R.-M., N.B., K.O. and T.K.; visualization, L.R.-M. and T.K.; supervision, K.O. and T.K.; project administration, T.K.; funding acquisition, T.K. All authors have read and agreed to the published version of the manuscript.

Funding: The authors gratefully acknowledge the financial support of the European Regional Development Fund via the Mobilitas Pluss (project MOBERA1) of the Estonian Research Council and base financed project of EULS PM180260 TIBT. NB would like to acknowledge the European Union's Horizon 2020 research and innovation program under grant agreement No 668997.

European Union
European Regional
Development Fund

Investing
in your future

Acknowledgments: We would like to acknowledge Vahur Rooni for determining the composition of the raw Napier grass (fiber analysis).

Conflicts of Interest: The authors declare no conflict of interest.

References

1. OECD/IEA. *Key World Energy Statistics*; IEA Publishing: Paris, France, 2017; pp. 1–97. Available online: www.iea.org/t&c (accessed on 6 August 2019).
2. U.S. Energy Information Administration. *IEA Country Analysis Brief*; IEA: Washington, DC, USA, 2016.
3. OECD/IEA. *Africa Energy Outlook: A Focus on Energy Prospects in Sub-Saharan Africa*; IEA: Paris, France, 2014; Volume 242.
4. Rocha-Meneses, L.; Raud, M.; Orupõld, K.; Kikas, T. Second-generation bioethanol production: A review of strategies for waste valorisation. *Agron. Res.* **2017**, *15*, 830–847.
5. Roj-Rojewski, S.; Wysocka-Czubaszek, A.; Czubaszek, R.; Kamocki, A.; Banaszuk, P. Anaerobic digestion of wetland biomass from conservation management for biogas production. *Biomass Bioenergy* **2019**, *122*, 126–132. [CrossRef]
6. Lazarevic, D.; Martin, M. Life cycle assessment calculative practices in the Swedish biofuel sector: Governing biofuel sustainability by standards and numbers. *Bus. Strategy Environ.* **2018**, *27*, 1558–1568. [CrossRef]
7. Sassanelli, C.; Rosa, P.; Rocca, R.; Terzi, S. Circular economy performance assessment methods: A systematic literature review. *J. Clean. Prod.* **2019**, *229*, 440–453. [CrossRef]
8. D'Adamo, I.; Falcone, P.M.; Ferella, F. A socio-economic analysis of biomethane in the transport sector: The case of Italy. *Waste Manag.* **2019**, *95*, 102–115. [CrossRef] [PubMed]
9. Ben-Iwo, J.; Manovic, V.; Longhurst, P. Biomass resources and biofuels potential for the production of transportation fuels in Nigeria. *Renew. Sustain. Energy Rev.* **2016**, *63*, 172–192. [CrossRef]
10. Da Silva, P.P.; Cerqueira, P.A.; Ogbe, W. Determinants of renewable energy growth in Sub-Saharan Africa: Evidence from panel ARDL. *Energy* **2018**, *156*, 45–54. [CrossRef]
11. Kemausuor, F.; Adaramola, M.S.; Morken, J. A Review of Commercial Biogas Systems and Lessons for Africa. *Energies* **2018**, *11*, 2984. [CrossRef]
12. Mohammed, I.Y.; Abakr, Y.A.; Mokaya, R. Biofuel and valuable products recovery from Napier grass pre-processing: Process design and economic analysis. *J. Environ. Chem. Eng.* **2019**, *7*, 102962. [CrossRef]
13. Narinthorn, R.; Choorit, W.; Chisti, Y. Alkaline and fungal pretreatments for improving methane potential of Napier grass. *Biomass Bioenergy* **2019**, *127*, 105262. [CrossRef]
14. Anderson, W.F.; Dien, B.S.; Masterson, S.D.; Mitchell, R.B. Development of Near-Infrared Reflectance Spectroscopy (NIRS) Calibrations for Traits Related to Ethanol Conversion from Genetically Variable Napier Grass (*Pennisetum purpureum* Schum.). *BioEnergy Res.* **2019**, *12*, 34–42. [CrossRef]
15. Negawo, A.T.; Teshome, A.; Kumar, A.; Hanson, J.; Jones, C.S. Opportunities for Napier Grass (*Pennisetum purpureum*) Improvement Using Molecular Genetics. *Agronomy* **2017**, *7*, 28. [CrossRef]
16. Meiramkulova, K.; Bayanov, A.; Ivanova, T.; Havrland, B.; Kára, J.; Hanzlíková, I. Effect of different compositions on anaerobic co-digestion of cattle manure and agro-industrial by-products. *Agron. Res.* **2018**, *16*, 176–187. [CrossRef]
17. Tsai, M.-H.; Lee, W.-C.; Kuan, W.-C.; Sirisansaneeyakul, S.; Savarajara, A. Evaluation of different pretreatments of Napier grass for enzymatic saccharification and ethanol production. *Energy Sci. Eng.* **2018**, *6*, 683–692. [CrossRef]
18. Suntivarakorn, R.; Treedet, W.; Singbua, P.; Teeramaetawat, N. Fast pyrolysis from Napier grass for pyrolysis oil production by using circulating Fluidized Bed Reactor: Improvement of pyrolysis system and production cost. *Energy Rep.* **2018**, *4*, 565–575. [CrossRef]
19. Wang, Q.; Sun, J.; Zhang, C.; Xie, G.-J.; Zhou, X.; Qian, J.; Yang, G.; Zeng, G.; Liu, Y.; Wang, D. Polyhydroxyalkanoates in waste activated sludge enhances anaerobic methane production through improving biochemical methane potential instead of hydrolysis rate. *Nature* **2016**, *6*, 19713. [CrossRef]
20. Zeng, S.; Yuan, X.; Shi, X.; Qiu, Y. Effect of inoculum/substrate ratio on methane yield and orthophosphate release from anaerobic digestion of *Microcystis* spp. *J. Hazard. Mater.* **2010**, *178*, 89–93. [CrossRef]
21. Wanjala, B.W.; Obonyo, M.; Wachira, F.N.; Muchugi, A.; Mulaa, M.; Harvey, J.; Skilton, R.A.; Proud, J.; Hanson, J. Genetic diversity in Napier grass (*Pennisetum purpureum*) cultivars: Implications for breeding and conservation. *AoB Plants* **2013**, *5*, plt022. [CrossRef]
22. Singh, B.P.; Singh, H.P.; Obeng, E. Elephantgrass. In *Biofuel Crops: Production, Physiology and Genetics*; Singh, B.P., Ed.; CABI: Wallingford, UK, 2013.

23. Sawasdee, V.; Pisutpaisal, N. Feasibility of Biogas Production from Napier Grass. *Energy Procedia* **2014**, *61*, 1229–1233. [CrossRef]
24. Janejadkarn, A.; Chavalparit, O. Biogas production from Napier grass (Pak Chong 1) (*Pennisetum purpureum* × *Pennisetum americanum*). In Proceedings of the 2013 2nd International Conference on Material Science and Engineering Technology, London, UK, 16–17 November 2013; Volume 856, pp. 327–332.
25. Liu, Y.-K.; Chen, W.-C.; Huang, Y.-C.; Chang, Y.-K.; Chu, I.M.; Tsai, S.-L.; Wei, Y.-H. Production of bioethanol from Napier grass via simultaneous saccharification and co-fermentation in a modified bioreactor. *J. Biosci. Bioeng.* **2017**, *124*, 184–188. [CrossRef]
26. Wongwatanapaiboon, J.; Kangvansaichol, K.; Burapatana, V.; Inochanon, R.; Winayanuwattikun, P.; Yongvanich, T.; Chulalaksananukul, W. The Potential of Cellulosic Ethanol Production from Grasses in Thailand. *J. Biomed. Biotechnol.* **2012**, *2012*, 1–10. [CrossRef] [PubMed]
27. Ferella, F.; Cucchiella, F.; D'Adamo, I.; Gallucci, K. A techno-economic assessment of biogas upgrading in a developed market. *J. Clean. Prod.* **2019**, *210*, 945–957. [CrossRef]
28. Raud, M.; Olt, J.; Kikas, T. N2 explosive decompression pretreatment of biomass for lignocellulosic ethanol production. *Biomass Bioenergy* **2016**, *90*, 1–6. [CrossRef]
29. Owen, W.F.; Stuckey, D.C.; Healy, J.B.; Young, L.Y.; McCarty, P.L. Bioassay for monitoring biochemical methane potential and anaerobic toxicity. *Water Res.* **1979**, *13*, 485–492. [CrossRef]
30. Angelidaki, I.; Alves, M.; Bolzonella, D.; Borzacconi, L.; Campos, J.L.; Guwy, A.J.; Kalyuzhnyi, S.; Jenicek, P.; van Lier, J.B. Defining the biomethane potential (BMP) of solid organic wastes and energy crops: A proposed protocol for batch assays. *Water Sci. Technol.* **2009**, *59*, 927–934. [CrossRef]
31. Cioabla, A.E.; Ionel, I.; Dumitrel, G.-A.; Popescu, F. Comparative study on factors affecting anaerobic digestion of agricultural vegetal residues. *Biotechnol. Biofuels* **2012**, *5*, 39. [CrossRef]
32. Rocha-Meneses, L.; Ferreira, J.A.; Bonturi, N.; Orupõld, K.; Kikas, T. Enhancing Bioenergy Yields from Sequential Bioethanol and Biomethane Production by Means of Solid–Liquid Separation of the Substrates. *Energies* **2019**, *12*, 3683. [CrossRef]
33. FAO. Natural Resources—Biomass Potential Assessment: BEFS RA Tool. Available online: http://www.fao.org/energy/bioenergy/bioenergy-and-food-security/assessment/befs-ra/natural-resources/en/ (accessed on 29 September 2019).
34. FAO. Food and Agriculture Organization of the UN. *Pennisetum purpureum*. Available online: http://ecocrop.fao.org/ecocrop/srv/en/home (accessed on 29 September 2019).
35. Pereira, L.E.T.; Paiva, A.J.; Geremia, E.V.; da Silva, S.C. Regrowth patterns of elephant grass (*Pennisetum purpureum* Schum) subjected to strategies of intermittent stocking management. *Grass Forage Sci.* **2015**, *70*, 195–204. [CrossRef]
36. Sawanon, S.; Sangsri, P.; Leungprasert, S.; Sinbuathong, N. Methane Production from Napier Grass by Co-digestion with Cow Dung. In *Energy Solutions to Combat Global Warming*; Zhang, X., Dincer, I., Eds.; Springer International Publishing: Cham, Switzerland, 2017; pp. 169–180. [CrossRef]
37. Abila, N. *Biofuels Adoption in Nigeria: Analysis of Sustainability and Policy Issues*; University of Vaasa: Vaasa, Finland, 2014.
38. Rocha-Meneses, L.; Bergamo, T.S.F.; Kikas, T. Potential of cereal-based agricultural residues available for bioenergy production. *Data Brief* **2019**, *23*, 103829. [CrossRef]
39. Haegele, M.T.; Arjharn, W. The effects of cultivation methods and planting season on biomass yield of Napier grass (*Pennisetum purpureum* Schumach.) under rainfed conditions in the northeast region of Thailand. *Field Crops Res.* **2017**, *214*, 359–364. [CrossRef]
40. Manouchehrinejad, M.; Yue, Y.; de Morais, R.A.L.; Souza, L.M.O.; Singh, H.; Mani, S. Densification of Thermally Treated Energy Cane and Napier Grass. *BioEnergy Res.* **2018**, *11*, 538–550. [CrossRef]
41. Chukwu, M.A. *A GIS Based Approach to Investigating the Potential of Herbaceous Bioenergy Feedstocks for Cellulosic Bioethanol Production in Nigeria*; Newcastle University: Newcastle Upon Tyne, UK, 2018.
42. Cook, B.G.; Pengelly, B.C.; Brown, S.D.; Donnelly, J.L.; Eagles, D.A.; Franco, M.A.; Schultze-Kraft, R. *Tropical Forages: An Interactive Selection Tool. Web Tool*; CSIRO: Canberra, Australia; DPI&F(Qld): Queensland, Australia; CIAT: Cali, Colombia; ILRI: Nairobi, Kenya, 2005.
43. Mohammed, I.Y.; Abakr, Y.A.; Kazi, F.K.; Yusup, S.; Alshareef, I.; Chin, S.A. Comprehensive Characterization of Napier Grass as a Feedstock for Thermochemical Conversion. *Energies* **2015**, *8*, 3403–3417. [CrossRef]

44. ECN. TNO Biomass & Energy Efficiency. Phyllis2, Database for Biomass and Waste: Sugarcane Bagasse. Available online: https://phyllis.nl/ (accessed on 29 September 2019).
45. Sturm, A.; Müller, K.; Upasena, S. *A Manual for the Preparers and Users of Eco-efficiency Indicators*; United Nations Conference on Trade and Development: Geneva, Switzerland, 2004.
46. Hamzah, N.; Tokimatsu, K.; Yoshikawa, K. Solid Fuel from Oil Palm Biomass Residues and Municipal Solid Waste by Hydrothermal Treatment for Electrical Power Generation in Malaysia: A Review. *Sustainability* **2019**, *11*, 1060. [CrossRef]
47. Bappah, M.; Bradna, J.; Velebil, J.; Malatak, J. The potential of energy recovery from by–products of small agricultural farms in Nigeria. *Agron. Res.* **2019**, *17*. [CrossRef]
48. Nascimento, S.A.; Rezende, C.A. Combined approaches to obtain cellulose nanocrystals, nanofibrils and fermentable sugars from elephant grass. *Carbohydr. Polym.* **2018**, *180*, 38–45. [CrossRef]
49. Rocha-Meneses, L.; Ivanova, A.; Atouguia, G.; Ávila, I.; Raud, M.; Orupõld, K.; Kikas, T. The effect of flue gas explosive decompression pretreatment on methane recovery from bioethanol production waste. *Ind. Crops Prod.* **2019**, *127*, 66–72. [CrossRef]
50. Yi, J.; Dong, B.; Jin, J.; Dai, X. Effect of increasing total solids contents on anaerobic digestion of food waste under mesophilic conditions: Performance and microbial characteristics analysis. *PLoS ONE* **2014**, *9*, e102548. [CrossRef]
51. Agrawal, R.; Bhadana, B.; Mathur, A.S.; Kumar, R.; Gupta, R.P.; Satlewal, A. Improved Enzymatic Hydrolysis of Pilot Scale Pretreated Rice Straw at High Total Solids Loading. *Energy Res.* **2018**, *6*. [CrossRef]
52. Luna-delRisco, M.; Normak, A.; Orupõld, K. Biochemical methane potential of different organic wastes and energy crops from Estonia. *Agron. Res.* **2011**, *9*, 331–342.
53. Meegoda, J.N.; Li, B.; Patel, K.; Wang, L.B. A Review of the Processes, Parameters, and Optimization of Anaerobic Digestion. *Int. J. Environ. Res. Public Health* **2018**, *15*, 222. [CrossRef]
54. Montgomery, L.F.R.; Bochmann, G. *Pretreatment of Feedstock for Enhanced Biogas Production*; Baxter, D., Ed.; IEA Bioenergy Task 37—Energy from Biogas; IEA Bioenergy: Paris, France, 2014; ISBN 978-1-910154-05-2.
55. Phuttaro, C.; Sawatdeenarunat, C.; Surendra, K.C.; Boonsawang, P.; Chaiprapat, S.; Khanal, S.K. Anaerobic digestion of hydrothermally-pretreated lignocellulosic biomass: Influence of pretreatment temperatures, inhibitors and soluble organics on methane yield. *Bioresour. Technol.* **2019**, *284*, 128–138. [CrossRef] [PubMed]
56. Pessoa, A., Jr.; Mancilha, I.M.; Sato, S. Acid hydrolysis of hemicellulose from sugarcane bagasse. *Braz. J. Chem. Eng.* **1997**, *14*, 291–297. [CrossRef]
57. Rocha-Meneses, L.; Raud, M.; Orupõld, K.; Kikas, T. Potential of bioethanol production waste for methane recovery. *Energy* **2019**, *173*, 133–139. [CrossRef]
58. Binod, P.; Kuttiraja, M.; Archana, M.; Janu, K.U.; Sindhu, R.; Sukumaran, R.K.; Pandey, A. High temperature pretreatment and hydrolysis of cotton stalk for producing sugars for bioethanol production. *Fuel* **2012**, *92*, 340–345. [CrossRef]

sustainability

MDPI

Article

Role of Waste Collection Efficiency in Providing a Cleaner Rural Environment

Florin-Constantin Mihai [1,*] and Adrian Grozavu [2]

1 Department of Research, Faculty of Geography and Geology, Alexandru Ioan Cuza University, Carol I Blvd, Nr. 20A, RO-700505 Iasi, Romania
2 Department of Geography, Faculty of Geography and Geology, Alexandru Ioan Cuza University, Carol I Blvd, Nr. 20 A RO-700505 Iasi, Romania; adriangrozavu@yahoo.com
* Correspondence: mihai.florinconstantin@gmail.com

Received: 30 October 2019; Accepted: 26 November 2019; Published: 2 December 2019

Abstract: The exposure of rural communities to illegal waste dumping practices associated with the lack of or poor waste collection schemes prior to the closure of rural dumpsites under EU regulations and the role of collection efficiency afterward in reducing this critical environmental threat constitutes a key issue in rural Romania. The present study reveals huge amounts of household uncollected waste released into the natural environment outside the official statistics of rural dumpsites. Despite the expansion of waste collection coverage towards rural areas since 2010, the problem of illegal dumping practice is difficult to solve. The improvement of collection efficiency, better law enforcement, and surveillance of environmental authorities coupled with educational and environmental awareness are necessary steps to combat this bad practice. A circular economy paradigm must be enacted in rural regions through separate collection schemes and to improve cost-efficient alternatives, such as home composting, and traditional and creative reuse practices, particularly in less developed regions.

Keywords: rural area; waste management; pollution; environment; recycling; circular economy

1. Introduction

Uncollected wastes across rural communities are susceptible to uncontrolled disposal via open dumping or open burning practices, with direct impacts on environmental factors (air–water–soil nexus) and public health. Rural areas are often neglected by formal waste management services due to a complex of factors, such as geographical barriers, sparse settlements, low population densities, poorer socioeconomic conditions, long distances from urban areas, transportation costs, etc. The characteristics of household waste are variable across different households, villages, regions, and countries [1,2].

Collection rates of wastes generated may significantly vary from one country to another as less than 50% in the case of low-income countries, 50% to 80% in the case of middle-income countries, and over 90% in the case of high-income countries but are rarely 100% [3].

Illegal waste dumping of solid waste raises many problems even in developed countries [4,5], transition economies [6,7], or developing countries, where rural areas are frequently exposed to such environmental threats [8]. The increasing amounts of waste generated across the globe raise more difficulties in dealing with proper waste management activities at the regional and local scale involving urban or rural municipalities [9,10]. The old non-compliant landfills are replaced by new regional integrated waste management facilities, which must include rural communities [11,12].

Solid waste collection schemes cover only part of the rural population and the burning of waste and animal feed with food scraps seems to be prevalent options in rural communities, as is the case in Brazil, for example [13]. The spatial and temporal distribution of rural waste characteristics can be extremely non-homogenous in emerging economies [14]. Organic waste could provide a source of biomethane for cities [15], but for rural areas, such initiatives are scarcely seen in Eastern Europe [16], where animal feed and home composting are traditional routes for organic fraction beside landfills or illegal dumping practices [17]. New EU members struggle to mitigate waste dumping practices across rural settlements and to provide reliable waste management services [18]. These countries are the worst performers in terms of municipal waste management practices [19]. However, older EU member states (e.g., Spain) are still facing the problem of illegal dumping practices in rural areas and regional authorities must take proper actions to deal with it [20]. Open dumping practices were a widespread option across rural Romania because of the poor facilities and lack of investments in this sector. Some improvements have been seen since EU adhesion in 2007, but rural waste dumping practices remain a serious environmental threat. Romania has significant gaps between urban and rural areas in terms of socio-economic development, where distant rural communities from urban areas are exposed to serious poverty and social exclusion issues. The North-East Region has one of the lowest per capita gross domestic product (GDP) at current market prices by EU regions (NUTS2) during 2007–2016 despite an increasing trend in the later years [21]. Under such circumstances, waste management activities should pay special attention to rural communities, particularly in the case of a peripheral region at the EU eastern border that is prone to illegal dumping practices.

The aim of the present study was to reveal the exposure of rural communities in the North-East Region of Romania to illegal waste dumping practices associated with the lack of or poor waste collection schemes prior the closure of rural dumpsites under EU regulations and to point out the role of collection efficiency afterward in reducing this critical environmental threat in rural Romania, supported by activities that promote a rural circular economy framework. In this regard, several objectives were further taken into consideration: (i) To point out the major gaps between the amounts of uncollected household waste based on poor rural waste collection coverage (during 2003–2009) compared to those reported to be disposed of in the wild dumps (2010); (ii) a multi-scale approach at the county and rural municipality levels (commune) combined with relevant collection efficiency scenarios for middle-income countries supported by spatial analysis in order to reveal the magnitude of waste dumping practices in a peripheral EU region; (iii) to calculate the amounts of rural uncollected household waste at the county level during 2010–2016 as a further primary source for illegal waste dumping practices; (iv) spatial analysis of uncollected household waste (2012 vs. 2015) at the commune level in Neamt county, based on collection efficiency derived to the latest available data on collection rates provided by environmental authorities; and (v) to support the traditional activities of organic waste fraction (e.g., home composting, animal feed) and the transition towards a rural circular economic framework by promoting the 3, 6, or 9 Rs policy (reduce, reuse, repair, recovery, refurbish, repurpose, remanufacture, recycle, refuse) at household and community levels. This study argues that official statistics regarding uncontrolled waste disposal practices must be confronted with sound estimation methods of uncollected waste flow to better understand the potential pollution issues within the study area and to explain the geographical disparities.

2. Materials and Methods

2.1. Study Area

The North-East Region of Romania covers 36.850 sq.km (representing 15.46% of the territory of the country), is equivalent to a NUTS-2 region with 3.3 million inhabitants, and includes six counties (equivalent to the NUTS3 regions), such as Botosani, Iasi, Suceava, Neamt, Vaslui, and Bacau, and 46 urban areas (Figure 1).

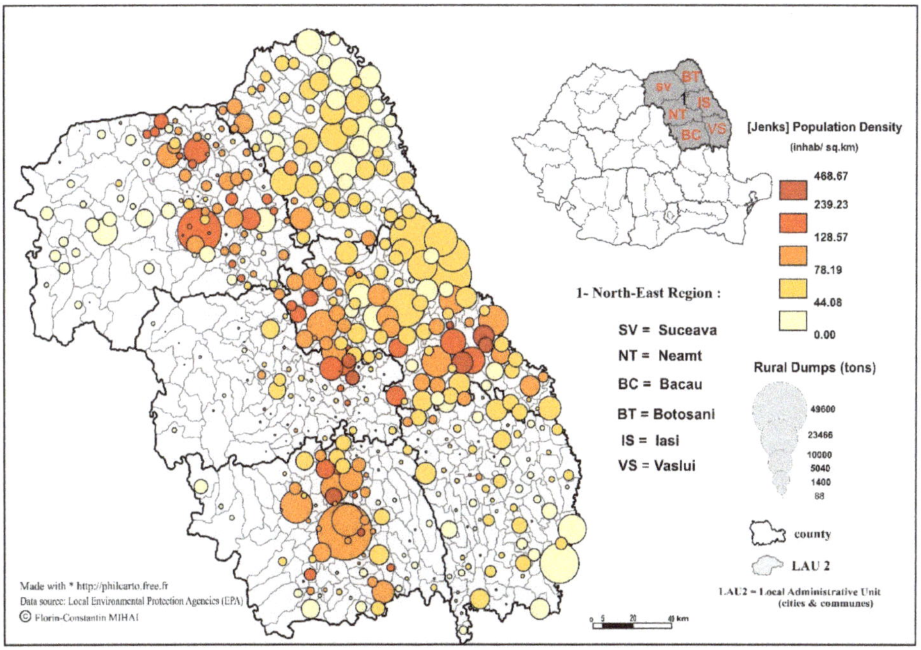

Figure 1. Spatial analysis of waste amounts disposed of in rural dumps.

NUTS 2 are the basic regions of the application of regional policies in EU, including those related to the environment and waste management sectors, but in Romania, such regions have no governmental responsibilities. On the other side, each county is ruled by a County Council, which supervises the implementation of such policies at the local administrative unit level (cities and communes equivalent to the LAU-2 level). The geographical conditions of the North-East Region are given by a mountainous (Eastern Carpathians) sector (28% of the territory) in the western part, a subcarpathian zone (12%) in the central area, and a plateau zone (60%), which entirely covers the eastern counties of the region, such as the Botosani, Iasi, and Vaslui counties [22]. Most of the population lives in rural areas (58%) according to the Population Census from 2011, in 506 communes with 2361 villages. Therefore, a sound rural waste management sector should be a crucial environmental objective in the study area.

2.2. The Closure and the Monitoring Process of Wild Dumps Parameters

The lack and poor coverage of waste collection services (WCSs) across rural municipalities has contributed to the disposal of rural household waste in wild dumps. These sites are uncontrolled, without any environmental protection measures, threatening the local environment and public health. Local environmental protection agencies and National Environmental Guard via County Commissariats inventoried these sites between 2009–2010 with the aid of local municipalities. According to the Government Decision no. 345 regarding the landfill of waste, all rural dumpsites should be closed and rehabilitated until July 2009. Data concerning dumpsite volumes are counted at the rural municipality level (commune). The maps we obtained reveal some spatial patterns within the North-East Region, which are further examined in the results and discussion sections. Dumpsites volume data expressed in cubic meters are based on pile volume estimations by determining the area of the base and then multiplying it by the average height of the pile. In many cases, the base of a pile resembles a rectangle where the area is the length times width (L × W). There is no information about weighing such sites; in fact, few urban landfills have weighing systems in Romania and most waste statistics are based on volume estimations provided by waste operators taking into account the garbage truck capacity. In the case of Iasi county, the average height of the dump is provided, and the volume is calculated using the rectangle geometry. The conversion of the volume data of wild dumps in kilograms is performed using a specific density of 400 kg/m^3.

Wild dumps are frequently smaller than 1 ha with a sparse distribution across the surroundings. The commingled wastes are not compacted or soil covered, and the density of waste is lower than conventional urban landfills (700–900 kg/m^3). Some communes had no reported dumps on their administrative territory despite the poor coverage of WCS in rural areas during 2003–2009. In other cases, poor data about their area (sq.m) is available. The monitoring process of these wild dumps scattered across rural areas was performed by local authorities under the supervision of environmental institutions. This is the most comprehensive empirical data about wild dumps at the commune level in Romania. Therefore, the year 2010 is the best option to analyze the underestimation level of rural waste dumping practices in the context of poor waste management facilities from previous years at the regional scale (NUTS2).

2.3. Assessment of Household Waste Generated and Uncollected

The paper estimated the amounts of household waste generated and uncollected at the county level based on the per-capita waste generation rate as follows:

$$Q_{hwu}\ (t.yr^{-1}) = P_{noWCS} \times Grw \times 365/1000, \quad (1)$$

where Q_{hwu} is the amount of household waste generated and uncollected by waste operators ($t.yr.^{-1}$); P_{noWCS} is the number of inhabitants with no access to WCS; and Grw is the per-capita waste generation rate in rural areas (kg. $inhab.day^{-1}$).

The paper used three rural per-capita waste generation rates, such as: 0.31 $kg.inab.day^{-1}$ as a specific regional rate [23], 0.4 ($kg.inhab.day^{-1}$) as the national flat rate [24], and 0.5 $kg.inhab.day^{-1}$ as an above-national-average rate. These amounts of household waste generated are related as a ratio to the total amounts of household waste disposed in wild dumps. Local environmental protection agencies calculate the amounts of municipal waste generated and uncollected by waste operators in rural areas using a waste generation rate of 0.4 $kg.inhab.day^{-1}$ as suggested by environmental authorities [25], but the data is not available at the commune level. The waste collection coverage rates are not broken down per local administrative unit level (cities and communes); therefore, waste statistics are aggregated at the county level in environmental reports. This fact limits the possibility of evaluating the uncollected household waste flow across the communes of a wider geographical area, but collection efficiency scenarios could fill this gap. This formula was applied in the case of counties and communes where waste collection coverage is not 100%.

The share of dumpsites (total amount of waste disposed of in dumps at the county level) as the ratio of total household waste generated and uncollected was determined for each county to reveal the magnitude of this practice. In this particular case, the timeline covers 7 years (2003–2009) where few rural inhabitants have access to formal WCSs, and waste dumping practices were a widespread option among rural communities until the closure of rural dumpsites in 2009–2010. The uncollected household waste was further calculated at the county level (2010–2016) and commune level (Neamt county as a case study, 2012 vs. 2015) derived from rural inhabitants without access to WCSs, and on the other hand, uncollected household waste related to the gaps of waste collection schemes based on the lower and upper ranges of collection efficiency scenarios specific to middle-income countries like Romania. The use of these three waste generation rates indicates different perspectives of waste dumping practice from each county to another.

The role of the similar fraction as household waste fraction generated by economic agents and the local institutions is further discussed. Collection efficiency scenarios were used to reveal, on the one hand, that the amounts of uncollected household waste are much larger than those disposed of in the wild dumps (2010), and on the other hand, to point out that rural communities are still exposed to illegal waste dumping practices.

2.4. Worst- vs. Best-Case Scenario Analysis

No waste collection services scenario (noWCS) was used to calculate the amounts of household waste generated and uncollected in each commune during a year (2010) based on the number of inhabitants provided by the Population Census 2011. In this scenario, the number of inhabitants with no access to WCS is equal to the population of each commune.

This scenario was correlated with the total waste disposed in the dumps at the commune scale to reveal the underestimation level of waste dumping practices, particularly in the western counties of the region. There is no available data at the rural municipal level (commune) concerning waste collection coverage for 2004–2009, only at the county level. This is the reason why the scenario analysis must be taken into consideration at the local administrative level (LAU2 = commune). The "best-case scenario" refers to the amounts of household waste generated by the rural population without access to WCS. For rural municipalities, where collection coverage is 100% (according to the environmental or local authorities), a full collection efficiency with no illegal dumping practices was assumed.

2.5. Collection Efficiency Scenarios (Low and Upper Ranges)

Field observations point out that even rural communities with a full waste collection coverage are facing waste dumping practices, suggesting that collection efficiency is not 100%. This fact is confirmed by local authorities, such as Manastirea Casin commune (Bacau county), where collection efficiency was 30% in 2010 and by previous publications [26,27].

Two scenarios were taken into consideration, such as WCS40 (collection efficiency is 40% as a low range) and WCS70 (collection efficiency is 70% as an upper range), which are more realistic than the previous worst- and best-case scenarios. These scenarios combine the amounts of uncollected household waste fed by two main sources: (i) Rural inhabitants without access to WCSs (Equation (1)) and (ii) the amounts of uncollected household waste derived from low (40%) or upper collection efficiency (70%) ranges of those inhabitants connected with such services as follows:

$$\text{Qhwut} = (\text{Qhwp} - \text{Qhwp} \times 0.4) + \text{Qhwu}, \tag{2}$$

where Qhwut is the total amounts of uncollected household wasteby formal WCS, and Qhwp is the amounts of household waste generated by population with access to WCS using the per-capita generation rate given in Section 2.3.

$$\text{Qhwut} = (\text{Qhwps} - \text{Qhwps} \times 0.7) + \text{Qhwu}. \tag{3}$$

These are consistent with collection rates for middle-income countries (like Romania) ranging between 50% and 80% [3], with the mention that rural communities are expected to have a lower collection efficiency than urban areas due to following factors: sparse settlements and lower density, poorer socioeconomic conditions, geographical isolation, scattered waste collection points, low collection frequency, large distances from landfills, recycling, and waste treatment facilities, etc. Thus, lower (40%) and upper ranges (70%) were taken into consideration to calculate the rural uncollected household waste flow at the county level derived from the gaps in the rural waste collection schemes.

2.6. Collection Efficiency Based on the Rural Household Collection Rate

The current rural waste dumping practices following the closure of rural wild dumps in 2009–2010 were examined in our study, with a particular focus on Neamt county. The most recent local environmental report stipulates that despite a significant increase of waste collection coverage among rural residents (5.24 times, from 53,089 in 2009 to 278,167 inhabitants in 2015), the collection rate of household waste by waste operators is much lower (1.5 times), suggesting serious gaps in the rural waste collection schemes across the county [28].

In this case, collection efficiency (Cef) was determined using the ratio of the collection rate calculated on a per-capita basis (kg.inhab.day^{-1}) during 2010–2015 (latest data available) by a local environmental protection agency to national and regional waste generation rates as shown in Table 1.

Table 1. Ratio of rural household collection rate to national and regional generation rates.

Year	Rural Collection Rate	Grw = 0.4 Cef (%)	Grw = 0.31 Cef (%)
2010	0.252	63	40
2011	0.200	50	64.51
2012	0.205	51.25	66.12
2013	0.130	32.5	42
2014	0.152	38	49
2015	0.146	36.5	47%

The average rural collection rate for the period 2010–2015 was 0.18 kg.inhab.day^{-1} in Neamt county, which has a ratio of 45% of the national rural waste generation rate (0.4 kg.inhab.day^{-1}) and 58% in case of the regional generation rate (0.31 kg.inhab.day^{-1}). These values are consistent with previous low and upper ranges scenarios (40–70%), but the regional waste generation rate was further taken into consideration, resulting in a collection efficiency of 60 (WCS60) in rural Neamt county. This is a different approach, but it can be applied in rural regions where data about rural collection rates are available and they must be below the national waste generation rates stipulated in environmental reports. Rural waste dumping practices were further analyzed in 2012 (where some communes are not covered by WCS) and 2015, where all communes are served by public or private waste operators. The amounts of uncollected household waste were calculated for both years using the equation from Section 2.3 and applying WCS60 as follows:

$$\text{Qhwut} = (\text{Qhwps} - \text{Qhwps} \times 0.6) + \text{Qhwu}. \quad (4)$$

The amounts of uncollected household waste from rural inhabitants without access to WCS were determined for 2012. In the case of 2015, amounts of uncollected household waste derived mainly from the gaps in waste collection systems (WCS60). Spatial analysis revealed rural regions most exposed to illegal dumping practices in 2012 and 2015.

3. Results and Discussion

3.1. Geographies of Dumpsites

The total amounts of waste disposed of in the wild dumps are 1.403 million tons at the regional level with larger amounts disposed in Iasi county (552,102.8 t) and lowest in Neamt county (35,318 t). Figure 1 points out the geography of dumps at the regional scale as follows:

- Eastern counties of the North-East Region (Botosani, Iasi, Vaslui) that overlap on the Moldavian Plateau have a homogenous higher density of population and large amounts of waste disposed of in wild dumps; and
- The western counties of the region (Suceava, Neamt, Bacau) have a low density of population and smaller dumpsites in the mountain sector (Eastern Carpathians—the western half of counties) and high density and larger amounts of dumps in the proximity of the corridor valleys of Suceava, Moldova, and Siret rivers.

The subcarpathian depression sector, which is a favorable geographical area for the development of human settlements, has a high density and larger amounts disposed of in the dumps (Neamt and Bacau counties). However, peripheral areas and distant rural communities from urban centers are less populated. That is the case of rural communities from the eastern part of Bacau county, southeast of Neamt county, and western and central areas of Vaslui county. The variation of the total dump capacity (t) is significant from each commune to another, ranging from smaller wild dumps (<100 t) to larger than 30,000 t. A diverse geographical distribution is observed between and within counties as shown in Figure 2. The waste dumping amounts expressed as per capita provide an insightful geographical comparison between rural municipalities.

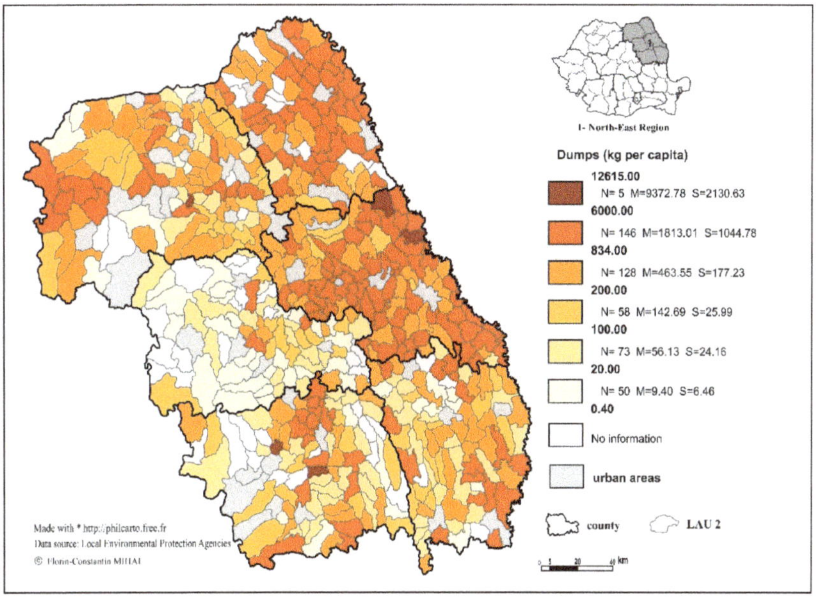

Figure 2. Per-capita analysis of waste amounts from dumps at the commune level in 2010.

A strong variation is observed in the western counties where the landscape varies, such as mountain areas, subcarpathian depressions and hills, valleys, and plateau areas with particular socio-economic features. The lower values of dumps (<100 kg.inhab) are found in 123 rural municipalities, particularly in the mountain sector of western counties. The regional average of the study area is 834 kg per capita per total dump capacity reported at the commune level. There are 151 communes with values above this regional average, with a particular focus across Iasi and Botosani counties.

A rural inhabitant generates 113.15 kg.inhab.yr^{-1} of household waste if the per-capita waste generation rate is 0.31 kg.inhab.day^{-1}, 146 kg.inhab.yr^{-1} according to national average rate, or 182.5 kg.inhab.yr^{-1} if the generation rate is above the national flat rate (0.5 kg.inhab.day^{-1}). In all three cases, the amount of household waste generated is less than 200 kg.inhab.yr^{-1}.

The map in Figure 2 reveals that several rural communities reported lesser amounts of household waste disposed of in wild dumps than those generated by one inhabitant in a year, in the context of poor waste collection coverage at the regional level. In fact, there are 181 rural communities in this situation providing solid arguments towards a poor monitoring process of waste dumping practices, and on the other hand, a higher susceptibility of river dumping practices in mountain and subcarpathian areas combined with backyard burning practices [27,29]. Such waste disposal routes could explain the lower values than the regional average (<800 kg.per capita) of the western counties, but there are 50 communes with values even below 20 kg.per capita/dump/commune. In such cases, there is no doubt that open dumping practices are heavily underestimated across rural communities, with this issue being further analyzed in Section 3.3.

Floodplains and riverbeds are frequently exposed to the illegal dumping of solid waste because of improper waste management facilities in rural areas.

The amounts of waste disposed of in riverbeds are diverted from local wild dumps exposed to floods. Also, wild dumps located on floodplains are exposed to flash floods, which transport the wastes into downstream localities [30]. The same river dumping practices occur in rural Poland as shown by Malinowski et al., [31] along with the Wisłok and Lubatówka river courses. Illegal dumpsites were also detected mainly in rural areas close to agricultural land in the Canary Islands [32]. Municipal landfills create specific ecosystems where some plant species can be dangerous to surrounding agricultural lands [33], but rural dumpsites are much smaller with lower amounts of waste disposed of and the closed sites are often covered by ruderal species.

Eastern Europe is prone to illegal dumping practices because waste collection coverage is not 100%, especially in rural areas, as confirmed in post-soviet countries, such as Ukraine, Belarus, Georgia, Moldova, and Russia [34]. The lack of a waste-sorting culture, poor infrastructure, and landfill prevalence are additional issues that such countries are facing [35].

Open burning is another waste disposal option of households' uncollected waste across rural communities. Combustible wastes accumulate in open piles (backyards, roadsides, or floodplains) containing mixed fractions, such as biowaste (food waste, garden waste, wood), plastics, textiles, paper and cardboard, and occasionally hazardous items (electronic waste, batteries, etc.) or sawdust. River dumping and open burning practices could divert a certain part of uncollected household waste, decreasing the amount of waste in dumpsites. This data seems to be questionable at the local scale due to the high number of communes that have reported lower volumes of dumpsites within their administrative area.

3.2. *Poor Waste Collection Services Contribute to Large Amounts of Uncollected Household Waste*

The lack of waste collection services in rural areas was the norm in the North-East Region of Romania prior to EU accession (2007) as Figure 3 shows. Such services were non-existent in Vaslui county during 2003–2010, 1% to 2% in Botosani county (2003–2007), less than 5% in Iasi county (2003–2008), and less than 10% in Suceava county (2003–2006). Neamt county has a constant range (9–11%) during 2003–2008, with an increase of 15% in 2009. Open dumping was a widespread practice across rural communities until July 2009. Local authorities were obliged to close such dumpsites and on the other hand, to establish their own waste management services or to delegate this amenity towards a private waste operator. Rural population coverage is more than 50% only in Suceava (71, 24%) compared to Vaslui (0.07%) in 2009. Rural communities have been exposed to unsound waste management practices, such as open dumping, river dumping, and open burning of household waste.

The expansion of WCSs towards rural areas has emerged since 2008 with a peak in 2009–2010. Botosani and Suceava have the highest collection coverage rates after the closure of dumpsites followed by Iasi county, and in the later years by Neamt and Bacau counties. Vaslui county represents the worst case situation during the full timeline analysis (2003–2016), facing serious illegal waste dumping and open burning practices across rural communities due to the lack of waste collection schemes.

Local dumpsites were the main option for household waste disposal across rural communities in the eastern counties compared to the western half of Bacau, Neamt, and Suceava. Eastern Carpathians favored the development of human settlements along the river valleys (Bistrita, Trotus, Moldova) and its tributaries. Such open dumps were often located in the proximity of riverbanks, but river dumping practices were more widespread disposal practices among mountain localities [30]. Such localities impose particular challenges for the waste management sector in terms of waste collection, transport, and location of waste treatment facilities [36].

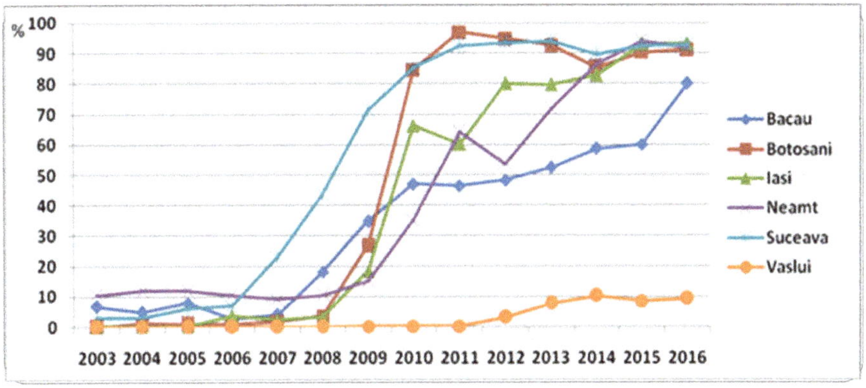

Figure 3. Rural population coverage with waste collection services (WCSs) 2003–2016.

Poor waste collection coverage contributed to large amounts of uncollected household waste during 2003–2009 across rural municipalities being susceptible to be uncontrolled disposal in the surroundings of wild dumps. The total amount calculated is 1.55 MT (0.31 kg.per capita.day^{-1}) or 2 MT (0.4 kg.per capita.day^{-1}) across the North-East region. At first glance, the regional value of uncollected household waste (1.55 MT) is closer to those disposed of in the dumps (1.4 MT) suggesting that dumps represent 90.5% of disposal practice of household waste in rural areas.

However, at the county level, there are significant differences concerning the ratio of dumps in total uncollected household waste, ranging from 14% in Neamt county to 164% in Iasi county as shown in Table 2. Firstly, dumps cover a poor share of uncollected household waste, suggesting an improper monitoring process of rural dumps performed by environmental and local authorities across rural areas of Neamt county. On the other hand, river dumping and open burning practices could mitigate the amounts of waste disposed of in local dumps, particularly in the mountain sector of Suceava, Neamt, and Bacau counties. Wild dumps are more consistent with the extra-Carpathian areas of the North-East Region, particularly in depression and plateau areas as shown in Figure 1. Secondly, there are two waste generation sources at the commune level that could contribute to open dumping practices: Inhabitants via uncollected household waste by waste operators and the economic agents (shops, pubs, institutions, local companies) that generate similar wastes, which feed the uncollected waste flow if there are no waste collection facilities across rural municipalities. Most of the waste generated in rural areas is provided by households (80%) and economic agents (20%), as suggested by master plans for waste management systems [37]. The basic waste indicators vary from one commune to another at the local scale as revealed in Neamt county [26]. This variation is common across rural communities because of non-homogenous social-economic, demographic, and geographic conditions.

Han et al. [1] found that in rural China, the characteristics of the household waste in towns or central villages were similar to those in cities but were different from those in common villages (the smallest type of community). In urban areas, the share of similar waste is expected to increase, particularly in large cities where business and public institutions are more developed.

If economic agents (20%) are included as contributors to open dumping practices, the per-capita generation rate at the commune level increases from 0.31 to 0.4 kg.inhab.day^{-1} (regional average) and from 0.4 to 0.5 kg.inhab.day^{-1} (national flat rate).

The resulting values decrease the share of dumps in the total uncollected waste at the county level, particularly for Iasi and Botosani counties. The regional average rate better explains the contribution of households (rural population) to waste dumping practices; the national flat rate (WGR = 0.4) and the upper rate (WGR = 0.5) are consistent if economic agents are taken into consideration at the county level. Since there are poor coverage rates of WCS across the study area during 2003–2009, the contribution of economic agents to open dumping practices should not be ignored. Field observations reveal the fact that even rural localities covered by WCSs are still susceptible to illegal waste disposal practices due to the improper behavior of local residents, poor collection frequency, inadequate waste collection infrastructure, sanitation fees, etc.

Table 2. The ratio of uncollected household waste from rural dumps at the county level using different waste generation rates (WGRs).

County	Rural Dumps (t)	Kg Per Capita	Qhwu_t (2003_09) WGR = 0.31 kg.inhab.day	% Qhwu of DUMPs	Qhwu_t (2003-09) WGR = 0.4	% Qhwu of Dumps	Qhwu_t (2003-09) WGR = 0.5	% Qhwu of Dumps
Bacau	213,376.8	536.51	276,405.97	77.19	356,652.86	59.82	445,816.08	47.86
Botosani	280,280	1043.02	210,087.83	133.41	271,081.07	103.39	338,851.34	82.71
Iasi	552,102.8	1243.39	335,359.8	164.62	432,722.32	127.58	540,902.91	102.07
Neamt	35,318	99.84	248,553.09	14.20	320,713.66	11.01	400,892.08	8.8
Suceava	190,176	464.08	262,276.52	72.50	338,421.32	56.19	423,026.65	44.95
Vaslui	132,466	487.29	218,048.05	60.75	281,352.32	47.08	351,690.40	37.66
North-East	**1,403,719.6**	654.16	**1,550,731.28**	90.51	**2,000,943.59**	70.15	**2,501,179.48**	56.12

3.3. Assessment of Rural Waste Dumping Underestimation Level According to Scenario Analysis

The data on dumpsite volumes at the EU region level does not cover the huge amounts of uncollected household waste during one year if noWCS are provided, as shown by the maps in Figure 4. In this scenario, there are 217,903.591 tons of uncollected household waste (WGR = 0.31 kg.inhab.day^{-1}), which represents 15.5% of the total amounts reported to be disposed of in total dumps. The ratio of uncollected household waste in one year is more than 100% of rural dumpsites capacities reported by 130 communes (most of them located in Neamt county), between 75% and 100% in another 30 communes, and only in 37 communes the ratio is less than 5%.

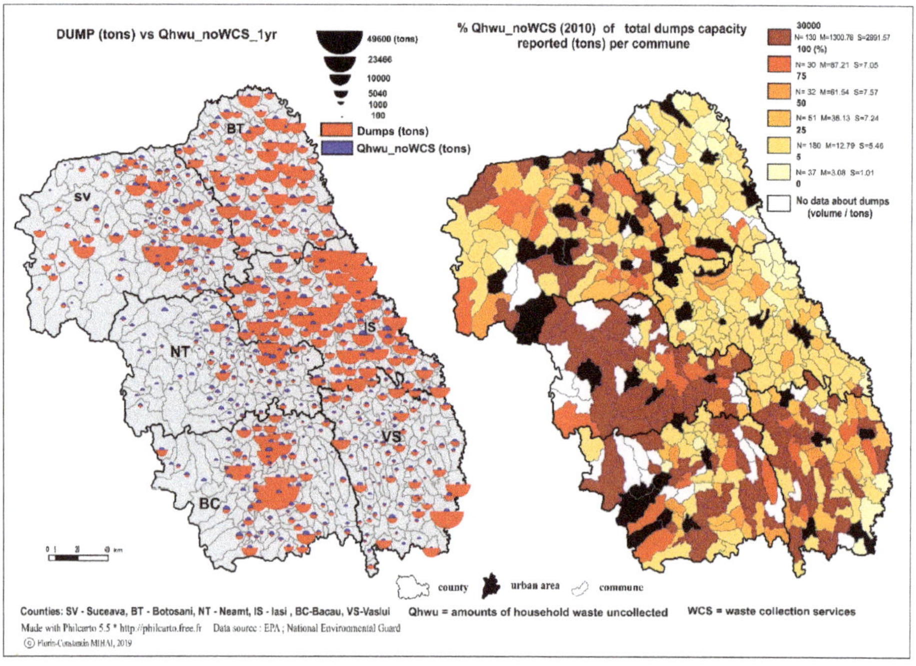

Figure 4. Household waste uncollected using noWCS scenario related to rural dumps. NoWCS = no access to waste collection services.

Open dumping practices seem to be seriously underestimated in the case of 190 rural municipalities with incomplete data about rural dumpsites parameters across their administrative areas (Suceava, Neamt, Bacau, and Vaslui counties).

Waste diversion from wild dumps via river dumping and open burning of household waste could not cover all amounts of uncollected household waste. Home composting is also a diversion route in the case of biowaste fraction from wild dumps even if it is performed at the household level in open piles.

Food waste has a lower degree in rural areas of Czech Republic based on traditional recovery options, such as self-provision, cooking at home, and animal feeding [38].

A similar situation is valid across rural communities of the North-East Region, particularly in villages that are more distant to urban areas. Improper law enforcement and monitoring of illegal waste disposal practices leads to a poor assessment of waste dumping dimensions across rural communities. The same issue is highlighted in rural Poland, where the number of uncontrolled dumping sites revealed in the official statistics is underestimated and research on illegal waste disposal cannot be based on them [39].

Despite the fact that the regional database of wild dumps is the most comprehensive so far, this paper demonstrates that there are significant amounts of waste uncollected and uncovered by the dumpsites capacities reported by the local authorities, particularly in Neamt, Bacau, Suceava, and Vaslui counties.

Figure 5 shows that 226 communes (yellow polygons_right map) across the North-East Region have full coverage of WCS in 2010 with a better extension in Botosani, Iasi, and Suceava counties.

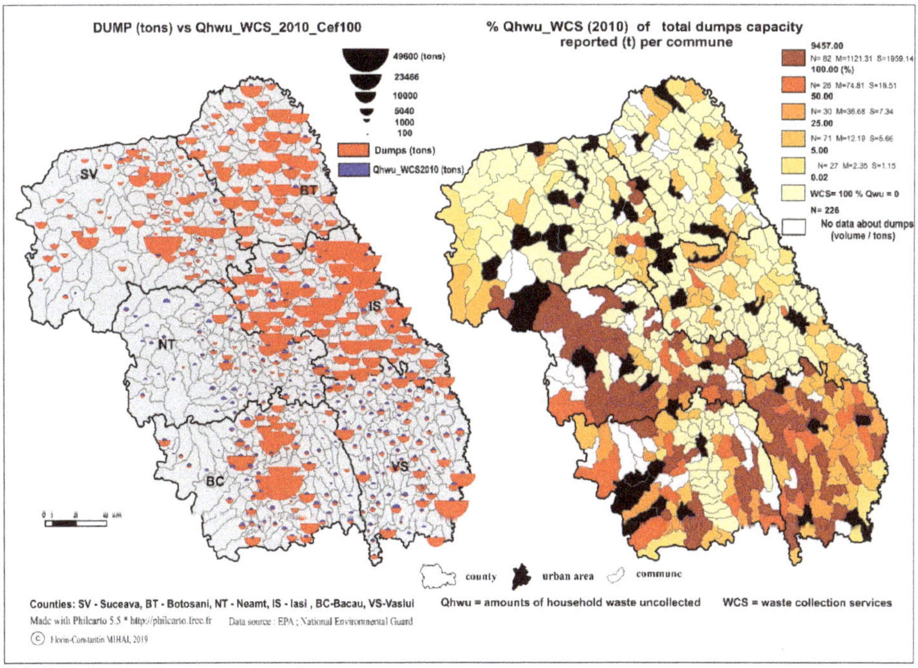

Figure 5. Household waste uncollected based on waste collection coverage rates in 2010 related to rural dumps (Cef = 100%).

In such cases, the amounts of uncollected household waste are null since there are no inhabitants without access to such services, suggesting a full collection efficiency (100%) as opposed to the noWCS scenario.

However, field observations show that even such communes are still facing illegal dumping practices, pointing out serious gaps in current rural waste management facilities. The illegal dumping of waste occurs even in high-income countries, such as England, where improvements in waste management, distribution facilities, and legal factors (law enforcement and prosecution actions of local councils), are required to combat this environmental threat [40].

The same actions need to be addressed in Romania both in urban and rural areas. Furthermore, if only the population unserved by WCS is taken into consideration at the commune level, there are several rural communities (82) that reported fewer amounts of waste disposed in dumps than those generated and uncollected in 2010 as shown in Figure 4. Most of the rural municipalities from Neamt, Bacau, and Vaslui counties are in this situation, only four communes in Suceava county, and none in Iasi and Botosani counties. In the case of Vaslui county, all communes have large amounts of uncollected household waste due to the lack of WCSs in rural areas in 2010. Thus, there are over 30 communes where the ratio of uncollected household waste in 2010 surpasses the total amounts disposed in the dumps from previous years. In this regard, the collection efficiency is a key factor to be considered for further estimations. Figure 6 shows a more realistic perspective than Figure 5 where the amounts of household waste generated and uncollected per commune are larger due to an inefficient waste collection system.

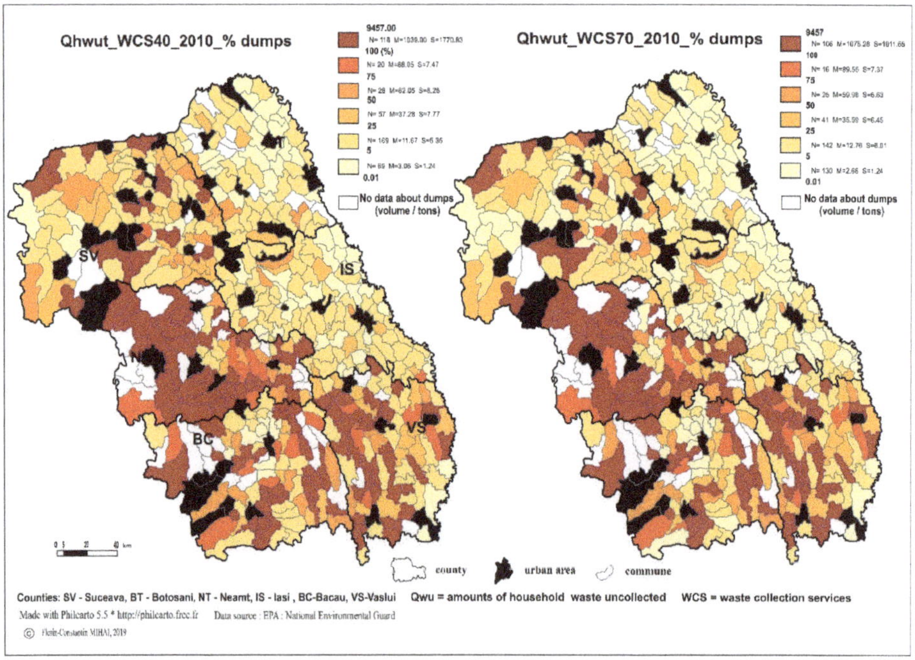

Figure 6. Household waste uncollected in 2010 based on low and upper collection efficiency scenarios related to rural dumps.

This fact is confirmed by previous studies [26,27] and by field observations. The main spatial patterns are still valid across these scenarios where the magnitude of waste dumping practices is seriously underestimated across Neamt, Vaslui, Bacau, and Suceava counties.

There are 116 (WCS40) and 106 (WCS70) rural municipalities that generate in one year more uncollected household waste than that reported as disposed of in local dumps; 20 (WCS40) and 16 (WCS70) communes where the dump capacity should be filled over 75% as shown in Figure 5. On the opposite side, a higher collection efficiency leads to a larger number of communes (130), which contribute less than 5% of total local dumps compared to 69% in the case of poorer efficiency (40%—low range).

This study demonstrates that even with a reasonable collection efficiency (WCS70), such as un upper range of middle-income countries like Romania in rural areas, the amounts of uncollected household waste could fill over 50% of the local dumps in only one year across 147 communes. These data resulted from such scenarios that argue that most of the rural waste dumping practices are out of official records without any knowledge about their repercussions to the natural environment or to public health issues. Furthermore, collection systems and treatment are still lacking in rural Romania and regulations are not still in action [41]. Capital investment in rural waste management services should be increased in low-income regions to relieve the burden of local municipalities as suggested by Cao et al. [42].

3.4. Assessment of Uncollected Household Waste after the Closure of Rural Dumpsites (2010–2016)

After the closure of rural dumpsites in 2009–2010, the expansion of waste collection coverage towards rural areas started to emerge, thus the amounts of household waste generated and uncollected by rural inhabitants without access to formal waste management sector have decreased since 2010 in the North-East Region from 109,141.79 tons to 48,998 tons in 2016 as shown in Figure 7. The total amount (540,849 tons) of uncollected household waste during 2010–2016 is one of the primary sources for environmental pollution by uncontrolled waste disposal activities (e.g., wild dumps, freshwater pollution, open burning practices, etc.).

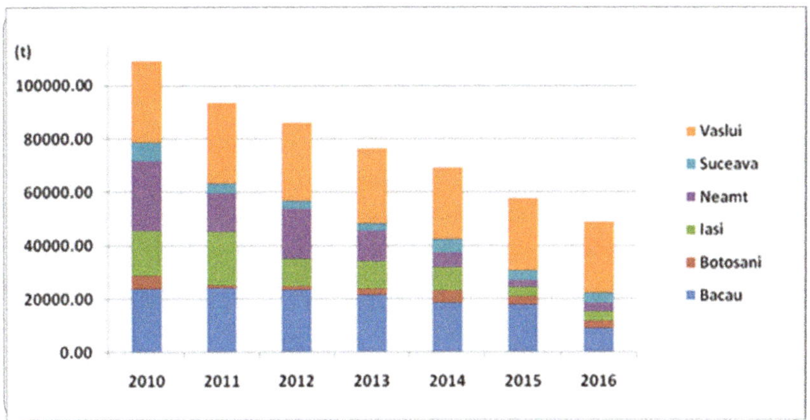

Figure 7. Household waste generated by rural population without access to WCSs during 2010–2016 in the North-East Region (data source: EPA environmental reports—author compilation).

Better waste collection coverage rates of rural areas across Iasi, Botosani, and Suceava counties led to lower amounts of uncollected household waste during this period. Neamt and Bacau counties made some progress in the latter years, but the situation in rural areas of Vaslui is still the worse of all the region. The rural waste collection coverage was under 10% in 2016 in this county, therefore, the natural environment around rural settlements was significantly exposed to illegal dumping or open burning practices. In fact, 199,127.8 t of household waste was generated and uncollected in this county during 2010–2015 as a ratio of 36.81% of the North-East Region. Bacau county contributed 138,238.5 t of uncollected household waste and Botosani had the least amount, being under 20,000 t.

Full coverage of the rural population to waste collection schemes is expected in the following years due to the implementation of regional integrated municipal waste systems in each county of the region. Such systems stipulate the construction of one to two regional sanitary landfills (serving both urban and rural areas), transfer stations, and sorting and composting plants [24]. However, the delays associated with the construction of these new regional sanitary landfills, bureaucracy, tender process, and court decision have prolonged the waste management infrastructure crisis in Neamt, Bacau, Vaslui, and Suceava counties. The low and upper collection efficiency scenarios were further applied at the county level to determine the extra amount of household waste generated and uncollected in rural areas as an additional source to illegal dumping practices. Therefore, Table 3 points out that gaps in the waste collection schemes during 2010–2016, irrespective of low or upper collection efficiency rates, indicate that the total amounts of household waste cumulated surpass one million tons during 2010–2016. The cumulation of household waste generated by the rural population without access to WCS with the low range of collection efficiency of those covered by waste operators reveals huge amounts of household waste in each county, ranging from 144,274 t in Botosani County to 325,527 t in Vaslui County. These wastes are susceptible to uncontrolled disposal in the natural environment. The upper range reveals the key role played by better collection efficiency in rural areas, saving 511,410.85 t of uncollected household waste at the North-East region level compared to the lower range (WCS40). In both cases, Bacau and Vaslui counties cumulated over 200,000 t of uncollected household waste.

Table 3. Rural uncollected household waste flow based on collection efficiency scenarios during 2010–2016.

County (2010–2016)	Hwu_noWCS (t)	Hwu_no WCS + WCS40 (t)	Hwu_noWCS + WCS70 (t)	Hwu_noWCS + WCS60 (t)_NT
Bacau	138,238.56	326,908.88	232,573.72	264,018.77
Botosani	19,293.31	144,274.46	81,783.89	102,614.08
Iasi	74,315.99	291,862.03	183,089.01	219,346.68
Neamt	81,385.53	249,097.05	165,241.29	*193,193.21*
Suceava	28,487.96	226,000.81	127,244.39	160,163.20
Vaslui	199,127.82	325,527.66	262,327.74	283,394.38
North East Region (total)	**540,849.18**	**1,563,670.89**	**1,052,260.04**	**1,222,730.32**

Hwu_noWCS = household waste generated and uncollected of the population without access to WCS.

The collection efficiency based on the collection rate in Neamt county was applied to test the uncollected household waste flow as a middle range of the North-East Region. In this scenario, Bacau, Iasi (as the largest rural population at North-East Region level), and Vaslui counties generate the largest amounts of uncollected household waste. In the latter case, the unserved population is the biggest contributor in every situation to be taken into consideration.

Testing different parameters of collection efficiency scenarios reveals, on the one hand, that rural communities can generate large amounts of uncollected household waste, which can pollute the natural environment and on the other hand, the improvement of household waste capture by formal waste management systems is a crucial factor besides the full coverage of the rural population to waste collection schemes.

3.5. Rural Waste Dumping Practices in Neamt County: A Comparative Analysis 2012–2015

The expansion of WCS towards rural areas has emerged since the closure of rural dumpsites in 2009, but illegal waste dumping practices still occur nowadays. In 2012, there were seven communes without access to formal WCS and several rural municipalities with partial coverage of such services. Figure 8 shows the uncollected household waste by inhabitants without access to sanitation services in 2012 (red fraction of the pie chart) compared to 2015, where all communes are connected to waste collection schemes. Thus, the population unserved by WCS generated 6434.9 tons of 17,236.7 total tons of uncollected household waste in rural areas in 2012. In the latter case, the illegal dumping practices are associated with a poorer collection efficiency supported by field observations and previous studies, and on the other hand, by low collection rates during 2010–2015 as shown in Table 1. In 2015, rural communities generated 15,892.4 tons of uncollected household waste based on the WCS60 scenario. The amounts of the uncollected household waste range between 134 and 1153 tons at the commune level, taking into account both years.

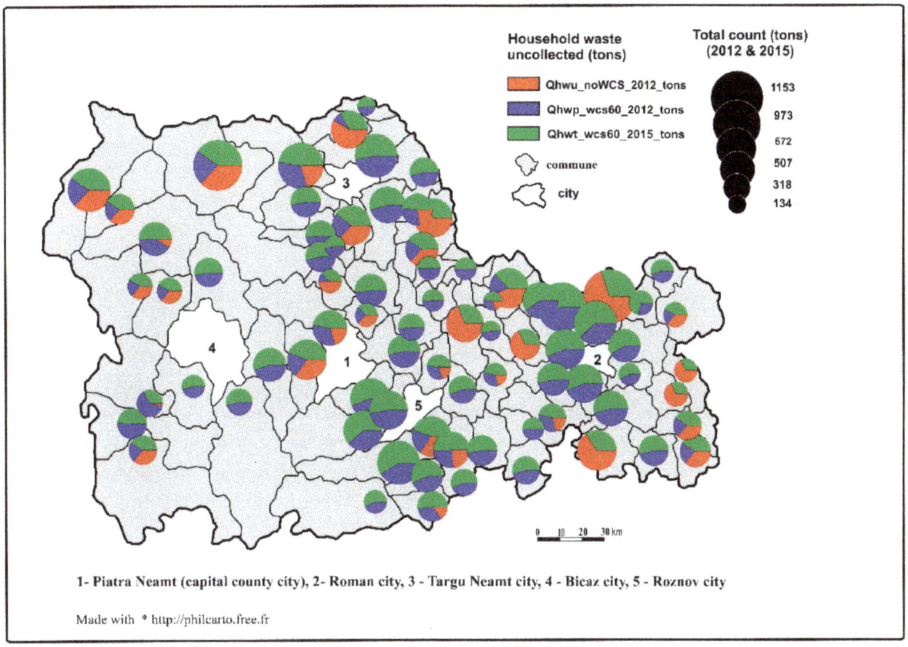

Figure 8. Uncollected household waste in rural areas of Neamt County in 2012 and 2015.

More than 30 communes did not have full coverage of WCS in 2012 (blue fraction of the pie chart), which, combined with a collection efficiency of 60%, led to larger amounts of households' uncollected waste being susceptible to uncontrolled disposal in comparison to 2015.

The most vulnerable rural areas to illegal dumping practices are situated in the eastern and south-eastern parts of the county outside of those seven communes with no such services in 2012 (without a blue section of the pie chart). Furthermore, well-populated communes located in the south of Piatra Neamt city (county capital) generate large amounts of uncollected household waste prone to illegal waste dumping practices. Most of the waste operators signed contracts with local authorities rather than directly with inhabitants, thus gaps are expected in waste collection schemes. This fact could explain the lower collection rates during 2010–2015 despite the total rural waste collection coverage being 94% in 2015 at the county level. The higher collection, transportation, and landfill costs caused by the closure of non-compliant landfills from Targu Neamt, Bicaz, and Roman cities are transferred into rural sanitation fees paid by the rural population served. In this context, some people refuse to pay for waste management services and wastes generated are improperly disposed of via wild dumps or open burning practices [29].

The above situations reveal the routes for illegal waste dumping practices despite the presence of waste operators in rural areas or even full coverage of the population to such services.

4. Development of the Rural Circular Economy Framework

A circular economy is becoming a key strategic framework for EU sustainability being dedicated to several actions to achieve decoupling from the current linear economy model [43].

The circular economy involves a multi-sectoral approach and complex interactions between various stakeholders [44], where industry, agriculture, commerce, and tourism can make the transition to such a model at regional levels [45] besides a reliable solid waste management system. New recycling targets are set for the overall municipal waste fraction (65% as the recycling rate by 2035) and 70% for recycling 70% of packaging waste by 2030 and special targets for some special packaging materials for plastics (55%), paper/cardboard (85%), glass (75%), and ferrous metals (80%) to be fulfilled by all EU) [46]. Romania must upgrade as soon as possible the current waste management systems to cover both urban and rural areas to separate collection schemes, sorting stations, composting plants, transfer stations, and regional sanitary landfills in order to successfully achieve these new EU targets related to circular economy policies.

4.1. New Regional Integrated Waste Management Systems

Rural areas must be integrated into regional waste management systems where the main facilities are frequently located around the cities. Different rural areas within a county will be connected to transfer stations of urban areas in the proximity. On such sites, recyclables will be sorted and processed to be further sold to recycling companies. The residual waste (mixed fraction) with poor recycling potential will be transported to the regional sanitary landfill site. In the first stage, all communes within a county must be connected to waste collection schemes provided by public services or private waste operators. Secondly, the source-separated collection facilities via collection points (e.g., dry recyclables) or from door-to-door schemes are basic steps to stimulate recycling operations. Waste collection frequency should be at least every week for residual waste and no more than 2 weeks for dry recyclables (plastics, metals, glass, paper/cardboard).

Collection points must be carefully located across rural communities taking into account the distances from households and the collection points. In fact, door-to-door collection schemes seem to be more efficient in mountainous areas or rural settlements displayed along the watercourse and their tributaries [26]. Collection points are more feasible for compact and populated rural areas, particularly in the proximity of urban areas. Special waste streams, such as e-waste, used tires, bulky waste, construction, and demolition waste, batteries and accumulators, end-of-life vehicles, and hazardous items, must be collected through special collection campaigns or brought to urban recycling centers by individuals. In this regard, environmental and local municipalities should initiate environmental awareness events about the critical role played by special waste collection events for such types of waste. Local economic agents and public institutions must manage their own packaging waste stream or delegate a specialized waste operator to collect and further process this waste stream as part of the extended producer responsibility scheme). Some rural economic agents could serve as a local collection point for such special waste streams (e.g., batteries and accumulators, e-waste, used oil, etc.) in partnership with recycling companies. A source-separated waste collection based on four waste fractions has been compulsory since 1 July 2019 according to the updated waste management law [47], at least in the case of plastics, metals, paper and cardboard, and glass beside the residual waste of the municipal waste stream. Furthermore, these waste fractions must be reached by December 31 2020, a level for reuse and recycling at least 50% of the total mass generated. This target is hard to achieve in rural areas where separate collection schemes are just being implemented. The landfill fee will increase to 80 lei per ton (1 leu = 4.7 EUR) in 2020 as a measure to discourage the landfill of waste and to fund recycling and recovering initiatives through the Environmental Fund Administration. The regional waste management plans must be updated at each county level of the North-East Region according to the new National Waste Management Plan [24].

4.2. Home Composting and Animal Feed

These are traditional routes for biowaste fraction of municipal waste stream across rural communities. In rural Romania, subsistence agriculture still prevails among households, thus biowaste is regarded as a cheap resource for obtaining natural fertilizers for farming activities. The older habits use animal manure combined with garden waste and food waste (vegetables) to make compost on open piles. However, this is a rude technique performed on direct soil, which can pollute the local environment through emissions to air, soil, and groundwater bodies. New composting bins and special platforms for the storage of organic waste should be implemented via regional waste management systems following the steps provided in guidelines.

Composting plays a key role in the rural circular paradigm due to the high share of organic waste in the MSW stream. Also, the Landfill Directive 1999/31/EC requires the reduction of biodegradable waste to be disposed of in urban landfills; therefore, home composting activities or centralized composting facilities must treat most biowaste flows fed by rural communities. Besides composting activities, animal feed (bones, meat, other food items, crop residues as fodder) is another key alternative for rural communities. Home composting and animal feed are key alternatives for less developed regions and sparsely populated rural settlements in managing organic wastes [48]. Rural–urban linkages could stimulate biowaste prevention and organic farming. As an example, a food waste diversion program was initiated by retailers and restaurants (hotels), which is sorted and sent to compost in a rural bio farm (Ciocanesti, Dimbovita County). This initiative collected 621 tons of organic waste, producing 595 tons of compost, Another 26 tons of vegetables and fruits have been saved and donated and this project delivered 5200 meals to elderly people, those with disabilities, or homeless people [49].

4.3. Community Waste Management and Creative Reuse of Waste Items

Distant rural localities from urban centers face more challenges in managing their MSW stream due to the reluctance of waste operators to cover such areas and supplementary costs related to the transportation of waste collected towards recycling and disposal facilities. In this context, rural communities must implement traditional (e.g., home composting, animal feed, recovery and reuse of waste items at the household level) and innovative routes (e.g., upcycling or creative reuse, refurbishment of computers and other IT equipment) to combat illegal dumping and open burning practices and to avoid landfill of the MSW stream as much as possible. Figure 9 shows the traditional routes and formal waste management routes to make the transition from linear to circular economy model and to combat major environmental threats associated with improper waste management activities. There is a guide *Making Waste Work* that can help rural communities of low- and middle-income countries (including rural Romania) manage their waste using simple and low-cost techniques and foster local recycling enterprises and a local economy [50].

Urbanization process, construction sector, and the expansion of infrastructure (roads, public utilities, etc.) are expected to increase in the following years in Romania. The rural areas will be vulnerable to a huge amount of construction and demolition wastes (C&DW) if there is not sufficient treatment capacities. Mobile crushing plants could be an optimal solution for rural communities to deal with C&DW flows. This waste stream has a high potential for reuse, recovery, and recycling activities under circular economy prospects as new building materials for both urban and rural areas [51].

Rural creative reuse has started to be observed in some rural municipalities: polyethylene terephthalate (PET)bottles are used to decorate the gates of pubs; plastics bottles caps are used to build household gates according to the local traditional customs (e.g., Blaga village, Iasi County). Various waste streams (plastics, paper/cardboard, wood, textile, e-waste, etc.) are reused to create new kinds of items useful in households. This activity could be an additional source of income but will imply challenges related to the provision, transport, storage, and delivery of products.

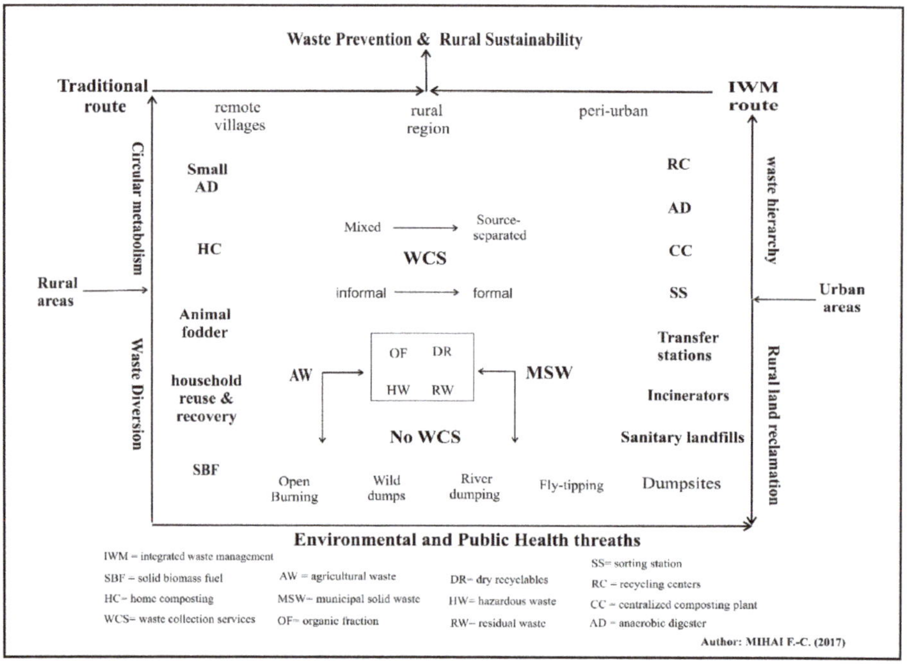

Figure 9. Pathways towards waste prevention and rural sustainability. Source: Mihai and Taherzadeh 2017 (CC-BY license) [2].

A wide range of activities related to upcycling can be performed with the support provided by specialized organizations, such as http://reciclarecreativa.ro/.. At the EU level, there is a policy handbook to stimulate creative partnerships through upcycling activities that was created in 2014 [52]. However, the impact of upcycling is limited so far in rural areas, but such practices could spread the environmental awareness and zero waste concept towards a larger audience supported also by schools, mass-media, social media, local stakeholders, non-governmental organizations (NGOs), etc. Internet coverage across rural areas has emerged in the last years, thus inhabitants could learn about upcycling activities and how to embrace waste prevention initiatives under the zero waste paradigm. The zero waste concept emerges at the European level (https://zerowasteeurope.eu/) with the national organization from the EU (including Romania) and non-EU countries. Zero waste, defined as "the conservation of all resources by means of responsible production, consumption, reuse and recovery of products, packaging, and materials without burning, and with no discharges to land, water, or air that threaten the environment or human health" https://zerowasteeurope.eu/what-is-zero-waste/, is supported by Zero Waste International Alliance. However, this zero-waste concept seems to emerge in cities but such a concept must be adapted to diverse features of rural regions. In this context, the role of NGOs could be significant in consolidating practices of 3, 6, or 9Rs (reduce, reuse, repair, recovery, refurbish, repurpose, remanufacture, recycle, refuse) in rural communities.

An example of e-waste recycling activities combined with social inclusion is the WISE WEEE project, which aims to keep the maximum value of products in the country using local labor of marginalized groups (women and men with a disability, chronic diseases, family, justice, or poverty issues, addictions, etc.) from Bucharest city [53]. These types of social enterprises could be reliable alternatives for rural communities of the North-East Region, which are more vulnerable to social exclusion associated with lack of investments, job opportunities, and poverty issues. Education and environmental awareness campaigns among pupils and students seem to be key factors in the long term concerning the adoption of a zero-waste lifestyle to prevent waste generation as much as possible at the household level and to consolidate the circular economy in urban and rural areas [54,55].

5. Conclusions

The lack of WCSs prior to the closure of rural dumpsites (2003–2009) contributed to large amounts of uncollected household waste in each county of the study area, ranging from 335,359.8 tons in Iasi county to 210,087.83 tons in Botosani county. The closure process of rural wild dumps (2009–2010) provided the most comprehensive database at North-East Region level concerning the volumes of such sites but the paper points out serious gaps at the local scale (LAU2) within a county or between western and eastern counties of this peripheral EU region. The ratio of open dumping practices of total uncollected household waste is higher in eastern counties (70–80%) than mountainous areas of Suceava, Neamt, and Bacau counties, where river dumping practices (including plastic pollution) could be a widespread alternative option as pointed out in a previous study [27,30].

Several rural communities (181 communes) disposed less than 200 kg/inhab.year^{-1} in wild dumps (as reported values), which is almost equivalent to the amount generated by one person if rural waste generation is 0.31, 0.4, or even 0.5 kg.inhab.day^{-1}. The environmental pollution dimension associated with rural waste dumping practices is seriously underestimated taking into account only the gross empirical data resulting from the closure procedure of reported wild dumps. The maps combined with scenario analysis revealed that 130 rural municipalities generate, in one year, more wastes than that reported as dumped on the surroundings from previous years (noWCS scenario). Furthermore, 82 communes generated more household waste than that disposed of in rural dumps and the other 26 rural communities generated more than 50% of the total dump capacity per commune in the best-case scenario where the collection efficiency was 100%. Despite the fact that no rural WCS were provided in Vaslui county during 2009–2010, 30 communes generated in 2010 more household wastes than those disposed of in dumps in previous years. This poor situation prevailed during 2010–2016, where 199,127.8 tons of household waste were generated and uncollected as a ratio of 36.81% of the North-East Region. The extension of full WCSs towards rural communities emerged during 2010–2016 as a basic step to avoid the illegal dumping of solid waste, but it is not a sufficient factor. However, the amount of household waste generated by the rural population without access to WCSs decreased to 540,849 tons (2010–2016) compared to 1,550,731 tons prior to the closure of rural dumpsites (2003–2009). Collection efficiency is not expected to be 100% across rural municipalities and more uncollected household waste is leaking into the natural environment as suggested by the low and upper ranges of collection efficiency scenarios (WCS40 and WCS70) specific to the case of a middle-income country like Romania.

The total amount of uncollected household waste derived from the population without access to WCSs combined with that due to gaps in the waste collection schemes could reach over 1 MT of uncollected household waste at the North-East Region level, irrespective of the collection efficiency scenario used. These amounts of household waste are primary sources of waste-related pollution in rural areas besides other possible waste streams (e.g., construction and demolition waste, agricultural wastes). The rural waste dumping practices may vary in terms of the type and magnitude at different geographical scales from one county to another or between villages of a commune. This was confirmed in the case of Neamt county, where the rural collection rate was below the regional waste generation rate during 2012–2015 (average 0.18 kg vs. 0.31 kg.inhab.day^{-1}) and the calculated collection efficiency was 60%. The poor collection rates performed by waste operators highlight the current gaps in the rural waste collection schemes, which feeds illegal waste dumping practices. The paper estimated 33,129.1 tons of uncollected household waste in 2012 and 2015 prone to waste dumping practices across rural communities of Neamt county.

The paper points out that the traditional routes (home composting, animal feed, household recovery of waste items) must be further improved and supported by the rural community besides formal regional integrated waste management systems coupled with innovative projects or activities that stimulate creative reuse, the zero waste concept, and social solidarity.

Further investigations are necessary to reveal the exposure of rural communities towards unsound waste dumping practices across the transition and developing countries and to examine cost-efficient options towards a rural circular economy.

Author Contributions: F.-C.M.—developed the conceptualization of the paper and the methodology, gathered the data, performed the analysis and figures, writing the first draft of the manuscript. A.G.—literature review and revision of the manuscript draft

Funding: The APC is supported by Department of Geography, Faculty of Geography and Geology. This research work was supported by a grant of the Alexandru Ioan Cuza University of Iasi, within the Research Grants program, Grant UAIC, code GI-UAIC-2017-06.

Conflicts of Interest: The author declares no conflict of interest. The funders had no role in the design of the study; in the collection, analyses, or interpretation of data; in the writing of the manuscript, or in the decision to publish the results.

References

1. Han, Z.; Liu, Y.; Zhong, M.; Shi, G.; Li, Q.; Zeng, D.; Zhang, Y.; Fei, Y.; Xie, Y. Influencing factors of domestic waste characteristics in rural areas of developing countries. *Waste Manag.* **2018**, *72*, 45–54. [CrossRef] [PubMed]
2. Mihai, F.-C.; Taherzadeh, M.J. Introductory Chapter: Rural Waste Management Issues at the Global Level. In *Solid Waste Management in Rural Areas*; Mihai, F.-C., Ed.; IntechOpen: Rijeka, Croatia, 2017. [CrossRef]
3. Hoornweg, D.; Bhada-Tata, P. *What a Waste: A Global Review of Solid Waste Management, Urban Development Series Knowledge Papers*; World Bank: Washington DC, USA, 2012; Available online: http://documents.worldbank.org/curated/en/2012/03/16537275/waste-global-review-solid-wastemanagement (accessed on 15 March 2012).
4. Triassi, M.; Alfano, R.; Illario, M.; Nardone, A.; Caporale, O.; Montuori, P. Environmental pollution from illegal waste disposal and health effects: A review on the "Triangle of Death". *Int. J. Environ. Res. Public Health* **2015**, *12*, 1216–1236. [CrossRef] [PubMed]
5. Borrell, R.J.; Rodríguez, F.R.; Monedero, A.L.L. Factor analysis and geographic information system for determining probability areas of presence of illegal landfills. *Ecol. Ind.* **2014**, *37*, 151–160. [CrossRef]
6. Sedova, B. On causes of illegal waste dumping in Slovakia. *J. Environ. Plan Man.* **2016**, *59*, 1227–1303. [CrossRef]
7. Stanisavljević, N.; Ubavin, D.; Batinić, B.; Fellner, J.; Vujić, G. Methane emissions from landfills in Serbia and potential mitigation strategies: A case study. *Waste Manag. Res.* **2012**, *30*, 1095–1103. [CrossRef] [PubMed]
8. Zeng, C.; Niu, D.; Zhao, Y. A comprehensive overview of rural solid waste management in China. *Front. Environ. Sci. Eng.* **2015**, *9*, 949–961. [CrossRef]
9. Taherzadeh, M.J.; Rajendran, K. Factors Affecting the Development of Waste Management. Experiences from Different Cultures. In *Waste Management and Sustainable Consumption: Reflections on Consumer Waste*; Ekström, K.M., Ed.; Routledge: Abingdon, UK, 2015; pp. 67–88.
10. Poldnurk, J. Optimisation of the economic, environmental and administrative efficiency of the municipal waste management model in rural areas. *Resour. Conserv. Recycl.* **2015**, *97*, 55–65. [CrossRef]
11. Stanic-Maruna, I.; Fellner, J. Solid waste management in Croatia in response to the European Landfill Directive. *Waste Manag. Res.* **2012**, *30*, 825–838. [CrossRef]
12. Panaretou, V.; Malamis, D.; Papadaskalopoulou, C.; Sotiropoulos, A.; Valta, K.; Margaritis, M.; Plevri, A.; Moustakas, K.; Loizidou, M. Implementation, and evaluation of an integrated management scheme for MSW in selected communities in Tinos Island, Greece. *Waste Biomass Valor.* **2016**. [CrossRef]
13. De Morais Lima, P.; Paulo, P.L. Solid-waste management in the rural area of BRAZIL: A case study in Quilombola communities. *J. Mater. Cycles Waste Manag.* **2018**, *20*, 1583–1593. [CrossRef]
14. Wu, X.; Yue, B.; Huang, Q.; Wang, Q.; Li, Z.; Wang, Y.; Yu, J. Investigation of the physical and chemical characteristics of rural solid waste in China and its spatiotemporal distributions. *Environ. Sci. Pollut. Res.* **2018**, *25*, 17330–17342. [CrossRef] [PubMed]

15. Cucchiella, F.; D'Adamo, I.; Gastaldi, M. Sustainable Italian Cities: The Added Value of Biomethane from Organic Waste. *Appl. Sci.* **2019**, *9*, 2221. [CrossRef]
16. Florkowski, W.J.; Us, A.; Klepacka, A.M. Food waste in rural households supports for local biogas production in Lubelskie Voivodeship. *Resour. Conserv. Recycl.* **2018**, *136*, 46–52. [CrossRef]
17. Ciura, D.; Łukasiewicz, M.; Malinowski, M. Analysis of morphological composition of wastes deposited on illegal dumping sites located in the area of Olsztyn district. *Infrastruct. Ecol. Rural Areas* **2017**, 1301–1315. [CrossRef]
18. Macias, A.; Piniarski, W. Municipal Solid Waste Management Problems on a Local Scale: A Case Study from Rural Poland. *Pol. J. Environ. Stud.* **2016**, *25*, 1623–1632. [CrossRef]
19. Castillo-Giménez, J.; Montañés, A.; Picazo-Tadeo, A.J. Performance in the treatment of municipal waste: Are European Union member states so different? *Sci. Total Environ.* **2019**, *687*, 1305–1314. [CrossRef]
20. Hidalgo, D.; López, F.; Corona, F.; Martín-Marroquín, J.M. A novel initiative to counteract illegal dumping in rural areas of Valladolid Province. Environ. *Sci. Pollut. Res.* **2019**. [CrossRef]
21. European Commission. Regions and Cities Illustrated (RCI). Available online: https://ec.europa.eu/eurostat/cache/RCI/#?vis=nuts2.economy&lang=en (accessed on 12 October 2019).
22. ADR Nord-Est 2013 Regional Development Strategy of Nort-East 2014–2020. Available online: http://www.adrnordest.ro/user/file/pdr/v3/strategie%20RNE%202014-2020%20aprilie%202013.pdf (accessed on 14 January 2018). (In Romanian).
23. Ciuta, S.; Apostol, T.; Rusu, V. Urban and Rural MSW Stream Characterization for Separate Collection Improvement. *Sustainability* **2015**, *7*, 916–931. [CrossRef]
24. National Waste Management Plan (Version 5, 2 November 2018). Available online: http://mmediu.ro/app/webroot/uploads/files/PNGD_vers5.pdf (accessed on 14 January 2018). (In Romanian).
25. National Environment Protection Agency (NEPA). *The State of the Environment Report in 2016*; NEPA: Bucharest, Romania, 2017.
26. Mihai, F.C. Waste collection in rural communities: Challenges under EU regulations. A case study of Neamt County, Romania. *J. Mater. Cycles Waste Manag.* **2018**, *20*, 1337–1347. [CrossRef]
27. Mihai, F.-C. Rural plastic emissions into the largest mountain lake of the Eastern Carpathians. *R. Soc. Open Sci.* **2018**, *5*, 172396. [CrossRef]
28. Environment Protection Agency of Neamt County. *The State of the Environment Report in 2017*; Protection Agency of Neamt County: Neamt County, Romania, 2018.
29. Mihai, F.C.; Banica, A.; Grozavu, A. Backyard burning of household waste in rural areas. Environmental impact focusing on air pollution. In Proceedings of the 19th International Multidisciplinary Scientific GeoConference on Ecology, Economics, Education and Legislation SGEM, Albena, Bulgaria, 28 June–7 July 2019; Volume 19, pp. 55–62. [CrossRef]
30. Mihai, F.C.; Minea, I.; Grozavu, A. Assessment of waste dumping practices in mountain creeks. In Proceedings of the 18th International Multidisciplinary Scientific GeoConference on Ecology, Economics, Education and Legislation SGEM, Albena, Bulgaria, 2–9 July 2018; Volume 18, pp. 89–96. [CrossRef]
31. Malinowski, M.; Wolny-Koladka, K.; Jastrzebski, B. Characteristics of Illegal Dumping Sites–Case Study: Watercourses. *Infrastruct. Ecol. Rural Areas* **2015**, *4*, 1475–1484.
32. Quesada-Ruiz, L.; Rodriguez-Galiano, V.; Jordá-Borrell, R. Identifying the main physical and socioeconomic drivers of illegal landfills in the Canary Islands. *Waste Manag. Res.* **2018**. [CrossRef] [PubMed]
33. Vaverková, M.D.; Winkler, J.; Adamcova, D.; Radziemska, M.; Uldrijan, D.; Zloch, J. Municipal solid waste landfill–Vegetation succession in an area transformed by human impact. *Ecol. Eng.* **2019**, *129*, 109–114. [CrossRef]
34. Skryhan, H.; Shilova, I.; Khandogina, O.; Abashyna, K.; Chernikova, O. Waste management in post-soviet countries: How far from the EU? *Detritus* **2018**, *3*, 193–203. [CrossRef]
35. Fedotkina, O.; Gorbashko, E.; Vatolkina, N. Circular Economy in Russia: Drivers and Barriers for Waste Management Development. *Sustainability* **2019**, *11*, 5837. [CrossRef]
36. Semernya, L.; Ramola, A.; Alfthan, B.; Giacovelli, C. Waste management outlook for mountain regions: Sources and solutions. *Waste Manag. Res.* **2017**, *35*, 935–939. [CrossRef] [PubMed]
37. MPCT-Master. *Plan for Integrated Waste Management System in Constanta County*; Louis Berger: Morristown, NJ, USA, 2016.

38. Sosna, D.; Brunclíkov, L.; Galeta, P. Rescuing things: Food waste in the rural environment in the Czech Republic. *J. Clean Prod.* **2019**, *214*, 319–330. [CrossRef]
39. Jakiel, M.; Bernatek-Jakiel, A.; Gajda, A.; Filiks, M.; Pufelska, M. Spatial and temporal distribution of illegal dumping sites in the nature protected area: The Ojców National Park, Poland. *J. Environ. Plan Man.* **2018**. [CrossRef]
40. Liu, Y.; Kong, F. Santibanez Gonzalez, EDR. Dumping, waste management, and ecological security: Evidence from England. *J. Clean Prod.* **2017**, *167*, 1425–1437. [CrossRef]
41. Ferronatoa, N.; Rada, E.C.; Portillo, M.A.G.; Cioca, L.I.; Ragazzi, M.; Torretta, V. Introduction of the circular economy within developing regions: A comparative analysis of advantages and opportunities for waste valorization. *J. Environ. Manag.* **2019**, *230*, 366–378. [CrossRef]
42. Cao, S.; Xu, D.; Liu, S. A Study of the Relationships between the Characteristics of the Village Population Structure and Rural Residential Solid Waste Collection Services: Evidence from China. *Int. J. Environ. Res. Public Health* **2018**, *15*, 2352. [CrossRef] [PubMed]
43. European Commission. Closing the loop—An EU Action Plan for the Circular Economy. 2015. Available online: https://eurlex.europa.eu/legalcontent/EN/TXT/?uri=CELEX:52015DC0614 (accessed on 27 October 2019).
44. Rosa, P.; Sassanelli, C.; Terzi, S. Towards Circular Business Models: A systematic literature review on classification frameworks and archetypes. *J. Clean. Prod.* **2019**, 117696. [CrossRef]
45. Falcone, P.M. Green investment strategies and bank-firm relationship: A firm-level analysis. *Econ. Bull.* **2018**, *38*, 2225–2239.
46. European Parliament. Directive (EU) 2018/852 of the European Parliament and of the Council of 30 May 2018 amending Directive 94/62/EC on packaging and packaging waste. Official Journal of the European Union L150/141. Available online: https://eur-lex.europa.eu/legal-content/EN/TXT/?uri=uriserv:OJ.L_.2018.150.01.0141.01.ENG&toc=OJ:L:2018:150:TOC (accessed on 10 October 2019).
47. Emergency Ordinance No. 74/2018 for amending and supplementing Law No. 211/2011 regarding the waste regime, of Law No. 249/2015 regarding the management of packaging and packaging waste and the Government Emergency Ordinance No. 196/2005 regarding the Environmental Fund.
48. Mihai, F.C.; Ingrao, C. Assessment of biowaste losses through unsound waste management practices in rural areas and the role of home composting. *J. Clean. Prod.* **2018**, *172*, 1631–1638. [CrossRef]
49. AFF. Activity Report. 2018. Available online: https://static1.squarespace.com/static/5a463ececd39c39db5dbfc31/t/5d0b545759148f000129b0fb/1561023600224/AFF+2018+Raport+Activitate+_Ro+_+Pagina+cu+Pagina.pdf (accessed on 27 October 2019).
50. WasteAid UK Making Waste Work: A Toolkitt Retrieved 29 October 2019. Available online: https://wasteaid.org/toolkit/making-waste-work/ (accessed on 29 October 2019).
51. Mihai, F.-C. Construction and demolition waste in Romania: The route from illegal dumping to building materials. *Sustainability* **2019**, *11*, 3179. [CrossRef]
52. European Agenda for Culture. Policy Handbook on the Promotion of Creative Partnerships. 2014. Available online: https://ec.europa.eu/assets/eac/culture/library/reports/creative-partnerships_en.pdf (accessed on 10 October 2019).
53. Ateliere Fara Frontiere. Wise WISE. Available online: https://issuu.com/atelierefarafrontiere/docs/wise_weee_booklet (accessed on 10 October 2019).
54. Saseanu, A.S.; Gogonea, R.-M.; Ghita, S.I.; Zaharia, R.Ş. The Impact of Education and Residential Environment on Long-Term Waste Management Behavior in the Context of Sustainability. *Sustainability* **2019**, *11*, 3775. [CrossRef]
55. Laurenti, R.; Martin, M.; Stenmarck, Å. Developing Adequate Communication of Waste Footprints of Products for a Circular Economy—A Stakeholder Consultation. *Resources* **2018**, *7*, 78. [CrossRef]

sustainability

MDPI

Article

Exploring the Environmental Performance of Urban Symbiosis for Vertical Hydroponic Farming

Michael Martin [1,2,*], Sofia Poulikidou [1] and Elvira Molin [1,2]

[1] IVL Swedish Environmental Research Institute, Life Cycle Management and Sustainable Society, Valhallavägen 81, 114 27 Stockholm, Sweden; sofia.poulikidou@ivl.se (S.P.); elvira.molin@ivl.se (E.M.)

[2] KTH Royal Institute of Technology, Department of Sustainable Development, Environmental Science and Engineering (SEED), Teknikringen 10b, 114 28 Stockholm, Sweden

* Correspondence: michael.martin@ivl.se; Tel.: +46-107-886-681

Received: 25 October 2019; Accepted: 26 November 2019; Published: 27 November 2019

Abstract: Vertical farming has emerged in urban areas as an approach to provide more resilient food production. However, a substantial share of the material requirements come from outside their urban environments. With urban environments producing a large share of residual and waste streams, extensive potential exists to employ these material and energy streams as inputs in urban farming systems to promote more circular economy approaches. The aim of this article is to assess the environmental performance of employing residual material flows for vertical hydroponic farming in urban environments in order to support more circular, resilient, and sustainable urban food supply. Life cycle assessment (LCA) is used to assess replacing conventional growing media and fertilizers with urban residual streams. Paper, compost, and brewers' spent grains were assessed for replacements to conventional gardening soil employed in the studied system. Biogas digestate was also assessed as a replacement for conventional fertilizers used in the recirculating water bath. The results suggest that large environmental performance benefits are illustrated when conventional growing media is replaced. Although not as significant, employing fertilizers from residual urban streams also leads to large potential benefits, suggesting the two residual streams have the potential for more circular hydroponic systems.

Keywords: urban symbiosis; food; hydroponic; industrial symbiosis; urban farming; life cycle assessment (LCA); horticulture; circular economy

1. Introduction

Urban farming has been identified by a number of authors to provide promising solutions to secure food supplies, produce more sustainable food and reduce pressure on agricultural land by shifting food production to urban environments [1–5]. Urban farming encompasses a number of methods and approaches; although vertical and hydroponic farming have become popular options worldwide in recent years; see e.g., [1,6,7]. This is primarily promoted for its potential to extend the seasonal availability of regional foods, especially in Northern Europe [2,8,9]. The methods for vertical urban farming are typically defined by horticultural practices in controlled environments less affected by outside factors, typically employing LED lighting, controlled atmospheric conditions and hydroponic systems for nutrient and water management. These are commonly located within the urban environment, or in peri-urban settings. Furthermore, many urban environments have unutilized spaces which have led to the further promotion of such vertical farming methods [5,10–12].

Much of the literature available on urban vertical farming points to the expectations and technical solutions for these growing systems [3,6,13]. Much less literature is available outlining case studies, findings from development practices and business models required, in addition to the resource and sustainability of these systems, as vertical farming applications and research is still gathering momentum [4]. As such, advocates of vertical farming claim that these farming techniques can reduce environmental impacts from conventional production systems, increase productivity, significantly reduce transportation; offering many advantages to traditional greenhouses and agriculture [10,14]. However, studies reviewing the sustainability of these claims are limited [15–18].

Furthermore, few studies review the link these innovative urban farming techniques to their urban systems. Many of the previous studies review, with traditional linear approaches; employing conventional fertilizers, growing media and energy requirements. While these systems are being extensively expanded in urban environments, the potential for the use of urban residual material and energy is important to assess to promote a circular economy through industrial symbiosis [9,19]. Recently, several authors have explored approaches to integrate urban agricultural systems with urban systems to develop symbiotic networks; see e.g., [10,17,20–23]. Through symbiotic development, employing concepts from industrial symbiosis, the firms can collectively collaborate for shared management of resources; creating local circular economies, resilience and revenue [10,24,25]. Industrial symbiosis (IS), a research topic which applies concepts to promote collaboration between firms for exchanging energy, utilities, materials, or services. As such, it can create mutual benefits and valorized processes and has seen considerable interest and growth in recent years due to the popularity of the circular economy [24,26,27]. Despite the term implying that industrial production and practices are of primary importance, this limitation is not exclusive and exchanges may extend beyond the industrial setting with surrounding systems to include agriculture, horticulture, forestry, fisheries, and other municipal and urban systems [19,28]; extending the bounded geographical proximity generally associated with the concept. In previous assessments, significant resource and environmental impact reductions compared to linear approaches have been outlined by employing residual materials from urban sources and industrial firms through industrial and urban symbiosis [17,21,29,30].

The study is based on previous work by the authors [31], and expanding this to review the potential of more urban symbiosis to employ several urban residual streams. The aim of this study is to assess the environmental implications of employing residual material flows for vertical hydroponic farming in urban environments in order to support circular, resilient and sustainable urban food supply.

2. Materials and Methods

The following sections outline the case study system assessed, the methodology for reviewing the environmental performance and information about the theoretical scenarios for urban symbiosis.

2.1. The Case Study

The assessment is based on the annual production from a vertical hydroponic farming system, Grönska Stadsodling 365, in the south of Stockholm, producing 60,000 plants in pots annually. The system produces a variety of leafy greens and herbs (e.g., basil, cilantro, mint, and salad), sold to regional supermarkets and distributors. For this study, it is assumed that only basil is produced, as basil represents the majority of outputs from the system [11].

2.2. Life Cycle Assessment Method

The environmental performance assessment uses life cycle assessment methodology for symbiotic systems based on recommendations provided in [32] using physical allocation to partition impacts between products and by-products for firms involved in the symbiotic exchanges. The sensitivity to this choice is also tested in the analysis. While the studied scenarios review cases for urban symbiosis with several firms, in this study, only the impacts for the vertical farming firm are reviewed. This is motivated by the scope to explore the implications of employing urban residual streams for vertical hydroponic farming and not reviewing an industrial symbiosis network.

The functional unit employed for the environmental assessment is the annual production of basil available to consumers in a pot with growing medium and packaging (i.e., 60,000 plants), see depiction in the Supplementary material, Figure S1. The study is limited to the production and final availability of the plants to consumers. Thus, the study is conducted using a cradle-to-gate perspective, including all upstream processes in the cultivation, such as the production of the pot systems, seeds, soil and fertilizers, and packaging materials. No waste handling of the pots or waste was included in the assessment as the aim is to review the influence of using residual materials (see Figure 1).

The LCA for the different scenarios was conducted in the OpenLCA software. For this study, the CML 2014 [33] life cycle impact assessment (LCIA) method was employed. The impact categories included in this study include GWP (100)—global warming potential (measured in kg CO_2-eq), EP—eutrophication potential (measured in kg PO_4-eq), AP—acidification potential (measured in kg SO_2-eq), ABD—depletion of abiotic resources—fossil fuels (measured in MJ) and human toxicity (kg 1,4-dichlorobenzene eq.). These impact categories were chosen as they provide a review of the regional, global and resource implications of food systems. Life cycle inventory (LCI) data was obtained from LCI databases such as Ecoinvent [34] and relevant data and input from literature.

2.3. Scenarios

2.3.1. Baseline (Current Production System)

The baseline scenario is based on previous work [31] and modeled to represent the current production system at Grönska (in 2018). In this scenario, the plants are grown in pots made of primarily paper and peat; referred to hereafter as paper pots. This was modeled based as a mix of peat and paper fibers, assumed to be similar corrugated paper product production based on data from Ecoinvent [34]. Gardening soil is employed as the growing medium in the baseline case [31]. Data for the materials and environmental impacts of gardening soil from the Swedish market were obtained from [35]. The fertilizer used for the hydroponic system is blended into the water bath and recirculated. Data for the fertilizers were provided by producers. Only major nutrients were included and modeled, which included nitrogen (N), phosphorus (P), and potassium (K). All LCI data for fertilizers was obtained from Ecoinvent [34]; see Table 1 and Supplementary Material for further details. The final products are packaged in the paper pots with gardening soil and wrapped in a waxed covered paper with labels; see Figure S1 in the Supplementary materials.

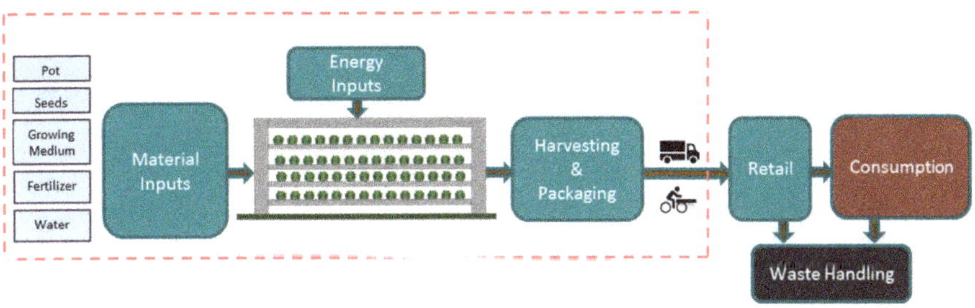

Figure 1. System boundaries of the study (Dashed line represents the system boundaries).

The transportation of the final products to retail, primarily to supermarkets in the Stockholm area is also included. In the case study, all transportation of plants was performed by cargo bike and electric vehicles; each encompassing 50% of the total deliveries, as the market is primarily local. The distance traveled annually for deliveries by the electric vehicle was assumed to be roughly 1390 km. Other transportation of the raw materials was assumed to be transported by truck, with distances outlined in Table 1. Data for transportation was provided by datasets in Ecoinvent [34].

The infrastructure employed in the vertical farming system, including LED fixtures, structures for the growing platforms, pumps, trays, tubing, heating, control units, and timers are also included in the assessment. See Table 1 and Supplementary Material for further information. All energy for the vertical farm, including electricity for lighting the LED fixtures, ventilation, pumps, and heating is included. For the operations, it is assumed that the ventilation systems is running 24 h per day and the LED fixtures roughly 12 h per day. The Swedish electricity mix and Nordic electricity mix were used for comparison and sensitivity to the choice; see analysis below. As outlined in [31] heating is regulated by an external heating unit during colder months and heat from the building (from district heating system) was not taken into account as the vertical farm is located in the basement, employing an unused space in an office building; while also producing residual heat from the LEDs that is sufficient for maintaining a constant temperature for production [11,22].

Table 1. Material and energy inputs for the annual production in the baseline scenario.

Main Category	Process/Flow	Amount	Unit	Transport (km)	Lifetime (Years)
Infrastructure	Steel Structure	242	kg	100	30
	LEDs	8640	units	100	15
	Trays (PET)	36	kg	100	15
	Tubing/Other Plastics	10	kg	100	5
	Pumps	2	units	100	10
	Heater and Other Electronics	3	units	100	10
Raw materials	Paper Pot	223	kg	100	-
	Seeds	6	kg	100	-
	Growing Medium (Soil)	12,350	kg	50	-
	Nitrogen (N)	10	kg	100	-
	Phosphate (P)	12	kg	100	-
	Potassium (K)	14	kg	100	-
	Paper	449	kg	100	-
	Wrapping Paper	38	kg	50	-
	Label	480	m^2	50	-
	Water	144,890	liters	-	-
Energy Inputs	Lighting	26,490	kWh	-	-
	Ventilation	490	kWh	-	-
	Heating and Electronics	3290	kWh	-	-
	Pumps	2190	kWh	-	-
Outputs	Plants	60,000	plants	1390	-

2.3.2. Symbiotic Scenarios

Vertical farming systems can benefit from the use of many urban residual materials. This includes wastewater, carbon dioxide, heating and cooling, and packaging. In the scenarios which review the use of urban residual streams, only the growing media and fertilizers are reviewed; see Figure 2. This was done considering they were found more feasible with the existing production methods and require less add-on technologies and infrastructure, see a review of potential options for urban symbiosis for the case study vertical farm in [36], previous literature [22], and based on communication with the case study firm [2]. Furthermore, these flows were shown to have a large impact on the overall environmental impacts in a previous study of the baseline scenario [31] and therefore, were explored further.

The scenarios, labeled Circular A-D represent different theoretical configurations of these urban resource circularity pathways for vertical hydroponic farming; assuming they produce similar outputs as the baseline scenario with the altered material configurations. This includes single or combined approaches for using urban resources. See further details in the proceeding text, Table 2, and Figure 2 for a depiction of these scenarios. In the scenarios Circular A–Circular D, equivalent volumes (m^3) of growing media derived from residual urban materials were used to replace conventional gardening soil. These include a combination of compost, shredded recycled paper (in Circular A and C), and combined with dried brewers' spent grains (BSG) (in Circular B and Circular D) from local breweries. The growing media mixtures, containing both nutrients and fiber were assumed to produce similar growing results in the hydroponic system employed. The mixtures were identified for their potential to provide nutrients and a fibrous base in the hydroponic systems. Allocation of impacts to the brewers' spent grains was based on economic allocation in the LCI dataset for dried grains from ethanol production [34], resulting in only 2.3% of the impacts being allocated to brewers' spent grains. Drying of the grains was also included in the assessment. For the recycled paper, no impact resulting from the paper was allocated to the product, only the collection and treatment (shredding) of the paper. Composting emissions were based on LCI data from [34] for compost. It was assumed that the transportation of BSG to the vertical farm required a distance of no more than 20 km due to geographical proximity. For the compost and paper, this was increased to 40 km to account for increased transportation of collecting the materials in the urban setting.

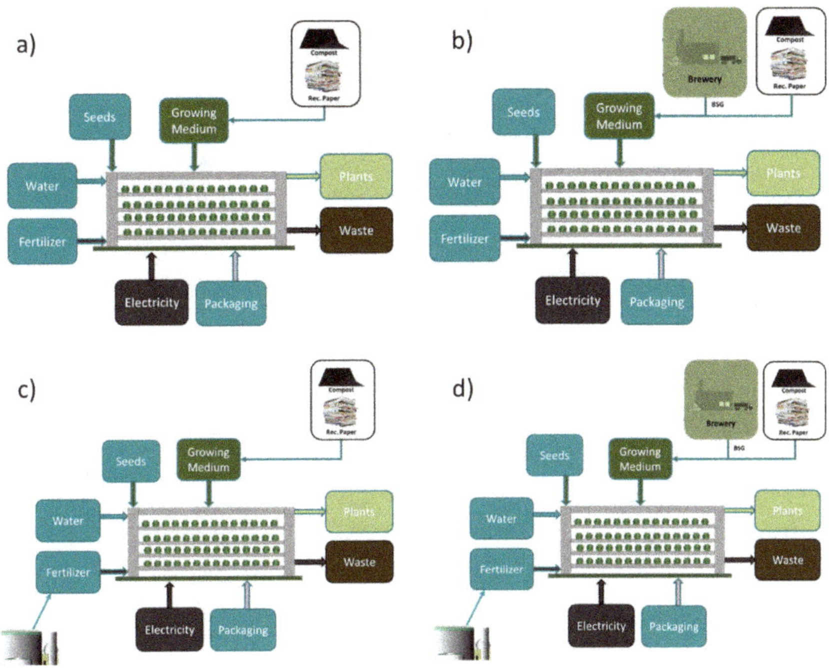

Figure 2. Depiction of circular scenarios A–D (shown in **a**–**d**) for vertical hydroponic systems using resources from urban environments; (**a**) depicting Circular A, (**b**) Circular B, (**c**) Circular C and (**d**) Circular D

In the scenarios Circular A-Circular D, equivalent volumes (m^3) of growing media derived from residual urban materials were used to replace conventional gardening soil. These include a combination of compost, shredded recycled paper (in Circular A and C), and combined with dried brewers' spent grains (BSG) (in Circular B and Circular D) from local breweries. The growing media mixtures, containing both nutrients and fiber were assumed to produce similar growing results in the hydroponic system employed. The mixtures were identified for their potential to provide nutrients and a fibrous base in the hydroponic systems. Allocation of impacts to the brewers' spent grains was based on economic allocation in the LCI dataset for dried grains from ethanol production [34], resulting in only 2.3% of the impacts being allocated to brewers' spent grains. Drying of the grains was also included in the assessment. For the recycled paper, no impact resulting from the paper was allocated to the product, only the collection and treatment (shredding) of the paper. Composting emissions were based on LCI data from [34] for compost. It was assumed that the transportation of BSG to the vertical farm required a distance of no more than 20 km due to geographical proximity. For the compost and paper, this was increased to 40 km to account for increased transportation of collecting the materials in the urban setting.

Conventional fertilizer was also substituted for a concentrated biofertilizer. The biofertilizer is produced from biogas digestate and concentrated through water removal. The biofertilizer is sourced from a regional biogas producer (and tested in Circular C and D) and mixed into the water bath. Figures from the nutrient blend are obtained from [37,38] for digestate from co-digestion plants employing large shares of food waste and other biological urban residual streams. The application of the biofertilizer was assumed to require a similar nutrient content as the conventional fertilizer. However, as outlined in [39], the availability of certain nutrients in biofertilizers from digestate may be a limiting factor for their employment and may not fully substitute conventional fertilizers. As such, additional phosphorous and potassium from conventional fertilizers were added to nutrient blend as the biofertilizer employed required additional input of these nutrients, while ammonium was assumed to meet requirements. Allocation of impacts to the biofertilizer were based on economic allocation, which resulted in no impact being allocated to the biofertilizer, as it does not typically result in a profit for co-digestion plants in Sweden [40,41]. The transportation distance for the biofertilizer was assumed to be 30 km from the nearest co-digestion plant. Further details on the nutrient amounts can be found in the Supplementary Material.

Table 2. Comparison of the different material flows for the baseline vs. circular scenarios.

	Baseline	Circular A	Circular B	Circular C	Circular D
Growing Medium	Conv. Soil	Paper and Compost	BSG, Paper, Compost	Paper and Compost	BSG, Paper, Compost
Fertilizer	Conv. Fertilizers	Conv. Fertilizers	Conv. Fertilizers	Biofertilizer + Conv. Fertilizer	Biofertilizer + Conv. Fertilizer

3. Results and Analysis

The results indicate potential environmental benefits for circular employment of residual materials for vertical hydroponic farming. As illustrated in and Table 3 and Figure 3, large reductions in greenhouse gas (GHG) emissions are possible. However, no significant change in the other reviewed environmental impact categories is illustrated. As further exemplified in Figure 4, the results point to the growing media as the primary beneficial material for reducing GHG emissions. All scenarios with growing media from residual sources have largely reduced GHG emissions; with the scenarios utilizing a blend compost and paper showing the largest reductions (e.g., scenarios Circular A and C); with GHG emissions by over 60% and 62% compared to the baseline scenario respectively. Circular C scenario, which illustrated the largest emissions reductions, is primarily due to the reduction of impacts from the growing medium. The impacts from the growing media employed in Circular B and D are only slightly higher (50 kg CO_2-eq annually) compared to Circular A and C; see also Table 3. Replacing conventional fertilizers with biofertilizer also illustrated GHG emission reductions compared to conventional fertilizer (reducing the impact of the fertilizers by roughly 90 kg CO_2-eq annually) for the Circular C and D scenarios, although the reductions were not as substantial compared to other inputs. See also Supplemenatry Material, Table S6 for further details.

Table 3. Comparison of the environmental impacts of the Baseline and Circular scenarios. GHG—Greenhouse gas emissions, Acid.—Acidification, Eutrop.—Eutrophication, Human Tox—Human Toxicity, Abiotic Res. Dep.—Abiotic Resource Depletion.

	GHG	Acid.	Eutrop.	Human Tox.	Abiotic Res. Dep.
	(kg CO_2-eq)	(kg SO_2-eq)	(kg PO_4-eq)	(kg 1,4 DCB-eq)	(MJ eq.)
Baseline	5241	15.16	204.8	6458	32,261
Circular A	2089	13.77	204.4	6338	29,100
Circular B	2179	14.38	204.7	6373	29,945
Circular C	2000	13.30	204.2	6291	28,655
Circular D	2090	13.91	204.6	6326	29,501

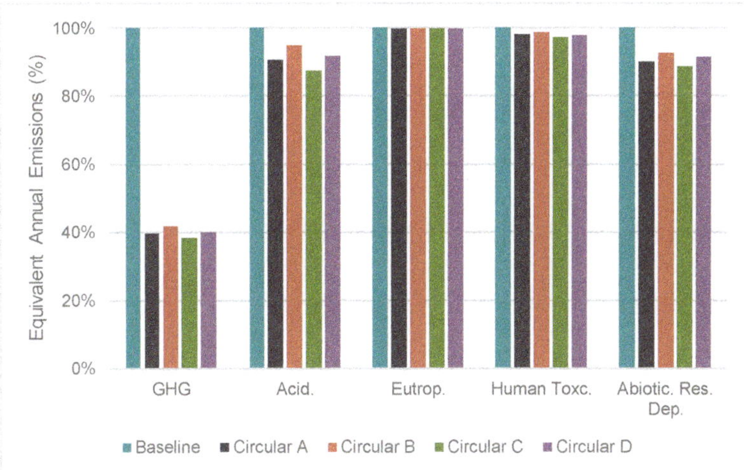

Figure 3. Comparison of the environmental impact categories for the Baseline and Circular scenarios reviewed, normalized to Baseline Scenario.

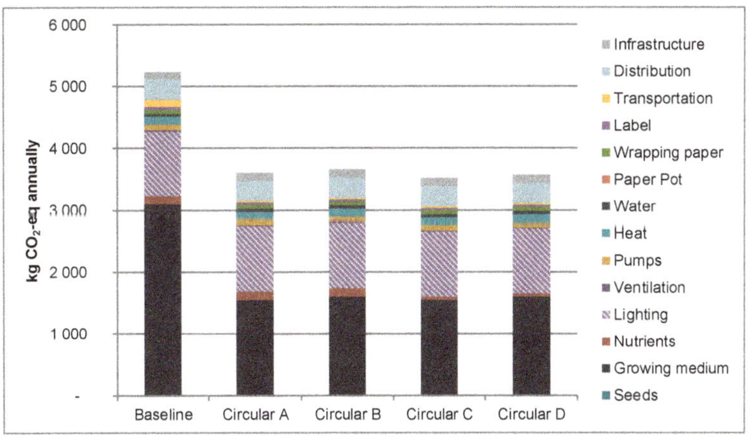

Figure 4. Review of the annual GHG emissions for the hydroponic system separated into different categories of material and energy inputs (measured in kg CO_2-eq annually).

While the GHG emissions reductions are dominated by the growing media, the acidification impacts are due primarily to the electricity use in lighting and the wrapping paper used in the final product. The overall acidification impacts are only slightly reduced by substituting the gardening soil with residual materials. It is further reduced, only slightly, by the use of biofertilizers, see Figure 5.

Eutrophication impacts are also dominated by the paper pots used in the final product and the distribution of the final plants. Therefore, as illustrated, the use of residual products had little effect on reducing the emissions from fertilizers and growing media employed, see Figure 6.

Human toxicity impacts are also dominated by the processes related to the paper pot, the infrastructure employed and the lighting. Once again, no pronounced reductions in human toxicity impacts can be illustrated from the residual use of materials to replace conventional fertilizers and growing media, see Figure 7.

The abiotic resource depletion shows a marked reduction from the baseline scenario from the reduced transportation involved in using available urban residual materials; the only impact category to show such a significant reduction. Thereafter, the use of abiotic resources is also reduced considerably by the replacement of conventional gardening soils with urban residual materials, see Figure 8.

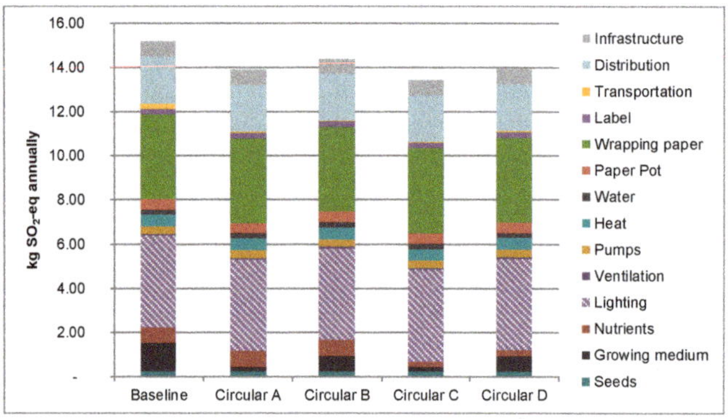

Figure 5. Review of the annual acidification impacts for the hydroponic system separated into different categories of material and energy inputs (measured in kg SO_2-eq annually).

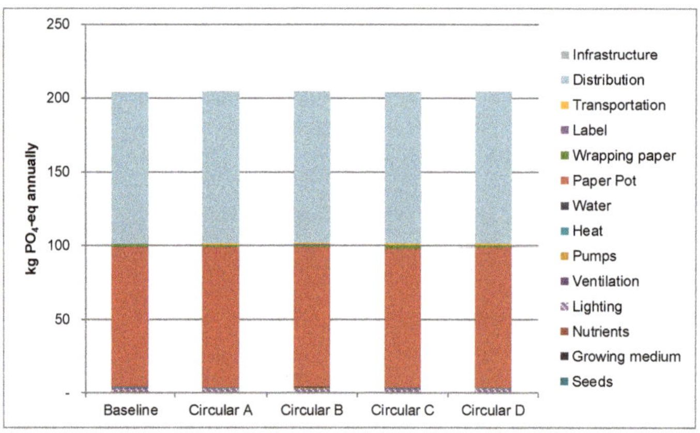

Figure 6. Review of the annual eutrophication impacts for the hydroponic system separated into different categories of material and energy inputs (measured in kg PO_4-eq annually).

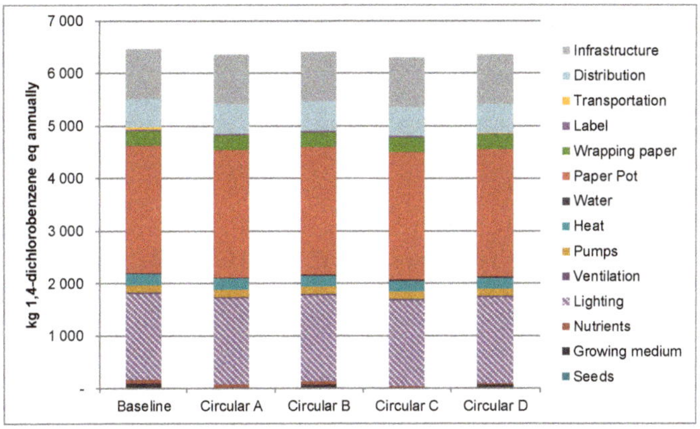

Figure 7. Review of the annual human toxicity impacts for the hydroponic system separated into different categories of material and energy inputs (measured in kg 1,4 dcb-eq annually).

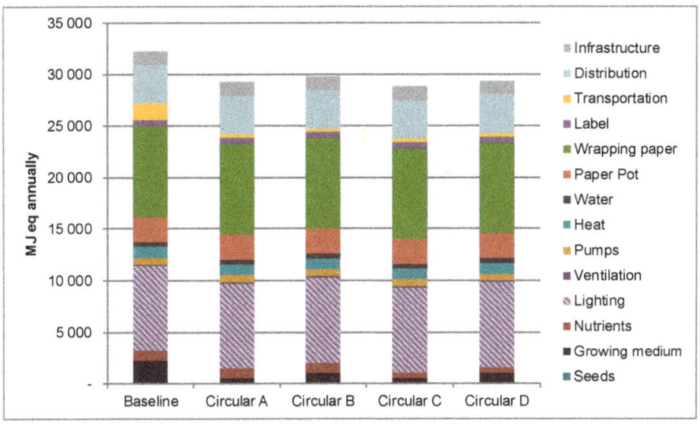

Figure 8. Review of the annual abiotic resource depletion for the hydroponic system separated into different categories of material and energy inputs (measured in MJ-eq annually).

3.1. Growing Media

While no significant change in the overall environmental impacts in other environmental impact categories other than GHG emissions were highlighted, Table 4 illustrates the implications for the environmental impacts for the use of residual materials as growing media. Again, large reductions are illustrated for GHG emissions, with all circular scenarios reducing the GHG emissions by over 3 tonnes CO_2-eq annually. Furthermore, reductions of over 70% are illustrated for acidification, human toxicity, and abiotic resource depletion. The scenarios, Circular A and Circular C show the largest potential environmental impact reductions; see Table 4.

In order to identify the sensitivity to this choice, comparisons were made for the baseline scenario and one of the circular scenarios employing different growing medium blends. A growing medium containing an increased amount of peat was employed to compare with the blend currently used (labeled Baseline (Incr. Peat). This was done as conventional gardening soils contain larger shares of peat than what is used in the case studied [35]. Furthermore, as Circular B and D had a large share of BSG (i.e., 80%), the sensitivity to the share of BSG was also reviewed by assuming it could be increased to 100%.

Table 4. Environmental impacts from growing media reviewed in the different scenarios.

	GHG	Acid.	Eutrop.	Human Tox.	Abiotic. Res. Dep.
	(kg CO_2-eq)	(kg SO_2-eq)	(kg PO_4-eq)	(kg 1,4 DCB-eq)	(MJ eq.)
Baseline	3087	1.30	0.44	101	2173
Circular A	21.7	0.11	0.03	9	322
Circular B	63.9	0.39	0.20	25	683
Circular C	21.7	0.11	0.03	9	322
Circular D	63.9	0.39	0.20	25	683

As illustrated in Figure 9, the GHG emissions may be sensitive to the choices made in the modeling. Increasing the amount of peat could increase the emissions by roughly 30%, with an increase in growing medium emissions of over 1000 kg CO_2-eq annually, with a notable effect when comparing with the circular scenarios. If BSG was assumed to make up 100% of the share of the growing medium in the Circular B scenario, the impacts would increase by 20%, or roughly 20 kg CO_2-eq annually. For the overall system´, this has little effect and only a slight increase in emissions for the BSG due to an increase in drying required for the added amount of BSG.

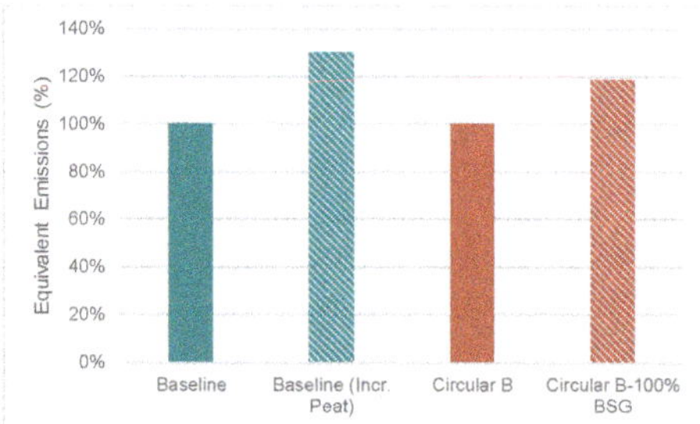

Figure 9. Sensitivity to choices made in modeling the growing medium (measured in %).

3.2. *Fertilizers*

Despite being less significant for the overall emissions of the vertical farming system, the use of biofertilizer from regional residual materials also led to reductions in nearly all impact categories for the Scenarios Circular C and D employing biofertilizer. As illustrated in Figure 10, over 60% reductions in emissions of greenhouse gases, acidification and human toxicity impacts resulted from employing biofertilizer. Eutrophication impacts were reduced by over 50%, while the abiotic resource depletion was reduced by over 40%, see further details in Tables S6–S10 in the Supplementary material for further details. As illustrated, this provides a discernible reduction in impacts compared to those from conventional fertilizer use in the baseline scenario; see Figure 10.

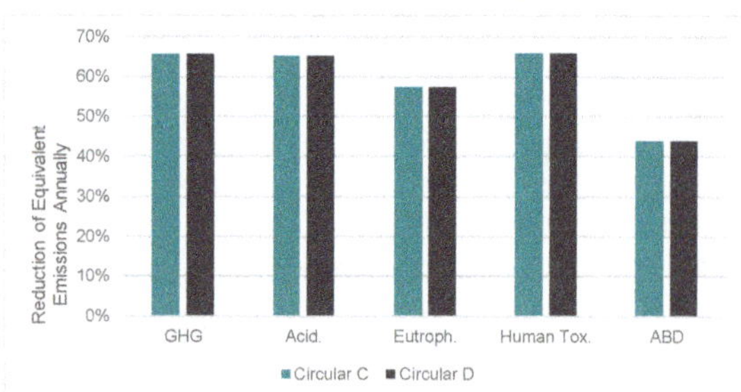

Figure 10. Reduction of emissions for different impact categories (illustrated in % reduction) for the use of biofertilizer in the Circular C and Circular D scenarios compared to the impacts from conventional fertilizers in the baseline scenario.

3.3. Influence of Methodology

As the life cycle assessment followed the approach for employing LCA to review the environmental performance of IS networks, employing the physical allocation method as outlined in [32], the results could be sensitive to this choice. For example, many previous studies have employed the system expansion approach as outlined in [32]; see e.g., [19,35,42]. However, this study, due to the magnitude of the materials being employed, employs only the physical allocation method. This choice of methodology could have an affect on theo overall impacts allocated to the final product, due to the physical allocation of impacts to the residual materials used in the vertical hydroponic farm. The sensitivity to this methods is illustrated in Figure 11.

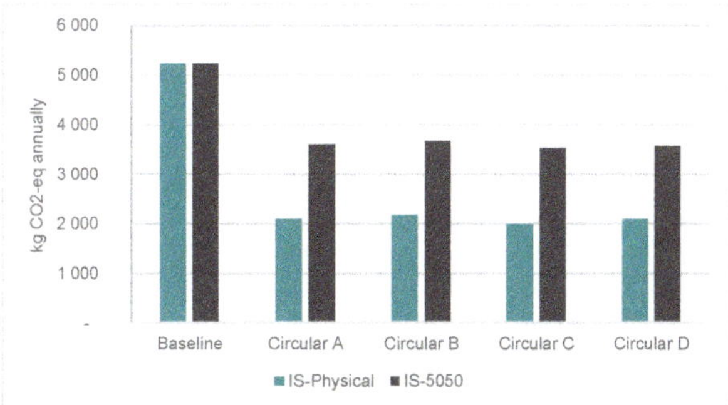

Figure 11. Sensitivity to chosen method for allocation (or avoidance) for exchanges of materials. IS-Physical refers to physical allocation and IS-5050 refers to the system expansion method outlined in [32].

As illustrated, the overall GHG emissions can be influenced by the choice of method to allocate or avoid allocation employing different methods. The 50/50 method outlined in [32] illustrates higher impacts. For example, in each scenario the 50/50 methodology increases the annual GHG emissions by over 1400 kg CO_2-eq. This is due to the fact that the hydroponic farm is on the receiving end of the synergies. It is therefore burdened with half the impact of the conventional raw materials for these exchanges and any upgrading impacts for their processing before use. In the employed method, i.e., applying physical allocation, impacts are allocated to the by-products used in the hydroponic farm based on their economic value, see more in [32]. Due to the fact that the by-products employed have little economic value, their impacts are reduced, illustrated in Figure 11 above.

3.4. Energy

Also, of importance is the processes employing energy, where a considerable share of the impacts can be attributed to the electricity used for different processes; primarily due to lighting, see also [31]. A sensitivity analysis for the electricity mix is reviewed subsequently. The sensitivity to the electricity mix employed for energy employed in the different processes was also reviewed; see Table 5. In this study, the Swedish electricity mix was employed. However, if the Nordic electricity mix was used, the overall impacts would be considerably increased. By using the Swedish mix, compared to the Nordic mix, in the circular scenarios (i.e., A–D) the emissions are nearly halved. The same is true for the GHG emissions per edible kg of plants produced; exemplifying the importance of this choice. See Supplementary material for a listing of the LCI data used in all scenarios, including datasets for Nordic and Swedish electricity mixes.

Table 5. Review of the sensitivity of the GHG emissions to the choice of electricity mix (Comparing the Nordic mix to the Swedish mix). Shown in annual GHG emissions.

F.U.	Electricity Mix	Baseline	Circular A	Circular B	Circular C	Circular D
Annual Impact	Nordic Mix	7219	3985	4005	3850	3870
(kg CO_2-eq/year))	Swedish Mix	5241	2089	2179	2000	2090

4. Discussion

As the results from this study show, urban environments have the potential to provide resilient, sustainable and competitive food systems through symbiotic networks. This can be done by exploring the potential to employ residual streams to directly reduce the environmental impacts associated with traditional material and energy flows for vertical hydroponic farming systems. The following sections provide a discussion of the results in relation to other studies and potential improvements to improve more symbiotic development.

4.1. Urban Symbiosis

The results indicate that environmental performance benefits, primarily GHG emission reductions, are possible through synergies with urban firms. Similar findings have been suggested in previous research through integration with utilities and waste heat [17,20,22] and claims in further studies (see e.g., [3,4,10]). For example, Chance et al. [10] review the material flows and social implications of an urban symbiotic network for hydroponic systems and stipulate on the sustainability of the system, although no quantitative were developed. Marchi et al. [23] also explore the possibility of employing symbiotic networks to improve horticulture, focusing primarily on the potential economic benefits. Few assessments of the environmental performance of such potential urban symbiosis networks are available in the literature, pointing to the novel results provided in this study. However, the benefits of such systems are not limited to environmental performance improvements. The urban symbiosis, and due to the relative geographical proximity, can provide many opportunities for shared learning; leading to human and social capital development [10,43]

4.1.1. Residual Products for Growing Media

The results suggest that the growing media has a substantial contribution to the environmental performance of the system. Replacing conventional soil containing a large shares of peat, with other media was shown to reduce the environmental impacts greatly. Similar results were also found in [44], also suggesting that using industrial by-products can improve the sustainability of their systems. Several previous reviews have studied the potential of residual products as growing medium, showing extensive viability for a number of different horticultural applications, also suggesting minimal effect on the plant production see, e.g., [44–47]. As [48] suggests, materials with high cellulosic content are a good source of organic matter, including e.g., municipal compost, paper waste, brewer's spent grain and paper mill waste. For traditional potted plants, these materials have been utilized up to 100 percent of the substrate used in the growing media, although blends of these have also proven important to take into account the different characteristics (e.g., salts, pH and moisture retention (ibid). However, employing residual products, may require added infrastructure for handling in automated processes for e.g., filling the pots; and also require further assessment to meet standards and requirements in the industry [49]. While this study did not assess these parameters more in detail, further research may be needed and testing in the case study systems will be required to maintain economic viability. Sparked by the potential impact of growing media on horticulture sustainability, recently, there has also been a push to harmonize assessments of growing media sustainability, despite the lack of studies available in the area [50].

While this study reviews the use of brewing industry residues, residual products from the brewing industry are not currently explored to their fullest potential [51,52]. This is especially true for small-scale breweries, which may not have handling processes to deliver by-products and wastes in an efficient manner. While there are a few large-scale breweries in Sweden with well-developed markets for by-products, small-scale breweries have been increasing in number, from roughly 10 in 2008 to over 340 in 2018 [1], and lack efficient handling methods for their by-products, increasing the need to manage resources more sustainably. Additionally, the use of by-products and waste handling is also quite divergent amongst producers. While many large-scale producers may currently use their by-products for low-value applications, i.e., to produce animal feed or even fuel for boilers [9,10], it is unclear how much of the small-scale producers handle their by-products, providing a potential revenue stream for this residual stream, although this may entail added infrastructure and processes to upgrade these to a marketable product.

4.1.2. Fertilizer

The results suggest that biofertilizers from biogas plants could offer a sustainable alternative to conventional fertilizers. Few studies have reviewed the use of biogas residues for hydroponic farming [39], although the material is widely employed in traditional agriculture [53–57]. Furthermore, hydroponic farming could provide a new market for biogas plants, where the market for this residual product has been identified as a bottleneck in their production system [40,58]. While this study assumes that the product is available, upgrading and further infrastructure may be needed to extract and include nitrification of the digestate for use in hydroponic farms [39].The results of this study illustrate that identifying and influencing the use of fertilizers can also improve hydroponic systems. Recent research suggests that the impacts associated with applications of conventional fertilizers for urban farming (e.g., in hydroponic systems) is important to take into account, influencing the overall life cycle impacts of the system [18].

4.1.3. Energy

As illustrated, electricity for the different processes was found to be a major influencing input, primarily a result of LED lighting systems employed, which accounted for the largest share (over 80%) of GHG emissions from the energy use. These results concur with previous studies, which illustrate that the control of the systems, e.g., through energy consumption for artificially maintained climatic and light regimes, constitute a significant contribution to the environmental impacts of such systems; see e.g., [9,10,15].

Furthermore, as reviewed in this study, the choice of LCI data used for the electricity in the assessment has a substantial influence on the overall impacts. Similar results were tested in a study by Romeo, Vea, and Thomsen [15]. The assessments in this study reviewed only the use of Swedish electricity mix, compared to the Nordic electricity mix. However, by purchasing more sustainable electricity from the market, e.g., from only renewable sources, the impacts may be significantly lower.

4.2. *Extending the Synergies*

While this study reviews the pilot case for a limited production of 60,000 plants per year, the case study firm has expanded production. With the new setup and increased number of LEDs, the hydroponic farm may have issues with excess heat [11,22]. As such, the residual heat could be utilized in the district heating system, and improve the efficiency of the LEDs and district heating network; see e.g., further elaboration in [22] with specific application in a Swedish context. Improving energy efficiency may also take place through synergies with other urban systems and buildings, e.g., by powering the LEDs with solar energy. These can be placed on the roofs of the occupied buildings for operations or on other buildings in proximity to the production site, which has also been stipulated in several previous assessments to reduce impacts and demand for grid electricity [59–61].

As outlined previously, many urban residual streams can be used for growing media; although many of these require drying and further processing before they can be used in current processes and machines for automated filling of the pots. Synergies with small-scale breweries be explored further to dry BSG. Small-scale breweries are also large consumers of energy and have an abundance of residual heat which is not used further; which can also be explored to dry the product [62,63]. The excess heat from the breweries may also be used in place of the electric heaters used in the case study [22], in case of expansion. However, the amount of heat required was not found to be important in the scale of production explored in this study, as it is primarily used during colder months (as the LEDs provide enough heat), it was out of scope in this study. However, previous studies have shown this to greatly benefit larger systems, see e.g., [22]. In addition to previously described material and energy synergies with the brewing industry, the carbon dioxide produced during fermentation may be used to expedite plant production. Similar studies have shown this to be possible [30], although again, these utility synergies were not explored in this study due to the scope and size of the production system. However, in the current system, which has expanded considerably, the use of carbon dioxide may be interesting to expedite growing and revenue.

While this study builds on theoretical potential for synergies between different firms in an urban context, it should be noted that the identification and reviews of viable options for further synergies is often not enough to lead to successful symbiotic development [64–66]. The vertical farming representatives alone will require support which can help with the success of synergy options. This can come from more hands-on facilitation to develop dialogues between the firms involved in these residual synergies. Many researchers have suggested that facilitation is key for successful industrial and urban symbiosis networks [19,28,67–69]; where trust, above all, has been identified as a critical resource to allow for industrial symbiosis to be feasible [70–73].

4.3. Limitations

This study includes a number of limitations which may influence the results. As illustrated in the analysis, the results may be sensitive to data choices; this is shown for the electricity LCI data employed. Several datasets were not available, e.g., forming of the paper pots and drying of the brewers' spent grains and assumptions on comparable processes were made. With hydroponic systems, it is also important to include water consumption, as a hallmark of the system is the limited use of water. However, few datasets and LCIA methods allow for such assessments; thus it was not included.

The chosen environmental impacts were also included as they are representative for studies of conventional agriculture. However, few studies have been made which review impacts other than GHG emissions and thus the results for these additional indicators cannot be compared with more than a few previous studies [15,31]. We recognize also that the vertical hydroponic system can offer many other benefits regionally [10], although this assessment was only confined to environmental impacts. Finally, while this study was made on a theoretical potential of these substrates and their output, it is important to note that a number of studies have been conducted for using residual materials with good results for the production of different types of plants and leafy greens [21,44,45] and the synergies could also be extended to review the impact of utility synergies (e.g., heat, carbon dioxide and water) [22,23,74].

5. Conclusions

Vertical hydroponic farming methods have emerged in urban areas worldwide to viably produce and sustain urban populations with sustainable food supplies. This study has reviewed the potential of employing urban residual streams to create a more circular vertical hydroponic system in Stockholm. Through symbiotic development, the results point to the potential to improve the environmental performance of these systems. This is achieved by employing residual streams for growing media, bio-based fertilizers and reducing transportation of raw materials. Overall, the largest environmental performance improvements come from the replacement of conventional gardening soil with residual materials for the growing media, i.e., recycled paper, compost and brewers' spent grains, reducing the GHG emissions from the entire system annually by over 60%. The impacts from fertilizers can also be reduced by employing biofertilizers, reducing fertilizer GHG emissions by over 66%. Furthermore, as similar to previous studies, the results also address a number of processes to improve the sustainability of these systems and many further synergies to improve the performance of vertical hydroponic farming through urban symbiosis.

Supplementary Materials: The following are available online at http://www.mdpi.com/2071-1050/11/23/6724/s1.

Author Contributions: M.M. has contributed to the project design, life cycle assessment, and the majority of the writing of the manuscript. E.M. and S.P. contributed with a primary role in data collection for the baseline and circular scenarios and to the life cycle assessment.

Funding: This project was funded through a grant for research on developing more resource-efficient vertical hydroponic systems with Grönska through the Swedish Environmental Protection Agency and additional support was provided from Stiftelsen IVL to complete the final writing of the manuscript.

Acknowledgments: The authors would like to thank Petter, Robin, Natalie and Ingrid at Grönska Stadsodling 365 for their support and input for this project. Special gratitude is also owed to Erik Johannes for his support in data collection assessment of potential circularity scenarios. We would also like to acknowledge the support and input from the anonymous reviewers for their contribution to developing this paper.

Conflicts of Interest: The authors declare no conflict of interest.

References

1. Despommier, D. The Rise of Vertical Farms. *Sci. Am.* **2009**, *301*, 80–87. [CrossRef] [PubMed]
2. Goldstein, B.; Hauschild, M.; Fernández, J.; Birkved, M. Testing the environmental performance of urban agriculture as a food supply in northern climates. *J. Clean. Prod.* **2016**, *135*, 984–994. [CrossRef]
3. Eigenbrod, C.; Gruda, N. Urban vegetable for food security in cities. A review. *Agron. Sustain. Dev.* **2015**, *35*, 483–498. [CrossRef]
4. Thomaier, S.; Specht, K.; Henckel, D.; Dierich, A.; Siebert, R.; Freisinger, U.B.; Sawicka, M. Farming in and on urban buildings: Present practice and specific novelties of Zero-Acreage Farming (ZFarming). *Renew. Agric. Food Syst.* **2014**, *30*, 43–54. [CrossRef]
5. Cockrall-King, J. *Food and The City: Urban. Agriculture and the New Food Revolution*; Prometheus Books: New York, NY, USA, 2012.
6. Kozai, T.; Niu, G. Chapter 1—Introduction. In *Plant Factory, Kozai, T., Niu, G., Takagaki, M., Eds.*; Academic Press: San Diego, CA, USA, 2016; pp. 3–5. [CrossRef]
7. Kozai, T. Resource use efficiency of closed plant production system with artificial light: Concept, estimation and application to plant factory. *Proc. Jpn. Acad. Ser. B Phys. Biol. Sci.* **2013**, *89*, 447–461. [CrossRef] [PubMed]
8. Graamans, L.; Baeza, E.; van den Dobbelsteen, A.; Tsafaras, I.; Stanghellini, C. Plant factories versus greenhouses: Comparison of resource use efficiency. *Agric. Syst.* **2018**, *160*, 31–43. [CrossRef]
9. Molin, E.; Martin, M. *Assessing the Energy and Environmental Performance of Vertical Hydroponic Farming, IVL Research Report*; C299. IVL; Swedish Environmental Research Institute: Stockholm, Sweden, 2018.
10. Chance, E.; Ashton, W.; Pereira, J.; Mulrow, J.; Norberto, J.; Derrible, S.; Guilbert, S. The Plant—An experiment in urban food sustainability. *Environ. Progr. Sustain. Energy* **2018**, *37*, 82–90. [CrossRef]
11. Grönska. Grönska Stadsodling 365. Available online: http://www.gronska.se (accessed on 11 November 2018).
12. AeroFarms. AeroFarms. Available online: www.aerofarms.com (accessed on 8 September 2018).
13. Eaves, J.; Eaves, S. Comparing the Profitability of a Greenhouse to a Vertical Farm in Quebec. *Can. J. Agric. Econ./Revue Canadienne D'agroeconomie* **2018**, *66*, 43–54. [CrossRef]
14. Benke, K.; Tomkins, B. Future food-production systems: Vertical farming and controlled-environment agriculture. *Sustain. Sci. Pract. Policy* **2017**, *13*, 13–26. [CrossRef]
15. Romeo, D.; Vea, E.B.; Thomsen, M. Environmental Impacts of Urban Hydroponics in Europe: A Case Study in Lyon. *Procedia CIRP* **2018**, *69*, 540–545. [CrossRef]
16. Kulak, M.; Graves, A.; Chatterton, J. Reducing greenhouse gas emissions with urban agriculture: A Life Cycle Assessment perspective. *Landsc. Urban Plan.* **2013**, *111*, 68–78. [CrossRef]

17. Sanjuan-Delmás, D.; Llorach-Massana, P.; Nadal, A.; Ercilla-Montserrat, M.; Muñoz, P.; Montero, J.I.; Josa, A.; Gabarrell, X.; Rieradevall, J. Environmental assessment of an integrated rooftop greenhouse for food production in cities. *J. Clean. Prod.* **2018**, *177*, 326–337. [CrossRef]
18. Llorach-Massana, P.; Muñoz, P.; Riera, M.R.; Gabarrell, X.; Rieradevall, J.; Montero, J.I.; Villalba, G. N2O emissions from protected soilless crops for more precise food and urban agriculture life cycle assessments. *J. Clean. Prod.* **2017**, *149*, 1118–1126. [CrossRef]
19. Martin, M.; Harris, S. Prospecting the sustainability implications of an emerging industrial symbiosis network. *Resour. Conserv. Recycl.* **2018**, *138*, 246–256. [CrossRef]
20. Sanyé-Mengual, E.; Martinez-Blanco, J.; Finkbeiner, M.; Cerdà, M.; Camargo, M.; Ometto, A.R.; Velásquez, L.S.; Villada, G.; Niza, S.; Pina, A.; et al. Urban horticulture in retail parks: Environmental assessment of the potential implementation of rooftop greenhouses in European and South American cities. *J. Clean. Prod.* **2018**, *172*, 3081–3091. [CrossRef]
21. Dorr, E.; Sanyé-Mengual, E.; Gabrielle, B.; Grard, B.J.P.; Aubry, C. Proper selection of substrates and crops enhances the sustainability of Paris rooftop garden. *Agron. Sustain. Develop.* **2017**, *37*. [CrossRef]
22. Gentry, M. Local heat, local food: Integrating vertical hydroponic farming with district heating in Sweden. *Energy* **2019**, *174*, 191–197. [CrossRef]
23. Marchi, B.; Zanoni, S.; Pasetti, M. Industrial Symbiosis for Greener Horticulture Practices: The CO2 Enrichment from Energy Intensive Industrial Processes. *Procedia CIRP* **2018**, *69*, 562–567. [CrossRef]
24. Chertow, M.R. Industrial symbiosis: Literature and taxonomy. *Ann. Rev. Energy Environ.* **2000**, *25*, 313–337. [CrossRef]
25. S.A.W. The Structure, Function, and Evolution of a Regional Industrial Ecosystem. *J. Ind. Ecol.* **2009**, *13*, 228–246. [CrossRef]
26. Lombardi, D.R.; Laybourn, P. Redefining Industrial Symbiosis. *J. Ind. Ecol.* **2012**, *16*, 28–37. [CrossRef]
27. Martin, M.; Eklund, M. Improving the environmental performance of biofuels with industrial symbiosis. *Biomass Bioenerg.* **2011**, *35*, 1747–1755. [CrossRef]
28. Mirata, M.; Carlsson, P.; Harris, S.; Martin, M.; Fornell, R.; Hackl, R.; Källqvist, T.; Dalväg, E.; Broberg, S. *International and Swedish State of Play in Industrial Symbiosis: A Review with Proposals to Scale up Industrial Symbiosis in Sweden*; Linköping University: Linköping, Sweden, 2018.
29. Fisher, S.; Karunanithi, A. Contemporary comparative LCA of commercial farming and urban agriculture for selected fresh vegetables consumed in Denver, Colorado. In Proceedings of the 9th International Conference on Life Cycle Assessment in the Agri-Food Sector, San Francisco, CA, USA, 8–10 October 2014.
30. Dias, G.M.; Ayer, N.W.; Khosla, S.; Van Acker, R.; Young, S.B.; Whitney, S.; Hendricks, P. Life cycle perspectives on the sustainability of Ontario greenhouse tomato production: Benchmarking and improvement opportunities. *J. Clean. Prod.* **2017**, *140*, 831–839. [CrossRef]
31. Martin, M.; Molin, E. Environmental Assessment of an Urban Vertical Hydroponic Farming System in Sweden. *Sustainability* **2019**, *11*, 4124. [CrossRef]
32. Martin, M.; Svensson, N.; Eklund, M. Who gets the benefits? An approach for assessing the environmental performance of industrial symbiosis. *J. Clean. Prod.* **2015**, *98*, 263–271. [CrossRef]
33. Guinée, J.B. *Handbook on Life Cycle Assessment: Operational Guide to the ISO Standards*; Kluwer Academic Publishers: Dordrecht, The Netherlands, 2002.
34. Ecoinvent. *Ecoinvent version 3.4*; Ecoinvent: Zurich, Switzerland, 2017.
35. Martin, M. Evaluating the environmental performance of producing soil and surfaces through industrial symbiosis. *J. Ind. Ecol.* **2019**. [CrossRef]
36. Johannes, E.; Martin, M. *Potential for Urban. Symbiosis with Vertical Hydroponic Farming*; IVL Swedish Environmental Research Institute: Stockholm, Sweden, 2018.
37. Gasum. *Biofertilizer From Biogas Digestate. Discussions on the Nutrient Content*; Gasum: Espoo, Finland, 2018.
38. Martin, M.; Wetterlund, E.; Hackl, R.; Holmgren, K.M.; Peck, P. Assessing the aggregated environmental benefits from by-product and utility synergies in the Swedish biofuel industry. *Biofuels* **2017**, *1*, 1–16. [CrossRef]
39. Strandmark, E. *Biogödsel Som Kvävekälla i Hydroponisk Tomatproduktion*; SLU, Sveriges lantbruksuniversitet; Fakulteten för landskapsarkitektur, trädgårds-och växtproduktionsvetenskap, Institutionen för biosystem och teknologi: Uppsala, Sweeden, 2019.

40. Martin, M. Potential of biogas expansion in Sweden: Identifying the gap between potential studies and producer perspectives. *Biofuels* **2015**, *6*, 233–240. [CrossRef]
41. Martin, M.; Parsapour, A. Upcycling wastes with biogas production: An exergy and economic analysis. In Proceedings of the Venice Symposium 2012, Fourth International Symposium on Energy from Biomass and Waste, Venice, Italy, 12–15 November 2012.
42. Martin, M. Quantifying the environmental performance of an industrial symbiosis network of biofuel producers. *J. Clean. Prod.* **2015**, *102*, 202–212. [CrossRef]
43. Velenturf, A.P.M.; Jensen, P.D. Promoting Industrial Symbiosis: Using the Concept of Proximity to Explore Social Network Development. *J. Ind. Ecol.* **2016**, *20*, 700–709. [CrossRef]
44. Barrett, G.E.; Alexander, P.D.; Robinson, J.S.; Bragg, N.C. Achieving environmentally sustainable growing media for soilless plant cultivation systems—A review. *Sci. Hortic.* **2016**, *212*, 220–234. [CrossRef]
45. Chrysargyris, A.; Stavrinides, M.; Moustakas, K.; Tzortzakis, N. Utilization of paper waste as growing media for potted ornamental plants. *Clean Technol. Environ. Policy* **2018**. [CrossRef]
46. Christoulaki, M.; Gouma, S.; Manios, T.; Tzortzakis, N. Deployment of Sawdust as Substrate Medium in Hydroponically Grown Lettuce. *J. Plant. Nutr.* **2014**, *37*, 1304–1315. [CrossRef]
47. Verhagen, J.B.G.M.; Boon, H.T.M. *Classification of Growing Media on Their Environmental Profile*; Food and Agrigultural Organisation (FAO): Rome, Italy, 2008; pp. 231–238.
48. Chong, C. Experiences with Wastes and Composts in Nursery Substrates. *Am. Soc. Horic. Sci.* **2005**, *15*, 739. [CrossRef]
49. Martin, M. *Assessing the Environmental Implications of a Regional Industrial Symbiosis Network for Innovative Products. IVL Research Report C297.*; Swedish Environmental Research Institute: Stockholm, Sweden, 2018.
50. Blonck. Development of Life Cycle Assessment (LCA) standard for growing media sector in Europe. Available online: http://www.blonkconsultants.nl/2019/04/30/development-of-life-cycle-assessment-lca-standard-for-growing-media-sector-in-europe/?lang=en (accessed on 4 April 2019).
51. Enweremadu, C.C.; Waheed, M.A.; Adekunle, A.A.; Adeala, A. The Energy Potential of Brewer's Spent Grain for Breweries in Nigeria. *J. Eng. Appl. Sci.* **2008**, *3*, 175–177.
52. Santos, M.; Jiménez, J.J.; Bartolomé, B.; Gómez-Cordovés, C.; del Nozal, M.J. Variability of brewer's spent grain within a brewery. *Food Chem.* **2003**, *80*, 17–21. [CrossRef]
53. Surindra, S. Potential of domestic biogas digester slurry in vermitechnology. *Bioresour. Technol.* **2010**, *101*, 5419–5425. [CrossRef]
54. Meier, M.S.; Stoessel, F.; Jungbluth, N.; Juraske, R.; Schader, C.; Stolze, M. Environmental impacts of organic and conventional agricultural products–Are the differences captured by life cycle assessment? *J. Environ. Manag.* **2015**, *149*, 193–208. [CrossRef]
55. Brännvall, E.; Zamora, C.B.; Sjöblom, R.; Kumpiene, J. Effect of industrial residue combinations on availability of elements. *J. Hazardous Mater.* **2014**, *276*, 171–181. [CrossRef]
56. Vaneeckhaute, C.; Meers, E.; Michels, E.; Ghekiere, G.; Accoe, F.; Tack, F.M.G. Closing the nutrient cycle by using bio-digestion waste derivatives as synthetic fertilizer substitutes: A field experiment. *Biomass Bioenerg.* **2013**, *55*, 175–189. [CrossRef]
57. Vaneeckhaute, C.; Meers, E.; Michels, E.; Buysse, J.; Tack, F.M.G. Ecological and economic benefits of the application of bio-based mineral fertilizers in modern agriculture. *Biomass Bioenerg.* **2013**, *49*, 239–248. [CrossRef]
58. Olsson, L.; Fallde, M. Waste(d) potential: A socio-technical analysis of biogas production and use in Sweden. *J. Clean. Prod.* **2014**. [CrossRef]
59. Hussin, N.S.M.; Amin, N.A.M.; Safar, M.J.A.; Majid, M.S.A.; Nasir, N.F.M. Smart hydroponic system with hybrid power source. *J. Telecommun. Electron. Comput. Eng.* **2018**, *10*, 35–39.
60. Siregar, S.; Sari, M.I.; Jauhari, R. Automation system hydroponic using smart solar power plant unit. *J. Teknol.* **2016**, *78*, 55–60. [CrossRef]
61. Ureña-Sánchez, R.; Callejón-Ferre, Á.J.; Pérez-Alonso, J.; Carreño-Ortega, Á. Greenhouse tomato production with electricity generation by roof-mounted flexible solar panels. *Sci. Agric.* **2012**, *69*, 233–239. [CrossRef]
62. Ainsworth, P.; İbanoğlu, Ş.; Plunkett, A.; İbanoğlu, E.; Stojceska, V. Effect of brewers spent grain addition and screw speed on the selected physical and nutritional properties of an extruded snack. *J. Food Eng.* **2007**, *81*, 702–709. [CrossRef]

63. Mussatto, S.I.; Dragone, G.; Roberto, I.C. Brewers' spent grain: Generation, characteristics and potential applications. *J. Cereal Sci.* **2006**, *43*, 1–14. [CrossRef]
64. Chertow, M.; Park, J. Scholarship and Practice in Industrial Symbiosis: 1989–2014. In *Taking Stock of Industrial Ecology*; Clift, R., Druckman, A., Eds.; Springer International Publishing: Cham, Switzerland, 2016; pp. 87–116. [CrossRef]
65. Walls, J.L.; Paquin, R.L. Organizational Perspectives of Industrial Symbiosis:A Review and Synthesis. *Organ. Environ.* **2015**, *28*, 32–53. [CrossRef]
66. Martin, M.; Svensson, N.; Eklund, M.; Fonseca, J. Production synergies in the current biofuel industry: Opportunities for development. *Biofuels Future Sci.* **2012**, 545–554. [CrossRef]
67. Zhu, J.; Ruth, M. The development of regional collaboration for resource efficiency: A network perspective on industrial symbiosis. *Comput. Environ. Urban. Syst.* **2014**, *44*, 37–46. [CrossRef]
68. Mirata, M.; Hamilton, I. *Organizational and Institutional Influences on Industrial Symbiosis: The case of Econova and its Synergistic Partnerhips*; Linköping University Research Report; Linköping University: Linköping, Sweeden, 2018.
69. Harris, S.; Mirata, M.; Broberg, S.; Carlsson, P.; Martin, M. *A Roadmap for Increased Uptake of Industrial Symbiosis in Sweden*; IVL: Stockholm, Sweden, 2018; Volume 2018, p. 20.
70. Laybourn, P.; Lombardi, R. The Role of Audited Benefits in Industrial Symbiosis: The UK. National Industrial Symbiosis Programme. *Meas. Control* **2007**, *40*, 244. [CrossRef]
71. Golev, A.; Corder, G.D.; Giurco, D.P. Barriers to Industrial Symbiosis: Insights from the Use of a Maturity Grid. *J. Ind. Ecol.* **2015**, *19*, 141–153. [CrossRef]
72. Wolf, A.; Eklund, M.; Soderstrom, M. Towards cooperation in industrial symbiosis: Considering the importance of the human dimension. *Prog. Ind. Ecol. Int. J.* **2005**, *2*, 185–199. [CrossRef]
73. Chertow, M.R. "Uncovering" industrial symbiosis. *J. Ind. Ecol.* **2007**, *11*, 11–30. [CrossRef]
74. Martin, M. *Valorization of By-Products and Raw Material Inputs in the Biofuel Industry*; Report from an f3 project; The Swedish Knowledge Centre for Renewable Transportation Fuels: Göteborg, Sweden, 2013.

sustainability

MDPI

Article

Corporate Environmental Responsibility and Firm Information Risk: Evidence from the Korean Market

Daeheon Choi [1], Chune Young Chung [2,*], Dongnyoung Kim [3] and Chang Liu [4]

1. College of Business Administration, Kookmin University, 77 Jeongneung-ro, Seongbuk-gu, Seoul 02707, Korea; dhchoi@kookmin.ac.kr
2. School of Business Administration, College of Business and Economics, Chung-Ang University, 84 Heukseok-ro, Dongjak-gu, Seoul 06974, Korea
3. College of Business Administration, California State University San Marcos, 333 S. Twin Oaks Valley Rd., San Marcos, CA 92096, USA; dkim@csusm.edu
4. College of Business Administration, California State University, Sacramento, 6000 J Street, Sacramento, CA 95819, USA; chang.liu@csus.edu

* Correspondence: bizfinance@cau.ac.kr

Received: 29 October 2019; Accepted: 18 November 2019; Published: 19 November 2019

Abstract: Despite the potential benefits of a firm's corporate environmental commitment to its information environment, few empirical studies examine the relationship between corporate environmental responsibility (CER) and firm information risk in emerging markets. In such markets, better corporate transparency and less information asymmetry are becoming increasingly important owing to firms' poor governance structures, the lack of protection for investors, the substantial participation of unsophisticated individual investors, and so on. Using a comprehensive sample of firms engaged in CER for the period from 2005 to 2016, we find that a firm's CER score has a negative effect on measures of firm information risk in the emerging Korean market, which is characterized by poor corporate governance and a strong influence of owner–managers. Furthermore, our results show that the negative relationship between CER and information risk is more pronounced for firms with higher uncertainty (lower transparency). Thus, we conclude that CER enhances a firm's information environment by reducing investors' information risk.

Keywords: corporate environmental responsibility; information risk; earnings quality; *chaebol*; corporate governance

JEL Classification: G32; G34

---

1. Introduction

Traditionally, environmental protection has largely been a government responsibility with the private sector simply reacting to government regulations, sanctions, and incentives. However, as human activities continue to affect the earth's climate, corporate environmental responsibility (CER) is receiving increasing attention and private corporations are expected to assume more active roles in protecting the environment [1–3]. Stern [3] shows that the benefits of early action on climate change outweigh the costs. Despite some skepticism about the benefits of CER [4], Margolis and Walsh [5] and Orlitzky et al. [6] suggest that CER helps to create a competitive advantage and improves financial performance. Wahba [7] also provides evidence that firms that care for their environment are valued by the market. Thus, firms are expected to increasingly support CER activities.

Information about a firm's CER performance related to shareholder returns is particularly important. Recent studies show that increasing numbers of investors are seeking reliable information about CER activities through public or private channels. Related studies document that such investors actively utilize this information in their investment decisions. Despite the growing importance of information on firms' CER activities to investors, however, few studies examine how investors use this information to assess a firm's operations and value. In particular, studies have found little evidence on whether information about CER activities, as conveyed by a manager or third-party entities, benefits investors by reducing corporate uncertainty risk. To the extent that a firm's CER activities reflect the manager's proclivity to be a moral agent, the firm should also have greater information transparency and lower information risk [8].

Recent studies do investigate whether firm-specific information risk influences pricing decisions in capital markets (Traditional financial theory argues that the firm-intrinsic information property does not affect pricing decisions because intrinsic risk can be eliminated through diversified investments. However, several studies, including Merton's [9] incomplete information models, Diamond and Verrecchia's [10] liquidity effect models, and the asymmetric information models of Admati [11] and Brennan et al. [12], support the notion that the firm-intrinsic information property influences the expected rate of return.). In particular, empirical accounting studies use earnings quality as a substitute for firm-specific information risk to analyze the relation between earnings quality and the cost of capital [13–17]. Most studies find a negative correlation between the cost of capital and earnings quality, and Easley and O'Hara [18] and Lambert et al. [19] establish theoretical systems to explain the negative correlation between the quality of accounting information and the cost of capital. Easley and O'Hara [18] posit the existence of information asymmetry among investors. Less-informed investors demand return premia on firms with high information asymmetry (i.e., high information risk), because they recognize their informational disadvantages relative to better-informed investors. In contrast, Lambert et al. [19] consider information precision rather than information asymmetry. Specifically, they define information precision as the average accuracy of an investor's future cash flow prediction.

Francis et al. [16,17] empirically demonstrate the theoretical concepts of Easley and O'Hara [18] and Lambert et al. [19] by analyzing the effect of accruals quality (AQ) on the cost of capital and stock returns, where AQ serves as a proxy for firm-level information risk (precision or asymmetry). They find that the costs of debt and capital are greater for firms with poor AQ than they are for firms with good AQ. Furthermore, stock returns change significantly as the degree of AQ changes. Numerous follow-up studies consider whether AQ is a risk factor, with mixed results. Some researchers find that AQ significantly influences the cost of capital and the pricing decision [13,20–23], whereas others find no evidence of such an influence [24–28].

Building on the results of prior studies regarding the information role of CER activities, we hypothesized that socially responsible firms are more likely to gain the market's trust, thus reducing the level of information risk between the firm and its stakeholders. Here, socially responsible firms are those that commit to active environmental engagement and transparency and do not withhold adverse news related to their environmental policies. Specifically, we investigated whether CER activities can reduce information risk in emerging capital markets, such as that of South Korea. Using a sample of 2,314 observations of firms listed on the Korea Exchange for the period from 2005 to 2016, we found that corporate environmental activity is negatively related to firm information risk. In addition, these relationships are more evident for firms whose stocks are traded frequently by individual investors and for firms controlled by an owner–manager. Overall, this study shows how CER enriches the information environment surrounding a firm. To the best of our knowledge, this study is the first to present empirical evidence substantiating the effect of CER on information risk in Korea.

2. Variables and Methodology

Our sample consisted of 2314 firm-year observations covering all nonfinancial companies listed on the Korea Exchange for the period from 2005 to 2016. In particular, we used the CER scores provided by the Korea Economic Justice Institute (KEJI) and developed by the Citizens' Coalition for Economic Justice (CCEJ) as a proxy for a firm's CER activities. The KEJI's CER score is the single most credible metric and is widely used in academic research. It is also used to determine the annual Good

Corporation Awards provided by the CCEJ. We extracted accounting, financial, stock, and trading volume data from 1999 to 2015 from FnGuide's DataGuidePro (FnGuide is a representative company in Korea that provides accounting, financial, stock price, and trading volume data along with analyst consensuses and economic references. DataGuidePro is the firm's data extraction system. Many institutions, companies, and researchers in Korea use DataGuidePro to analyze Korean companies; see http://www.fnguide.com/). We included only firms with fiscal years ending in December to unify the measuring time, and we excluded outliers. We also excluded firms with no collectible financial, stock, or trading volume data.

We adopted the approach developed by Francis et al. [16,17], who measured firm-level information risk using accounting earnings quality. Francis et al. [16,17] measured the past volatility of abnormal accruals for individual firms and defined firms with greater AQ volatility as having higher information risk. They estimated abnormal accruals (v_{it}) by conducting a regression analysis from year *t4* to year *t* using the annual industry-specific model given by Equation (1), and they then calculate the standard deviation of the abnormal accruals. Francis et al. [16,17] define AQ as the standard deviation of abnormal accruals over the previous five years. In Equation (1), $TCA_{i,t}$ indicates the total current accruals of firm *i* in year *t*; we measured total current assets as follows:

$$TCA_{i,t} = \Delta CA_{i,t} - \Delta CL_{i,t} - \Delta Cash_{i,t} + \Delta STDEBT_{i,t},$$

where $\triangle CA_{i,t}$ is the change in the current assets of firm *i* from year *t*−1 to year *t*, $\triangle CL_{i,t}$ is the change in the current liabilities of firm *i* from year *t*−1 to year *t*, $\triangle Cash_{i,t}$ is the change in the cash and cash-convertible assets of firm *i* from year *t*−1 to year *t*, and $\triangle STDEBT_{i,t}$ is the change in the current liabilities of firm *i* from year *t*−1 to t.

A_{it} is the average total assets of firm *i* across years *t* and *t*−1; CFO_{it} is the cash flow from firm *i*'s operations in year *t*; $\triangle REVi_t$ is firm *i*'s sales in year *t*−1 deducted from sales in year *t*; PPE_{it} is the gross property, plant, and equipment value of firm *i* at the end of year *t*; and v_{it} is the residual of Equation (1).

$$\frac{TCA_{it}}{A_{it}} = \varnothing_0 + \frac{\varnothing_1 CFO_{i,t-1}}{A_{it}} + \frac{\varnothing_2 CFO_{it}}{A_{it}} + \frac{\varnothing_3 CFO_{it+1}}{A_{it}} + \frac{\varnothing_4 \Delta REV_{it}}{A_{it}} + \frac{\varnothing_5 PPE_{it}}{A_{it}} + v_{it} \quad (1)$$

$$\therefore AQ_{i,t} = \sigma(\hat{v}_{i,t}).$$

In addition, Francis et al. [16,17] contend that the volatility of abnormal accruals can be determined by the fundamental or innate risk factor in an individual firm's operating activities and the discretionary risk factor incurred by a manager's opportunistic earnings management. Thus, they decomposed AQ into two components and analyzed each component's effect on the cost of capital. They first used the relationship between individual firm-level operating risk factors (e.g., firm scale, cash flow volatility, sales volatility, the business cycle, and the frequency of loss) and AQ to estimate the innate component and then allocated the remainder to the discretionary component. We applied Francis et al.'s [16,17] methods by dividing AQ into innate and discretionary components. Then, we investigated the effects of CER on these components.

Innate AQ is the predicted value of Equation (2), and discretionary AQ is the residual. In Equation (2), AQ_{it} represents the AQ of firm *i* in year *t*; $SIZE_{it}$ is the size of firm *i* at the end of year *t*, defined as the log of the firm's market capitalization in units of one million won; $\sigma(CFO)_{it}$ indicates the cash flow volatility, calculated as the standard deviation of the firm's adjusted operating cash flows with respect to its total assets from year *t*−4 to year *t*; $\sigma(Sales)_{jt}$ denotes sales volatility, which is the standard deviation of adjusted sales with respect to total assets from year *t*−4 to year *t*; $OperCycle_{it}$ is the operating cycle of firm *i* in year *t*, calculated as the log of the sum of days of accounts receivable and days of inventory; and $NegEarnRatio_{it}$ is the number of losses that occurred within the firm over the previous five years (as a percentage).

$$AQ_{it} = \beta_0 + \beta_1 SIZE_{it} + \beta_2 \sigma(CFO)_{it} + \beta_3 \sigma(Sales)_{it} + \beta_4 OperCycle_{it} + \beta_5 NegEarnRatio_{jt} + \varepsilon_{it} \quad (2)$$

$$InnateAQ_{it} = \hat{AQ}_{it}$$

$$DiscAQ_{it} = AQ_{it} - \hat{AQ}_{it}.$$

Specifically, we employed Fama-MacBeth [29] cross-sectional regressions to investigate the influence of corporate environmental activity on information risk while controlling for other explanatory variables that may affect information risk in a multivariate regression setting. Based on the related studies described in the previous section, we employed the following control variables, for which detailed descriptions are available on request: Total assets (T_Asset_t), financial leverage (F_Lev_t), the return on assets (ROA_t), the market-to-book-value ratio (MTB_t), revenue growth (RG_t), the standard deviations of revenue and of operating cash flow (SD_Rev_t, SD_OCF_t, respectively), firm age (F_Age_t), and R&D expenses (RND_t). Lastly, *Ind_D* is a dummy variable that takes a value of one if a firm's stock is part of the KOSPI 200 and a value of zero otherwise. Chung et al. [30] show that KOSPI 200 firms are generally *chaebol* affiliates; thus, weak corporate governance is more likely to concern outside shareholders for such firms than it does for non-KOSPI 200 firms.

3. Results

Table 1 presents the mean, standard deviation, 5th percentile, 25th percentile, median, 75th percentile, and 95th percentile values of the key variables. We find that the variables related to information risk exhibit large standard deviations, implying that informational transparency varies significantly among Korean firms. In addition, *CER* ranges from 3.954 to 8.232 with an average of 5.453 and a standard deviation of 0.834, indicating significant cross-sectional variation in corporate environmental engagement. The wide distributions of information risk and *CER* in our sample allow us to analyze the extent to which corporate environmental activities affect a firm's information risk.

Table 1. Descriptive statistics.

Variable	Mean	Std. Dev.	5th Pctl.	25th Pctl.	Median	75th Pctl.	95th Pctl.
AQ	0.093	0.068	0.000	0.046	0.073	0.119	0.360
DiscAQ	−0.006	0.057	−0.212	−0.042	−0.023	0.017	0.234
InnateAQ	0.091	0.042	−0.065	0.059	0.077	0.134	0.292
CER	5.453	0.834	3.954	4.124	5.321	6.872	8.232
T_Asset	19.123	1.521	17.211	18.101	18.871	19.345	22.871
F_Lev	0.4871	0.213	0.141	0.291	0.414	0.651	0.801
ROA	0.002	0.212	−0.241	−0.019	0.031	0.058	0.135
MTB	5.331	0.987	4.312	5.232	5.639	6.612	7.422
RG	0.271	4.812	−0.391	−0.078	0.081	0.201	0.692
SD_Rev	0.171	0.179	0.000	0.071	0.131	0.224	0.476
SD_OCF	0.071	0.059	0.000	0.028	0.049	0.091	0.161
F_Age	3.381	0.587	2.412	2.971	3.424	3.698	4.125
RND	0.015	0.039	0.000	0.000	0.002	0.013	0.071
Ind_D	0.201	0.412	0.000	0.000	0.000	0.000	1.000

Notes: This table presents the mean, standard deviation, 5th percentile, 25th percentile, median, 75th percentile, and 95th percentile values of the variables based on a sample of 2,314 observations of firms listed on the Korea Exchange for the period from 2005 to 2016. The variables are winsorized at the 1% and 99% levels, following Ayers et al. [31].

Because it takes time for corporate engagement to influence a firm's information environment, we regressed the variables related to information risk on lagged *CER*. Table 2 shows our baseline results. Column 1 shows that lagged *CER* is inversely related to AQ at the 1% significance level, implying that corporate environmental effort enhances a firm's information quality. In Columns 2 and 3, we find from the magnitudes of the coefficients of lagged *CER* in both models that the effect of *CER* on innate information risk is more pronounced than that on discretionary risk is. Hence, our results show that corporate environmental engagement mitigates the risk related to managerial discretionary behaviors and improves a firm's innate informational environment.

Table 2. Effect of corporate environmental engagement on information risk.

Variables	*AQ*	*DiscAQ*	*InnateAQ*
Intercept	0.0124 **	0.0154 ***	0.0212 **
	(2.52)	(3.41)	(2.85)
CER_{t-1}	−0.0312 ***	−0.0241 ***	−0.0469 ***
	(−4.31)	(−3.07)	(−5.87)
T_Asset_{t-1}	−0.0053 ***	−0.0043 ***	−0.0059 ***
	(−4.31)	(−4.63)	(−4.77)
F_Lev_{t-1}	0.0541 ***	0.0559 ***	0.0548 ***
	(8.31)	(8.27)	(8.36)
ROA_{t-1}	−0.0598 ***	−0.0539 ***	−0.0598 ***
	(−6.36)	(−6.16)	(−6.33)
MTB_{t-1}	0.0145 ***	0.0144 ***	0.0147 ***
	(5.48)	(5.46)	(5.53)
RG_{t-1}	−0.0012	−0.0011	−0.0011
	(−0.44)	(−0.44)	(−0.45)
SD_Rev_{t-1}	0.0122 ***	0.0121 ***	0.0127 ***
	(5.13)	(5.34)	(5.23)
SD_OCF_{t-1}	0.1124 ***	0.1198 ***	0.1129 ***
	(6.86)	(6.92)	(6.80)
F_Age_{t-1}	−0.0217 ***	−0.0215 ***	−0.0215 ***
	(−3.05)	(−4.94)	(−3.06)
RND_{t-1}	0.0357	0.0347	0.0366
	(0.32)	(0.31)	(0.32)
Ind_D	−0.0153 ***	−0.0154 ***	−0.0154 ***
	(−4.46)	(−3.74)	(−4.52)
Adjusted R^2	0.2312	0.1923	0.2787
Observations	2314	2314	2314

Notes: This table shows the estimated results of regressing information risk on lagged corporate environmental responsibility scores using Fama–MacBeth cross-sectional regressions. The values in parentheses are *t*-statistics adjusted for Newey–West autocorrelation with three lags [32]. ***, **, and * denote statistical significance at the 1%, 5%, and 10% levels, respectively.

In Table 3, we provide two robustness checks to further corroborate our findings. First, to examine the informational heterogeneity among the sample firms, we divided the firms into two subgroups based on R&D expenses (*RND*) in each year (Aboody and Lev [33] show that firms with higher RND derive more firm value from intangibles and unique products, leading to greater information asymmetry between executives and outside shareholders). Firms with zero (nonzero) R&D expenses are likely to exhibit low (high) information asymmetry. Then, we regressed the information risk variables on the lagged independent variables for each subsample of firms. Column 1 shows the results for firms with nonzero R&D expenses and indicates that *CER* is significantly negatively associated with *AQ*. However, Column 2 shows that this negative relationship is not statistically significant for firms with zero R&D expenses. This result implies that corporate environmental efforts have a greater effect for firms with more information uncertainty. Considering the magnitude and statistical significance of the results for the subsamples of firms in Columns 1 and 2, we can conclude that the effect of passive-monitoring institutions is more pronounced for firms with high information asymmetry, which is an important characteristic of *chaebols*.

Table 3. Robustness tests.

Variable	AQ			
	Top *RND*	Bottom *RND*	*Chaebol*	*Non-Chaebol*
Intercept	0.0242 **	0.0312	−0.0232	0.0871 ***
	(3.21)	(1.53)	(−0.89)	(6.71)
CER_{t-1}	−0.0608 ***	−0.1051	−0.0638 ***	−0.0352
	(−4.57)	(−1.57)	(−5.06)	(−1.56)
T_Asset_{t-1}	−0.0056 ***	−0.0031	−0.0076 ***	−0.0058 ***
	(−5.27)	(−0.53)	(−4.96)	(−3.52)
F_Lev_{t-1}	0.0578 ***	0.0485 ***	0.0421 ***	0.0411 ***
	(8.44)	(6.10)	(7.10)	(4.44)
ROA_{t-1}	−0.0573 ***	−0.0693 ***	−0.0717	−0.0591 ***
	(−6.86)	(−7.32)	(−0.50)	(−5.03)
MTB_{t-1}	0.0212 ***	0.0134 ***	0.0177 ***	0.0133 ***
	(5.51)	(6.13)	(5.97)	(3.43)
RG_{t-1}	−0.0008	−0.0005	−0.0021	−0.0005
	(−0.27)	(−0.22)	(−0.56)	(−0.12)
SD_Rev_{t-1}	0.0088 ***	0.0054 ***	0.0069 ***	0.0097 ***
	(5.07)	(3.33)	(3.31)	(4.52)
SD_OCF_{t-1}	0.1453 ***	0.1577*	0.3133 ***	0.2981 ***
	(7.49)	(2.23)	(6.25)	(7.30)
F_Age_{t-1}	−0.0131 ***	−0.0159 ***	−0.0121 *	−0.0123 ***
	(−4.98)	(−4.50)	(−2.11)	(−4.62)
RND_{t-1}	0.0198	0.0176	0.1234	0.1312
	(0.58)	(0.45)	(0.72)	(0.19)
Ind_D	−0.0155 ***	0.0143	−0.0147 **	0.0123
	(−3.42)	(1.51)	(−3.24)	(0.32)
Adjusted R^2	0.0987	0.0981	0.0728	0.0629
Observations	1489	825	925	1389

Notes: This table shows the results of considering additional settings to corroborate the baseline findings. We provide the estimated results of regressing information risk on lagged corporate environmental responsibility scores using the Fama–MacBeth cross-sectional regression approach. The bottom *RND* (R&D expenses) subsample of firms includes those with zero *RND* and, thus, has more firm-year observations than the top *RND* subsample of firms. *Chaebol* and *Non-Chaebol* denote subsamples of *chaebol*-affiliated and non-*chaebol*-affiliated firms, respectively. The values in parentheses are *t*-statistics adjusted for Newey–West autocorrelations with three lags [32]. ***, **, and * denote statistical significance at the 1%, 5%, and 10% levels, respectively.

Next, we considered the information quality in *chaebol* and non-*chaebol* firms. *Chaebols* own many of the financial and non-financial firms in Korea and thus have a significant effect on the Korean economy. Their influence on their affiliates is bolstered through internal business dealings, cross-debt guarantees, and reciprocal shareholdings [34]. Because *chaebols* are mainly controlled by family members, self-interested behavior is often observed. For example, the controlling shareholders of *chaebol*-affiliates tend to divert corporate resources to affiliated targets that benefit from the acquisitions to the detriment of other outside shareholders [35]. The boards of *chaebol* affiliates largely comprise associates of the *chaebol* families, compromising the transparency of the firms' decision-making [36]. Overall, *chaebols* are prone to poor corporate governance and are characterized by high information asymmetry between management and outside shareholders. In the institutional context of the Korean market, improving the quality of a firm's information and environment through active environmental engagement, which provides trust and transparency to stakeholders, may be more effective for *chaebol*-affiliated firms. Columns 3 and 4 show the results when we divide the sample into subgroups of *chaebol*-affiliated firms and non-*chaebol* firms. The regression results show that the negative coefficient of *CER* is statistically significant only for *chaebol*-affiliated firms. Hence, this analysis supports our conjecture that the effect of corporate environmental engagement on information risk should be more important for firms with poor governance and opaque information. The results in Table 3 corroborate our main finding that *CER* plays an important role in reducing a firms' information risk.

4. Conclusions

We examined whether corporate environmental responsibility reduced firm information risk in the Korean market during the period from 2005 to 2016. We found a negative relationship between corporate environmental activity and information risk. In addition, this relationship is more evident for firms whose stocks are traded frequently by individual investors and for firms that are essentially controlled by an owner–manager. Overall, this study demonstrates the effects of corporate environmental responsibility on a firm's information environment.

Our empirical results provide further evidence that environmental protection and economic growth are not conflicting objectives. CER engagement serves as an important mechanism through which corporate managers in emerging economies can reduce information risk, mitigate the degree of adverse selection, and increase shareholder value. Investors should also look for signs of CER activities that are indicative of a firm's commitment to social responsibility and information transparency. As economic activities intensify and impose increasingly greater impacts on the environment, governments may encourage private corporations to self-regulate and incentivize them to take on more voluntary CER initiatives.

In particular, this study broadly adds to the recent literature in sustainability examining corporate social responsibility (CSR) activities and firm performance. Loh, Thomas, and Wang [37] document that sustainability reporting practice is positively associated with firm value based on Singapore-listed companies. In addition, Singh, Sethuraman, and Lam [38] show that such a positive relationship between sound CSR practices and firm value holds in Hong Kong and China as well. Recently, Hategan and Curea-Pitorac [39] also corroborate the positive influence of CSR activities on firm value. Importantly, Kim, Park, and Lee [40] show that the CSR-Firm value nexus is largely influenced by ownership structure in a firm based on the Korean market.

However, this study is subject to several caveats regarding the empirical estimation. First, our estimator might be biased owing to a potential endogeneity problem. Possible treatments to endogeneity could be performing a robustness test using instrumental variables and lagged independent/dependent variables. Alternatively, setting up a dynamic model could be useful. Second, introducing an exact channel through which corporate investment in CER can affect corporate financial performance might yield more comprehensive results. Lastly, our results were obtained using a sample of South Korean firms; we should emphasize that caution must be exercised before the implications are generalized to all emerging markets. We leave the verification of our results in other markets to future work.

Author Contributions: C.Y.C. designed the research. C.Y.C. performed the research and analyzed the data. C.Y.C. and C.L. wrote the paper. D.C. and D.K. revised the paper. All authors read and approved the final manuscript.

Funding: This work was supported by the research program of Kookmin University in Korea.

Acknowledgments: We would like to thank the editor and the two reviewers for their helpful comments and suggestions.

Conflicts of Interest: The authors declare no conflict of interest.

References

1. Mazurkiewicz, P. *Corporate Environmental Responsibility: Is a Common CSR Framework Possible?* Working Paper; World Bank: Washington, DC, USA, 2004.
2. Pachauri, R.K.; Reisinger, A. *Climate Change 2007. Synthesis Report. Contribution of Working Groups I, II, and III to the Fourth Assessment Report*; Intergovernmental Panel on Climate Change (IPCC): Geneva, Switzerland, 2008.
3. Stern, N. *The Economics of Climate Change: The Stern Review*; Cambridge University Press: Cambridge, UK, 2007.
4. Weitzman, M.L. A review of the Stern Review on the economics of climate change. *J. Econ. Lit.* **2007**, *45*, 703–724. [CrossRef]
5. Margolis, J.D.; Walsh, J.P. *People and Profits? The Search for a Link Between a Company's Social and Financial Performance*; Psychology Press: New York, NY, USA, 2001.

6. Orlitzky, M.; Schmidt, F.L.; Rynes, S.L. Corporate social and financial performance: A meta-analysis. *Organ. Stud.* **2003**, *24*, 403–441. [CrossRef]
7. Wahba, H. Does the market value corporate environmental responsibility? An empirical examination. *Corp. Soc. Responsib. Environ. Manag.* **2008**, *15*, 89–99. [CrossRef]
8. Dhaliwal, D.; Radhakrishnan, S.; Tsang, A.; Yang, Y. Voluntary nonfinancial disclosure and the cost of equity capital: The initiation of corporate social responsibility reporting. *Account. Rev.* **2011**, *86*, 59–100. [CrossRef]
9. Merton, R.C. A simple model of capital market equilibrium with incomplete information. *J. Financ.* **1987**, *42*, 483–510. [CrossRef]
10. Diamond, D.W.; Verrecchia, R.E. Disclosure, liquidity, and the cost of capital. *J. Financ.* **1991**, *46*, 1325–1359. [CrossRef]
11. Admati, A.R. A noisy rational expectations equilibrium for multi-asset securities markets. *Econom. J. Econom. Soc.* **1985**, *53*, 629–657. [CrossRef]
12. Brennan, M.J.; Chordia, T.; Subrahmanyam, A. Alternative factor specifications, security characteristics, and the cross-section of expected stock returns. *J. Financ. Econ.* **1998**, *49*, 345–373. [CrossRef]
13. Aboody, D.; Hughes, J.; Liu, J. Earnings quality, insider trading, and cost of capital. *J. Account. Res.* **2005**, *43*, 651–673. [CrossRef]
14. Botosan, C.A. Disclosure level and the cost of equity capital. *Account. Rev.* **1997**, *72*, 323–349.
15. Botosan, C.A.; Plumlee, M. Assessing alternative proxies for the expected risk premium. *Account. Rev.* **2005**, *80*, 21–53. [CrossRef]
16. Francis, J.; LaFond, R.; Olsson, P.; Schipper, K. Cost of equity and earnings attributes. *Account. Rev.* **2004**, *79*, 976–1010. [CrossRef]
17. Francis, J.; LaFond, R.; Olsson, P.; Schipper, K. The market pricing of accruals quality. *J. Account. Econ.* **2005**, *39*, 295–327. [CrossRef]
18. Easley, D.; O'Hara, M. Information and the cost of capital. *J. Financ.* **2004**, *59*, 1553–1583. [CrossRef]
19. Lambert, R.; Leuz, C.; Verrecchia, R. Accounting information, disclosure and the cost of capital. *J. Account. Res.* **2007**, *45*, 385–420. [CrossRef]
20. Barth, M.; Konchitchki, Y.; Landsman, W.R. Cost of capital and earnings transparency. *J. Account. Econ.* **2013**, *55*, 206–224. [CrossRef]
21. Bhattacharya, N.; Ecker, F.; Olsson, P.; Schipper, K. Direct and mediated associations among earnings quality, information asymmetry, and the cost of equity. *Account. Rev.* **2012**, *87*, 449–482. [CrossRef]
22. Kim, D.; Qi, Y. Accruals quality, stock returns, and macroeconomic conditions. *Account. Rev.* **2010**, *85*, 937–978. [CrossRef]
23. Ogneva, M. Accrual quality, realized returns, and expected returns: The importance of controlling for cash flow shocks. *Account. Rev.* **2012**, *87*, 1415–1444. [CrossRef]
24. Cohen, D. Does information risk really matter? An analysis of the determinants and economic consequences of financial reporting quality. *Asia Pac. J. Account. Econ.* **2008**, *15*, 69–90. [CrossRef]
25. Core, J.; Guay, W.; Verdi, R. Is accruals quality a priced risk factor? *J. Account. Econ.* **2008**, *46*, 2–22. [CrossRef]
26. Khan, M. Are accruals mispriced? Evidence from tests of an intertemporal capital asset pricing model. *J. Account. Econ.* **2008**, *45*, 55–77. [CrossRef]
27. McInnis, J. Earnings smoothness, average returns, and implied cost of equity capital. *Account. Rev.* **2010**, *85*, 315–341. [CrossRef]
28. Mohanram, P.; Rajgopal, S. Is PIN priced risk? *J. Account. Econ.* **2009**, *47*, 226–243. [CrossRef]
29. Fama, E.F.; MacBeth, J.D. Risk, return, and equilibrium: Empirical tests. *J. Polit. Econ.* **1973**, *81*, 607–636. [CrossRef]
30. Chung, C.Y.; Sul, H.K.; Wang, K. *Geographic and Market Proximity: Which one Matters? Working Paper*; Chung-Ang University: Seoul, Korea, 2017.
31. Ayers, B.C.; Ramalingegowda, S.; Yeung, P.E. Hometown advantage: The effects of monitoring institution location on financial reporting discretion. *J. Account. Econ.* **2011**, *52*, 41–61. [CrossRef]
32. Newey, W.K.; West, K.D. Automatic lag selection in covariance matrix estimation. *Rev. Econ. Stud.* **1994**, *61*, 631–653. [CrossRef]
33. Aboody, D.; Lev, B. Information asymmetry, R & D, and insider gains. *J. Financ.* **2000**, *55*, 2747–2766.
34. Chang, S.J.; Hong, J. Economic performance of group-affiliated companies in Korea: Intragroup resource sharing and internal business transactions. *Acad. Manag. J.* **2000**, *43*, 429–448.

35. Bae, K.H.; Kang, J.K.; Kim, J.M. Tunneling or value added? Evidence from mergers by Korean business groups. *J. Financ.* **2002**, *57*, 2695–2740. [CrossRef]
36. Chang, S.J. Ownership structure, expropriation, and performance of group-affiliated companies in Korea. *Acad. Manag. J.* **2003**, *46*, 238–253.
37. Loh, L.; Thomas, T.; Wang, Y. Sustainability reporting and firm value: Evidence from Singapore-listed companies. *Sustainability* **2017**, *9*, 2112. [CrossRef]
38. Singh, P.J.; Sethuraman, K.; Lam, J.Y. Impact of corporate social responsibility dimensions on firm value: Some evidence from Hong Kong and China. *Sustainability* **2017**, *9*, 1532. [CrossRef]
39. Hategan, C.-D.; Curea-Pitorac, R.-I. Testing the correlations between corporate giving, performance and company value. *Sustainability* **2017**, *9*, 1210. [CrossRef]
40. Kim, W.S.; Park, K.; Lee, S.H. Corporate social responsibility, ownership structure, and firm value: Evidence from Korea. *Sustainability* **2018**, *10*, 2497. [CrossRef]

sustainability

MDPI

Article

The Role of Renewables in a Low-Carbon Society: Evidence from a Multivariate Panel Data Analysis at the EU Level

Mihail Busu

Faculty of Business Administration in Foreign Languages, Bucharest University of Economics Studies, 010374 Bucharest, Romania; mihail.busu@fabiz.ase.ro

Received: 26 July 2019; Accepted: 20 September 2019; Published: 25 September 2019

Abstract: Low carbon emission has a major positive impact on our society. Due to the importance of reducing carbon emission levels, factors that contribute significantly towards reducing carbon emission levels have attracted the interest of academics and researchers in the field. In this paper, the author develops a multiple linear regression analysis to examine the relationship between renewable energy consumption, biofuel production, resources productivity, bioenergy productivity, the level of urbanization and population and their impact on total carbon dioxide (CO_2) emissions. Data was collected from the European Statistical Office (EUROSTAT) and four statistical hypotheses were validated through a regression model with panel data using the statistical software EViews 11. The study was conducted for 27 European Union (EU) countries during 2008 to 2017. The author's findings indicate that renewables have a direct and positive influence on the levels of CO_2 emissions, as opposed to population growth and urbanization. These findings suggest that public policy should be directed towards increasing the use of renewables in EU countries, while the level of urbanization and the population growth add more restrictions in the modelling equation of the impact on CO_2 emissions.

Keywords: carbon emissions; renewable energy; biofuels; productivity; resources; panel data; EU

---

1. Introduction

The Member States of the United Nations Framework Convention on Climate Change (UNFCCC) concluded the Paris Agreement to combat climate change and to intensify the actions needed for a sustainable transition towards a low-carbon future. Energy consumption will need to grow, taking into account the possibilities for achieving greater energy efficiency and for controlling greenhouse gas emissions in general, through the application of new technologies on terms which make such an application economically and socially beneficial.

The use of energy from green resources generates multiple concerns for academics as well as for the governments, in order to find the best solution to answer to the challenge of climate change. Ratifying the Paris Agreement and enforcing it by as many countries as possible would create the premise for achieving a low-carbon society.

Nowadays, the real problem is how to reduce CO_2 emissions and one of the solutions is the increasing use of renewables.

The aim of this study is to analyze the impact of renewables, biofuels, resources, bioenergy, urbanization and population on CO_2 emissions for a panel of 27 EU countries, between 2008 and 2017. To achieve this objective, a multiple linear regression model was used with the Pooled Least Square (PLS) method and the analysis was performed using EViews 11.0 software.

A description of the indicators used in the research model is shown in Figures 1–6. Thus, Figure 1 reveals the levels of CO_2 emissions in European Union (EU) countries, between 2007 and 2017.

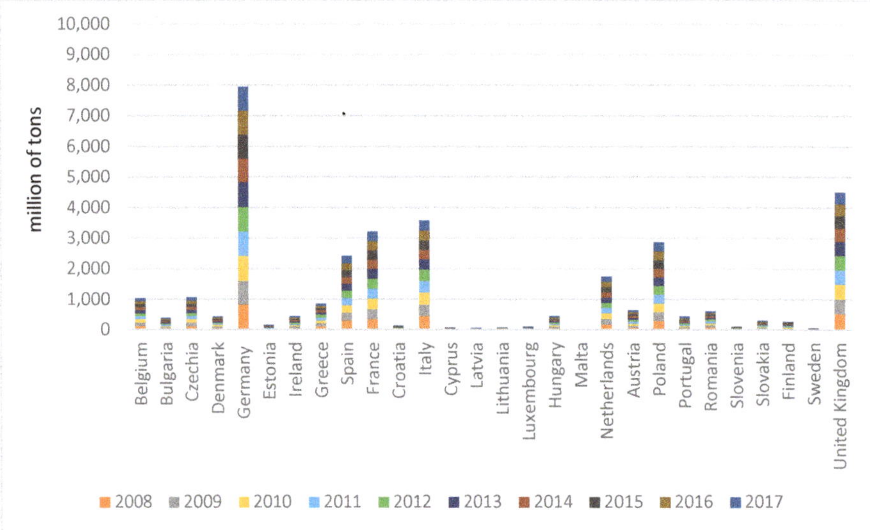

Figure 1. CO_2 emissions, in millions of tons, in European Union (EU) countries between 2008 and 2017. Source: Eurostat [1].

The energy available in the European Union comes from energy produced in the EU and from energy imported from third countries. In 2017, the EU produced approximately 45% of its own energy, while 55% was imported. In 2017, the energy mix in the EU, meaning the range of energy sources available, was mainly made up of five different sources: petroleum products (including crude oil), natural gas, solid fossil fuels, renewable energy and nuclear energy. In Figure 2, the share of each type of energy at the EU level is shown.

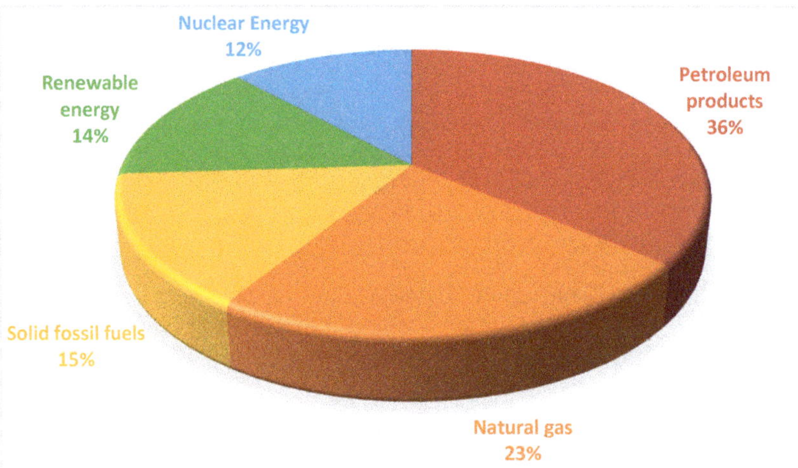

Figure 2. Energy mix produced in the EU in 2017. Source: Eurostat [1].

From this figure, we can see that renewable energy produced in the EU only counted for 14% of total energy production.

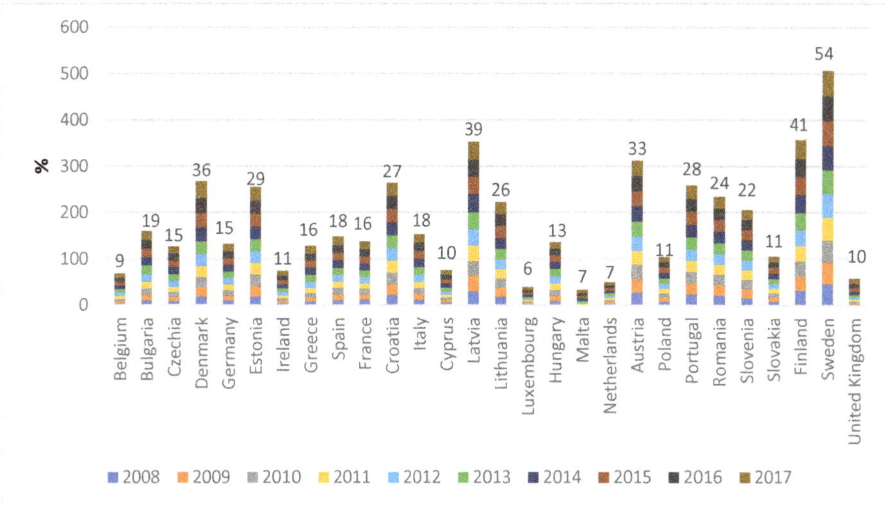

Figure 3. The percentages (%) of renewable energy in total energy consumption at the EU level, between 2008 and 2017. Source: Eurostat [1].

From the graph above, we can see that the highest level of renewable energy at the EU level in the past ten years was in Sweden (54%), Finland (41%) and Latvia (39%), while the lowest were in the Netherlands (7%), Malta (7%) and Luxembourg (6%).

Figure 4 presents the evolution of biofuel production in EU countries.

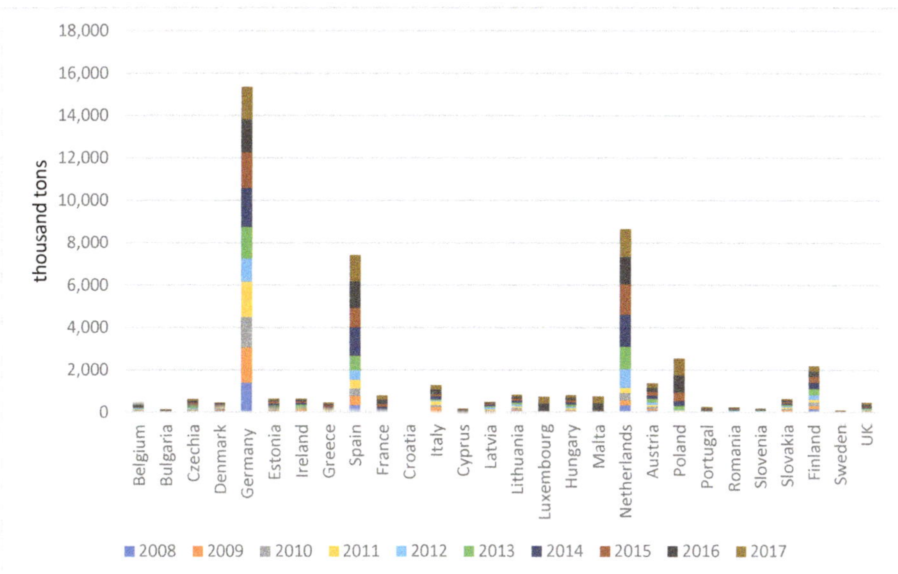

Figure 4. Biofuel production, in thousand tons, in the selected countries, between 2008 and 2017. Source: Eurostat [1].

Figure 4 reveals the fact that the countries with the highest biofuel production, from 2010 to 2016, were Germany, the Netherlands and Spain, while Sweden, Croatia and Bulgaria came last.

Resource productivity is computed as the quotient between gross domestic product (GDP) and domestic material consumption (DMC). DMC corresponds to the total amount of materials directly used by the economy of a country. It is defined as the annual quantity of raw materials extracted from the internal territory of the selected economy, minus all physical exports, plus all physical imports [1]. In Figure 5, we can see the resource productivity in EU countries.

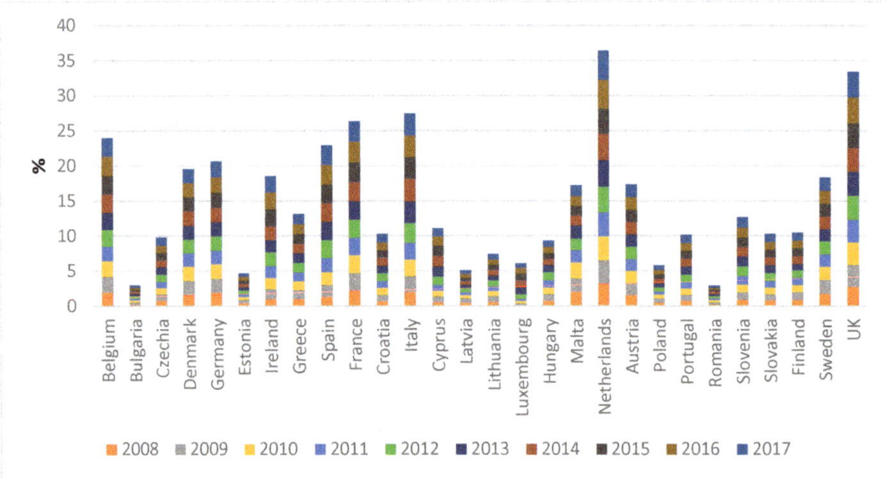

Figure 5. Resources productivity (%) at the EU level, between 2007 and 2017. Source: Eurostat [1].

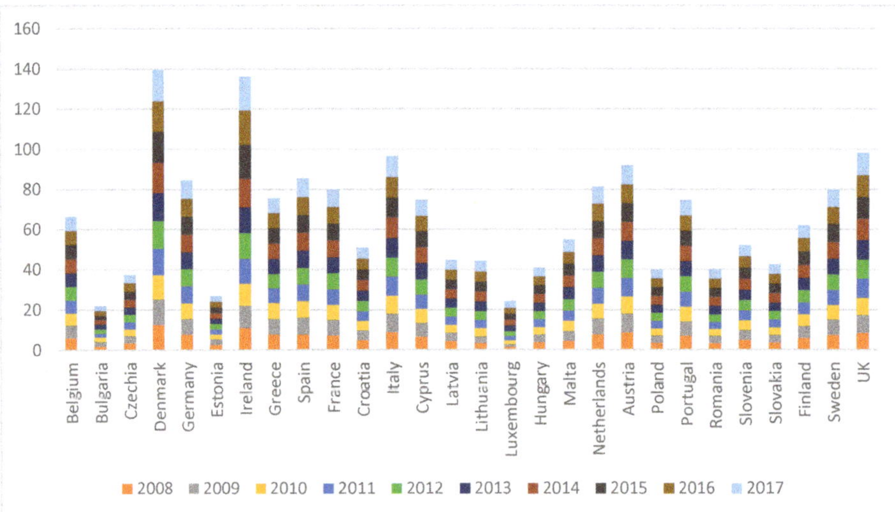

Figure 6. Bioenergy productivity (euro/kg) at the EU level, between 2008 and 2017. Source: Eurostat [1].

From the figure above, we can see that the Netherlands, UK and Italy were the top three countries from the EU with the highest level of the indicator 'resources productivity', from 2007 to 2017. At the same time, the countries with the lowest level of resources productivity were Estonia and Bulgaria.

The last indicator evaluated at the EU level is bioenergy productivity. This indicator results from the division of the GDP by the gross inland consumption of energy for a given calendar year [1]. It measures bioenergy productivity in terms of efficient consumption and provides a picture of the degree of decoupling of energy use from growth in GDP. The unit measure is euro/kg.

This graph reveals the fact that, from 2007 to 2016, Denmark, Ireland and UK were the top three countries regarding bioenergy productivity at the EU level. At the same time, the Czech Republic, Estonia and Bulgaria were the three countries with the lowest levels of bioenergy productivity.

This research paper is structured as following. Firstly, it highlights the macroeconomic key indicators that are relevant for CO_2 emissions at the EU level. Then, an evaluation of the panel data multiple linear regression model is conducted. Finally, the research hypotheses are presented and tested. Limitations of the study, further research and conclusions are summarized in the last section of the article.

2. Literature Review and Hypotheses Development

According to scientists and experts, traditional energy resources (crude oil or coal) will soon be exhausted. Furthermore, the experts at the Paris Agreement Conference of Parties (COP) declared that the fossil fuels age is over as such. On the other hand, the dependence on energy resources is still quite strong in most countries of the world, while the levels of CO_2 emissions are increasing constantly. Thus, actualizing the necessity for developing and increasing the share of renewable energy in the overall energy balance should be a goal for all EU countries in order to lower their CO_2 emissions. Additionally, this development priority corresponds with the Sustainable Development Goals (SDG) 2030, which have been accepted by the world's leading countries.

It should be noted that, according to the COP 21 Report, the countries had agreed "to undertake rapid reductions thereafter, in accordance with the best available science, so as to achieve a balance between anthropogenic emissions by sources and removals by sinks of greenhouse gases in the second half of this century, on the basis of equity and in the context of sustainable development and efforts to eradicate poverty" [2]. Moreover, they agreed to support, develop, and enlarge the share of renewable energy and to develop economies with zero net emissions as soon as possible. In practice, this means that the countries are going to increase their shares of renewable energy and are supposed to decrease their CO_2 emissions.

Previous research studies have analyzed the relationship between CO_2 emissions and renewable energy. Ben Aissa et al. [3] stated that renewable energy consumption had a positive and direct impact on CO_2 reduction for a sample of 11 African countries. Other studies argued that the main contributor of CO_2 emissions is the increasing levels of urbanization and population growth [4–6]. Kumar et al. [7] and Dietz et al. [8] concluded that renewable energy use has a positive impact on the decreasing levels of carbon dioxide emissions. Apergis and Payne [9] assessed the correlation between resources productivity and increasing levels of CO_2 emissions in a study of The Organization for Economic Cooperation and Development (OECD) countries, using a panel data analysis. Shafiei and Salim [10] examined EU countries, concluding that an increase in the use of biofuels and renewable energy would lead to a decrease in CO_2 levels.

Other research papers underlined that there is inequality and an asymmetric relation between poor and rich countries on CO_2 environmental impact [11,12]. The authors studied the effect of the consumption of biofuel energy on CO_2 emissions and concluded that the variation depends on country development in the world economic system. Moreover, they have investigated the relationship between renewable energy consumption, population growth and their impact on total CO_2 emission efficiency (CO_2 per GDP unit).

The relationship between renewables and a low-carbon society was considered by many researchers. It was demonstrated that there is a close link between the use of renewables and the reduction of CO_2 emissions [13,14]. The authors concluded that renewables have an extremely important role in a low-carbon society.

Moreover, while some researchers [15–17] argue that the use of biofuels and bioenergy have a strong impact on the reduction levels of CO_2, other economists [18–20] conclude that resources productivity and energy efficiency have a higher impact on CO_2 emissions. Nevertheless, while some authors [21–23] argued that bioenergy productivity and biofuel production have a direct and significant impact on decreasing the levels of CO_2 emissions, other researchers [24,25] concluded that population and urbanization levels have a significant and negative impact on decreasing the levels of CO_2 emissions. An assessment [24] of the European renewable energy source (RES) trajectory towards 2020, starting from historical values and through common scientific methods, laid down a new approach to evaluate RES performance in Europe. The proposed framework is based on three indicators: the share of energy from RESs in gross final energy consumption, RES primary production per capita and the gross final consumption of RES per capita. Other researchers [25] analyzed the financial issues that might prevent the investment decisions of green companies. Their conclusions indicate that effective policy interventions should ensure that objectives are orientated towards the long term with the aim of reducing the risks perceived by financial institutions in funding biomass producers. Based on a Fully Modified Ordinary Least Square (FMOLS) regression model analysis, Singh et al. [26] argue that renewable energy production is associated with a positive and statistically significant impact on economic growth in both developed and developing countries for the period 1995–2016. Starting with the analysis based on a Malaysian Case Study, Takeda et al. [27] showed that electricity from renewables has greater adverse impact on workers from the supply chain than the conventional electricity mix, in view of the social aspects countered.

In 1997, Kaya and Yokobory [28] introduced "The Kaya identity", which states that the total emission levels of the greenhouse gas carbon dioxide can be expressed as a product of four factors: human population, GDP per capita, energy intensity (per unit of GDP), and carbon intensity (emissions per unit of energy consumed). This method was used by many researchers. Wu et al. [29] used Kaya to decompose the contribution of potential driving forces on aviation CO_2 emissions. In another study [30], the authors focused their attention on the Shandong Province in China as an example to determine the drivers for the carbon density by using an extended Kaya identity and a logarithmic mean Divisia index model (LMDI) with two layers. They concluded that there are eight positive driving factors of carbon density during the period 2000–2015, including traffic congestion, land urbanization and seven negative driving factors, with reference to industrialization, energy intensity and economic structure. Nevertheless, the increasing levels of population and urbanization in recent decades generated high levels of CO_2 emissions. Moreover, Wu et al. [31] introduced an urbanization factor into the Kaya identity, and three simulations were conducted to forecast the carbon footprint and to explore the effects of the energy use paradigm shift policy. Based on the Kaya identity, increasing biomass energy reduces the energy CO_2 footprint and causes overall fossil CO_2 emissions to fall. The Kaya identity also states that population is an important factor of the increasing levels of CO_2 emissions. In this view, it is straight forward to assume that population causes CO_2 emissions. Other economists [32] argue that a shift to renewable energy sources reduces the sources of CO_2 emissions. Hence it is reasonable to assume that renewable energy is one of the causing factors of CO_2 reduction. Biofuels are also used in the transportation sector, a cause of high levels of CO_2 emissions. It is therefore reasonable to assume that one factor to decrease the levels of CO_2 emissions is the use of biofuels. According to Wang et al. [33], urbanization is an important factor in the growth of carbon emissions, as the city is a dense area of carbon emissions. Likewise, we could consider that urbanization is one of the causing factors of CO_2 emissions. Zha et al. [34] provide a methodology for decomposing the per capital CO_2 emissions into Kaya factors and two interaction terms. The authors demonstrate that resource productivity is one of the factors causing a decrease in CO_2 emissions. It is then reasonable to consider that resource productivity is one of the drivers that determines the reduction of CO_2 emissions.

All these studies confirm that, while urbanization and population growth could increase CO_2 emissions, renewables represent the drivers for the decrease in the levels of CO_2 emissions.

Taking into account the theoretical framework depicted in this section, the research hypotheses will be defined.

In order to analyze the impact of independent variables on the dependent variable, four statistical assumptions were formulated in Table 1. Since we have six independent variables in our model, we will test our model for multicollinearity, because some other factor, not included in our analysis, might be the cause of all studied factors.

Table 1. Research hypotheses of this study.

	Hypotheses
H_1	Renewable energy use at the EU level has a significant and strong impact on CO_2 emissions.
H_2	Biofuel production at the EU level has a significant and strong impact on CO_2 emissions.
H_3	Resources productivity has a significant impact on CO_2 emissions.
H_4	Bioenergy productivity is strongly correlated to the levels of CO_2 emissions.
H_5	Urbanization level in EU countries has a significant impact on CO_2 emissions.
H_6	Population level in EU countries has a significant impact on CO_2 emissions.

These statistical hypotheses will be tested and validated by a multiple linear panel data regression model, which will be described in the next section.

3. Research Method

3.1. Sample Description

In the econometric analysis, seven indicators were used—one dependent variable (CO_2 emissions) and six independent factors (renewable energy consumption, biofuel production, resources productivity, bioenergy productivity, level of urbanization and population). Data was collected from EUROSTAT, between 2008 and 2017.

3.2. Dependent and Independent Variables

A description of the dependent variable in the model (Y) and the six independent variables (X_1–X_6) is shown in Table 2.

Table 2. Descriptive statistics of variables in the model.

Variable	Name	Definition	Unit
(Y)	CO_2	The total CO_2 emissions in each EU country, measured in millions of tons	Millions of tons
(X_1)	Renewable	The rate of renewable energy in total energy consumed. This indicator represents the percentage (%) of renewable energy in total energy consumption at the EU level	Percentages (%)
(X_2)	Biofuels	Total production of biofuels in EU countries	Thousand tons
(X_3)	Resources	The quotient between gross domestic product (GDP) and domestic material consumption (DMC)	Percentages (%)
(X_4)	Bioenergy	This indicator results from the division of the GDP by the gross inland consumption of bioenergy for a given calendar year	Euro/kg
(X_5)	Urbanization	The percentage of urban population in the total population	Millions
(X_6)	Population	The total population in each EU country	Millions

3.3. Research Methodology

Starting with the empirical results as described, this research paper is focused on the following question: "What is the impact of the renewables on a low-carbon society at the EU level?". To answer this question, the author estimates which of the six independent factors, namely, renewable energy use, biofuel production, resources productivity, bioenergy productivity, population and urbanization, has a more significant impact on the dependent variable of the multiple linear regression model. As the research studies mentioned above, these independent variables are some of the main factors to describe the levels of CO_2 emissions. While the promotion of renewable energy is widely advocated as an effective solution to the mitigation of CO_2 emissions, increasing the quantities of biofuel production could lead to lowering CO_2 emissions. A biofuel is a fuel that is produced through contemporary processes from biomass. Biofuels could be used for transport as well as for heat and electricity. It is important to quantify the influence of each driver, based on the specific quantities defined (quantities of biofuels, as such). Resource productivity is the quantity of good or service (outcome) that is obtained through the expenditure of unit resource. Resource productivity is a key concept used in sustainability measurement in an attempt to decouple the direct connection between resource use and environmental degradation with an important impact on CO_2 emissions.

According to Croissant and Millo [35] and Baltagi [36], the F-test should be used to test the validity of the Pooled Model from the intended Fixed-Effects model against the Static Panel Data Models. To perform this test, unrestricted and restricted models are required.

$$\text{Restricted model}: Y_i = \alpha + X_i\beta_i + u_i,\ \text{(all intercepts are restricted to be the same)} \tag{1}$$

$$\text{Unrestricted model}: Y_i = \alpha_i + X_i\beta_i + u_i; H_0 : \alpha_i = \alpha; H_0 : \alpha_i \neq \alpha \tag{2}$$

where:

- Y_i = the dependent variable;
- X_i = independent variables;
- α_i, β_i = parametric coefficients;
- u_i = error term;
- $i = \overline{1, N}$.

If the null hypothesis is rejected; it will be $\alpha i \neq \alpha$. In such a case, a classical model is accepted, and a solution would be made by using the pooled data technique. Conversely, the Fixed-Effects model will be valid.

The Hausman test is performed to compare the Random-Effects and Fixed-Effects models. According to Wang et al. [37], random effects are preferred under the null hypothesis due to the higher efficiency.

- H_0: There is no correlation between independent variables and unit effects;
- H_1: There is a correlation between independent variables and unit effects.

Also, in order to make a choice between the Pooled Method and the Random Models, Lagrange Multiplier Breusch–Pagan Test is used [38]. The null and the alternative hypothesis that the variance of random effects is zero is as follows:

$$H_0 : \sigma_u^2 = 0; H_1 : \sigma_u^2 \neq 0,$$

where σ_u^2 is the variance of the Random-Effects model.

The results of the econometric analysis will be presented in the results section.

4. Results

A description of the dependent and independent variables used in the model; the mean, median and standard deviation are shown in Table 3. These measures of central tendency are indicators of how close the data points are to a normal distribution. In cases where the data has a standard normal distribution, the median and the mean values approximate each other [39]. From Table 3, we can see that for all variables in the model, the median and mean have close values. Hence, we could assume that all variables in the model are normally distributed.

Table 3. Descriptive statistics of variables in the model.

Variable *	Mean	Median	Standard Deviation	N
CO_2 (Y)	122.343	120.233	12.134	27
Renewable (X_1)	17.322	15.345	3.302	27
Biofuels (X_2)	234.654	230.645	56.563	27
Resources (X_3)	352.765	344.891	12.547	27
Bioenergy (X_4)	34.541	32.653	7.329	27
Urbanization (X_5)	23.524	26.344	5.347	27
Population (X_6)	543.8761	540.239	0.0987	27

* Y = CO_2 emissions—represent the total CO_2 emissions in each EU country; X_1 = Renewable—the rate of renewable energy in total energy consumed; X_2 = Biofuels—biofuel production in each EU member state; X_3 = Resources—represents resources productivity; X_4 = Bioenergy—represents the bioenergy productivity at the EU level; X_5 = Urbanization—the degree of urbanization in the total population; X_6 = Population—represents the total population (in millions) in each EU country. Source: Data analysis was performed by the author using EViews 11.0 (EViews, 2017).

The matrix of correlations was calculated to test the presence of multicollinearity among the independent variables used in the regression model. According to Weinberg and Carmeli [40], in a multiple regression model, there are no multicollinearity problems if the correlation coefficients among the independent variables are less than ±0.30. Since the correlation coefficients between the explanatory variables in Table 4 are smaller than ±0.30, we could conclude that there are no multicollinearity problems among the variables.

Table 4. The correlation matrix.

Variable	Y	X_1	X_2	X_3	X_4	X_5	X_6
Y	1						
X_1	0.687	1					
X_2	0.702	0.044	1				
X_3	0.545	0.088	0.053	1			
X_4	0.612	0.132	0.176	0.054	1		
X_5	0.785	0.129	0.080	0.072	0.105	1	
X_6	0.856	0.188	0.094	0.097	0.118	0.132	1

Source: Data analysis was performed by the author using EViews 11.0.

After reporting descriptive statistics for the variables used in the model, the Lagrange Multiplier (LM) Breusch–Pagan Test F-test and Hausman Test were performed to verify whether the method used in our analysis of the model in Equation (1) has random effects, fixed effects or pooled data.

The F test statistical results are shown in Table 5. The null hypothesis H_0 is accepted since the probability value (Prob. = 0.321) is greater than the threshold of 0.05. Hence, we conclude that the Fixed-Effects Model would not be suitable for our analysis.

Table 5. The Fixed-Effects F-Test.

F Statistics	4.16
Probability	0.321

The Hausman Test, Chi-square statistic and *p*-value are shown in Table 6.

Table 6. The Hausman Test.

Chi-Square Statistic	1.7982
Chi-Square Statistic Probability	0.8975

Since the *p*-value (Probability) is greater than the 0.05 threshold, we fail to reject the null hypothesis and conclude that there is a correlation between the independent variables and unit effects. Hence, the validity of the fixed model is rejected.

Now, to make a choice between the Pooled Method and the Random Models, the Lagrange Multiplier Breusch–Pagan Test will be used.

The values of the Breusch–Pagan Test are given in Table 7.

Table 7. The Random-Effects Test.

	Cross Section	Time	Both
Coefficients	28.18	46.432	87.95
Probability	0.091	0.756	0.064

Since all probability values (Probability) in the above table are less than the threshold value 0.05, we conclude that the H_0 hypothesis is accepted. Hence, we conclude that the Random-Effects Model would not be suitable for our analysis. Therefore, the pooling data techniques of the model in Equation (1) would be appropriate.

The regression equation used to test the four statistical hypotheses would be performed using the Pooled Least Square Method. This method will be used to estimate the impact of renewables on CO_2 emissions the EU level, between 2008 and 2017.

For the quantitative analysis, CO_2 emissions were considered as the dependent variable (y) influenced by a set of six independent factors (regressors), namely, the renewable energy rate (x_1), biofuel production (x_2), resources productivity (x_3), bioenergy productivity (x_4), urbanization (x_5) and population (x_6), as independent variables. Multiple linear regression analysis covered the following stages: the development of the regression model, estimating model parameters and checking the accuracy of the results.

Analyzing the levels of CO_2 emissions during 2008–2017 at the EU level, according to the independent variables, the following results were obtained for the multiple regression function using the multifactorial linear regression model (see Table 8):

Table 8. Impact of renewable energy, biofuel production, resource productivity, bioenergy productivity, urbanization and population on CO_2 emissions at the EU level.

Dependent Variable: CO_2
Method: Pooled least squares
Sample: 2008 2017
Total panel observations: 270
CO_2 = C(1) + C(2)*RENEWABLE + C(3)*BIOFUELS+ C(4)*RESOURCES + C(5)*BIOENERGY+C(6)*URBANIZATION+C(7)*POPULATION

	Coefficient	Std. Error	*t*-Statistic	Prob.
C	23.9335	91.346	3.12376	0.0092
RENEWABLE (X1)	−0.654523	1.543	4.243033	0.0098
BIOFUELS (X2)	−0.983504	1.762	4.762098	0.0153
RESOURCES (X3)	−0.567837	1.073	5.120943	0.0082
BIOENERGY (X4)	−0.805490	1.476	6.092085	0.0027
URBANIZATION (X5)	1.665434	1.814	6.165498	0.0090
POPULATION (X6)	1.734502	1.654	7.109345	0.0085
R-squared	0.778297	Mean dependent variables		7.21987
Adjusted R-squared	0.693918	S.D.[2] dependent var		0.80932
S.E.[1] of regression	0.098723	Akaike info criterion		1.98345
Sum squared residual	1.503963	Schwarz criterion		1.87403
Log likelihood	104.4508	Hannan–Quinn criterion		1.98765
Durbin–Watson stat	2.1174520			
Prob (F-statistic)	0.0000000			

[1] S.E. = standard error; [2] S.D. = standard deviation.

The results of the econometric analysis reveal that the model is valid, and all independent variables are significant for the model. Moreover, most of the variation of the dependent variable is explained by the model. The main result of the current paper is that renewable energy consumption, biofuel production, resources productivity and bioenergy productivity are positive and significant factors of CO_2 emissions at the EU level, while the level of urbanization and population have a negative and strong impact on CO_2 emissions in EU member states.

The negative coefficient of variable X1 reveals that the renewable energy variable has a negative and significant effect on CO_2 emission, and a one-unit increase in the rate of renewable energy in total energy consumed will lead to a decrease in CO_2 emission rates by 0.654, which is congruent with the findings achieved by [41]. Also, the negative coefficient of X2 means that biofuel production has a negative and strong impact on CO_2 emissions, and a one-unit increase in biofuel production will lead to a decrease in CO_2 by 0.983, which is in line with [42]. Moreover, the negative coefficient of X3 explains that resources productivity has a negative and strong effect on the decrease in CO_2 emissions, which confirms the study by [43]. The negative coefficient of X4 reveals that bioenergy productivity has a negative and significant effect on CO_2 emission. This indicates that a one-unit increase in bioenergy productivity will lead to a decrease in CO_2 emissions by 0.805, which confirms the work of Proskurina et al. [44]. Also, the positive coefficient of X5 means that urbanization has a positive and significant effect on CO_2 emissions. This indicates that a one-unit increase in the rate of urbanization will lead to an increase in CO_2 emissions rates by 1.665, which is incongruent with the findings of [45]. Finally, the positive coefficient of X6 in Table 8 reveals the fact that population has a positive and significant effect on CO_2 emission. This indicates that a one-unit increase in population will lead to an increase in CO_2 emission rates by 1.734. This result is in line with the work of [46].

Since the value of R-squared in Table 6 is 0.778, we conclude that 77.8% of the variability of the dependent variable is explained by the variation of the independent variables in the model. Moreover, the Durbin–Watson (DW) Test indicates that there are no autocorrelation problems between the explanatory variables in the model since the value of the statistical test is DW = 2.11, which is very close to 2, and leads to the conclusion that the errors are not auto-correlated. The inverse correlation between the renewables and carbon dioxide emissions is confirmed, while urbanization and population growth are proportional with increasing levels of carbon emissions.

Collinearity will be tested with the Variance Inflection Factor (VIF) test. The results are shown in Table 9.

Table 9. The Variance Inflection Factor (VIF) test for collinearity.

Variance Inflation Factors
Date: 9 May 2019 Time: 09:32
Sample: 2008 2017
Included observations: 270

Variable	Coefficient Variance	Uncentered VIF	Centered VIF
C		6.956	NA
RENEWABLE	1.543	2.508	1.348
BIOFUELS	1.762	2.876	1.876
RESOURCES	1.073	2.012	1.012
BIOENERGY	1.476	2.817	1.817
URBANIZATION	1.814	2.265	1.265
POPULATION	1.654	1.983	1.103

C = constant; Source: Data analysis was performed by the author using EViews 11.0.

Since all the VIF values corresponding to the independent variables are between 1 and 5, we could conclude that the model does not have collinearity problems.

From Table 8, we observe that the model estimation results are statistically significant at a significance level of 95% for all six explanatory variables in the model, as their corresponding *p*-values (Prob.) are smaller than the 0.05 threshold.

In Table 10 we could see the results of the validation of the statistical hypotheses.

Table 10. Validation of the statistical hypotheses.

Hypothesis	Validated (Yes/No)
H_1	Yes
H_2	Yes
H_3	Yes
H_4	Yes
H_5	Yes
H_6	Yes

Thus, according to the statistical analysis results, all four statistical assumptions were valid.

5. Discussion

In this section, we discuss the multiple linear factor analysis results using the Pooled Least Squares (PLS) method. The method was used in this study to make an estimation of the impact of the renewables on low carbon emissions at the EU level.

The relationship between the levels of CO_2 emissions and renewables has received attention in recent economic literature. Multiple linear regression model parameters used in this study were estimated by PLS, and the analysis was performed using EViews 11.0 software.

The multiple regression analysis concluded that the model was valid and correctly specified and the renewables were significant indicators of low carbon levels in all 27 EU countries, since the values of the estimated coefficients of the regression model were significantly different than zero and most of the variation of CO_2 emissions in EU countries was explained by the model. The results of the paper confirm recent studies of renewable energy impact on low carbon levels [47–53]. In addition, the novelty of this study resides in the fresh outlook taken for a set of 27 EU countries for the period 2008–2017, in order to assess the interaction between renewables and CO_2 emissions. Finally, the results of the regression model validate the statistical hypothesis, mainly related to the significant and strong effect of resources productivity on low carbon emissions, confirming the EU statement that a 30% increase in resource productivity by 2030 would lead to an increase in GDP by 1 percentage point [54]. These results are consistent with the study by Puigcerver-Peñalver [55], who developed a regression model for CO_2 emissions, which was partly explained by resources productivity and population growth.

The conclusions of our analysis were consistent with the work of Marques [56], who developed a multiple linear regression model to determine the factors of the low carbon levels of EU member states, partly explained by the levels of urbanization and renewable energy use. The results are also connected to other studies [57,58], which underline that an important step of achieving a low-carbon society is to increase the use of renewables. The authors argued that bioenergy productivity, resources productivity and renewable energy are important factors of low carbon levels and sustainable development.

The multiple regression analysis performed in this study demonstrates the impact of the independent factors, i.e., renewables, on the dependent levels of CO_2 emissions. As such, as a way of example, we conclude that resources productivity and renewable energy use play a greater role in terms of the impact of low carbon emissions compared to the impact of renewable energy on CO_2 emissions. Moreover, the Kaya identity helped us to determine a casualization between the independent factors and CO_2 emissions. It was shown that increasing biomass correlates with decreasing fossil CO_2. It therefore seems reasonable to assume that one of the driving forces behind decline in fossil CO_2 emissions has been increasing biomass usage.

6. Conclusions

The European Commission Report on environmental policy confirms Europe's commitment to lead global climate action and presents a vision that can lead to achieving net zero greenhouse gas emissions by 2050. In 2018, the EU adopted legislation aiming to reduce its greenhouse gas emissions by at least 40% by 2030, as compared to 1990. When the agreed EU legislation is fully implemented, the cut to EU emissions is estimated to reach approximately 45% by 2030.

Reducing the levels of CO_2 emissions requires constant and significant investments in the renewable energy infrastructure in order for EU countries to develop towards meeting the EU climate change objectives. For instance, the Nordic countries have implemented the "Circular Public Procurement in the Nordic Countries" (CIPRON), which is a process expected to provide conditions and criteria that can stimulate energy and material savings and close material loops, spread innovative solutions and create markets for clean solutions. Moreover, the Nordic countries have implemented alternative energy use with direct impact on lowering CO_2 emissions.

This paper contributes to the results of the scientific research on the evaluation of the benefits achieved by using renewables for a low-carbon society. Building a climate-friendly, low-carbon society and economy is a big challenge, but also a huge opportunity. Increasing the rates of renewable energy in total energy consumption at the EU level, the production of biofuels in all EU countries, and having better resources productivity and bioenergy productivity in all member states are the main factors of a low-carbon society.

This study could count for regional, local and national public authorities from all the EU member states involved in law making, as well as for companies, which could develop their business plans according to the predicted effects of reducing carbon dioxide emissions for their benefits.

This quantitative analysis was based on the data values of EU macroeconomic indicators over a period of 10 years and, therefore, the main limitation of this study is associated with the length of the time period used in the econometric research. Thus, future research should be conducted for longer time periods, which may reveal a better picture of the econometric model applied for the analyzed macroeconomic indicators.

To conclude, we observe that the econometric model on CO_2 emissions was valid and accurately specified, and that the factors of renewable energy, biofuel production, resources productivity and bioenergy productivity were significant factors of CO_2 emissions for the EU member states. This was due to the fact that these drivers registered significant values for the estimated coefficients, significantly different from zero, and that the model explained most of the variation in the CO_2 emissions of the EU member states. This paper adds to the recent studies of the impact of renewables on CO_2 emissions at the EU level [59–62].

Practical implications of government, private and civil society actors to develop low-carbon societies have gained increasing attention in the EU in recent years. While policy makers and a range of non-state actors have long championed the need for individual responses to climate change through shifts in attitudes and behavior, the past five years have witnessed an increasing emphasis on (area-based) communities as the means through which a low carbon transition should be achieved by the government-based programs, civil society involvement and grassroots schemes.

Funding: This research received no external funding.

Conflicts of Interest: The author declares no conflict of interest.

References

1. Eurostat. Available online: http://ec.europa.eu/eurostat (accessed on 30 June 2019).
2. COP 21 Report. 2015. Available online: https://www.gouvernement.fr/en/cop21 (accessed on 5 September 2019).
3. Aïssa, M.S.B.; Jebli, M.B.; Youssef, S.B. Output, renewable energy consumption and trade in Africa. *Energy Policy* **2014**, *66*, 11–18. [CrossRef]
4. Poumanyvong, P.; Kaneko, S. Does urbanization lead to less energy use and lower CO_2 emissions? *A cross-country analysis. Ecol. Econ.* **2010**, *70*, 434–444.
5. Zhang, C.; Lin, Y. Panel estimation for urbanization, energy consumption and CO_2 emissions: A regional analysis in China. *Energy Policy* **2012**, *49*, 488–498. [CrossRef]
6. Martínez-Zarzoso, I.; Maruotti, A. The impact of urbanization on CO_2 emissions: Evidence from developing countries. *Ecol. Econ.* **2011**, *70*, 1344–1353. [CrossRef]
7. Kumar, B.; Asadi, M.; Pisasale, D.; Sinha-Ray, S.; Rosen, B.A.; Haasch, R.; Abiade, J.; Yarin, A.L.; Salehi-Khojin, A. Renewable and metal-free carbon nanofibre catalysts for carbon dioxide reduction. *Nat. Commun.* **2013**, *4*, 2819. [CrossRef]
8. Dietz, M.E. Low impact development practices: A review of current research and recommendations for future directions. *Water Air Soil Pollut.* **2007**, *186*, 351–363. [CrossRef]
9. Apergis, N.; Payne, J.E. Renewable energy consumption and economic growth: Evidence from a panel of OECD countries. *Energy Policy* **2010**, *38*, 656–660. [CrossRef]
10. Shafiei, S.; Salim, R.A. Non-renewable and renewable energy consumption and CO_2 emissions in OECD countries: A comparative analysis. *Energy Policy* **2014**, *66*, 547–556. [CrossRef]
11. Heil, M.T.; Wodon, Q.T. Inequality in CO_2 emissions between poor and rich countries. *J. Environ. Dev.* **1997**, *6*, 426–452. [CrossRef]
12. Duro, J.A. Weighting vectors and international inequality changes in environmental indicators: An analysis of CO_2 per capita emissions and Kaya factors. *Energy Econ.* **2013**, *39*, 122–127. [CrossRef]
13. Dogan, E.; Seker, F. Determinants of CO_2 emissions in the European Union: The role of renewable and non-renewable energy. *Renew. Energy* **2016**, *94*, 429–439. [CrossRef]
14. Li, R.; Su, M. The Role of Natural Gas and Renewable Energy in Curbing Carbon Emission: Case Study of the United States. *Sustainability* **2017**, *9*, 600. [CrossRef]
15. Busu, M. Adopting Circular Economy at the European Union Level and Its Impact on Economic Growth. *Soc. Sci.* **2019**, *8*, 159. [CrossRef]
16. Gomiero, T. Are Biofuels an Effective and Viable Energy Strategy for Industrialized Societies? *A Reasoned Overview of Potentials and Limits. Sustainability* **2015**, *7*, 8491–8521.
17. Salman, B.; Ong, M.Y.; Nomanbhay, S.; Salema, A.A.; Sankaran, R.; Show, P.L. Thermal Analysis of Nigerian Oil Palm Biomass with Sachet-Water Plastic Wastes for Sustainable Production of Biofuel. *Processes* **2019**, *7*, 475. [CrossRef]

18. Hou, Y.; Iqbal, W.; Muhammad Shaikh, G.; Iqbal, N.; Ahmad Solangi, Y.; Fatima, A. Measuring Energy Efficiency and Environmental Performance: A Case of South Asia. *Processes* **2019**, *7*, 325. [CrossRef]
19. Hsiao, W.L.; Hu, J.L.; Hsiao, C.; Chang, M.C. Energy Efficiency of the Baltic Sea Countries: An Application of Stochastic Frontier Analysis. *Energies* **2019**, *12*, 104. [CrossRef]
20. Cucchiella, F.; D'Adamo, I.; Gastaldi, M. Future Trajectories of Renewable Energy Consumption in the European Union. *Resources* **2018**, *7*, 10. [CrossRef]
21. Lage, S.; Gojkovic, Z.; Funk, C.; Gentili, F.G. Algal Biomass from Wastewater and Flue Gases as a Source of Bioenergy. *Energies* **2018**, *11*, 664. [CrossRef]
22. Al-Esawi, N.; Al Qubeissi, M.; Kolodnytska, R. The Impact of Biodiesel Fuel on Ethanol/Diesel Blends. *Energies* **2019**, *12*, 1804. [CrossRef]
23. Banga, J.R.; Menolascina, F. Computational Methods Enabling Next-Generation Bioprocesses. *Processes* **2019**, *7*, 214. [CrossRef]
24. Busu, C.; Busu, M. How Does Renewable Energy Impact Carbon Emissions? An Eu Level Analysis. In Proceedings of the 11th International Management Conference "The Role of Management in the Economic Paradigm of the XXIst Century, Bucharest, Romania, 2–4 November 2017; pp. 502–510.
25. Busu, M. Assessment of the Impact of Bioenergy on Sustainable Economic Development. *Energies* **2019**, *12*, 578. [CrossRef]
26. Singh, N.; Nyuur, R.; Richmond, B. Renewable Energy Development as a Driver of Economic Growth: Evidence from Multivariate Panel Data Analysis. *Sustainability* **2019**, *11*, 2418. [CrossRef]
27. Takeda, S.; Keeley, A.R.; Sakurai, S.; Managi, S.; Norris, C.B. Are Renewables as Friendly to Humans as to the Environment?: A Social Life Cycle Assessment of Renewable Electricity. *Sustainability* **2019**, *11*, 1370. [CrossRef]
28. Kaya, Y.; Yokobori, K. (Eds.) *Environment, Energy, and Economy: Strategies for Sustainability*; United Nations University Press: Tokyo, Japan, 1997.
29. Wu, C.; Liao, M.; Liu, C. Acquiring and Geo-Visualizing Aviation Carbon Footprint among Urban Agglomerations in China. *Sustainability* **2019**, *11*, 4515. [CrossRef]
30. Dong, F.; Li, J.; Zhang, Y.-J.; Wang, Y. Drivers Analysis of CO_2 Emissions from the Perspective of Carbon Density: The Case of Shandong Province. *China Int. J. Env. Res. Public Health* **2018**, *15*, 1762. [CrossRef] [PubMed]
31. Wu, Y.; Luo, J.; Shen, L.; Skitmore, M. The Effects of an Energy Use Paradigm Shift on Carbon Emissions: A Simulation Study. *Sustainability* **2018**, *10*, 1639. [CrossRef]
32. Nakicenovic, N.; Alcamo, J.; Grubler, A.; Riahi, K.; Roehrl, R.A.; Rogner, H.H.; Victor, N. *Special Report on Emissions Scenarios (SRES), a Special Report of Working Group III of the Intergovernmental Panel on Climate Change*; Cambridge University Press: Cambridge, UK, 2000.
33. Wang, F.; Gao, M.; Liu, J.; Qin, Y.; Wang, G.; Fan, W.; Ji, L. An Empirical Study on the Impact Path of Urbanization to Carbon Emissions in the China Yangtze River Delta Urban Agglomeration. *Appl. Sci.* **2019**, *9*, 1116. [CrossRef]
34. Zha, D.L.; Zhou, D.Q. The Inequality about Provincial Energy Efficiency and Its Related CO_2 Emission: Decomposition Based on Kaya. *Syst. Eng.* **2007**, *11*, 65–71.
35. Croissant, Y.; Millo, G. Panel data econometrics in R: The plm package. *J. Stat. Softw.* **2008**, *27*, 1–43. [CrossRef]
36. Baltagi, B.H. Forecasting with panel data. *J. Forecast.* **2008**, *27*, 153–173. [CrossRef]
37. Wang, W.; Cao, W.J.; Chen, J.M. Dynamic Relation Analysis On Employment, Wages and Income Gap of Urban Residents In China For Panel Data Model As The Tool. In *Sustainable Development, Proceedings of the 2015 International Conference*; Zhu, L., Ouadha, A., Eds.; World Scientific Publications: Singapore, 2015; pp. 435–443.
38. Block, J. Long-Term Orientation of Family Firms: An Investigation of R&D Investments, Downsizing Practices, and Executive Pay. Wiesbaden: Gabler, 2007. Available online: https://link.springer.com/book/10.1007/978-3-8349-8412-8 (accessed on 18 March 2019).
39. Chang, N.-B. Economic and policy instrument analyses in support of the scrap tire recycling program in Taiwan. *J. Environ. Manag.* **2008**, *86*, 435–450. [CrossRef] [PubMed]
40. Weinberg, D.; Carmeli, A. Exploring the Antecedents of Relationship Commitment in an Import–Export Dyad. In *New Perspectives in International Business Research*; Emerald Group Publishing Limited: Bingley, UK, 2008; pp. 113–137.

41. Khan, M.W.A.; Panigrahi, S.K.; Almuniri, K.S.N.; Soomro, M.I.; Mirjat, N.H.; Alqaydi, E.S. Investigating the Dynamic Impact of CO_2 Emissions and Economic Growth on Renewable Energy Production: Evidence from FMOLS and DOLS Tests. *Processes* **2019**, *7*, 496. [CrossRef]
42. Lazarevic, D.; Martin, M. Life cycle assessment calculative practices in the Swedish biofuel sector: Governing biofuel sustainability by standards and numbers. *Bus. Strategy Environ.* **2018**, *27*, 1558–1568. [CrossRef]
43. Chen, S.; Yan, F.; Wu, R. Capital deepening, productivity promotion and CO_2 emission in China. *Financ. Trade Econ.* **2010**, *12*, 111–119.
44. Proskurina, S.; Junginger, M.; Heinimö, J.; Vakkilainen, E. Global biomass trade for energy–Part 1: Statistical and methodological considerations. *Biofuels Bioprod. Biorefining* **2019**, *13*, 358–370. [CrossRef]
45. Busu, M.; Nedelcu, A. Sustainability and Economic Performance of the companies in the renewable energy sector in Romania. *Sustainability* **2017**, *10*, 8. [CrossRef]
46. Dietz, T.; Rosa, E.A. Effects of population and affluence on CO_2 emissions. *Proc. Natl. Acad. Sci. USA* **1997**, *94*, 175–179. [CrossRef]
47. D'Adamo, I. The Profitability of Residential Photovoltaic Systems. A New Scheme of Subsidies Based on the Price of CO_2 in a Developed PV Market. *Soc. Sci.* **2018**, *7*, 148. [CrossRef]
48. Gámez-García, D.C.; Saldaña-Márquez, H.; Gómez-Soberón, J.M.; Arredondo-Rea, S.P.; Gómez-Soberón, M.C.; Corral-Higuera, R. Environmental Challenges in the Residential Sector: Life Cycle Assessment of Mexican Social Housing. *Energies* **2019**, *12*, 2837. [CrossRef]
49. Kircher, M. Bioeconomy: Markets, Implications, and Investment Opportunities. *Economies* **2019**, *7*, 73. [CrossRef]
50. Mengal, A.; Mirjat, N.H.; Walasai, G.D.; Khatri, S.A.; Harijan, K.; Uqaili, M.A. Modeling of Future Electricity Generation and Emissions Assessment for Pakistan. *Processes* **2019**, *7*, 212. [CrossRef]
51. D'Adamo, I.; Rosa, P. Current state of renewable energies performances in the European Union: A new reference framework. *Energy Convers. Manag.* **2016**, *121*, 84–92. [CrossRef]
52. Falcone, P.M.; Sica, E. Assessing the opportunities and challenges of green finance in Italy: An analysis of the biomass production sector. *Sustainability* **2019**, *11*, 517. [CrossRef]
53. da Graça Carvalho, M.; Bonifacio, M.; Dechamps, P. Building a low carbon society. *Energy* **2011**, *36*, 1842–1847. [CrossRef]
54. Biber-Freudenberger, L.; Basukala, A.; Bruckner, M.; Börner, J. Sustainability performance of national bio-economies. *Sustainability* **2018**, *10*, 2705. [CrossRef]
55. Puigcerver-Peñalver, M.C. The impact of structural funds policy on European regions growth. A theoretical and empirical approach. *Eur. J. Comp. Econ.* **2007**, *4*, 179–208.
56. Marques, A.C.; Fuinhas, J.A.; Manso, J.P. Motivations driving renewable energy in European countries: A panel data approach. *Energy Policy* **2010**, *38*, 6877–6885. [CrossRef]
57. Roman, A.-G.; Mocanu, M.; Hoinaru, R. Disclosure Style and Its Determinants in Integrated Reports. *Sustainability* **2019**, *11*, 1960. [CrossRef]
58. EU. Regulation (EC) No 2150/2002 of the European Parliament and the Council on Waste Statistics. 2002. Available online: http://www.kluwerlawonline.com/abstract.php?id=EELR2003019 (accessed on 23 December 2018).
59. Dogan, E.; Seker, F. The influence of real output, renewable and non-renewable energy, trade and financial development on carbon emissions in the top renewable energy countries. *Renew. Sustain. Energy Rev.* **2016**, *60*, 1074–1085. [CrossRef]
60. Karmellos, M.; Kopidou, D.; Diakoulaki, D. A decomposition analysis of the driving factors of CO_2 (Carbon dioxide) emissions from the power sector in the European Union countries. *Energy* **2016**, *94*, 680–692. [CrossRef]
61. Kök, A.G.; Shang, K.; Yücel, Ş. Impact of electricity pricing policies on renewable energy investments and carbon emissions. *Manag. Sci.* **2016**, *64*, 131–148. [CrossRef]
62. Bento, J.P.C.; Moutinho, V. CO_2 emissions, non-renewable and renewable electricity production, economic growth, and international trade in Italy. *Renew. Sustain. Energy Rev.* **2016**, *55*, 142–155. [CrossRef]

sustainability

MDPI

Article

The Role of Public Participation in Environmental Governance: Empirical Evidence from China

Jin Guo * and Junhong Bai

School of Business, Nanjing Normal University, Nanjing 210023, China
* Correspondence: guojin0901@njnu.edu.cn; Tel.: +86-025-8589-8095

Received: 22 July 2019; Accepted: 26 August 2019; Published: 28 August 2019

Abstract: As an essential stakeholder of environmental resources, the public has become the third force which assists in promoting environmental governance, together with local governments and polluting enterprises. In this paper, we construct a mediation model and a 2SLS (Two Stage Least Square) model to illustrate the role of public participation based on inter-provincial panel data of China from 2011 to 2015. The results indicate that the advantages of handling informational asymmetry and enhancing social supervision are the two logical starting points of involving public participation in environmental governance. As the public has no executive power, they can participate in environmental governance in an indirect way by lobbying local governments' environmental enforcement of polluting enterprises. In addition, their deterrent of polluting enterprises can also generate effects similar to local governments' environmental enforcement, and such a deterrent will help promote environmental governance directly. At the present time in China, the effects of public participation in environmental governance are mainly reflected in the form of back-end governance, while the effects of front-end governance are not remarkable enough. This research is of great significance in perfecting China's environmental governance system by means of arousing and expanding the public's rights to participate in environmental governance.

Keywords: public participation; environmental governance; information asymmetry; social supervision; back-end governance; front-end governance; Chinese case

1. Introduction

Environmental problems are troubling the sustainable economic development of the whole world. Following the theory of public economics, government intervention serves as an appropriate way to avoid a "tragedy of the commons" in the environmental area caused by market failure. Therefore, a kind of top-down environmental governance system led by the government and accompanied by the participation of polluting enterprises has been established in many countries [1,2]. However, the effects of this practice in many regions are far from satisfactory. Instead, this authoritarian environmentalism is suffering from a low efficiency caused by government failure [3,4]. Environmental problems are typically complex, and have an effect on multiple actors and agencies. Therefore, it is necessary to clarify other stakeholders' involvement so as to rebuild the environmental governance system [5]. An optional and widely mentioned stakeholder is the public [5–8].

The industrial revolution has not only brought great progress to human society, but also brought increasingly severe environmental pollution problems. Thereupon, the practices of public participation in environmental governance are staged in many countries. Here are some typical cases: During the four days from December 5 to December 8 in 1952, the Great Smog of London caused thousands of people to suffer from lung diseases or even die. After that, the public's environmental awareness played a leading role in the air pollution control campaign. Finally, the promulgation of the Clean Air Act in 1956 marked that the residents' supervision of polluting enterprises had obtained a formal legal status [9]. In the 1960s, Japan's industrialization triggered serious environmental pollution, which brought about various public diseases, such as mercury poisoning and asthma. The affected masses launched large-scale protest marches and legal proceedings, and even spontaneously established civil organizations to oppose polluting enterprises and lobby local governments. Eventually, the 64th interim parliament, also known as the congress on public diseases, was convened in 1970 and a series of laws and regulations were issued to put restrictions on the behaviors of enterprises. In the year of 1962, a book titled "Silent Spring" written by Rachel Carson was published in America and aroused an enormous public response. On 22 April 1970, an environmental protection parade involving 20 million citizens was regarded as the prologue of public participation in environmental governance in America, and later, this day was celebrated worldwide as Earth Day [10].

After China's reform and opening-up in 1978, more emphasis was put on government-oriented regulations concerning environmental governance [11,12]. However, this situation is changing with the awakening of its people's environmental consciousness. In 2011, a tropical storm caused a dam break in a chemical industry park in the city of Dalian, leading to pollution of the p-Xylene. A few days later, a large-scale demonstration broke out, which forced the relocation of this chemical industry park [13]. In 2012, in protest against a sewage disposal project that was dumping wastewater into the sea, a public petition broke out in the city of Nantong, which forced the local government to permanently cancel this kind of sewage disposal project [14]. In response to the public's enthusiasm, the Chinese government has also come to recognize the considerable role of public participation in environmental governance. In 2014, China's newly revised environmental protection law was promulgated, and it clearly pointed to setting up a litigation system for public interest in environmental protection. According to this litigation system, the Supreme People's Court of China had tried 1635 environmental public interest lawsuits by the end of 2017 [15]. In 2015, its Ministry of Ecology and Environment also promulgated a politic document titled "Measures for Public Participation in Environmental Protection", aimed at protecting the rights of public participation in environmental governance. Two years later, in the report of the 19th National Congress of the Communist Party of China, its state leaders pronounced the construction of a multi-agent environmental governance system with the participation of all stakeholders, including local governments, enterprises, social organizations, and the public [16].

According to the statements above, it is explicitly shown that public participation functions as an indispensable force in environmental governance. However, there are still many questions to answer. Firstly, as the public has no executive power, what are the logical starting points and paths of public participation in environmental governance? Secondly, as there are great debates concerning the consequences of public participation [6], how can we effectively evaluate its effects in environmental governance? In order to respond to these questions, this paper illustrates the role of public participation by constructing a mediation model and a Two Stage Least Square (2SLS) model based on inter-provincial panel data of China from 2011 to 2015.

The structure of this paper is as follows. Section 2 briefly reviews previous studies. Section 3 describes the theoretical foundation and path hypotheses. Section 4 explains the empirical strategy and data. Section 5 carries out empirical analyses. Section 6 presents the conclusions. Section 7 provides discussions for policy design.

2. Literature Review

2.1. Concept and Developing Stages of Public Participation

Public participation in governance covers either the direct or indirect involvement of stakeholders in decision-making of policies, plans, or programs that appeal to them [17]. Its development has gone through two stages, including the stage of passive participation and the stage of active participation. To some extent, the public's passive participation means voting with their feet. Tiebout [18] held the view that the public could express their dissatisfaction with local public services by migration to choose a better living environment. Banzhaf and Walsh [19] provided strong empirical support for the notion that households voted with their feet in response to changes in environmental quality. In fact, passive participation is a kind of threaten-to-leave mechanism, which has played a central role in the theory of local public affairs for centuries.

With the rise of democracy, Hirschman [20] proposed another form of public participation by means of petition and protest, namely, voting with their hands. The public's active participation is functioning as a major part of the environmental justice movement [21]. Compared with the threaten-to-leave mechanism, this appealing mechanism can contribute to similar governance effects. More importantly, through active participation, the public can transfer the negative externality of environmental pollution to polluting enterprises, instead of bearing it by themselves.

2.2. Advantages and Challenges of Public Participation

A large number of theoretical studies have emerged to elaborate the multiple advantages of involving public participation in environmental governance, such as improving the understanding of environmental events [22,23], enhancing social cohesion [24,25], and advancing the rationality and quality of decision-making [26,27]. Kanu et al. [28] argued that greater attention to public participation during the Environmental Impact Assessment (EIA) process can lead to the formulation of projects that deliver more social benefits, fewer environmental costs, and greater economic and financial benefits. Chen and Han [29] claimed that public participation could enhance the public's environmental awareness, mobilize multiple forces to reconcile the conflicts among multiple interest groups, supervise corporate environmental behavior, and overcome the shortcomings of government unilateral decision-making. In short, the involvement of public participation is beneficial to enhancing environmental governance's effectiveness by improving the quality of decisions and perfecting their implementation [30–32].

There are also some case studies supporting the success of public participation in environmental governance. Based on the thematic reports and policy recommendations of the China Council for International Cooperation on Environment (CCICED), Enserink and Koppenjan [33] verified the correlation between environmental governance and public participation, indicating that public participation would bring about a sustainable urbanization process. By citing a case in Poland, Cent et al. [34] reached a conclusion similar to Enserink and Koppenjan [33]. Based on 239 typical cases around the world, Beierle [31] demonstrated that public participation could not only improve environmental policy, but also played an important educational role in helping resolve the conflicts and mistrust related to environmental issues. By studying three energy and natural resource management cases (i.e., sustainable energy systems in Austria, energy transition in Southeast England, and sustainable management of the Urdaibai River Basin in Northern Spain), Garmendia and Stagl [22] presented the framework of public participation for sustainability and social learning. Using the data from a survey administered to 215 stakeholder groups worldwide and separately, 69 case studies of specific stakeholder engagement, Akhmouch and Clavreul [35] shared the experiences and lessons that had emerged from engaging stakeholders in the OECD (Organization for Economic Co-operation and Development) Water Governance Initiative. By reviewing the motivations, purposes, designs, and outcomes of public engagement in climate change policy and water resource management in Alberta, Canada, Adkin et al. [36] pointed out that political leadership and the interactions between civil society actors were shown to be important to promote environmental governance.

Public participation in environmental governance also faces many challenges. Fischer and Young [37] pointed out that a lack of expertise prevented the public from effectively participating in the debate on environmental governance decision-making. As a result, their opinions would be over ruled by existing privileges and groups [38,39]. Due to the lack of a systematic approach and an inadequate public administration system, Marzuki [40] also claimed that the public participation process was sometimes threatened by bureaucratic constraints, which contributed to the exclusion of the public from the process of participatory governance. Fung [41] listed three challenges for successful participatory governance: the absence of systematic leadership, the lack of a popular or elite consensus, and the limited scope and power of participatory innovations. Yakubu [42] insisted that successfully achieving public participation goals relied on an equitable process, but it faced many barriers, such as a lack of financial resources and participation skills.

2.3. Opposite Views of Involving Public Participation

During the past decades, the governance of environmental problems has evolved to cover a wider range of stakeholders in more extensive open discussions. However, there have also been great debates concerning the consequences of public participation [6], and there have been signs that the participatory agenda has started to lose its momentum and justification because of the disappointment of actual achievements [43]. From an empirical perspective, Newig and Fritsch [27] and Drazkiewicz et al. [44] pointed out that more effective policy-making cannot be guaranteed with the involvement of public participation, which might even lead to inferior decisions and poor implementations when citizens without professional knowledge or experience are involved. Wang and Di [45] carried out a survey covering 85 townships and interviews with 151 township leaders in China, whose statistical results showed that no significant improvement was seen in environmental quality with the involvement of public participation. He et al. [46] used panel data in China to test the relationships between external pressures and corporate environmental behaviors, but the results did not confirm that social pressure was a statistically significant source of environmental improvement. Fung [41] evaluated the three potential values of public participation to advance democratic governance (i.e., effectiveness, legitimacy, and social justice). Nevertheless, the results did not exhibit an obvious effect of public participation. Based on panel data of 31 Chinese provinces from 2004 to 2015, Wu et al. [47] investigated the impact of public participation on environmental performance, showing that environmental petitions were significantly correlated with environmental pollutants, but the conclusions were not robust.

In response to the inconsistency between theoretical studies and empirical studies, some scholars have provided explanations for the unremarkable effects of public participation in environmental governance. Webler and Tuler [7] revealed that there might have been different perspectives as to what was viewed as appropriate, indicating that limited agreements and strong differences in opinions caused huge obstacles to the efforts of achieving social justice through public participation. According to interviews with professionals involved in participation in environmental governance, Wesselink et al. [43] also found that differences and potential conflicts had restricted the development of public participation. Although public participation could be used as an important goal in formulating responses to the risks of environmental pollution, Few et al. [48] still argued that there would be fundamental challenges to be faced in its practice, many of which were related to power. Eden [49] pointed out that the scientific construction of environmental issues often meant that such participation in policy-making was difficult when the public was not considered as scientifically "expert".

It can be seen that theoretical studies and some case studies both support the effectiveness of public participation in environmental governance, while the findings of many empirical studies have failed to prove its success. That is to say, the methodology of empirical studies may not be applicable enough. By introducing a mediation model and a 2SLS model to modify the methodology, this paper has confirmed the role of public participation with empirical evidence from China. The contributions of this paper lie in the following aspects: firstly, we expound the theoretical logic of involving public participation in environmental governance by analyzing its advantages of handling informational asymmetry and enhancing social supervision; secondly, the public's indirect participation path and direct participation path are proposed and examined by constructing a mediation model; thirdly, the endogeneity bias is alleviated by choosing public participation's instrumental variables to carry out a 2SLS regression; and fourthly, we further classify public participation into Complaints and Proposals to discuss their heterogeneity.

3. Theoretical Foundation and Path Hypotheses

3.1. Theoretical Foundation

3.1.1. Solving Information Asymmetry

Enterprises' discharge of industrial pollutants is the primary cause of environmental pollution [50,51]. However, enterprises' polluting behaviors are usually concealed, such as late-night blowdown, underground blowdown, and trans-regional blowdown [52]. Despite the installation of devices to dispose industrial pollutants, they are just used for dealing with the government's environmental inspections, which have also been constantly reported by news media [53,54]. Although new environmental monitoring methods, such as big data, drones, and remote control systems, have been piloted in some areas [47,55], regular inspections and sudden inspections remain the two major approaches for local governments to obtain enterprises' discharge information [56]. However, in practice, regular inspections tend to be formalistic, resulting in inadequate substantial deterrent effects on polluting enterprises, while the high cost of sudden inspections restrains both the frequency and the scope of monitoring.

In view of these issues, it is difficult for local governments to obtain real-time information on enterprises' emissions. Severe information asymmetry arises between polluting enterprises and local governments [57], revealing the first defect in the top-down environmental governance system [58].

Public participation has multiple advantages in dealing with information asymmetry [59], and therefore, public participation will function as an optimal means to make up for this defect for the following reasons [60]. Firstly, compared with the limited members in local governments' environmental protection department, public participation involves a much broader mass base. Secondly, in contrast to the high cost of local governments' monitoring, public participation can operate at almost zero cost. Monitoring polluting enterprises does not have to be the public's intentional or systematic behavior, but instead, it can be viewed as an incidental part of their daily life. Thirdly, in comparison to the hysteresis of local governments' monitoring, public participation presents better timeliness, which can even prevent pollution before the outbreak of environmental problems.

Based on the above statements, we argue that the first logical starting point of involving public participation in environmental governance is that it can effectively deal with the problem of informational asymmetry between polluting enterprises and local governments [58].

3.1.2. Improving Social Supervision

There are three supervision forms of environmental governance, namely administrative supervision by local governments, judicial supervision by judiciary authorities, and social supervision by the public. As a kind of authoritarian environmentalism, the top-down environmental governance system has to rely on administrative supervision.

However, the administrative supervision also faces government failure. For example, in China, the assessment and promotion system for local officials is mainly based on indicators related to GDP, and consequently, the promotion needs of local officials are likely to overlap with the profit demand of polluting enterprises [61]. As a result, this government failure may result in institutional rent-seeking and collusion between polluting enterprises and local governments and weaken the effectiveness of local governments' administrative supervision, revealing another defect in the top-down environmental governance system [56].

Making up for this defect depends on social supervision, which mainly originates in public participation [62]. Compared with local governments' administrative supervision, social supervision by the public has the following advantages. Firstly, social supervision is characterized by external monitoring. Therefore, public participation can function as an external force to break the collusion between local governments and polluting enterprises [63]. Secondly, social supervision is characterized by numerous participants and multiple channels, so that polluting enterprises are unable to avoid supervision by rent-seeking or cutting off the diffusion of public opinions [24]. Thirdly, social supervision can permanently keep polluting enterprises under the high pressure of environmental protection [22].

Based on the above statements, we argue that the second logical starting point of involving public participation in environmental governance is that it can effectively improve social supervision, which can be used as a necessary supplement for the administrative supervision of local governments [64].

3.2. Path Hypotheses

3.2.1. Indirect Path Relies on Local Governments' Environmental Enforcement

Owing to the advantages of handling informational asymmetry and enhancing social supervision, public participation has consolidated its theoretical foundation in environmental governance. However, it should be noted that as the public does not have any executive power, public participation may not directly bring about real constraints on polluting enterprises.

Fortunately, in practice, polluting enterprises still pay much attention to public opinions. This is because the public can lobby local governments' attention by disclosing the information of enterprises' polluting behaviors. Under the pressure of public opinion, local governments will impose severe environmental enforcement on polluting enterprises. Therefore, we propose the first path hypothesis of public participation in environmental governance and we will prove it using empirical evidence in Section 5.

Hypothesis 1: As the public does not have any executive power, they can participate in environmental governance in an indirect way by lobbying local governments' environmental enforcement of polluting enterprises.

3.2.2. Direct Path Relies on Deterring Enterprises from Pollution

Meanwhile, we also argue that local governments' value should be reflected not only in its real environmental enforcement, but also in its potential enforcement capability. In other words, polluting enterprises are well aware that once their polluting behaviors are exposed by the public, they are bound to be punished by local governments' severe environmental enforcement. In that case, polluting enterprises will optimize their producing behaviors in advance so as to prevent the occurrence of these predictable punishments. Therefore, we propose the second path hypothesis of public participation in environmental governance and we will prove it using empirical evidence in Section 5.

Hypothesis 2: Under the premise of effective local governments, public participation's deterrent of polluting enterprises can also generate effects similar to local governments' environmental enforcement, which will then promote environmental governance directly.

Based on the above theoretical foundation and path hypotheses, the framework of public participation in environmental governance is plotted in Figure 1, from which we can clearly see modification to the top-down environmental governance system by public participation.

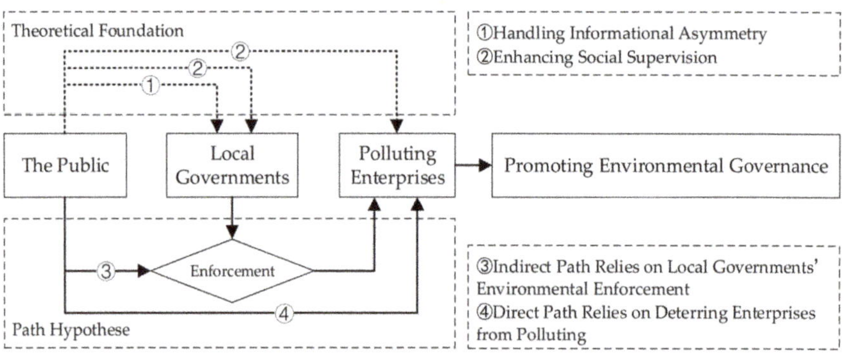

Figure 1. The framework of public participation in environmental governance.

4. Empirical Strategy and Data

4.1. Empirical Strategy

4.1.1. Benchmark Model

To demonstrate the effects of public participation in environmental governance, we need to begin with a benchmark model. The regression is given by the following:

$$\ln(pollution_{it}) = \alpha + \beta \ln(public_{it}) + \sum \Upsilon \boldsymbol{X} + \lambda_i + \eta_t + \varepsilon_{it} \quad (1)$$

where $pollution_{it}$ denotes the level of environmental pollution in province i at time t, $public_{it}$ denotes the level of public participation, $\boldsymbol{X}$ refers to a set of control variables, λ_i is the province dummy, η_t is the time dummy, and ε_{it} is an error term. The logarithm of all variables is applied to alleviate heteroscedasticity and nonlinearity.

Parameter β captures the elasticity of public participation to environmental pollution, which is expected to be significantly negative, indicating that public participation can reduce environmental pollution and improve environmental governance.

The basic formula to quantify $pollution_{it}$ is given by the following:

$$pollution_{t,j} = \sum\nolimits_{j=1,2,3} \frac{pollutant_{it}^{j}}{\sum_{j=1}^{j=30} pollutant_{it}^{j}} \Big/ 3 \quad (2)$$

where $j = 1, 2, 3$, denotes the three major industrial pollutants, i.e., industrial wastewater, industrial waste gas, and industrial waste residue. It has to be noted that the three pollutants are weighed by the industrial added value to avoid overestimating parameter β in heavily industrialized provinces.

4.1.2. Two Sub-Types of Public Participation

It is obvious that there are two forms for the public to create a better environment, which are Complaints and Proposals. The difference between them is that the former focuses on the back-end governance of erupted environmental issues, while the latter focuses on the front-end governance of pollution threats that have not yet erupted.

In order to shed light on the heterogeneity between the two sub-types of public participation, Equation (1) can be reconstructed as follows:

$$\ln(pollution_{it}) = \alpha + \beta_1 \ln(complaint_{it}) + \beta_2 \ln(proposal_{it}) + \sum \Upsilon \boldsymbol{X} + \lambda_i + \eta_t + \varepsilon_{it} \quad (3)$$

Parameters β_1 and β_2 capture the heterogeneous effects of environmental governance between Complaints and Proposals.

4.1.3. Local Governments' Mediation Effect

In Section 3.2, we pointed out that the public can participate in environmental governance in an indirect path by lobbying local governments' environmental enforcement of polluting enterprises. In order to verify this hypothesis, we take local governments' environmental enforcement as a path variable and the mediation model is constructed as follows:

$$\ln(pollution_{it}) = \alpha + \beta' \ln(public_{it}) + \rho \ln(government_{it}) + \sum \Upsilon \boldsymbol{X} + \lambda_i + \eta_t + \varepsilon_{it} \quad (4)$$

where $government_{it}$ denotes the level of local governments' environmental enforcement in province i at time t, and parameter ρ captures its impact on environmental pollution. Parameter β' captures the new elasticity of public participation to environmental pollution after the path variable is added to the model.

The mediation model has been widely adopted in psychological research [65]. Moreover, due to its good performance in analyzing functional routes between economic variables, the mediation model has also been applied to recent economic studies [66,67]. In this paper, the variation between parameter β' and parameter β is taken into account. If the absolute value of parameter β' decreases after the addition of the path variable, i.e., $|\beta'| < |\beta|$, and parameter ρ is also significantly negative, it indicates that the public relies on local governments' environmental enforcement to participate in environmental governance.

In fact, the mediation effect of the path variable in Equation (4) is the sharing of public participation's effect in Equation (1). Therefore, if parameter β' still passes the significance test after the addition of the path variable, it means that local governments' environmental enforcement cannot completely replace the effect of public participation, which suggests that public participation can also participate in environmental governance without lobbying local governments' environmental enforcement. As mentioned in Hypothesis 2, the effect of the deterrent of public participation on polluting enterprises is also likely to promote environmental governance directly.

In addition, to verify the mediation effect, it is also necessary to examine the relationship between public participation and local governments' environmental enforcement by Equation (5).

$$\ln(government_{it}) = \alpha + \delta \ln(public_{it}) + \sum \boldsymbol{\Phi Z} + \lambda_i + \eta_t + \varepsilon_{it} \tag{5}$$

Parameter δ should be significantly positive, indicating that a higher level of public participation tends to cause harsher environmental enforcement by local governments.

4.1.4. Instrumental Variables to Alleviate Endogeneity Bias

Heavy pollution may trigger the public's stronger willingness to participate in environmental governance. In consequence, there may be a bidirectional causality between public participation and environmental pollution. Meanwhile, as public participation is an abstract concept with difficulties in quantification, measurement errors are inevitable in public participation. Taking these problems into consideration, we adopt instrumental variables (IV) to alleviate endogeneity bias.

Since public participation has been sub-divided into Complaints and Proposals, we choose the level of residents' education as the instrumental variable for Complaints, and choose the number of each province's National People's Congress (NPC) deputies as the instrumental variable for Proposals. The two instrumental variables are selected on the basis of the following reasons. Firstly, residents with a higher education tend to pay more attention to environmental quality and have a better sense of social responsibility to prevent enterprises from polluting the environment. The National People's Congress is a landmark for the public to make proposals to governments. Therefore, the two instrumental variables satisfy the correlation hypotheses with the endogenous variables. Secondly, there is no direct causal relationship between residents' education level and industrial pollutants. The number of each province's NPC deputies is distributed based on the population size, ethnic groups, and genders, as well as some other demographic characteristics. Therefore, the two instrumental variables satisfy the exogenous hypotheses with the explained variable.

Based on the two instrumental variables, a Two Stage Least Square (2SLS) model is constructed as follows:

$$first\ stage:\ \ln(public_{it}) = \alpha + \theta_1 \ln(education_{it}) + \theta_2 \ln(deputy_{it}) + \varepsilon_{it} \tag{6}$$

$$second\ stage:\ \ln(pollution_{it}) = \alpha + \beta'' \ln(\widehat{public_{it}}) + + \sum \boldsymbol{\Upsilon X} + \lambda_i + \eta_t + \varepsilon_{it} \tag{7}$$

where $education_{it}$ denotes the level of residents' education and $deputy_{it}$ denotes the number of each province's NPC deputies. In the first stage, the regressions of the two instrumental variables to the endogenous variables are carried out, in which the fitted values of public participation are obtained, i.e., $\widehat{public_{it}}$. In the second stage, the fitted values of public participation are employed to conduct the regression to environmental pollution. Parameter β'' captures the amendatory impact of public participation on environmental pollution by alleviating endogeneity bias.

4.2. Data

4.2.1. Public Participation

Data concerning public participation among China's 30 provinces has been collected and kept by the Ministry of Ecology and Environment (MEE) in the China Environmental Yearbook [68]. In this paper, five indicators are selected to measure the level of public participation in each province. Respectively, they are complaints by telephone and the Internet, accusation letters, petitions, proposals from the NPC, and proposals from the CPPCC.

Specifically, the level of each province's public participation is measured by the sum of all the five indicators. In terms of the two sub-types of public participation, the sum of the first three indicators is used to measure Complaints and the sum of the last two indicators is used to measure Proposals. It has to be noted that the five indicators are weighed by their population in each province to avoid the overestimation of small provinces.

The year of 2011 is set as the starting year, because in the previous years, complaints from the Internet were not included in the China Environmental Yearbook [68]. However, at present, the Internet has become an increasingly important channel for the public to participate in environmental governance.

4.2.2. Environmental Pollution

Data concerning the three industrial pollutants (i.e., wastewater, waste gas, and waste residue) is extracted from the database of the Institute of Public and Environmental Affairs (IPE), which is a non-profit environmental research organization registered in Beijing, China. This created a database of environmental information since 2006. The basic formula employed to quantify each province's environmental pollution is given by Equation (2) in Section 4.1.1.

4.2.3. Path Variable, Instrumental Variables, and Control Variables

As for the path variable, the proportion of enterprises subject to environmental penalties is used to measure the level of local governments' environmental enforcement. The records of enterprises' environmental penalties are extracted from the IPE Database.

As for the two instrumental variables, the ratio of residents with a college diploma or above to the population aged 6 or above is used to measure the level of residents' education in each province. Data concerning residents' educational background is collected from the annual sample survey of population carried out by the National Bureau of Statistics of China. The number of each province's NPC deputies is extracted from the 11th and 12th NPC reports.

Previous studies have indicated that deindustrialization tends to reduce the discharge of pollutants to improve environmental quality [69], but local governments' investment in environmental governance will be restrained by budgetary deficits [70]. Therefore, these factors are included as control variables in this paper. Respectively, they are measured by the annual change in the proportion of industrial added value to each province's GDP, and the ratio of the fiscal gap to fiscal revenue. Table 1 presents the descriptive statistics of all variables.

Figure 2 presents the unconditional correlation between public participation and environmental pollution, showing that there is an obvious negative correlation between them. Figure 3 presents the unconditional correlations between the two sub-types of public participation and environmental pollution. The finding in Figure 1 is still true for Complaints, but is not suitable for Proposals. In contrast, there is a positive correlation between Proposals and environmental pollution.

Table 1. The descriptive statistics of variables.

Indicator	Obs.	Mean	S.D.	Min.	Max.
public participation (per 10,000 persons)	150	18.093	11.820	5.441	87.802
complaints (per 10,000 persons)	150	17.848	11.801	5.272	87.490
telephone or Internet complaints	150	40,042.53	42,664.02	1190	267,461
accusation letters	150	4198.74	4142.214	110	25,272
petitions	150	1648.393	1279.466	58	6852
proposals (per 10,000 persons)	150	0.245	0.191	0.036	1.662
proposals from NPC	150	229.967	181.567	11	1196
proposals from CPPCC	150	353.933	490.309	11	5567
environmental pollution	150	3.00	1.963	0.643	10.849
industrial waste water (million tons)	150	711.825	570.685	67	2463
industrial waste gas (billion cubic meters)	150	2240.691	1607.14	167.6	7912.1
industrial waste residue (million tons)	150	108.785	96.858	3.86	455.76
government enforcement	150	30.149	18.084	3.145	93.477
education level	150	11.731	6.217	4.992	39.939
NPC deputies	150	87.873	42.800	19	181
industrial structure	150	−1.272	1.790	−8.722	3.153
budgetary deficit	150	0.113	0.031	0.064	0.220
provinces	30				
years	5				

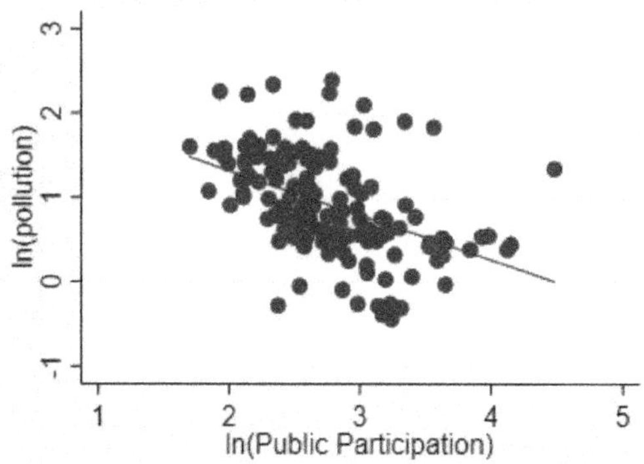

Figure 2. The unconditional correlation between public participation and environmental pollution.

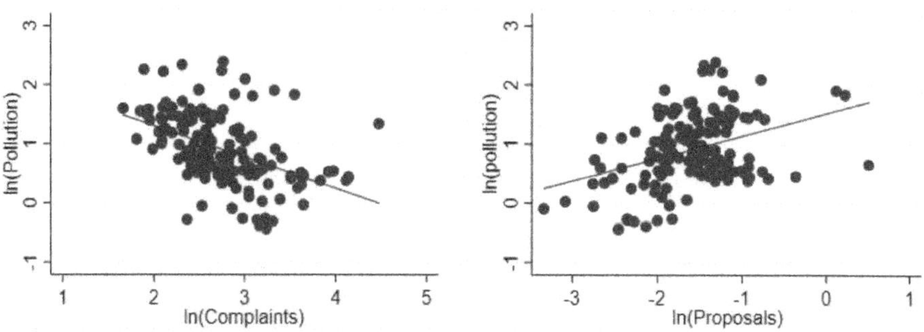

Figure 3. The unconditional correlations between the two sub-types of public participation and environmental pollution.

5. Empirical Findings

5.1. Benchmark Estimation Results

The benchmark estimation results are reported in Table 2. In Model (1)–(2) and Model (3)–(4), different lag periods of the explained variable are considered. Public participation is sub-divided into Complaints and Proposals in Model (2) and Model (4). The robust standard error is applied to alleviate heteroscedasticity and control the fixed effects of each province.

Table 2. The baseline estimation results of public participation to environmental pollution.

Variable	Pollution		Lag1. Pollution	
	Model (1)	Model (2)	Model (3)	Model (4)
public participation	−0.1163 ** (−2.63)		−0.1464 *** (−2.81)	
complaints		−0.1025 ** (−2.14)		−0.1477 ** (−2.73)
proposals		−0.0532 (−1.13)		0.0074 (0.16)
industrial structure	0.0033 (0.38)	0.0017 (0.19)	0.0281 *** (3.41)	0.0280 *** (3.31)
budgetary deficit	0.0138 (0.18)	0.0001 (0.00)	−0.0068 (−0.11)	−0.0053 (−0.09)
_cons.	1.1811 *** (3.31)	1.1163 *** (3.15)	1.4176 *** (5.58)	1.4228 *** (5.45)
F.E.	YES	YES	YES	YES
obs.	150	150	120	120
R-sq.	0.0887	0.1039	0.2861	0.2899

Note: *t*-value in parentheses. *, **, and *** denote significance at the 10%, 5%, and 1% level, respectively.

In Model (1), it can be seen that public participation has a negative and significant estimated coefficient, i.e., $\beta = -0.1163$, which indicates that improving public participation significantly contributes to reducing the discharge of industrial pollutants. In terms of the marginal effect, a one-standard-deviation improvement (i.e., 4.43%) in public participation causes a 0.52% reduction in the discharge of industrial pollutants. In Model (2), the estimated coefficient of Complaints is negative and statistically significant at the level of 5%, i.e., $\beta_1 = -0.1025$, while the estimated coefficient of Proposals does not pass the significance test. These results indicate that the two sub-types of public participation present heterogeneous effects on environmental governance, which are almost consistent with the pattern shown in Figures 1 and 2.

At the present time in China, back-end governance is the major form of public participation in environmental governance, while the form of front-end governance remains at a low level and fruitless. It implies that the public has paid much more attention to the environmental issues that have erupted and seriously affected their daily lives. On the other hand, as to environmental threats that have not yet erupted, the public has not shown an active willingness of participation. There are two possible explanations for this. Firstly, from the perspective of the public, back-end governance has a better mass foundation because polluting enterprises interfere with the public's interests and environmental pollution reduces the quality of their lives. Secondly, from the perspective of polluting enterprises, they will not take the public's proposals seriously because these proposals are not compulsory. As a result, the form of front-end governance has limited constraints on polluting enterprises.

Compared with Model (1)–(2), similar results are demonstrated in Model (3) and Model (4) with one-period-lagged environmental pollution, but their estimated coefficients are much higher and more significant. In Model (3), the same increase (i.e., 4.43%) in public participation causes a 0.65% reduction in the discharge of industrial pollutants, which is much higher than the result of 0.52% in Model (1). This finding is consistent with the reality. In practice, there is a hysteresis between the public's participation and the acquisition of practical results. Meanwhile, in Model (4), the estimated coefficient of Complaints remains negative and statistically significant, while the estimated coefficient of Proposals does not pass the significance test. This finding has further verified that the form of back-end governance is much more efficient than the form of front-end governance in contemporary China.

In terms of the control variables, the regression results indicate that deindustrialization is conducive to improving environmental quality, which implies that China's industrialization has overly depended on the resource input and has exhibited a serious negative externality on the environment. However, there is no direct causal relationship between the budgetary deficit and environmental governance.

5.2. Estimation Results of the Mediation Effect

In Table 3, we examine the relationship between public participation and local governments' environmental enforcement. In Model (5) and Model (6), the regression results indicate that a higher level of public participation and Complaints tends to bring about tougher environmental enforcement by local governments. However, no significant impact of Proposals is exerted on local governments' environmental enforcement. According to these findings, it is shown that, compared with front-end governance, the form of back-end governance has a greater potential to arouse a more significant response from local governments.

Table 3. The estimation results of public participation to local governments' environmental enforcement.

Variable	Environmental Enforcement	
	Model (5)	**Model (6)**
public participation	0.3292 ** (2.23)	
complaints		0.2721 * (1.70)
proposals		0.2309 (1.25)
_cons.	2.3037 *** (5.67)	2.8298 *** (4.39)
F.E.	YES	YES
obs.	150	150
R-sq.	0.0488	0.0718

Note: *t*-value in parentheses. *, **, and *** denote significance at a 10%, 5%, and 1% level, respectively.

Table 4 reports the mediation effect of local governments' environmental enforcement. In Model (7) and Model (8), the estimated coefficients of local governments' environmental enforcement do not pass the significance test. Considering the hysteresis between public participation and practical results, we take one-period-lagged environmental pollution as the explained variable in Model (9) and Model (10). Indications based on the estimation results are as follows: Firstly, the estimated coefficients of local governments' environmental enforcement are negative and statistically significant at the level of 5%, which implies that tougher environmental enforcement by local governments is beneficial to reducing the discharge of industrial pollutants; secondly, the regression of public participation in Model (9) has a significantly negative estimated coefficient, i.e., $\beta' = -0.1298$, and the absolute value of parameter β' shows a slight decline compared with $\beta = -0.1464$ in Model (3). At the same time, the estimated coefficient of Complaints in Model (10) is significantly negative, with its absolute value declining similarly when compared with that in Model (4), i.e., $|\beta_1' = -0.1298| < |\beta_1 = -0.1477|$.

The results above have verified Hypothesis 1 proposed in Section 3.2.1. As the public has no executive power, they can participate in environmental governance in an indirect way by means of lobbying local governments' environmental enforcement of polluting enterprises.

Table 4. The mediation effect of local governments' environmental enforcement.

Variable	Pollution		Lag1. Pollution	
	Model (7)	Model (8)	Model (9)	Model (10)
public participation	−0.1103 *** (−3.01)		−0.1265 *** (−3.69)	
complaints		−0.0985 *** (−2.68)		−0.1298 *** (−3.77)
proposals		−0.0491 (−1.33)		0.0175 (0.53)
local governments' enforcement	−0.0254 (−0.99)	−0.0207 (−0.80)	−0.0570 ** (−2.37)	−0.0583 ** (-2.41)
industrial structure	0.0015 (0.20)	0.0003 (0.04)	0.0217 ** (2.52)	0.0215 ** (2.50)
budgetary deficit	0.0265 (0.33)	0.0114 (0.14)	0.0054 (0.07)	0.0097 (0.12)
_cons.	1.1873 *** (3.37)	1.1261 *** (3.19)	1.4821 *** (4.30)	1.5007 *** (4.32)
F.E.	YES	YES	YES	YES
obs.	150	150	120	120
R-sq.	0.0963	0.1088	0.3299	0.3352

Note: t-value in parentheses. *, **, and *** denote significance at a 10%, 5%, and 1% level, respectively.

In addition, despite the significant mediation effect of local governments' environmental enforcement, parameter β' still passes the significance test after adding the path variable to Model (10). It means that local governments' environmental enforcement is unable to completely replace the effect of public participation in environmental governance, which further verifies the reasonability of Hypothesis 2 proposed in Section 3.2.2. That is to say, the effect of the deterrent of public participation on polluting enterprises can also generate effects similar to local governments' environmental enforcement, which will help promote environmental governance directly.

5.3. 2SLS Estimation Results with IV

Based on Hausman's test of the endogeneity, it can be found that there is a significant endogenous relationship between public participation and environmental pollution. Therefore, instrumental variables (IV) are applied to alleviate endogeneity bias. Table 5 reports 2SLS estimation results with instrumental variables, and the first stage regressions are reported in its lower half. In addition, we take one-period-lagged environmental pollution in Model (11)–(13) in view of the hysteresis.

In Model (11), by taking the level of residents' education and the number of each province's NPC deputies as instrumental variables, the significance test of public participation's estimated coefficient achieves further improvement. Its absolute value also realizes a large rise from $|\beta = -0.1464|$ in Model (3) to $|\beta'' = -0.4542|$. However, the F statistic of the weak IV test is less than the threshold of 10, which means that the two instrumental variables fail to pass the weak identification test. In addition, the regression results in the first stage show that the estimated coefficient of NPC deputies does not pass the significance test. In Model (12), public participation is sub-divided into Complaints and Proposals, but their estimated coefficients to environmental pollution also fail to pass the significance test and the F statistic of the weak IV test still fails to pass the threshold.

Due to the facts above, the sub-type of Proposals is eliminated in public participation, and accordingly, the instrumental variable of NPC deputies is also removed from Model (13). After that, the F statistic of the weak IV test increases to 14.28, indicating that residents' education level passes the weak identification test. In Model (13), the estimated coefficient of Complaints is significantly negative, with an absolute value realizing a large increase from $|\beta_1 = -0.1477|$ in Model (4) to $|\beta_1'' = -0.4442|$. The same increase (i.e., 4.43%) in public participation causes a 1.97% reduction in the discharge of industrial pollutants, almost three times more than that in Model (4). Based on this finding, a conclusion is drawn that the effect of public participation on promoting environmental governance can be further enhanced by introducing residents' education level as the instrumental variable to alleviate its endogeneity bias.

Table 5. The Two Stage Least Square (2SLS) estimation results of public participation to environmental pollution with instrumental variables.

Variable	**Pollution**		
	Model (11)	**Model (12)**	**Model (13)**
public participation	−0.4542 *** (−3.07)		
complaints		0.0036 (0.00)	−0.4442 *** (−3.07)
proposals		−2.0138 (−0.05)	
industrial structure	0.0261 ** (2.23)	0.0063 (0.01)	0.0256 ** (2.21)
budgetary deficit	0.1170 (0.93)	−0.3632 (−0.03)	0.1128 (0.90)
_cons.	1.7199 *** (3.38)	−0.5334 (−0.01)	1.7024 *** (3.39)
F.E.	YES	YES	YES
obs.	120	120	120
R-sq.	0.3661	0.2891	0.3677
Hausman Endogeneity Test	0.00	0.00	0.00
Weak IV Test	7.29	0.00	14.28
Anderson-Rubin Wald Test	0.00	0.00	0.00

The First Stage of Regression

Variable	**Public Participation**	**Complaints**	**Proposals**	**Complaints**
education level	0.7523 *** (3.15)	0.7637 *** (3.15)	0.1711 (0.66)	0.7559 *** (3.16)
NPC deputies	−0.3117 (−0.33)	−0.2827 (−0.29)	−0.1105 (−0.11)	
industrial structure	0.0107 (0.41)	0.0099 (0.38)	−0.0075 (−0.27)	0.0107 (0.41)
budgetary deficit	0.3523 (1.44)	0.3527 (1.42)	−0.1604 (−0.60)	0.3669 (1.52)
_cons.	0.7825 (0.18)	0.6085 (0.13)	−0.7610 (−0.16)	−0.6609 (−0.56)
F.E.	YES	YES	YES	YES
obs.	120	120	120	120
R-sq.	0.1355	0.1358	0.0093	0.1349

Note: *t*-value in parentheses. *, **, and *** denote significance at a 10%, 5%, and 1% level, respectively.

6. Conclusions

Based on inter-provincial panel data of China from 2011 to 2015, the present study has confirmed the role of public participation in environmental governance by constructing a mediation model and a 2SLS model. The results indicate that the advantages of handing information asymmetry and enhancing social supervision have become the two logical starting points for involving public participation in environmental governance. As the public has no executive power, they can participate in environmental governance in an indirect way by means of lobbying local governments' environmental enforcement of polluting enterprises. In addition, public participation's deterrent effect on polluting enterprises can also generate effects similar to local governments' environmental enforcement, which will help promote environmental governance directly. At the present time in China, the effects of public participation in environmental governance are mainly reflected in the form of back-end governance, while the effects of front-end governance are not remarkable.

Regarding the puzzle of some other empirical studies that fail to prove the effectiveness of public participation in environmental governance [41,44–46], this paper also provides relevant explanations. Firstly, due to the heterogeneous effects on environmental governance between back-end governance and front-end governance, we argue that taking different types of public participation as a whole, while neglecting their differences, may be an important reason for this inconformity. Secondly, as the public relies on local governments' enforcement to participate in environmental governance, we also argue that neglecting this indirect participation path may also serve as an important explanation for the puzzle. Thirdly, as the bidirectional causality between public participation and environmental pollution tends to cause serious endogeneity bias, we hold the opinion that inadequate treatment of this endogeneity bias may essentially account for public participation's ineffectiveness.

7. Discussions

The present study contributes to a better understanding of the role of public participation in environmental governance in China. However, as a case exemplar of authoritarian environmentalism, the participation of Chinese citizens in its environmental governance remains inadequate [71–73]. In particular, unless environmental pollution has broken out and seriously affected their daily life, Chinese citizens will not take the initiative to participate in environmental governance [41]. Our findings are of great significance in perfecting China's environmental governance system by means of arousing and expanding the public's rights to participate in environmental governance.

Firstly, the present study points out that handling information asymmetry and enhancing social supervision are the two logical starting points for involving public participation in environmental governance. Therefore, we suggest that the Chinese government should standardize the disclosure of environmental information to ensure the public's right to know about, participate in, and supervise environmental issues. For example, interactive channels between the public and local governments should be expanded, particularly by widely applying smart phones, computers, and many other network terminal devices.

Secondly, the present study also reveals that residents' education level has a significant positive correlation with public participation. Hereby, it is necessary to stress the importance of improving residents' education level in China. As China is a populous country, this will be an arduous project and may not achieve a remarkable effect in a short period of time. We suggest that implementing this project should not be only restricted to compulsory education. Other methods, such as community publicity, Internet platforms, and public service advertising, should be fully utilized.

Thirdly, as a kind of pollutant source control, front-end governance is majorly exhibited in pollution pre-warning and cost saving. However, our conclusions indicate that the effects of front-end governance are not remarkable enough at the present time in China. Therefore, we hold the opinion that the Chinese government should attach more importance to cultivating its people's awareness of active participation. There is a lot of work to do, such as creating a ritual sense of making recommendations for its citizens, and establishing a visual platform for the public to check the progress of their suggestions.

Fourthly, it has to be noted that placing an emphasis on the role of public participation does not mean that we can neglect the roles of local governments and polluting enterprises. Therefore, to involve the public in the environmental governance system, the Chinese government also needs to pay attention to the coordination between the public, local governments, and polluting enterprises. In particular, tensions between the public and polluting enterprises have to be handled in an appropriate way. We suggest establishing a regular dialogue mechanism among all stakeholders. Under this mechanism, the public will be able to exercise their supervisory rights, and polluting enterprises will be offered adequate time to modify their production behaviors.

In addition, the present study also contains some defects, one of which is that the modes of public participation in environmental governance are far beyond the five indicators we have considered. In Section 5.3, the sub-type of Proposals and the instrumental variable of NPC deputies are eliminated from the 2SLS model due to the weak identification test. However, this elimination prevents us from shedding light on the effect of front-end governance. In Section 4.2, we constructed a comprehensive indicator by three major industrial pollutants to measure the level of environmental pollution. However, the public's feeling on different types of industrial pollutants may be different, then leading to different levels of public participation and different effects on environmental governance. Public participation in China may take on specific characteristics, forms, and degrees due to its own institution and culture, but the present study fails to make a comparative study between China and other countries. These defects will be further addressed in our subsequent studies.

Author Contributions: Conceptualization, J.G. and J.B.; data curation, J.G.; formal analysis, J.G.; methodology, J.B.; writing—original draft, J.G.; writing—review & editing, J.B. All authors read and approved this version. The authors appreciate the valuable comments of anonymous reviewers.

Funding: This work was supported by the National Natural Science Foundation of China (71803086) and the Social Science Foundation of Jiangsu in China (17JDB005).

Acknowledgments: We appreciate the constructive suggestions from peer reviewers and the help of editors. All remaining errors are ours.

Conflicts of Interest: The authors declare no conflict of interest.

References

1. Kostka, G.; Nahm, J. Central-local relations: Recentralization and environmental governance in China. *China Q.* **2017**, *231*, 567–582. [CrossRef]
2. Lo, K. How authoritarian is the environmental governance of China? *Environ. Sci. Policy* **2015**, *54*, 152–159. [CrossRef]
3. He, G.; Lu, Y.; Mol, A.P.J.; Beckers, T. Changes and challenges: China's environmental management in transition. *Environ. Dev.* **2012**, *3*, 25–38. [CrossRef]
4. Liu, L.; Zhang, B.; Bi, J. Reforming China's multi-level environmental governance: Lessons from the 11th Five-Year Plan. *Environ. Sci. Policy* **2012**, *21*, 106–111. [CrossRef]
5. Bäckstrand, K. Civic science for sustainability: Reframing the role of experts, policy-makers and citizens in environmental governance. *Glob. Environ. Politics* **2003**, *3*, 24–41. [CrossRef]
6. Bulkeley, H.; Mol, A.P.J. Participation and environmental governance: Consensus, ambivalence and debate. *Environ. Values* **2003**, *12*, 143–154. [CrossRef]
7. Webler, T.; Tuler, S. Four perspectives on public participation process in environmental assessment and decision making: Combined results from 10 case studies. *Policy Stud. J.* **2006**, *34*, 699–722. [CrossRef]
8. Newig, J. Does public participation in environmental decisions lead to improved environmental quality? Towards an analytical framework. *Int. J. Sustain. Commun.* **2007**, *1*, 51–71.
9. Zhang, D.; Liu, J.; Li, B. Tackling air pollution in China—What do we learn from the great smog of 1950s in London. *Sustainability* **2014**, *6*, 5322–5338. [CrossRef]
10. Taylor, B. Wilderness, spirituality and biodiversity in North America: Tracing an environmental history from Occidental roots to Earth Day. *Wilderness Myth. Relig. Approaching Relig. Spat. Cosmol. Ideas Wild Nat.* **2012**, *55*, 293.

11. Guo, J.; Xu, Y.; Pu, Z. Urbanization and its effects on industrial pollutant emissions: An empirical study of a Chinese case with the spatial panel model. *Sustainability* **2016**, *8*, 812. [CrossRef]
12. Wu, J.; Song, M.; Yang, L. Advances in energy and environmental issues in China: Theory, models, and applications. *Ann. Oper. Res.* **2015**, *228*, 1–8. [CrossRef]
13. Ravesteijn, W.; Liu, Y.; Yan, P. Responsible innovation in port development: The Rotterdam Maasvlakte 2 and the Dalian Dayao Bay extension projects. *Water Sci. Technol.* **2015**, *72*, 665–677. [CrossRef] [PubMed]
14. Jian, L.; Chan, C.K.C. Collective identity, framing and mobilisation of environmental protests in urban China: A case study of Qidong's Protest. *China Int. J.* **2016**, *14*, 102–122.
15. Zhou, Q. Report on the Work of the Supreme People's Court of China. Available online: http://news.cyol.com/content/2018-03/26/content_17051712.htm (accessed on 26 March 2018).
16. Zheng, S.; Kahn, M.E. A new era of pollution progress in urban China? *J. Econ. Perspect.* **2017**, *31*, 71–92. [CrossRef]
17. Quick, K.S.; Bryson, J.M. *Public Participation: Handbook on Theories of Governance*; Edward Elgar Publishing: Cheltenham, UK, 2016.
18. Tiebout, C.M. A pure theory of local expenditures. *J. Political Econ.* **1956**, *64*, 416–424. [CrossRef]
19. Banzhaf, H.S.; Walsh, R.P. Do people vote with their feet? An empirical test of environmental gentrification. *RFF Discuss. Paper No. 06-10* **2006**. [CrossRef]
20. Hirschman, A.O. *Exit, Voice, and Loyalty: Responses to Decline in Firms, Organizations, and States*; Harvard University Press: Cambridge, MA, USA, 1970.
21. Taylor, D.E. The rise of the environmental justice paradigm: Injustice framing and the social construction of environmental discourses. *Am. Behav. Sci.* **2000**, *43*, 508–580. [CrossRef]
22. Garmendia, E.; Stagl, S. Public participation for sustainability and social learning: Concepts and lessons from three case studies in Europe. *Ecol. Econ.* **2010**, *69*, 1712–1722. [CrossRef]
23. Jolibert, C.; Wesselink, A. Research impacts and impact on research in biodiversity conservation: The influence of stakeholder engagement. *Environ. Sci. Policy* **2012**, *22*, 100–111. [CrossRef]
24. Innes, J.E.; Booher, D.E. Reframing public participation: Strategies for the 21st century. *Plan. Theory Pract.* **2004**, *5*, 419–436. [CrossRef]
25. Muro, M.; Jeffrey, P. Time to talk? How the structure of dialog processes shapes stakeholder learning in participatory water resources management. *Ecol. Soc.* **2012**, *17*. [CrossRef]
26. Hogl, K.; Kvarda, E.; Nordbeck, R.; Pregernig, M. *Environmental Governance: The Challenge of Legitimacy and Effectiveness*; Edward Elgar Publishing: Cheltenham, UK, 2012.
27. Newig, J.; Fritsch, O. Environmental governance: Participatory, multi-level-and effective? *Environ. Policy Gov.* **2009**, *19*, 197–214. [CrossRef]
28. Kanu, E.J.; Tyonum, E.T.; Uchegbu, S.N. Public participation in environmental impact Assessment (EIA): A critical analysis. *Archit. Eng.* **2018**, *3*, 1.
29. Chen, C.X.; Han, L. Public Participation in water environment control: The status and experience of Shenzhen, Southern China. *Meteorol. Environ. Res.* **2018**, *9*, 70–79.
30. Bai, X.; McAllister, R.R.J.; Beaty, R.M.; Taylor, B. Urban policy and governance in a global environment: Complex systems, scale mismatches and public participation. *Curr. Opin. Environ. Sustain.* **2010**, *2*, 129–135. [CrossRef]
31. Beierle, T.C. *Democracy in Practice: Public Participation in Environmental Decisions*; Routledge: London, UK, 2010.
32. Reed, M.S. Stakeholder participation for environmental management: A literature review. *Biol. Conserv.* **2008**, *141*, 2417–2431. [CrossRef]
33. Enserink, B.; Koppenjan, J. Public participation in China: Sustainable urbanization and governance. *Manag. Environ. Qual. Int. J.* **2007**, *18*, 459–474. [CrossRef]
34. Cent, J.; Grodzińska-Jurczak, M.; Pietrzyk-Kaszyńska, A. Emerging multilevel environmental governance—A case of public participation in Poland. *J. Nat. Conserv.* **2014**, *22*, 93–102. [CrossRef]
35. Akhmouch, A.; Clavreul, D. Stakeholder engagement for inclusive water governance: "Practicing what we preach" with the OECD water governance initiative. *Water* **2016**, *8*, 204. [CrossRef]
36. Adkin, L.E.; Hanson, L.L.; Kahane, D.; Parkins, J.R.; Patten, S. Can public engagement democratize environmental policymaking in a resource-dependent state? Comparative case studies from Alberta, Canada. *Environ. Politics* **2017**, *26*, 301–321. [CrossRef]

37. Fischer, A.; Young, J.C. Understanding mental constructs of biodiversity: Implications for biodiversity management and conservation. *Biol. Conserv.* **2007**, *136*, 271–282. [CrossRef]
38. Blackstock, K.L.; Kelly, G.J.; Horsey, B.L. Developing and applying a framework to evaluate participatory research for sustainability. *Ecol. Econ.* **2007**, *60*, 726–742. [CrossRef]
39. Vedwan, N.; Ahmad, S.; Miralles-Wilhelm, F.; Broad, K.; Letson, D.; Podesta, G. Institutional evolution in Lake Okeechobee management in Florida: Characteristics, impacts, and limitations. *Water Resour. Manag.* **2008**, *22*, 699–718. [CrossRef]
40. Marzuki, A. Challenges in the public participation and the decision making process. *Sociol. I Prost. Sociol. Space* **2015**, *53*, 21–39.
41. Fung, A. Putting the public back into governance: The challenges of citizen participation and its future. *Public Adm. Rev.* **2015**, *75*, 513–522. [CrossRef]
42. Yakubu, O. Delivering environmental justice through environmental impact assessment in the United States: The challenge of public participation. *Challenges* **2018**, *9*, 9. [CrossRef]
43. Wesselink, A.; Paavola, J.; Fritsch, O.; Renn, O. Rationales for public participation in environmental policy and governance: practitioners' perspectives. *Environ. Plan. A* **2011**, *43*, 2688–2704. [CrossRef]
44. Drazkiewicz, A.; Challies, E.; Newig, J. Public participation and local environmental planning: Testing factors influencing decision quality and implementation in four case studies from Germany. *Land Use Policy* **2015**, *46*, 211–222. [CrossRef]
45. Wang, H.; Di, W. The World Bank. In *The Determinants of Government Environmental Performance: An Empirical Analysis of Chinese Townships*; World Bank Publication: Washington, DC, USA, 2002.
46. He, Z.X.; Xu, S.C.; Shen, W.X.; Long, R.Y.; Chen, H. Factors that influence corporate environmental behavior: Empirical analysis based on panel data in China. *J. Clean. Prod.* **2016**, *133*, 531–543. [CrossRef]
47. Wu, J.; Xu, M.; Zhang, P. The impacts of governmental performance assessment policy and citizen participation on improving environmental performance across Chinese provinces. *J. Clean. Prod.* **2018**, *184*, 227–238. [CrossRef]
48. Few, R.; Brown, K.; Tompkins, E.L. Public participation and climate change adaptation: Avoiding the illusion of inclusion. *Clim. Policy* **2007**, *7*, 46–59. [CrossRef]
49. Eden, S. Public participation in environmental policy: Considering scientific, counter-scientific and non-scientific contributions. *Public Underst. Sci.* **2016**, *5*, 183–204. [CrossRef]
50. Li, G.; Fang, C.; Wang, S.; Sun, S. The effect of economic growth, urbanization, and industrialization on fine particulate matter (PM2.5) concentrations in China. *Environ. Sci. Technol.* **2016**, *50*, 11452–11459. [CrossRef] [PubMed]
51. Stern, D.I.B. The Environmental Kuznets Curve. In *Companion to Environmental Studies*; Routledge: London, UK, 2018.
52. Bai, Z. Study on cross-boundary governance of water pollution in Huaihe River in China. *J. Sustain. Dev.* **2015**, *8*, 241. [CrossRef]
53. Hu, S.; Tang, W. Analysis on the formation and legislative prevention and control measures of groundwater pollution: A case study from Xinjiang, China. *Nat. Environ. Pollut. Technol.* **2017**, *16*, 393.
54. Luo, W.; Guo, X.; Zhong, S.; Wang, J. Environmental information disclosure quality, media attention and debt financing costs: Evidence from Chinese heavy polluting listed companies. *J. Clean. Prod.* **2019**, *231*, 268–277. [CrossRef]
55. Wu, Y.; Zhang, W.; Shen, J.; Mo, Z.; Peng, Y. Smart city with Chinese characteristics against the background of big data: Idea, action and risk. *J. Clean. Prod.* **2018**, *173*, 60–66. [CrossRef]
56. Zhang, X. Implementation of pollution control targets in China: Has a centralized enforcement approach worked? *China Q.* **2017**, *231*, 749–774. [CrossRef]
57. Martínez-Ferrero, J.; Ruiz-Cano, D.; García-Sánchez, I.M. The causal link between sustainable disclosure and information asymmetry: The moderating role of the stakeholder protection context. *Corp. Soc. Responsib. Environ. Manag.* **2016**, *23*, 319–332. [CrossRef]
58. Zhang, L.; Mol, A.P.J.; He, G. Transparency and information disclosure in China's environmental governance. *Curr. Opin. Environ. Sustain.* **2016**, *18*, 17–24. [CrossRef]
59. Hart, R.A. *Children's Participation: The Theory and Practice of Involving Young Citizens in Community Development and Environmental Care*; Routledge: London, UK, 2013.

60. Tian, X.L.; Guo, Q.G.; Han, C.; Ahmad, N. Different extent of environmental information disclosure across Chinese cities: Contributing factors and correlation with local pollution. *Glob. Environ. Chang.* **2016**, *39*, 244–257. [CrossRef]
61. Wu, M.Q.; Chen, B. Assignment of provincial officials based on economic performance: Evidence from China. *China Econ. Rev.* **2016**, *38*, 60–75. [CrossRef]
62. Burton, P. Conceptual, theoretical and practical issues in measuring the benefits of public participation. *Evaluation* **2009**, *15*, 263–284. [CrossRef]
63. Jiang, D.; Zhang, J. Policy Analytics, Modelling, and Informatics. Public Administration and Information Technology. In *Competition and Collusion between Government and Businesses in Pollution Management: Analysis Based on Stochastic Differential Game*; Gil-Garcia, J., Pardo, T., Luna-Reyes, L., Eds.; Springer: Cham, Germany, 2018; pp. 407–427.
64. Kadushin, A.; Harkness, D. *Supervision in Social Work*; Columbia University Press: New York, NY, USA, 2014.
65. Judd, C.M.; Kenny, D.A. Process analysis: Estimating mediation in treatment evaluations. *Eval. Rev.* **1981**, *5*, 602–619. [CrossRef]
66. Cutler, D.M.; Lleras-Muney, A. Understanding differences in health behaviors by education. *J. Health Econ.* **2010**, *29*, 1–28. [CrossRef] [PubMed]
67. Reimer, M.N.; Haynie, A.C. Mechanisms matter for evaluating the economic impacts of marine reserves. *J. Environ. Econ. Manag.* **2018**, *88*, 427–446. [CrossRef]
68. Ministry of Ecology and Environment of the People's Republic of China. *China Environmental Yearbook*; China Forum of Environmental Journalists: Beijing, China, 2011–2015.
69. Yu, S.; Zheng, S.; Zhang, X.; Gong, C.; Cheng, J. Realizing China's goals on energy saving and pollution reduction: Industrial structure multi-objective optimization approach. *Energy Policy* **2018**, *122*, 300–312. [CrossRef]
70. Cheung, G.; Davies, P.J.; Trück, S. Transforming urban energy systems: The role of local governments' regional energy master plan. *J. Clean. Prod.* **2019**, *220*, 655–667. [CrossRef]
71. Beeson, M. The coming of environmental authoritarianism. *Environ. Politics* **2010**, *19*, 276–294. [CrossRef]
72. Gilley, B. Authoritarian environmentalism and China's response to climate change. *Environ. Politics* **2012**, *21*, 287–307. [CrossRef]
73. Zhu, X.; Zhang, L.; Ran, R.; Mol, A.P.J. Regional restrictions on environmental impact assessment approval in China: The legitimacy of environmental authoritarianism. *J. Clean. Prod.* **2015**, *92*, 100–108. [CrossRef]

sustainability

MDPI

Article

Aerobic Treatment of Waste Process Solutions from the Semiconductor Industry: From Lab to Pilot Scale

Francesco Ferella *, Valentina Innocenzi, Svetlana Zueva, Valentina Corradini, Nicolò M. Ippolito, Ionela P. Birloaga, Ida De Michelis, Marina Prisciandaro and Francesco Vegliò

Department of Industrial and Information Engineering and Economics, University of L'Aquila, 67100 L'Aquila, Italy

* Correspondence: francesco.ferella@univaq.it; Tel.: +39-0862-434238

Received: 27 June 2019; Accepted: 16 July 2019; Published: 18 July 2019

Abstract: Tetramethylammonium hydroxide (*TMAH*) is widely used as a solvent in the semiconductor industry. After the photo-impression process, it is necessary to remove the photoresist (PR) layer from the surface of the circuits; for this purpose, a *TMAH* solution is usually used. This chemical compound is highly toxic and corrosive and cannot be discharged into the environment. This study was carried out in collaboration with LFoundry (SMIC group), in order to prove the feasibility of biodegradation under aerobic conditions, using microorganisms coming from the LFoundry's wastewater treatment plant (WWTP) at different operating conditions. The feed composition was modified in order to add a small but increasing amount of *TMAH* and PR. The aim was to verify if the increase of *TMAH* concentration was harmful to bacteria. The feed stream, containing *TMAH* and PR, was the only carbon source for the metabolism of the aerobic microorganisms. The results of this study demonstrated an effective biological degradation of *TMAH* and showed a total removal efficiency of more than 99.3%, with a final concentration of 7 mg/L. Moreover, the kinetic parameters of the Monod model were also calculated. The results obtained from the experimental campaign were used to design a pilot plant that will treat around 25 L/h of waste *TMAH*/PR solution.

Keywords: tetramethylammonium hydroxide; *TMAH*; anaerobic digestion; photoresist; wastewater

1. Introduction

In several production processes, special chemical compounds are often used; such chemicals cannot be easily replaced with other ones, as no substances with similar physicochemical properties are available so far. This is the case of *TMAH*, which is a quaternary ammonium salt extensively used in the semiconductor industry.

The problem lies in the high toxicity for the biota, as demonstrated by various studies [1,2]. The exposure to *TMAH* causes harmful effects on human health, whether ingested or inhaled: being very corrosive is harmful to both the mucous membranes and the skin in general. If *TMAH* is ingested, it causes burns and ulcers [3]. The acute *Daphnia similis* toxicity test demonstrated that the 48-h lethal concentration 50 (LC50) of *TMAH* is only 0.75 mg/L. The acute toxicity of $N\text{-}NH_4^+$ to *Daphnia similis* varied with the pH of the collected wastewater: the 48h LC50 values were found to vary in the range of 18.5–155 mg/L from pH 7.0 to pH 6.5 [2].

Mori et al. [4] also studied the *TMAH* effects on the aquatic environmental: the tests were carried out on seaweed and freshwater fish, in particular, the microalga *Pseudokirchneriella subcapitata*, the bacterium *Vibrio fischeri*, the fresh fish *Oryziaslatipes* (or rice fish) and the microcrustacean *Daphnia magna*. The results highlighted a strong impact on the development of these organisms because of *TMAH* in high concentration. The damage varies depending on the exposure level and can also lead to the death of the organisms; for this reason, it is necessary to treat it before discharging.

Adsorption is an effective technique that can be used to remove the *TMAH* molecule. In particular, graphene oxide (GO) was tested in the adsorption of *TMAH* in different operating conditions; it was demonstrated that the adsorption capacity is around double to that of granular (GAC) and powdered (PAC) activated carbon [5] as well as zeolite Na-Y [6].

The adsorption of *TMAH* was also tested with ion-exchange resins like Amberlite IR-120 and Dowex HCR-W2 [7]. The adsorption with different kinds of activated carbon was also studied by Prahas et al. [8]; other studies were performed to evaluate mesoporous silicate materials or strongly and weakly acidic cation exchange resins, as well as electrodialysis in the removal of such a molecule [9–11].

Catalytic oxidation is another interesting technique investigated in the past for the removal of *TMAH*. Suitable catalysts, usually based on active metals like Pd-V_2O_5-WO_3or Pt supported on titania-silica or alumina, were used [12]. Catalytic oxidation involves the catalyzed reaction of *TMAH* to TMA^+ and the further decomposition of TMA^+ to nitrogen, water, and carbon dioxide [13].

Membrane distillation is another effective treatment for the removal of *TMAH* and the recovery of process water in the nano-electronics industry [14].

Different authors have studied the biological degradation of *TMAH*, both in anaerobic and aerobic conditions, but the biological treatment of such waste solutions is still difficult in standard activated sludge plant [15].

Few studies investigated the treatment of waste solutions containing *TMAH* by biological processes in up-flow anaerobic sludge blanket (UASB) reactors with *Methanosarcina* and *Methanomethylovorans* bacteria: removal yields of around 90% were achieved, together with 90% of methane production [15,16]. Lei et al. [15] showed that effective removal is carried out under aerobic conditions in sequencing batch reactors (SBR). Hence, the anaerobic methanogenic degradation of *TMAH* was fully demonstrated in a batch operating mode with a 1000 mg/L synthetic solution, where the appropriate substrate composition was added. The specific *TMAH* degradation rate and the half-saturation constant of the enriched methanogens were 39.5 mg *TMAH*/gVSS·h and 820 mg/L, according to the Monod kinetics for *TMAH* degradation. The concentration of sulphides higher than 20 mg/L showed a heavy inhibition and slowed down the specific *TMAH* degradation rate of *Methanomethylovorans* and *Methanosarcina* [17].

An interesting study was carried out by means of real wastewater from a full-scale methanogenic UASB reactor that treats the sewage from the manufacturing of thin-film transistor liquid crystal displays (TFT-LCD). The batch trials demonstrated that *Methanomethylovorans hollandica* and *Methanosarcina mazei* are the dominant methanogens in the UASB responsible for *TMAH* degradation. In anaerobic conditions, the UASB sludge achieved a specific degradation rate of 9.5 mg *TMAH*/gVSS·h, even when the original concentration of *TMAH* was 1500 mg/L [18]. Aerobic batch trials were also investigated, and the results showed a maximum specific degradation of 8.8 mg *TMAH*/gVSS·h with an initial *TMAH* of 145 mg/L, but inhibition occurred when the *TMAH* concentrations reached 150 mg/L [18].

Anaerobic conditions were also tested by Liu et al. [19]. The anaerobic treatment of waste solution containing 340 mg/L of *TMAH* at room temperature was conducted in lab-scale experiments, where the methane conversion yield of *TMAH* reached nearly 90%.

Autotrophic nitrogen removal over nitrite in a continuous anoxic up-flow bioreactor was investigated by Chen et al. [20]. Such a process was used to treat synthetic wastewater containing *TMAH* in a concentration range of 200–1000 mg/L. The nitrogen average removal yield was always greater than 90% in all the trials, with a peak of 98% after a retention time of around 4.3 days. Trimethylamine and methylamine were the main biodegradation intermediates detected in the solution.

Great attention is paid to waste solutions from the semiconductor industry in those countries where many factories are located, in particular, China, Taiwan, South Korea, and Japan. This is demonstrated by the high percentage of scientific papers dealing with such a topic that comes from the aforementioned countries. Instead, Europe and the USA seem not to be aware of this problem, and this has resulted in a lack of research. The present study assesses the biological treatment in a laboratory-scale aerobic reactor of a liquid waste stream containing tetramethylammonium hydroxide (*TMAH*)/photoresist blend. The results were then used to design a pilot-scale plant with a capacity of 25 L/h in continuous operation mode. The goal of the paper was to minimize the concentration of *TMAH* in the treated sewage released into the environment, considering the toxicological aspects and looking for the best biological technique; in particular, the objective was focused on the efficiency of the aerobic degradation as a function of the feed composition, optimized for such purpose. The novelty of the present research lies in the aerobic degradation of *TMAH* in high concentration (around 1800 mg/L) with specialized microorganism strains, using a second waste stream as a carbon source.

2. Materials and Methods

2.1. Feed Composition

The wastewater (R1), provided by the company that manufactures semiconductors (LFoundry, Avezzano, Italy), contains 1600–2000 mg/L of *TMAH*, and the relevant pH is usually in the range of 12–13. The European Waste Code (EWC) of such a solution is 11 01 12. The *TMAH* solution was neutralized by 5 mol/L H_2SO_4 solution to pH 7, that is a value suitable for the microbial growth.

For a correct and optimal bacterial growth, the following two streams were added to the *TMAH* waste solution:

- a photoresist solution (R2), EWC 14 06 03. This solution is an additional waste stream produced by the manufacturing processes of LFoundry: it is a mixture of organic substances, mainly 1-methoxy-2-propanol, with a total organic carbon (TOC) concentration of around 615 g/L. It was added as a source of carbon, in order to supply the optimal C/N ratio for the bacterial metabolism, that should be 20 by weight [21]. Such a ratio is indeed too low, around 3.5 in the *TMAH* molecule, thus the second waste stream R2 was added to the previously mentioned stream R1;
- a growth medium, whose composition is shown in Table 1.

Table 1. Composition of the growth medium.

Compound	Concentration (mg/L)
$CuCl_2$	140
Na_2MoO_4	250
$NaHCO_3$	820
K_2HPO_4	210
$MgSO_4$	510
$FeCl_3$	110
Yeast Extract	12

The amount of the mixture of *TMAH* and PR effluents was calculated by solving the following mass balance given by the equation system:

$$V_1 + V_2 = V_{TOT} \tag{1}$$

$$\frac{C_1 \times V_1 + C_2 \times V_2}{C_{N-TMAH} \times V_1} = \frac{20}{1} \tag{2}$$

where C_1 is the carbon mass concentration in *TMAH* solution, 1.1 g/L; C_2 is the carbon mass concentration in the photoresist solution, 615 g/L; $C_{N\text{-}TMAH}$ is the nitrogen mass concentration in the *TMAH* molecule, 0.31 g/L; V_1 is the volume of the *TMAH* solution R1; V_2 is the volume of the photoresist solution R2; and V_{TOT} is the total volume of the wastewater treated in the reactor. The total volume of the wastewater blend solution treated in the lab-scale bioreactor was set to 3 L.

2.2. Biological Tests

The seeding activated sludge was taken from the wastewater treatment plant located in the LFoundry's site, that usually treats all the sewage coming from toilets, cleaning of some process equipment from the process and the canteen. The activated sludge, containing neither *TMAH* nor photoresist, was stored in wide neck plastic bottles. They were kept under a fume hood and left open—in contact with atmospheric air—for 14 days, to allow the complete oxidation of residual organic matter. Thus, the substrate, whose composition is listed in Table 1, was added. The feeding for the reactor was obtained by mixing 1.93 L of *TMAH* residue, 20 mL of photoresist, and 50 mL of culture mineral medium. The experimental reactor was kept at room temperature (20 ± 2 °C), stirred at 70 rpm with air-oxygen saturation. Colony counts, Lowry's protein assay, and the biodiversity indexes were calculated according to the methods detailed in Moretti et al. [22]. Colony count was performed on Luria–Bertani enriched medium and AGAR-*TMAH* selective medium. Lowry's protein assay was carried out on lysate cells to assess the biomass production, hence the bacterial DNA was extracted from the samples. The biodiversity indexes, in particular, the range-weighted richness, functional organization, Simpson diversity index, and Simpson evenness index, were evaluated. Main genus representation in sequence reads were *Comamonas* (18.3 ± 5.7%), *Pseudomonas* (18.1 ± 5.3%), *Stenotrophomonas* (12.3 ± 3.1%), and *Brevundimonas* (11.4 ± 3.8%), while others sequence reads were spread in various groups belonging to families *Sphingomonadaceae* (8.1 ± 1.0%), *Sphingobacteriaceae* (4.05 ± 2.2%), *Methylophilaceae* (4.05 ± 3.18%), *Xanthobacteraceae* (3.30 ± 0.14%), *Xanthobacter* (2.55 ± 0.07), and *Rhodococcus* (1.90 ± 0.57%). The microorganism community was inoculated and adapted quickly to the change of nutrients, and stabilized over a new equilibrium state within a week when in the constant presence of *TMAH* and any further perturbation did not change the community structure. The biomass enrichment was obtained by means of some sequential batches, according to the sequence: (1) Batch T, from day 1 to day 6 (2 L of inoculum and 2 L of feeding solution); (2) Batch R, from day 7 to day 12, Batch A from day 13 to day 18, and Batch M from day 19 to day 24: at the beginning of each batch from the 7–24th day, 1 L of activated sludge coming from the previous batch was left in the reactor and fed with 2 L of feeding solution; (3) Batch M, from day 25 to day 30, where 1 L of activated sludge resulting from Batch M was added to 2 L of distilled water and 50 mL of mineral culture medium [22].

The biological results showed an organized and stable community over time, even in the long run, composed of specialized species that were also the best selected for the desired function. After that, the biomass was concentrated by gravity and stored at 4 °C in order to be used as inoculum for the two batch cycles.

The biological tests were carried out in a bioreactor BIOSTAT® B (Sartorius, Goettingen, Germany) (Figure 1) in batch operating mode. The process conditions for the tests were: temperature 25 °C, pH 7, stirring speed 70 rpm, oxygen flow-rate of 2.0 L/min, controlled and regulated by the control unit of the bioreactor, whose nominal capacity was 3.5 L.

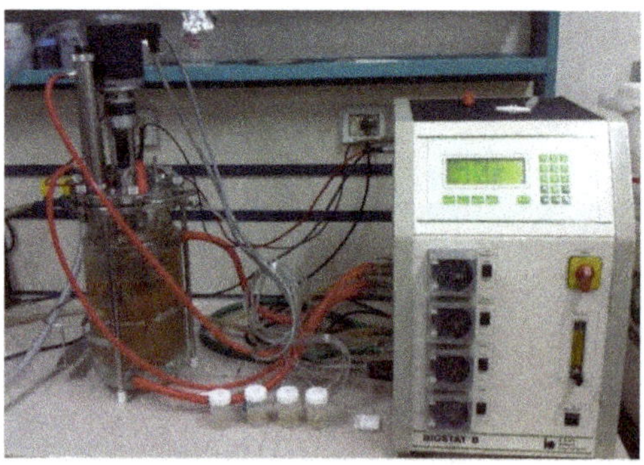

Figure 1. BIOSTAT®B and its control unit.

Two sequential batch cycles were carried out; such cycles were consecutive in order to confirm the results with different waste solution samples. At the end of the first cycle, mixing and aeration were switched off, so that the biomass could settle; thus, the supernatant was removed by a peristaltic pump and disposed of, whereas the settled biomass was centrifuged in order to remove the remaining solution. Afterward, the fresh mixture (2678 mL of *TMAH* +22 mL of PR solutions) was added together with 300 mL of growth medium and the recycled biomass. At the end of each cycle, the total volume of the *TMAH*/PR wastewater mixture and growth medium was removed and disposed of. The concentration of *TMAH*, after dilution with the photoresist and sludge, was 1780 mg/L and 1625 mg/L for batch cycle 1 and 2, respectively. The batch time for each cycle was 21days, whereas the solid retention time (SRT) was 42 days. The composition of the two solutions, after blending, is listed in Table 2.

Table 2. Composition of the solutions for the two batch tests.

Parameter	Batch 1 (mg/L)	Batch 2 (mg/L)
pH	7.20	6.95
COD	5085	4863
TMAH	1780	1625
$NH_4{}^+$	75	62
F^-	0.04	0.02
$NO_3{}^-$	<0.01	<0.01
Cl^-	0.09	0.06
Sb, As, Cd, Cr, Hg, Ni, Pb, K, Se, Cu	<0.01	<0.01
Na	0.55	0.71

The mixture's pH was adjusted to the optimal value (i.e., 7) by the addition of H_2SO_4 (96%wt) or NaOH (35%wt) from the initial value of 12.4.

Every day, one sample of 100 mL was collected and centrifuged at 5000 rpm. The supernatant was used to determine the pH (Seven Compact pH-meter, Mettler Toledo), *TMAH* (Ion Chromatograph Dionex DX5000), and ammonium ion (Nessler's reagent method) concentrations, whereas the total suspended solids (TSS) were determined after drying of the settled material at 105 °C for 24 h.

The sample's volume was refilled by the addition of the growth medium. The kinetic parameters of the Monod model were also calculated for the design of the pilot bioreactor [21].

3. Results and Discussion

3.1. Kinetic Model

It was assumed that the kinetics of the microorganism population could be represented by the Monod model (Equation (3)):

$$\mu = \frac{\mu_{max} \times S}{K_S + S} \tag{3}$$

where μ is the specific growth rate of the microorganisms (h^{-1}), μ_{max} is the maximum specific growth rate (h^{-1}), S is the concentration of the limiting substrate for growth (mg/L), and K_S is the half-velocity constant, that is, the value of S corresponding to μ/μ_{max} = 0.5 (mg/L). The specific growth rate (μ) was calculated from an overall mass balance for the biomass at stationary conditions.

One single batch test was sufficient to derive the specific growth rate, by solving the system of linear first order differential equations:

$$\frac{dX}{dt} = \mu \times X \tag{4}$$

$$\frac{dS}{dt} = -\sigma \times X \tag{5}$$

$$\frac{dP}{dt} = \pi \times X \tag{6}$$

where X, S, and P are the concentrations of microorganisms (mg/L), *TMAH* (mg/L), and ammonium ion (mg/L), respectively, and μ, σ, and π are the specific growth rate, substrate consumption rate, and product generation rate (h^{-1}). These three equations have to be coupled with the well-known Monod (Equation (3)), Pirt (Equation (7)), and Luedeking–Piret (Equation (8)) equations:

$$\sigma = \frac{1}{Y^{G}_{X/S}} \times \mu + m \tag{7}$$

$$\pi = \alpha \times \mu + \beta \tag{8}$$

where the coefficients m and β are null (product associated to the growth), the biomass yield $Y^{G}{}_{X/S}$ is 0.34 g of biomass per g of substrate, and α = 0.2 g of ammonium per g of biomass (experimental values). The detailed calculation can be found in Innocenzi et al. [21]. Such an approach allows the fitting of substrate depletion data versus time to the integrated Monod equation by using nonlinear regression, which is advantageous since μ_{max} and K_S may be calculated from a single progress curve [23].

From the analysis of the data collected from the tests carried out with the bench bioreactor, the following kinetic parameters were calculated:

- $\mu_{max} = 0.0425 \pm 0.0034\ h^{-1}$;
- $K_S = 800 \pm 51$ mg/L.

These data were used to design the optimal configuration of the biological equipment for the pilot plant.

3.2. Biological Tests

Figure 2 shows the pH, NH_4^+, *TMAH* and TSS trends for each batch cycle. From Figure 2, the following conclusions can be inferred:

- the pH value changed during each cycle: it increased to alkaline values and then came back towards neutral values after several days. This was apparently due to a buffering effect of the growth medium;
- NH_4^+ concentration increased with time: this was a clear indication of the *TMAH* degradation and indeed started after the adaptation period of 36–48 h;
- the *TMAH* concentration trend showed a rapid degradation and a further decrease toward zero, after the adaptation period. It is possible to hypothesize that, after nearly two days, the *TMAH* was adsorbed on the biomass and, afterward, was gradually decomposed, reaching concentrations very low if compared to the initial one. The final *TMAH* concentration obtained in the two batch cycles was 7 and 4 mg/L;
- the biomass concentration increased up to the tenth/eleventh day, but after that, it was rather constant, at around 1300–1500 mg/L.

Figure 3 shows the *TMAH* degradation and the resulting NH_4^+ production for each cycle; the *TMAH* removal was higher than 99%, and this confirms the effectiveness of the biological process carried out in the experimental campaign. Hu et al. [18] stated that the aerobic sludge with a concentration of 2000 mg/L can gradually decompose *TMAH*, after several hours of inhibition, but the reduction in such ability usually occurs when the *TMAH* concentration reaches 150 mg/L. Instead, Lei et al. [15] found that an acclimated aerobic sludge reduces the inhibitory effect of *TMAH* up to 300 mg/L, but the aerobic process is not recommended for wastewater containing more than 1000 mg/L of such a molecule. Nevertheless, the 14-day acclimated strains were able to degrade higher concentrations of *TMAH*.

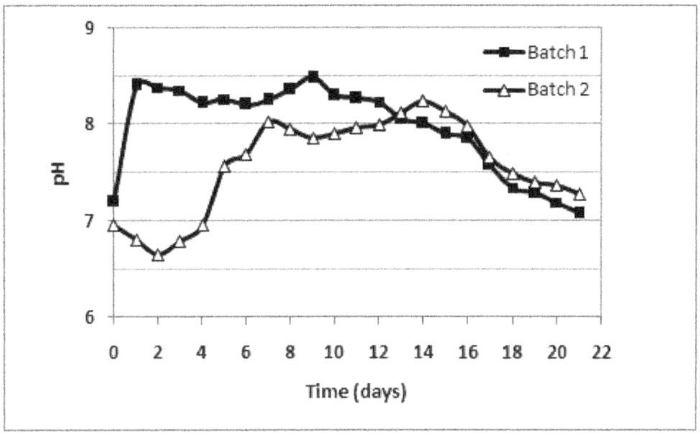

(a)

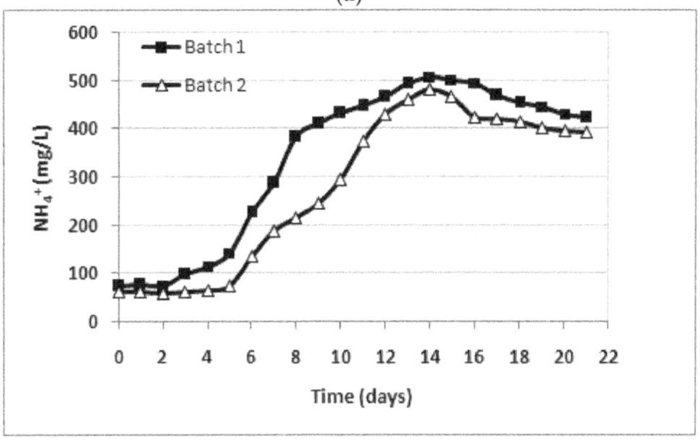

(b)

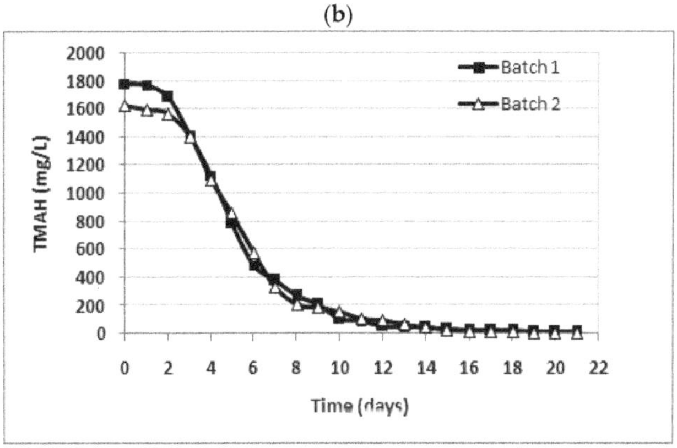

(c)

Figure 2. *Cont.*

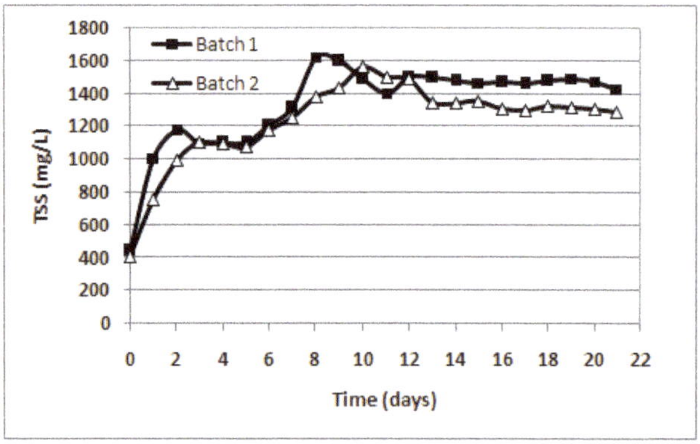

(d)

Figure 2. pH (**a**), NH_4^+ (**b**), *TMAH* (**c**),and TSS (**d**) trends for the effluent in batches 1 and 2.

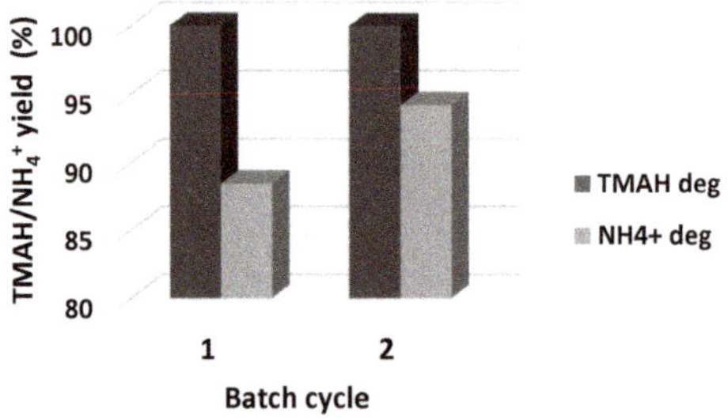

Figure 3. Degradation and NH_4^+ ion production for each cycle.

Comparing these results with those obtained in other prior experiments, where the feeding conditions were different (i.e.,1.5 L of *TMAH*/PR mixture feed (1.488 mL of *TMAH* mixed with 12 mL of PR) plus 1.5 L of growth medium, with a *TMAH* concentration of 992 mg/L), it is possible to observe that the increase in the initial *TMAH* concentration from 992 mg/L to 1780 g/L does not cause harmful effects on bacteria: as a matter of fact, the population of the microorganisms did not show any slowdown in their metabolic activity. The results of such tests are reported in Figure 4: six batch cycles were carried out with the same procedure described in Section 2.2 (25 °C, stirring at 70 rpm, 2 L/min of O_2, batch time 21 days). The final *TMAH* concentration was in the range of 2–5 mg/L.

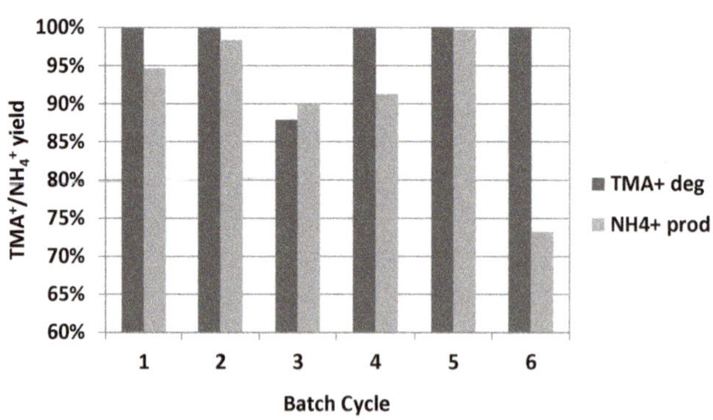

Figure 4. Degradation and NH_4^+ ion formation for previous experiments with different feed condition (50% waste solution (*TMAH*-PR)/50% growth medium), *TMAH* C_0= 992 mg/L.

4. Pilot Plant

At the moment, LFoundry neutralizes the *TMAH* by H_2SO_4 and NaOH, and the solution passes through an ion exchange resin filter from which the *TMAH* is stripped by another solution: in this manner, the *TMAH* can be concentrated and the resulting volume is lower. This solution is thus stored in a big tank and sent to an external plant authorized for the treatment of such waste. In addition, LFoundry also owns a conventional activated sludge system that already treats the wastewater from toilets, the canteen, the solution from which the *TMAH* is removed (from the ion-exchange) and other process wastewaters. Hence, the aim of LFoundry is to construct an upstream plant that can treat such particular liquid stream, instead of being disposed of externally, saving a significant amount of the annual operating costs relevant to the waste treatment.

The Monod model was used to design the pilot-scale bioreactor. The design was optimized by applying the minimization of the total volume, using three reactors in series [24].

Such a configuration, in continuous operating mode, is composed of three bioreactors in series that allow a remarkable saving in the total volume required for the treatment of the *TMAH*/PR solution. The volume of each bioreactor is indeed around 1.1 m^3 (total volume 3.3 m^3), whereas the volume of one single bioreactor would have been 10 m^3. The pilot plant is housed in two 40 ft standard containers and can treat three types of industrial effluents produced by LFoundry: line 1 treats the *TMAH*/PR mixed stream by the biological process, whereas line 2 (BOE) and line 3 (SEZ) treat other two waste streams containing high concentrations of nitrates, fluorides, and acetic acid. The first container includes one neutralization reactor, a storage tank and three biological reactors in series; the second container houses the equipment to treat the other two waste solutions by using physicochemical operations, in particular, one reactor, a plate and frame filter, and some tanks to store the effluents before and after the treatments. Some pictures of the pilot plant are shown in Figure 5.

(a) (b) (c)

Figure 5. 40 ft container housing the pilot plant (**a**), storage tank (**b**), and the three bioreactors (**c**).

The pilot-scale tests began in the winter 2018 and are currently being carried out for optimization purposes; the overall results will be published as soon as the experimental campaign ends. Nonetheless, a preliminary design of the full-scale plant was also carried out, considering that the amount of the *TMAH*/photoresist mixture currently produced at LFoundry is 6300 t/year. The optimized configuration with three reactors in series, 30 m^3 each, with pumps, two tanks for neutralization and final storage, PLC, and control devices, electricals, and more, will require an investment of around € 1.64 million. The total operating costs were estimated to be nearly 90 €/t, lower than the current cost paid for the external disposal of such solutions, that amounts to 140 €/t. The payback time is 4.75 years. LFoundry will evaluate the possibility of constructing the fully automated plant once a more accurate economic analysis, based on the pilot-scale data, is available.

5. Conclusions

The experiments carried out with *TMAH*/PR wastewater showed that the aerobic biological treatment is able to remove the *TMAH* molecule. In the present case, the mixture was composed of 10% of growth medium and 90% of *TMAH*/PR wastewater, while in other previous experiments, such a composition was 50% growth medium and 50% *TMAH*/PR. For each cycle that lasted 21 days, the *TMAH* concentration was reduced to 4–7 mg/L, with removal yields greater than 99.3%: this means that the microorganism populations already present in the sludge from the LFoundry's WWTP can adapt their metabolism and use the *TMAH* as substrate, when photoresist, another waste solution, is dosed as carbon source. Moreover, the optimal composition of the growth medium and all the process parameters like pH, temperature, O_2flow-rate, and stirring were optimized. The kinetic parameters of the Monod model were also obtained in order to design the pilot plant, whose capacity was set at 25 L/h. The adapted microorganisms were thus used for the inoculum in the pilot plant, where three bioreactors in series were chosen in order to reduce the total volume required by the process. The volume of each reactor is around 1.1 m^3. The pilot-scale experimental campaign is currently being carried out.

Author Contributions: Conceptualization, I.D.M. and M.P.; Methodology, S.Z.; Experimental Tests, V.I., N.M.I., V.C. and S.Z.; Analytical Measurements, V.I., S.Z., I.P.B. and N.M.I.; Investigation, I.P.B.; Data Curation, V.I.; Writing—Original Draft Preparation, F.F.; Writing-Review and Editing, F.F. and N.M.I.; Supervision, M.P. and F.V.; Project Administration, V.C. and I.D.M.; Funding Acquisition, F.V.

Funding: This research was funded by the EUROPEAN COMMISSION, grant number LIFE15 ENV/IT/000332, Project LIFE BITMAPS (http://www.lifebitmaps.eu/).

Acknowledgments: Authors kindly acknowledge the LFoundry's personnel for their precious help and work in the characterization of the samples and in the pilot-plant tests.

Conflicts of Interest: The authors declare no conflict of interest.

References

1. Lin, C.C.; Yang, C.C.; Ger, J.; Deng, J.F.; Hung, D.Z. TMAH poisoning. *Clin. Toxicol.* **2010**, *48*, 213–217. [CrossRef] [PubMed]
2. Lee, C.Y.; Wang, L.M.; Ngo, M.H.; Chen, T.H.; Cheng, H.H. Acute toxicity assessment of TFT-LCD wastewater using *Daphnia similis* and *Cyprinus carpio. Process Saf. Environ. Protect.* **2016**, *104*, 499–506. [CrossRef]
3. Lee, C.H.; Wang, C.L.; Lin, H.F.; Chai, C.Y.; Hong, M.Y.; Ho, C.K. Toxicity of tetramethylammonium hydroxide: Review of two fatal cases of dermal exposure and development of an animal model. *Toxicol. Ind. Health* **2011**, *27*, 497–503. [CrossRef] [PubMed]
4. Mori, I.C.; Arias-Barreiro, C.R.; Koutsaftis, A.; Ogo, A.; Kawano, T.; Yoshizuka, K.; Inayat-Hussain, S.H.; Aoyama, I. Toxicity of tetramethylammonium hydroxide to aquatic organisms and its synergistic action with potassium iodide. *Chemosphere* **2015**, *120*, 299–304. [CrossRef] [PubMed]
5. Chang, S.; Lin, K.Y.A.; Lu, C. Efficient adsorptive removal of tetramethylammonium hydroxide (TMAH) from water using graphene oxide. *Sep. Purif. Technol.* **2014**, *133*, 99–107. [CrossRef]
6. Chang, S.; Lu, C.; Lin, K.Y.A. Comparisons of kinetics, thermodynamics and regeneration of tetramethylammonium hydroxide adsorption in aqueous solution with graphene oxide, zeolite and activated carbon. *Appl. Surf. Sci.* **2015**, *326*, 187–194. [CrossRef]
7. Shu, H.Y.; Chang, M.C.; Liu, J.J. Cation resin fixed-bed column for the recovery of valuable TMAH reagent from the wastewater. *Process Saf. Environ. Prot.* **2016**, *104*, 571–586. [CrossRef]
8. Prahas, D.; Liu, J.C.; Ismadji, S.; Wang, M. Adsorption of tetramethylammonium hydroxide on activated carbon. *J. Environ. Eng.* **2012**, *138*, 232–238. [CrossRef]
9. Kelleher, B.P.; Doyle, A.M.; O'Dwyer, T.F.; Hodnett, B.K. Preparation and use of a mesoporous silicate material for the removal of tetramethylammonium hydroxide (TMAH) from aqueous solution. *J. Chem. Technol. Biotechnol.* **2001**, *76*, 1216–1222. [CrossRef]
10. Nishihama, S.; Takatori, K.; Yoshizuka, K. Separation and recovery of tetramethylammonium hydroxide with zeolitic adsorbents. *Ion Exch. Lett.* **2011**, *3*, 1–6.
11. Citraningrum, H.M.; Liu, J.C.; Chern, J.M. Removal of tetramethylammonium hydroxide from solution using ion exchange. *IEEE Trans. Semicond. Manuf.* **2013**, *26*, 214–220. [CrossRef]
12. Hirano, K.; Okamura, J.; Taira, T.; Sano, K.; Toyoda, A.; Ikeda, M. An efficient treatment technique for TMAH wastewater by catalytic oxidation. *IEEE Trans. Semicond. Manuf.* **2001**, *14*, 202–206. [CrossRef]

13. Wang, C.W.; Liang, C. Oxidative degradation of TMAH solution with UV persulfate activation. *Chem. Eng. J.* **2014**, *254*, 472–478. [CrossRef]
14. Noor, I.; Coenen, J.; Martin, A.; Dahl, O.; Aslin, M. Experimental investigation and techno-economic analysis of tetramethylammonium hydroxide removal from wastewater in nanoelectronics manufacturing via membrane distillation. *J. Membr. Sci.* **2019**, *579*, 283–293. [CrossRef]
15. Lei, C.N.; Whang, L.M.; Chen, P.C. Biological treatment of thin-film transistor liquid crystal display (TFT-LCD) wastewater using aerobic and anoxic/oxic sequencing batch reactors. *Chemosphere* **2010**, *81*, 57–64. [CrossRef]
16. Chang, K.F.; Yang, S.Y.; You, H.S.; Pan, J.R. Anaerobic treatment of tetramethylammonium hydroxide (TMAH) containing wastewater. *IEEE Trans. Semicond. Manuf.* **2008**, *21*, 486–491. [CrossRef]
17. Hu, T.H.; Whang, L.M.; Huang, C.Y. Methanogenic degradation of tetramethylammonium hydroxide by *Methanomethylovorans* and *Methanosarcina*. *J. Hazard. Mater.* **2018**, *357*, 180–186. [CrossRef]
18. Hu, T.H.; Whang, L.M.; Liu, P.W.G.; Hung, Y.C.; Chen, H.W.; Lin, L.B.; Chen, C.F.; Chen, S.K.; Hsu, S.F.; Shen, W.; et al. Biological treatment of TMAH (tetra-methyl ammonium hydroxide) in a full-scale TFT-LCD wastewater treatment plant. *Bioresour. Technol.* **2012**, *113*, 303–310. [CrossRef]
19. Liu, B.; Yoshinaga, K.; Wu, J.H.; Chen, W.Y.; Terashima, M.; Goel, R.; Pangallo, D.; Yasui, H. Kinetic analysis of biological degradation for tetramethylammonium hydroxide (TMAH) in the anaerobic activated sludge system at ambient temperature. *Biochem. Eng. J.* **2016**, *114*, 42–49. [CrossRef]
20. Chen, S.Y.; Lu, L.A.; Lin, J.G. Biodegradation of tetramethylammonium hydroxide (TMAH) in completely autotrophic nitrogen removal over nitrite (CANON) process. *Bioresour. Technol.* **2016**, *210*, 88–93. [CrossRef]
21. Innocenzi, V.; Zueva, S.; Prisciandaro, M.; De Michelis, I.; Di Renzo, A.; Mazziotti Di Celso, G.; Vegliò, F. Treatment of TMAH solutions from the microelectronics industry: A combined process scheme. *J. Water Process Eng.* **2019**, *31*, 100780. [CrossRef]
22. Moretti, G.; Matteucci, F.; Saraullo, M.; Vegliò, F.; Del Gallo, M. Selection of a very active microbial community for the coupled treatment of tetramethylammonium hydroxide and photoresist in aqueous solutions. *Int. J. Environ. Res. Public Health* **2018**, *15*, 41. [CrossRef] [PubMed]
23. Robinson, J.A.; Tiedje, J.M. Nonlinear estimation of Monod growth kinetic parameters from a single substrate depletion curve. *Appl. Environ. Microbiol.* **1983**, *45*, 1453–1458. [PubMed]
24. McDuffie, N.G. *Bioreactor Design Fundamentals*, 1st ed.; Butterworth-Heinermann: London, UK, 1991.

sustainability

MDPI

Review

Main Dimensions in the Building of the Circular Supply Chain: A Literature Review

Rocío González-Sánchez [1,*], Davide Settembre-Blundo [1,2], Anna Maria Ferrari [3] and Fernando E. García-Muiña [1]

1 Department of Business Administration (ADO), Applied Economics II and Fundaments of Economic Analysis, Rey-Juan-Carlos University, 28032 Madrid, Spain; davide.settembre@gresmalt.it (D.S.-B.); fernando.muina@urjc.es (F.E.G.-M.)
2 Gruppo Ceramiche Gresmalt, Via Mosca 4, 41049 Sassuolo, Italy
3 Department of Sciences and Methods for Engineering, University of Modena and Reggio Emilia, 42122 Reggio Emilia, Italy; annamaria.ferrari@unimore.it
* Correspondence: rocio.gonzalez@urjc.es; Tel.: +34-91-4887-786

Received: 29 February 2020; Accepted: 15 March 2020; Published: 20 March 2020

Abstract: Circular economy is an alternative to the traditional production model and has therefore attracted a great deal of attention from researchers. The change in the production system is accompanied by new logistical needs related both to resources and waste and to the distribution and recovery of products. The circular supply chain involves return processes and the manufacturer intends to capture additional value in the supply chain. In this paper, value chains have been mapped to visualize the links and interactions between the different stages and actors to understand the complexities of these systems and to make informed decisions. For this reason, and based on thorough literature review, the final objective of this work is to achieve a conceptual framework to study circular supply chain, which uses the main theoretical perspectives in strategic management literature. Four dimensions have been identified to support the development of these new supply chains—greater intensity in the relationships established in the supply chain, adaptation of logistics and organizational, disruptive and smart technologies, and a functioning environment. It can be concluded that to develop a new relationship capacity will allow for reaching more frequent, closer relationships with more actors. These relationships will be developed within an adapted organizational and logistical framework that is framed in new business model archetypes. However, dimensions related to the business environment such as sectoral, legislative, and fiscal frameworks must be incorporated.

Keywords: circular supply chain (CSC); circular supply chain management (CSCM); circular economy; sustainability; literature review; value creation

1. Introduction

The requirement to cover a constantly growing globalized demand in a sustainable way, implies an adequate and efficient management of supply chain operations [1]. Certain sectors, such as the automotive industry, have a complex supply chain network responsible for much of the environmental degradation in their value chain [2]. Concerned with improving sustainability in their supply chains to enhance their operational, economic, and social responsibility performance, many companies have begun to incorporate new or recycled materials, cleaner technologies, and new organizational and logistical practices [3,4].

Numerous papers support the importance of effective supply chain management for the economy of many countries. The development of policies and actions that achieve a more efficient and sustainable supply chain will allow better results, through the design of cost-efficient schedules, facilitating the flow, supporting "just-in-time" deliveries within supply chains, adopting 3R (reduce/reuse/recycle), and improving sustainability of the operations [3,5]. Management of the total cost in the supply chain must consider aspects such as transport costs, penalties for delays, costs for emissions, etc. Many of these costs not only have an impact on the profit and loss account, but also affect the sustainability of the supply process [6,7]. In fact, to facilitate processes within supply chains, reducing associated delays and improving the sustainability of supply chain operations, many distribution companies began to apply new systems and new techniques, as the dual-channel supply chains in which the manufacturer uses both vertical integration online and an offline intermediary [7], or the cross-docking technique that provides the fast flow of products from inbound trucks to assigned outbound trucks [1,3].

Integration and cooperation between production operations and transport enables improved performance and sustainability in the supply chain [6]. Sustainability need be reached through the network of corporation. This implies the involvement and coordination of the different actors of the supply chain, including manufacturers, logistics companies, distribution facility operators, and retailers [3,7]. Consequently, it is important to consider behavior at both the individual and organizational level. It is recommended that a strong mechanism be designed to motivate all members of the supply chain to participate in a joint sustainability effort that incorporates several types of perspectives [4]. So, [7] propose a sustainable risk-sharing contract which could distribute profits between channel members and coordinate the system under a fixed risk-sharing degree.

"The holistic shift from traditional supply chain to sustainable supply chain has been practiced in different industries for many years" [2] (p. 1). However, the application of the principles of the circular economy to the functioning of the supply chain, requires organizations to redesign their chains under a new approach [8]. The circular economy (CE) is an alternative paradigm to the current and dominant production model called "take-make-waste-dispose" [9–12] that causes a high amount of waste and an inability to regenerate the resources used. Therefore, CE can be considered an attempt to respond to a productive system based on the incessant development of economies of scale that will enable a continuous and growing demand for new products and services to be satisfied. Accordingly, through a programmed obsolescence [13], the life cycle of products launched on the market is reduced, which leads us to a "society based on waste".

In opposition, the CE would consider transforming the models of production and consumption oriented towards products, to models oriented towards solutions. Along these lines, various studies reconsider the management of materials and products or services, experimenting with how to extend their useful life, reuse them, re-manufacture or recycle them along the value chain from cradle to cradle [14–17]. It would imply a reduction in the production and consumption of raw materials [18]. Consequently, circular supply chain (CSC) promotes transformation from a linear to a circular model of flow of products [19]. The aim would be to provide a coherent framework for redesigning systems to enable a restorative economy, based on a benefit from the flow of resources and products over their lifetime, limiting the material input to society [20–22]. Thus, environmental management positively influences operational performance [23]. Change in the production system is accompanied by new logistical needs related both to resources and waste and to the distribution and recovery of products. Thus, the network of organizations involved in the supply chain establishes upward and downward linkages in the different processes and activities, so it is necessary to achieve a necessary integration [24]. The CSC involves "return processes and the manufacturer intends to capture additional value and further integrate all activities in the supply chain" [25] (p. 3).

The possibility of achieving a more sustainable economic system has attracted the attention of both researchers and other stakeholders, which has been reflected in a significant increase in articles published in recent years in international journals indexed in the top positions of recognized databases [26]. However, research on supply chain development in the field of circular economy is fragmented between several research streams [26,27]. Although the field of supply chain research is well established, further research is needed on the adaptation of the chain to the principles of circular economy [28,29]. This paper conducts a systematic literature review (SLR) on the CSCs. However, there are still numerous areas of research that require further study [15,16], which could be gathered around two fundamental pillars—their conceptualization and implantation [30].

Circular supply chain has become a strategic variable for organizations, going beyond environmental aspects. There is also an important route widening the focus of study and considering the social and economic scenarios that affect the different stakeholders, in a broad sense [31], as most of the research on practices in the sphere of change towards a more sustainable productive system has been developed [16]. It is necessary to define a new range of specific actions to adequately implement the circular economy principles to supply chains, for which the adoption of systemic innovations is necessary.

To achieve these goals, the present research addresses the following main research questions:

1. What is the definition of circular supply chain? What other terms are used as synonyms and what differential aspects can be established?
2. What theories of strategic management could be applied to the analysis of the circular supply chain that would make it easier to frame the practices to be carried out?
3. What are the dimensions that allow the design of circular supply chains? What kind of challenges do they pose?

The paper is structured as follows. After this introduction, the paper presents a description of the methodology used to select previous literature and a brief definition of the circular supply chain. Next, fundamental criteria to consider when designing specific actions in the design and implementation of supply chains. Finally, findings, conclusions, and future lines of research are presented.

2. Materials and Methods

To understand a phenomenon, it is necessary to build a theoretical basis. Similarly, to innovate and create new possibilities to empirically reconstruct phenomena, it is also necessary to go beyond the current theoretical frameworks [32]. The building of a theory is a slow and progressive process of construction. The first contributions are not very specific, but as it is studied in depth, the theoretical framework establishes the dimensions that give it its identity. A systematic review of the literature has been carried out as it allows for the evaluation and interpretation of all available research that is relevant to a particular research question in a thematic area. It is a suitable method for structuring the conceptual basis of the novel research topic [33]. Building a correct theoretical base allows the development of useful action models. It allows us to summarize the existing evidence, and therefore, to capture the existing knowledge for its development. In addition, through this type of review some gaps in current research can be identified to define future areas of research.

Systematic review of the literature is a form of secondary study that uses a well-defined methodology. For this, the next step is to define the search protocol, the terms to be searched, the combinations of terms, the search strategy used for each source and how the results of each search will be recorded. The phases of this research begin with the formulation of the research questions, after which the articles were located in the databases with the highest coverage for the researched topic: Scopus. The literature review was conducted between November 2019 and February 2020. The keywords used in the search were "circular supply chain"; "green supply chain" AND "circular economy"; and "closed-loop supply chain" AND "circular economy", according to the following steps. The first search was made through the main term—"circular supply chain"—in the title, abstract, keywords, and the main text of the papers. This first search was completed with the terms associated—green supply chain and closed-loop supply chain—when the article is associated to the CE, if the journal has no results from the first search or only one paper. Limiting the literature search to the one in which authors choose to explicitly mention CE, ensures that only relevant content has been included [34]. To corroborate the suitability of the selected papers, in a second round, the theoretical development of the paper was analyzed in detail.

Based on Ferreira Gregorio, Pié, and Terceño´s study [35], we considered the main journals with the highest impact on Scopus—Q1 and Q2—with the greatest number of papers published on circular economy. The six main journals with the greatest impact in the categories directly related to the analyzed concept were used in the search (*Journal of Cleaner Production; Sustainability; Resources, Conservation and Recycling; Production Planning and Control; Journal of Industrial and Production Engineering*; and *Ecological Economics*). In two of them no results were found—*Journal of Industrial and Production Engineering* and *Ecological Economics*—and new two of great impact were incorporated—*Production Planning and Control*; and *Resources* (Table 1).

Table 1. Sources of information.

Journal	Number of Documents	Ranking/Impact SCOPUS 2018	Category
Journal of Cleaner Production	19	Q1/1,62 (SJR)	Engineering industrial and manufacturing engineering; environmental science; industrial and manufacturing engineering; renewable energy, sustainability and the environment
Sustainability (Switzerland)	19	Q2/0,55 (SJR)	Geography, planning and development; management, monitoring, policy and law
Production Planning and Control	7	Q1/1,43 (SJR)	Business, management and accounting strategy and management; computer science; computer science applications; decision sciences management science and operations research; engineering industrial and manufacturing engineering
Resources, Conservation and Recycling	3	Q1/1,54 (SJR)	Waste management and disposal
Journal of Industrial Ecology	1	Q1/1,49 (SJR)	Environmental science; social sciences
Resources	1	Q2/0,65 (SJR)	Environmental science; management, monitoring, policy and law nature and landscape conservation

The first six journals in order of the number of publications are *Journal of Cleaner Production; Sustainability; Production Planning and Control; Resources, Conservation and Recycling; Journal of Industrial Ecology*; and *Resources*. The most relevant papers linking supply chain and circular economy were selected gathering a core sample of 50 papers taken into account for the purpose of content analysis. Figure 1 shows the distribution of articles in the various journal.

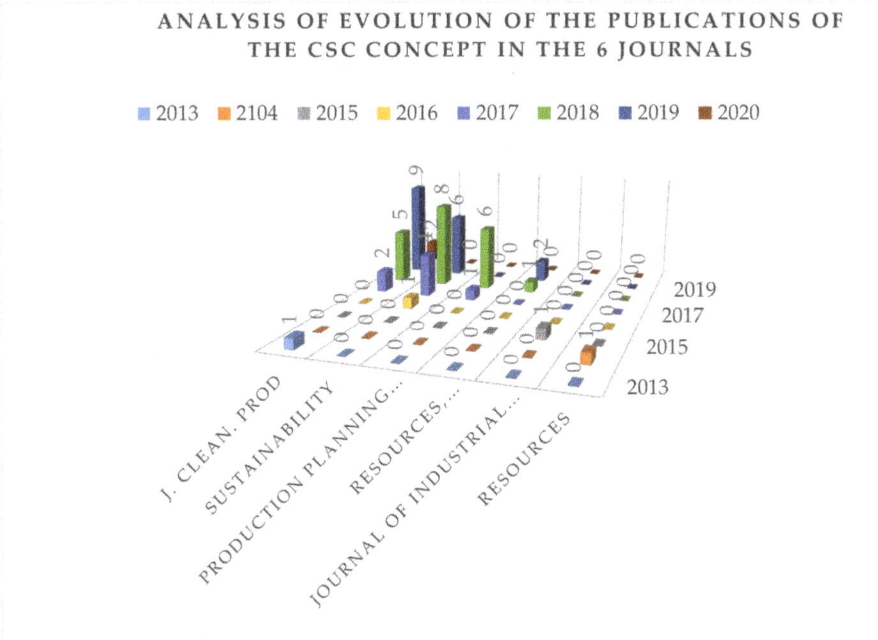

Figure 1. Analysis of the evolution of the publication of the 'circular supply chain' concept in the journals under study.

The journals with the majority of publications related to circular supply chain are *Journal of Cleaner Production* and *Sustainability*, each with 19 articles. The year 2018 is the one with the highest number of articles, followed very closely by 2019. The temporal evolution of the 50 scientific texts analyzed in the years between 2013 and 2020 offers an ascending evolution. It is remarkable the exponential growth of the publication of articles related to circular supply chain since 2017.

3. The Conceptualization of Circular Supply Chain

Many papers consider Pearce and Turner as the authors who first coined the term CE in the early 1990s [16,24,30,36]. Pearce and Turner in their seminal work [37] (p. 67) considered that "scientists tend to define pollution differently from economists." In this assertion it can be established one of the main reasons that leads these authors to expose in the 90s the need to reconcile economy and environment, expanding the horizons of the economy. It implies, therefore, the passage from a linear and open economy to a circular and closed model. An industrial system that is restorative or regenerative by intention and design.

The starting point is that economic growth is directly related to flows of materials and energy [38]. The classical linear economy is based on the manufacture of short-lived products, planned obsolescence, economies of scale, and the consequent growing consumer demand for new products. While the CE is based on the consideration of the negative externalities that the consumption of resources originates [9]. Therefore, CE is focused on how to avoid, minimize, restore, and/or compensate stakeholders [39,40]. The application of circularity in the supply chain has two main pillars. One is based on extending the durability of products or increasing the amount of remanufacturing, repair, renovation, and recycling cycles. The second would be the extension of the period of time during which the materials are kept in use [41].

It is necessary to rethink the productive system, in such a way that CE can focus on the three Rs (reduction, reuse, and recycling), the 6Rs (reuse, recycle, redesign, remanufacture, reduce, recover), or the 9Rs (refuse, reduce, reuse, repair, refurbish, remanufacture, repurpose, recycle, recover) to achieve greener but also more efficient production processes, which would make them more profitable for organizations [39,42–45]. Accordingly, CE has traditionally been associated with "sustainability" [30,46–49]. It understands industry from a restorative and regenerative perspective by intention and design [3]. In this sense, it would mean the attempt to dissociate economic growth from the indiscriminate consumption of resources and goods [37], through practices that allow for optimizing the industrial system. The circular economy considers the supply chain as a critical element for its implementation, which requires the acceptance of all actors involved [50]. However, the application of practices related to other organizations is much more complex than when applied simply at the organizational level [51].

Through circular supply chains it is possible not only to reduce the production of waste, but also to achieve self-sustaining production systems in which materials are returned to the production cycle [52]. Circular supply chains apply to both the manufacturing and service sectors [53]. Various terms have been wrongly used in the literature to talk about the application of the paradigms of the circular economy—reverse supply chain, close-loop chain or open-loop chain, and green supply chain. However, it is essential to consider the main characteristics of these different types of supply chains, since although they cannot be considered as circular supply chains, they have contributed to their constitution.

3.1. *Reverse Supply Chain*

Reverse supply chain management has been developed as an adaptation of circular economy principles to supply chain management. Indeed, a reverse supply chain includes activities dealing with product design, operations, and end-of-life management in order to maximize value creation over the entire lifecycle through value recovery of after-use products either by the original product manufacturer or by a third party. Reverse supply chains are either open-loop or closed-loop [52,54]. Although the recovery of products at the end of their useful life is considered to be an environmentally friendly activity, such recovery requires an energy cost and generates pollution from the transport and subsequent treatment of the products that must be considered [55].

3.2. *Closed-loop Chain vs. Open-loop Chain*

Open-loop supply chains involve materials recovered by parties other than the original producers who are capable of reusing these materials or products. On the other hand, closed-loop supply chains deal with the practice of taking back products from customers and returning them to the original manufacturer for the recovery of added value by reusing the whole product or part of it [54]. Closed-loop supply chains expanding on reverse logistics, include remanufacturing, reuse, repair, refurbishment, and recycling [56]. They require considerable investment in resources, and then development of a collection system which takes back the product at its end-of-life [41]. Open-loop chains involve materials from several producers and closed-loop chains focus on one particular manufacturer [52].

3.3. *Green Supply Chain:*

Green supply chains engage suppliers and customers to foster environmental cooperation that will result in gains associated with both environmental and economic performance [26]. As opposed to traditional supply chain, "green supply chain management is characterized by greenness in product design, selection and purchase of raw materials, production, distribution of final products, and after sale services" [8] (p. 1284).

Two approaches can be considered when developing practices in green supply chains, based on monitoring and collaboration. In the monitoring approach, the purchasing company sets the standard for evaluating suppliers and their products. When based on the collaborative approach, buyers are required to be directly involved in improving the environmental performance of suppliers, focusing on long-term objectives [23].

These terms appear in literature and are used interchangeably in several papers. However, as demonstrated, there are important differences to consider between these concepts (Figure 2). Circular supply chain is a step beyond closed supply chains and green supply chains. Firstly, it expands the number of actors in the chain by also considering sectors other than that of origin. Secondly, the relationships between actors also change. Customers can return the product or its waste to any actor in the value chain of the production system within the industry sector, or with different industrial sectors [27].

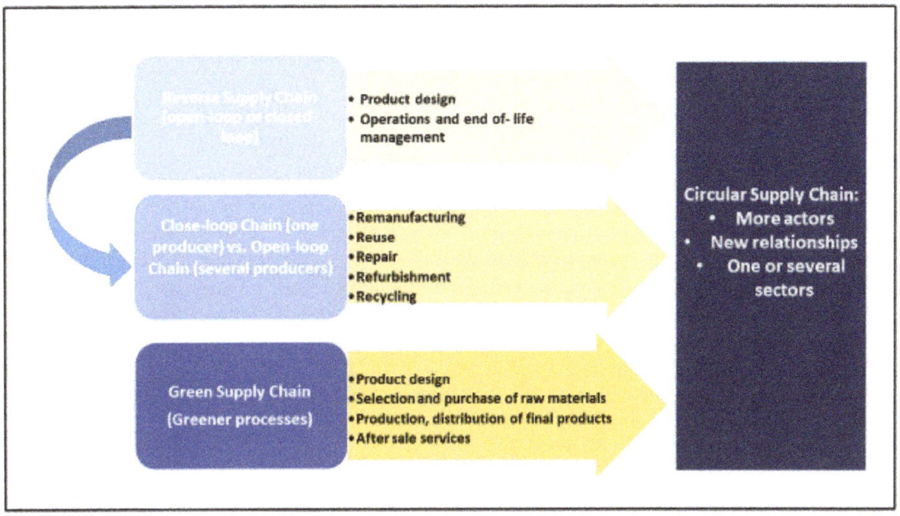

Figure 2. Contribution of the main terms related to the circular supply chain.

However, the theoretical concept needs to be translated into reality through strategies and guidelines that allow a more rational productive system to be achieved [44,57]. Six stages of maturity have been established based on a logic sequence of general management activities—problem identification, objective and intervention activities development activities, implementation and operation activities, and monitoring activities [58] (p. 23). Therefore, circular supply chain would be a guide for mapping the necessary key activities, potential challenges, and available resources so that the company can proactively develop individual and organizational tools to achieve its economic, social, and environmental objectives [30]. In such a situation, the company must rethink both the strategic activities of the company and the relationships established with external partners [59]. Therefore, we find a transformation of the value chain of the companies that wish to adopt the circular approach [44].

4. Building the Circular Supply Chain: Dimensional Design

4.1. Circular Supply Chain Management (CSCM)

Geissdoerfer et al. [60] (p. 714) define "the configuration and coordination of the organizational functions marketing, sales, R&D, production, logistics, IT, finance, and customer service within and across business units and organizations to improve operative effectiveness and efficiency of the system and generate competitive advantages." Circular supply chain management (CSCM) offers a compelling perspective that includes the vision of a zero-waste economy and the restorative and regenerative cycles designed based on circular thinking.

For this restoration and regeneration of materials to achieve the vision of zero waste, business model and supply chain designs must be adapted with the participation of a wide range of stakeholders [27]. For them, distributors must be considered from a broader perspective, since they are no longer considered only as the company's suppliers—closed-loop—but also as others in the same sector—open-loop, same sector—and even in other sectors—open-loop, cross sector [61]. Decision making in supply chain management should be done with the estimation of different types of costs. This estimation generally depends on several factors that make up the supply chain [62], which will be analyzed from the main theoretical perspectives in strategic management literatures.

4.2. Theoretical Perspectives in Strategic Management Literature

The resource-based view (RBV) [63–65] contributes to a better understanding of how the company as a whole works, as well as the resources and competencies fundamental for the company to redesign its operations in response to a change in competitive conditions. "Companies need certain dynamic capabilities and organizational routines to deal with the increased complexity of managing innovation from a sustainable perspective" [66] (p. 225). The capacities, routines, and resources included in the business model must allow, on the one hand, the detection of opportunities with the objective of obtaining valuable knowledge about the business habitat [67], and on the other hand, seizure through organizational capacities to take advantage of recognized opportunities and create value from them [68]. Both must achieve the implementation of new products, services, or processes [66]. Therefore, "RBV is considered as an adequate theoretical framework to understand whether specific resources applied to the CE by businesses are relevant for closing production loops without affecting the level of competitiveness" [69] (p. 3).

Industrial ecology (IE) can be defined as a policy with the aim of reducing the amount of waste creation by examining the flows of materials and energy in industrial systems as closing the material flow loop efficiently [70,71]. "The IE enables understanding how the industrial system works, how it is regulated, and what interactions it presents, to restructure it in order to make it similar to natural systems" [72] (p. 2). For all that, circular supply chain incorporates concepts and ideas from IE.

The agency theory will also condition how it operates, since the company (who act as principal) must ensure that the different primary stakeholders (customers or suppliers) will behave in accordance with the contractual terms established. These terms should enable the achievement of business objectives related both to the provision of sustainable services and to the sale and recovery of products at the end of their useful life [31,73]. It must therefore consider temporal aspects that would be related to the technical life of the product and the duration of the cycle of use of the same one [72]. The value chains can be mapped to visualize the linkages and interactions between the different stages and chain actors to understand the complexities of such multi-actor systems and make informed decisions regarding the coordination and balance among stakeholders of a supply chain [74,75]. For this reason, [45] consider that greater intensity is required in the relationships established in the supply chain and with customers. It implies a change of focus, focusing on the life cycle of the product and not on the quantity of the product produced.

Strategic networks are stable inter-organizational links which are of importance to the company and which express these links through various forms, such as strategic alliances or long-term buyer-supplier partnerships [76]. The network perspective is of great relevance for understanding value creation in the circular economy due to the importance of the networks that are formed between companies, their suppliers, their customers, and other relevant partners [60].

The configuration of the network in terms of density and centrality [77] and the importance of governance mechanisms such as trust. Other sources of value in strategic networks include shortened time to market [78], enhanced transaction efficiency, reduced asymmetries of information, and improved coordination between the firms involved in an alliance [76]. It seeks "to change organizational mindsets to facilitate collaborative knowledge development and sharing, the creation of shared visions, and collaborative value propositions" [79] (p. 23).

In the context of institutional theory, companies incorporate social legitimacy through adopting the norms and social traditions predominant in their environment [23]. Powerful institutions have an option of implementing policies which boost organizations and the population to adopt a practice [80]. The environment of the circular economy is governed by new rules and customs that revolutionize social, cultural, and political models.

From the main theoretical perspectives of strategic management literature, we propose four main dimensions that would allow us to classify the main factors found in the literature review (Figure 3). In the following sections we will carry out a detailed analysis of these dimensions and their variables, to finally propose a conceptual model to support the design and implementation of circular supply chains.

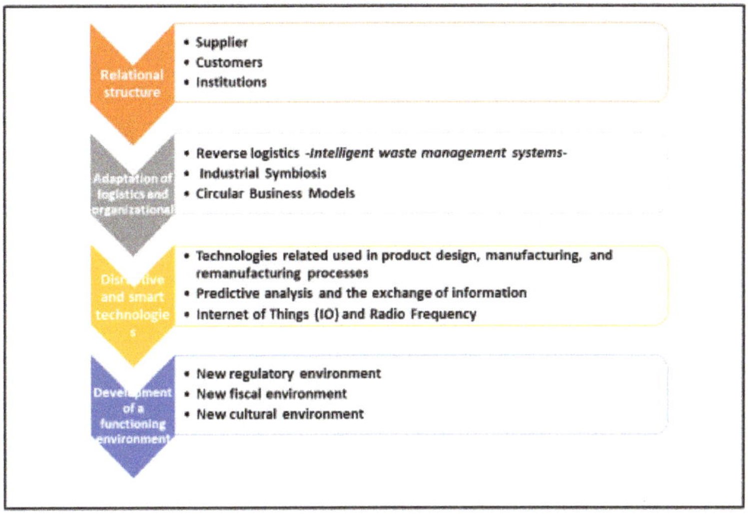

Figure 3. Main dimensions in the design of circular supply chains.

4.3. Relational Structure

There are different actors involved in the supply chain with different organizational management structures [81]. Current configurations of the supply chain must be redesigned to implement the exchange of waste and industrial by-products considering the principles of the circular economy [56]. This problem involves "a variety of stakeholders, demands behavioral changes, and requires a complete rethinking of the current waste management systems and the dominant linear economic model" [82] (p. 1). Circular thinking must be applied at all stages of the supply chain and go beyond the boundaries of the sector [27]. This involves different stakeholders from a broader perspective than has been done in the traditional supply chain. It is not only a question of change in the productive system, but also of incorporating relations between the agents involved. Collaboration in the supply chain enables a network of actors to be connected in their supply chain by managing the transparency of data, flows and exchanges of material, responsibilities, predictability, and benefit sharing [4,83].

"Supply chain management involves different actors and a socio-ecological system which explains tensions and driving forces in the management of the supply chain" [50] (p. 4). Sharing a vision of the future in CE, in particular in an early stage, makes it possible to achieve clear collective goals and serves as inspiration, motivation, and direction [83]. Cooperation between internal or external stakeholders in the supply chain will also facilitate the exchange of information, whereas industrial symbiosis networks facilitate the need for exchange of by-products, materials and energy between producers [41,84]. There are environmental considerations for circular supply chain design that consider the flow of materials and energy between different companies, allowing the formation of an industrial system of symbiotic exchange of resources and waste products [85]. The company leading the process will be a crucial actor in the supply chain, as its decisions will have a cascading effect on the other actors.

Furthermore, it can serve as a reference when it comes to transferring sustainable practices into the productive process [50]. For all these reasons, it is necessary to study the new relationships that are established with all the players involved in the circular supply chain.

4.3.1. Suppliers

"Suppliers, as the first layer of the supply chain network, pose a great impact on environmental pollution" [62] (p. 1). In addition, the relationship with suppliers becomes closer, in such a way that efficient management of resources is shared. It is essential to make a correct selection of the suppliers to guarantee lower costs of treatment of the materials and a lower environmental impact, reducing the distribution centers and the vehicles used. Therefore, it is necessary to create a framework to structure the decision-making problems and use the methods to decide between multiple alternatives [62]. The selection process can be completed with further development of suppliers to improve the performance of the existing supplier [2].

One problem to consider is the inventory–location and routes [62,86], so it would be convenient to consider a smaller number of trips and with shorter routes. The routes for a fleet of vehicles could be optimized with regard to costs and emissions [55]. New tools can be used for this purpose, such as novel diploid evolutionary algorithm for the truck scheduling problem [3]. The direct impact of both direct transport—transport between the buyer and the first-tier supplier—and indirect transport—transport following the trade operations between different geographical markets—by suppliers in the circular supply chain should be considered in the environmental impact [86]. So, it is recommended to favor local suppliers located in the final markets in order to reduce the costs of indirect transport in the circular supply system [62,86].

There are additional criteria in the selection of suppliers' waste handling activity they affect to estimate the net environmental impact. Reducing the pre-deposition of waste in landfills, avoids producing additional emissions. In addition, it is important to consider the level of usability of the waste with respect to the virgin raw material. Poor usability would lead to additional emissions and changes in productivity [86].

4.3.2. Customers

In the linear economy, customers are the final link in the supply chains, playing a passive role. In the circular economy, among other actors in the supply chain, customers are required to take an active part in the recovery of products and the recycling of waste materials [87]. The customer becomes a key participant in the strategic network that is developed in the circular economy, so it is essential to promote loyalty and satisfaction to establish a longer-term relationship. "Firms have been increasingly influenced by customers' ethical values and ecological thinking, pushing them to address environmental management practices" [2] (p. 4). Companies applying the principles of the circular economy in their supply chain should share common objectives and cooperate with customers to encourage green purchasing behavior [8].

However, within the framework of the circular economy, it is necessary to further evolve customer behavior and values to reduce the environmental impact of products in the usage stage [2]. The transition to CE requires changes in the behavior of customers both in their consumption and in the treatment of the waste they produce. These changes can be brought about through the implementation of awareness campaigns and education for sustainability [27].

In this context, the ownership of the product that the company has manufactured does not end with the sale of it. In fact, the productive system must contemplate the reincorporation of the product to the productive process. In this sense, the useful life of the products acquires a new dimension. For this reason, we can consider a change of model in which the sale is associated to the utility of the product, and not to the naked property of the same one. A collaborative consumption model needs to be developed for improved interaction among customers, suppliers, and retailers to access to products rather than ownership of products [19]. For that reason, it is necessary to consider, in diverse industries, other commercial relations with clients beyond sales [1]. Thus, customers could participate actively by sharing their solutions and by providing feedback [50]. "Supply chains can become sustainable and improve their economic and socio-environmental performance by motivating customer behavior toward green consumption patterns, which, in turn, motivate producers and suppliers to change their operations" [55] (p. 652). Customers' behavior directly affects the capacity of the market. In the supply chain, in order to influence such behavior, it should consider the difference between the cost of the warranty for new products and remanufactured products and extend the customers' utility function from the consumer's perspective, optimizing warranty period decisions [88].

Another tool when it comes to influencing customer behavior is the design of proper reward programs. In contrast to the prevailing assumption of customer preference for monetary compensation as driver to participate, current papers have shown that customers may prefer rewards associated with facilitating the collection process of waste or products [87]. Integrating the customer behavior approach into the supply chain would lead to a more evolved model that they have called the extended sustainable supply chain, which considers both environmental factors and strategies for change [55].

4.3.3. Institutions

Institutional pressure is considered to be the influence exerted by the institutional environment through social norms, rules, and/or culture. This pressure has a significant positive impact on supply chain relationship management and sustainable supply chain design [85]. Governments could promote public demand of sustainable products and a greater involvement to support the implementation of circular economy practices [50]. They can develop appropriate policies, guidelines, plans, measures, and targets for the long-term promotion of the CE and sustainable society [89,90].

Government intervention with respect to the application of dynamic intervention mechanisms or subsidies should be conditioned by the preferences of clients or consumers [91]. "Many governments around the world have also introduced a series of remanufacturing policies and regulations to encourage and guide enterprises to focus on the source of sustainable development" [92] (p. 16).

In view of the above, we propose the following proposals related to external relations.

Proposition 1 (P_1). Collaboration within the supply chain network positively affects environmental and economic performance of circular supply chains.

$P_{1.1.}$ Correct selection of the suppliers positively affects environmental and economic performance of circular supply chains.

$P_{1.2.}$ Designing tools to influence customer behavior positively affects environmental and economic performance of circular supply chains.

$P_{1.3.}$ Institutional pressure through social norms, rules, and/or culture positively affects environmental and economic performance of circular supply chains.

4.4. Adaptation of Logistics and Organizational Management

The change implied by the application of the principles of circular economy in the supply chain requires the adaptation of the organization, in general, and of production, in particular. For this purpose, three fundamental related concepts are analyzed—reverse logistic, industrial symbiosis, and circular business models.

Reverse logistics are fundamental to the application of CE principles in supply chain logistics, both in achieving greater extraction of product value and in the reuse of materials or products [27]. All members in the supply chain must be involved for the true operationalization of reverse logistics [93]. The literature review also relates that reverse logistics is a key component of remanufacturing [94]. "Remanufacturing is emerging as one of the closed-loop supply chain approaches for the circular economy but it is beneficial and successful only if the products are designed for remanufacturing.

Remanufacturing is the only circular business model which provides the latest feature and warranty to the products" [90] (p. 2). The technique allows commodities to be moved from where they have been consumed to the place where they will be processed to capture value or appropriate disposal; aspects such as packaging or the geographical dispersion of points of consumption are essential [80,89]. The focus would be on efficient packaging design strategies abiding regulations and utilizing end-of-life of packaging material [34].There is a need for a systemic approach in understanding the relationship between packaging and supply due to the significant global footprint of multiple product physical supply chains [80].

Associated with reverse logistics, the adaptation of waste management systems must also be developed. Intelligent waste management systems involve both infrastructure and management aspects, but also aspects related to the behavior of citizens, product designers, producers, and policy makers. The functions in this system consider from the design of the products or services to the end-of-life management [82,95]. The involvement of the main actors is essential to control or to decrease waste generation [36,82]. So, the capacities analyzed must be completed with the relational capacity that considers a wide range of interests of the different stakeholders, both internal and external. As for suppliers and customers, the relational capacity must turn them into strategic factors, managing to develop "supply loops" in such a way that the company can choose suppliers offering better-performing materials, or recover products, components, and materials used and incorporate them back into the productive system in a systematic way [46,66,73,96].

Within this relational capacity we find the industrial symbiosis that favors the transformation of waste from a process into input or raw material between companies that work together, whether or not they belong to the same industry [44]. This could mean that linking value chains would require new governance structures—incentive intensity, administrative control, autonomous adaptation, and coordinated adaptation—with hybrid and hierarchical characteristics to better face with the interdependencies resulting from current transactions [97].

Finally, a new business model is required to develop more integrated systems that enable moving from products toward associated services and reuse practices. The circular business model implementation encourages the design of circular or reverse supply chains, allowing products at the end of their life cycles to reenter the supply chain as production [81]. So, a circular business model could provide managerial practices for design and implementation of supply chain [29]. There are a wide number of business model archetypes that can be used as a starting point [29,98]. Some studies propose some business models that favor the implementation of circular supply chains. For example, [29,95,99,100] confirm that product service systems (PSS) business models have the potential to trigger and enhance the circularity features of supply chains, which can be complemented by other tools, such as the sustainable value analysis tool, to assist practitioners.

It should be considered that reuse needs to be developed in a profound way, both considering the characteristics of the material itself, as well as its quality or usefulness, and analyzing aspects of the market. There are differences between sustainable business models and circular business models, since the latter not only create sustainable value, but also involve dynamic and continuous management, allowing the loops of resources to be modified [20,30]. To reach this, structural, cultural, and social change must be achieved. "Shifting toward a circular model may offer enormous opportunities, including cost savings through waste reduction, better supply chain management, lower sensitivity to resource price volatility, and longer, better relationships with customers" [31] (p. 4). In relation to the work to be done on relationships, [72] state that promoting collaboration between external and internal stakeholders is part of the model.

Then, our proposals are defined as follows:

Proposition 2 (P_2). The adaptation of organizational and productive structures positively affects environmental and economic performance of circular supply chains.

P2.1. Reverse logistic positively affects environmental and economic performance of circular supply chains.

P2.2. Industrial symbiosis positively affects environmental and economic performance of circular supply chains.

P2.3. Circular business models positively affect environmental and economic performance of circular supply chains.

4.5. The Use of Disruptive and Smart Technologies

Considering the complexity of applying the circular economy approach to the supply chain, the sector requires a deliberate and detailed monitoring system which should be adaptive to technological changes [5,34,101]. The new smart technologies allow the development of new functionalities necessary for productive and management change [58].

Industry 4.0 term is used for the fourth industrial revolution incorporating factors such as the Internet of Things (IoT), augmented reality, additive manufacturing (AM), big data, cloud computing, simulation, industrial automation, and cybersecurity [102]. As far as technology is concerned, there is still a long way to go. Smart enabling technologies in a circular framework can help both to facilitate efficient monitoring, collection, separation and transport of waste for value recovery and proper disposal, as in recent years, to data acquisition and communication technologies [82]. Current material recovery technologies are opportune to control phases by penalizing incorrect behaviors [5],

We can consider different typologies according to the objective sought in the supply chain. Firstly, those technologies related used in product design, manufacturing, and remanufacturing processes to a reduction of production costs and to achieve more sustainable operations—such as augmented reality technology, intelligent robots, or 3D printing for CSCM [92]. For example, those related to extending the life cycle of products, eliminating programmed obsolescence. Similarly, the rapid development of network technology has also allowed the development of the electronic channel, with the advantages of fewer intermediaries and greater efficiency in control and lower inventory risk [91].

Secondly, new technological tools now allow predictive analysis and the exchange of information with stakeholders. Developing computer tools based on collaborative platforms building waste analytics to report in the supply chains is important to ensure that the value of materials is sustained within the economic circle [24]. So, it is necessary to go deeper into the functions of big data in circular supply chain management, as they allow for predictive analysis of supply chain sustainability performance [27,103].

Thirdly, the Internet of Things (IO) and radio frequency; through the Internet of Things (IO) and the Internet of services, information is monitored, controlled, and transferred, orienting the actions to be developed. Industry 4.0 has enabled the design, planning, and operation of sustainable supply chains that ensure the incorporation of environmental protection into supply management [53]. Identification technologies (Radio Frequency Identification (RFID), Near Field Communication (NFC) sensors, Global Positioning System (GPS), etc.) can be used to improve traceability and to improve product life cycle information management [20]. These technologies facilitate real-time data collection and inform effective decision-making in restoration activities [82].

Achieving more economical and targeted technologies can facilitate processes in circular supply chains, since the exchange of technologies and the innovation that makes it possible to improve the operation of the whole chain [89]. Supported by this technological revolution, are new theoretical concepts of relevance. The integration of Industry 4.0 in the circular economy allows the optimization of the use of resources and energy by implementing disruptive technologies, although it is in its early stages [27,53].

All these arguments encourage us to propose that:

Proposition 3 (P_3). Smart technologies implemented with sustainable practices positively affect environmental and economic performance of circular supply chains.

4.6. Development of a Functioning Environment: New Regulatory, Fiscal, and Cultural Environment

Circular supply chains take on a global character, however, economic viability will depend on government support in their implementation [52], which implies having to manage legislation from different regions and their corresponding regulations [50]. It would be necessary to reach a systematic regulation and policy system, with better interactions among policy makers, governments, industry, and society [28]. An absence of firm legislative mechanism affects the manufacturing firm's decisions to incorporate eco-friendly solutions to their operations [19]. "Due to the lack of regulatory pressures, organizations tend to continue the status quo of waste management, which is often a neglected part of supply chain operations management" [82] (p. 5).

Stricter government regulations around the world will place responsibility on all actors in the supply chain for implementing the necessary measures, for example, facilitating the adoption of reverse logistics initiatives. Establishing shared responsibility laws for waste management would involve manufacturers, retailers, government, waste pickers, and customers, which would facilitate both collaboration between actors and the attribution of responsibilities [93]. Government regulations need to prescribe clear guidelines for operating within each step of the supply chain and enforce penalties for non-compliance [84]. In summary, it would be desirable, in order to encourage the implementation of circular supply chains, that regulatory intervention at government and European Commission level brings clarity to the law so that it does not prevent CE collaboration [41].

Sectoral agreements are critical instruments as formalization is expected to encourage companies in the supply chain to implement, for example, logistics systems for waste [93]. This fact is important if we consider that sectors can act as important transmission centers between suppliers and consumers in the global network, providing additional information [104]. Whereas in circular supply chains there is a need for greater collaboration at a horizontal level between supply chains and between different industry sectors, therefore cross-sectoral standards are required through legislation, beyond the voluntary cooperation that arises at company level [41]. However, in order to properly design policy interventions in specific sectors through supply chains, affected communities must first be identified [104].

A lack of economic benefits in the short run can be understood as the increasing short-term cost [19]. In addition, many organizations find it difficult to obtain financial resources to improve their waste management, especially if they deal with it on an individual basis, as this prevents them from achieving scale economies [82]. In this sense, it is key to carry out correct fiscal management by the corresponding institutions, so that, for example, recycling can be encouraged by exempting recycled products and even post-consumer waste from taxes [89]. In this line, it would also play a role to consider subsidies that encourage the use of renewable energy, penalizing those that are more polluting [5].

Finally, the cultural environment that frames the application of the principles of the circular economy must be considered. Cultural changes in both society and business must be considered. The lack of environmental education and the protection in the adult generation is reflected in mentalities, habits, and behaviors that often do not take into account protection of the environment, and behavior that is difficult to change [82].The development of a new organizational culture is essential for the implementation of greener supply chains [19]. Developing an organizational culture can overcome the lack of human resource capabilities that can be a crucial obstacle to achieving implementation of the circular supply chain.

Based on all the above arguments, we formulate the following proposals:

Proposition 4 (P_4). The design of a new legislative, fiscal, and cultural framework positively affects environmental and economic performance of circular supply chains.

P$_{4.1.}$ Legal requirements to include the CE principles positively affects environmental and economic performance of circular supply chains.

P$_{4.2.}$ The design of fiscal tools positively affects environmental and economic performance of circular supply chains.

P$_{4.3.}$ The development of a new cultural framework that facilitates the flow of knowledge in social and business environments, positively affects environmental and economic performance of circular supply chains.

As a conclusion of the literature analysis, a theoretical model has been drawn. Figure 4 provides a graphic depiction of the proposed analysis model. The different blocks of the model are correlated with each other by the propositions enunciated in the theoretical framework and built on the basis of the analysis of the literature. The strategic objective of the model takes up the challenge arising from the research question: What are the dimensions that allow the design of circular supply chains? What kind of challenges do they pose?

Four fundamental dimensions have been identified when developing and implementing circular supply chains—greater intensity in the relationships established in the supply chain, adaptation of logistics and organizational, disruptive and smart technologies, and a functioning environment. These dimensions apply both within the organization and in its environment. For this reason, the total commitment of the different actors involved—organizations, clients, institutions, etc.—is necessary.

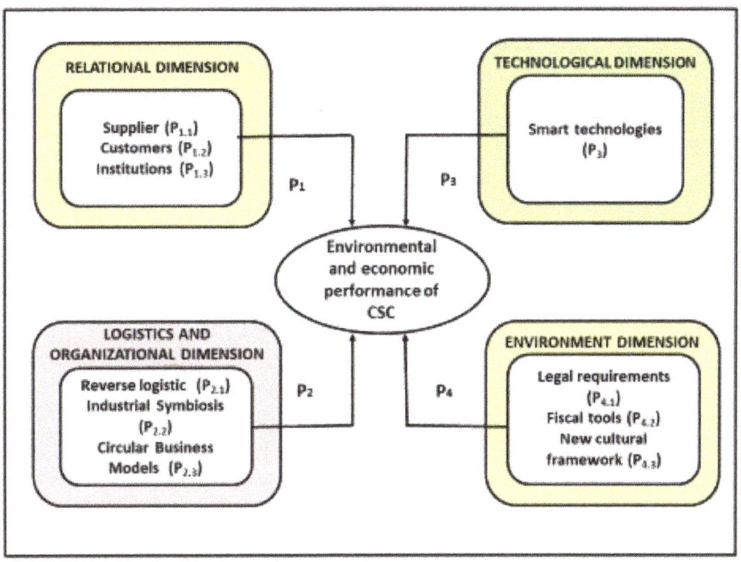

Figure 4. Conceptual model for the integration of circular economy into supply chains.

To summarize, Table 2 shows the definitions, configurations and enablers of the supply chains associated with the circular economy by the main papers analyzed.

Table 2. Summary of the concept 'circular supply chain' in the main articles analyzed.

Authors	Denomination	Definition	Configurations (C) or indicators (I) tools	Enablers (E) or Inhibitors (I)
Chu et al. (2017) [23]	Green supply chain	A set of practices that combines environmental issues with supply chain (SC) management in order to guarantee environmental compliance and promote the environmental capability.	Environmental performance, environmental management systems, environmental audits, demand for greener products, useful information, technical assistance, and joint development of products (I).	Institutional pressures—government, customer, and competitor pressures (I).
De Angelis et al. (2017) [41]	Circular supply chain	The embodiment of circular economy (CE) principles within supply chain management.	Shift from product ownership; structural flexibility and start-ups in regional/local loops; open and closed material loops in technical and biological cycles; closer collaboration; and public and private procurement in the service industry (C).	N.A.
Masi et al. (2017) [26]	Circular supply chain	A critical unit of action for the implementation of the CE because of the necessity for joint effort beyond organizational boundaries to involve external coordination with upstream partners.	Eco-industrial parks, environmental or green SCs, and closed-loop SCs (C).	Financial, technological, societal, informational, and institutional (E).
Geissdoerfer et al. (2018) [60]	Circular supply chain	The supply chain that allows to close, narrow, slow down, intensify, and dematerialize resource loops.	Value proposition in terms of economic, environmental, and social value the firm aim at delivering; creation and delivery system with focus on the role of the business in closing the loop of the product life cycle; and value captured by the various stakeholders.	Economic, environmental, and social goals; proactive stakeholders management; and long-term perspective (E).
Kazancoglu et al. (2018) [8]	Green supply chain	It provides the resource optimization and it is seen as a solution to solve environmental problems and consumption patterns within the whole supply chain.	Environmental performance; economic/ financial performance; operational performance; logistics performance; organizational performance; and marketing performance (I).	N.A.
Leising et al. (2018) [83]	Circular supply chain collaboration	It enables connecting a network of actors in their supply chain by managing data transparency, material flows and exchanges, responsibilities, predictability, and sharing benefits.	Actor learning; networks dynamics; business model; and visions (C).	N.A.
Mangla et al. (2018) [19]	Circular supply chains	Application of reuse, recycling, and remanufacturing to circular model of flow of products, by-products, and waste.	N.A.	Driving barriers; linkage barriers; autonomous barriers; and dependent barriers (I).
Mishra et al. (2018) [98]	Closed-loop supply chain (CLSC)	The design, control, and operation of a system to maximize value creation over the entire life cycle of a product.	Circular design; business model design; forward and reverse supply chain.	Strategic leadership for CE enabled CLSC program, systems, and training program; chemical hazards; and legislation circularity scorecard (E).

Table 2. *Cont.*

Authors	Denomination	Definition	Configurations (C) or indicators (I) tools	Enablers (E) or Inhibitors (I)
Prosman and Sacchi (2018) [86]	Circular supply chains	A leap towards a more environmentally friendly economy that includes forward supply chains and reverse activities.	Supplier selection criteria—induced transport; affected waste handling activity; and usability of discarded products.	N.A.
Vlajic et al. (2018) [105]	Circular supply chains	Concept that considers value recovery in the context of circular flows, as well as those elements that might affect their creation.	Product residual value; quantities available for recovery; value from recovery; and markets for recovered (I) products.	N.A.
Yang et al. (2018) [99]	Circular supply chains/closed-loop supply chain	The design, control, and operation of a system to maximize value creation over the entire life cycle of a product with dynamic recovery of value from different types and volumes of returns over time.	Product-service systems business models—power of the inner circle; power of circling long; power of cascaded; and power of pure circles (C).	N.A.
Coenen et al. (2019) [58]	Closed-loop supply chain	It serves the circular economy because developments such as climate change and resource scarcity have become serious issues in global politics.	Six maturity stages—based on the well-known capability maturity framework and the concept of double-loop learning.	N.A.
Daú et al. (2019) [53]	Supply chain 4.0	It, by bringing the disruptive technologies together in their supply chains, brings together, in addition to Industry 4.0 technologies, sustainable practices.	Time, infrastructure, cost, and institutional (C).	Smart technologies (E).
de Oliveira et al. (2019) [89]	Circular supply chain	It is based on sustainable supply chain narratives, including reverse logistics, sustainable supply chain management (SSCM), and closed-loop supply chains (CLSC).	Reverse logistics, sustainable supply chain management (C), and closed-loop supply chains (C).	Logistics and economic challenges, technology and innovation, consumer knowledge and legislation (E).
Duan et al. (2019) [91]	E-channel closed-loop supply chain network (E-CLSCN)	Closed-loop process of resources-production-consumption-collection-remanufacturing under the e-channel to emphasize the simultaneous improvement of social and environmental benefits to realize the sustainable development of economy and society, while achieving economic benefits.	Multi-period CLSCN (C).	Social and government participation (E), uncertain factors (I), and consumers' behavior (E).
Farooque et al. (2019) [27]	Circular supply chain	The integration of circular thinking into the supply chain and its surrounding industrial and natural ecosystems.	Focused on product-level circularity or focused on value-based assessment of resource efficiency and CE related performance of supply chain actors (I).	Geographic and industrial contexts (E).
Meherishi et al. (2019) [80]	Sustainable packaging in supply chain management (SPSCM).	Use of packaging layers and associated waste along the supply chain.	Circular economy design; new business models; reverse cycles.	Government policies; collaboration between players; incentives to players in the supply chain to adopt circular. economy practices (E).

Table 2. *Cont.*

Authors	Denomination	Definition	Configurations (C) or indicators (I) tools	Enablers (E) or Inhibitors (I)
Niu et al. (2019) [92]	Design for remanufacture (DfRem)-driven closed-loop supply chain	It affects both the manufacturing process of the initial product and the recycling and remanufacturing processes of subsequent waste products.	Design for remanufacture (DfRem)-driven two-stage; and multi-period modeling processes (C).	Industry 4.0 (E).
Taghikhah et al. (2019) [55]	Extended sustainable supply chain (ESSC)	The ESSC framework assumes that other managerial techniques should also be employed, with a focus on the social dimension, on education, motivation, nudging, and persuasion as part of development towards sustainability.	Green consumers behavior—environmental behavior factors; and strategies for behavior change (C).	N.A.
Zhang et al. (2019) [82]	Circular supply chain	A transition to CE requires a paradigm shift to an innovative and more sustainable supply chain ecosystem.	Smart waste management, and smart enabling technologies.	The lack of regulatory pressures; the lack of environmental education and culture of environmental protection; and the lack of market pressures and demands (I).
Zhu et al. (2019) [88]	Closed-loop supply chain	It enables waste products to be professionally restored to the same quality and performance as new products and is considered to be the most valuable product recycling method.	Decentralized or centralized decision system (C).	Warranty services (E).
Govindan et al. (2020) [62]	Circular closed-loop supply chain	Incorporating circular economy (CE) into their supply chain network to extend the sustainability frontier by reducing the need for virgin materials, which contributes to the circulation of resources.	Supplier selection; and supply chain network design.	Decision-making methods (E).
Hussain and Malik (2020) [56]	Circular supply chain	The future high performing state given the CE's established links with strong sustainability.	N.A.	Collaboration within supply chain network; and supply chain configuration (E).
Singhal, et al. (2020) [90]	Circular supply chain (CSC)	CSC helps organizations in making efficient use of resources and results in increased value to the society.	Design for remanufacturing; management prescience; collection strategy; and purchase intention (C).	N.A.

Source: Own elaboration from other studies.

5. Discussion and Conclusions

The current competitive environment requires companies to be innovative in their production systems and to rethink the current use of resources and waste management. Circular productive systems must produce higher yields by using fewer resources, but also entail fewer emissions [106]. This circularity also extends to companies' supply chains, because of the key role it plays in their performance. Therefore, the adaptation of supply chains to the paradigm of the circular economy is attracting the interest of researchers. Based on a systematic review of the literature, a conceptual model has been proposed that includes the main dimensions for the development and implementation of circular supply chains.

5.1. Theoretical Contribution

Although there is increased interest from researchers since 2017, there is significant conceptual confusion. The use of terms that do not have the same meaning makes it difficult to establish a conceptual framework. These terms have been the basis for the establishment of the circular supply chain, but this term is a further step in the application of sustainability in supply chains.

There is a lack of theoretical basis from the perspective of business management or social aspects, since research has mainly focused on production and operations [31]. For all these reasons, it is interesting to apply certain theories from the field of strategic management—resource-based view, industrial ecology, agency theory, strategic networks, and institutional theory—in order to convert the circular supply chain into a favorable instrument that allows managing its resources and strategic capacities as well as its influence on the creation and maintenance of competitive advantages.

5.2. Practical Contribution

Providing action guidance to companies would promote success in incorporating the circular philosophy into supply chain systems, both intra-company and beyond company boundaries. The proposed model explores the impact of certain variables on the functioning and performance of circular supply chain operations. In order to facilitate decision-making, these variables have been classified into fundamental dimensions based on strategic management. Four dimensions have been identified to support the development of these new supply chains: (1) greater intensity in the relationships established in the supply chain, (2) adaptation of logistics and organizational, (3) disruptive and smart technologies, and (4) a functioning environment.

Regarding the establishment of a new framework of relationships (Proposition 1), successful circularization will require integrated synergistic actions by all actors and sectors involved and supported by improved flows of knowledge [107]. The development of a relational capacity is also essential. Relationships are closer, more frequent, and with new actors. Therefore, new rules of the game must be established that take into account the particularities of this new paradigm. Achieving a model of adoption of the full circular would imply its application both internally and externally, involving suppliers and customers in their internal activities [28].

In addition, the company needs to adapt both logistically and organizationally (Proposition 2). Reverse logistics encourage the return of material via the producer and industrial symbiosis favors the exchange of waste between industrial partners. But the transformation goes much further. It requires the design of circular business models [108]. Circular business models are a more complex and narrow type of business model innovation than sustainable business model, since the latter not only create sustainable value, but also involve dynamic management of the loops of resources. Consequently, achieving archetypes through business models of CE, which are recognized at both the meso and micro levels, would allow the development of a common framework [96].

The new technologies allow the development of new functionalities necessary for productive and management change [58]. The main role of information and communication technologies is the application of push and saving impacts to optimize the economic processes of production, consumption and circulation. So, technology development toward a circular economy in three fundamental aspects (Proposition 3): (1) The production, for example recycling of waste, high-efficiency incinerators and cogeneration systems, product design, manufacturing, and remanufacturing processes; (2) the stakeholders, for example predictive analysis and the exchange of information; and (3) the information, so through the Internet of Things (IO) and the Internet of services, information is monitored, controlled, and transferred.

As a final point, the environmental dimensions, whose relationship to the circular supply chain has been established in the Proposition 4. Through long-term agreements [15], the establishment of reward systems [58], and the achievement of financial and legal commitments [109], the company can capture value. Because of the need for collaboration between different actors, there is a need to employ a multidisciplinary system in solving problems where actors can be held responsible for others for their tasks and deliveries [83]. A holistic framework helps companies ensure they are more environmentally-conscious in circular supply chain activities and provides a roadmap in terms of environmental, economic, logistical, operational, and organizational activities [16] to adopt circular supply models effectively. The new framework is also more complex, and thus more difficult to apply than the original one.

5.3. Limitations and Directions of Future Research

This literature review has some limitations. Further research is needed to determine the applicability of these insights, since the greater weight in the analyzed articles has a marked theoretical or case study character. The second limitation is related to the search phase, where we limit our search to articles published in the selected journals, and skip other journals. We have only reviewed publications in English, so research published in other languages has not been analyzed in this study. Thirdly, as mentioned in this paper, there is a need to look more deeply, not only at the direct relationship between the dimensions and the CSC, but also at the moderating effects that the dimensions have on the relationships of the other dimensions to the results.

Finally, this paper presents a proposal when designing circular supply chains, however this proposal needs to be tested in different scenarios. Circular economy models, although popular, have not been fully tested [110]. The ability to fully map the relationships between the different dimensions and their effects on the performance of the circular supply chain will be of great interest in making practical recommendations for obtaining the highest possible return on investment.

Author Contributions: Conceptualization, R.G.-S. and D.S.-B.; data curation, A.M.F.; formal analysis, R.G.-S. and F.E.G.-M.; investigation, D.S.-B.; methodology, A.M.F.; project administration, F.E.G.-M.; supervision, F.E.G.-M.; writing—original draft preparation, R.G.-S.; writing—review and editing, R.G.-S. and F.E.G.-M. All authors have read and agreed to the published version of the manuscript.

Funding: This research was funded by the European Union under the LIFE Program, grant number: LIFE16 ENV/IT/000307 (LIFE Force of the Future).

Acknowledgments: The authors would like to acknowledge the editor and the two anonymous reviewers for their helpful suggestions to improve the paper.

Conflicts of Interest: The authors declare no conflict of interest.

References

1. Theophilus, O.; Dulebenets, M.A.; Pasha, J.; Abioye, O.F.; Kavoosi, M. Truck Scheduling at Cross-Docking Terminals: A Follow-Up State-Of-The-Art Review. *Sustainability* **2019**, *11*, 5245. [CrossRef]
2. Masoumi, S.M.; Kazemi, N.; Abdul-Rashid, S.H. Sustainable Supply Chain Management in the Automotive Industry: A Process-Oriented Review. *Sustainability* **2019**, *11*, 3945. [CrossRef]
3. Dulebenets, M.A. A Diploid Evolutionary Algorithm for Sustainable Truck Scheduling at a Cross-Docking Facility. *Sustainability* **2018**, *10*, 1333. [CrossRef]
4. Dong, C.; Li, Q.; Shen, B.; Tong, X. Sustainability in Supply Chains with Behavioral Concerns. *Sustainability* **2019**, *11*, 4051. [CrossRef]

5. D'Adamo, I.; Gastaldi, M.; Rosa, P. Recycling of end-of-life vehicles: Assessing trends and performances in Europe. *Technol. Forecast. Soc. Chang.* **2020**, *152*, 119887. [CrossRef]
6. Guo, F.; Liu, Q.; Liu, D.; Guo, Z. On Production and Green Transportation Coordination in a Sustainable Global Supply Chain. *Sustainability* **2017**, *9*, 2071. [CrossRef]
7. Zhu, L.; Ren, X.; Lee, C.; Zhang, Y. Coordination Contracts in a Dual-Channel Supply Chain with a Risk-Averse Retailer. *Sustainability* **2017**, *9*, 2148. [CrossRef]
8. Kazancoglu, Y.; Kazancoglu, I.; Sagnak, M. A new holistic conceptual framework for green supply chain management performance assessment based on circular economy. *J. Clean. Prod.* **2018**, *36*, 82–1299. [CrossRef]
9. Beu, D.; Ciugudeanu, C.; Buzdugan, M. Circular Economy Aspects Regarding LED Lighting Retrofit—From Case Studies to Vision. *Sustainability* **2018**, *10*, 3674. [CrossRef]
10. Blomsma, F.; Brennan, G. The Emergence of Circular Economy: A New Framing Around Prolonging Resource Productivity. *J. Ind. Ecol.* **2017**, *21*, 603–614. [CrossRef]
11. Siyambalapitiya, J.; Zhang, X.; Liu, X. Is Governmentality the Missing Link for Greening the Economic Growth? *Sustainability* **2018**, *10*, 4204. [CrossRef]
12. Veleva, V.; Bodkin, G. Corporate-entrepreneur collaborations to advance a circular economy. *J. Clean. Prod.* **2018**, *188*, 20–37. [CrossRef]
13. Mont, O. Innovative approaches to optimising design and use of durable consumer goods. *Int. J. Prod. Dev.* **2008**, *6*, 227–250. [CrossRef]
14. McDonough, W.; Braungart, M. *Cradle to Cradle: Remaking the Way We Make Things*; North Point Press: New York, NY, USA, 2002.
15. Korhonen, J.; Nuur, C.; Feldmann, A.; Birkie, S.E. Circular economy as an essentially contested concept. *J. Clean. Prod.* **2018**, *175*, 544–552. [CrossRef]
16. Merli, R.; Preziosi, M.; Acampora, A. How do scholars approach the circular economy? A systematic literature review. *J. Clean. Prod.* **2018**, *178*, 703–722. [CrossRef]
17. Núñez-Cacho, P.; Molina-Moreno, V.; Corpas-Iglesias, F.A.; Cortés-García, F.J. Family Businesses Transitioning to a Circular Economy Model: The Case of "Mercadona". *Sustainability* **2018**, *10*, 538. [CrossRef]
18. Martinho, F.C.G.; Picado-Santos, L.G.; Capitão, S.D. Feasibility Assessment of the Use of Recycled Aggregates for Asphalt Mixtures. *Sustainability* **2018**, *10*, 1737. [CrossRef]
19. Mangla, S.; Luthra, S.; Mishra, N.; Singh, A.; Rana, N.; Dora, M.; Dwivedi, Y. Barriers to effective circular supply chain management in a developing country context. *Prod. Plan. Control* **2018**, *29*, 551–569. [CrossRef]
20. Bocken, N.M.P.; de Pau, I.; Bakker, C.; van der Grinten, B. Product design and business model strategies for a circular economy. *J. Ind. Prod. Eng.* **2016**, *33*, 308–320. [CrossRef]
21. Mehr, J.; Jedelhauser, M.; Binder, C.R. Transition of the Swiss Phosphorus System towards a Circular Economy—Part 1: Current State and Historical Developments. *Sustainability* **2018**, *10*, 1479. [CrossRef]
22. Sinclair, M.; Sheldrick, L.; Moreno, M.; Dewberry, E. Consumer Intervention Mapping—A Tool for Designing Future Product Strategies within Circular Product Service Systems. *Sustainability* **2018**, *10*, 2088. [CrossRef]
23. Chu, S.H.; Yang, H.; Lee, M.; Park, S. The Impact of Institutional Pressures on Green Supply Chain Management and Firm Performance: Top Management Roles and Social Capital. *Sustainability* **2017**, *9*, 764. [CrossRef]
24. Akinade, O.O.; Oyedele, L.O. Integrating construction supply chains within a circular economy: An ANFIS-based waste analytics system (A-WAS). *J. Clean. Prod.* **2019**, *229*, 863–873. [CrossRef]
25. Guide, V.D.R.; Harrison, T.P.; Van Wassenhove, L.N. The Challenge of Closed-Loop Supply Chains. *Interfaces* **2003**, *33*, 3–6. [CrossRef]
26. Masi, D.; Day, S.; Godsell, J. Supply chain configurations in the Circular Economy: A systematic literature review. *Sustainability* **2017**, *9*, 1602. [CrossRef]
27. Farooque, M.; Zhang, A.; Thürer, M.S.; Qu, T.; Huisingh, D. Circular supply chain management: A definition and structured literature review. *J. Clean. Prod.* **2019**, *228*, 882–900. [CrossRef]
28. Homrich, A.S.; Galvao, G.; Abadia, L.G.; Carvalho, M.M. The circular economy umbrella: Trends and gaps on integrating pathways. *J. Clean. Prod.* **2018**, *175*, 525–543. [CrossRef]
29. Rosa, P.; Sassanelli, C.; Terzi, S. Towards Circular Business Models: A systematic literature review on classification frameworks and archetypes. *J. Clean. Prod.* **2019**, *236*, 117696. [CrossRef]
30. Geissdoerfer, M.; Savaget, P.; Bocken, N.M.P.P.; Hultink, E.J. The Circular Economy—A new sustainability paradigm? *J. Clean. Prod.* **2017**, *143*, 757–768. [CrossRef]

31. Lahti, T.; Wincent, J.; Parida, V. A Definition and Theoretical Review of the Circular Economy, Value Creation, and Sustainable Business Models: Where Are We Now and Where Should Research Move in the Future? *Sustainability* **2018**, *10*, 2799. [CrossRef]
32. Reichertz, J. Abduction: The logic of discovery of grounded theory. *Forum Qual. Soz.* **2009**, *11*, 1–16.
33. Kitchenham, B. *Procedures for Performing Systematic Reviews, TR/SE-0401*; Keele University: Keele, UK, 2004.
34. Kalmykova, Y.; Sadagopanb, M.; Rosado, L. Circular economy—From review of theories and practices to development of implementation tools. *Resour. Conserv. Recycl.* **2018**, *135*, 190–201. [CrossRef]
35. Ferreira Gregorio, V.; Pié, L.; Terceño, A. A Systematic Literature Review of Bio, Green and Circular Economy Trends in Publications in the Field of Economics and Business Management. *Sustainability* **2018**, *10*, 4232. [CrossRef]
36. Ghisellini, P.; Cialani, C.; Ulgiati, S. A review on circular economy: The expected transition to a balanced interplay of environmental and economic systems. *J. Clean. Prod.* **2016**, *114*, 11–32. [CrossRef]
37. Pearce, D.; Turner, R.K. *Economics of Natural Resources and the Environment*; Johns Hopkins University Press: Baltimore, MD, USA, 1990.
38. Kirchherr, J.; Reike, D.; Hekkert, M. Conceptualizing the circular economy: An analysis of 114 definitions. *Resour. Conserv. Recycl.* **2017**, *127*, 221–232. [CrossRef]
39. Avdiushchenko, A. Toward a Circular Economy Regional Monitoring Framework for European Regions: Conceptual Approach. *Sustainability* **2018**, *10*, 4398. [CrossRef]
40. Van Buren, N.; Demmers, M.; van der Heijden, R.; Witlox, F. Towards a Circular Economy: The Role of Dutch Logistics Industries and Governments. *Sustainability* **2016**, *8*, 647. [CrossRef]
41. De Angelis, R.; Howard, M.; Miemczyk, J. Supply Chain Management and the Circular Economy: Towards the Circular Supply Chain. *Prod. Plan. Control* **2017**, *29*, 425–437. [CrossRef]
42. Liu, L.; Liang, Y.; Song, Q.; Li, J. A review of waste prevention through 3R under the concept of circular economy in China. *J. Mater. Cycles Waste* **2017**, *7*, 1–10. [CrossRef]
43. de Mattos, C.A.; de Albuquerque, T.L.M. Enabling Factors and Strategies for the Transition Toward a Circular Economy (CE). *Sustainability* **2018**, *10*, 4628. [CrossRef]
44. Fonseca, L.; Domingues, J.; Pereira, M.; Martins, F.; Zimon, D.; Fonseca, L.M.; Domingues, J.P.; Pereira, M.T.; Martins, F.F.; Zimon, D. Assessment of Circular Economy within Portuguese Organizations. *Sustainability* **2018**, *10*, 2521. [CrossRef]
45. Lewandowski, M. Designing the business models for circular economy—Towards the conceptual framework. *Sustainability* **2016**, *8*, 43. [CrossRef]
46. Molina-Moreno, V.; Leyva-Díaz, J.C.; Sánchez-Molina, J.; Peña-García, A. Proposal to Foster Sustainability through Circular Economy-Based Engineering: A Profitable Chain from Waste Management to Tunnel Lighting. *Sustainability* **2017**, *9*, 2229. [CrossRef]
47. Oncioiu, I.; Căpuşneanu, S.; Türkeș, M.C.; Topor, D.I.; Oprea Constantin, D.-M.; Marin-Pantelescu, A.; Hint, M.S. The Sustainability of Romanian SMEs and Their Involvement in the Circular Economy. *Sustainability* **2018**, *10*, 2761. [CrossRef]
48. Zambon, I.; Colantoni, A.; Cecchini, M.; Mosconi, E.M. Rethinking Sustainability within the Viticulture Realities Integrating Economy, Landscape and Energy. *Sustainability* **2018**, *10*, 320. [CrossRef]
49. Nußholz, J.L.K.; Rasmussen, F.N.; Milios, L. Circular building materials: Carbon saving potential and the role of business model innovation and public policy. *Resour. Conserv. Recycl.* **2019**, *141*, 308–316. [CrossRef]
50. Muñoz-Torres, M.J.; Fernández-Izquierdo, M.Á.; Rivera-Lirio, J.M.; Ferrero-Ferrero, I.; Escrig-Olmedo, E.; Gisbert-Navarro, J.V.; Marullo, M.C. An Assessment Tool to Integrate Sustainability Principles into the Global Supply Chain. *Sustainability* **2018**, *10*, 535. [CrossRef]
51. Masi, D.; Kumar, V.; Garza-Reyes, J.A.; Godsell, J. Towards a more circular economy: Exploring the awareness, practices, and barriers from a focal firm perspective. *Prod. Plan. Control* **2018**, *29*, 539–550. [CrossRef]
52. Genovese, A.; Acquaye, A.A.; Figueroa, A.; Koh, S.L. Sustainable supply chain management and the transition towards a circular economy: Evidence and some applications. *Omega* **2017**, *66*, 344–357. [CrossRef]
53. Daú, G.; Scavarda, A.; Scavarda, L.F.; Portugal, V.J.T. The Healthcare Sustainable Supply Chain 4.0: The Circular Economy Transition Conceptual Framework with the Corporate Social Responsibility Mirror. *Sustainability* **2019**, *11*, 3259. [CrossRef]
54. French, M.L.; LaForge, R.L. Closed-loop supply chains in process industries: An empirical study of producer re-use issues. *J. Oper. Manag.* **2006**, *24*, 271–286. [CrossRef]

55. Taghikhah, F.; Voinov, A.; Shukla, N. Extending the supply chain to address sustainability. *J. Clean. Prod.* **2019**, *229*, 652–666. [CrossRef]
56. Hussain, M.; Malik, M. Organizational enablers for circular economy in the context of sustainable supply chain management. *J. Clean. Prod.* **2020**, *256*, 120375. [CrossRef]
57. Su, B.W.; Heshmati, A.; Geng, Y.; Yu, X.M. A review of the circular economy in China: Moving from rhetoric to implementation. *J. Clean. Prod.* **2013**, *42*, 215–227. [CrossRef]
58. Coenen, J.; van der Heijden, R.; van Riel, A.C.R. Making a Transition toward more Mature Closed-Loop Supply Chain Management under Deep Uncertainty and Dynamic Complexity: A Methodology. *Sustainability* **2019**, *11*, 2318. [CrossRef]
59. Denyer, D.; Tranfield, D. Producing a systematic review. In *The Sage Handbook of Organizational Research Methods*; Buchanan, D.A., Bryman, A., Eds.; Sage Publications Ltd.: Thousand Oaks, CA, USA, 2009; pp. 671–689.
60. Geissdoerfer, M.; Morioka, S.M.; de Carvalho, M.M.; Evans, S. Business models and supply chains for the circular economy. *J. Clean. Prod.* **2018**, *190*, 712–721. [CrossRef]
61. Weetman, C. *A Circular Economy Handbook for Business and Supply Chains: Repair, Remake, Redesign, Rethink*; Kogan Page: London, UK, 2017.
62. Govindan, K.; Mina, H.; Esmaeili, A.; Gholami-Zanjani, S.M. An Integrated Hybrid Approach for Circular supplier selection and Closed loop Supply Chain Network Design under Uncertainty. *J. Clean. Prod.* **2020**, *242*, 118317. [CrossRef]
63. Wernerfelt, B. A resource-based view of the firm. *Strateg. Manag. J.* **1984**, *5*, 171–180. [CrossRef]
64. Barney, J. Firm resources and sustained competitive advantage. *J. Manag.* **1991**, *17*, 99–120. [CrossRef]
65. Grant, R.M. The Resource-Based Theory of competitive advantage: Implications for strategy formulation. *Calif. Manag. Rev.* **1991**, *34*, 114–135. [CrossRef]
66. Mousavi, S.; Bossink, B.; van Vliet, M. Dynamic capabilities and organizational routines for managing innovation towards sustainability. *J. Clean. Prod.* **2018**, *203*, 224–239. [CrossRef]
67. Teece, D.J. Explicating dynamic capabilities: The nature and microfoundations of (sustainable) enterprise performance. *Strateg. Manag. J.* **2007**, *28*, 1319–1350. [CrossRef]
68. Teece, D.J. Dynamic Capabilities: Routines versus Entrepreneurial Action. *J. Manag. Stud.* **2012**, *49*, 1395–1401. [CrossRef]
69. Portillo-Tarragona, P.; Scarpellini, S.; Moneva, J.M.; Valero-Gil, J.; Aranda-Usón, A. Classification and Measurement of the Firms' Resources and Capabilities Applied to Eco-Innovation Projects from a Resource-Based View Perspective. *Sustainability* **2018**, *10*, 3161. [CrossRef]
70. Ranta, V.; Aarikka-Stenroos, L.; Mäkinen, S.J. Creating value in the circular economy: A structured multiple-case analysis of business models. *J. Clean. Prod.* **2018**, *201*, 988–1000. [CrossRef]
71. Laurenti, R.; Singh, J.; Frostell, B.; Sinha, R.; Binder, C.R. The Socio-Economic Embeddedness of the Circular Economy: An Integrative Framework. *Sustainability* **2018**, *10*, 2129. [CrossRef]
72. Sumter, D.; Bakker, C.; Balkenende, R. The Role of Product Design in Creating Circular Business Models: A Case Study on the Lease and Refurbishment of Baby Strollers. *Sustainability* **2018**, *10*, 2415. [CrossRef]
73. Matos, S.; Silvestre, B. Managing stakeholder relations when developing sustainable business models: The case of the Brazilian energy sector. *J. Clean. Prod.* **2013**, *45*, 61–73. [CrossRef]
74. Laubscher, M.; Marinelli, T. Integration of circular economy in business. In Proceedings of the Conference; Going Green-Care Innovation 2014, Vienna, Austria, 17–20 November 2014.
75. Lüdeke-Freund, F.; Gold, S.; Bocken, N. A Review and Typology of Circular Economy Business Model Patterns. *J. Ind. Ecol.* **2018**, *23*, 36–61. [CrossRef]
76. Gulati, R.; Nitin, N.; Zaheer, A. Strategic Networks. *Strateg. Manag. J.* **2000**, *21*, 203–215. [CrossRef]
77. Freeman, L.C. Centrality in Social Networks Conceptual Clarification. *Soc. Netw.* **1979**, *1*, 215–239. [CrossRef]
78. Kogut, B. The network as knowledge: Generative rules and the emergence of structure. *Strateg. Manag. J.* **2000**, *21*, 405–425. [CrossRef]
79. Brown, P.; Bocken, N.; Balkenende, R. Why Do Companies Pursue Collaborative Circular Oriented Innovation? *Sustainability* **2019**, *11*, 635. [CrossRef]
80. Meherishi, L.; Narayana, S.A.; Ranjani, K.S. Sustainable packaging for supply chain management in the circular economy: A review. *J. Clean. Prod.* **2019**, *237*, 117582. [CrossRef]

81. Albuquerque, T.L.M.; Mattos, C.A.; Scur, G.; Kissimoto, K. Life cycle costing and externalities to analyze circular economy strategy: Comparison between aluminum packaging and tinplate. *J. Clean. Prod.* **2019**, *234*, 477–486. [CrossRef]
82. Zhang, A.; Venkatesh, V.G.; Liu, Y.; Wan, M.; Qu, T.; Huisingh, D. Barriers to smart waste management for a circular economy in China. *J. Clean. Prod.* **2019**, *240*, 118198. [CrossRef]
83. Leising, E.; Quist, J.; Bocken, N. Circular Economy in the building sector: Three cases and a collaboration tool. *J. Clean. Prod.* **2018**, *176*, 976–989. [CrossRef]
84. Salim, H.; Stewart, R.A.; Sahin, O.; Dudley, M. Drivers, barriers and enablers to end-of-life management of solarphotovoltaic and battery energy storage systems: A systematic literature review. *J. Clean. Prod.* **2019**, *211*, 537–554. [CrossRef]
85. Zeng, H.; Chen, X.; Xiao, X.; Zhou, Z. Institutional pressures, sustainable supply chain management, and circular economy capability: Empirical evidence from Chinese eco-industrial park firms. *J. Clean. Prod.* **2017**, *155*, 54–65. [CrossRef]
86. Prosman, E.J.; Sacchi, R. New environmental supplier selection criteria for circular supply chains: Lessons from a consequential LCA study on waste recovery. *J. Clean. Prod.* **2018**, *172*, 2782–2792. [CrossRef]
87. Borrello, M.; Caracciolo, F.; Lombardi, A.; Pascucci, S.; Cembalo, L. Consumers' Perspective on Circular Economy Strategy for Reducing Food Waste. *Sustainability* **2017**, *9*, 141. [CrossRef]
88. Zhu, X.; Yu, L.; Li, W. Warranty Period Decision and Coordination in Closed-Loop Supply Chains Considering Remanufacturing and Consumer Behavior. *Sustainability* **2019**, *11*, 4237. [CrossRef]
89. de Oliveira, C.T.; Luna, M.M.M.; Campos, L.M.S. Understanding the Brazilian expanded polystyrene supply chain and its reverse logistics towards circular economy. *J. Clean. Prod.* **2019**, *235*, 562–573. [CrossRef]
90. Singhal, D.; Tripathya, S.; Jena, S.K. Remanufacturing for the circular economy: Study and evaluation of critical factors. *Resour. Conserv. Recycl.* **2020**, *156*, 104681. [CrossRef]
91. Duan, C.; Xiu, G.; Yao, F. Multi-Period E-Closed-Loop Supply Chain Network Considering Consumers' Preference for Products and AI-Push. *Sustainability* **2019**, *11*, 4571. [CrossRef]
92. Niu, S.H.; Zhuo, H.; Xue, K. DfRem-Driven Closed-Loop Supply Chain Decision-Making: A Systematic Framework for Modeling Research. *Sustainability* **2019**, *11*, 3299. [CrossRef]
93. Guarnieria, P.; Cerqueira-Streita, J.A.; Batista, L.C. Reverse logistics and the sectoral agreement of packaging industry in Braziltowards a transition to circular economy. *Resour. Conserv. Recycl.* **2020**, *152*, 104541. [CrossRef]
94. Subramoniam, R.; Huisingh, D.; Babu, R. Remanufacturing for the automotive aftermarket-strategic factors: Literature review and future research needs. *J. Clean. Prod.* **2009**, *17*, 1163–1174. [CrossRef]
95. Emmanuel-Ebikake, O.; Sassanelli, C.; Terzi, S. PSS design through Design for Supply Chain: State of the art review. In Proceedings of the 28th CIRP Design Conference, Nantes, France, 23–25 May 2018.
96. Oghazi, P.; Mostaghel, R. Circular Business Model Challenges and Lessons Learned—An Industrial Perspective. *Sustainability* **2018**, *10*, 739. [CrossRef]
97. Maaß, O.; Grundmannm, P.H. Governing Transactions and Interdependences between inked Value Chains in a Circular Economy: The Case ofWastewater Reuse in Braunschweig (Germany). *Sustainability* **2018**, *10*, 1125. [CrossRef]
98. Mishra, J.L.; Hopkinson, P.G.; Tidridge, G. Value creation from circular economy-led closed loop supply chains: A case study of fast-moving consumer goods. *Prod. Plan. Control* **2018**, *29*, 509–521. [CrossRef]
99. Yang, M.; Smart, P.; Kumar, M.; Jolly, M.; Evans, S. Product-service systems business models for circular supply chains. *Prod. Plan. Control* **2018**, *29*, 498–508. [CrossRef]
100. Sassanelli, C.; Rossi, M.; Pezzotta, G.; Pacheco, D.J.P.; Terzi, S. Defining lean product service systems features and research trends through a systematic literature review. *Int. J. Prod. Lifecycle Manag.* **2019**, *12*, 37–61. [CrossRef]
101. Ali, S.H. Social and Environmental Impact of the Rare Earth Industries. *Resources* **2014**, *3*, 123–134. [CrossRef]
102. Nascimento, D.L.M.; Alencastro, V.; Quelhas, O.L.G.; Caiado, R.G.G.; Garza-Reyes, J.A.; Tortorella, G.L. Exploring Industry 4.0 technologies to enable circular economy practices in a manufacturing context: A business model proposal. *J. Manuf. Technol. Manag.* **2018**, *30*, 607–627. [CrossRef]
103. Dubey, R.; Gunasekaran, A.; Childe, S.J.; Papadopoulos, T.; Luo, Z.; Wamba, S.F.; Roubaud, D. Can Big Data and Predictive Analytics Improve Social and Environmental Sustainability? *Technol. Forecast. Soc. Chang.* **2017**, *144*, 534–545. [CrossRef]

104. Liang, S.; Feng, Y.; Xu, M. Structure of the Global Virtual Carbon Network: Revealing Important Sectors and Communities for Emission Reduction. *J. Ind. Ecol.* **2015**, *19*, 307–320. [CrossRef]
105. Vlajic, J.V.; Mijailovic, R.; Bogdanova, M. Creating loops with value recovery: Empirical study of fresh food supply chains. *Prod. Plan. Control* **2018**, *29*, 522–538. [CrossRef]
106. Strauch, S.M.; Wenzel, L.C.; Bischoff, A.; Dellwig, O.; Klein, J.; Schüch, A.; Wasenitz, B.; Palm, H.W. Commercial African Catfish (Clarias gariepinus) Recirculating Aquaculture Systems: Assessment of Element and Energy Pathways with Special Focus on the Phosphorus Cycle. *Sustainability* **2018**, *10*, 1805. [CrossRef]
107. Withers, P.J.A.; Doody, D.G.; Sylvester-Bradle, R. Achieving Sustainable Phosphorus Use in Food Systems through Circularisation. *Sustainability* **2018**, *10*, 1804. [CrossRef]
108. Braun, A.; Kleine-Moellhoff, P.; Reichenberger, V.; Seiter, S.T. Case Study Analysing Potentials to Improve Material Efficiency in Manufacturing Supply Chains, Considering Circular Economy Aspects. *Sustainability* **2018**, *10*, 880. [CrossRef]
109. Bocken, N.; Short, S.; Rana, P.; Evans, S. A literature and practice review to develop Sustainable Business Model Archetypes. *J. Clean. Prod.* **2014**, *65*, 42–45. [CrossRef]
110. D'Adamo, I.; Falcone, P.M.; Ferella, F. A Socio-Economic Analysis of Biomethane in the Transport Sector: The Case of Italy. *Waste Manag.* **2019**, *95*, 102–115. [CrossRef]

sustainability

MDPI

Review

A Structured Literature Review on Obsolete Electric Vehicles Management Practices

Idiano D'Adamo [1] and Paolo Rosa [2,*]

1 Department of Law and Economics, Unitelma Sapienza—University of Rome, Viale Regina Elena 295, 00161 Roma, Italy; idiano.dadamo@unitelmasapienza.it

2 Department of Management, Economics, and Industrial Engineering, Politecnico di Milano, Piazza Leonardo da Vinci, 32, 20133 Milano, Italy

* Correspondence: paolo1.rosa@polimi.it; Tel.: +39-02-2399-9537

Received: 6 November 2019; Accepted: 2 December 2019; Published: 3 December 2019

Abstract: The use of electricity for transportation needs offers the chance to replace fossil fuels with greener energy sources. Potentially, coupling sustainable transports with Renewable Energies (RE) could reduce significantly both Greenhouse Gas (GHG) emissions and the dependency on oil imports. However, the expected growth rate of Electric Vehicles (EVs) could become also a potential risk for the environment if recycling processes will continue to function in the current way. To this aim, the paper reviews the international literature on obsolete EV management practices, by considering scientific works published from 2000 up to 2019. Results show that the experts have paid great attention to this topic, given both the critical and valuable materials embedded in EVs and their main components (especially traction batteries), by offering interesting potential profits, and identifying the most promising End-of-Life (EoL) strategy for recycling both in technological and environmental terms. However, the economics of EV recycling systems have not yet been well quantified. The intent of this work is to enhance the current literature gaps and to propose future research streams.

Keywords: obsolete electric vehicles; ELV management; circular economy; structured literature review

1. Introduction

The transportation sector is one of the main reasons for global warming. About one-third of the global energy demand and one-sixth of global Greenhouse Gas (GHG) emissions come from transport [1], mainly because of fossil fuels [2,3]. Given the increasing number of catastrophic events caused by climate changes, international institutions have decided to reconsider the way vehicles can move with a lower impact on the environment. Trying to answer to these trends, automotive manufacturers have been pushed towards the development of innovative technologies for the sustainable mobility of people and things [4,5], and this has also followed the circular economy concept [6,7]. Hence, Electric Vehicles (EVs) were developed under many forms, like BEVs (Battery Electric Vehicles), HEVs (Hybrid Electric Vehicles), PHEVs (Plug-in Hybrid Electric Vehicles), REEVs (Range Extended Electric Vehicles), FCEVs (Fuel Cell Electric Vehicles) and FCHEVs (Fuel Cell Hybrid Electric Vehicles). Each of them employs electricity in a different way in order to move [8,9]. Electric cars can be broadly classified into full electric and hybrid ones [10,11]. An EV moves only through an electric motor, whereas an HEV moves either with an electric motor or a conventional combustion motor. A battery stores the extra energy, by capturing it with regenerative braking systems. In a PHEV, the batteries can be loaded with additional grid electricity. In a REEV, either an internal combustion engine or the grid electricity charges the battery. A FCEV (or FCHEV) embeds a hydrogen tank and a fuel cell as a source of energy [12]. From a structural perspective, they can be considered a type of HEV, in which the fuel cell replaces the internal combustion engine. Using atmospheric oxygen and compressed gaseous hydrogen supplied from the on-board tank, the fuel cell generates electricity, which powers the vehicle's electric motor [13].

According to the Global EV Outlook of the Electric Vehicle Initiative (EVI) and the International Energy Association (IEA), the global EVs exceeded 5.1 million in 2018, up 2 million from the previous year. China is the world's largest electric car market with 2.3 million units, followed by Europe (1.2 million units) and the USA (1.1 million units). This outlook defines the future global electric car sales in 2030 by considering two potential scenarios: 23 million units in the New Policies Scenario and 43 million units in the EV30@30 Scenario (Figure 1) [10].

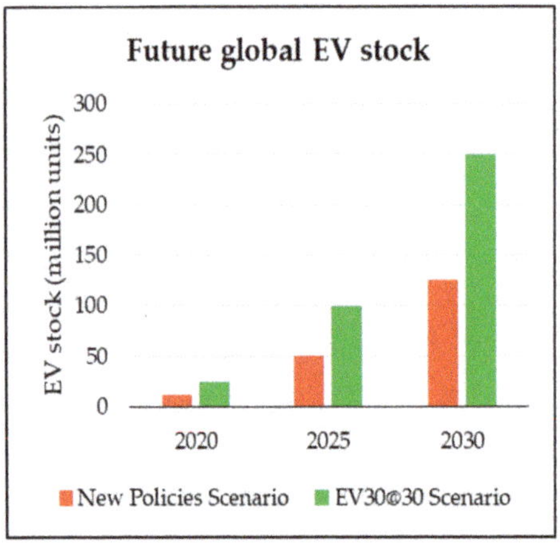

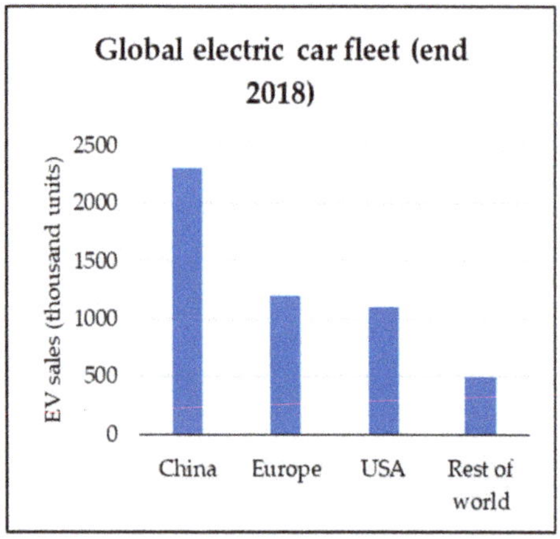

Figure 1. Global EV stock in 2020–2030 period and global EV sales in 2018 [10].

Several studies already assessed the higher sustainability of EVs compared with common Internal Combustion Engine Vehicles (ICEVs) [14–16]. However, EVs are not immune from criticism. Generally, their weight is higher than ICEVs (because of batteries, electric motors, power electronics, etc.), their range of action is limited and recharging infrastructures are lacking [11,17,18]. Furthermore, one of the most important issues related to EVs is that, given their higher complexity, they are very difficult to recycle [19–24]. In order to summarize the available knowledge and provide evidence for the main gaps that are still waiting for innovative answers, a structured literature review is proposed in this work.

The paper is organized as follows. Section 2 presents the topic conceptualization and classification, describes the research methodology and assesses the framework of analysis. Section 3 shows the literature review metrics adopted and proposes an overall view on results. Section 4 shows a discussion on the relevant topics analyzed by proposing a critical perspective. Finally, Section 5 presents some concluding remarks.

2. Materials and Methods

2.1. Topic Conceptualization and Classification

Renewable Energies (REs), sustainable transportation and waste management strategies have assumed a central role in the last decades, not only in theoretical terms, but also in practice [25,26]. Citizens, firms and governments are extremely interested in creating economic opportunities and preserving the environment. Their combination could potentially reduce the environmental impact of every human activity and offers interesting chances for new businesses [27]. Among waste management strategies, there is great attention paid towards recycling [28–31]. An assessment of the knowledge on EVs gives us the chance to put together all these points.

2.2. Research Methodology and Framework of Analysis

In order to assess the whole knowledge on EVs, a systematic literature review was implemented. After a deep survey, a list of papers selected through the most popular scientific works search engines (e.g., Google ™ Scholar, Web of Science ™, Sage ™, Science Direct ™, Springer ™, MDPI ™, Emerald ™, Scopus ™, Taylor & Francis ™ Online and Wiley ™ Online Libraries) have been evaluated [32]. All of the selected scientific documents have been published between 2000 and 2019. They have been provided by adopting a series of combinations of two keywords like "recycling" and "electric vehicle" that have been researched in the titles, abstracts and keywords of papers. After a deep reading of all the papers, a structured literature review was performed, and the main results are summarized below. The output of the searching process in terms of number of works published by year is proposed in Figure 2. The number of total documents (n° 171) reveals the considerable attention devoted to these topics, especially from 2015 onwards, with about 67% of documents concentrated between 2015 and 2019. Documents pertain to n° 100 scientific journals with impact factor, n° 27 scientific journals without impact factor, n° 28 proceedings of scientific conferences, n° 10 scientific reports, n° 4 industrial reports and n° 2 book chapters.

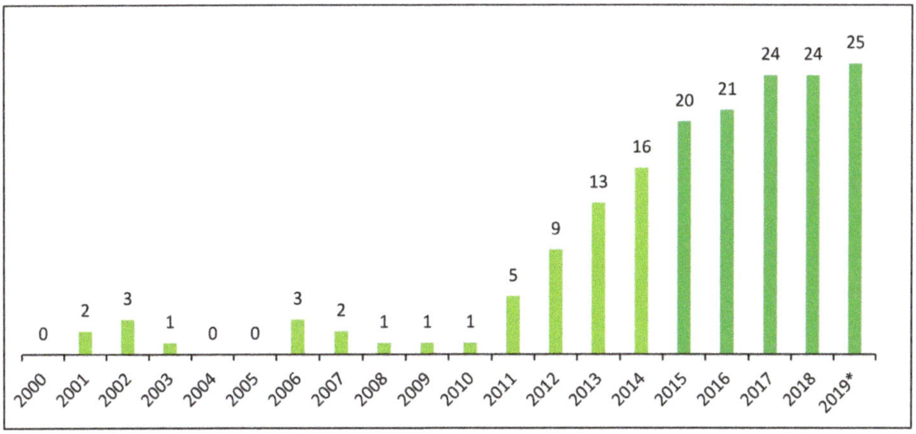

Figure 2. Historical series of published papers from 2000 up to 2019 (partial).

The growth trend reached its peak during the last year examined. The 2019 data are partial, but greater than the previous years. The last available data speak about a new record of EVs on the road, with a global EV stock of about 5.1 million vehicles in 2018, up 2 million from the previous year [10].

Figure 3 displays the geographical distribution of documents, where the institution of the first author was considered as reference. This distribution is concentrated in China, the USA and Germany. These countries cover about 50% of the total number of published articles.

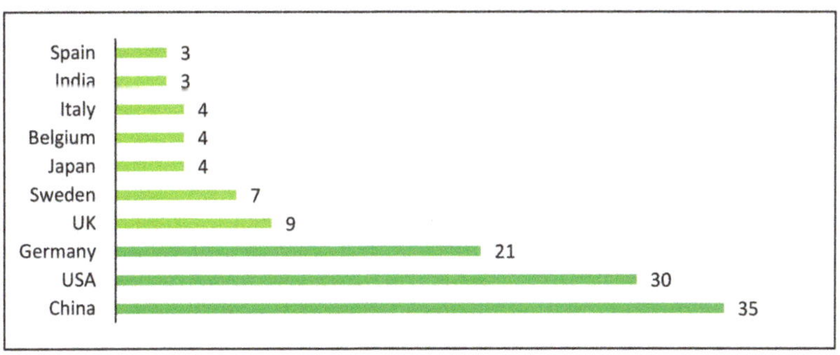

Figure 3. Geographical distribution of published papers.

China occupies the first position with n° 35 documents, followed by the USA with 30 documents, coinciding with their role in the automotive market. In fact, China was the global leader in EV manufacturing from 2016 onwards [33–35], while the USA occupied this role till 2015 [36]. Interestingly, Germany has a lower stock of EVs than other countries, but a high relevance in the European automotive sector and has a high involvement of the government towards the research and diffusion of EVs [37]. There are several perspectives from which EVs and recycling were addressed by the literature (Figure 4) [38]. In macroscopic terms, the EV End-of-Life (EoL) strategy is the most discussed topic. Among these strategies, recycling is the best solution (n° 52 documents). The second most discussed topic is the environmental evaluation of EVs (n° 40 documents), performed to underline the advantages of moving towards sustainable goals [39], while the economic and social benefits of EV recycling are not well assessed by the experts. In addition, several authors dedicated great attention to a specific EV component (batteries) [40].

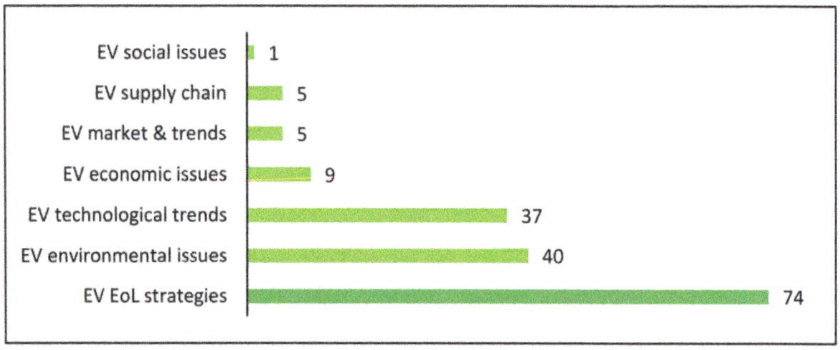

Figure 4. Macro topics of published papers.

The analysis of macro topics highlights that research on EVs follow a multidisciplinary strategy. About the research methodology, it is broadly based on the analytical approach (n° 129 documents). Theoretical, survey and case studies are very limited, with 37, 3 and 2 documents, respectively. In the following section, each macro topic is discussed in detail.

3. Results

The structured literature review showed that articles pertaining to the obsolete EV management practices could be classified in three types:

- Works on EV disassembly (see Section 3.1);
- Works on EV recycling (and reuse, just for batteries)—(see Section 3.2);
- Works on EV remanufacturing (see Section 3.3).

In addition, considering only EV recycling, the three pillars of sustainability are explored as well:

- Works on EV recycling environmental issues (see Section 3.4);
- Works on EV recycling economic issues (see Section 3.5);
- Works on EV recycling social issues (see Section 3.6).

3.1. EV Disassembly

When considering a traditional ELV dismantling process, disassembly is the second activity, after fluids and hazardous systems decontamination, done by car dismantlers on obsolete vehicles. It represents a high value stage for car dismantlers, given that disassembled components (if in good conditions) can usually be resold as spare parts on the secondary market. For EV disassembly, the main elements taken into account by experts are batteries, electric engines and power electronics (see Table 1).

Table 1. Focus of EV disassembly-oriented papers.

Author	Battery	Engine	Electronics
[41]	x		
[42]	x		
[43]		x	
[44]			x
[45]			x

For the batteries, disassembly is done (after discharging) immediately before either recycling or remanufacturing. Given the lack of information in product variants, battery disassembly is done manually. Only two examples have been found in literature [41,42]. Here, the authors present a concept for a battery disassembly workstation where operators are assisted by robots. While persons perform more complex tasks, robots perform simple and repetitive tasks, such as removing screws and bolts from cases. A similar approach is proposed also by [43], but focusing on EV electric engines.

Finally, other experts focus on power electronics [44,45]. Here, a robotized workstation is proposed for the automatic disassembly of electronic components from EV batteries before their final recycling. An identification of the profitability of recycling such electronic components is also provided.

One of the first steps of EoL management is disassembly, typically requiring several time/cost consuming processes. It depends on the costs and risks related to the ability to separate the sub-components from the whole product as to whether disassembly is viable or not. From a technological point of view, manual procedures are usually adopted, explaining the low number of papers focusing on this topic.

3.2. EV Recycling

The EVs market is one of the most interesting fields from the recycling point of view. A generic EV embeds lots of key materials (almost 25 kg per car) inside different subsystems and components, offering great recycling potentials. Some important examples are represented by traction batteries, electric drive motors and power electronics [46]. The production of electric cars is expected to grow rapidly, reaching 20 million cars by 2020 [36]. By assuming a mean life of a car of 10 years, there will be an enormous amount of EVs to be recycled by 2030. From these data, it is clear that the strategic importance can be assumed by a preventive decision about alternative sustainable treatments for this waste flow. In particular, the use of industrial symbiosis can minimize material wastage and environmental burdens [23]. A comparison among recycling methods is proposed by some authors [47], in which the final result defines the role of recycling policies that aim to incentivize battery collection and emissions reductions (Table 2).

Table 2. Focus of EV recycling-oriented papers.

Author	Battery (Reuse/Recycle)	Magnets	Electronics	Fuel Cells
[48]	x			
[49]	x			
[50]	x			
[51]	x			
[52]	x			
[53]	x			
[54]	x			
[55]	x			
[18]	x			
[42]	x			
[56]	x			
[57]	x			
[21]	x			
[58]	x			
[50]	x			
[59]	x			
[60]	x			
[61]	x			
[62]	x			
[63]	x			
[64]	x			
[65]	x			
[66]	x			
[67]	x			
[68]	x			
[69]	x			
[70]	x			
[71]	x			
[72]	x			
[73]	x			
[42]	x			
[74]	x			
[75]		x		
[76]		x		
[77]		x		
[78]		x		
[79]		x		
[80]		x		
[46]			x	
[81]			x	
[82]				x
[13]				x

Recycling is an opportunity to close the loop of EVs, which aims to reach sustainability goals. However, specific recycling pillars are proposed in the next sub-sections. One of the main results from this review is the significant number of papers focusing on this EoL option. Certainly, reuse is a better solution in terms of the waste hierarchy, but it is not always feasible from a technical point of view. Recycling processes, instead, are suitable to satisfy the circular economy model. Material circularity requires the development of secondary markets where critical and special metals can re-enter in the raw materials cycle. As the authors express, in order to support this development, the economic side must be always taken into account when new technological options are selected.

3.2.1. EV Battery Recycling

The EoL management of EV batteries is one of the most discussed issues in literature. Broadly speaking, EoL strategies can be distinguished in three categories: reuse, remanufacturing and recycling. Literature works are focused on the pros and cons related to each battery technology from both technical, environmental and economic perspective [83–86]. Other authors focus on both a kind of technology (usually Li-ion) and the management of materials embedded in batteries [87–90] (Tables 3–5). Considering the economic perspective, the cost of EV batteries plays a critical role in determining the commercial viability of EVs, not only during their usage, but also at the end of their useful life. Spent batteries maintain a relevant market value as manufacturers can extract critical materials from key components (e.g., cells and power electronics), typically through hydrometallurgical processes. This topic is investigated from multiple perspectives in literature (see Table 2).

Table 3. Focus of EV battery reuse-oriented papers.

Author	Environmental	Economic	Technical
[48]	x		
[49]		x	
[50]		x	
[51]		x	
[52]			x
[53]			x

Table 4. Focus of EV battery recycling-oriented papers.

Author	Current State	Predictions	Technologies
[54]	x		
[55]	x		
[18]	x		
[42]	x		
[56]		x	
[57]		x	
[21]		x	
[58]		x	
[50]		x	
[59]			x
[60]			x
[61]			x
[62]			x
[63]			x
[64]			x
[65]			x
[66]			x
[67]			x
[68]			x
[69]			x
[70]			x
[71]			x
[72]			x
[73]			x
[42]			x
[74]			x

Table 5. Technologies supporting EV battery recycling processes.

Author	Hydrometallurgy	Biometallurgy	Mechanical	Mixed
[59]	x			
[60]	x			
[61]	x			
[62]	x			
[63]	x			
[64]	x			
[65]	x			
[66]	x			
[67]	x			
[68]	x			
[69]	x			
[70]		x		
[71]		x		
[72]			x	
[73]			x	
[42]				x
[74]				x

One way to manage obsolete EV batteries is represented by reuse. Given the short lifetime of an EV battery (quantified by many experts as 8–10 years—or the period where the battery capacity reduces to 80% of the original one), their reuse is seen by experts as a reasonable and sustainable strategy, before opting to recycle [48]. Better performances can be obtained by reusing EV batteries together with Renewable Energy (RE) sources in stationary applications. Because of this, several business perspective are proposed in the literature, either under the form of Product-Service Systems (PSSs) [49], dedicated EU regulations [50] or are considered industrial symbiosis [51]. However, the most effective way to manage obsolete EV batteries seems to be a combination of both reuse and recycling practices [52,53].

Several papers have been written about EV battery recycling in the last decades. In general terms, EV battery recycling follows the same process exploited for recovering any type of e-waste, with disassembly, shredding, separation and refining as the main process steps. Depending on the technologies employed during refining (chemical or mechanical ones), it is possible to reach different material recovery performances.

From the current state of the art perspective on EV battery recycling, some works are available in literature, but none of them consider this topic in a broad perspective. Some experts focus on the EV battery design stage by considering the economic and environmental strategies supporting the sustainable treatment of these products [54]. Others follow the same logic, but focus on either a specific type of EV battery [55], national context [18] or recycling method [42].

From the prediction perspective, the focus is on critical materials embedded into EV batteries, either in terms of current availabilities, projected mining capacity or forecasted demands [56]. These assessments are usually presented under the form of decision-support tools [57] or generic simulation platforms [21]. Finally, other experts assess the introduction of EV batteries recycling on current ELV regulations by taking as reference either the Umicore battery recycling process [58] or the Chinese context [50].

From a technological perspective, EV battery recycling is a well-assessed topic in literature, with a prevalent role for the hydrometallurgical process, given its high performances in terms of materials recovery. Some authors describe it through a review on the evolution of chemical recovery technologies [59,60]. Others prefer to focus on either a specific chemical process [61,69], separation processes [66–68], EV battery type [62], leaching agent [63] or recovered material [64,65]. A promising sub-category of hydrometallurgical processes is represented by biological ones. However, only two works have been found in literature on this topic, and both of them focus on organic leaching agents [70,71]. The mechanical process is another way to recover EV batteries. However, in this case, only two works have been found in literature [72,73]. Finally, other experts put together both chemical and mechanical processes, by employing all their benefits [42,74].

3.2.2. EV Magnet Recycling

After EV batteries, EV magnets are the second element discussed in literature. Several works present innovative ways to recover Rare Earth Elements (REEs) from obsolete magnets, either coming from mixed sources [75] or specific waste streams (including magnets from HEVs) [76–78]. Other works quantify present and future amounts of recovered REEs from specific HEV components [79]. Finally, different recycling approaches for recycling magnets from HEVs are compared [80].

3.2.3. EV Power Electronics Recycling

As evidenced by the authors many times for common ELVs, in the similar case of EVs, the recovery of electronic components is still in its infancy [46]. Even if electronics in EVs are even more present than in ICEVs, neither industry, nor politics, nor scientists consider its recovery to be an important issue, preferring to focus on batteries (see the previous Sections 3.2 and 3.2.1). The only paper found in literature on this topic compares, both in economic and environmental impact terms, two different ways to recycle EV power electronics, by exploiting either traditional ELV recovery processes or coupling them to a dedicated plant [81].

3.2.4. Fuel Cells Recycling

Another focus related to EVs is the recycling of fuel cells. Given the difficulty of the BEV's ability to cover long distances, FCEVs will surely take part of the market in future car sales. This way, a percentage of future obsolete EVs will be constituted by FCEVs. Unfortunately, also in this case, only two articles have been found in literature. The first one assesses the effects of a probable update of the current EU ELV Directive towards the recovery of fuel cells [82]. The second one investigates the potential contribution offered by the recycling of FCEVs for meeting the current platinum demand of Europe [13].

3.3. *EV Remanufacturing*

The remanufacturing of components coming from obsolete cars is a well-assessed business. However, from an EV perspective, the literature considers of only EV battery remanufacturing. Considering the few papers focusing on that, EV battery remanufacturing is discussed in terms of either overall process [91], economic performances (compared with reuse/recycling ones) [92,93] or real application cases [94].

3.4. *EV Environmental Issues*

The diffusion of EV technologies is strictly related with energy storage technologies [95]. This way, the environmental analysis has been historically focused on the use phase of EVs. However, many components of EVs (e.g., electronics, magnets and batteries) embed critical raw materials. In this way, experts have started to assess the positive environmental impact associated with EV recycling (as a more sustainable alternative than landfilling), both in terms of GHG emissions reduction [20], electricity mix generation technologies [96], secondary resources recovery (specifically REEs [97], critical metals [12] and lithium [98]) and policy measures that ensure the availability of materials [33].

3.5. *EV Economic Issues*

An important result coming from the present work is that economic issues of EV recycling systems are not well assessed. In particular, the following gaps have been evidenced [99]:

- Scarcity of studies assessing the potential value of different EV battery technologies [100,101];
- Low EV battery recycling rates given the focus of recycling plants on high-volumes [102];
- Translation of expected environmental benefits into real economic benefits [103].

3.6. EV Social Issues

Social issues related with EVs are rarely assessed by the experts, mainly in terms of the social influence on eco-innovation adoption. For this topic, just one paper [104] underlined the importance of interpersonal social influence, opinion leadership and personal norms on eco-innovation adoption.

4. Discussion

Satisfying human needs in the most sustainable way (and without further impacting the climate) is the greatest challenge of the 21st century. The experts demonstrated in several works that both renewable energies and waste management strategies (either individually or together) can guarantee improvements in this sense [105–107]. Obsolete EV management practices represent a good example because several types of data (e.g., EV configurations, battery energy sources, electrical machines, charging systems, optimization techniques) are required [108,109].

From one side, EVs represent the answer of car manufacturers towards international directives that, for decades, have been asking for greener and more sustainable vehicles [34,110,111]. Hence, their reuse, remanufacturing and recycling is considered by many authors as a potential solution to several environmental challenges, like resource scarcity, sustainable economic growth and waste management [112,113]. From this side, some quantitative analyses are available [114,115]. However, given the great uncertainty related with either global volumes (see Table 1 for details), growth rates and the general evolution of the EV market, it is very difficult to have reliable estimates, even by adopting the most advanced simulation tools [116,117]. Therefore, none of the most recent works on ELVs investigate how EVs could influence future ELV trends. These data are of utmost importance not only for car manufacturers, but also for policymakers [118]. Based on these data, industries (especially those involved at EoL stage) could decide how to improve their plants' recovery performances, especially for low-volume materials. Instead, politicians could monitor illegal ELV flows and sustain the EV market expansion through optimized subsidy policies.

From a second perspective, the management of EV components (e.g., batteries, electric motors and electronic components) presents some knowledge gaps. The literature is full of articles considering batteries and electric motors to be promising components worth recycling [119]. However, power electronics could also increase the overall profitability, but few works assessed and quantified it [120,121]. This way, current recycling technologies must be improved if companies involved in ELV reverse logistic chains are willing to gather the highest profit from EVs [122–125]. Contrarily, the risk is the same encountered by companies when managing electronic components of ICEVs. Also, this change will be needed in terms of a legislative re-thinking of current regulations and procedures, by offering a concrete support to actors willing to enter into current ELV recovery chains [126]. Here, innovative directives, environmental requirements and technologies able to manage obsolete EVs are urgently needed [127].

From a third perspective, recycled metals represent the most interesting source of both economic and environmental benefits, given the huge amounts embedded in EVs. However, limiting the recycling process to cathode materials will play a negative effect on the EV battery recycling economics and the environmental impact [128]. This way, neither reward-penalty mechanisms nor subsidy policies will be sufficient [129]. The only way to increase profitability will be to consider the most valuable elements embedded in EVs, like power electronics and magnets.

Results coming from the work underlined, like the adoption of new technologies, can increase the efficiency and effectiveness of entire recycling processes towards more sustainable practices. At the same time, economic aspects related to recycling processes seem to not be well analyzed by the literature, and the main variables affecting their profitability are not well understood. These elements, together with the break-even point expressed in terms of the number of ELVs recycled per year, represent some interesting research areas for the future.

5. Conclusions

Currently, automotive manufacturers are investing big amounts of money on EVs, and the market is characterized by big growth trends and economic opportunities. However, environmental advantages could be obtained only if EVs can be really green, either in terms of the type of energy source exploited (i.e., powered by RE sources) or by considering different EoL strategies and by following the circular economy paradigm. From this last perspective, the current work shows lots of papers studying new ways to recycle EVs. Some of them are focused on the disassembly of whole cars, some on reuse of the components, some on reverse logistic chains and others on remanufacturing of components. However, lots of experts focus on EV battery recycling, especially Li-ion ones. Given their weight and content in critical materials, a battery is considered to be one of the prevalent elements to recover from EVs. However, we think that EVs can present other interesting components that are worth recycling, usually not considered by both scientific and industrial experts.

In order to avoid what currently happens during the recycling of ICEVs, the present paper wanted to assess the existing literature on EV recycling, trying to evidence current lacks in knowledge and to open issues for potential improvements. They can be summarized in: (i) limited estimates of future ELV streams, (ii) limited assessment of relations among stakeholders within the reverse logistic chain, (iii) limited studies on economic issues, (iv) absence of social analyses and (v) limited case studies considering the three sustainability pillars together.

Results highlight six considerations: (i) the topic is multidisciplinary and actual; (ii) economic evaluation is needed to develop the ELV recycling sector; (iii) the role of power electronics is not investigated into detail; (iv) the applicability of Circular Economy (CE) models on ELVs is feasible; (v) the pivotal role of recycling activities within CE models is verified and (vi) both waste management and renewable energy management can support the development of sustainable activities.

Author Contributions: Conceptualization, I.D. and P.R.; methodology, I.D. and P.R.; formal analysis, I.D.; data curation, P.R.; writing—original draft preparation, I.D. and P.R.; writing—review and editing, I.D. and P.R.; visualization, I.D.; supervision, P.R.

Funding: This research received no external funding.

Conflicts of Interest: The authors declare no conflict of interest.

Acronyms

BEV	Battery Electric Vehicle	GHG	Greenhouse Gas
CE	Circular Economy	HEV	Hybrid Electric Vehicle
ELV	End of Life Vehicles	ICEV	Internal Combustion Engine Vehicle
EoL	End of Life	IEA	International Energy Association
ESS	Energy Storage System	LIB	Lithium Ion Battery
EU	European Union	PCB	Printed Circuit Board
EV	Electric Vehicle	PHEV	Plug-in Hybrid Electric Vehicle
EVI	Electric Vehicle Initiative	RE	Renewable Energy
FCEV	Fuel Cell Electric Vehicle	REE	Rare Earth Elements
FCHEV	Fuel Cell Hybrid Electric Vehicle	REEV	Range Extended Electric Vehicle

References

1. IRENA. *Biogas for Road Vehicles Technologu Brief*; IRENA: Abu Dhabi, UAE, 2018.
2. Tan, X.; Zeng, Y.; Gu, B.; Wang, Y.; Xu, B. Scenario Analysis of Urban Road Transportation Energy Demand and GHG Emissions in China—A Case Study for Chongqing. *Sustainability* **2018**, *10*, 2033. [CrossRef]
3. Lu, M.; Xie, R.; Chen, P.; Zou, Y.; Tang, J. Green Transportation and Logistics Performance: An Improved Composite Index. *Sustainability* **2019**, *11*, 2976. [CrossRef]

4. Martin, M.; Røyne, F.; Ekvall, T.; Moberg, Å. Life cycle sustainability evaluations of bio-based value chains: Reviewing the indicators from a Swedish perspective. *Sustainability* **2018**, *10*, 547. [CrossRef]
5. Sovacool, B.K.; Kester, J.; Heida, V. Cars and kids: Childhood perceptions of electric vehicles and sustainable transport in Denmark and the Netherlands. *Technol. Forecast. Soc. Chang.* **2019**, *144*, 182–192. [CrossRef]
6. Saidani, M.; Yannou, B.; Leroy, Y.; Cluzel, F. Heavy vehicles on the road towards the circular economy: Analysis and comparison with the automotive industry. *Resour. Conserv. Recycl.* **2018**, *135*, 108–122. [CrossRef]
7. Fuso Nerini, F.; Slob, A.; Engström, R.E.; Trutnevyte, E. A Research and Innovation Agenda for Zero-Emission European Cities. *Sustainability* **2019**, *11*, 1692. [CrossRef]
8. Álvarez Fernández, R. A more realistic approach to electric vehicle contribution to greenhouse gas emissions in the city. *J. Clean. Prod.* **2018**, *172*, 949–959. [CrossRef]
9. Zhang, Y.; Han, Q. Development of electric vehicles for China's power generation portfolio: A regional economic and environmental analysis. *J. Clean. Prod.* **2017**, *162*, 71–85. [CrossRef]
10. IEA. *Global EV Outlook 2019—Scaling-Up the Transition to Electric Mobility*; IEA: London, UK, 2019.
11. EEA. *Electric Vehicles in Europe*; EEA: Copenhagen, Denmark, 2016.
12. Grandell, L.; Lehtilä, A.; Kivinen, M.; Koljonen, T.; Kihlman, S.; Lauri, L.S. Role of critical metals in the future markets of clean energy technologies. *Renew. Energy* **2016**, *95*, 53–62. [CrossRef]
13. Wittstock, R.; Pehlken, A.; Wark, M. Challenges in Automotive Fuel Cells Recycling. *Recycling* **2016**, *1*, 343–364. [CrossRef]
14. Lave, L.B.; MacLean, H.L. An environmental-economic evaluation of hybrid electric vehicles: Toyota's Prius vs. its conventional internal combustion engine Corolla. *Transp. Res. Part D Transp. Environ.* **2002**, *7*, 155–162. [CrossRef]
15. Offer, G.J.; Howey, D.; Contestabile, M.; Clague, R.; Brandon, N.P. Comparative analysis of battery electric, hydrogen fuel cell and hybrid vehicles in a future sustainable road transport system. *Energy Policy* **2010**, *38*, 24–29. [CrossRef]
16. Correa, G.; Muñoz, P.; Falaguerra, T.; Rodriguez, C.R. Performance comparison of conventional, hybrid, hydrogen and electric urban buses using well to wheel analysis. *Energy* **2017**, *141*, 537–549. [CrossRef]
17. Graditi, G.; Langella, G.; Laterza, C.; Valenti, M. Conventional and electric vehicles: A complete economic and environmental comparison. In Proceedings of the ICCEP 2015—5th International Conference on Clean Electrical Power: Renewable Energy Resources Impact, Taormina, Italy, 16–18 June 2015; pp. 660–665.
18. Wang, W.; Wu, Y. An overview of recycling and treatment of spent LiFePO4 batteries in China. *Resour. Conserv. Recycl.* **2017**, *127*, 233–243. [CrossRef]
19. Manzetti, S.; Mariasiu, F. Electric vehicle battery technologies: From present state to future systems. *Renew. Sustain. Energy Rev.* **2015**, *51*, 1004–1012. [CrossRef]
20. Hao, H.; Qiao, Q.; Liu, Z.; Zhao, F. Impact of recycling on energy consumption and greenhouse gas emissions from electric vehicle production: The China 2025 case. *Resour. Conserv. Recycl.* **2017**, *122*, 114–125. [CrossRef]
21. Tang, Y.; Zhang, Q.; Li, Y.; Wang, G.; Li, Y. Recycling Mechanisms and Policy Suggestions for Spent Electric Vehicles' Power Battery -A Case of Beijing. *J. Clean. Prod.* **2018**, *186*, 388–406. [CrossRef]
22. Larcher, D.; Tarascon, J.-M. Towards greener and more sustainable batteries for electrical energy storage. *Nat. Chem.* **2015**, *7*, 19–29. [CrossRef]
23. Mathur, N.; Deng, S.; Singh, S.; Yih, Y. Evaluating the environmental benefits of implementing Industrial Symbiosis to used electric vehicle batteries. *Procedia CIRP* **2019**, *80*, 661–666. [CrossRef]
24. Qiao, Q.; Zhao, F.; Liu, Z.; He, X.; Hao, H. Life cycle greenhouse gas emissions of Electric Vehicles in China: Combining the vehicle cycle and fuel cycle. *Energy* **2019**, *177*, 222–233. [CrossRef]
25. Rosa, P.; Terzi, S. Comparison of current practices for a combined management of printed circuit boards from different waste streams. *J. Clean. Prod.* **2016**, *137*, 300–312. [CrossRef]
26. Singlitico, A.; Goggins, J.; Monaghan, R.F.D. The role of life cycle assessment in the sustainable transition to a decarbonised gas network through green gas production. *Renew. Sustain. Energy Rev.* **2019**, *99*, 16–28. [CrossRef]
27. Zeng, X.; Li, J.; Liu, L. Solving spent lithium-ion battery problems in China: Opportunities and challenges. *Renew. Sustain. Energy Rev.* **2015**, *52*, 1759–1767. [CrossRef]
28. Cucchiella, F.; D'Adamo, I.; Rosa, P.; Terzi, S. Automotive printed circuit boards recycling: An economic analysis. *J. Clean. Prod.* **2016**, *121*, 130–141. [CrossRef]

29. D'Adamo, I.; Rosa, P.; Terzi, S. Challenges in waste electrical and electronic equipment management: A profitability assessment in three European countries. *Sustainability* **2016**, *8*, 633. [CrossRef]
30. Amato, A.; Becci, A.; Birloaga, I.; De Michelis, I.; Ferella, F.; Innocenzi, V.; Ippolito, N.M.; Pillar Jimenez Gomez, C.; Vegliò, F.; Beolchini, F. Sustainability analysis of innovative technologies for the rare earth elements recovery. *Renew. Sustain. Energy Rev.* **2019**, *106*, 41–53. [CrossRef]
31. Cheng, C.; Lin, C.; Wen, L.; Chang, T. Determining environmental costs: A challenge in a governmental e-waste recycling scheme. *Sustainability* **2019**, *11*, 5156. [CrossRef]
32. Webster, J.; Watson, R.T. Analyzing the Past to Prepare for the Future: Writing a Literature Review. *MIS Q.* **2002**, *26*, xiii-xiii.
33. Du, J.; Ouyang, M.; Chen, J. Prospects for Chinese electric vehicle technologies in 2016–2020: Ambition and rationality. *Energy* **2017**, *120*, 584–596. [CrossRef]
34. Zhang, X.; Liang, Y.; Yu, E.; Rao, R.; Xie, J. Review of electric vehicle policies in China: Content summary and effect analysis. *Renew. Sustain. Energy Rev.* **2017**, *70*, 698–714. [CrossRef]
35. IEA. *Global EV Outlook 2016—Beyond One Million Electric Cars*; IEA: London, UK, 2016.
36. IEA. *Global EV Outlook 2017—Two Million and Counting*; IEA: London, UK, 2017.
37. Wolff, S.; Madlener, R. Driven by change: Commercial drivers' acceptance and efficiency perceptions of light-duty electric vehicle usage in Germany. *Transp. Res. Part C Emerg. Technol.* **2019**, *105*, 262–282. [CrossRef]
38. Zeng, X.; Duan, H.; Wang, F.; Li, J. Examining environmental management of e-waste: China's experience and lessons. *Renew. Sustain. Energy Rev.* **2017**, *72*, 1076–1082. [CrossRef]
39. Choma, E.F.; Ugaya, C.M.L. Environmental impact assessment of increasing electric vehicles in the Brazilian fleet. *J. Clean. Prod.* **2017**, *152*, 497–507. [CrossRef]
40. Peters, J.F.; Baumann, M.; Zimmermann, B.; Braun, J.; Weil, M. The environmental impact of Li-Ion batteries and the role of key parameters—A review. *Renew. Sustain. Energy Rev.* **2017**, *67*, 491–506. [CrossRef]
41. Wegener, K.; Andrew, S.; Raatz, A.; Dröder, K.; Herrmann, C. Disassembly of electric vehicle batteries using the example of the Audi Q5 hybrid system. *Procedia CIRP* **2014**, *23*, 155–160. [CrossRef]
42. Zhang, J.; Li, B.; Garg, A.; Liu, Y. A generic framework for recycling of battery module for electric vehicle by combining the mechanical and chemical procedures. *Int. J. Energy Res.* **2018**, *42*, 3390–3399. [CrossRef]
43. Bdiwi, M.; Rashid, A.; Putz, M. Autonomous disassembly of electric vehicle motors based on robot cognition. In *Proceedings of the ICRA 2016—IEEE International Conference on Robotics and Automation*; IEEE: Stockholm, Sweden, 2016; pp. 2500–2505.
44. Li, J.; Barwood, M.; Rahimifard, S. Robotic disassembly for increased recovery of strategically important materials from electrical vehicles. *Robot. Comput. Integr. Manuf.* **2018**, *50*, 203–212. [CrossRef]
45. Li, J.; Barwood, M.; Rahimifard, S. An automated approach for disassembly and recycling of Electric Vehicle components. In Proceedings of the IEVC 2014—IEEE International Electric Vehicle Conference, Florence, Italy, 17–19 December 2014; pp. 1–6.
46. Elwert, T.; Goldmann, D.; Römer, F.; Buchert, M.; Merz, C.; Schüler, D.; Sutter, J. Current Developments and Challenges in the Recycling of Key Components of (Hybrid) Electric Vehicles. *Recycling* **2015**, *1*, 25–60. [CrossRef]
47. Ciez, R.E.; Whitacre, J.F. Examining different recycling processes for lithium-ion batteries. *Nat. Sustain.* **2019**, *2*, 148–156. [CrossRef]
48. Canals Casals, L.; Amante García, B.; Aguesse, F.; Iturrondobeitia, A. Second life of electric vehicle batteries: Relation between materials degradation and environmental impact. *Int. J. Life Cycle Assess.* **2017**, *22*, 82–93. [CrossRef]
49. Bräuer, S. They Not Only Live Once—Towards Product- Service Systems for Repurposed Electric Vehicle Batteries. In *Proceedings of the MKWI 2016—Multikonferenz Wirtschaftsinformatik*; Nissen, V., Stelzer, D., Straßburger, S., Fischer, D., Eds.; Technische Universität Ilmenau: Ilmenau, Germany, 2016; Volume 4, pp. 1299–1310.
50. Xie, Y.; Yu, H.; Ou, Y.; Li, C. Business Model for Recycling Traction Battery. In Proceedings of the MEITA 2015—International Conference on Materials Engineering and Information Technology Applications, Qingdao, China, 28–29 November 2015; pp. 176–180.
51. Cusenza, M.A.; Guarino, F.; Longo, S.; Mistretta, M.; Cellura, M. Reuse of electric vehicle batteries in buildings: An integrated load match analysis and life cycle assessment approach. *Energy Build.* **2019**, *186*, 339–354. [CrossRef]

52. Pagliaro, M.; Meneguzzo, F. Lithium battery reusing and recycling: A circular economy insight. *Heliyon* **2019**, *5*, 1–7. [CrossRef] [PubMed]
53. Ioakimidis, C.S.; Murillo-Marrodán, A.; Bagheri, A.; Thomas, D.; Genikomsakis, K.N. Life Cycle Assessment of a Lithium Iron Phosphate (LFP) Electric Vehicle Battery in Second Life Application Scenarios. *Sustainability* **2019**, *11*, 2527. [CrossRef]
54. Gaines, L. The future of automotive lithium-ion battery recycling: Charting a sustainable course. *Sustain. Mater. Technol.* **2014**, *1*, 2–7. [CrossRef]
55. Sonoc, A.; Jeswiet, J.; Soo, V.K. Opportunities to improve recycling of automotive lithium ion batteries. *Procedia CIRP* **2015**, *29*, 752–757. [CrossRef]
56. Sonoc, A.; Jeswiet, J. A review of lithium supply and demand and a preliminary investigation of a room temperature method to recycle lithium ion batteries to recover lithium and other materials. *Procedia CIRP* **2014**, *15*, 289–293. [CrossRef]
57. Liu, S.; Gong, D. Modelling and simulation on recycling of electric vehicle batteries—Using Agent approach. *Int. J. Simul. Model.* **2014**, *13*, 79–92. [CrossRef]
58. Tytgat, J. The recycling efficiency of Li-ion EV batteries according to the European Commission Regulation, and the relation with the end-of-life vehicles directive recycling rate. In Proceedings of the EVS27—2013 World Electric Vehicle Symposium and Exhibition, Barcelona, Spain, 17–20 November 2013; Volume 6, pp. 1039–1047.
59. Chagnes, A.; Pospiech, B. A brief review on hydrometallurgical technologies for recycling spent lithium-ion batteries. *J. Chem. Technol. Biotechnol.* **2013**, *88*, 1191–1199. [CrossRef]
60. Zeng, X.; Li, J.; Singh, N. Recycling of spent lithium-ion battery: A critical review. *Crit. Rev. Environ. Sci. Technol.* **2014**, *44*, 1129–1165. [CrossRef]
61. Chen, X.; Ma, H.; Luo, C.; Zhou, T. Recovery of valuable metals from waste cathode materials of spent lithium-ion batteries using mild phosphoric acid. *J. Hazard. Mater.* **2017**, *326*, 77–86. [CrossRef]
62. Heelan, J.; Gratz, E.; Zheng, Z.; Wang, Q.; Chen, M.; Apelian, D.; Wang, Y. Current and Prospective Li-Ion Battery Recycling and Recovery Processes. *JOM J. Miner. Met. Mater. Soc.* **2016**, *68*, 2632–2638. [CrossRef]
63. Ku, H.; Jung, Y.; Jo, M.; Park, S.; Kim, S.; Yang, D.; Rhee, K.; An, E.-M.; Sohn, J.; Kwon, K. Recycling of spent lithium-ion battery cathode materials by ammoniacal leaching. *J. Hazard. Mater.* **2016**, *313*, 138–146. [CrossRef] [PubMed]
64. Moradi, B.; Botte, G.G. Recycling of graphite anodes for the next generation of lithium ion batteries. *J. Appl. Electrochem.* **2016**, *46*, 123–148. [CrossRef]
65. Zhang, W.; Liu, Z.; Xia, J.; Li, F.; He, W.; Li, G.; Huang, J. Preparing graphene from anode graphite of spent lithium-ion batteries. *Front. Environ. Sci. Eng.* **2017**, *11*, 1–8. [CrossRef]
66. Zhang, X.; Xue, Q.; Li, L.; Fan, E.; Wu, F.; Chen, R. Sustainable Recycling and Regeneration of Cathode Scraps from Industrial Production of Lithium-Ion Batteries. *ACS Sustain. Chem. Eng.* **2016**, *4*, 7041–7049. [CrossRef]
67. Li, H.; Corneal, L.M.; Standridge, C.R. Effects of acid concentration, temperature, and time on recycling of post-vehicle-application lithium-ion batteries of varying chemistries. *Mater. Renew. Sustain. Energy* **2015**, *4*, 1–5. [CrossRef]
68. Zeng, X.; Li, J. Innovative application of ionic liquid to separate Al and cathode materials from spent high-power lithium-ion batteries. *J. Hazard. Mater.* **2014**, *271*, 50–56. [CrossRef]
69. Raugei, M.; Winfield, P. Prospective LCA of the production and EoL recycling of a novel type of Li-ion battery for electric vehicles. *J. Clean. Prod.* **2019**, *213*, 926–932. [CrossRef]
70. Li, L.; Fan, E.; Guan, Y.; Zhang, X.; Xue, Q.; Wei, L.; Wu, F.; Chen, R. Sustainable Recovery of Cathode Materials from Spent Lithium-Ion Batteries Using Lactic Acid Leaching System. *ACS Sustain. Chem. Eng.* **2017**, *5*, 5224–5233. [CrossRef]
71. Xin, Y.; Guo, X.; Chen, S.; Wang, J.; Wu, F.; Xin, B. Bioleaching of valuable metals Li, Co, Ni and Mn from spent electric vehicle Li-ion batteries for the purpose of recovery. *J. Clean. Prod.* **2016**, *116*, 249–258. [CrossRef]
72. Cheng, Y.-P.; Li, Y.; Jiang, S.; Xie, H.-Q. The recovery of lithium cobalt oxides from spent Li-ion batteries and its electrochemical performances. In Proceedings of the ICPRE 2016—2016 IEEE International Conference on Power and Renewable Energy, Shanghai, China, 21–23 October 2016; pp. 204–208.
73. Diekmann, J.; Hanisch, C.; Froböse, L.; Schälicke, G.; Loellhoeffel, T.; Fölster, A.-S.; Kwade, A. Ecological Recycling of Lithium-Ion Batteries from Electric Vehicles with Focus on Mechanical Processes. *J. Electrochem. Soc.* **2017**, *164*, A6184–A6191. [CrossRef]

74. Yun, L.; Linh, D.; Shui, L.; Peng, X.; Garg, A.; LE, M.L.P.; Asghari, S.; Sandoval, J. Metallurgical and mechanical methods for recycling of lithium-ion battery pack for electric vehicles. *Resour. Conserv. Recycl.* **2018**, *136*, 198–208. [CrossRef]
75. Lixandru, A.; Venkatesan, P.; Jönsson, C.; Poenaru, I.; Hall, B.; Yang, Y.; Walton, A.; Güth, K.; Gauß, R.; Gutfleisch, O. Identification and recovery of rare-earth permanent magnets from waste electrical and electronic equipment. *Waste Manag.* **2017**, *68*, 482–489. [CrossRef] [PubMed]
76. Bandara, H.M.D.; Mantell, M.A.; Darcy, J.W.; Emmert, M.H. Rare Earth Recycling: Forecast of Recoverable Nd from Shredder Scrap and Influence of Recycling Rates on Price Volatility. *J. Sustain. Metall.* **2015**, *1*, 179–188. [CrossRef]
77. Bandara, H.M.D.; Darcy, J.W.; Apelian, D.; Emmert, M.H. Value analysis of neodymium content in shredder feed: Toward enabling the feasibility of rare earth magnet recycling. *Environ. Sci. Technol.* **2014**, *48*, 6553–6560. [CrossRef]
78. Rademaker, J.H.; Kleijn, R.; Yang, Y. Recycling as a strategy against rare earth element criticality: A systemic evaluation of the potential yield of NdFeB magnet recycling. *Environ. Sci. Technol.* **2013**, *47*, 10129–10136. [CrossRef]
79. Yano, J.; Muroi, T.; Sakai, S. Rare earth element recovery potentials from end-of-life hybrid electric vehicle components in 2010-2030. *J. Mater. Cycles Waste Manag.* **2015**, *18*, 655–664. [CrossRef]
80. Elwert, T.; Goldmann, D.; Roemer, F.; Schwarz, S. Recycling of NdFeB Magnets from Electric Drive Motors of (Hybrid) Electric Vehicles. *J. Sustain. Metall.* **2016**, *3*, 108–121. [CrossRef]
81. Bulach, W.; Schüler, D.; Sellin, G.; Elwert, T.; Schmid, D.; Goldmann, D.; Buchert, M.; Kammer, U. Electric vehicle recycling 2020: Key component power electronics. *Waste Manag. Res.* **2018**, *36*, 311–320. [CrossRef]
82. Handley, C.; Brandon, N.P.; van der Vorst, R. Impact of the European Union vehicle waste directive on end-of-life options for polymer electrolyte fuel cells. *J. Power Sources* **2002**, *106*, 344–352. [CrossRef]
83. Kaushal, R.K.; Nema, A.K.; Chaudhary, J. Strategic exploration of battery waste management: A game-theoretic approach. *Waste Manag. Res.* **2015**, *33*, 681–689. [CrossRef] [PubMed]
84. Xing, Y.; Ma, E.W.M.; Tsui, K.L.; Pecht, M. Battery Management Systems in Electric and Hybrid Vehicles. *Energies* **2011**, *4*, 1840–1857. [CrossRef]
85. Hu, Y.; Cheng, H.; Tao, S. Retired Electric Vehicle (EV) Batteries: Integrated Waste Management and Research Needs. *Environ. Sci. Technol.* **2017**, *51*, 10927–10929. [CrossRef] [PubMed]
86. Liu, D.; Song, Y.; Li, L.; Liao, H.; Peng, Y. On-line life cycle health assessment for lithium-ion battery in electric vehicles. *J. Clean. Prod.* **2018**, *199*, 1050–1065. [CrossRef]
87. Richa, K.; Babbitt, C.W.; Gaustad, G. Eco-Efficiency Analysis of a Lithium-Ion Battery Waste Hierarchy Inspired by Circular Economy. *J. Ind. Ecol.* **2017**, *21*, 715–730. [CrossRef]
88. Richa, K.; Babbitt, C.W.; Gaustad, G.; Wang, X. A future perspective on lithium-ion battery waste flows from electric vehicles. *Resour. Conserv. Recycl.* **2014**, *83*, 63–76. [CrossRef]
89. Soo, V.K.; Peeters, J.R.; Paraskevas, D.; Compston, P.; Doolan, M.; Duflou, J.R. Sustainable aluminium recycling of end-of-life products: A joining techniques perspective. *J. Clean. Prod.* **2018**, *178*, 119–132. [CrossRef]
90. Xu, C.J.; Zhang, W.; He, W.; Li, G.; Huang, J.; Zhu, H. Generation and management of waste electric vehicle batteries in China. *Environ. Sci. Pollut. Res.* **2017**, *24*, 20825–20830. [CrossRef]
91. Ramoni, M.O.; Zhang, H.-C. End-of-life (EOL) issues and options for electric vehicle batteries. *Clean Technol. Environ. Policy* **2013**, *15*, 881–891. [CrossRef]
92. Foster, M.; Isely, P.; Standridge, C.R.; Hasan, M.M. Feasibility assessment of remanufacturing, repurposing, and recycling of end of vehicle application lithium-ion batteries. *J. Ind. Eng. Manag.* **2014**, *7*, 698–715. [CrossRef]
93. Kampker, A.; Heimes, H.H.; Ordung, M.; Lienemann, C.; Hollah, A.; Sarovic, N. Evaluation of a Remanufacturing for Lithium Ion Batteries from Electric Cars. *Int. J. Mech. Mechatron. Eng.* **2016**, *10*, 1922–1928.
94. Liu, W.-W.; Zhang, H.; Liu, L.-H.; Qing, X.-C.; Tang, Z.-J.; Li, M.-Z.; Yin, J.-S.; Zhang, H.-C. Remanufacturing cathode from end-of-life of lithium-ion secondary batteries by Nd:YAG laser radiation. *Clean Technol. Environ. Policy* **2016**, *18*, 231–243. [CrossRef]
95. Hannan, M.A.; Hoque, M.M.; Mohamed, A.; Ayob, A. Review of energy storage systems for electric vehicle applications: Issues and challenges. *Renew. Sustain. Energy Rev.* **2017**, *69*, 771–789. [CrossRef]
96. Wu, Z.; Wang, M.; Zheng, J.; Sun, X.; Zhao, M.; Wang, X. Life cycle greenhouse gas emission reduction potential of battery electric vehicle. *J. Clean. Prod.* **2018**, *190*, 462–470. [CrossRef]

97. Riba, J.R.; López-Torres, C.; Romeral, L.; Garcia, A. Rare-earth-free propulsion motors for electric vehicles: A technology review. *Renew. Sustain. Energy Rev.* **2016**, *57*, 367–379. [CrossRef]
98. Ziemann, S.; Müller, D.B.; Schebek, L.; Weil, M. Modeling the potential impact of lithium recycling from EV batteries on lithium demand: A dynamic MFA approach. *Resour. Conserv. Recycl.* **2018**, *133*, 76–85. [CrossRef]
99. Wang, X.; Gaustad, G.; Babbitt, C.W.; Bailey, C.; Ganter, M.J.; Landi, B.J. Economic and environmental characterization of an evolving Li-ion battery waste stream. *J. Environ. Manag.* **2014**, *135*, 126–134. [CrossRef]
100. Wang, X.; Gaustad, G.; Babbitt, C.W.; Richa, K. Economies of scale for future lithium-ion battery recycling infrastructure. *Resour. Conserv. Recycl.* **2014**, *83*, 53–62. [CrossRef]
101. Price, B.; Dietz, E.; Richardson, J. Life cycle costs of electric and hybrid electric vehicle batteries and End-of-Life uses. In Proceedings of the EIT 2012—IEEE International Conference on Electro/Information Technology, Indianapolis, IN, USA, 6–8 May 2012; pp. 1–7.
102. Kibira, D.; Jain, S. Impact of Hybrid and Electric Vehicles on Automobile Recycling Infrastructure. In Proceedings of the WSC'11—2011 IEEE Winter Simulation Conference, Phoenix, AZ, USA, 11–14 December 2011; pp. 1072–1083.
103. Huth, C.; Kieckhäfer, K.; Spengler, T.S. Make-or-buy strategies for electric vehicle batteries-a simulation-based analysis. *Technol. Forecast. Soc. Chang.* **2015**, *99*, 22–34. [CrossRef]
104. Jansson, J.; Nordlund, A.; Westin, K. Examining drivers of sustainable consumption: The influence of norms and opinion leadership on electric vehicle adoption in Sweden. *J. Clean. Prod.* **2017**, *154*, 176–187. [CrossRef]
105. Garcia-Muiña, F.; González-Sánchez, R.; Ferrari, A.; Settembre-Blundo, D. The Paradigms of Industry 4.0 and Circular Economy as Enabling Drivers for the Competitiveness of Businesses and Territories: The Case of an Italian Ceramic Tiles Manufacturing Company. *Soc. Sci.* **2018**, *7*, 255. [CrossRef]
106. D'Adamo, I.; Falcone, P.M.; Ferella, F. A socio-economic analysis of biomethane in the transport sector: The case of Italy. *Waste Manag.* **2019**, *95*, 102–115. [CrossRef]
107. Garcia-Muiña, F.E.; González-Sánchez, R.; Ferrari, A.M.; Volpi, L.; Pini, M.; Settembre-Blundo, C.; Settembre-Blundo, D. Identifying the Equilibrium Point between Sustainability Goals and Circular Economy Practices in an Industry 4.0 Manufacturing Context Using Eco-Design. *Soc. Sci.* **2019**, *8*, 241. [CrossRef]
108. Un-Noor, F.; Padmanaban, S.; Mihet-Popa, L.; Mollah, M.N.; Hossain, E. A comprehensive study of key electric vehicle (EV) components, technologies, challenges, impacts, and future direction of development. *Energies* **2017**, *10*, 1217. [CrossRef]
109. Kawamoto, R.; Mochizuki, H.; Moriguchi, Y.; Nakano, T.; Motohashi, M.; Sakai, Y.; Inaba, A. Estimation of CO2 Emissions of Internal Combustion Engine Vehicle and Battery Electric Vehicle Using LCA. *Sustainability* **2019**, *11*, 2690. [CrossRef]
110. Ferrão, P.; Amaral, J. Assessing the economics of auto recycling activities in relation to European Union Directive on end of life vehicles. *Technol. Forecast. Soc. Chang.* **2006**, *73*, 277–289. [CrossRef]
111. Li, Y.; Lim, M.K.; Tan, Y.; Lee, S.Y.; Tseng, M.-L. Sharing economy to improve routing for urban logistics distribution using electric vehicles. *Resour. Conserv. Recycl.* **2019**, *153*, 1–13. [CrossRef]
112. Lieder, M.; Rashid, A. Towards circular economy implementation: A comprehensive review in context of manufacturing industry. *J. Clean. Prod.* **2016**, *115*, 36–51. [CrossRef]
113. Gaustad, G.; Krystofik, M.; Bustamante, M.; Badami, K. Circular economy strategies for mitigating critical material supply issues. *Resour. Conserv. Recycl.* **2018**, *135*, 24–33. [CrossRef]
114. Zubi, G.; Dufo-López, R.; Carvalho, M.; Pasaoglu, G. The lithium-ion battery: State of the art and future perspectives. *Renew. Sustain. Energy Rev.* **2018**, *89*, 292–308. [CrossRef]
115. Stoycheva, S.; Marchese, D.; Paul, C.; Padoan, S.; Juhmani, A.; Linkov, I. Multi-criteria decision analysis framework for sustainable manufacturing in automotive industry. *J. Clean. Prod.* **2018**, *187*, 257–272. [CrossRef]
116. Krishna Mohan, T.V.; Amit, R.K. Dismantlers' dilemma in end-of-life vehicle recycling markets: A system dynamics model. *Ann. Oper. Res.* **2018**, 1–29. [CrossRef]
117. Rosa, P.; Terzi, S. Improving end of life vehicle's management practices: An economic assessment through system dynamics. *J. Clean. Prod.* **2018**, *184*, 520–536. [CrossRef]
118. Gu, H.; Liu, Z.; Qing, Q. Optimal electric vehicle production strategy under subsidy and battery recycling. *Energy Policy* **2017**, *109*, 579–589. [CrossRef]

119. Hoyer, C.; Kieckhäfer, K.; Spengler, T.S. Impact of Mandatory Rates on the Recycling of Lithium-Ion Batteries from Electric Vehicles in Germany. In Proceedings of the LCE 2013—20th CIRP International Conference on Life Cycle Engineering, Singapore, 17–19 April 2013; pp. 543–548.
120. Khodier, A.; Williams, K.S.; Dallison, N. Challenges around automotive shredder residue production and disposal. *Waste Manag.* **2018**, *73*, 566–573. [CrossRef]
121. Cucchiella, F.; D'Adamo, I.; Rosa, P.; Terzi, S. Scrap automotive electronics: A mini-review of current management practices. *Waste Manag. Res.* **2016**, *34*, 3–10. [CrossRef] [PubMed]
122. Hoyer, C.; Kieckhäfer, K.; Spengler, T.S. Technology and capacity planning for the recycling of lithium-ion electric vehicle batteries in Germany. *J. Bus. Econ.* **2015**, *85*, 505–544. [CrossRef]
123. Zhou, F.; Wang, X.; Lim, M.K.; He, Y.; Li, L. Sustainable recycling partner selection using fuzzy DEMATEL-AEW-FVIKOR: A case study in small-and-medium enterprises (SMEs). *J. Clean. Prod.* **2018**, *196*, 489–504. [CrossRef]
124. Ai, N.; Zheng, J.; Chen, W.-Q. US end-of-life electric vehicle batteries: Dynamic inventory modeling and spatial analysis for regional solutions. *Resour. Conserv. Recycl.* **2019**, *145*, 208–219. [CrossRef]
125. Reinhardt, R.; Christodoulou, I.; Gassó-Domingo, S.; Amante García, B. Towards sustainable business models for electric vehicle battery second use: A critical review. *J. Environ. Manag.* **2019**, *245*, 432–446. [CrossRef]
126. Mayyas, A.; Steward, D.; Mann, M. The case for recycling: Overview and challenges in the material supply chain for automotive li-ion batteries. *Sustain. Mater. Technol.* **2018**, *17*, 1–13. [CrossRef]
127. Qiao, Q.; Zhao, F.; Liu, Z.; Hao, H. Electric vehicle recycling in China: Economic and environmental benefits. *Resour. Conserv. Recycl.* **2019**, *140*, 45–53. [CrossRef]
128. Tang, Y.; Zhang, Q.; Li, Y.; Li, H.; Pan, X.; Mclellan, B. The social-economic-environmental impacts of recycling retired EV batteries under reward-penalty mechanism. *Appl. Energy* **2019**, *251*, 1–16. [CrossRef]
129. Hendrickson, T.P.; Kavvada, O.; Shah, N.; Sathre, R.; Scown, C.D. Life-cycle implications and supply chain logistics of electric vehicle battery recycling in California. *Environ. Res. Lett.* **2015**, *10*, 1–10. [CrossRef]

MDPI
St. Alban-Anlage 66
4052 Basel
Switzerland
Tel. +41 61 683 77 34
Fax +41 61 302 89 18
www.mdpi.com

Sustainability Editorial Office
E-mail: sustainability@mdpi.com
www.mdpi.com/journal/sustainability

CPSIA information can be obtained
at www.ICGtesting.com
Printed in the USA
LVHW071703160820
663340LV00032B/927

9 783039 364558